# THE LETTERS AND PRIVATE PAPERS OF WILLIAM MAKEPEACE THACKERAY

## VOLUME II

LONDON : HUMPHREY MILFORD
OXFORD UNIVERSITY PRESS

THE LETTERS AND PRIVATE PAPERS OF

# *William Makepeace*
# THACKERAY

Collected and edited by

*Gordon N. Ray*

In four volumes

*Volume II: 1841–1851*

HARVARD UNIVERSITY PRESS

Cambridge, Massachusetts

1945

PRINTED AT THE HARVARD UNIVERSITY PRINTING OFFICE

CAMBRIDGE, MASSACHUSETTS, U.S.A.

# CONTENTS OF VOLUME II

# ILLUSTRATIONS IN VOLUME II

*(The name of the owner of each illustration taken from the original is noted in parenthesis.)*

# ILLUSTRATIONS

LETTERS, 1841–1851

TO EDWARD FitzGERALD
10 JANUARY 1841

*Address:* Edward Fitz-Gerald Esq^re | Geldestone Hall | Beccles. | England.
*Postmark:* 14 JA 1841. Hitherto unpublished.

Avenue S^te Marie. Faubourg du Roule
10. January. 1841.

My dear old Edward. Your letter though it has not been answered till now gave me a great pleasure — I think your's are the only letters that were always welcome to me, for they always contain something hearty w^h makes me happier when I am happy, and consoles me when I am dull. This blow that has come upon me has played the deuce with me that is the fact, and I don't care to write to my friends and pour out lamentations w^h are all the news I have to tell.

I saw my dear little woman yesterday for the first time for six weeks, since w^h time she has been at Esquirol's [1] "famous Maison de Santé". Esquirol is dead since she went there, & the place conducted by his nephew, who is likewise a famous man in his profession. He says *Elle doit guérir,* and I think so too: at first she was in a fever and violent, then she was indifferent, now she is melancholy & silent and we are glad of it. She bemoans her condition and that is a great step to cure. She knows everybody and recollects things but in a stunned confused sort of way. She kissed me at first very warmly and with tears in her eyes, then she went away from me, as if she felt she was unworthy of having such a God of a husband. God help her.

My father mother and cousin are all going off to Italy in this

---

[1] Jeanne Etienne Dominique Esquirol (b. 1772), the great alienist, had died on December 2, 1840. At this time there was no place in Europe where the mentally afflicted were more competently treated than in his clinic. His theory of insanity may be studied in *Des Maladies mentales considérées sous les rapports médical, hygiénique, et médico-légal* (1838).

dreadful weather, to meet a brother of the governor's ² who has just come after 20 years from India — a noble fellow who adores my mother, and thinks my father the best man in the world, and has fallen in love with my cousin whom he knew when she was 4 years old, and who has fallen in love with him too as young ladies will do who are five and twenty and love letter writing. There is something very affecting in his simple admiration of her — Miss Mary writes him verses forsooth and he says 'they are the finest verses I ever read in my life' and that she must not with all her talents & accomplishments look down upon a poor illiterate soldier *grey headed* (grey headed with a dash) & 50 years' old. Then he grieves because a pair of diamond earrings that he had ordered at Delhi were not ready when he came away. Mary is a capital girl, and quite ready to jump down his throat, and so it will be a match. My poor mother is going though it breaks her heart to part with the children — and my Grandmother & I are to keep house: that is she keeps house & I live in it. Since my calamity, I have learned to love all these people a great deal more — my mother especially God bless her who has such a tender yearning big heart that I begin to cry when I think of her: and when I see her with the children, cleaving to them, am obliged to walk off for the sight is too much for me. When you read Titmarsh's letters to Miss Smith ³ wʰ I trust you will buy, as 7 1/2d out of the 2/6 will come to me — you will read a pretty incident about her and the children apropos of the Napoleon procession, I don't know what the rest of the book is scarcely for I saw no proofs and wrote as hard as I could.

Dicky Milnes is here — and I have got to like him very much almost. He is amazingly clever, and very kind-hearted he does not talk big, and if he affects to take an extraordinary degree of interest in the person before him, why it's a good affectation at any rate, and better than the common cursed indifference.

A couple of months hence I shall ask you to pay my wife's pension for a month, a heavy sum £ 20: but it is a comfort to have her

² Colonel Charles Carmichael-Smyth.
³ *The Second Funeral of Napoleon.* The "pretty incident" to which Thackeray refers comes at the beginning of the third letter (*Works*, IV, 696–697).

at the very best place, and after giving her a trial there of 6 or 7 months or so, we may look out for a cheaper abode for her if it please God to keep her still ill.

As soon as I am alone with my Grandmother I intend to flare up and write a novel — about something, I don't know what yet but have a fancy for the reign of Henry V.[4]

You must remember me very kindly to Kerrich and your sister who has been so good as to like her brother's old friend. God bless you my dear Edward I'm writing this at the Club, where a score of bawling Frenchmen are smoking and playing billiards — I don't know or speak to 1 of them, but it is very amusing to come here from time to time, and watch their ways. ⟨. . .⟩ [5]

[4] In a letter to Bentley, the publisher, which may be tentatively dated November, 1840, when Thackeray visited London, Barham writes: "Thackeray called here yesterday; wants to be busy, so I recommended him to treat with you for a three vol. historical novel, which he is very well inclined to do. From his reading I think he would succeed, especially if, as I suggested, it were of the Queen-Hoo Hall style, illustrated by his own woodcuts of costume, caricature, &c. in the livelier parts." (Richard Harris Dalton Barham, *Life and Letters of the Rev. Richard Harris Barham*, 2 vols., London, 1870, II, 112). Thackeray appears to have thought well of Barham's suggestion concerning *Queen-hoo Hall* (1808), a romance of life in fifteenth century England by the antiquary Joseph Strutt (1749-1802) to which Sir Walter Scott added a concluding chapter, for shortly after he settled in Paris for the winter, he began a novel of his own, laid in the same period. The seven chapters and fragment of an eighth which he completed during the next few months are printed in *Centenary Works* (XXV, 3-41) under the title "The Knights of Borsellen." He carried his romance no further, but in later years he often contemplated returning to it, and had he lived longer, he would probably have completed it. His notes for "The Knights of Borsellen," some of which appear in *Centenary Biographical Introductions*, XXV, xlii, and *Centenary Works*, XXV, 43-46, are preserved in the Harvard College Library.

[5] The signature has been cut away. Lady Ritchie (*Biographical Introductions*, V, xiii-xiv) writes of the period in her father's life that followed this letter: "He was almost alone; his parents had been called away by family affairs; my baby-sister and I were deposited with our great-grandmother, Mrs. Butler, who certainly thought us inconveniently young. . . .

"I can remember being taken to see him in his lodgings, early of a morning. Very often he was dressing, and it was a privilege to see him shave, better still to watch him drawing pictures or tearing little processions of pigs with curly tails out of paper. Sometimes he was writing, and to my surprise and annoyance could not tear out little pigs."

194. TO MRS. PROCTER
21 JANUARY 1841

Published in part, *Biographical Introductions*, V, xiv. My text is taken from a transcript given Lady Ritchie by George Murray Smith.

4 Avenue St Marie,
Faubourg du Roule,
Paris.
21 January, 1841.

My dear Mrs Procter,

Our Milnes who is going away tomorrow will I hope bear this with him, — it is only to thank you for writing so kindly to me who have had so many troubles of late as to be very glad and sigh for sympathy and consolation. I saw Miss Montague's marriage [6] in the paper, and was about to write to you for I knew with what pain you looked forward to it — but I found my letter when half done did not contain a word of sympathy for you, and only a long selfish account of my own particular sorrows, and so tore it up. Don't be angry if I tell you that on reading your letter I felt glad that somebody else was miserable and lonely. For my own misfortunes Milnes will tell you all about them. They were pretty severe at first — not now, and I feel ashamed of myself for not being more lastingly sorry. See, it always comes to this, and I am just doing what I tore up the last letter for, whenever any one else asks me to feel for them I begin prating about myself.

I have got to like Milnes very much indeed. He is quite simple and affectionate and eager to do good offices. He has introduced me to a charming little woman here, so pretty and clever and kind, fresh out of the country, and that is a charm, Madam, too for blasés dogs like me who have exhausted every pleasure and dissipation in the magnificent turmoil of a Great Coram Street.

Thank you for your kind pains about the book. I have seen many reviews of it — an important work which was compiled in four

[6] Mrs. Procter's step-sister.

days: the Ballad [7] being added to it as an after-thought. It is the deuce that poetry or rhymes, and never was an unfortunate fellow so plagued. For a whole week you would have fancied me a real poet — having all the exterior marks of one — with a week's beard, a great odour of tobacco, a scowling ferocious thoughtful appearance, I used to sit all day meditating, nail-biting and laboriously producing about twenty lines in twelve hours. Are all poets in this way? How wise Procter was to leave it for the gay science of law, in which a fellow has but to lie back in a Windsor chair and read interesting leases and settlements with 'five guineas' written on the title page. I hope Titmarsh will produce as much.

How well the Times [8] found him out! The article is very smart I think and complimentary too: and best of all will make people curious to get the book. I have 7 1/2 d out of each half-crown.

| 100 copies. | = | 750 pence | = | £3 : 2 : 6 |
|---|---|---|---|---|
| 1000 copies | = | 7500 " | = | £31 : 5 : 0 |
| 10000 copies | = | 75000 " | = | £312 : 10 : 0 |
| 100000 copies | = | 750000 " | = | £3125 : : |

One hundred copies have already been sold, so that you see my fortune is very clear. As for the Athenaeum [9] I give it up. Why will men drink so much water-gruel and wear lambs' wool stockings, and be so squeamish. Fiddle-de-dee. The great Forster [10] too has made a mistake. There is not a word in praise of John Bull. Give me the jolly old times, though even that is liable to error. I don't believe Titmarsh has a bit higher opinion of himself than he has of the rest of the world: nor does he much conceal his opinion of the one or the other. Please to read the account of the family

[7] "The Chronicle of the Drum."

[8] There is a shrewd and friendly half column on *The Second Funeral of Napoleon* in *The Times* of January 19.

[9] The critic for *The Athenaeum* (January 16, p. 53) holds that Thackeray's book is "a mere (though very imperfect) newspaper report of proceedings, better reported in fifty other forms and places."

[10] Forster describes Thackeray's letters to Miss Smith as "sensible, instructive, [and] amusing" and finds "The Chronicle of the Drum" to be a "serious ballad of considerable power," marred by "a most John Bullish Franco-mania" (*Examiner*, January 17, p. 37).

procession: my dear old mother is the heroine of it. God bless her: in these latter days I have learned to love and admire her more cordially than anything else I know of. The great heart of God Almighty must yearn as he looks down upon this woman, who lies awake all night thinking for us and loving us all.

Dear Mrs Procter, will you excuse all this strange talk. And believe me in spite of it,

Most faithfully yours,

W. M. Thackeray.

195.
## TO EDWARD FɪᴛᴢGERALD
JANUARY ? 1841 [11]

Published in part, *Biographical Introductions*, IX, xli.

*   *   *

This letter is written at the Club, 20 Frenchmen singing chattering and smoking, w$^h$ must acc$^t$ for the décousu state of it, and for some of the conceit. Had I been alone I might have disguised it better, and humbugged it into almost an appearance of modesty. One fellow is singing

*   *   *

He [12] has introduced me to a charming little woman here a Lady ⟨. . .⟩ [13] from Norfolk, with a dear little Irish accent, and a delightful fresh kind of enthusiasm w$^h$ charms me. She has an old husband whom you will know at once, when I tell you that the other day at dinner he told us with perfect gravity how Brummel asked George 'to ring the bell', and meeting H. R. H in the Park afterwards asked his companion 'Who's your fat friend? — ' O sancta simplicitas [14] What a number of Norfolk turkies must this

---

[11] The date of this letter is determined by its similarity in content to that of January 21.

[12] Milnes.

[13] This name is irrecoverably overscored.

[14] Words uttered by John Huss (1373–1415), "at the stake, seeing an old peasant bringing a faggot to throw on the pile" (*Oxford Dictionary of Quotations*; London, 1941, p. 548).

old boy have eaten to keep him up to the telling of stories like
those! — The old fellow is 65 years old, and told me that only
that night he had a dream about being flogged at Charter-House —
There is something touching in this I think about wʰ Mʳ William
Wordsworth might make a poem if he chose.

*     *     *

conceit of poor ⟨. . .⟩ ¹⁵ himself much better than the persons he
writes about. I dont believe your dictum as to the propriety of leaving humbug to drop off of itself. Every body writes it up, it has the
newspapers the House of Lords and all the toadies and lickspittles
in the world on its side — let us at least say a word or two to show
it up: if it be but to show people it is humbug else the stupid
Britons will go on fancying it is God's truth: and it is time that
their stupid superstition, that infernal

196.       TO MRS. CARMICHAEL-SMYTH
27 FEBRUARY–6 MARCH 1841

Published in part, *Biographical Introductions*, V, xviii-xix.

My dearest Mammy. We are on the look out for letters from
Naples wʰ are to contain the great news I presume. for whats the
use of delaying these matters, and allowing poor lovers to pine? ¹⁶
I suppose you will go on to Rome & see the wonders there as why
shouldn't you, after the lovyers have had a spell of honey-moon.
How I should like to see the same places, but that I daresay you
have often thought of ere this. As for us we are going on in the old
way, I seem to work very hard but don't get much done. All the
week I have been busy with etchings for the new edition of Yellowplush,¹⁷ & have been to Ivry twice between times, & shall go again

---

¹⁵ At this point about eight words are cut away.
¹⁶ Mary Graham and Colonel Carmichael-Smyth were married on March 4,
1841.
¹⁷ The first volume of Thackeray's *Comic Tales and Sketches*, listed among
"Publications Received" in *The Spectator* of April 24 (p. 402).

tomorrow. No improvement to speak of the little woman is a little more active, reads out, speaks a little of a night, and yesterday when I was going away pressed me by words to stay — wʰ is always something. We had a long walk in the country. Her remarks were those of a child: she noticed things however a good deal horses, fowls, &c. — it was carnival time, and the fools of the place were making a great braying of trumpets and parading after the fashion of the fools here. Anny was 1 of the latter, you should hear her remarks about the show: the Hamertons took her to see it. They are most constant visitors to the old lady, and a great comfort really. We get on famously, She does not like the monthly expences much, wʰ amount to near 600 fr., but there is no means of lightening them in any way just now, and I'm not going to play delicacy.

Mʳˢ Crowe is going with her 2 girls to the I of Wight Why the juice only knows, she will spend at the very least 100 £ and the juice only knows too how her husband gets that — for Bess Hamerton & I have agreed that he can't possibly spend less than 1000 a year. I wish I knew the way of getting it.

I am getting dreadfully bitten with my old painting mania; and as soon as I have written that famous book you know of, & made a few hundred pounds make a vow to the great Gods that I will try the thing once more. Meanwhile I have put the novel aside as I think I told you, to get if poss: something ready agˢᵗ April for Mʳˢ T.

Titmarsh has sold 140 copies, & be hanged to it: the donkeys of a public don't know a good thing when they get it. It has however been hugely praised by the press — and will serve to keep my name up though a failure — thus you know that General Moran when he retreated through the Black Forest, General Moore, General Massena & others made themselves illustrious by their reverses — fiddlestick: what is the use of writing such stuff to you? — it's the result of the infernal cross fire — A fortnight ago I lost my penknife and bought a new one — yesterday I found the old 1 and gave the new one to the engraver who is filing my plates for me — to day I have lost the tother knife Is it not too bad? Such a man of

MARY GRAHAM, AFTERWARDS MRS. CHARLES CARMICHAEL

*(From a sketch by Thackeray)*

an engraver as I have found! [18] I wish you could see him. He is abᵗ 28 has not a spark of genius: works 14 hours a day, never breakfasts except off cheese & bread in his atelier, dines in the same way, never goes out, makes about 3000 francs a year, has a wife & child & is happy the whole day long — the whole house is like a cage of canaries, nothing but singing from night till morning. It goes to my heart to hear his little wife singing at her work — what noble characters does one light on in little nooks of this great world! — I can't tell you how this man's virtue and simplicity affects me. Bon Dieu to think of one's own beastly gormandizing egotism after this — I am trying however to correct some and yesterday walked to Ivry from the Barrier & back, and there with Isabella, & then from the Louvre, all to save 3 francs — There's virtue, my god, & think of Marvy toiling for 365 5090 hours

$$\frac{14}{1440}$$
$$365$$

in a year, never grumbling, never exceeding, and always having a 5 franc piece — for a brother-artist in distress.

Another instance of virtue. I wouldn't drink any brandy & water yesterday.

Why was not this sent a week ago? I forget why because GM I think had just dispatched a sheet, and I thought I would keep mine, and so dawdled and dawdled.

This last bit is written on the 6 March, yours & Marys letter just come in, God bless you all. I think of my dearest Mammy who is lonely now; but I am very glad for Polly's sake. Depend on it the virtues of that girl some of them that is, want independence to bring them out. What I hope & pray is that she will sufftˡʸ respect and admire her husband. Her Devonshire friends flattered Polly & did her no good. but when she gets into the world on her own — I beg your pardon you know what I mean — she'll get that nonsense out of her.

[18] See *Memoranda*, Louis Marvy.

197.                           TO MRS. PROCTER
                              19 MARCH 1841

*Address:* Mrs Procter, | Grove End Place, | Regent's Park, | London. | England. Extracts published, *Biographical Introductions*, V, xv. My text is taken from a transcript given Lady Ritchie by George Murray Smith.

                                                    Avenue St Marie,
                                                    Paris.
                                                    March 19, 1841.
My dear Mrs Procter,

I fell into the arms of our lusty Reeve yesterday at the Exhibition, and we agreed to dine together on Sunday — and we talked about our friends in London, and he told me how Chorley had compelled him, Reeve, to give up the wearing of waistcoats, and then we talked of you and Procter and I determined to send you off a little note immediately by way of apology for my last one which you must have thought written by a madman. Indeed it was written by a very miserable fellow who was quite unaccustomed to that kind of mood and is not a whit happier now, only he bears his little griefs more composedly. What won't a man bear with a little practice! Ruin, blindness, his legs off, dishonour, death of dearest friends, and what not. As the cares multiply —— don't know whether this sentence is left unfinished because I don't know how to finish it or because it is a shame to begin such dissertations to a lady who merits more graceful treatment from me.

What shall I tell you? Last night there were at the least two hundred thousand persons of both sexes disguised in various costumes, dancing madly from ten until five this morning: [19] as I suppose the Bishop of London [20] was at Drury Lane when he cried out so against the French rabble. Did his Lordship dance with his apron on? It would have been a fine sight and a pretty subject for

[19] This masked ball is described in "Shrove Tuesday in Paris" (*Works*, XIII, 566–572).
[20] Charles James Blomfield (1786–1857) was Bishop of London from 1828 to 1856.

a picture. Odry says in one of the farces, "I saw a beautiful carp in the market to-day, and when I go next week I am determined to buy it." I was just on the point of covering this paper with a picture of the Bishop dancing, but have put it off till next week or till the next exhibition, or till the next time that I venture to send you a letter. Indeed I have hardly the impertinence to despatch such nonsense as this. Part of the nonsense must be laid to the account of my Grandmamma for whom I have been cutting slices of plum cake all the morning apropos of the marriage of my cousin who has just taken a husband at Naples; and a very good one too: but it is very hard for a man of my dignity to be obliged to cut up plum cake and pack it in bits of paper and eat little crumbs of it slyly every now and then, and to know for a certainty that I shall be unwell for having eaten it. All these things press on my mind and prevent me from writing as sensibly as otherwise under more favourable circumstances I might.

⟨Reeve⟩ says the whole town is talking of me, and my new book. Oho, thought I, they *have* found it out, have they? That ballad about the Drum in spite of poor Chorley is beginning to be liked, and those Napoleon letters — well, they have been a long time finding out the merit of them. No such thing: it appears the whole town is talking about my new novel of Cecil.[21] O just punishment of vanity! How I wish I had written it — not for the book's sake but for the filthy money's, which I love better than fame. The fact is I am about a wonderful romance,[22] and oh, I long for the day when the three volumes shall be completed — not for the fame's sake again, but for the disgusting before-mentioned consideration.

Dear Mrs Procter, please not to read any of the foregoing part of this, but to light at once upon the conclusion which contains the whole cream and gist of my note, and that is I hope you are very well, I hope your husband is very well and all the little people: and I am always,

> Yours most truly,
>
>          W. M. Thackeray.

[21] By Mrs. Gore, published in 1841.
[22] See above, No. 193.

For the benefit of two rascally Governments that we cannot care a farthing for.[23]

As economy is the order of the day, and it is always cheap to sponge on one's friends, will you please to put a 1 d stamp on the enclosed and send it on its way? It seems a sin to tempt Providence and throw away 1/7 d.

198.                    TO MRS. PROCTER
                        5 APRIL 1841

Extract published, *Biographical Introductions*, V, xv. My text is taken from a transcript given Lady Ritchie by George Murray Smith.

                                    Avenue St Marie Fbg du Roule,
                                            April 5, 1841.

My dear Mrs Proctor,

All this week I have been thinking of your kind letter, and indeed last Monday it was a very near chance indeed that I did not bound off by the coach and take you and Procter at your word, and absorb ink and other liquors which he tempted me with. Indeed it would have been very pleasant to look out in that little green garden of yours, and see how Miss Nanny has grown, and admire the pear blossom (Leigh Huntish this) and then admire Procter asleep on the sofa, and then think what a wonderful good dinner I had had, and then talk in a certain agreeable jocose sneering good-humoured scandalous sentimental sort of way with a certain lady that makes the best tea and the best jokes in the world. O, but it would have been a pleasant holiday for a poor devil, like your humble servant, who nevertheless heartily thanks God that he never took any such thing.

For instead of going to London, I went to see my dear little patient at Ivry, and as the doctors there honestly confessed that they could do nothing for her, determined to try — what? — the medicine that is administered in the Opera of the Eliseri d'Amore: [24]

---

[23] This postscript is written on the outside of the letter.
[24] By Donizetti, first performed in 1832.

and off I took the little woman a pleasant walk across the fields to a pleasant little gudgeon house on the river, where we had a dinner and she took two glasses of the elixir which I devoted myself to finish. It did her a great deal of good and made her eyes sparkle, and actually for the first time these six months the poor little woman flung herself into my arms with all her heart and gave me a kiss, at which moment of course the waiter burst in. This only served to mend matters for the lady went off in a peal of laughter, the first these six months again, and since then I have had her at home not well, nor nearly well, but a hundred times better than she was this day week: when I got your letter which made me think of going to London, which proved to me that I ought to go to Ivry, which induced me to try the experiment of the champagne, which caused my wife to give me a kiss, which brought the waiter into the room, which made my wife laugh, like the Princess Badroulboudour [25] and so on. I told the waiter the circumstances of the case, and that the caress to which he had been privy was one that although it would not probably have been given had I been aware that his eye was at the keyhole, was still an embrace authorized, nay enjoined, by the strictest regulations of morality. The beast did not believe a word of the story but what care I? Only let her get well and I shall be the happiest man in the world. Ye Gods how I will venerate champagne — I always did.

You see now, dear Mr and Mrs Procter, why it is impossible that I should accept your polite invitation — indeed it was a great deal more than polite, it was very kind and friendly, and there is a remark, Madam, which you will allow me to intrude upon you which is that it is almost worth a man's while to be downcast and unhappy for a time that he may get his friends' kindness and sympathy. He relishes it so: and I think the liking for it remains afterwards: at least now I feel a hundred per cent happier than when I got your offer, and enjoy it really as much almost as if I had accepted it.

[25] Daughter of the Sultan of China and the wife of Aladdin, of Arabian Nights fame.

Goodbye, dear Mrs Procter, and believe me always most truly yours and Procter's,

W. M. T.

199.          TO EDWARD FitzGERALD
6 APRIL 1841

*Address:* Edward FitzGerald Esq^re | Geldestone Hall | Beccles. *Readdressed:* Boulge Hall | Woodbridge. *Postmark:* 6 AP 1841. Published in part, *W. M. Thackeray and Edward Fitzgerald*, ed. Shorter, pp. 18-19.

\* \* \*

it to M^rs Carlyle. It is capital wicked fun to vex the French about it.[26]

How does the Naseby business go on, and the marriage at the end thereof? [27] It is a fine thing depend upon it, in spite of all the woes and trouble attendant on it: not that you have any need to have your heart softened, it is warm & kind enough already, but it completes a man's faculties somehow, and lets him into secrets unknown to bachelors, especially that fine one of loving children, for w^h to be sure you have a great aptitude; as every other big-hearted man — stuff & nonsense — I am quite tired and only writing

\* \* \*

what. I will lie down on my bed, smoke a segar & read a curious fine book Michelets History of France.[28] and so ⎯⎯ my dear old Edward. Oh stop, I must send you a charade by a young lady. I am sure I ought to get the pocket book for it.

[26] Probably the affair of the Vengeur. See *Memoranda*, Thomas Carlyle.

[27] Among other residences the FitzGerald family owned a house at Naseby Woolleys, near Cromwell's battlefield, where FitzGerald spent a good part of his early life. It is possible that he was endeavoring to persuade his mother to turn this property over to him, so that he might marry Miss Charlesworth. See above, No. 88.

[28] The first five volumes of Michelet's *Histoire de France*, carrying the chronicle to 1461, were published between 1835 and 1841.

Charade by a lady of fifteen.

I am first in the last, in the last I am found
In the flower you'll find me though not in the ground.
Not seen in the rose in the lily I'm hid
Not seen in the eye, yet (strange!) in the lid.
In the palace I lurk, In the castle am seen
Yet banished (alas!) from the cot on the green.
Deep hit in the violets bosom I dip
Im the very first thing to be found on your lip
Though not known to the river Im found in its flow
Unseen in the breezes Im still in their blow
Not felt in the fire, I'm part of the coal
And am aye the last thing that is found in the bowl.
When you look to your right though of me you're bereft
I'm the very first thing that you meet on your left
I always am heard in the toll of the bell
And am lying like truth at the end of a well.
Though absent when dinner & breakfast you munch
You'll certainly own that Im present at lunch.
Yes, yes I am never away from your meals
You have me alike in soles salmon and eels.
In mutton beef chickens although I am missed
Yet in lamb & in fowls & in veal I exist
Is a lady without me — dont deign to accost her
You'll find her a bold begging letter impostor
I'm twice in your pillow though not in your bed
Say gentles my name for my riddle is read.

                                Amelia Jane.

I want this to be tried upon a young person of average intellect.

\*   \*   \*

200.          TO MRS. CARMICHAEL-SMYTH
                        APRIL 1841

Hitherto unpublished. *Endorsed:* 15. April. 1841.

My ⟨deares⟩t Mammy. G M was writing a letter t'other day
and I suppose told you of my news: how Isabella is no longer an
inmate of Ivry house but at this minute seated very comfortably by
my side wonderfully better I think for her removal. She talks
twice as much interests herself ⟨. . .⟩ [29]

never did at Ivry. I thank God that I took her away as I did — it
was only with the notion of carrying her to dinner and back again,
but when at dinner she said she w^d like to go to the play, and so here
she has been for a week. In a few days she & I shall go to sleep at
M^rs Spencer's most probably who will take charge of the young
woman during the day at the rate of 300 francs a month. She is to
keep a servant out of this, and I don't think could be expected to
do it for less.

But the little woman put on such a pitiful look when I talked of
sending her away from me: & is so happy and so really affectionate
with me, that leave her I will not, it w^d be a sin to throw away the
chance of good I may do her and plunge her in ⟨. . .⟩ [30]

novel again: though I have very much cooled on it
and lost the best part of six weeks work w^h consisted in reading
more than in writing; all the reading & ardor I shall have to get
up again: Well, never mind, so long as the little woman gets round
again. What wonderful luck I have had sure enough, in having
you and GM, & dear old Polly's purse to go to when my own was
dry, and a shelter for my little ones. Indeed I tremble to think
how matters *might* have been without you. However this is sentiment with a vengeance. M^r Rothschild might want a shilling if the
bank broke, or the Duke of Devonshire be begging for dinner if

[29] About twenty words have here been cut from the letter.
[30] About thirty words have here been cut from the letter.

there were a revolution, and though my chances of starvation are a great deal nearer, yet a gentleman has no right to disquiet himself upon such speculations as these.

Isabella & I walk out a good deal, and I spend hours of my time reading novels: very profitable isn't it. Good old Stevens has pulled a tooth out of her jaw as big as an ink-bottle, and sundry others are to follow she does not so much as cry O; though the pain must be terrific. You should hear me shout & yell for a twentieth part of the pain.

What shall I tell you? Yesterday going to a shop for a novel a French shop for an English novel, I talked for a long time with the woman in as good French as her own I believe, but when I said that I wanted an English novel: she said 'Ah, Monsieur can not read French' (I had nearly spoiled the joke) ⟨but⟩ its not a very good one. Truly you should have heard the prim patronizing way in w^h the woman made the blunder. To day at the pastrycook's we heard an Englishman say that he for his part hang him would never go in a French vessel, curse them they all go to the bottom ⟨. . .⟩ [31]

John Bull prejudices think how they are shared by millions of our countrymen, who mistake their insolence and conceit for patriotism. When will we get to the end of this humbug, and be simple and charitable? — Stop. I will go instantly and write at the very least a guinea's worth of disquisition upon the above two characters: making wholesome remarks for both nations. [32]

I dont know how many days ago the above was written but thank God my news are still good: and my dear little woman continues to get on. I don't mean to say that she is much better to day than yesterday: but she is evidently happy ⟨. . .⟩ [33]

Yesterday she had Anny for 1/2 an hour on her knee, telling her

[31] About twenty words have here been cut from the letter.
[32] See "On Men and Pictures" (*Works*, XIII, especially pp. 376–379), which appeared in *Fraser's Magazine* for July. Thackeray must have received a good deal more than a guinea for his remarks.
[33] About twenty-five words have here been cut from the letter.

a story: she could not remember it all: but it was a satisfaction to me to see this weakness and that she felt she was at fault: — We will have her back again please God — and it is an inexpressible happiness to me to have her away from that lonely place, and to see her even as she is.

My dearest Mammy's letter has just come in, & written in low spirits that she must not feel: for indeed now that I have my wife back I forget all about former discomforts. If she had stopped for a century at that place she would never have been well. It was horrid to see wild fierce women rambling about in the garden: and when I saw the difference between Pussy & them I felt how wrong it was to keep her in such company.

The Spencer arrangement has not come off, but Isabella passes the day there 5 times a week, and I fetch her home in the evening, and she does not give the least trouble. We have had only 1 stubborn fit in the fortnight, and very little rambling — not of the idée fixe kind but of a loose gentle harmless nature. I have had a talk with Skiers who was very wise: & with Crowe's german Doctor very wise too, who recommended moral treatment: medicines that would open her bowels.

## 201.          TO MAJOR CARMICHAEL-SMYTH
### 25 APRIL 1841

*Address:* Major Carmichael Smyth. | Poste Restante | Florence | Italie. Hitherto unpublished.

My dear Father. The enclosed scrap is for Mother: and I really think the project mentioned in it of compounding with the Con. creditors [34] in that would be of the greatest good — to me at least: and to dear Mother too whose heart is twisted round those little children of mine and who will never be happy till she has them under her wing. When Great Coram S$^t$ lease is out, we ought [to] take a bigger house with a garden for the Infantry: and there is no reason why we should not be all decently happy. My poor little

[34] See above, No. 164.

woman will not be thoroughly restored to me, for long long months to come: but her affections are now somewhat awakened; — it w$^d$ be a sin to crush them again: in an Asylum, or even to take from her her fair chance of recovering them by placing her away from us.

As for the Constitutional or for any other definitive arrangement there is no hurry in course. Here I am in clover, happier than I have been for many months back with the poor little woman mending, ⟨and⟩ perfectly quiet, and every now & then affectionate: and have done enough work to keep my hand off the Devil's tail for some time to come: now I can get back to the novel; it will be a long affair but can't be better done anywhere than here. When it's done: will be plenty of time to go to Ireland. Meanwhile I hope you and Mammy, and my Uncle and Aunt Charles will have your pleasure, and specially that M$^{rs}$ Smyth the elder won't take on, and fancy her poor dear interesting son too unhappy.

God bless you all. I dont know the day of the month but it is a Sunday, and M$^{rs}$ Thack & I are going to have a walk with this scrap to the Magdalen Church & post office for w$^h$ we are just in time so no more from your affectionate Son

W M T.

On reflection it is the 25$^{th}$

If you see the Colonel [35] please thank him for a double letter containing nothing. Also has come a very pathetic one from his serv$^t$ hoping for the return of his dear Colonel: but it is dated in December last. Ashurst's [36] letter is 10 April.

[35] Colonel Shawe.
[36] William Henry Ashurst of Ashurst and Son, 137 Cheapside (*Post Office London Directory*, 1847), the Major's solicitor.

202.                         TO MRS. PROCTER
                           28 MAY–5 JUNE 1841

Published in part *Biographical Introductions*, V, xv-xviii. My text is taken
from a transcript given Lady Ritchie by George Murray Smith.

                              Avenue St Marie. Fbg du Roule,
                                28 May 1841. — that is 5 June.
My dear Mrs Procter,

Please when you write not to give me any accounts whatever of
any gaieties in which you indulge, or any sort of happiness falling
to the share of you or anyone else. But if anybody meets with an
accident, is arrested, ruined, has a wife run away with, if Chorley
falls ill and is marked with the small pox, do be so kind as to write
me off word immediately, and I will pay the post cheerfully. The
only welcome intelligence in your letter is that the Austins have
lost a good deal of money, and Procter £1,100. Ah, say I, he takes
guinea stalls and buys water-colours, does he? Well, well, we shall
have him down as one of us soon: in the slough of despair —
Despair, Madam, is the word — Byronish — I hate mankind, and
wear my shirt collars turned down.

Now absurd as this seems on the part of a man naturally, I believe, kind-hearted: there is upon my word and honour a kind of
truth in it. When I hear of bad luck happening to people, I am
glad, that's the fact, and I am sure that the generosity or kindness
with which one endeavours sometimes to relieve a man that has
fallen into misfortune is often the result of one's personal good
spirits and gratification at the contrast between the sufferer and
one's self.

Is not that a turning down of shirt collars with a vengeance?
and a pretty return for what I know is sincere sympathy and good
will on your part? But let me declare solemnly and with my hand
on my waistcoat (it is a great deal too hot to wear one by the way,
so let us say at once, like Knowles, 'on the hearrrt') that I don't
mean to accuse the bo sex of any unworthy feeling of the sort. You
are not selfish like us brutes, but always kind and feeling for poor

fellows in the days of their ill-luck. As a proof, did not two old ladies [37] toil up to this distant quarter the other day, two old ladies, one of them lame, and the thermometer at 85 for both of them, out of sheer kindness and pity for my situation? Men will not perform any such sacrifices — only one has called upon me in the eight months we have been here: and he came for some purpose of his own. As for my misfortunes they are not so great as they seem: no man can afford to be miserable for nine months together at the illness of a person ever so dear to him. We get indifferent that's certain, but if bound to remain with the sick person constantly, profoundly ennuyé. For about six weeks I was my wife's sole attendant, and almost broke down under the slavery: — well, a woman whom I have hired to do that work, does it with the utmost cheerfulness for ten francs a week, and never thinks about being miserable at all.

My wife will get well, I hope and believe; perhaps not for a year, perhaps in a month. There is nothing the matter with her except perfect indifference, silence and sluggishness. She cares for nothing, except for me a little, her general health has greatly improved: her ideas are quite distinct when she chooses to wake from her lethargy. She is not unhappy and looks fresh, smiling and about sixteen years old. To-day is her little baby's birthday. She kissed the child when I told her of the circumstance, but does not care for it.

You have seen a great deal more of Madame Rachel [38] in a week than I have, often as I have been here, the only time I ever saw her was once with Milnes in an atrocious piece called Marie Stuart: she made the most however of that unfortunate but deservedly decapitated sovereign. This week, for the first time these six months, I determined to try and amuse myself at the play, and paid twenty-five sous like a man to the pit, to see Mademoiselle Déjazet.

[37] The Miss Hamertons.
[38] Elisa Félix (1821–1858), called Rachel, the celebrated tragic actress. She had made her début at the Théâtre Français in 1838 (she had appeared in another Parisian theater the year before), and she first appeared in *Marie Stuart*, a French adaptation of Schiller's tragedy, on December 22, 1840.

This young creature who is neither so innocent nor so good looking as Vestris,[39] but on the other hand incomparably older and
cleverer, chose to act the part of a young girl of sixteen, in a little
muslin frock and pinafore, with trousers and long braided hair like
the Misses Kenwigs; [40] when this hideous leering grinning withered
old painted simpering wretch came forward, do you know I was
seized with such a qualm as to shout out: "Why — she is too ugly,"
and I was obliged to stride over 10,000 people in a most crowded
pit in order to get rid of the sight of her. Is it that one is growing
moral? par hazard in one's declining years, or only more difficult?
There were hundreds of people in the house perfectly satisfied and
charmed: nay, many young wicked fellows casting I have no doubt
eyes of fire towards this hideous old grinning wretch. Ah, happy
days of youth! I once knew a man who was in love with Mrs
Vedy [41] that female Methusalem, or let one say at once that
Methusalemess, who leads the festive dance at Covent Garden.

*[sketch]*

What delights me beyond measure is the Controversy between
Macready and Heraud [42] in the Monthly Magazine. It is a wonderful magazine: and the editor a man of a noble madness and
dullness.

Thank you about Peter Priggins.[43] O, but a man has a good
lesson sometimes for his naughty pride and vanity. I read the book
the other day and I declare was quite awe-stricken by the immense
vulgarity of it. I know I am not very genteel [44] — indeed Fraser's
head shopman says: "Mr T. is a man of talent but everything he

[39] Though the scandalous *Memoirs of Mme. Vestris* (1826; 1839) are un-
trustworthy, the lady was neither innocent nor particularly handsome. Both
she and Mlle. Déjazet were born in 1797.
[40] See chapter 14 of *Nicholas Nickleby*.
[41] A sketch by Thackeray of Mrs. Vedy ten years earlier is reproduced in
Volume I (Appendix II).
[42] John Abraham Heraud (1799–1887), editor of *The New Monthly
Magazine* between 1839 and 1842.
[43] Theodore Hook's *Peter Priggins, The College Scout*, 3 vols., London,
1841 (but the novel is really by J. T. J. Hewlett).
[44] The transcript reads *jointed*.

does is so atrociously vulgar" — very good, but is it as vulgar as
Peter Priggins? I declare I don't think so, — I fancy I could not
be if I tried: from lack of a great quality that Peter has, like his
Editor, Theodore Hook, of admiring certain things that are essentially mean and low. There is one sentiment in Priggins that I
can't express sufficient admiration of. It is said of some young
fellow who has been drunk all night and all morning and all the
day before (indeed the book is filled from beginning to end with
drunkenness) — as for Tom, says Peter, "GOOD beer *always*
made him sober." [45] Do you see the immensity of the sentiment?
I never can hope to think about beer in that way, that awful, respectful way. BEER, what an immense word, what a grand coarseness about it! Ah, but I should like to drink some — some Hodson's
Pale Ale, in neat little frisky bottles, uncorked by a neat-handed
Phillis [46] in a sunshiny parlour, where I have had before this some
of the pleasantest, gayest, comfortablest dinners in the world. The
parlour I mean belongs to a Gothic Cottage near the Roman Catholic Chapel in the Regent's Park, and the master of the house often
goes to sleep after dinner. Well, I am really sorry now that he
has lost his money: having arrived at good humour by writing six
pages of nonsense, and thinking about all the kindness and pleasure
I have had from you. (I find I have been writing on a torn half
sheet of paper.) Will you pardon me for taking such liberties as
writing on torn smoke-smelling paper, and not addressing you in a
more respectuous and well-bred way? A genteeler soul would
never have dared to allude to Hodson's ale, in writing a letter to a
lady: at the very most I know Chorley would not have hinted at
anything beyond Maraschino, or allowed that he cared for aught
except a pleasant conversation and a dish of green tea. [47]

I have to ask another pardon too for introducing my friend
O'Donnel to you. He is one of the best friends I have, but a man
extremely uncouth and matter-of-factish, and going to your house I

[45] "Let him be drunk as he will," Mr. Wydeawake remarks of Tripes (*Peter
Priggins*, II, 95), "a jug of *good* beer always sobers him."
[46] Milton, "L'Allegro," l. 86.
[47] This joke had its origin in Chorley's review of *The Paris Sketch Book*.
See above, No. 170.

think that both you and he will feel that he is out of place, so indeed I had no business to take such a liberty as to give him credentials. But he heard me discoursing about the pleasantness of your hospitality and asked me for a letter, as he is going to be quite alone in London. You won't like him, and I knew it when I wrote, but did not dare say so to him, and so committed upon you who have no means of resisting or resenting a still greater *bévue*. He has a thousand of the very best qualities but not the most necessary one of being pleasant. Why had I not the sense to say "No" to him at once? Alfred Tennyson, if he can't make you like him, will make you admire him, — he seems to me to have the cachet of a great man. His conversation is often delightful, I think, full of breadth manliness and humour: he reads all sorts of things, swallows them and digests them like a great poetical boa-constrictor as he is. Now I hope, Mrs. Procter, you will recollect that if your humble servant sneers at small geniuses, he has on the contrary a huge respect for big ones, or those he fancies to be such. Perhaps it is Alfred Tennyson's great big yellow face and growling voice that has had an impression on me. Manliness and simplicity of manner go a great way with me, I fancy: there is a man here for instance whom on the strength of a great pair of eyebrows and a good manner, and a dexterous silence, I have persisted in considering as a man of genius, or near it, for these ten years past, and am only and with a great deal of pains beginning to be undeceived.

Was ever such a dirty piece of paper seen, or such a stupid letter full of nonsensical egotism? — the fact is for the dingy state of the paper: I have only got a little table three feet by two, and as there are a bundle of manuscripts, a bottle of ink that will upset, a paint box and water, several dry lumps of bread for rubbing out with, portfolios, drawings, segars, sealing wax, the whole of my *ménage*, and so sure as this letter is discontinued for a moment, so sure does it tumble into a puddle of ink, or another of water, or into a heap of ashes. Well, I have not the courage to clear the table, nor indeed to do anything else, for I have had ten months of wretchedness, and truth to tell am quite beaten down. I don't know when I shall come round again — not until I get a holiday and that mayn't

be for months to come: my father and mother being away in Italy
and who knows when they will come back.  Meanwhile I can't
work, nor write even amusing letters, nor talk of anything else but
myself which is bearable sometimes when Ego is in very good
health and spirits, but odious beyond measure when he has only to
entertain you with his woes.

Yesterday I had a delightful walk with a painter from ⟨. . .⟩ [48]
to Saint Germain, through charming smiling countries that seem
to be hundreds of leagues away from cities: — psha — this sentence was begun with a laudable intent of relieving you from the
wearisome complaints of the last paragraphs but it is in vain.  Allow
me then, dear Mrs. Procter, to shut up the scrawl altogether, and
to give a loose to dulness in privacy — it can't be enjoyed properly
in company.  In spite of which I am always yours and Procter's,

Most truly,

W. M. T.

203.    TO RICHARD MONCKTON MILNES
10 JULY 1841 [49]

My text is taken from Reid's *Life of Lord Houghton*, I, 263.

Saturday, 10th July, 1841.
Stockton-on-Tees.

My dear R. M. M., — You have inflicted upon me the most

[48] At this point the original is torn.
[49] This letter was written from South Durham, where Thackeray was visiting John Bowes Bowes.  With the aid of Thackeray's "Notes on the North
What-d'ye-Callem Election.  Being the Personal Narrative of Napoleon Put-
nam Wiggins, of Passimaquoddy" (*Fraser's Magazine*, September and October,
1841, pp. 352–358 and 413–427) it is possible to trace his movements on this
excursion almost from day to day.  The curious style of these travel notes is
explained by the fact that Thackeray used them as a vehicle for the burlesque
of Nathaniel P. Willis which he had for some time been planning.  See above,
No. 148.
Bowes had invited his friend to visit him at his country seat during the
General Election of 1841.  Thackeray accordingly set out from London for
the north country one day late in June.  He arrived in Darlington ("Stuffing-

cruel blow possible; [50] for I had hoped to come to you on Monday, staying Tuesday, and be-offing Wednesday; for I must have two days in London, and be back in Paris on Sunday. I shall look out for you Monday at the Grand Jury room at York, and regret heartily that I am not allowed to have a couple of days' quiet talk with you in your paternal groves, after the cursed racket of this infernal election. I shall not of course conceal from you that the Tories in this Division have met with a heavy blow and great discouragement [51] . . . If I do not call you by your right address on the cover, it is because you persist in addressing me as John, whereas my name is

William Thackeray.

---

ton" in his "Notes") from York on the afternoon of Friday, June 25, and proceeded to Streatlam Castle ("Britton Hall") that evening. There he remained with Bowes ("Francis Britton") until July 13, enjoying the pleasures of life on a great estate. He was present on Tuesday, July 6, at Bowes's nomination to parliament by his friend Mr. Witham ("Mr. Hartington"). Bowes was a Whig ("green and white") and had as his colleague Lord Harry Vane (1803–1891), later (1864) fourth Duke of Cleveland, whom Thackeray calls "Lord George Cramley." The only Conservative ("pink") candidate was Mr. Farrer ("Mr. Bouncer"). The poll was set for Friday and Saturday, July 9 and 10, and on these days Thackeray visited with his friend the principal towns of South Durham, among them Hartlepool ("Cockleton"), Darlington, and Stockton-on-Tees (*Times*, July 8). Both the Whig nominees were returned.

[50] Milnes had written to defer Thackeray's visit to Fryston Hall in Yorkshire, his father's country seat, because he had been called unexpectedly to York to serve on the Grand Jury. Thackeray found it possible to prolong his stay in England and spent the week following July 13 at Fryston. He travelled there from York with William Frederick Pollock (1815–1888), later (1870) second Baronet, who writes: "As we walked up on a fine summer afternoon to the then front of the house, Milnes and his father were standing at the door, the latter in a dressing-gown and smoking a cigar. He at once, after a hospitable greeting, gave one to each of us, and added, 'You may smoke anywhere in this house — in your bedrooms, if you please — and Mrs. Milnes does not mind it in her drawing-room. Only you must not smoke in Richard's room, for he doesn't like it.' Thackeray turned to Milnes and said, 'What a father is thrown away upon you!' When we were saying good-bye at the end of our visit, Thackeray thanked Mr. Milnes for the pleasure it had given him, and said, 'Your house, sir, combines the freedom of the tavern with the elegance of the chateau.' " (*Personal Remembrances*, I, 177)

[51] Milnes was a conservative.

On second thought I won't call you Thomas Milnes, Esq., as I intended, lest mistakes should arise, and you should be deprived of this letter.

204.                 TO JAMES FRASER
                        24 JULY 1841

*Address:* James Fraser Esq^re | Streatly. | by Reading. *Postmarks:* 24 JY 1841, READING JY 25 1841. Hitherto unpublished.

Saturday. July something. 1841.
My dear Fraser

Your invitation was very kind, and I should have been delighted to accept it but my time is run out; and I am bound to be back with my poor wife on Wednesday at Paris. I sh^d have been glad to talk both gossip & business with you.

The first part of the business is this. I think on the 1^st August the magazine will owe me some 17 or 18 £ will you let me know how much: I want to make up £17 " 10. for my landlord whose rent was due 1 July.

Next. I have in my trip to the country, found materials (rather a character) for a story, that I'm sure must be amusing.[52] I want to write & illustrate it, and as you see how Harry Lorrequer succeeds both in the Dublin Magazine & out of it,[53] why should not my story of BARRY-LYNN (or by what name so ever it may be called) answer in as well as out of Regina. Suppose for instance you were to give a sheet & a half per month that sheet and a half could be stretched into two sheets for the shilling number by transposing (or whatever you call it) the type: and the book would thus make a handsome saleable volume at the end of the year. My subject I am sure is a good one, and I have made a vow to chasten and otherwise popularize my style. Thus I could have 20 guineas a month from you and a farther chance of profit from the sale of

[52] *The Memoirs of Barry Lyndon.* See *Memoranda,* John Bowes Bowes.
[53] Charles Lever's *Confessions of Harry Lorrequer* (1839) and *Charles O'Malley* (1841) were both originally published in *The Dublin University Magazine.*

the single numbers. Were we to come to a bargain I would not of course begin until 3 numbers of the tale were in hand: with the plates &c.

This is all the business I have to talk to you about: You see that 12 guineas a sheet is small pay for prime stuff: at least without a chance of anything more; and this more we might both of us make I should hope without much fear. Think over this please. it certainly seems to me between you & me that there is as much stuff in M⁚ Titmarsh as in almost the best of the people now writing comicalities, and why shouldn't he turn out successful? — I mean, pecuniarily so.

Let me have a line at Paris if you like my plan or if you have any other plan, or if you can manage to raise my contribution in some way to a price wʰ a man likes to work for: for it is but human nature as you know when Blackwood & Bentley are offering big prices to be hankering after Blackwood & Bentley.

Enough. I was very glad indeed to see your favorable account of yourself. I hope you will continue to progress,[54] and that once more we shall have some meetings in the little parlor where I promise & vow to act decently.

I shall have a goodish paper describing what I saw at the Elections [55] ready for you by 10 August at latest. 15 pages or so. — in a new & taking way.

> Goodbye dear Fraser, always yours gratefully.
> W M T.

I shall be in town for Parliament — in a month.


205.                    DIARY
          27 JULY–11 AUGUST 1841

Hitherto unpublished.

Oh Lord God — there is not one of the sorrows or disappointments of my life, that as I fancy I cannot trace to some error crime

---

[54] Fraser died in October.
[55] See above, No. 203.

or weakness of my disposition. Strengthen me then with your help, to maintain my good resolutions — not to yield to lust or sloth that beset me: or at least to combat with them & overcome them sometimes.

Above all O Gracious Father, please to have mercy upon those whose well-being depends upon me. O empower me to give them good and honest example: keep them out of misfortunes w^h result from my fault: and towards them enable me to discharge the private duties of life — to be interested in their ways & amusements, to be cheerful & constant at home: frugal & orderly if possible. O give me your help strenuously to work out the vices of character w^h have born such bitter fruit already:

July 27. Arrived this morng from Boulogne outside very crowded & uncomfortable. Found the wife very glad to see me, and the dear little ones very well & happy. Thank God for the kindness of those who have stood in such good stead by them. Mother's letter about Graeffenberg [56] came w^h I answered, and after going in quest of diligence fares &c found a hydropathic physician who spoke very well indeed ab^t Isabella's case. She passed the evening at the Spencer's whither I went in search of her, after paying a visit to our friends upstairs. My heart feels very humble & thankful for God's kindness towards these beautiful children, and I do humbly pray that I may be kept in a mood for seriously considering & trying to act up to my duty. How much would my powers of mind alone gain from something like regularity, & how determinedly ought I to strive to win it!

July 28. My wife I fancy a little better — certainly better — very little feeling, but a little memory and justness of speech — Drew all the morning or else read Marriotts Joseph Rushbrook [57] a good natured manly sort of book — walked with I to the Rue de Londres & back again, by the Parc of Monsieaux that looks green & pretty, & on the plain of Menceaux, hearing the steam-engines.

After dinner talked to her, and read article on Bowes' election —

[56] A village in Silesia, where a hydrotherapic sanatorium was established in 1838.
[57] Captain Marryat's *Joseph Rushbrook or the Poacher* (1841).

found in my portfolio an article written 2 months ago, of w^h the existence was completely forgotten, & so saw more & more the utility of keeping some memorandum. Wrote till 12. and thought of a good plan for some weekly-paper articles — skits on newspaper paragraphs for the week. Mem. remember Punch's Parliament.[58] The children all day delightful. O God, O God give me strength to do my duty

Thursday 29. Did nothing all day until 3 except try to make a burlesque sonnet. Rec^d D^r Reich & a gentleman who came about Eliza's character. Anny went with M^rs Spencer to see the fête. At 2 went to read the papers, and at 3 by the railroad to S^t Germains where the good Crowes had a kind dinner for us. Read Mathilde,[59] the extreme fashionableness of w^h will form a good subject for imitation. In the Gazette des Tribunaux an excellent acc^t of a man converted from Protestantism rec^d with open arms by all sorts of monk-houses and robbing each. O'D [60] at S^t Germains much better than in London — came back with him at 10/11 — the lamps of the Arc d'Etoile seen flaring bright most part of the way.

August 6. The first two or three of these days past in writing or idling of a morning, & carousing of an evening with Stevens. More letters from my mother relative to the Sudopathic plan: and I have had a couple of interviews with D^r Weincke a clever personable man, but whose system is frightfully complicated. We began it on Thursday morning my wife sweating for 4 hours. The same to day, and baths and walks afterwards occupying the greater part of the day. On Tuesday she was pretty well, the next day exceedingly violent so much so that I was compelled to remain with her from then until now.

Read in the paper the news of M^rs Blechynden's death. It is the sorest point I have on my conscience never to have taken notice of her.

---

[58] Possibly an idea for a contribution to *Punch*, the first number of which had appeared on July 17. See below, No. 219.

[59] A novel by Eugène Sue, first published in 1841.

[60] O'Donnell.

Read a novel of Emile Souvestre: [61] no good except in the beginning, and sent off to day Friday the article on the S. D. Election. The Morning Post very flattering to Men & Coats.[62]

11. My mother's letters have at last had their effect and we are now bound for Germany. These days have been spent in passport-hunting & other such preparations: pray Heaven that the treatment may be beneficial.

After her violence my wife is considerably better. Looked over in these days the letters from Belgium that I had written last year at this time [63] — & found as usual, that I had clean forgotten them. They came upon me quite as strange compositions, and seemed clever and amusing. Such a complete want of memory have I, that even an election squib written at Bowes's had passed clean out of my mind. The more necessity then for keeping a journal of all doings, writings, & readings.

Is it necessary to remember that yesterday 9 I & Jim Thackeray [64] dined together, and had some admirable claret & champagne.

Remember to make the ballad about Richard II.[65] & that of the Jewish wife.

[61] The most recent book by this prolific novelist (1806–1854) was *Mémoires d'un sans-culotte bas-breton* (1841).

[62] An article by Thackeray in *Fraser's Magazine* for August, 208–217.

[63] See above, No. 177.

[64] Thomas James Thackeray.

[65] These notes would appear to concern *Rebecca and Rowena*, which Thackeray did not write for some years. Richard II figures in this Christmas book, and Rebecca might be vaguely described as a Jewish wife, though she becomes a Christian before her wedding in Thackeray's tale.

206.                    TO MRS. RITCHIE
                        19 AUGUST 1841

*Address:* M^rs Ritchie | Albany Street | Regent's Park.  Published in part, *Some Family Letters of W. M. Thackeray,* pp. 21–23.  *Endorsed:* W^m Thackeray 19 Aug 1841.

Thursday. 19 August.

My dear Aunt.

You will see by this address [66] to what an out of the way place I have brought my poor little patient.  It is however one of the most beautiful places in the world, a fine air, and a kind of genteel hospital set up for the cure of almost all complaints by means of sweating & cold water.  Gouts & rheumatisms & other inflamatory ills go off here as if by magic.  People begin at four o'clock in the morning to be wrapped up in blankets, where they lie & melt for four hours, then come shower-baths, plunging baths, hip-baths, all sorts of water taken within & without, and at the end of a certain number of months: they rise up & walk.  I have a strong hope that under this strange regimen my dear little patient will recover her reason.  My mother is here whose presence is the greatest possible comfort to me, and with her for a short time my cousin with her husband Charles Smyth.  They are 2 of the noblest people God ever made: and are as generous as I ever knew people — they have given me 500 £, w^h with 500 £ more that just falls into me through the death of poor M^rs Blechynden, puts me out of the reach of fortune for some years to come, and removes the horrible care and fear of want w^h has been hanging over me in the past year since my wife's affliction.

When I wrote to you about money matters last September, you may remember I said I never should have applied to M^r Ritchie, except at the last extremity, and here thank God that extremity is removed, and with it, not the least painful of the many painful necessities that have oppressed me in this unhappy year: so that now

---

[66] Thackeray's address does not appear in the letter.  He was writing from a sanatorium located in the former Convent of Marienburg, built in 1738, near Boppard on the Rhine.

at any rate I shall be able when I come to London, not to sneak away from the dearest friends I have in it. God bless them all. What a deal of care has this generosity of Mary Smyth's removed from me!

My uncle Charles Thackeray [67] wrote me from Calcutta, begging me to continue if possible the annuity M$^{rs}$ Blechynden had. I shall make arrangement; but it is not fair I think that the daughter sh$^d$ have as much as was allotted for the support of daughter & mother, and I hope my Aunt Halliday will help in supporting her brothers grandchild. She is rich I believe, at least has a handsome income — and no one at any rate can say as much for me.

My dear little wife is just stepped out of half an hour's ice-cold hip bath, and is smiling and looking very comfortable, *warm* & sensible. She says I am to remember her most kindly to you, and sends her love to Charlotte & Jane — and now as it's time to take her half an hour's brisk walk w$^h$ always follows the bath, I shall shut this letter up, and am always dear Aunt, yours most affectionately

W M Thackeray.

207.      TO EDWARD FITZGERALD
13 SEPTEMBER–OCTOBER 1841 [68]

*Address:* (Edw)ard Fitz-Gerald Esq$^r$ | 39 Portland Place | LONDON. Hitherto unpublished.

Heidelberg. October something. 1841.

My dear Edward I wonder whether I shall ever be able to fill this enormous sheet of paper. You must know it has just been brought to me by a fat landlord in a comical cap, along with a pint of very sour wine, and if I have made his eyebrows very queer, it

---

[67] A Calcutta barrister (1794–1846?), *Genealogy* (61), who had been in India since 1823. Mrs. Bayne (*Memorials*, p. 501) learned from Mrs. Ritchie that "he was full of wit and talent, handsome and agreeable, and devoted to his father whom he nursed in a dangerous illness. He fell a victim to the demon of drink, then so fashionable in India."

[68] This letter is reproduced in facsimile as the frontispiece to this volume.

is not because I wish to persist in that old wicked trick of making queer eyebrows but because nature has given him such a pair, and how can I help it? I wonder where my dear old Edward is at this writing — it's half a year nearly since I heard from you. I am writing in an arbour of an inn at Boppart on the Rhine — where I have been for a month with my poor little woman, under the care of a famous water-doctor in these parts, who cures everything by means of sweating, & bathing. At five o'clock in the morning M$^{rs}$ Thack begins to sweat in blankets, at eight they pour buckets of water over her, at twelve she takes an enormous douche for five minutes, at five sweating again, and more buckets of ice-cold water. Well, she has been doing this for a month and the upshot is that she is so extraordinarily better, that I do begin to think we are at last to have her well. She *is* in fact all but well, and at last, thank God for it, laughs talks and is happy. It is this day year [69] that her malady declared itself first: and though she is not yet quite like other people, yet when I remember how bad she has been, and was but a month ago, my dear old fellow I am ready to jump for joy. The first days she would not stand the immense sluicing of the water-pipe, and I was obliged to go in with her. It would have made a fine picture — M$^{rs}$ Thack in the condition of our first parins, before they took to eating apples, and the great Titmarsh with nothing on but a petticoat lent him by his mother, and far too scanty to cover that immense posterior protuberance with w$^{h}$ nature has furnished him. I'm the contrary of a cherubim that's the fact. This is rare witty stuff to write isn't it? Well I have nothing else to say — and am really with all the year's sufferings quite used up. When my wife is well she must set to work & take care of me I think. My father & mother are here, and the latter as you may fancy an immense comfort to me. God bless the dear old tender loving soul — it's worth while to be unhappy for a time — to find how such admirable creatures tend and suffer with one. The Governor though by Heaven's blessing perfectly well, nevertheless for the love of science gets up every morning at four, sweats for 4 hours, douches, forswears wine at dinner, douches again, and con-

[69] September 13. See above, No. 182.

cludes the day's amusements by sitting for nearly an hour in a tub of icy-cold water. In the last twenty years he has been successively a convert to Abernethy's blue-pills, of w<sup>h</sup> he swallowed pounds — to Morison's ditto — w<sup>h</sup> he flung in by spoonsfuls to S<sup>r</sup> John Long to whom he paid 100 guineas for rubbing an immense sore on & then off his back, to Homeopathy w<sup>h</sup> put the nose of all other systems of medicine out of joint, and finally to Hydrosudopathy — agst w<sup>h</sup> dont let me say a word. It has been the means of setting my dear little wife in her senses again.

Here comes the landlord with his eyebrows, and his two daughters to take their supper in the arbour — I wish that my Ned, were here in his stead reposing his head, underneath the grape vine; and in spite of the fleas (most [70] annoying are these) here taking his ease, on the Banks of the Rhine, Here are gardens and bowers, here are churches & towers, w<sup>h</sup> I copy for hours, in a sketchbook so fine — thick orchards one sees, & Plantations of Peas, but be hanged to the fleas on the Banks of the Rhine. You can't though you try, see a cloud in the sky, but only can spy the sun in his shine, or the moon through the trees, like a round Cheshire cheese, illumines the fleas on the Banks of the Rhine. Ah here could I spend, a time without end, by the side of my friend that best friend of mine.

I forget what it was that stopped the impromptu — I couldn't get on with it most likely, and it was written in grand summer weather near a month ago. Since then I haven't been fit to write: my wife not so well: quite as reasonable but excessively violent & passionate w<sup>h</sup> the Doctors say is a good sign. Well it worked upon me very much, & a week ago I was obliged to go away, thinking that a tour might do me good, but no such thing: I am now on the tour, as miserable as the deuce and if I write to you it's because I want to take refuge from cursed loneliness & low spirits Thanks for your letter my dear old man, the sight of your hand writing is always a comfort to me — My God, how I wish I had you to be with me. Will you go to Italy with me & my wife this winter? If

---

[70] Thackeray here begins a new page, at the top of which he writes: "Continuation of the Impromptyou)".

you will, I'll go: if not I must go back to Paris, and shall set upon a
novel [71] of w.ᶜʰ I have an idea: a famous good plan if I can but keep
my tail sufficiently up: but I have no amusement at Paris, nobody
to talk to, and home, I am very ashamed to confess bores me.
There is that stupid old Governor of mine: we are always on the
point of quarreling, though we never do. He is a worthy man however, & the dear old Mother an angel of a woman.

I have written the first act of — a tragedy,[72] of all things in the
world: and in blank verse too for Macready ⟨to⟩ spout. I wish I
might put it in prose the subject is very good. ⟨. . .⟩ [73]

Ah what a pleasure it would be to have you & old Morton, and
jaw about the Fine Arts. I wanted to go to Munich, and see the
modern Germans, for the purpose of exposing them; but haven't
the heart, & am just going back again, to the poor little wife. If
you won't come to Italy will you come to Paris for the winter? I
have another long weary winter before me. Pish. Psha. Fiddle-
deedee & nonsense. I've made much improvement in sketching:
& have done 1 or 2 walnut trees to admiration — it's nothing but
practice, and care. This is the very last model of my favorite German student He has adopted a little of the French fashions of late
as I see with pain. I'm quite of your opinion about Farquhar, he's
the only fellow among them. ⟨He was⟩ something more than a
mere comic tradesman: and has a grand drunken diabolical fire in
him.

What I have seen of the German illuminated school [74] is donkey-
ism — poor *precieuse* stuff. with a sickening sanctified air. Here's
the paper filled up, & it still wants 1/2 an hour of the coach. What
shall I say? — Yes — I saw Fanny Buttler,[75] & Adelaide K at Frankfurt A. looking very well: but Fanny I did not even know, she was
changed so — as dirty as a housemaid, and in a housemaid's cos-

[71] *Barry Lyndon.*
[72] The manuscript of this unpublished tragedy has not been preserved.
[73] About six lines have here been cut away.
[74] The "pre-Raphaelite" painters of Germany, led by J. F. Overbeck (1789–1869) and Peter von Cornelius (1783–1867).
[75] Mrs. Pierce Butler, better known as Fanny Kemble, accompanied by her sister Adelaide.

tume. She won't forgive me for not knowing her, & would hardly speak to me in consquints. Ah Yellowplush! where are the days when you lived & laughed. If I don't mind I shall be setting up for an unacknowledged genius, & turn as morbid as Bulwer. God bless you.

Direct if within a fortnight to Marienberg. Boppart. Rhine.

208.　　　　　　TO MRS. RITCHIE
　　　　　　15 OCTOBER 1841

*Address:* M<sup>rs</sup> Ritchie | Boulogne Sur Mer. | France. *Postmarks:* BOPPARD 15, BOULOGNE 19 OCT. 1841. Hitherto unpublished.

＊　　＊　　＊

little scandal?

Johnny [76] is to have a cadetship M<sup>r</sup> Jaffray tells me: [77] it will cost your tender heart to part from him: but what a fine provision! Four years ago the⟨re was a⟩ little fellow with us, that was brought up by the charity of his fri⟨ends⟩ and his mother a Major's widow — a Major in the guards was out in a sort of bettermost service — the little man got a cadetship 2 years back, and has just sent home a handsome sum out of his savings to his mother. Now, please God, I don't mean that you are to be any such mother of any such son: but it's a fine thing to see a well-disposed lad acting for himself, and fighting the world bravely: and I don't mind telling you that I think Johnny has a mother at home, who spoils him. Well — from abusing my mother-in-law behind her back, I am beginning to fall foul of my aunt and cousin to their faces — isn't it better that I should stop at once, especially as through the exercise of this abuse, the great sheet of paper has come to an end? You will excuse the last part of the letter, dear Aunt, I'm sure, for the sake of the good

[76] John Ritchie, later a Lieutenant in the Indian army, sailed with his brother William for Calcutta in September, 1842.

[77] We learn from William Ritchie's daughter, Mrs. Warre-Cornish (*Some Family Letters*, p. 23) that Mrs. John Richmond Jaffray was "the mother of handsome Arthur Jaffray, Thackeray and my father's contemporary and friend, who constantly welcomed them in Eaton Square." The Jaffrays lived at 28 Eaton Square (*Royal Blue Book*, 1846).

news in the first — Give my love to all, and ask William to write me a line to Paris, if he is with you.

Always affectionately yours<br>
W M Thackeray.

209.    TO WILLIAM HARRISON AINSWORTH
7 JANUARY 1842

*Address:* W. H. Ainsworth Esq^re | Kensal Manor-House | Harrow-Road. *Post-mark:* JA 7 1842. Hitherto unpublished.

My dear Ainsworth

I was very sorry too, as how shouldn't a man be who has a taste for Port-wine and good company?

Since then, I have been very bad & in bed for a couple of days: but I am vastly better now, & if quite set up by Saturday will not fail to come down. — Once more I must leave the visit conditional and at the same time delicately request you to name your hour.

I have been scribbling the letter to day w^h you desire, & hope it will turn out pretty well.[1] I wish I could stop in London and do more for you: but unlucky fortune carries me away.

I don't think anything of Mahony's writing for Bentley; he may have written that song[2] — & a poor one too. — a long time since: he has had, too, former connexions with the Miscellany. Of this however and more we will talk, please God, on Saturday, if I don't come I'm ill — but by the name of all you hold most sacred name the hour.

Yours ever<br>
W M T.

[1] Thackeray may be referring either to his "Sultan Stork," which appeared in the initial number of *Ainsworth's Magazine*, February, 1842, pp. 33–38, or, more probably, to a personal letter which Ainsworth had asked him to write.

[2] "The Mistletoe. A Dithyramb. By Father Prout," *Bentley's Miscellany*, January, 1842, pp. 111–112. Ainsworth was understandably distressed to find his old friend Mahony writing for the principal rival of his forthcoming magazine. The complicated story of their ensuing quarrel is related in S. M. Ellis, *William Harrison Ainsworth and His Friends*, 2 vols., (London and New York, 1911), II, 17–33.

210.      TO GEORGE WILLIAM NICKISSON [3]
        6 FEBRUARY 1842

*Address:* M: Nickisson | 215 Regent Street. *Postmark:* 7 FEBR 42. Hitherto unpublished.

                     11 Avenue Fortunée. Sunday.
Dear Nickisson.

Please have the 2 cuts [4] handsomely and faithfully engraved, & placed across the 2 columns.

              Yrs—    W M T.


211.        TO MRS. SPENCER
          10 FEBRUARY 1842

Hitherto unpublished. My text is taken from a draft in Thackeray's hand, endorsed by him "M:ʳˢ Spencer. 10 Feb.," which is owned by Mrs. Fuller.

My dear Madam.

To day my wife goes to take up her residence with D: Puzin at Chaillot. She seems to like the notion very much, and will have kind attention & rational society: for only one of the Doctor's many patients is in her condition.

Will you please to break this intelligence to M:ʳˢ Shawe, whose sensibilities might suffer by an abrupt announcement & the sight of my handwriting? M:ʳˢ Shawe will soon be able to visit her daughter, or to be visited by her, whenever her feelings admit her to take such an indulgence. I grieve to hear from Miss Shawe that M:ʳˢ Shawe was agitated by poor Isabella's visit on Tuesday: the former lady wondered that Isabella *should have been allowed to go out* in such a state of agitation, — if M:ʳˢ Shawe shares in that wonder as is not improbable, I can only assure her that Isabella went to see her quite against my wish, for I was obliged to accompany her, & this

[3] A bookseller and publisher who was proprietor and, apparently, editor of *Fraser's Magazine* from 1841 to 1848.
[4] For "Dickens in France," *Fraser's Magazine*, March, 1842, 342–352.

brought on myself a task w.ʰ I wish carefully to avoid, —that of ever seeing M.ʳˢ Shawe.

Enclosed is a letter written some days ago relative to M.ʳˢ Shawe's refusal to take charge of her daughter: I am sorry to trouble you with this kind of correspondence; but am compelled to *préciser* every one of my transactions with my wife's mother, in order that I may be able to show her relations when I go to Ireland in the Spring, what my real conduct with regard to her has been, — it has been somewhat misunderstood by M.ʳˢ Shawe's family and I hope to be able to prove that *I* at least have not failed in my duty to the poor girl.

As for that lady's own behavior, I now possess a series of documents in her handwriting, and

I am dear Madam Y.ʳˢ &c.


212.        TO CHAPMAN AND HALL
            25 FEBRUARY 1842

*Address:* Mess.ʳˢ Chapman & Hall. | 186 Strand | London. | Angleterre. *Postmarks:* PARIS 26 FEVR. 42, 1 MR 1842. Hitherto unpublished.

11 Avenue Fortunée. Beaujon. Paris.
Feb 25. 1842.

My dear Sirs

A friend carries to London to day the article w.ʰ I promised you — 1/2 that is: for I have only been able to get down to the Revolution of July; ⁵ & must keep L. P for another number.

I should like very much to do for you an article on Victor Hugo's Rhine: w.ʰ might be made smart, & would be easy writing. The restoration took me 5 weeks of very hard labor, & caused me a trouble of w.ʰ I had no idea when I undertook the work.

Please to let me know if you can give space to a sheet about Hugo this month — you could have it by the 10.ᵗʰ: if *not* be so good as to

---

⁵ For this article and that on Hugo, see below, Appendix VIII. Thackeray's survey of the early years of Louis Philippe's reign was never written. His notes for it are preserved in the Harvard College Library.

send the enclosed note to Fraser's. — for if the thing be not done soon, it will be assuredly caught up elsewhere.

The weather is fine, & I look forward with pleasure to the Irish trip in Spring.

Very faithfully yrs<br>W M Thackeray.

213.     TO EDWARD FɪᴛᴢGERALD
9 MARCH 1842

*Address:* Edward Fitz-Gerald Esq^re | 39 Portland Place | LONDON. *Post-mark:* MR 18 1842. Extract published in *Biographical Introductions*, V, xxii.

9 March. 1842

My dear Edward. Indeed I ought to have written long ago: but have been hard at work ever since I came back, and out of working times hating the sight of a pen — Thank you for your letter. The poor little woman is getting better & better — much better since I parted from her, w^h I was obliged to do on returning for she was past my management. She is close by at Chaillot, perfectly happy, obedient and reasonable. I see her of course continually — but it makes my heart sick to be parted from her; and every now and then turns up something, some reminiscence of old times or some simple thing w^h she says, & w^h knocks me quite down, and makes me cry like a child. I get melancholy too being with the children, they are not half the children without their mother — A man's grief is very selfish certainly, and it's our comforts we mourn.

Well it is probable I should have talked to you of something more amusing, but for a cursed headache w^h prevents me from working to any advantage, and so you get the refuse. I began a letter some time back that was lugubrious too, for I was very much shocked with reading in an old Galignani the result of that fatal Niger Expedition, and thought of that kind gentle sister of your's suffering & being unhappy.[6] By Jove what a lucky fellow Kerrich

---

[6] FitzGerald's sister Andalusia, later (1844) Mrs. Francis de Soyres, had been engaged to Captain Bird Allen, a brother of John Allen. Captain Allen

is to have a wife and a great family and a chance to give all his affections full play. I hope your sister will be with him a good deal, his cheerful house will be the best consoler

What have I been doing — writing articles &c and have been to the play a good deal: it is always sure to be pleasant here. It is a great comfort to be able to like the theatre once again, and be amused by little sparkling frisky pieces. Yesterday I had a ticket to hear what they call a Stabat Mater [7] by Rossini wʰ is here making a great noise. It is very beautiful, there are 10 concerted pieces, Tamburini especially admirable, and to crown all a very good box. So I stayed away and dined off cold beef & soupe maigre, with my friend Collignon the artist, & his wife who is charming. Such a little active innocent smiling kindly creature. He a very clever fellow out of his profession, and sometimes in it, but not often. Au reste the loyalest stanchest man possible: it is quite fine to see him and his wife breasting poverty together, and indeed their soupe maigre is admirable.

What stuff and nonsense this is to write to you. I have read no novels or good books to talk of, but scores of volumes of history, in the most owllike solemn way, and by way of amusement Victor Hugo's new book on the Rhine. He is very great, and writes like a God Almighty. — about this book I've been trying to write to day & only squeezed out one lousy page.

He says some fine things — wiz looking at the stars, he says that the night is as it were the normal colour of heaven — There is something awful in it — a dark-blue eternity glittering all over with silent watchful stars. Is it nonsense or the contrary? — I know what Venables wᵈ say: that the dark blue is all gammon, being an optical effect & so on — but still it's rather awful, and I feel certain that time & space are dark blue. Of course calling to mind the well-known passage of the Sacred Writer of Putney [8] — 'the old bl —

---

went to Africa in 1840 as a member of the Niger Expedition and died of fever on October 25 of the following year (Grier, *John Allen*, pp. 70–77).

[7] First performed on January 7, 1842, in Paris. Antonio Tamburini (1800–1876) was a famous basso.

[8] In the first paragraph of Clarke's *Library of Useless Knowledge* (see above, No. 130), Athanasius Gasker announces that he was born in Putney, and he

b — b — y, the old pl — th — ric & w — nt — n st — r. What you say of that Scoundrel Yates, next, naturally comes into my thoughts — There is something awful about him too. Gracious God what a stupendous impudence! He is a fellow who would put his hands up the petticoats of an angel. I have had several distinct laughs over the Cyprian Courtezans & the pas seductif. One can see it, and that enormous Yates leering at the side-scene. I wish I had known it last month, when in a very dull paper about a piece called Nicholas Nickl⟨eby⟩ of course I fell to thinking of him as Mantalini 9 — This was written (that is not this, but the last sentence) full ten minutes ago — ever since I have been thinking of Yates — are you doing so now at the present moment? Tis midnight, the wind is banging and bursting doors and shutters open — I pity the poor mariner &c. — Well the thoughts of our friend have put me into a good humour: the first fit of the sort to day. Let's go to bed, and excuse me dear old fellow for writing this stupid letter, perhaps I won't send it — but I'm glad to have had a talk with you, even though about nonsense — Mon Dieu, en

avons nous déja parlé dans notre temps?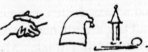

later exclaims, refuting the rumors of his death that had circulated during the long period of his retirement: "Ye men of England! I LIVE! Yes — the 'Old Blue Baby!' 'the old plethoric and wanton star!'" (p. 50) The first of these names, it should be explained, derives from the disastrous catastrophe of Gasker's lecture on *The Sexes of Facts* at Pedaster House, a severely Evangelical school for young ladies. He has occasion to display a picture of "the Monstrous Fact: which was an irregularly formed, and enormous, transparent, dark blue, naked, Baby, sitting cross-legged, upon a sack of Embden Groats, cursing and swearing, and throwing about religious tracts," and this representation is at once recognized as a likeness of Mrs. Earlygrave, the mistress of Pedaster House (p. 46). It is only by good fortune that Gasker escapes unarmed in the riot that follows.

9 "Can France, I thought, produce a fop equal to Yates? Is there any vulgarity and assurance on the Boulevard that can be compared to that of which, in the character of Mantalini, he gives a copy so wonderfully close to Nature?" ("Dickens in France," *Works*, V, 755)

214.      TO MRS. CARMICHAEL-SMYTH
10 MAY 1842

Hitherto unpublished.

Tuesday — May 10.

My dearest Mammy. Your letter was most welcome as you may think with all the good news of big & little, and pray God I shall continue [from] you to hear such, and that you won't have to leave the children, but get well as is best, in their company.

What my probabilities are I dont quite know as yet — but I have 5 weeks work before me, and then will come the great Irish question to be resolved, w$^h$ will depend upon my having money or not. If I have enough, I will go I think. If not I have some other work offered me, w$^h$ w$^d$ be both profitable & pleasant, but I expect I shall be home-sick by that time — indeed have had one or two pretty severe fits of that complaint already. Bess's letter and your's however are famous remedies for it: and I've had a line from Isabella too w$^h$ was written without dictation, and has comforted me hugely.

They are all here fixed upon departure, and will be with you without fail I think. Mary makes me angry from a most exaggerated terror and hatred that she has got of G. M; but I'm sure she wants to see you, and that her heart is in the right place. Only she is excessively fond of domination and first-fiddle-playing, and this I do think is the reason why she has preferred Coram S$^t$ to Paris.$^{10}$ Her Doctor has inspired me with much disgust, a clever smooth fellow who flatters her so much as to make me vomit — Hering $^{11}$ is his name. To day they have been to M$^r$ Travers with the child,$^{12}$ w$^h$ is enormously fat & fine, and w$^h$ will be operated on

---

$^{10}$ Thackeray was living with Colonel and Mrs. Carmichael-Smyth, who on August 17 dropped the surname of Smyth by royal license, at 13 Great Coram Street.

$^{11}$ William Hering, surgeon, 38 Mortimer Street, Cavendish Square; Benjamin Travers, surgeon, 12 Bruton Street, Bond Street (*Post Office London Directory*, 1847).

$^{12}$ Charles Henry Edward ("Chéri") Carmichael-Smyth (d. 1895), later Carmichael, who was born on January 9, 1842.

for *two* cataracts at the end of the year — The poor little fellow has been unlucky indeed. Charles has had bad news from India — Bruce & Shand have failed, and another house in w^h he had a little money, is likewise on the go. Whereupon though he had made up his mind to go to Devonshire & to see Mark,[13] he has given up all thoughts of leaving home: & is not sorry I think in his heart to have any excuse for staying by the side of his adored — So poor Mark writes up a pathetic letter of the dinner he had prepared, lamb & a lobster, tarts gooseberry & rhubarb, and all the children jumping for joy to see their Uncle Charles — M^rs Mark is just gone back to her husband — but very loth to move I thought: nay possibly not gone yet, for I left her on the point of starting only, and her heart may fail her, on acc^t of the blessed baby, or for some other reason. Mary is a capital mother up early in the nursery, and ceaselessly busied about the infant: and I already foresee Jealousies regarding it — She'll say you love mine better, as sure as fate — and I think you will to, for they're of a different sort: but that's neither here nor there — God bless the dear little ones, & the granny who loves them — your account of the country does my heart good.

Will you tell Crowe with regard to my letter — that I left in his secrétaire, a packet containing spoons &c belonging to Reeves with all that gentleman's letters: that I suppose is the Greek of w^h you write for I forget anything else in the letter.

I took a week's pleasuring, but am now got into pretty decent work of mornings, and am about one or two things that I should have ⟨. . .⟩ [14]

[13] Captain Mark Wood Carmichael-Smyth (1801–1872), a younger brother of the Major's and formerly an officer in the Madras cavalry. He married Marianne Hutton (d. 1890) in 1831 and had three children.

[14] The final pages of this letter have been lost.

215.        TO WILLIAM EDWARD HICKSON [15]
                16 MAY 1842

Hitherto unpublished.

13 G<sup>t</sup> Coram S<sup>t</sup> Russell Sq<sup>e</sup>
16 May. 1842

Dear Sir

"Modern English Comedies' would be a good subject for a light article in the Westminster. Have you room for July, and can we come to terms? [16]

You were good enough to write to me last year for contributions: your letter did not reach me till many weeks after & found me on the Rhine. I am only just returned to London, and shall be glad if the Review can afford to purchase me, to sell myself & wits as far as they go —

faithfully y<sup>rs</sup> dear Sir

W M Thackeray.

216.        TO MRS. CARMICHAEL-SMYTH
                21 MAY 1842

*Address:* M<sup>rs</sup> Carmichael Smyth. | Rue des Arcades | S<sup>t</sup> Germain en Laye | France. *Postmarks:* 21 MY 1842, ST-GERMAIN-EN-LAYE 23 MAI 42. Hitherto unpublished.

My dearest Mammy. I can only afford you half a sheet, dividing the two francs between you and my wife, to whom please dispatch the enclosed.[17] It was a comfort to hear that you had been to see her, and found her pretty well: and that the little ones God bless them were flourishing too, and you all in the fresh air of S<sup>t</sup> Germains. Charles & Mary seem making serious preparations for moving, and will be with you pretty early in June. I wonder how I shall stand being quite alone. I think pretty well; for I have as much society out of doors as I want and only too much hospitality

---

[15] Hickson (1803-1870) edited *The Westminster Review* from 1840 to 1846.

[16] See below, No. 217.

[17] This letter has not been preserved.

& good feeding. As for work there seems so much of it here, and of such variety that I have only to pick & choose, and make in a certain way, a decent income. Whether I shall go to Ireland or not remains like everything else in suspense — but that rascally 120£ [18] is hanging over me and will take a long time to pay off. What else have I got to say? all the dinners &c are chronicled in Isabella's letter and the rest of the days are spent pretty well in working and dawdling about. Your letter is just come in, thank God for it, and to hear that you are all so well. As for Anny's reading and writing, why trouble her? The fresh air is best, and plenty of fun with her playmates.

By the bye I have had a visit from M[r] Hickman who talks confidently has invited Nokes and Crucifix, and wants the ex-proprietors to meet together and palaver concerning the payment of his claim.[19] He asked me to join with D[r] Black and request M[r] Ashurst to *give up the deed*, papers &c relative to the Con: & it is evident that he is at fault somewhere. Now I think G.P. had better request Ashurst to hand over the boxes to Charles (or better still, to an indifferent person who might give them to Charles who might carry them over to Paris — I went to see Black at a place he appointed but found an empty house and the people knowing nothing about him. He is now I believe a sort of hanger-on of Molesworth, Leader & Co, whom I heard speaking very highly of him.

Did I send my love to Bess for the letter she wrote me? Indeed I was very thankful for it, as for any scrap of information ab[t] the poor little woman — not but that I am quite easy concerning her: feeling that she's happier away from us than with us.

Whats the rest of the news? Mary has been a little peeking I believe; she bids me say that she'll write very soon — tomorrow I think she said. for this is written at the Club. Charles is busy trying to get up a subscription for the Caubul sufferers [20] — and has ad-

---

[18] See above, No. 179.

[19] For this development in the legal action threatened by the creditors of *The Constitutional*, see above, No. 164.

[20] The most disastrous episode of the first Afghan War was the retreat of a British garrison driven out of Kabul in November and eventually massacred (January, 1842). Of the 3,000 men only a few escaped.

vertized the carriage to be sold a great bargain 75 guineas with the harness. How many pairs of sheets did you order me when last here to bring over? — not surely *nine* pairs, the horrible mad cook here says nine, I believe only four, and she has no doubt no doubt carried off the others. They are fine housekeepers — worse than we were I think such dirt & cobwebs on the walls, suffered so calmly! — only every now & then Charles for consistency's sake, goes to the kitchen and makes a row. Mary had a mesmeric sitting the other day — and was sent to sleep, but not sound: to day the experiment was to be repeated — the magnetized & worthy man. Fiddledee! what stuff to be writing about, and yet it is of a piece with all the rest of the letter. So Farewell, and God bless all — and tell me plenty of stories about the children. W M T.

217.        TO WILLIAM EDWARD HICKSON
                       26 MAY 1842

Hitherto unpublished. *Endorsed:* W M Thackeray My 26/42.

13 G! Coram S!

Dear Sir

I am sure you will sympathize with my grief in being obliged to say that the sum proposed by you is too small. I hope to make at least twenty guineas out of the dramatists of the Victorian Age.[21]

Faithfully yrs. dear Sir

W M Thackeray.

218.        TO CHAPMAN AND HALL
                       4 JUNE 1842

Hitherto unpublished.

13 G! Coram S!
Sat? 4 June.

My dear Sirs

I send you a receipt on t'other side: but have of course too much confidence in your sense of justice to suppose that you would think

[21] Thackeray does not appear to have written this article.

of paying 4 sheets of shuperb writing [22] with 40£ — The restoration alone cost me 6 weeks labor, & the reading of many scores òf books. However we'll talk more on this subject another time.

Yrs ever

W M Thackeray.

Received of Messr⁵ Chapman & Hall twenty pounds on acc⁴ of articles furnished to the Foreign Quarterly Review

W M Thackeray.

London 4 May [23] — 1842.

219.        TO MRS. CARMICHAEL-SMYTH
                 11–? JUNE 1842 [24]

*Address:* M⁷ˢ Carmichael Smyth | Rue des Arcades | S⁴ Germain-en-Laye | France. Hitherto unpublished.

Southborough n⁷ Tunbridge Wells.<br>11 June 1842.

My dearest Mammy I came down here on Tuesday as I threatened, and if I dont keep my other promise of writing you an immense long letter: it is because I have written myself out in the last 4 days, so hard have I been at work — Near 25 £ worth, that's a fact: but it's a sort of thing that one could not keep up: and its better economy to write oftener & less. It's the pleasantest greenest place in the world,[25] pleasant woods close at hand, fields on the

[22] Thackeray's two identified contributions to *The Foreign Quarterly Review* for July, "The Last Fifteen Years of the Bourbons" (384–420) and "The German in England," (370–383) total fifty pages. A sheet is equivalent to sixteen magazine pages.

[23] A mistake for Saturday, June 4.

[24] This letter was begun on June 11 and finished shortly before June 24, when Thackeray left London for Wales.

[25] "Oh, my dear Mr. Beney, of the Hand and Sceptre Inn, Southborough, near Tunbridge Wells," Thackeray wrote some two weeks later from a bad hotel in Hereford, "how I envied your snug smiling green parlour, your unostentatious ducks and green peas, your pretty garden and sparkling cider, your kind, bustling welcome, as well to travellers who preferred the genteel part of your house, as to him who alighted at your tap. Oh, BENEY! how I yearned

other side very quiet & happy to walk in, and Tunbridge Wells 3 miles off, which I examined with a queer sort of feelings. That lovely cottage we used to inhabit [26] has gone to heaven; so has old Gramp the riding master, his son taking his place now the father is in another & better world. Cottages have grown upon the common: and as for the house at Penshurst w$^h$ I thought rather a splendid affair, it is finer outside, but in the most woebegone condition within. I looked out for my old friend the dead man with the worms and was very near missing him strange to say: the fact is he has got up and changed his place from the gallery where he used to be to a front room: of course carrying all his worms with him. Penshurst is a royal country much more grand & picturesque than this — but even this look out of a green common with old oak trees, and a road with merry-looking gigs gingling up and down is better than Coram Street. & that bell at Coram Street, and that unhappy little room where I never can remain five minutes without some one rattling at the door, w$^h$ I've vainly locked. Charles & Mary will think me very ungrateful — Amen. But all the same I admire him more than ever. I never saw such delightful humility, and carelessness of self. Mary's Doctor is not such a humbug as I first thought him, but has really I believe a strong admiration for that young lady. — I wonder [what] makes me ill-pleased at these vulgar people admiring her? — Upon my word I don't think so but the style of thing is distasteful to me — Well, bating jealousy on her part, w$^h$ you told me of, and of w$^h$ I have seen some curious instances — she is a good fellow; She is as jealous of your love for me, and found a letter t'other day, w$^h$ I read too — from her to you — in w$^h$ she pointed out that *I* had formed other ties, but *she* was all your's she feels ashamed of it now, and spoke of it: I told her that she had to use a genteel phrase *pitched it too strong*: — she is of a passionate temper, and fancies those explosions of love in w$^h$ she indulged formerly rather creditable and indicative of immense

---

for the Hand and Sceptre Inn, in that huge genteel hotel!" ("Cockney Travels," *Centenary Works*, [XXVI], 116)

[26] In the summer of 1823, when Thackeray, his mother, and his step-father passed the long vacation in Tunbridge Wells. See above, No. 7.

sensibility — it was all temperament. A person does not love you
more because she hugs the breath out of your body. She is jealous
of me & the G M.; says that I flatter her Bon dieu! and that *she*
couldn't do what I do: and she has told me twice or thrice very
kindly of the sums the old lady has given me: making tolerably
long calculations in favor of G M's generosity. The fact is she is
not pleased in her heart at having received G M's 100£: and is
always making comparisons — measuring herself with this person
& that: and fighting hard to maintain her old self-esteem. I don't
think that *h*emales have that sort of spirit generally. — or perhaps
I'm trying to run her down myself because of the 500£. What's
all this scandal? — the fact is, somehow, that she doesn't *agree* with
me: and so be so good as to burn this if I don't burn it myself, w$^h$ is
just as likely. Ah! there was more nobleness and simplicity in that
little woman that neither of you knew, than I've seen in most people
in this world. God help her, and if ever he pleases to restore her
to me mend both of us. It was pleasant walking about here in the
fields on Thursday & thinking of Annie: my dear little girl, I hear
her voice a dozen times a day, and when I write to her, it's a days
work — blubbering just as I used to do when I left you to go to
school — not from any excess of affection filial or paternal as I very
well know; but from sentiment as they call it — the situation is
pathetic. Look what a sentimental man Sterne was, ditto Coleridge
who would have sent his children to the poor house — by Jove,
they are a contemptible, impracticable selfish race, Titmarsh included and without any affectation: Depend upon it, a good honest
kindly man not cursed by a genius, that doesn't prate about his
affections, and cries very little, & loves his home — he is the real
man to go through the world with. Look at G P. and his steadiness
of heart, with love for working-days as well as Sundays: how much
superior that sort of enduring character and manliness is, to all our
flashy touch-and-go theorizing about love — Shall I pay you some
more compliments about him? — it seems indecent: only I know
you like to have it told you, that I feel respect and attachment for
him, and so there's an end on't.

It's a strange thing too that I should fill a page with abuse of

Polly, and choke after three lines of praise of G P: but it's awfully hard to say what you think in the complimentary way, whereas the scandal slips out quite naturally — It is I suppose the satirical propensity and be hanged to it: now Charles could write a folio of kind things about people, and never say a bad word.

Whether I go to London tomorrow or not depends upon the state of the bill here — my extras have been 1 pint cyder, 1 glass gin daily — no wine except one day a pint — and scribble scribble all day. The last thing in Frazer [27] has made a sort of hit: and I've been writing for the F. Q. and a very low paper called Punch,[28] but that's a secret — only its good pay, and a great opportunity for unrestrained laughing sneering kicking and gambadoing. Likewise I've done for Ainsworth 2 little articles [29] for Fraser 3 long ones, so that I've not been idle since I've been away — wʰ is a story by the way: but here there is so much stir, bustle and blood flowing, that the work is done in 1/2 the time. Fraser has paid my wife's last month & has enough for the 2 next, and it will be a great pleasure to me if I can go to Ireland with my own earnings, and without touching Mary's money.

And now Madam having written a great deal more than I had any business to I shall respectfully wish you good night: and read

[27] "Fitz-Boodle's Confessions" in the June issue of *Fraser's Magazine*, pp. 707–721.

[28] Thackeray's first identified contribution to *Punch* appeared on June 18, 1842 (see below, Appendix VIII), his last on September 23, 1854. Between 1844 and 1851 he was the magazine's leading writer. See M. H. Spielmann's authoritative account of this connection in his *History of "Punch"* (London, 1895), pp. 303–326, and the same author's *Hitherto Unidentified Contributions of W. M. Thackeray to "Punch"* (New York and London, 1899). Some additions to Spielmann's full but not exhaustive bibliography will be found in Appendix XII below.

[29] The second part of "Sultan Stork" was published in *Ainsworth's Magazine* in May, "An Exhibition Gossip" in June. Thackeray's work for *Fraser's Magazine* probably consisted of "Professions. By George Fitz-Boodle" in the July number (pp. 43–60), "Fitz-Boodle's Confessions. Miss Löwe" in the October number (pp. 395–405), and "Fitz-Boodle's Confessions. Dorothea" in the number for January, 1843 (pp. 76–84). The two "Confessions" are stories rather than articles, however, and Thackeray may be referring to papers that have not as yet been identified.

Vols II & III of Anne of Geierstein [30] — I got it at the old library on the Pantiles (they're called Parade now) where when you & G P went to town I got the Italian [31] — God bless all — and my dear litle ones.

My dearest Mammy. This has been lying in the port folio for some days and should have been properly burned — but until I am away again, I shall not have another chance to write you a long letter, & please you burn this and not me.

I am now pretty well fixed upon departure for Ireland, having collacuted with Chapman & Hall The other young people, viz Charles & Mary talk of setting off on Tuesday next, but I hardly think she'll be strong enough — she looks pale, but well and handsome I think — Today Ive been paying visits and woe's me out of six found five at home. Old Turner composing a sermon, M[rs] Bitcherdear and others — she was almost pleasant though, & Constantia a pretty girl. Your letter made me have that dismal sort of gladness w[h] you know of. I wish I could see you all before I go, my dear old Mammy & children. Thank God for their all being so happy, as I intend to be directly I'm out of the tea-parties, visiting jobs, and endless racket of this place. Farewell.

W M T.

[30] *Anne of Geierstein: or The Maiden of the Mist* (1829), one of Sir Walter Scott's last novels.

[31] *The Italian, or the Confessional of the Black Penitents* (1797), the famous *roman noir* by Mrs. Radcliffe. When Thackeray visited Tunbridge Wells in 1860, this recollection of 1823 came again to his mind. He remembered a dark room in "a little house hard by on the Common here, in the Bartlemytide holidays. The parents have gone to town for two days: the house is all his own, his own and a grim old maid-servant's, and the little boy is seated at night in the lonely drawing-room, poring over 'Manfroni, or the One-handed Monk,' so frightened that he scarcely dares to turn round." (*Works*, XII, 228) It will be observed that with the lapse of time *The Italian* has given place to another Gothic romance by Mary-Anne Radcliffe, a quite different writer not to be confused with her more famous rival. Thackeray owned at the time of his death a set of *The Novel Newspaper* (1839-1840), the first volume of which contained, along with three other novels, *Manfrone; or, The One-Handed Monk* (*Howe Proofs*, p. 519), originally published in 1828.

220.          TO JOHN FORSTER
                22 JUNE 1842

Hitherto unpublished.

                                13 Coram S$^t$ 22 June.
Dear Forster.

Lest I should not see you before I go, this is to proffer thanks for received hospitality, & to wish you on the other hand a merited prosperity. I shall go to Ireland by Wales, w$^h$ country I find lies on the way of the former land, and w$^h$ I may as well discover en route.[32]

I wish I could have stopped to be one of the welcomers to Dickens [33] — to whom I needn't ask you on his return to present my respectful homages.

What do you think? Such has been the influence of time and example upon me, that I got your friend the Barnets' poems,[34] for the purpose of praising them — but this, alas, is humpawsable; never mind, I'll wait until he does something good & *then* you shall see.

Have you seen the bust of the Editor of the Foreign Quarterly Review at Suffolk Street? [35] — I found him out many weeks since. Prosperity to both say I with all my heart.

                Truly yours dear Forster
                    W M Thackeray.

---

[32] It appears from Thackeray's account of his tour in "Cockney Travels" (*Centenary Works*, XXVI, 93–124) that he left London on Friday, June 24, for Bristol, where he spent the night. On Saturday he proceeded to Chepstow. There he remained until Monday morning, when he went on by coach to Hereford, stopping at Tintern Abbey *en route*. Monday night was passed at Hereford. On the following day he continued by way of Shrewsbury, Llangollen, and Chester to Liverpool, where he arrived on Wednesday, June 29. By Monday, July 4, he was in Dublin.

[33] On Dickens's return from America.

[34] Sir Edward Bulwer-Lytton's *Eva, The Ill-omened Marriage and Other Poems* (1842).

[35] At the exhibition of the British Artists' Society, 6½ Suffolk Street.

221.        TO MRS. CARMICHAEL-SMYTH
                26 JUNE 1842 [36]

*Address:* M^{rs} Carmichael Smyth. | Rue des Arcades | à S^t Germain-en-Laye |
France. *Postmarks:* 26 JUNE 1842, ST-GERMAIN-EN-LAYE 30 JUIN
42. Hitherto unpublished.

My dearest Mammy. Please to send the enclosed half [37] to my
wife — it's a shame that I've left you so long without a letter, and
now you'll see that the great journey is actually begun; in a queer
circumbenditory way that is — for I was in hopes to have had a
glimpse of Wales as well as of Ireland, making my pen pay my
expenses at least in the former place. This I shall do but sight-
seeing and writing too occupy a deal of time for a man of my lazy
habits, and very seldom can I do either. Mary & Charles talk of
setting off on Tuesday, the poor old house was so overrun by the
Mohicans that I was obliged to go & sleep at the Hummuns [38] for
at last they drove me quite wild. Indeed the whole town was dis-
tracting & the only quiet place I found there was the club. In going
about this wonderful country you would fancy I was wild too for it
makes me swear & jump & sing & break out into the most fantastical
pranks of pleasure but it is a very wholesome excitement and sets
the mind in a pious proper frame of mind not like the debauchery
of cities: and makes one wonder & grow a little humble. I wish I
had a companion though to share the pleasure, FitzGerald or Morton or Tennyson: who is a growler but a man of genius. Well in
Ireland there will be no doubt companions enough.

I promised Black to apply once more to G. P regarding the
authorization to let Crucifix & Spratt have access to the Constitutional papers [39] and for what share-holders there may be I told
Crucifix between us two there was no one else, that if publicly

[36] Thackeray wrote this letter from Chepstow on the Sunday after he left
London.
[37] This letter has not been preserved.
[38] The Old Hummuns Hotel in Covent Garden. There is a drawing of the
"Mohicans" below, No. 224.
[39] See above, No. 164.

pressed with regard to the debts of the paper I should fight off &
deny all liability but that if any compromise could be come to I
would pay off my share by instalments as I could; and I believe the
whole matter might be arranged for 500£ or 600£ and it would be
better that we should pay a portion of this, than that the cursed
debt should hang over us for ever, and leave us in endless insecurity.
Hickman has saved his limitation statute, & so have the others by
making application to be paid: and paid it must be by one person or
the other, & not a shilling's worth if any of our little property will
be secure until that nasty claim is settled.

.So now I have done a part of my duty at least; Black's address is
at the Middlesex Reform Association's Chambers John Street
Adelphi

My wife's letter first made me very sick & disheartened, and then
I thought I understood it and could follow the train of thought if
a train you can call it. I can't help thinking still but that she is im-
proving, and am very glad above all to see that she desires to see
me & hear of me. God help us both and bring her back to me. I
think this is all I have to say for when I get to thinking of her &
the little ones I fall into the dumps: though thankful all the while
that they have my dear Mother to be a mother to them. How
thankful indeed oughtn't I to be — Well, the next best thing to do
after that is not to think of the matter at all, but to try & write a
good book, and see if I can put myself in some way to earn a secure
& decent living. So now shut up, & good night — I've been sight
seeing & walking & writing all this fine Sunday. God bless all.
W M T.

## 222.  TO THE REV. RICHARD HARRIS BARHAM [40]
### 1 JULY 1842

Hitherto unpublished.

opposite Liverpool.  July 1.  1842

Dear Barham.

Just before I left London, a man who is possessed of a good deal
of money and is also of a literary turn wrote to me that he wished
to see me on literary matters, whereupon instantly conjecturing
that he was about to start a Magazine out of w^h some plunder might
be had by the deserving, I delayed my departure saying of course
that I would be glad to further his plans.

What do you think the rich man wanted?  Why, pulling out of

[40] Thackeray had first met Barham (1788–1845), author of *The Ingoldsby
Legends* (1840–1847), at the Garrick Club many years earlier.  Much of
Barham's verse appeared in *Bentley's Magazine*, the proprietor of which was
his old schoolfellow Richard Bentley (1794–1871), and one of his best *mots*
concerns the christening of this publication.  "The magazine was originally
intended to have been called 'The Wits' Miscellany.'  'Why,' urged Barham,
when the change of title was suggested to him, 'why go to the other extreme?'"
(*Dictionary of National Biography* III, 189)  Bentley and his rival Henry
Colburn (d. 1855), publisher of *The New Monthly Magazine*, are portrayed
in *Pendennis* as Bacon and Bungay.

his pocket a huge bundle of papers of his own composition he wanted me to get them inserted in some magazine.

He had not only his own papers but those [of] a friend w$^h$ he wished to place. Now the friend's case is a very different one. This latter a M$^r$ Church, has been a gentleman all his life living upon a good income w$^h$ suddenly has quitted him through some West India failure. He is wofully pinched for money, according to his friend's account an extraordinary clever fellow, a good writer, humourous & a scholar.

Under such circumstances declining the rich mans proposal altogether, I advised him to tell the poor one to write some smart magazine tales, w$^h$ if they were up to the mark, would be pretty sure of a market, in the magazines of Great Britain among the contributors of w$^h$ wit learning & gentility are rare.

If any papers come to Bentley with M$^r$ Church's name will you get them put under the Editor's eye? — to stand or fall of course as their merit warrants. I am sure you will do so much "to help a fellow creature in distress" (as the great dramatic poet remarks) if you have the power or the opportunity.

I am so far on the road to Ireland w$^h$ country I am going to discover.

Always yours dear Barham

very much obliged

W M Thackeray.

It is a curious fact that both Boz & Titmarsh reached Liverpool the same day: [41] but the journals have not taken notice of the arrival of the latter. Gross jealousy!

[41] Dickens arrived in Liverpool aboard the packet-ship George Washington on the morning of June 29. He had sailed from New York three weeks earlier. (*Times*, June 30)

223.            TO EDWARD FɪᴛᴢGERALD
                     4 JULY 1842

Published in part, *Biographical Introductions*, V, xxiii-xxiv; facsimile in *The Cornhill Magazine*, XXXI (1911), 31-34.

> Shelburne Hotel
> Stephen Greed
> Dublud.
> July 4. 1842.

My dear old Yedward — I am just come after a delightful tower to Chepstow, Bristol Hereford, Srowsbry, Chester, Liverpool, Llangollen, and Wales in general — I found your dismal letter [42] waiting on arrival here — What the deuce are you in the dumps for? Dont flatter yourself but that I'll get on very well without you. Such a place as this hotel itself! — enough to make a chapter about [43] — such filth, ruin and liberality — o my dear friend pray heaven on bended kneee that tonight when I go to bed I find no (Turn over) 𝕩 𝕩 𝕩 . —Have you remarked that the little ones of all sting worst?

---

[42] FitzGerald's letter to Thackeray has not been preserved, but its tenor may be judged from his note to Pollock of June 24: "There is that poor fellow Thackeray gone off to Ireland: and what a lazy beast I am for not going with him. But except for a journey of two days, I get dull as dirt. I wish somebody had gone with him. But he will find lots of companions in Ireland." (*Letters and Literary Remains*, ed. Wright, I, 142)

[43] Thackeray devotes a few paragraphs to the Shelburne Hotel in chapter I of *The Irish Sketch Book*.

I wanted to give you an idea of the splendor of the chamber-maid at Chthlangothlen — the most sumptuous creature ever seen — yellow haired brown eyed dazzling fair with a neck like a marble pillar, and a busk  o heavens! —

I wrote a poem in the Llangollen album as follows

*a better glass nor a better Pipe*
*I never had in all my life*

Sam^l. Rogers.

Likewise a series of remarks by Thos Moore, beginning — 'There is a little yellow bird frequenting the cataracts of the Tigris where it empties itself into the Tabreez lake &c. What nonsense is all this to write — well, but the fact is I am just disjointed after the [voyage] my legs rocking about like a tipthy bal from the effeketh of the thteamer and I can't get to put down a sentence decently, and shan't be able for a couple of days or so. But I just wanted to shake hands with somebody however far across the water.

Your Uncle's [44] letter I've sent off (he has been very good naturedly to call & see if I had arrived) with my card pronounced here with that shuperfine elegance 'kyard' — Stuff there I go again, well there I go again. — Its a queer state of mind to be sure. Godblessyou. **W M T.**

P S. I wish you could see the apotheosis of William IV represented on the ceiling of the coffee-room such a picture! I shall get a most accurate copy of it fixing up easels telescopes &c.

[44] Peter Purcell of Halverstown, who is the "Mr. P———" of the second chapter of *The Irish Sketch Book*. FitzGerald's father was born Purcell but took the name of FitzGerald after the death of his wife's father, John Fitz-Gerald.

224.              TO CHAPMAN AND HALL
                      4 JULY 1842

Hitherto unpublished.

                                        Shelburne Hotel
                                    Stephen's Green. Dublin
                                        July 4, 1842.

My dear Sir[s].

   If you have an occasion to send to Paris will you kindly send
an F. Q. R. to the care of M<sup>r</sup> Crowe Rue 29 Juillet No 5. for my
mother (M<sup>rs</sup> Carmichael-Smyth). — I caught a glimpse of the
Review at Liverpool, and have no difficulty in finding out the name
of the author of the 1<sup>st</sup> article [45] in it. — Crowe I suppose is the
writer of the last. The classical vein is a good one: for w<sup>h</sup> purpose
Venables is your man. He is one of the finest scholars in England.

   I have been only here 6 hours, and see quite enough for a good
long chapter already, and have bought a fine new blank book, at
w<sup>h</sup> I have looked once or twice with great respect. I came through
Wales & have concocted a little article for Fraser,[46] just to get my
hand in — with nothing about Ireland in it of course.

   If your correspondent here is worth knowing will you send me a
letter to him. I thought I would write to say that actually & at
last I was in the country, and please God to get through it and the
book without farther delay or hindrance.

   If you light upon any pleasant German or French book that may
be reviewed without trouble or consultation of other works, please
keep it for me — travelling is expensive and I shall be glad to help
my purse along. — Mind also that the article (to come) on Louis
Philippe belongs to me. The author of Article I is a clever man
(as every body knows who knows my friend John Forster) but not

   [45] "The Reign of Terror: Its Causes and Results" was the opening article in
the July number of *The Foreign Quarterly Review* (275–308). In the Harvard College Library copy the article is ascribed to Bulwer-Lytton.
   [46] Probably "Cockney Travels," which was not published, however, until
1911, *Harper's Monthly Magazine*, June, 3–19.

conversant with France like your obedient serv![.] — and though the Louis Philippe article will take much time, & bring no profit, I want to do it, for reputation's sake. I don't think at all small beer of the Restoration — to w[h] you gave a good title.

Present my cordial homages to Dickens. I was at Liverpool when he was there, & knew nothing of that news, until he was on his way to London. Always my dear Sirs truly yrs

W M Thackeray.

225. TO CHAPMAN AND HALL
23 JULY 1842

Hitherto unpublished.

Cork.[47] Saturday. July 23. 1842.

Dear Sirs

Will you be kind enough to send me my balance in as many five pound notes as possible, directed to me at M[rs] Mac Oboy's. No 30 Patrick Street Cork.

Faithfully yrs

W M Thackeray.

[47] The reader may find the following outline of Thackeray's travels convenient for use with the map at the end of this volume. The references in Thackeray's *Works* are to *The Irish Sketch Book*.

After a few days in Dublin (*Works*, V, 271–290), Thackeray set off for southern and western Ireland. Passing through Rathcoole, Naas, Kilcullen, Carlow, and Waterford (pp. 291–319), he arrived in Cork shortly before July 23. He spent several days in Cork (pp. 320–346) before going on through Bandon, Skibbereen, Bantry, Glengariff, and Kenmare (pp. 347–370) to Killarney (pp. 371–384), which he reached on August 15. From Killarney he went by way of Tralee, Tarbert, Limerick, and Gort (pp. 385–420) to Galway (pp. 403–443). He then returned to Dublin through Clifden, Westport, Tuam, Ballinasloe, and Maynooth (pp. 444–482).

Thackeray passed the month of September in Dublin, visiting Wicklow just before the thirtieth (pp. 483–497) and the county meetings just after the thirtieth (pp. 498–509).

October he devoted to northern Ireland. He saw Dundalk, Belfast, Glenarm, and Ballycastle (pp. 510–542), and returned by way of Coleraine, Londonderry, Strabane, Enniskillen, and Virginia (pp. 543–571). After a few days in Dublin (pp. 572–582), he departed for London on November 1.

I have received Dickens' suckular [48] and shall be delighted to act against the Americans in any way he thinks fit.

226.                TO CHAPMAN AND HALL
                        28 JULY 1842

Hitherto unpublished. *Endorsed:* "Mr. MacOboys 30 Patrick S. Cork."

Cork. 28 July. 1842.

My dear Sirs

Your agreeable notes have just come to hand. I shall stay here or hereabouts till I get an answer from you, having plenty of work to do. I have been on a very pleasant journey, and hope please God to give a decent account of it. Let us pray that you may publish *two* decent books of travels [49] this year.

In regard of Louis Philippe I can do nothing sure without books to consult: for one must have an authority for every word that is said. A fortnight however will suffice for the article as I have the subject pretty well already, & you must give me this at Paris *at the latest day possible* — otherwise my book here will be spoiled.

I met a very good fellow [50] at Mʳ Lever's house in Dublin, who

[48] Concerning international copyright, printed in *The Examiner* of July 16 and in other periodicals.

[49] The other was Dickens's *American Notes*, published by Chapman and Hall in October.

[50] Major Frank Dwyer, who has left an elaborate account of the dinner given by Lever (see *Memoranda*) at which he was introduced to Thackeray: "His manner was at first reserved, earnest, and quiet; rather a disappointment, perhaps, to those who may have expected some external manifestation of his supposed humouristic proclivities; what was most observable seemed to be, that he was, himself, carefully observing and desirous of not being drawn out, at least, not prematurely. Conversation languished, as usual, during the *mauvais quart d'heure*, but revived after the soup had been disposed of. Lever threw up some political straw to ascertain how the wind blew: Thackeray praised some *fricandeau de veau*, of which he had partaken, a thing rarely seen on Irish tables, and the *chef-d'oeuvre* of Lever's German servant, who was cook and butler rolled up into one; which led to mention being made of the artistical arrangements of the kitchen at the Reform Club. This was just what was wanted: we then knew of course what Thackeray's politics were; . . . [He] adopted the liberal ideas of that period to their fullest extent, and the immediate object of his visit to Ireland was to write up something in the

has lived long in hungary — having been in the Austrian service) — he fell foul of poor Miss Pardoe [51] for some of her blunders and seems to know the country well. I suggested to him that if he

---

interests of his party — the coming question of the day was the repeal of the Corn Laws; there was also something to be ascertained about Maynooth, and a faint shadowing forth of what has, since then, been known as 'Upas-tree felling.' Lever's politics at this time were of a very different character. . . .

"As dinner proceeded, and after the ladies had retired, the two protagonists began to skirmish, endeavouring to draw each other out. Neither knew much of the other beyond what could be gleaned from their published works. Thackeray had as yet written only under an assumed name or anonymously; it was not so easy to get at him through his writings: Lever on the contrary had put his name to one or two works of so marked a character, that it seemed quite natural to connect his own individuality with that of some of his earlier heroes, who were, as we know, somewhat flighty and eccentric. The conversation had been led by Lever to the subject of the battle of Waterloo . . . Thackeray soon joined in; he did not pretend to know anything about the great battle, but he evidently wished to spur on Lever to identify himself with Charles O'Malley . . . [Thackeray] seemed always to wish to betray every Irishman he met into boasting in some shape or on some subject; he often reminded me of the agent's provocations of the continental police in this respect. . . . [Lever], quickly perceiving his antagonist's game, . . . met his feints with very quiet, but perfectly efficacious parries. It was highly interesting, and not a little amusing to observe how these two men played each a part, seemingly belonging to the other; Thackeray assuming what he judged to be a style of conversation suitable for Lever, whilst the latter responded in the same sarcastic and sceptical tone, proper to an English tourist in Ireland.

"French and German literature next came on the *tapis*. Thackeray seemed to value the last named more highly than the other. . . . [He] paid Lever the very handsome compliment of saying, that he would rather have written Lorrequer's English version of the Student song, 'The Pope he leads a happy life,' &c., than anything he had himself hitherto done in literature. . . . Passing on to French authors, full justice was done to the celebrities of the day: Dumas, Alphonse Karr, Balzac, George Sand, &c. Thackeray criticised the French theatre very sharply, and came out with a strong bit of humorous representation, which convulsed us with laughter. It had reference to some drama or opera, I forget what, in which the principal male character comes on the stage with a pirouette, and waving his hand in a majestic manner to a chorus, representing Jews in exile at Babylon, says, 'Chantez nous une chanson de Jérusalem.' Thackeray rose from his seat and did the thing, pirouette and all, most inimitably: by the way, he was fond of exhibiting his French pronunciation, also of caricaturing very cleverly that of his own countrymen, the English." (W. J. Fitzpatrick, *Life of Charles Lever*, 2 vols., London, 1879, II, 405–410)

[51] Julia Pardoe (1806–1862), author of *The City of the Magyar; or Hun-*

would write an article containing the information I would supply the fun and so we might both bear down upon that unfortunate virgin. He lives near Limerick whither I propose to bend my steps from this, by way of Bantry, Glengariff, Killarney, & the deuce knows where.

I shall be glad to have the honor of a letter from the mysterious Editor [52] of your Review, and wish it, the Proprietors, Editor and contributors the greatest prosperity possible.

Always faithfully yrs dear Sirs<br>W M Thackeray.

227.          TO MRS. CARMICHAEL-SMYTH
29 JULY 1842

*Address:* M<u>rs</u> Carmichael-Smyth. | Rue des Arcades | S<u>t</u> Germain-en-Laye | France. *Postmarks:* CORK JY 29 1842, ST-GERMAIN-EN-LAYE 3 AOUT 42. Extract published in *Biographical Introductions*, V, xxvii.

Cork. July 29, 1842.

My dearest Mammy. Your birthday compliment reached me only on Wednesday after following me about the country. It was a melancholy compliment and made me so with one thing and the other more dismal than I have been for many a day. What can be the meaning of the waywardness of the little one? Something that you wrote to me before frightened me very much, about the child's being fed like a little dog — I don't know why, for peevishness or nonsense would not frighten me in any other child. May God Almighty be good to us. It can't however be, for the child is intelligent, & affectionate, and oh pray heaven she may continue so, —

I have had some weary work here, going about to the old haunts, where I was with the poor little woman [53] — It is astonishing what memories the people have, a carman who drove me home recollected me perfectly, and made inquiries &c. I went to Grattan's

---

gary and its Institutions in 1839–40 (1840) and The Hungarian Castle (1842).

[52] See below, Appendix VIII.

[53] See Thackeray's letters of September and October, 1840.

Hill but could not find my dear little Nanny's friends Minny &
the rest, they were out with their mother — what a sickness the
place gave me! & this opposite door, where the mother used to
live!

This is certainly pleasant letter-writing. Well, I made a most
delightful trip with Peter Purcell and his family, as noble a fellow
as I ever came near, nothing but laughing & sunshine from morning
till night along the road and when I parted from them, I felt as if
I had known them all my life, and indeed I think I shall be sincerely attached to them for the rest of it. They are twice as hearty
and cordial these simple Irish people as our guindés English *enjoying* a great deal more, and liking themselves and others to be
happy.

From Waterford we went to Lismore a noble place w^h once belonged to that splendid robber Sir Walter Raleigh — a castle as
fine as Warwick nearly and a river near as beautiful as the Rhine —
Then from Lismore hither to the Agricultural Show: there were
grand doings for 3 days, a dinner then another dinner, then a ball
for 1400 persons, where I danced a quadrille without a single
blunder of consequence. But oh the disappointments of ambition!
this Agricultural Society has been the creation of Peter Purcell (by
the way I sent you a newspaper) — and he gave a silver cup and
200 to set the thing going, and when he arrived the Tories hardly
took notice of him and his cup. The Lord Lieutenant sent 100
guns, they roared thanks loyally, the Marquis of Downshire [54] put
his name down *but didn't pay the money*, the Mayor invited him
to a grand dinner asking Peter as one of the company. Downshire
at the public dinner talked about the *condescenscion* of gentlemen
mixing with farmers, and nothing he said could be more agreeable
than to see at proper periods, mind I say at proper periods, landed
gentlemen and their tenants meeting together — I could have flung
a leg of mutton at his head.

Otho Travers came to see me yesterday. He is grown quite old
& white-headed and has invited me to Lor Mount for tomorrow.

---

[54] Arthur Trumbull (1788–1845), third Marquess of Downshire. For an
account of the public dinner, see chapter 5 of *The Irish Sketch Book*.

I have been laying pen to paper as hard as possible since Sunday, taking advantage of a few days quiet to do lots of work. I hope youll like my articles the German,[55] and the last 15 years of the Bourbons in the Review. — they pay well near 1 £ a page. This is all sad disjointed stuff, but the fact is I am done up having been at it since 7 this morning and it's now just 5.

Please to make yourself easy about the drink. I am very moderate, drinking sherry and water after dinner and can't-abiding whiskey. I don't know what the young people have frightened you about with my London doings — It's the soda-water, and the not eating breakfast. Well soda water is a very pleasant drink: and as for wine by the way, I have breakfasted with Father Matthew [56] a fine fellow, simple straightforward manly and with *one idea*. He never lets a chance slip to get a convert, and says he w^d rather convert Peter Purcell than any man in Ireland. He took us to his burial ground, a pretty cemetery he has established in the vicinity of this place; and a young lady took us to a convent introducing us to a real live nun who took us over house, chapel, burial-place, cells &c — It gave one a strange turn, but I wont be eloquent about it, having already flared up in the journal. — I've no notes but write into a book at once when I've time.

I went away with the Purcells to Youghal and back thence to Cork again. Youghal a pretty town where Raleigh planted the first potato. Isn't that a sacred place? From this in about 4 days to Bantry, Glengariff, Limerick, Killarney and to see the Shannon. If you have not written just before this reaches you, write Post Office Killarney. I shall be there in 10 days from this, please God. And God take care of my children, and of those who are so good to them: and bless my dearest old Mother — prays her affectionate W M T.

[55] See above, No. 218.
[56] See chapter 6 of *The Irish Sketch Book*.

228.          TO MRS. CARMICHAEL-SMYTH
                    12-14 AUGUST 1842

*Address:* M^rs Carmichael:Smyth | Rue des Arcades | a S^t Germain en Laye |
pres Paris | France. *Postmarks:* KILLARNEY AU 15 1842, ST-GERMAIN-
EN-LAYE 19 AOUT 42. Hitherto unpublished.

My dearest Mammy, Your letters both reached me here no 2
yesterday on my arrival no 1 today, just after returning from a
*stag-hunt* w^h I hope will put you in a pretty flurry. But the fact is
the stag-hunt here is done on the water when it is done at all, but
we were for 4 hours in a dismal rain on the lake, and the juice a bit
of a stag made its appearance, though we heard much howling of
dogs in the mountain & even saw huntsmen with red coats rushing
through the wood.[57]

I arrived here last night after a charming rainy trip by Skibberian
Bantry. Glengariff & Kenmare and to show the beauty of Irish
cars yesterday I saw 3 tumbles off the carriage, one performed by a
man who hurt himself: one by me who didn't, and one by a pretty
woman, who was holding on very tight, for the fact is my arm was
round her waist (there's a gay young dog!) the car being squeezed
beyond all endurance & so on a sudden lurch of the road off we went
together. Nothing more beautiful than the country however was
ever seen, it is even more beautiful than this place, I think, w^h is
really too handsome. It seems as if it were set out for show.

I have made no such pleasant acquaintances as the Purcells since:
such people are not to be met with more than a few times in a man's
life, and as for fat Peter Purcell, I feel the warmest regard for him —
but at Glengariff I fell in with 5 men out of a yacht, with beards &
mustachios, pea-jackets and ferocious gold & velvet caps — Three
of them were attornies from Dublin it is quite a new breed: and I
hope to make some good out of them: we have been together all
day on the lake, where, thanks to the Macintosh that Charles gave
me, I was all day as dry as a chip. He has made some blunders

---

[57] See chapters 9 to 11 of *The Irish Sketch Book* for the stag-hunt and other
incidents mentioned in this letter.

about me. The last especially: but amen: if he were to accuse me of
picking pockets, I think he would be as near the mark. In London
I recollect he asked me 3 times whether I had left a note on W$^m$
Ritchie, and would not be satisfied with my answers until afterwards he enquired of W$^m$ Ritchie himself. It is curious this mistrust, and must arise from some crotchet for w$^h$ I'm sorry to say (or
glad) that I don't care a straw — I wish I had his home-loving
virtues though, and shall always admire them and him: if he were
as clever as he is simple & good & generous there would be no end
to him. I often think that in one's intercourse with men, w$^h$ creates
sympathies with some & antipathies with others, the party who
hates you, & he who loves you, are both right — (Two days after) —
Its a great mercy I fell asleep in the beginning of the above moral
sentence: that is to say pausing in the midst of it to consider the
vastness of the theme, Charles's singular mistrust & other weighty
matters I fell asleep, and next day spent the morning in bread
winning & the afternoon in pleasure: that is in going to see a race
w$^h$ was very amusing for about a quarter of an hour, but grew like
all other enjoyments to pall sadly and ended by downright disgust.
It was what they call a hurdle-race and one man had been carried
away half-killed, and in the second race a second fellow, a fine
spirited gentleman who was winning the race, failed on a hurdle,
was kicked in the head & loins by the falling horse, & was carried
away all but dead. So the bay-horse won, & there was a jolly ball
in the evening. I came away with a strong desire to have a basin &
be sick, but there were 10000 people left on the ground, and all
sorts of fun. To day I kept clear of the place, and went a pretty
drive, no prettier perhaps in the world to Mucruss Abbey, and by
the shores of two of the Killarney Lakes: they are prettier I think
from the land than from the water: then home to quill driving
again, and so it happens that whenever I begin to write to you, I
am always thoroughly done by the huge labors of the day.

And now lest I should carry the remainder of this from here to
Limerick & from Limerick to Galway, and thence to other unknown regions it is best to finish it to night & let the Cork post bear
it tomorrow morning whithersoever it will. I've not said any thing

about the little people, but the letter w$^h$ you apologized for was a very comfortable one indeed, thank God, and gave me great pleasure about poor little Marian whom I don't love as I ought. I am always thinking about Nanny but not of the little one God bless her; though for the first 3 months of her life I was immensely fond of her: but the mother makes half the children that's the truth: and I'm not ashamed to make the confession to you. God bless them, and all grandmothers, and indeed it will be a happy day when I get home again and see all the honest faces once more. As for money, mum is the word. I have spent 60£ in two months, & the juice knows how: except that with travelling waiters & inns & no great extravagance that I know of it costs 1£ a day but I have written double that sum: that's not counting the money I already owe on the book — w$^h$ is not a clear definition. Hume wrote me a kind letter saying Charles Thackeray was always in & out of drunkenness that he had called him a thief in one letter and proposed to write in his papers in the next, & concluded by promising to pay 100 this year. He says he is flourishing at Calcutta, where he may set up his papers: so I sent 4 bills on him to those scoundrelly Lubbocks who are India agents, & who sent me back the bills, not choosing to forward them for acceptance.

This place, the fact is is too handsome: and the loneliness by no means bearable. I feel disgusted with FitzGerald for not coming with me: but with a lazy habit perhaps the solitude is advantageous as it forces one to push on and tomorrow morning the travels begin again — from here to Tralee, & a place called Tarbert in the Shannon. I don't know where to tell you to write, but please God shall be in Dublin again in a fortnight — have a letter there to the Shelburne Hotel Stephen's Green — I sent off yesterday a letter to poor little Puss: and met a cousin of her's yesterday on the race course He evidently from his behaviour thinks me a dreadful reprobate, but what then? Let M$^{rs}$ Shawe have all the credit amongst her relations and who cares. Many a reputation has been made so: and now I can see you in a great fit of indignation that any saint should be so calumniated: but is it worth while setting the people right? — certainly one need not go and seek them for the purpose. In fact I had at one time indited a thundering letter for the family, but what's the use. Let things remain as they are. I warrant if any body leaves me ten thousand a year they would find me virtuous enough.

And now I cant find anything else to fill this vacant space but to pray God to bless my dear old Mother and the little ones, and all with you in that pretty drawing room. How I wish I could see, and in 6 weeks more please God I shall be there.

229.          TO MRS. CARMICHAEL-SMYTH
          31 AUGUST–1 SEPTEMBER 1842

*Address:* Mrs Carmichael-Smyth. | Rue des Arcades | a St Germain-en-Laye | France. *Postmarks:* SE 1 1842, ST-GERMAIN-EN-LAYE 5 SEPT. 42. Hitherto unpublished.

My dearest Mammy. I am just arrived at Dublin after a fortnight's pleasant trip, and thank God to get your letter & find all so well — As for Anny what is to be done? — I think whipping her will be put in practise, for where's a better cure for that sort of wilfulness and pride? With regard to my own delinquencies, I know I spend more than other people, but not in the proportion you suppose — Everybody's bill at an inn for a day is 10 or 11/ — Then comes the payment of servants, and then every other day coach-hire. To day 15/ yesterday 13/ and so on. But please God the money never shall be spent as you prophecy, and the portion I have drawn out shall be refunded. I don't look upon it as my own money upon this tour I shall use no more of it: nor desire to apply to it except I can pay it back, or except a violent necessity occur for making use of it.

I fear I shall be detained here some days with an article for Chapman & Hall other work delayed me similarly for 10 days last month, and then I will make quick work through the north of Ireland and complete the book at home — I have a volume written within a score of pages: and material for some more: but doubt about the success of the volumes through my own ignorance upon all practical subjects.

I went from Killarney to Tralee, from Tralee to Tarbert, from Tarbert up the Shannon to Limerick, thence to Galway, from Galway to Connemara, where I quartered myself on M$^r$ Martin's,[58] from Clifden through the Joyce country to Westport w$^h$ is far the most beautiful thing I have seen anywhere in Europe I think, and yesterday to Ballynasloe and to day home. Who do you think I met yesterday on the coach, but don't tell Bess.[59] There was a priest on the coach who talked about the County of Wicklow, and the guard said he was from the county, and asked him if he knew one Father Archer — so I asked the guard if *he* knew any of the Archers of Wicklow — 'Look on my boy, says he, and read my name,' — He is M$^{rs}$ Crowe's first cousin.[60] — and, Heaven forgive me, the first think I thought of was *the King's Messenger*. He says his grandfather was a man of large estate and spent most of it, that his father spent his share, and Captain Archer his, and that being thrown quite adrift on the world he gladly took a guard's place, and has filled it these thirty years. So that I have met M$^{rs}$ C's relations with a vengeance.

You will have seen poor Maginn's death [61] in the papers. I thought he could not live a week when I saw him in prison before leaving town, and his wife and children are of course without a penny — There'll be a subscription I suppose, and his works published & so on. He died of sheer drink I fear. By the way, I have kept clear of the whiskey, w$^h$ I found very unwholesome and not very pleasant — What dreadful stupid stuff is this I am writing, but I am tired out, having had no sleep last night for a flea, and nodding as I write this.

I caught the flea in my stocking, and passed in consequence, as all Europe will be glad to hear a favorable night. The rain has set in cats & dogs & so far the weather is good for me, for I can stop at home and finish my articles and could do no good travelling in such

[58] See chapters 17 and 18 of *The Irish Sketch Book*.
[59] Miss Hamerton.
[60] Mrs. Crowe was the former Margaret Archer, daughter of Joseph and Hester Archer of Newtown Mount Kennedy in the county of Wicklow (Sir Joseph Crowe, *Reminiscences*, p. 2).
[61] Maginn died on August 21.

a waterfall. We have no heat in this fair country like that you write of: it has been every day a cloak day and more than once I have regretted I had not a great coat too.

I have made as regards drawing half a dozen abominable attempts at landscapes, than w.ʰ many a child could do better; and shall confine the drawing for the book to figures almost entirely. How strange this is, I mean the bad landscape-drawing, in a person with an exceedingly strong perception of natural beauty. Buildings I can do smartly enough, but there are no buildings here: — only huts built of round stone, and sodded or strawed over — or tumble down modern houses, w.ʰ are more dismal than any other ruins. I don't think I cared much for Killarney, it is too fine and showy, and looks as if it were there on purpose to be admired, but Westport Bay is a miracle of beauty — and in Connemara I saw 1000 lakes of w.ʰ 10000 beautiful pictures might be made. Yesterday a man on the coach, quoted *by heart* a passage out of Titmarsh! How you would have admired him. It was all I could do not to embrace him, and say the Great Titmarsh is at this moment by your side. I find it is better and cheaper (economist!) to go to Inns than gentlemen's houses. The 5 days at Martins I did not write a word, being forced into innumerable excursions that lasted all day till dinner — one was a fishing excursion on the lakes — My & how the fish did jump! It was just as pleasant looking on, as fishing, the country & the people and the sport being quite strange and affording me plenty of amusement — the boatmen had a horrid contempt for me as you may imagine from my ignorance of sporting, but this did not make me very unhappy I believe. In Galway, a queer old town I passed 2 days scribing, 3 at Westport: at the same work — I have kept the towns to do at my leisure: but unless in going through the country I write of it the next day I find it is not near so well done — so much for all infamous memory.

It's a great blessing to hear that the baby thrives so at length. What are your intentions about the Winter, and do you move Southward? I have an offer of good & constant work in London (to write a history of England) but if the Tour succeeds shall be in no want of other employment,

And so, after this stupid letter, God bless all, and thank all once more for caring for my children when their father is out of sight. I won't be a bad father to them pray God, and declare that I would never have touched that money, had I not thought it was honestly my duty to do so. I'm glad you wrote though too for one so careless can't be reminded too often. Goodbye, dearest Mother. I'll write again before I leave this: and do you too soon. W M T.

230.        TO MRS. CARMICHAEL-SMYTH
            25–30 SEPTEMBER 1842

*Address:* M*ʳˢ* Carmichael Smyth. | Rue des Arcades | a S*ᵗ* Germain en Laye | France. *Postmarks:* SE 30 1842, ST-GERMAIN-EN-LAYE 5 OCT. 42. Hitherto unpublished.

My dearest Mammy. Since I received the dismal letter from G P. to say that you were ill once more with your rheumatic fever, I have been taking my pleasure as if nothing was the matter with you, and have been on a tour of a couple of days to Wicklow, that is as far as Glendalough w*ʰ* is 20 miles from the place where M*ʳˢ* Crowe's relations are. But if I tell you the trip would have been much pleasanter had I known you to be well, and not suffering with pain fever & want of rest, I don't think you will be told anything you required to know: and if God visits my dearest old mother with illness, it seems to me a sort of impertinence to pray for her relief: — a shoeblack might as well talk of using his interest with the Queen in behalf of some personage who in rank was a hundred degrees above him. Well, I will not pay you compliments, but indeed it will be a great happiness to me when I hear you are well again, and I hope to find a letter at the Post Office Belfast, to that effect: and God bless and guard you meanwhile. I was going to send you on a crowded sheet of paper, an immense long pert letter about the Wicklow tour,[62] killing 2 birds as the saying is — but the letter is a very dull one, and if it is but for half a dozen lines it's better to write to you than to send you specimens of manufacture.

[62] The manuscript of chapter 24 of *The Irish Sketch Book.*

To day a little child in its nurse's arms in Sackville Street, saw me and began shouting out 'Papa Papa' wʰ gave me such a turn of the stomach as never was — its a long long time since I have been away from the little people, but pray God the long time will soon be over now: 3 weeks more in the north and the job will be all but done; — done in a way that is the 2 volumes will be all but written; and the material ready, but I am beginning to find out now, that a man ought to be forty years in the country instead of 3 months, and *then* he wouldn't be able to write about it. I wonder who *does* understand the place? not the natives certainly, for the two parties so hate each other, that neither can view the simplest proceeding of the other without distrusting falsifying & abusing it. And where in the midst of all the lies that all tell, is a stranger to seek for truth? O Connell among the liars is the greatest liar of all however, and a man coming here as I did with a strong predisposition in favor of the Catholics, priests & all can't fail to get indignant at the slavish brutal superstition of the latter, and to become rather Toryfied so far. So I shall be abused by the Catholic Press for abusing the priests, and by the Tory papers for being a liberal and very unhappy be sure will this make me. And both parties will ask, what business has this bookseller's hack who is only fit to cut jokes and scribble buffooneries, to write about our country? — and both parties will be right too.

The Old Colonel [63] continues very comfortable in health. I dined there on Saturday a letter had just arrived from my mother in law stating that she hoped immediately to receive her dear child — of course. That little Corsilles is an odious conceited vulgar little wretch, and in order to show his consequence to me, bullied his poor little boy during dinner time in the most unjust & brutal way. It must be a hard thing for the poor old Colonel who has been used to refined and educated gentlemen all his life to be obliged to put up with such a snob for constant society and with the old ladies that form good old Miss Shawe's [64] twaddling old circle.

[63] Colonel Shawe. Corsilles was presumably a relative by marriage of the Shawes.
[64] No doubt Isabella's Aunt Mary, mentioned above, No. 101.

She is a very nice creature, kind simple and tender-hearted. I wish you could see the dinner-table though, and the awe in w<sup>h</sup> they all are of little humpey, who sate swaggering and bragging in the most wonderful way. He produced with a great manifesto a bottle of claret saying with a roguish look to the ladies 'I know the ladies are fond of clart? — and people were helped and he asked in triumph, ⟨Isn't⟩ it a fine sound wine? — Nobody dared tell the truth except me, that it was very bad, and why should one say otherwise to such a little self-sufficient creature?

As for Wicklow it is wonderfully beautiful, and having a companion this time, I actually made some long walks up hills to visit Lakes, Devils Glens &c — but this beauty though delightful to the eye is by no means profitable to the penny a lining trade: for one tries in vain to describe it — a cataract in print will answer for most cataracts & so on. I have spent much time fruitlessly over these descriptive subjects: w<sup>h</sup> shows clearly a great defect in a writer — it is the same with the pencil likewise.

I hear much praise of Thackeray of Dundalk [65] w<sup>h</sup> will be my

[65] The Rev. Elias Thackeray (1771–1854), *Genealogy* (32), was educated at Eton and Cambridge and came to Ireland in 1797 during the Rebellion as an officer in a regiment of dragoons. He took holy orders shortly after the Peace of Amiens in 1802 and was presented by Lord Roden with the Vicarage of Dundalk in the county of Louth. In 1824 Lord John Beresford, Archbishop of Armagh, gave him the valuable Rectory of Louth, six miles from Dundalk. Since the conscience of the church was not then awake to the evils of pluralism, he did not relinquish his earlier preferment. He was a very handsome man, who enjoyed great popularity among his parishioners. (*Memorials*, pp. 105–115)

Thackeray has left an account of his visit with this amiable clergyman in chapter 26 of *The Irish Sketch Book*. He grew very fond of "noble and dear old Elias" (*Works*, VI, 342) and after his death on April 29, 1854, wrote to Martin Thackeray, whose favorite brother Elias was, a letter of sympathy which I have not been able to trace but which is quoted in part by Lady Ritchie (*Biographical Introductions*, V, xxvi): "The world holds one good man the less, now your good brother has left it, after a life so noble, useful, and pious. I have always thought him one of the most fortunate of men; to have such a career, and such peculiar qualities suiting him for it — activity, benevolence, simplicity, faith, unselfishness, immense esteem from all round about him, who could not but love and honour him; what man could wish for a better fate in life; and if he was lucky here, he is now even more to be envied! The good deeds of his long life bear interest yonder. . . . One

first station after leaving this — tomorrow I must go to Maynooth, and then for a day to FitzGerald's brother [66] in the county Meath — the honestest fat fellow ever seen. He has turned Catholic and gobbles fish on Friday with the greatest piety.

Dearest Mother, Your letter is just come in — thank God to see the kind writing again maimed as it looks. I have luckily been detained here by money-matters, and by the arrival of Peter Purcell, and of an old college acquaintance who delayed me a day, and who I wish had been here earlier to show me the town w͟h he knows. FitzGerald has been lying idle & moping in the country, very sorry I think that he didn't join me, which the way I put the business he should have done. I have spent the past week reading & writing beginning to be very doubtful as to my success with this book.

Come to Paris I must of course. What I shall have to do will be done as well there as in London, for a month or more, and then we can talk of future movements, unless, as I think my dearest Mother should, you go to Aix for the winter, not wait through the spring. Why not pass the winter warmly, and why expose yourself to the colds & drafts of Paris?

Halverstown 30 September

I have left this letter open thinking & thinking about the children and whether I should take them or leave them with you who love them better than I do or as well I can't decide better today than 5 days since though I've been thinking of little else. It must rest upon your health    Why should you wait for the hot season to go to Aix when it is the winter you dread, and would suffer from most by remaining in Paris? This you and G P will consider.

---

would never think of being sorry for the death of such a man; at such years it was time that he should go and reap the fruit of his life. So I do not offer to condole with you on your brother's death; but I know you will believe in the sincere affection and honour in which I hold his memory, and that I like to think that such a man bore our name."

[66] Peter FitzGerald (1807–1875), described by Wright (*Life of Edward FitzGerald*, I, 30, and II, 160) as a kindly, rather simple-minded man, "with the conversation of a child," who had been converted to Catholicism by his wife.

As for the poor little woman that's another difficulty, I don't know of any place in London where I could place her to be so comfortable  Procter (who is a Lunacy Commissioner & knows them all) took me to his favourite place which makes me quite sick to think of even now.  He shook his head about other places.[67]

Ought I to write to my poor aunt? [68]  God help her, it is a frightful affliction for her, the poor tender-hearted soul, it is a shame to meddle with such a grief as that.  And I see my dear Mother's dread and terror lest Fate should seize upon *her* little ones.  Heaven guard them.  As long as they stay with you, you must tend them as you think best: and if ever I can believe, and if ever they come to live with me, I will treat them according to your plan too, but I must be made to believe first.  Meanwhile I am sure it's wrong to call other Doctors murderers though I've no business to lecture my old Mother.

I go to day to P. FitzGerald near Drogheda, thence by Dundalk and Rosstrevor coastwise to Belfast and the Giants' Causeway though I know I shall make nothing of the latter.  I shall come home inland, & be in Dublin on the 25$^{th}$ please God, in Paris on the 30 October: with the book such as it is all but done.  There I am engaged to do an article on Louis Philippe's reign, w$^h$ can be done either there or in London according as you determine to stay or go: but at Paris at any rate for a couple of months I shall be as well as in London.  Write to the Shelburne they will forward letters on, no place I shall go to will be more than 20 hours from Dublin. God bless all.

W M T.

[67] The treatment of the insane in Early Victorian England may be studied in the various *Reports of the Commissioners in Lunacy to the Lord Chancellor*, the parliamentary blue books upon which Charles Reade's *Hard Cash* (1863) is partially founded.

[68] Emily, Mrs. Ritchie's youngest child, had died shortly after September 1 (*Ritchies in India*, pp. 26 and 32).

231.              TO BRADBURY AND EVANS [69]
                  27 SEPTEMBER 1842

My text is taken from Spielmann's *History of "Punch,"* p. 310.

                                              Halverstown,
                                              Kildare,
Gentlemen,                                    Sept. 27, 1842.

Your letter containing an enclosure of £25, has been forwarded
to me, and I am obliged to you for the remittance. Mr. Lemon has
previously written to me to explain the delay, and I had also received a letter from Mr. Landells,[70] who told me, what I was
sorry to learn, that you were dissatisfied with my contributions to
"Punch." [71] I wish that my writings had the good fortune to
please everyone; but all I can do, however, is to do my best, which
has been done in this case, just as much as if I had been writing for
any more dignified periodical.

But I have no wish to continue the original agreement made
between us, as it is dissatisfactory to you and, possibly, injurious to
your work; and shall gladly cease Mrs. Tickletoby's Lectures,
hoping that you will be able to supply her place with some more
amusing and lively correspondent.

I shall pass the winter either in Paris or in London where, very
probably, I may find some other matter more suitable to the paper,
in which case I shall make another attempt upon "Punch." [72] —
Meanwhile, gentlemen, I remain, your very obedient Servant,

                              W. M. Thackeray.

[69] William Bradbury and Frederick Mullet ("Pater") Evans (d. 1870)
became proprietors of Punch on July 25, 1842. See Spielmann's *History of
"Punch,"* pp. 31–38.

[70] Ebenezer Landells (1808–1860), one of the founders of *Punch* and for
many years its engraver.

[71] "Miss Tickletoby's Lectures on English History," which appeared in
*Punch* from July 2 to October 1, 1842. It will perhaps escape the attention of
the modern reader that Miss Tickletoby's name is a variant, delicately modified
to suit her sex, of Dr. Swishtail's in *Vanity Fair.*

[72] Thackeray's next identified contribution to *Punch* was "The Sick Child,"
January 14, 1843.

232.         TO MRS. CARMICHAEL-SMYTH
                   ?-16 OCTOBER 1842

*Address:* Mrs Carmichael Smyth | Rue des Arcades | a St Germain En Laye |
France. *Postmarks:* COLERAINE, OC 18 1842, ST-GERMAIN-EN-LAYE
21 OCT. 42. Published in part, *Biographical Introductions*, V, xxiv-xxvii.

My dearest Mammy I think the last letter was after having
been at Halverstown put into the post on my way to FitzGerald's
brother in the County Meath — the honestest best creature that
ever was born. I stopped with him 3 days, on one going to see
Trim wh is near Laracor wh is the place where Swift's living was:
on another day to see Stone Castle a beautiful mansion belonging
to my Lord Conyngham, and on another to see the Boyne water
where as perhaps you have heard King William defeated King
James. Fitz's benevolence would have done you good to witness —
he thanked his coachman for driving us: his footman for bringing
in the tea-urn: and seemed to be bubbling over with good humour
and good will towards men, His wife a kind bigot of an Irishwoman
who made me a present of Wiseman's lectures [73] when I came away,
hearing me say I would like to read them, Wiseman you must
know is the great luminary of the R. Catholic church at present;
and my conviction after reading 1/4 his book is that he is as great
a hypocrite as ever lived.

From FitzGerald I went to Drogheda, where an hour was
enough to show the filthy squalid crawling l --- y town (see the
blot is come for using that word it is the true word) — to show the
dirty insecty town & suburbs, and the green old walls that Cromwell
battered. He put all the garrison (except about 200 the garrison
being 3000) to death here, and a great part of the inhabitants, bible
in hand, praising God, and talking of this crowning mercy. His
letter [74] to the Speaker of the H of Commons is a wonder of fanati-
cism and brutal simplicity.

[73] *Lectures on the Principal Doctrines and Practices of the Catholic Church*
(1836) by Nicholas Patrick Wiseman (1802–1865), later (1850) Archbishop
of Westminster, and Cardinal.
[74] Written from Dublin, September 17, 1649 (letter CV in Carlyle's *Oliver
Cromwell's Letters and Speeches*).

From Drogheda to Dundalk, where I went to old Thackeray, the most noble simple, humourous stupid delightful pious old fellow ever seen — Sir says he no person bearing the name of Thackeray must go through Dundalk without sleeping at my house: and though I represented that to remain at the Inn would be much more convenient, where I could smoke my cigar and write my page in quiet, there was nothing for it but to shift my quarters to his old dingy Vicarage: where he has a sick wife with rheumatism, and her sufferings made me think of my dear old Mother's, (it is true that allæopathy has been able to do nothing for her;) — and here the old gentleman ordered his curates to come and dine with me, and amused me all day taking me to Infant schools Hospitals and Institutions. Well, they were all delightful to see, especially the Infant Schools, God bless them, and the little ones singing in a way that makes the sternest ruffians cry — We went 1 day to Thackeray's living of Louth, the best in Ireland it was, worth 3000 £ a year, but now only half. But 1500 or 3000 this man never has a shilling at the year's end, and has no expenses or extravagances of his own. He must live on 500 and the rest goes to Schools, hospitals and the poor, and curates. I am sure God Almighty himself must be pleased to look down on honest Elias Thackeray, and ⟨when I⟩ hear of human depravity as applied to him and some others, can't believe ⟨it for⟩ the soul of me.

Have you remarked how stupid my letters are? Solitude creates a muzziness and incoherency in me, and I must get back to the little ones that's clear — I am never thinking of what I am writing about, all the time I was writing of Thackeray there was something else in my thoughts & so on — so that I feel what dreadful dull things my letters must be. Well from Armagh I went to Newry where a Doctor of Divinity gave me good claret for dinner and showed me. the savings banks, the Poorhouse, and the town in General — from Newry to Armagh, where the service of the Cathedral is wonderfully performed, and I looked at the Primate [75] with pleasure having heard of his noble generosity & bounty, and

[75] Richard Whately (1787–1863), Archbishop of Dublin from 1831 until his death.

from Armagh by the railroad hither: I was to have been off this morning, but that at breakfast with a gentleman to whom I had an introduction, something came up about some monstrous intrigues of the Roman Catholic priesthood so awful that I thought they would make a good chapter for the book, and that I was bound to stop and get at the truth of the business; well, thank God I shall have no chapter on that subject, the story told me by a Reverend Gentleman, Moderator of the Synod of Alstor, turns out to be a rank & monstrous falsehood — a little truth that is with 90/100 parts of lies — like M$^{rs}$ Shawes about somebody you know — but they are all so in this country; all exaggerating in abuse of each other — Not but that the priests are a disgusting body, and though I say thank God now as I ought if the truth must out, when I found the story against them was quite untrue, my first feeling was one of some mortification.

This is the only town properly speaking I have seen in Ireland, bustling, prosperous, busy, unhumbugging, the people are like the Scotch, the physiognomies quite altered, the country happy looking and thriving with neat houses and orchards and hedges — I ⟨am glad I⟩ have it for the end of my trip, and O I am glad the end of my trip is ⟨near.⟩ I have been heart-weary for months past that's the truth.

Coleraine Sunday I intended to have addressed the remainder of this, just for the look of the thing from the 'Giants Causeway' — but the place was so awful and lonely, that I was glad to run from it after a couple of hours visit — sea sickness in an infernal boat, tumbling and sprawling among rocks afterwards and a lonely dinner at a hotel situated over the colorful spot — a huge place with not a sole in it the last company being a corpse w$^h$ had just gone. I think the ghost was there still and got out of the place in a panic. It will make a capital chapter though, and that's something. The drive from Belfast along the coast is magnificent and I never enjoyed anything more in my life ⟨but I think⟩ I shall enjoy a visit to S$^t$ ⟨Germain⟩ still more. Meanwhile I dream of you ⟨and G P⟩ and the little ones every night, w$^h$ to be sure is not much comfort. I shall have done 5/6 of the book by the time I am with you, on

the 1 November please God, and shall have easy work with the
rest. Does G. P recollect a Colonel Cairnes [76] who was at Paris? —
Lever gave me a letter to him w^h I have just been to deliver 4
miles off at Port Rush — He is a great character by all accounts:
what they call here a *dust* w^h phrase Miss Elizabeth Hamerton will
be able to translate: but I think letters are rather a bore than otherwise — one can't work at the people's houses.

And so — (dinner has come off since the above and the fire is
just loaded with turf, and I'm going to try and set in for a night's
scribing: but first must say God bless my dearest old Mother and
all both little and tall at Saint Germain; A fortnight more please
God, and I won't be far from them.

If you have anything very pressing write to Dublin, the Shelburne, if not to London — I'll write once more too.

W M T.

233.                TO CHARLES LEVER
                   26 OCTOBER 1842

Hitherto unpublished.

                       Schelborne Hotel. Stéphens grin.
                       à Dublin ce 26 Octobre — 42

Arrivé dernièrement de Londres-Derri (ville assez considérable
du province d'Olster) le Chevalier de Titmarsh s'empresse d'offrir
ses hommages affectueux, a l'écrivain spirituel, au médecin dis-
tingué, — a l'aimable Lévèr!

Le séjour du Chevalier à Dublin ne sera que très court. En-
chainé (pauvre forçat de la Presse!) a son banc de travail, il n'aura
que peu d'instans à donner a l'amitié, a la société!

Combien lui sera t'il agréable, de renouveler quelques unes de
ces heures charmantes dont le souvenir lui est toujours si chèr!

[76] Colonel Cairnes was not the only representative of the military whom
Thackeray saw in northern Ireland. "He became a great favourite with the
officers of a regiment, then stationed at Newry," we learn from Major Dwyer
(Fitzpatrick, *Life of Charles Lever*, II, 415), "and was a frequent and welcome guest at their mess. Here . . . he got useful materials, and found
'sitters' for some of the events and characters introduced in the Brussels scenes
of 'Vanity Fair,' and on his return to Dublin from the North, I found that he
had got up a considerable stock of military characteristic and anecdote."

Tachons mon ami de rappeler ces doux momens! Qu'ils nous soient rendus encor une fois! Pour les âmes nobles, cher Lorréquèr, le Passé vit toujours: seul don du coeur dont la Fortune ne peut pas nous séparer, c'est un trésor a jamais inalterable pour nous. Accumulons sans cesse, mon ami, ces richesses généreuses! — et, comme l'agricole, qui, des moissons du herbe seulement, calcule achète les produits, — calculons, aimables avares! les chances du plaisir, tâchons d'accaparer l'avenir!

Demain, dans un mot, je serai libre pour DINER — oserai je démander à Madame votre épouse une place a sa table gracieuse et hospitalière? Samedi, mon spirituel camarade Varburton [77] (qui vous aime parce qu'il vous a vu) me prie de s'associer avec moi dans un petit projèt de repas valédictoire. Soyez bon, chèr Levèr quittez, pour ce jour seulement, une famille charmante, des bosquets solitaires — et rendez vous aux instances — aux adieux d'un ami! —

Notre diner sera servi à Kearns' Hotel: je prierai votre célèbre ami M. le Professeur de Bott,[78] de se joindre à nous: J'ai vu bien des misères dans ce pays, j'y ai moi-même passé bien de tristes heures; quittons le gaiment, cher ami, que les joies du réunion adoucissent la tristesse du départ!

Chevalier de Titmarsh

G. C. de l'ordre de l'Élépphant et du

chateau du Porc-et-Sifflet [79] &c &c.

[77] Eliot [i.e., Bartholomew Elliott George] Warburton (1810–1852), the Irish writer and traveller, whom Thackeray probably first met at Cambridge. Warburton matriculated at Queen's College in 1828, migrated to Trinity College in February, 1830, and received his B.A. and M.A. degrees in 1833 and 1837. Among his intimate friends were Milnes and John Kemble. He was called to the Irish bar in 1837, but his restless and adventurous temperament made the practice of law distasteful to him. In 1843 he went on the long excursion through Syria, Palestine, and Egypt which is described in the first and best known of his several books, *The Crescent and The Cross, or Romance and Realities of Eastern Travel* (1844). The circumstances of his death are noted below, No. 826.

[78] Dr. Isaac Butt (1813–1879), later leader of the Irish Home Rule party, who had held the chair of Political Economy at Dublin University from 1836 to 1841.

[79] Decorations appropriate to a Londoner. It was with difficulty that Thackeray's publishers dissuaded him from calling the account of his Irish tour "The Cockney in Ireland." See below, No. 248.

234.          TO MRS. CARMICHAEL-SMYTH
              · 28 OCTOBER 1842

*Address:* M^rs Carmichael-Smyth. | Rue des Arcades | a S^t Germain-en-Laye |
pres Paris | France. *Postmarks:* OC 28 1842, ST-GERMAIN-EN-LAYE
2 NOV. 42. Hitherto unpublished.

Dublin 28 October.

My dearest Mammy. The news on this scrubby half sheet wont
surprize you knowing how delays *will* take place spite of all
things — I can't get away from here until Tuesday night 1 Nov^r:
for the L. courts open that day, the new Lord Mayor is elected, and
I shall see some Dublin life worth looking at for the book.

I shall try [to] go round from Liverpool by way of York to see
the famous Quaker asylum there — a cheap and benevolent one: —
and then as for London I don't think I shall have much to keep me
there, before I go to my dear old cripple and the little ones.

That London must be the place eventually is quite clear: and I
think when the lease of Coram S^t is up I'll look out for a £40 house
in Regent's Park, Brodie for a housekeeper &c: but that's long
enough hence and who knows what may happen ere then? Charlie's
letter reached me at Derry w^h I reached from Coleraine, and where
I passed 3 pleasant days with Sir G. Hill [80] a relation of E Thackeray of Dundalk. Thence I went to Donegal, but the bad weather
at last overtook us: tempest, hail, snow & fury, and I posted back to
Dublin from Enniskillen and arrived on the 25^th. I've been hard
at work since, and the book is very near done — a clever book too,
but beside the point. If it will amuse people however, that is all I
ask, and I think Dickens's new book [81] w^h all the world is talking
about will in so far help me, as people who have read that & liked
it will like more reading of the same sort. If it succeeds, why then
* * * never mind the future. I am glad at any rate to have been
over the ground and to have seen the country, for this sort of ex-

[80] Sir George Hill (1804–1845), third Baronet, of Brooke Hall in the
county of Londonderry.
[81] *American Notes.*

perience involuntarily acquired & observation of manners & nature will always stand a man in stead. I have become bitten with a mania for *education,* and will certainly try and agitate a plan of cheap education for the middle classes. I saw at Templemoyle near Derry 70 boys, paying 10£ a year for board, as happy healthy & comfortable as any lads ever seen. They are at an Agricultural School, & pass 1/2 the day in the fields learning farming and 1/2 in the study, at Grammar, geography, mathematics surveying & so on — a noble plan.

The country, Protestant & Catholic is priest-ridden beyond all bearing, and is well to see, but as for living in it I would sooner live in a garret in dear old smoky London than a 50 windowed house here. The parties never cease quarreling — the society is under-educated — the priests as illiterate as boors — the clergy reading no profane literature — and shutting their eyes on this world for the next. — but this is God's world too, as well as the other and I am sure they have a right to enjoy this as well as Heaven itself.

Charles's letter brought me sad accts of poor Mary, & not much better of my dearest old Mother. Will she go Southwards for the winter? — or will she go & live at the Bains de Tivoli where the whole place is kept at a certain temperature? What a strange number of pros & cons there are in our circumstances! —

I was glad to see the gas-lights again, and my friends here jolly P. Purcell and his wife the gentlest charmingest creature. Lever and his children of whom I'm grown very fond in the absence of some-body else's children. God bless 'em and their kind guardians. I dine with Lever to day — tomorrow at the Kildare Street Club — Sunday with the old Colonel [82] I think, Monday with the Publisher & a literary party, and Tuesday after the Lord Mayors business, please God I'll cross the salt say to London     A line in Coram St would do me no harm.

Now I'm going to see the Workhouse: a school: and if time enough to drive 3 miles along the quay & pier to the Pigeon House God bless my dearest old Mother

W M T.

[82] Colonel Shawe.

235. TO RICHARD BENTLEY
10 DECEMBER 1842 [83]

My text is taken from a facsimile in *The Autographic Mirror*, III (1865), 15.

Dear B.

I want a copy of Walpole's letters and will have one if you choose to take it out in writing.

Yrs &c

W M Thackeray.

13 Great Coram S.ͭ 10 Dec.ʳ

236. TO MRS. CARMICHAEL-SMYTH
1 JANUARY 1843

*Address:* M.ͬˢ Carmichael-Smyth. | 81 Champs Elysées | Paris. *Postmark:* LE HAVRE 3 JANV 43. Hitherto unpublished.

Havre. Sunday.

My dearest Mammy. You'll see by the post-mark what good haste I've made. The boat advertised in Galignani to sail on Saturday, has been off the station these 6 months and a second boat wʰ was to have sailed on Saturday was delayed till the day before — do you understand that? — that is it ought by rights to have left Southampton on Friday whereas it left Havre on that day and has just come back again & won't start till tomorrow afternoon so I'm here till then.

I find as usual I have left some most important documents behind me. Luckily they are very light & will come by the post easy — these are some tracings [1] wʰ will be found in the pocket of a little black sketching book in my room. 2 of an Irish car, 1 of a

---

[83] The sixth and final volume of Bentley's edition of Walpole's *Letters*, edited by John Wright, is noticed in *The Spectator* of November 14, 1840, pp. 1097–98. Thackeray maintained a residence at 13 Great Coram Street from 1840 until 1843, but he was living there on December 10 only in 1842.

[1] Of illustrations for *The Irish Sketch Book*.

ANNE THACKERAY ABOUT 1843

*From a sketch by Thackeray*

ANNE THACKERAY AND HER FATHER ABOUT 1843
*From a sketch by Thackeray*

pair of lovers & a pig. the original drawings are there too but need not be sent. Please send off the others instanter per po:

How odd it is. The mania I have for working at inns! I have got a cheerful room at Wheeler's, and worked away for 4 hours yesterday or near it: I was up this morning at 8 o'c: breakfast over by nine snug fire comfortable everything — work away. Well: the reason I set off on Friday was that I might have the pleasure of thinking of you & the babes at high jinks during the evening night as I lay awake. But I did no such thing and slept I believe 13 hours out of the 16 the journey lasted.

G. M. when I came away gave me a sovereign for John: a genteel way of revoking her promise to pay him 12£ a year — however she begged me to go to the landlord of the house in G! Coram S! and say she would take it on the same terms for a year; as those folks are going somewhere in the Spring. & Bess Hamerton has promised not to leave her be she where ever she would. 'You can stay there too if you like', she said, 'as there will be plenty of room.' If this invitation extends to Isabella, it will be very well: with whom I am determined to live in Spring: — but I think it is very possible the old lady would like to house Charles & Mary: and perhaps the best answer to her proposal will be to discover that the landlord of Coram S! *wont* let the house for a year. I see there is a house in Easton Sq!ᵉ to be let for 80: this would be vastly more convenient, giving babes & children a clear air and an open walk.

I think Ive no more to say: except to give a kiss all round. Mind let the little ones go often to their mother — nothing is easier than to wait in the Court until the omnibus comes by, and to jump in it and so go through the mud. I took my wife a writing-book for wʰ she expressed a desire and left her very much pleased with it and promising to write. Try and put her in mind of the promise: but I don't care much about long letters from her — only a word or two —

So goodbye dearest Mother, & God Almighty bless all

W M T.

237.                    TO CHAPMAN AND HALL
                        19 JANUARY 1843 ²

*Address:* Mess.ʳˢ Chapman & Hall. | 186 Strand | London. | Angleterre. *Post-mark:* 19 1843. Hitherto unpublished.

> 81 Champs Elysées
> Paris. Thursday.

Dear Sirs

Examine well the enclosed page w.ʰ I send you — it is a no of a work in 25 numbers of w.ʰ the plates are almost all done: containing illustrations to the Fairy Tales. Each N.º here costs 10 sous: and the whole are to be sold for 10/.

Would it not be an admirable scheme in England and what do you think of FAIRY BALLADS by W. Thackeray? I would put these bits, humourous-pathetic verse, to suit the size of the plates, and the success I'm confident would be tremendous — I would rather have a share than money for my part of the enterprize.³

A good article might be done for the F. Q. R after the manner of those in the Westminster — 'The Paris Almanacks' — of a comic turn with the clichés of the wood-cuts. Will you authorize me to purchase such? briskly done, the Article would take more than Louis Philippe and Anaxagoras; I speak with respect of both.

Eugene Sues last novel Les Mysteres de Paris must be done with some such title as 'Thieve's Literature in France' — in a moral tone, with thanks for the cessations of the kind of thing in England: this I beg to book it is a striking article —

You will Im sure be glad to hear my wife is extremely better — all but herself again. This is the first spare minute I have had since my arrival to put pen to paper, but have just knocked up a little

---

² Thackeray's article with the running head, "Thieves Literature of France," reviewing *Les Mystères de Paris* by Eugene Sue, appeared in *The Foreign Quarterly Review* for April, 1843, pp. 231–249. This letter was written on Thursday, January 19, of that year.

³ Nothing came of this scheme, nor were any of the articles suggested in the next paragraph written.

garret, where I shall begin to work tomorrow — indeed I've been too happy until now. Always yours dear Sirs

W M Thackeray

I can think of nothing better than 'Irish Sketches' by W<sup>m</sup> T (M. A. T.) Author of &c — with many designs by the author.

238.　　　TO MARK LEMON

31 JANUARY 1843

*Address:* Mark Lemon Esq<sup>re</sup> | Wellington Street. | Strand. Hitherto unpublished.

G<sup>t</sup> Coram S<sup>t</sup> Tuesday 31 Jan.<sup>y</sup>

My dear Sir

I think the enclosed tragedy [4] will suit 'our eminent contemporary, [5] — But please let the authorship remain a secret between us.

Can you give me a call any morning, or where can I do the like for you? I am anxious to do all sorts of drawings, and think my hand is getting more accustomed to the work.

Faithfully yrs

W M Thackeray.

239.　　　TO GEORGE POTEMKIN PERRY

FEBRUARY 1843 [6]

*Address:* G. P. Perry Esq<sup>re</sup> | 5 John S<sup>t</sup> Adelphi. *Postmark:* FE ⟨. . .⟩ 18⟨43⟩. Hitherto unpublished.

My dear little fellow. I just got your card and welcome packet from Paris. Will you dine with me any day excep tomorrow at the

---

[4] See above, No. 207.

[5] Macready.

[6] The date is fixed by the fragmentary postmark and the reference to Perry in the next letter.

Garrick Club in King S[t] Covent Garden, and tell me news of all
my good friends across the O.

Yrs ever in a hurry

W M Thackeray.

13 G[t] Coram S[t] Brunswick Sq[re]
  I'm at home always till 3.


240.            TO MRS. CARMICHAEL-SMYTH
                16–20 FEBRUARY 1843

*Address:* M[rs] Carmichael Smyth | 81 Champs Elysées | Paris. | France. *Post-marks:* 20 FE ⟨1843⟩, 22 FEVR. 43 CALAIS. Hitherto unpublished.

Monday 20.

& several days before

One week follows another and when the time for writing comes
I always find myself in a hurry so this shall be begun betimes. That
is at ten o'clock one night so as to be ready for the post some days
hence. Well, what have I got to say, nothing but dinners dinners
until they were suddenly put an end to by a cold — and wonderful
to relate I have had no dinner these three days — no meat that is —
only po-eggs and tea: and the consequence is that if you & GP had
been homœopathizing me you would have said it was the greatest
cure ever known. I hope I shall be good to night when I am going
to an op, having on the brass buttons at this very minute. Here has
just come a half crown letter for you from M[rs] Waddell should
you like it to be sent on?

The printers of the book are abominably slow I cant get the stuff
out of their hands, and am still at my first 2 sheets. Meanwhile my
hands are pretty full of other work — w[h] grows upon one, but I am
sighing after the small people consumedly. It is all very well to
be jolly for a fortnight or a month but longer it's hard work. It's a
great comfort to have Fitz: and we dont see too much of each
other only at breakfast of mornings or for 1/2 an hour in the day to
laugh and smoke a cigar. We only talk nonsense: but that is the
best of talk and a good laugh the jolliest of luncheons.

And now for the great news HICKMAN has fixed his great gun [7] — a writ if you please — action for 715 in the Queens Bench &c — I wish he may get it — but all he wants is a compromise, and I intend to hold out a long time yet      I have been with General Fagan's attorney, a very clever old fellow, who telling me that H. had stopt proceedings against the General, I thought I would give him my job, and he has it for the moment. Tother General F has paid £40 and is off; and M^r Wright the attorney has given me such a piece of information as convinces me quite that H never can dare to support the action — as he must be cast if he does. I'm not at liberty to mention more — hem! You can't tell what a comfort the arrival of the writ was to me. Its like the tooth before you have it out — Nothing can be done till April so dont be afeard.

By the way Ive been bothered with tooth-ache, and tried another wonderful cure! M^r Kiddle [8] gave me a box of tooth-powder, and I have had no toothache since. He calls it conservative tooth-powder, and can't tell why it *should* cure but it does. This is wrote after the hop mentioned in page 1, where there was a grand meet, and supper by Gunter going on from 12 till 4 — the finest thing, and the most wholesome too: for it did me a world of good. To day I dine with Leech the Caricaturist,[9] I brought him up at Charter-house and he is a kind manly fellow.

Saturday. I wish Perry would send letters as they were directed. I find yours and Nanny's and my poor little woman's all here at the Reform-Club, where I am waiting for Procter with whom over a mutton-chop I shall talk of the Hickman business: he will super-intend the attorney for me, and determine whether or no I shall compromise.

Procter says (this is Monday) decidedly no, and thinks that Hickman will never bring his action. Well, I shan't break my heart if he doesn't: and so things must remain for a few days until we see what is done: when I'll report farther progress. Isabella's letter was very comfortable I think, though I don't understand the

[7] See above, No. 164.
[8] John Lambert Kiddle, chemist, 60 Lamb's Conduit Street (*Post Office London Directory*, 1847).        [9] See *Memoranda*.

passage about somnambulism: and I was glad to see the dear old Mammy's fist a little less shaky. What a strange uncertain way of life our's is! It seems fated that we are to make no plans at all. I must of course wait now until Hickmans business is over, before I settle whither to go. As for taking the house another year, the landlord wont do it, and moreover proposes to raise the rent — there is nothing that I have seen so good or so cheap. I wish I could afford 115 for High Row Knightsbridge with a garden that leads into Hyde Park: but it's preposterous.

Isn't [it] wonderful that here I'm actually pressed for time in spite of all the precautions! — The fact is I've been making verses and correcting proofs and writing letters all day at such a rate, that here's 5 o'clock come, and only time to say God bless all. The book is moving a good deal faster, and I really think a month now will finish it. They've spoiled my first chapter for me though (w^h you didn't see) by making me withdraw some personalities, agst the Catholics w^h might certainly have been dangerous. Isn't this dull stuff to tell about? — Well, I've only that and chronicles of dinners to talk about — eating all night scribing all day, and so goes the world God bless all once more. It does my heart good to hear that Anny likes school — Dingle Dingle here's the Bell! —

W M T.

241.            TO MRS. CARMICHAEL-SMYTH
                        MARCH? 1843
Hitherto unpublished.

My dearest Mammy. Your letter is just come in: and I thought it as well to write off to Dick straight, and tell him what the news were concerning the poor old lady. I am to dine with him tomorrow and went you may be sure to see Bess and get her news w^h and yours are good thank God: as for the 2 or 3 days per month it is nothing, it only shows how much better she is on other days.

Bess is magnificently lodged with a kind handsome exceedingly vulgar woman who drops her h's over one of the handsomest drawing rooms you ever saw: pillars, marble, stained glass hot & cold water all the way up the house, and luxuries and beauties innumerable. Squares upon Squares are springing up in the old quarter, and little Albion Street now lies shirking behind long rows of palaces, w$^h$ have well nigh got to Bayswater. That day I looked out for Sir James in Oxford Terrace,[10] but couldn't find him: however I suppose he will console himself at the delay.

The dinner-parties pour in rather too plentifully    I had 5 invitations for last Saturday; and a dinner every day in the week, the same this week; but the abuse of good dinners is wholesome in this respect that one grows used to the kind of life, and is not tempted to exceed. I've not had any soda-water this week: but my dear old Fitz and I have a cozy smoke at night over the fire; and the next day I get to work. It is curious that this racket agrees better with me than a quieter life and I have managed to write a good deal.

I've been making lots of drawings and the Punch people are beginning at last to find out that they are good. All the Irish blocks are spoiled: but no matter the public is too ignorant to know good from evil, and may possibly cry out that they are wonders.

As for Hickman I have intimated to him thro Black that I am not indisposed to compromise for 20£, and his letters after having been rampant are become quite mild & insinuating! I never answer any one of them; but shall gladly pay the 20£ to have the cust business over.

I sent off a long letter yesterday to Hume and his Star [11] w$^h$ is well spoken of here, and begins to make a stir; and have invented at least 4 schemes since I have been here for making immense sums of money — but let's wait till spring before thinking of making my fortune.

Where shall I go live? I've been looking to day at a house in Brunswick Sq$^e$ 100 a year not so big but cheerfuller than Coram

[10] Sir James Carmichael-Smyth, who was living with his mother at 95 Oxford Terrace (*Royal Blue Book*, 1843).

[11] Between 1843 and 1845 Thackeray wrote a series of London letters for *The Calcutta Star*, a newspaper founded in the former year by Hume, his sometime assistant on *The National Standard*. It should prove easy for anyone who has access to *The Calcutta Star* for these years to identify his contributions. There is an incomplete file of the journal in the Imperial Library at Calcutta.

Street, and with a wee bit of garden for the three children to play in — no 14 is just let for 90£ and not so good a house as mine — and the neighbouring houses are equally dear. Tomorrow I'm going to make an attack on the Brompton district

You'll let the M^rs have the other half sheet. It's as usual just post hour: and may God bless you all and thank my dearest Nanny for her letter.                    W. M. T.

Please send the note to Puzin.

242.          CHAPMAN AND HALL
          11 MARCH 1843

Hitherto unpublished.

Saturday. 11 March.

My dear Sirs

Will you beg M^r Landells to punch out the head of the enclosed young woman according to promise and give her a countenance something like the one I have drawn in pencil.

Here too are a couple more blocks, and only 3 more upon ⟨my⟩ word & honour are to follow — 1 O'Connell's head: a scene in Dublin, & another at the Giants' Causeway.

I find I am done out of no less than 50 pages by the size of the type &c. I bargained for 25 lines of 40 letters, and our page is 26 lines of 43. But your perspicacious generosity will bear this fact I'm sure in mind.

Yrs ever

W M Thackeray.

243.          TO MRS. CARMICHAEL-SMYTH
          MARCH 1843 [12]

Address: M^rs Carmichael Smyth. Hitherto unpublished.

My dearest Mammy. Hankey [13] will bring the heap of correspondence but no pinafores, for he goes by the mail and I could not

[12] This letter was written late in March, two or three days before the publication of the April number of *The Foreign Quarterly Review*.

[13] Captain Hankey, one of Thackeray's many friends in the Parisian English colony.

trouble him with such articles: besides those I looked at were not made like tothers and were dear I thought 4/ a piece. Cant you get them at Paris for that? Old John is clattering and banging among the chests & books and china, and the awful rubbish of the back-room; and I'm thinking of doing something or other: but who knows what? is it possible to decide upon anything in our strange circumstances. Suppose I take a house — I may be put in the Fleet on account of the Hickman business, or my wife mayn't be equal to come and live with me, or I mayn't have the heart to take the children from their Granny. It is the old story and be hanged to it.

They have not moved in the Hickman business any farther but it is not time yet: my friends inform me that the vis inertiæ is my best ally: but I see it must end in a compromise at last, for I am a shareholder & no mistake, and if I lose my case, what a mountain of costs come tumbling on my head. M$^r$ Morris has been with me about Charles's business: There will be not the least difficulty in getting his money out of pawn it appears, and unless he has written any letters to Hickman, no chance of proving the debt against him. But with our obstinacy, we have been all wrong. It would have been much cheaper to have compromised with the man for fifty or forty pounds than to have allowed this embarras to continue. What a pleasant letter! as I think over the various businesses I really see no end to them: but if end there be: it is clear to me that I must live in London, and work and not lose my place and my chances and be always on the move from one country to another. Here will I lay down the pen, and think and think about the future w$^h$ is not too much my habit — and fall back in a puzzle.

Here's a calculation     I have spent since July last

| Ireland | 110. |
|---|---|
| paid John | 65 |
| Painting &c | 35 |
| Isabella | 90. |
| Unpaid bills | 20. |
| House Rent | 50 |

370. besides private expences

I have 125£ left, and about 200 coming in from the book and unpaid articles. The childrens' nest egg is broken in upon as you say. but what was to be done else? There's nothing here except say 20£ of personal extravagance (and that is the outside mark) — that could have been avoided. I have earned the book call it 300£, and 110 elsewhere so that I have made rather more than I have spent. If I go on at the same rate: I can have the nest egg back in the course of the year please God: but then there will be Hickman's compromise & the lawyers to pay. Well sufficient for the day is the evil thereof.[14] Meanwhile there is plenty to be done here, and money to be made, by good will and energy: but it's only here. O that you would come and live at Boulogne!

Herewith is a letter for Anny,[15] and one for the little wife. I hope both are pleased with the picture-newspapers. They are excellent speculations, the man sold 100000 of the first number and has been making at the rate of 7000£ a year ever since. He was 5 years ago a clerk with 70£ a year, and then invented Parr's Pills a quack medicine of w$^h$ bread is said to be the chief compound. He made a fortune with this too. I had a great mind myself to have gambled a little in the Spanish last week I should have won 100£ if I had; they rose 2 per cent and will rise still according to all accounts, but it's best not to attack Fortune except in the legitimate way, of fighting her openly and to the face.

It did me good to see honest Hankey and hear his accounts of all. The book *must* be out in another month; they have called it Rambles in Ireland w$^h$ I think is a foolish name but I am too lazy to have my own way in the christening of it, and indeed the name does not matter a fig. In 3 more days had Hankey staid I could have sent you the 1$^{st}$ Volume and the F.Q.R. with 2 articles [16] that

---

[14] *St. Matthew*, 6, 34.

[15] The letter which follows this. Thackeray's letter to Isabella has not been preserved.

[16] Only one of these articles can be identified, that on *"Les Mystères de Paris* by Eugene Sue" (see above, No. 237). Robert S. Garnett in *The New Sketch Book* (London, 1906) printed no less than four articles from the April number of *The Foreign Quarterly Review* as Thackeray's, and the improbability of this wholesale attribution went unremarked because he erroneously as-

I've done this month: besides lots more work. I am very hard [at] it indeed now: from ten till 6 every day and then a good dinner, and then a good sleep: but I could not go on with this unless I had the fun in the evening, and the quantum of wine: — it is very brutal and unworthy but so it is. The dinner parties have dropped off now I have used all my friends up and indeed they were very good to last so long considering I have never the time or the grace to call. And so dearest Mammy I shall shut up and pray God bless all. It's a great blessing to think how well the children are getting on  When will they be ready for a move? Goodbye.

244.    TO ANNE THACKERAY
      MARCH 1843 [17]

*Address:* Miss Ann Thackeray | chez M. le Major Smyth | 81 Champs Elysées | à Paris. Hitherto unpublished.

  Though I have not written to my dearest Nanny, since I came away, I think about her many many times; and pray God for her and Baby and to make them both well and good. You will be well I hope in the spring when we will take a house by the seaside, and you can go into the fields and pick flowers, as you used to do at Margate: [18] before Mamma was ill and when Baby was only a little child in arms. Please God, Mamma will be made well one day too. How glad I shall be to see all my darlings well again: and there is somebody else who wants to see them again too and that is Brodie who longs to come back to them.

  She got your present, and was very much pleased: and so was Missy Allen with the sucre d'orge: and her Papa has written a little

---

signed three of the four articles to the July number in addition to that on Sue. The papers in which he finds Thackeray's hand are: "English History and Character on the French Stage," "Balzac on the Newspapers of Paris," and "George Herwegh's Poems." No doubt one of these — which, it would be risky to say — was written by Thackeray.

[17] This is the note to Annie mentioned in the preceding letter.

[18] In August, 1840.

book,[19] and has given me one of the copies of the book for you. Brodie also has brought a book for you, and another for Baby — indeed I shall be very glad to bring them.

Once Bess came to see me: and once I went to see her: and I have been to see your God-mamma [20] who gave you the red frock: but she is very very ill.

The other night as I was coming home I met in the street two little girls: and what do you think they were doing? —

Although one was no bigger than you, and the other not so big as Baby, they were singing little songs in the street, in hopes that some one would give them money: they said their mother was at home (that is the elder one said so, the younger was so little that she could not speak plain — only sing) — their mother was ill at home with three more children, and they had no bread to eat!

So I thought of my two dear little girls and how comfortable they were and how their Granny gave them good meals and their Grandmamma a nice house to live in: and I brought the little girls to M[r] Hill [21] the baker in Coram Street, and gave them a loaf and some money, and hope soon to give them some more. And this is all I have to say except God bless my dearest Nanny: and that I always say.

Papa.

I am just come home and have your letter and thank my dear little girl for her good news.

---

[19] Possibly the selection from Dürer's prints which Allen published as *The Gospel for the Unlearned* (Grier, *John Allen*, p. 59).

[20] Mrs. Sterling, who died on April 16, 1843.

[21] Alexander Hill, baker, Great Coram Street, Brunswick Square (*Robson's London Directory*, 1837).

245.        TO PERCIVAL LEIGH
               APRIL? 1843 [22]

Hitherto unpublished.

Dear Leigh

You did not write to say whether you can do the Irish Sketch
Book. it should be done if possible by Monday.

Please let me know by the bearer whether you will do it.

Yrs

W M T.


246.     TO GEORGE WILLIAM NICKISSON
              8 APRIL 1843

Published in *The Bookworm*, May, 1890, p. 172.

13 G$^t$ Coram S$^t$ April 8. 1843.

My dear Nickisson. I was at no loss in reading the amusing
'Illustrations of Discount' in the Magazine [23] to discover the name
of the author. Mr. Deady Keane shook me by the hand only a
fortnight since and at the very same time no doubt was writing the
libel on me w$^h$ appeared to my no small surprize in that very article.

[22] Thackeray seems to have written this note between Thursday, April 20,
and the following Monday. Despite his urgency *The Irish Sketch Book* was
not reviewed in *Fraser's Magazine* for May.

[23] The passage which offended Thackeray in this article runs as follows:
"The first person we met in the coffee-room [of the "Grubwell"] was Bill
Crackaway, one whom we have always looked upon as a bird of ill omen. His
long ungainly person is crowned with a face which Dame Nature must have
fashioned just after making a bad debt, and, therefore, in the worst of tempers.
A countenance of preternatural longitude is imperfectly relieved by a nose on
which the partial hand of Nature has lavished every bounty — length, breadth,
thickness, all but a — bridge; a mouth that seemed suddenly arrested in the act
of whistling, and, from its conformation, could only eliminate a sinister sneer,
but was physically incapable of the candour of an honest laugh, which, with
a most inhuman squint, gave a rare finish to the *os frontis* of this Corinthian
capital of our club.

"The first question this worthy lispingly asked of us was, 'Have you heard
the news?' To which, answering in the negative, he proceeded to inform us

I have advisedly let a week pass without deciding upon the course I ought to pursue. Few people (none that I have seen) know that the attack in question is levelled at myself, nor indeed have I any desire to make the public acquainted with that fact. But — as in a private house or an inn, if any person with no other provocation but that of drunkenness or natural malice, should take a fancy to call me by foul names, I should have a right to appeal to the host, and request him to have the individual so offending put out of doors — I may similarly complain to you that I have been grossly insulted in your Magazine.

Having written long in it; being known to you (please God) as an honest man and not an ungenerous one; I have a right to complain that a shameful and unprovoked attack has been made upon me in the Magazine, and as an act of justice to demand that the writer should no longer be permitted to contribute to Fraser.

If Mr. Deady Keane continues his contributions in any shape, mine must cease. I am one of the oldest and I believe one of the best of your contributors. A private individual I have been grossly abused in the Magazine, and must perforce withdraw from it unless I have your word that this act of justice shall be done me.

I make this demand not in the least as an act of retaliation against M$^r$ Keane, but as an act of justice w$^h$ I owe to myself, and w$^h$ is forced on me. At present at least it cannot be said that my anger is very revengeful or that his attack has rendered me particularly vindictive. It would be easy to fight him with the same weapons w$^h$ he uses, could I condescend to employ them: but I feel myself,

---

that Lord Edward Softhead had, to use our informant's expression, 'cut his stick and bolted.'

"'On what account?'

"'Oh! the bums are making some kind inquiries after him.'

"'And how much does he owe?' we asked.

"'Only 300,000*l.*' was the answer; 'but then, it is to the discounters, and I suppose, as he is rather green, he will not have touched more than 30 or 40,000*l.*'

"Now, as Crackaway added to the occupation of editor of a pseudophilosophical magazine the business of a bill-broker in the City, we take it for granted he knew something about these matters." (*Fraser's Magazine*, April, 1843, pp. 399–400)

and I hope one day he will discover, that they are unworthy of an honest man. If he only take care to let it be publicly known that it is his intention to abuse in the public prints any private individuals, whose personal appearance or qualities may be disagreeable to him, it is surprising how popular he will become, how his society will be courted, and his interests in life advanced.

But I am sure you will no longer allow him to exercise his office of satirist in your Magazine,[24] and hope (without the least wish to imply a threat) that for both our sakes, he will make no more attacks in print upon my person or my private character. Faithfully yrs dear Nickisson

W M Thackeray.

I have no copy of this letter: but should you send it to Mr. Keane, will you please to make one?

247.     TO PERCIVAL LEIGH [25]
20 APRIL 1843

*Address:* Percival Leigh Esq.[re] | M R C S. Hitherto unpublished.

Thursday 20.

Dear Leigh

Did Leech impart to you the modest service I want of you? A notice of half a dozen pages for Fraser will be accepted and acceptable. Not a puff you understand — hit as hard as you like but in a good natured way and so as not to break bones.[26]

[24] Thackeray continued to contribute to *Fraser's Magazine.* It may consequently be assumed that Nickisson dropped Keane.

[25] Percival Leigh (1813–1889) had been trained as a doctor at St. Bartholomew's Hospital, where his fellow-students included Leech, Albert Smith, and Gilbert A'Beckett. Not long after he became a Member of the Royal College of Surgeons in 1835, however, he abandoned medicine for journalism. He was on the staff of *Punch* from 1841 till his death, though he ceased to contribute in later years. Leigh, a genial man of scholarly tastes known as "The Professor" among his colleagues, was Thackeray's closest friend after Leech and Doyle among the *Punch* writers. See Spielmann's *History of "Punch,"* pp. 299–303.

[26] An article on "Titmarsh's Travels in Ireland" appeared in *Fraser's Magazine,* June, 1843, pp. 678–686.

The book is dedicated to M^r Lever: and the preface says that it was to have been called the Cockney in Ireland but for the remonstrances of the publisher w^h were so pathetic that the author was obliged to give way. In a *second edition* it is to be changed

I have the sheets all except the last  Will you — let me know if you can do the job *immediately* — & if not please return the important documents w^h must be sent to some other critic.

Yrs ever

W M Thackeray

I have been obliged to take the book away.

248.                    TO LAMAN BLANCHARD
                        21 APRIL 1843

My text is taken from Blanchard Jerrold's *The Best of All Good Company* (Boston, 1874), p. 166. Original not traced.

Dear Blanchard, — Not knowing the number of your row — not indeed certain whether it is Union Row or Place, I've sent by the Parcels Company the book, all but the last sheet, to the Examiner, to be forwarded to you.

It is dedicated to Mr. Lever, and the author will say in the preface that it was to have been called "The Cockney in Ireland," but for the pathetic remonstrances of the publishers.

And so Heaven speed it!

Ever yours,

Amelia.

I shall be in the Linden grove at the rising of the moon, and you will know me by a cherry-colored ribbon tied round the tail of my dog.

249.          TO MRS. CARMICHAEL-SMYTH
                    3 MAY 1843

*Address:* M<sup>rs</sup> Carmichael Smyth | 81 Champs Elysées | Paris. *Postmarks:*
3 MY 1843, 5 MAI 43 CALAIS. Hitherto unpublished.

My dearest Mammy. What a shame it has been that I didn't
write, I thought it was ⟨. . .⟩ [27] ten days ago: and have been waiting
day by day to tell you something was settled. Well nothing is
chambers are well nigh as dear as a house moving is awfully dear &
troubleso⟨me⟩ every house I see dearer than this and this a great
deal dearer than I ever thought it. I ⟨am⟩ bound by my lease it
appears to make good all dilapidations — 45£ if you please: With
25 for rent w<sup>h</sup> of course was inevitable. Add to this that M<sup>r</sup> Hickman has just announced his intention of going on with the trial — [28]
If I am cast it will cost me 400£ or else a bankruptcy so I have
offered 20 by way of compromise. He is perfectly authorized to
act in spite of the objections of wise Will — his bankruptcy was
annulled and there is no doubt as to his authority. Then will come
the delight of a new house and the expenses on getting in — by
Jupiter I don't know where it will all end. Pantechnicon as dear
as a house. Ye Gods assist an unfortunate literary man

All these things have been twisting and turning & bothering me
in addition to the old complaint: [29] and the perpetual botheration
of the book. The latter is over, & the complaint considerably more
quiet and relieved. A little sea-side will do me no harm     I don't
however want to leave town until I see how the book goes — and
till I have made if possible some arrangements for the future.
Blanchard has puffed me very handsomely already,[30] and those
who have read the book speak so well of it, that it may, please God,
turn out a success. Something afterwards must be done that is clear,
and we must determine whether the little ones are to stay abroad

[27] One or two words have crumbled away here.
[28] See above, No. 164.
[29] His stricture. See Appendix XXVIII.
[30] In *Ainsworth's Magazine*, May, 1843, pp. 435–438.

with their granny or at home with their father, and what is to come of the dear little —— Fiddlestick — the perplexities botherations & uncertainties are abominable — and indeed that's why I don't write.

My intent at present with regard to Hickman is to offer 30£ if he wont take 20£ if he wont take 30£ to go to Court at a certain expense of 20£ and the prospect of a bankruptcy at the last, and to make over the goods and chattels in some way as to secure them — As for my Grandmother & Mary the claim against them is absurd — I don't know how far Charles has committed himself: but of course the man relied on family feeling and that in case of a verdict against me, my relatives would come forward to bear me through. This is the pull he has over us all. Well there's no use in more talk or shilly shallying: the fact is I perceive I am writing nonsense — there's a huge row in the Club-room w$^h$ may account for a part of the same, added to the queer uncertainty under w$^h$ the whole business lies. What a sentence! — I am come into a private room & decent quiet and mean to state that it is my intention to compromise with Hickman in the best way I can: & that's the meaning of the above nonsense and also that while those who are abroad can afford to set the man at defiance, I at home must be for my own sake more submissive and pay reasonably rather than risk the other alternative.

I think if I've been silent for a fortnight you will be less annoyed now you know the reason why — the extreme puzzle I am in: but this can't last very much longer and then you shall have a more lucid letter. Your Roman packet came 2 days too late. And now I'll close this queer sheet: for I am in such a muzz as hardly to know what to write about. God bless all, and bless my dear little Nanny for the letter, how glad I shall be to see the velvet frocks! — W M T.

The agreement at Puzin's was for 26 francs.

250.      TO MRS. THACKERAY
3? MAY 1843 [31]

*Address:* M<sup>rs</sup> Thackeray. Hitherto unpublished.

My dearest little woman — I have a very bad excuse for not answering your kind letter, that I was waiting daily to say something about business, about the book, about the new house that I am going to take, and about some more matters. Well, all these things are as unsettled now as ever: and besides couldn't I have written even if they *were* unsettled? But you know how much business writing I have to do, & must be good-natured & pardon me.

Dear old M<sup>rs</sup> Sterling has gone to her long home and poor John has likewise met with a calamity in the loss of his wife, who died suddenly after her confinement the poor fellow only got the news of his mother's death a few hours before his second loss.[32] Old Sterling is very much affected: but you know his nature and that grief like his won't last very long.

I have at last finished the Irish book, w<sup>h</sup> is to be out tomorrow, and has already been famously reviewed by Blanchard in Ainsworth's Magazine. I have written to the Times people who have promised me a kind review,[33] and shall get plenty of puffing elsewhere. If the people will only buy the book as well as praise it my fortune is made. What else have I got to say? — I have been rather laid up with my old complaint [34] but am better now, and very very soon please God hope to see my dear little people once more. They say the town is very gay; but I have almost left off going to Operas and Theatres, and come home early, when FitzGerald & I have a pipe together and so go quietly to bed. It is delightful to have him in the house but I'm afraid his society makes me idle we sit and talk too much about books & pictures and smoke too many cigars.

[31] Thackeray probably sent this letter with that of May 3 to his mother.

[32] Sterling's wife died on the morning of April 18, two days after his mother passed away. His ordeal is described in Carlyle's *Life of John Sterling*, Part III, chapter 5.

[33] This promise was apparently not fulfilled.

[34] See Appendix XXVIII.

I don't think I have fallen in love with any body of late, except pretty M̲r̲s̲ Brookfield. M̲r̲s̲ Sartoris [35] has given up her tea-parties conversazioni and tableaux vivans being of this figure. 🙎 She is really as fat as Cottin [36] and twice as ugly, and if she is not to be confined till September, Heaven help us her babby will be a monster. Did I write to you about M̲r̲s̲ Procter's grand ball, and how splendid M̲r̲s̲ Dickens was in pink satin and M̲r̲ Dickens in geranium & ringlets? To night I am asked to no less than two balls, one to a publisher's lady; and one to an attorney's — and the probability is between ourselves that I shall go to neither. Every day I have been house hunting with all my might & main, and have found nothing at all so large & cheap as poor old glum Coram Street: but I want a garden for you and the little ones and a good air and a thousand other good things w̲h̲ can't be had except for more money than I fear I can muster — I've not sent you the paper because I've not written in it of late — but I was an ass for my pains, and you shall have it more regularly for the future — that is to say not for a very long future — for I hope I shall see my dearest little woman before three weeks be over. And so God bless you my love, and write me a line ever so short; it will always be worth a guinea to me — Your aff⟨te⟩ W M T.

251.        TO GEORGE POTEMKIN PERRY
                    5 MAY 1843

*Address:* George Potemkin Perry Esq̲r̲e̲ | 12 Rye Terrace | Peckham Rye.
*Postmark:* MY 5 1843. Hitherto unpublished.

                                13 Coram S̲t̲ )
                                                    5 May
                                Brunsw Sq̲r̲e̲ )

You *can* be of service to me. Send me for Evan's sake your London address, for I wish to confide to you the IRISH SKETCH BOOK for my mamma. It may be had of all publishers, w̲h̲ please to tell your friends.

[35] The former Adelaide Kemble.
[36] Elizabeth Cottin. See above, No. 12.

You are wrong as usual in supposing I have quitted Coram S$^t$ — nevertheless I am your fast friend

W M T.

Let me known instantaneously where I can send the packet.

252.          TO CHAPMAN AND HALL
                  15 MAY 1843 [37]

Hitherto unpublished.

Albion House. Brighton
Monday.

My dear Gents

Jerding promises a second notice in the L. G; and I think if a good advertisement were sent him with extracts from the compliments in the other periodicals — advantage might accrue to both sides. I read the Athenæum [38] no wonder: Forster — but I'll keep *that* for him & me: his article is splendid.

I came down here to be alone, & avoid good dinners and do some magazine work. If the papers have anything agreeable between this & Thursday, perhaps you will send them. I saw in the Tablet, an article of w$^h$ the first paragraph struck me as abusive so I did not proceed. It is a Catholic journal: & Titmarsh pitches into the priests so a return may be expected. But it would be ingenious to take any opinion of the Tablet (not too severe) and contrast it in an advertisement with a counter-opinion elsewhere. Thus. Titmarsh is perfectly fair (Examiner). Titmarsh is grossly prejudiced (Tablet) & so forth. But pray advertize magnificently.

Looking at the waves of the otion, I have I think hit upon (and executed part of) a little work w$^h$ may make a sensation: but of this anon.

Always yours dear Sirs
W M Thackeray.

[37] A first notice of *The Irish Sketch Book* appeared in *The Literary Gazette* on Saturday, May 13 (pp. 315–316), a second on May 20 (pp. 334–335). This letter was written on the intervening Monday. There was also a third notice in *The Literary Gazette* of May 27 (pp. 350–351).
[38] Over five columns are devoted to *The Irish Sketch Book* in *The Athenæum* for May 13, pp. 455–457.

253.        TO MRS. CARMICHAEL-SMYTH
20 MAY 1843

*Address:* ⟨M^rs Ca⟩rmichael Smyth | 81 Champs Elysees | Paris. *Postmark:*
20 MY 1843. Hitherto unpublished.

Direct to me at the
Saturday. Reform Club. 20 May

My dearest Mammy. I dont think the perplexities have de-
creased since I wrote last. I have been away to Brighton rather
unwell with an abcess occasioned by the old complaint and some
long walks w^h I took like an ass. It hung about me for 6 weeks
annoying me a good deal and causing general dullness stupidity
and so forth: but it has disappeared in the usual way and I'm now
quite a different man. The complaint itself does not annoy me, I
have gone a good way towards curing it, and see no reason to regret
having refused the aid of the Doctors. I sh^d have been well of the
other affair a month ago if I had followed my own way & not
theirs. But I won't bother you any more with this unsavory subject.

Old Coram S^t is dismantled, the House-Agent says he will take
in my furniture, and I have had to pay 70£ before walking out —
the other day while I was at Brighton, and seeing the bills up, a
gentleman called to look — the name was Hickman, and he made
some enquiries about the furniture — You said in your last letter,
that there was to be a general family compromise with him. Who
is to make it? Have any steps been taken regarding it? I wish to
know, because I must come to some compromise for myself: for the
state of doubt is intolerable, the expence of a law suit certain: and I
think there would be utter ruin at it's tail. He will be able to prove
that shares were taken in my name: and that I was a servant of the
company: acquiescing at any rate in the shares. So compromise at
any rate I will: and I shall begin on Wednesday morning next unless I hear from you before then. I called at Hicks's who had no
orders on the subject.

I am only waiting for this to come over: and thank God you are
determined on the warm salt baths — that is if they will do you

good, and why not as well as the mysterious baths elsewhere? I only wish you had fixed on Boulogne or Dieppe instead of Havre — Dieppe being prettier, better inhabited, and more likely to hold the person who would take care of the little woman: Boulogne gayer and more convenient in all respects except for the journey. If G.P. has made no selection, shall I go to Boulogne or Dieppe and look out a house for you? I would be sure to find some family besides who would take me & Isabella in. I thought you had removed her from Puzin, and so like a sneak sent no money: but here it is and all of the purest earnings. I am still about 100 ahead of the world, & may have 100 more from the book.

It is going pretty well. The Irish are in a rage about it. The Irish of my acquaintance: Boz has written me a letter of compliments, and the literary people like it generally very much. Not, I am afraid, White, who promises to review it in Blackwood, and pulled a very long face the other day when I met him.[39] He did not say a word however, and perhaps it was only my nervousness wh. saw the long face.

I have got my portmanteau packed with layers of stockings between the shirts for you: so be quick and let me know what you are bent on: what about Hickman, or Boulogne. I am sure from the 5 days I spent at Havre it is the dullest and most inconvenient town possible: and beg you to pause between that and t'other. While you are at the sea side, we can talk of what is to come next: and so God bless all

W. M. T.[40]

[39] The promised article in *Blackwood's Magazine* did not appear.

[40] The bottom half of the last leaf of this letter, which appears to have contained a postscript, has been cut away.

254.　　　　　TO JOHN FORSTER
25 MAY 1843 [41]

Hitherto unpublished.

Thursday. May 25.

My dear F.

I find the author of Ion [42] has engaged the house-dinner room at the G for tomorrow, and I am obliged to carry my young friends to a tavern. So I *haven't* asked Raymond to join my party, w^h will be a dull one; and I shall let our dinner stand over till next week.

Yrs unfaithfully

W M T.

255.　　　TO THE REV. WILLIAM BROOKFIELD
26 MAY 1843

My text is taken from *Mrs. Brookfield*, p. 123.

If you like two or three
Of your cronies to see
There's a swarry
To-morry
At Mitre court B.

256.　　　　　　　　　TO ?
29 MAY 1843

Hitherto unpublished. *Endorsed:* Rec^d May 29^th.

Reform Club. May 30.[43]
1843.

My dear Sir

I am afraid the drawing-scheme w^h you propose is one little likely to bring you profit. The market at Paris is stocked by thousands of

[41] Among possible years May 25 fell on Thursday only in 1843.
[42] Sir Thomas Noon Talfourd (1795–1854), a fellow member of the Garrick Club, whose *Ion* appeared in 1836.
[43] It would appear from the endorsement that this is a mistake for May 29.

artists — they care no more for an Englishman without a name
than for a Cherokee Indian; and copies of drawings are done so
plentifully and by such clever fellows, that you might go round
all the Drawing-shops and not sell one — A friend of mine who
copied with amazing dexterity made the attempt and could not get
a two franc piece for the best of his performances.

This is but cold comfort to give — It is best however to tell the
truth: and indeed if I were to choose, I would choose any place
rather than Paris for disposing of the goods you speak of —

I am very sorry to hear of your illness and should be very glad
indeed to know of any way in w^h I could further your views. BUT
— you know all that lies in *but*: and how hard it is in this world to
get over it.

Faithfully yrs, dear Sir<br>W M Thackeray.

I have no house in town — a bed room at the Hummums, and
pass my days at the Club — If you are passing any day this way, I
sh^d like to see the drawings very much BUT (as before) no more
know how to put you in the way of disposing of them, than I do
how to sell my own performances in that way.

257.    TO MRS. CARMICHAEL-SMYTH<br>10 AUGUST 1843

*Address:* M^rs Carmichael Smyth | 81 Champs Elysées | Paris. *Postmark:*
GRAVENHAGE 10. Hitherto unpublished.

After a deal of travelling we are at last come to a day's rest —
and now I may tell you of all the delights of the voyage.[44] Im-

---

[44] The reader may find the following outline of Thackeray's trip to the Low
Countries of service. He and his friend Stevens left Paris on Friday, August 4.
They passed through Cambrai on Saturday and stayed the night at Valenciennes. Sunday they travelled through Quiévrain and Brussels to Antwerp,
where they arrived at 2 P. M. Discovering the loss of his pocketbook, Thackeray returned to Brussels, but he was back in Antwerp by 10 that evening. On
Monday morning he and Stevens went on to Rotterdam. They spent Tuesday
there and continued to the Hague on Wednesday, August 9. August 12 found

primis I have lost my pocket-book with 20£ in it — that is, not the pocket-book, w^h was put into the Antwerp Post-office by the person who stole it, and who of course kept the 2 notes it contained. Well, that is not such a great evil, for the illustrious Stevens says he will bear the half of it: and to this I make no objection for he can well afford to do so. But as for seeing sights: it is in vain to try with such a compagnon de voyage, or indeed with almost any one — so as to turn the sights to any profit afterwards: I only know 3 people with whom a trip could be made useful to me.

We had to begin with the *bodkin* places in the Coach, w^h brought us after 20 hours to Cambrai, where we delayed 3 hours to get into another infernal machine w^h carried us to Valenciennes, where we arrived just in time to be too late for the rail-road, and so were forty hours on the road to ⟨Antwerp⟩ instead of 25, as in the old days before rail-roads were invented — In order to be in here the next morning we got up at three, fancy three!, and reached Quiévrain and then went in 8 hours to Brussels, and reached Antwerp at about 2, and there going to change my 10£ note — I managed to mislay my ⟨pocket-⟩book — I believe it was left in my room: for I missed it 5 minutes after my arrival — and so, fancying I had for-gotten it at Brussels, why I went back to Brussels again, and then from Brussels back to Antwerp again, and then up at 5 to go by the steamer to Rotterdam — so that all I saw of Antwerp was between 10 at night and 5 next morning, — viz. a double-bedded room and a good supper — not a single picture, to be seen nor sketch to be made for love or money.

Setting out by the Rotterdam steamer we had a fine opportunity of viewing the coast on each side, w^h is exceedingly picturesque as thus

and reached the place comfortably in time for supper, and a stroll afterwards through the tall bustling clean handsome comfortable

them still at the Hague. On August 17 they were about to leave for Ostend. Thackeray arrived in Paris on August 30, having spent most of the intervening period in Lille.

looking town,[45] where I longed to rig up a sketching apparatus, but of course had no time in the dark.

Yesterday we came on to this place: [46] through a very pleasing little country w.ʰ is not more variegated or undulating than a billiard table, and is speckled over with villages and little groves, and squat country houses, and cows innumerable. Every body what liked smoked in the diligence, w.ʰ I'm sure will make you long to come and travel in the country.

It is more than England — our bill at the Inn with no particular extravagance 18/per day, a florin to be paid everywhere, for every porter, commissioner, or glass of beer — and as you can't drink the water in this country — it is wonderful how one longs for it, and what a perpetual thirst travellers suffer under. The illustrious pays the bills with great splendor, and is magnificent in his interviews with waiters, travellers, and commissioners    They take him for a great man: and indeed he is as good and generous a fellow as can be. His two faults are his obstinacy in getting up 3 hours before it is necessary, and a persistance in dining in his own room and not at the table d'hôte — by w.ʰ we lose a good dinner and get a bad one badly served —

All the morning at last I have been picture-seeing — and saw the King of Holland in his own royal person smoking a segar, and superintending the papering of a new apartment in his "gallery" w.ʰ appears to be his passion just now. The palace is a poor little place, and the gallery is a tawdry, though comfortable & handsome affair: I saw four of the Illustrious's pictures in it, with their great names — that I recollect painters at 10 francs a day dibbling and varnishing over in his rooms — I suppose familiarity begets contempt for pictures as for anything else, certainly I could not admire these having seen them in dishabille at Stevens's, and knowing how clever he is at finding a pedigree for the works in his collection. The poor king seems to me to be greatly humbugged.

---

[45] The experiences of this evening in Rotterdam (and other events of the trip) are described in Thackeray's travel notes, published for the first time in Appendix IX.

[46] The Hague.

But in revenge, at the Public Gallery there are some half dozen of the finest pictures possible. I would give something to stop a week and copy them in water-colours and would pass the evenings sauntering in a little flat park with little trees & little canals, illuminated by a little round dumpy full moon, where Dutchmen and women saunter about, and seem very quiet and happy. There are Coffee-houses too here and there — grave old places, with little tables and pipes where people go and sit quite silent and drink a huge quantity of liquors that are brought by a dumb-waiter at a sign of the dumb guest of the Café. There are no other amusements, but a French opera thrice a week, and indeed I am inclined to think that this is just the stupidest royal residence of all the royal residences ⟨in⟩ Europe.

Yesterday I saw a little boy in wooden-shoes flying a kite (that waddled through the sky very lazily) Flying a kite and smoking a pipe. You see them squatted by the canals fishing with a straight rod, just as on the Dutch tiles,[47] and I have seen half a hundred of Gerard Dow's and Ostades already in the streets and along the road. Also I have seen a General walking about in grand uniform with stars epaulets, and a magnificent cocked hat and feather and 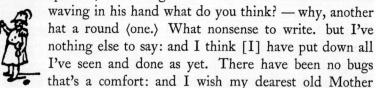 waving in his hand what do you think? — why, another hat a round ⟨one.⟩ What nonsense to write. but I've nothing else to say: and I think [I] have put down all I've seen and done as yet. There have been no bugs that's a comfort: and I wish my dearest old Mother could get such good nights sleep as falls to my share. Wasn't ⟨it a⟩ shame to come away and leave her suffering? It was in spite of all one can say to the contrary: I wish I could hear how you are: but I don't know where you are to write, and shall be back in a week probably (or if I can manage 4 or 5 days in Belgium alone) in 10 days. Seeing is certainly better than book-reading; it would be a good plan I think for a man in my trade to give up reading altogether for, say, a year: and see with nobody else's eyes but his own.

My dearest little woman As my mamma is of an anxious temperament and you are ⟨sup⟩posed to take things coolly, she is to have

[47] Compare below, Appendix IX.

the first reading of this letter, w$^h$ she will send on afterwards to you. It seems already about a year since I left home. I wonder is Anny grown much, and beg you to kiss her and baby for me: and so God bless all.

W M T.

Thursday.

258. TO WHOM IT MAY CONCERN
12 AUGUST 1843

*My text is taken from Thackeray in the United States, II, 135-136.*

Having, during a period of three days, had many opportunities of studying the character of Joseph:[48] the undersigned has great pleasure in recommending him to the travelling nobility and gentry of Great Britain. Joseph is active in body, gentlemanlike in manner: in the execution of commissions he is rapid, dexterous and faithful: he has many agreeable social qualities, and will often amuse the solitary tourist by appropriate anecdotes which he will recite over a glass of beer or wine at a Coffee-house, or will introduce as he conducts his client through the city: he is in a word everything that a Valet de place should be — conscientious, yet not squeamish, modest, willing, sober, discreet. Furthermore, it may be stated that he has a wife and six children; — though latter qualifications are such as he possesses in common with many other persons of far less merit, yet they are stated here, because, for the prayers of Meritorious Poverty British Benevolence has always a Kindly Ear: and because the stranger, in exercising his generosity towards Joseph, may have the satisfaction of thinking that he benefits at the same moment six little innocent invisible Josephs, whose daily dinner depends upon the exertions of their father.

Michael Angelo Titmarsh.

Done at the Hague, the 12th day of August, A. D., MDCCC-XLIII.

[48] We may be sure that this is not the Joseph of Thackeray's travel notes. As he elsewhere points out, "all commissioners are called Joseph."

P. S. — It may not perhaps be irrelevant to state, that the land-lord of the Marshal de Turenne possesses some of the finest Madeira in Europe.

259.          TO MRS. CARMICHAEL-SMYTH
                    17 AUGUST 1843

*Address:* Mʳˢ Carmichael-Smyth. | 81 Champs Elysées | Paris | Immediate.
*Postmark:* BELG. 18 AOUT 43. Hitherto unpublished.

Thursday Evening.

My dearest Mammy. Of all the failures in the world this ex-pedition has been the greatest putting the 20£ out of the question, I think I have not gained twopence worth of ideas in the course of the journey — I am coupled to an excellent fellow who pays the piper: but I must follow all his ways, am never free from him, and am looking at everything without the leisure to reflect on it: or indeed the time to see it. We breakfast ordinarily at 7 in the mutual bed-room, we go out to see old pictures at old picture-shops for hours we dine at 2 in the bed-room again. I am 1/2 wild with the life, & can't get away from my man. It seems hard to be writ-ing so about a good hearted generous creature at one's elbow who does everything in his power to make the journey comfortable.

We are short of money & S. writes to Paris to day for it. Please pop me a letter in the post on the same day you receive this — con-taining good news of all — and likewise a 10£ note, wʰ I hope may be found in one of the letters that have come for me in my absence. Will you open them & tell me in brief any news they contain? I have only written 3 pages in all the journey, I am wild with my jolly good man of the sea. I can't escape him: He wont let me see any one else or anything except in his company. I told him to go home without me leaving me a Napoleon until I could get money from home; no stay he will, and has ⟨spent⟩ all his money twice over (some 150£ with wʰ he set out) in pictures.

I wrote to Chapman & Hall for money wʰ they have in all probability but if not: G.P must try and lend it me: for this loss of the 20£ was a fatal business, & out of my control entirely: but if please God all is well — I am determined to see these towns alone once more and make something readable about them — a week would finish the job completely — O how I wish I had Morton & FitzGerald to look at the sights with me, instead of this worthy fellow: but I am not fit to live with any man that's the fact. God bless all. I have money at Fraser's for Isabella, for w^h D^r Puzin must wait until my return: & we have bought to day 2 pretty little rosaries for Anny & Baby at the Beguine convent.

We are going to Ostend now, so direct *instanter* to the Poste Restante there.

260.                TO AMÉDÉE PICHOT [49]
                       30 AUGUST 1843

*Address:* A M. | Monsieur Amédée Pichot | à Sèvres. *Postmarks:* PARIS 30 AOUT 43, SEVRES 30 AOUT 43. Facsimile in *L'Autographe* (1865).

                81 Champs Elysées. Paris — Mercredi.

Je ne puis vous rémercier qu'aujourdhui, mon cher M. Pichot, de vos deux obligeantes lettres. Je viens d'arriver à l'instant, d'un de ces grands Voyages, qui m'ont procuré ce beau titre de Lion Anglo-Hibernico-Batavo-Belgo que vous m'avez donne. Mais dans quelle position pour un lion me voyait on de retour dans *ma caverne*! Dompté, gardé a vue par un infâme Commissionaire des Menageries; (faute de pouvoir payer ma place à la Diligence) Je n'ai été qu'enfin rançonné par une cuisinière! [50] Aussi renoncé-je

---

[49] Pichot (1796–1877) was the author of several books on England, the editor for many years of the *Revue Britannique,* and the translator of Byron, Bulwer-Lytton, Dickens, Macaulay, Scott, and other English writers. He later made French versions of Thackeray's *Great Hoggarty Diamond* and *Book of Snobs.*

[50] Shortly after August 17 Thackeray left Stevens and set out alone for Paris. By the time he reached Lille, his funds were exhausted, and it is to this circumstance that we owe that memorable *cri du cœur,* "Titmarsh's Carmen Lilliense" (*Works,* XIII, 34–37):

> My heart is weary, my peace is gone,
>   How shall I e'er my woes reveal?
> I have no money, I lie in pawn,
>   A stranger in the town of Lille.

Relief arrived eight or ten days later in the form of a £10 note from Mrs.

à tout jamais, a mes titres léonins, et dès aujourdhui je cesse de mugir.

J'ai rapporté de la Belgique une inflammation d'yeux qui me fera garder la maison et l'ombre pendant quelques jours — Aussitot guéri, je m'empresserai de venir offrir mes respects à Madame Pichot, et de vous remercier pour vos hospitalités cordiales. J'aurai du avant de partir m'acquitter de ce devoir: mais mon voyage n'a été arreté, que deux heures avant mon depart, et j'ai quitté Paris sans avoir fait des adieux à mes amis, ni même à la police du Royaume.

Votre ami, M Prévost est il encore ici? Dans ce cas je lui donnerai avec plaisir une lettre pour Lever, et pour une autre personne qui pourra lui être utile a Dublin. Si M. Prévost parle notre langue, je pourrai aussi lui donner des recommendations pour quelques familles du pays, mais ce sont de personnes qui ne parlent guère le Francais, l'éducation étant fort peu à la mode dans l'Emerald Isle.

J'espère trouver Madame Pichot parfaitement remise de sa chute, and am always

My dear M. Pichot, most faithfully yours<br>W M Thackeray.

Vous pardonnerez les fautes de Francais d'un homme qui n'écrit *qu'avec un oeil.*[51]

---

Butler. This proved barely sufficient to get Thackeray to Paris, where he was ransomed from a coachman clamoring for his fare by Pauline, the Carmichael-Smyths' cook.

It should be noted that the date Thackeray assigns to his ballad ("Lille: Sept. 2, 1843") probably represents a guess made when he sent it to *Fraser's Magazine* on February 17 of the following year. He departed from Lille at the latest on August 29.

[51] Asked by Thackeray to point out the mistakes in this letter, Pichot replied: "Vous désirez, mon cher Titmarsh, que je fasse le pédagogue avec vous; volontiers, à condition que vous me rendrez la leçon, à la première lettre que je vous écrirai en anglais. 'Vous renoncez,' me dites vous, 'à votre rôle de lion;' (*Nolo leoniza i,* comme Walter Scott fait dire à son Gédédiah Cleisbotham); 'dès aujourd'hui vous cessez de *mugir* . . . parce que vous avez été rançonné par une cuisinière!' Si vous avez vraiment *mugi* c'est en votre qualité de fils de John Bull (Jean Taureau), dont vous êtes un des plus glorieux fils: mais ne

261.        TO MRS. CARMICHAEL-SMYTH
            26 SEPTEMBER 1843

*Address:* M<u>rs</u> Carmichael Smyth. | Rue S<u>t</u> Jacques 7. | à Montmorency. *Post-mark:* PARIS 26 SEPT 43. Hitherto unpublished.

Tuesday.

My dearest Mammy

G. P's letter finds me in the midst of a purge so that I can't come out to see the little reprobate to day: nor should I indeed like to be present at the correction w<u>h</u> ought to be administered to her. I wish indeed that for everything like brutality or violence or dis-obedience on the child's part, the rod should be applied to her: it is the only answer to such conduct, and you'll never keep up your authority without it. Pray do as G P advises: it is the shortest easiest and wholesomest of all corrections and will prevent I'm quite sure any scenes or conflicts for the future. Why hesitate? Every year the wilfulness will grow stronger, and your power to correct it less.

I sent you a sermon for Anny. pray pray ha⟨. . .⟩ [52] done. And God bless my poor old Mother. I don't ⟨. . .⟩ [53] words w<u>h</u> are more imagination ⟨. . .⟩ [54]

---

renoncez pas à *rugir.* 'Well roared, lion,' vous dirai je encore comme dans le *Songe d'une Nuit d'été,* car vous êtes un vrai lion, vous qui au lieu d'être *rançonné* par une cuisinière, avez reçu d'elle votre rançon épisode de votre histoire qui fera le pendant de la génerosité de votre tailleur, vous prêtant un billet de cinq cent francs lorsqu'il vous vit embarassée de lui solder son mémoire. Si le pauvre Goldsmith revenait au monde, il serait doublement jaloux de vous." (*L'Autographe*) For Thackeray's tailor, see the dedication to *The Paris Sketch Book* (*Works,* V, 3).

[52] About four words have here been torn away.
[53] About five words have here been torn away.
[54] The rest of the letter has been torn away.

262.    TO WILLIAM HARRISON AINSWORTH
27 SEPTEMBER 1843

*Address:* W. H. Ainsworth Esq^re | Lawson's Bedford Hotel | Rue S^t Honoré.
*Postmark:* Septembre 27 1843. Hitherto unpublished.

Wednesday.

My dear Ainsworth.

The enclosed fatal missive has just come from Stevens, and we must bear the disappointment as best we may. But remember that we have an engagement for Friday, and that you stand sponsor for M^rs Touchet [55] and your daughter in whose name you promised and vowed to *meet*. I have asked Pichot of the Britannic Review to meet you, and as on examining my state of furniture, I find my tea-spoon is all the plate in my possession, it has appeared just & fitting that we should dine at Véry's and not here. If the famous Lucrèce [56] is acted we might see that afterwards, or find some way of making the ladies spend a more cheerful evening than in a bachelor's room.

I shall call for you on Friday at *1/2 past 4*: and, shall notify to Gwilt the arrangement as it stands at present.

Yours ever

W M T.

[55] Mrs. James Touchet, Ainsworth's cousin by marriage.
[56] A tragedy by François Ponsard (1814–1867), written as a protest against the excesses of French romanticism. The contrast that Ponsard's drama afforded to Victor Hugo's *Les Burgraves* (1843) accounts in part for the great success which attended its first performance on April 22, 1843.

263.                    TO MRS. RITCHIE
                      13 OCTOBER 1843

*Address:* Madame Ritchie | à Villiers-le-Bel | près Sarcelles. *Postmarks:*
PARIS 14 OCT 43, VILLIERS LE BEL 14 OCT 43. Published in part,
*Biographical Introductions,* IV, xxxiii.

                              81 Champs Elysées.
                              Friday.
My dear Aunt.

Charlotte's hand-writing on William's letter had a very reproach-
ful look: and seemed to say 'Here is a letter for you but you don't
deserve it' — I ought to have written to you weeks ago, to explain
how it was that my little ones did not come to pay their promised
visit to you.

They are all at Montmorency, where they have been for this
month past: and as I go thither once or twice a week, and lose a
whole day in the journey to and fro, I can't afford to give up more
of my precious time, but am obliged to remain at home for the rest
of the week, working or pretending to work. I believe I am writing
a novel: [57] and shall be delighted when the day arrives when you
shall be able to read that remarkable production in print.

My little people are pretty well — Harriet especially, but Anny
suffers with a number of double teeth wʰ are about making their
appearance; my wife is provokingly well — so well I mean, that I
can't understand why she should not be quite well. I begin to fear
now that the poor dear little soul will never be entirely restored
to us.

William sends me very good news about 500£ wʰ a man owes
me at Calcutta, He (the debtor) sent a little remittance two
months since — and where is it now? — at the bottom of the Red
Sea with the Memnon. It is my usual luck. However the remittance is only delayed, and some months hence I shall get the dupli-
cates of the bills.

I hope the winter will bring you back to Paris — the view from

[57] *Barry Lyndon.*

your windows in the Rue d'Aguesseau is not very brilliant, but after all a good cheerful landscape of chimney-pots and walls is a better look out than naked trees and muddy lanes — to be sure I have no right to prejudge Villiers-le-Bel: — indeed ⟨you know⟩ that I have never seen it.

Yours dear Aunt affect⟨ionately⟩<br>W M Thackeray

264.        TO CHAPMAN AND HALL
10 NOVEMBER 1843

Hitherto unpublished.

Friday. 10 Nov<sup>r</sup><br>3 George Street<br>S<sup>t</sup> James Square

My dear Sirs

The German book will be a good one to have I think, and I can make an article combining that of Madame de Girardin, 'The lettres Parisiennes' & the new work of the immortal Grant.[58]

Yrs ever<br>W M Thackeray.

When I think about the ten guineas it is with a sinking of the heart. It is *too* low; and for the sake of human-nature & your property, I would recommend you to put a couple of guineas more upon the value of the article.

P. S. II. I enclose a letter for M<sup>r</sup> Delane with w<sup>h</sup> if you send a copy of the Sketch Book you will perhaps do no harm.[59]

[58] Thackeray's "New Accounts of Paris" (*Foreign Quarterly Review*, January, 1844, pp. 470–490) is devoted to *Paris im Frühjahr* by Heinrich Friedrich Ludwig Rellstab (1799–1860); *Lettres Parisiennes*, a series of feuilletons written for *La Presse* by Mme. Delphine de Girardin (1804–1855) under the name Vicomte de Launay; and *Paris and its People* by James Grant (1802–1879).

[59] Despite this appeal to Delane, *The Irish Sketch Book* was not reviewed in *The Times*.

265.   TO  THE  REV.  WILLIAM  BROOKFIELD ?
18 NOVEMBER 1843

Hitherto unpublished.

1  The enclosed letter [60] from Mͬ Procter will explain to my
revered friend why the undersigned thinks it his duty to break an
engagement, wʰ otherwise it would have been his pride to fulfil.

2.  The undersigned (in the discharge of the same painful obligation) has deemed it necessary to communicate to Mͬ Fitz-Gerald [61]
the note in question — and though not prepared from personal
communication to state what will be Mͬ FitzGeralds sentiments
upon a matter involving necessarily much delicate investigation, yet

[60] Procter's letter (the original of which is in the Berg Collection of the
New York Public Library) bears the date of November 18:

My dear Thackeray

Next Tuesday is my birthday — I shall be 27 on that day — Will you
& Messͬˢ Fitzgerald & Tennyson come & dine with me at 1/4 before 7,
therefore, on Tuesday. I shall try to get one or two men whom you all
know. And *I* mean to keep awake!

I know that neither Tennyson or Mͬ Fitzgerald will stand upon the
ceremony of receiving a separate note. Let me hear from you, as soon as
you can.

Yours ever
B W Procter.

Procter was born on November 21, 1787.

[61] Thackeray was in London "to have his eyes doctored," and FitzGerald
(*Letters and Literary Remains*, ed. Wright, I, 172) had come up from the
country to see him.

the Undersigned cannot help stating that he has counselled Mʳ FitzGerald to comply with the not unreasonable request of an amiable man.

3. This will necessarily involve a refusal of my reverend friend's invitation.

4. How will such a refusal be met? Will my reverend friend consider it as tantamount to a declaration of future non-intercourse, or will he rather commence first negotiations to arrange a dinner-party on some other day?

5. The undersigned would humbly suggest Wednesday as that day. For the following reasons.

1ˢᵗ Wednesday is the day immediately subsequent to Tuesday.

2ⁿᵈ On Wednesday the parties resiliating the contract as it at present stands are perfectly free to enter upon a new treaty.

6. The undersigned therefore reiterates his offer, and explains his perfect readiness to enter upon new negotiations.

He begs to offer to his reverend friend the assurances of his most profound

most devoted<br>& most sincere<br>Consideration<br>Titmarsh

Done at Pall-Mall
   L. S.
this 18 day of Novʳ 1843.


266.        TO MRS. CARMICHAEL-SMYTH
            24 NOVEMBER 1843

*Address:* Mʳˢ Carmichael Smyth | 81 Champs Élysées | Paris. *Postmarks:* 24 NO 1843, 26 NOV. 43 BOULOGNE. Hitherto unpublished.

My dearest Mammy. Although it is wrong to contradict one's own parents painful duty compels me in the present instance to give a flat denial to your last favor. I am not worse. I never was worse. I never was better in interior health, and my eyes is wonderfully improved — one quite well, the other all but restored and in the most interesting way to recovery. The painful mixture has been replaced by one more easy, and the job is such a good one I think that I shall let it go on. It took me 10 days to get into working habits, but now I am hard at it and with my hands for the moment awfully full. Alix Becher [62] has written in reply to your mysterious queries, and when Fitz goes away I shall be more free to go see him and my relatives. M<sup>r</sup> Bedingfield has favored me with a visit, and has charmed me as usual by his modesty and manly demeanour. You would have been pleased to hear him     Have you sent in a Comedy for the prize? says he — on w<sup>h</sup> I replied that I was not such a d — f — knowing perfectly well that the poor lad had forwarded a five-act masterpiece himself — on w<sup>h</sup> he said 'I think you could write *a farce* if you would but try' with a most wicked accent on the farce — and I think this is the most remarkable incident I have to relate — the world wags pleasantly enough. Breakfast with Fitz. Write at the Club dine with my friends and so on — It is quite curious to see how work falls in in London w<sup>h</sup> would be quite out of one's way at Paris: but I shall be back before Xmas P.G. and with my hands quite full for many months to come. Nobody talks about Ireland except the lawyers who are watching the shufflings and turnings of the O'Connell trial [63] — every one is full of the Corn-Law League w<sup>h</sup> is bidding fair to master the country. It will be a great and magnificent peaceful Revolution — the government of the country will fall naturally into the hands of the middle classes as it should do: and the Lords and country gentlemen will — only have their due share. They have had all till now: but I think Dicky Cobden has rung their knell, and I shouldn't wonder to see him Prime Minister of England

[62] Thackeray's cousin, Captain Alexander Bridport Becher (1796–1876) of the Royal Navy, who was employed in the Hydrographic Office from 1823 to 1865, edited *The Nautical Magazine* from 1832 to 1871. He lived at 29 Upper Gloucester Terrace.

[63] O'Connell's violent agitation for the repeal of the Corn Laws had led on October 14, 1843, to his arrest on charges of conspiracy, sedition, and unlawful assembly. His trial began on November 2, and on November 8 the Grand Jury brought in a true bill. On May 30, 1844, he was fined £2,000 and sentenced to a year in prison. (*Annual Register*, 1843–1844)

It is a wonder how one gets interested in these matters all of a sudden on smelling London fog — none of the French papers talk about the League and all are on O'Connell and yet the League is the great Fact of the day.

What do you think of this instance of Xtian forgiveness? Yesterday Nickisson shows me a letter from J. Wilks asking my address at Paris where he can put 100 a year into my pocket. Fancy that rascal O'Donnell printing old papers in Fraser's Magazine [64] — and bothering me to get them put in and to read them in

[64] At a meeting of "Our Club" about the year 1860 Thackeray told David Masson (*Memories of London in the Forties*, Edinburgh and London, 1908, pp. 245–248) the following story: "I'm quite at home with the Irish character! I know the Irish thoroughly. The best friend I ever had in the world — the nicest and most delightful fellow I ever knew in the world — was an Irishman. But, d'ye know, he was a great rascal! I'll tell you how he served me once. He was in low water, and was always coming to me to borrow a sovereign or two, when I hadn't many to spare. But he was such a dear delightful fellow, it was quite a pleasure to lend them to him. One day, however, he came to me and said, 'I say, Thack, you're a writer for magazines. Now, I've got a paper that I think would suit a magazine, and I wish you'd get it into one of them for me, because I'm hard-up at present, and a few guineas would come in handy.' I took his paper, and actually kept one of my own papers out of 'Fraser's Magazine' of the coming month, though it was rather a considerable sacrifice for me at the time, in order to get my friend's paper in. Oh! you've no idea what a nice delightful fellow that was! Well, the paper appeared; and it was perhaps a week or two after the beginning of the month before I next stepped into Fraser the publisher's shop. I thought Fraser looked rather glum when I went in; but I did not know the cause till he said, —

" 'Well, this is a pretty affair, Mr Thackeray!'

" 'What affair?' I asked.

" 'Why, that paper of your friend's, in this number!'

" 'What about it?' I said.

"He went to a drawer, and took out a newspaper clipping, and asked me to look at it. I did; and I found, to my horror, that my friend's paper was denounced as a barefaced plagiarism. It had been copied *verbatim* from an article that had appeared in some other periodical. The date and all other particulars were given.

"I was of course greatly annoyed, and indeed excessively angry; and I thought, 'Well, I must cut the fellow for ever; there's no getting on with him.' I took the clipping with me, and went straight to my friend's rooms, intending to blow him up, once for all, and have done with him. I showed him the clipping, and declared his behaviour to have been scandalous. What do you

MS. I'm sorry to say I felt a sort of satisfaction at this — it is a good pretense for having done with him. But this is after all not the way we must look at a starving and unsane man. For what were [we] taught to say forgive us our trespasses?

Did Isabella show Arthur Shawe's letter & the announcement of Henry's romantic marriage?

Ive nothing to say, and only wrote to ease your poor old doubting soul. And so God bless all, and good night.

W M T.

I went to see all the Allens the other day, and the little girls asked a great deal about Annie and whether baby was a good girl?

Shall I ask Brodie to come back? — that last oration of Justine's is really too bad.


267.      TO WILLIAM JERDAN
12 DECEMBER 1843

*Address:* W. Jerdan Esq^re | Great New Street | Fetter Lane. *Postmark:* 12 DE 1843. Hitherto unpublished.

27 Jermyn S^t 65
Tuesday.

My dear Jerdan

If you delight in performing good actions (as you notoriously do) pray insert the enclosed paragraph about a really clever novel,

---

think he did? He laughed in my face and treated the whole affair as a capital joke!

"That's how my Irish friend served me: but oh! he was the nicest friend, the dearest, most delightful fellow, I ever knew in the world."

[65] Thackeray's Jermyn St. lodgings, which he retained from late 1843 until April, 1845, are described in Vizetelly's *Glances Back through Seventy Years* (I, 249-250): "On calling at the address given me — a shop in Jermyn-street, eight or ten doors from Regent-street, and within a few doors of the present Museum of Geology — and knocking at the private entrance, a young lodging-house slavey in answer to my inquiries bade me follow her upstairs. I did so, to the very top of the house, and after my card had been handed in, I was asked to enter the front apartment, where a tall slim individual between thirty and thirty-five years of age, with a pleasant smiling countenance and a bridgeless nose, and clad in a dressing gown of decided Parisian cut, rose from

now in the course of publication by young Bedingfield [66] a grandson of old Doctor Turner, and my relative.

Pray do so, and count on the gratitude

of your Titmarsh.

### 268.    TO WILLIAM HARRISON AINSWORTH
### DECEMBER 1843? [67]

Published in part by Ellis, *Ainsworth*, II, 194. My text is taken from an American Art Association catalogue, April 23–24, 1917.

My dear Ainsworth:

There comes a note from Dickens who begs too for a remission of the dinner — as I can't have it without my two roaring [68] animals: and the play wouldn't be worth coming to with the part of Hamlet omitted — the great Titmarsh banquet is hereby postponed, to be held on some other occasion however with uncommon splendor.

Yrs. Ever.

W. M. T.

---

a small table standing close to the near window to receive me. When he stood up, the low pitch of the room caused him to look even taller than he really was, and his actual height was well over six feet. . . . The apartment was an exceedingly plainly furnished bedroom, with common rush seated chairs and painted French bedstead, and with neither looking-glass nor prints on the bare, cold, cheerless-looking walls. On the table from which Mr. Thackeray had risen, a white cloth was spread, on which was a frugal breakfast tray — a cup of chocolate and some dry toast — and huddled together at the other end were writing materials, two or three numbers of 'Fraser's Magazine,' and a few slips of manuscript." Though there is no reason to question the accuracy of Vizetelly's description, his first meeting with Thackeray cannot — as he asserts — have taken place in Jermyn Street. Thackeray lived at his Coram Street home until May, 1843, and the business of Vizetelly's interview was to engage him as a critic for the *Pictorial Times*, the initial issue of which, containing an article by Thackeray, appeared on March 18 of that year.

[66] *The Miser's Son.*

[67] It seems likely that Thackeray's dinner was planned to repay Dickens for one that he (*Letters*, ed. Dexter, I, 549) had given to Thackeray, Ainsworth, Maclise, Forster, and Cruikshank on December 9, 1843.

[68] American Art reads *waring.*

269.                    TO DANIEL MACLISE
                         DECEMBER 1843?

Published by W. Justin O'Driscoll, *Memoir of Daniel Maclise*, R. A. (London, 1871), p. 130.

Wednesday. 27 Jermyn S$^t$ [69]

My dear Maclise

Although from the lamentable state in wh I left you on Sunday evening you have probably quite forgotten your engagement to dine with me on Monday next; yet *I* for one will never shrink from my engagements, and in reminding you that the promise was made on your part, beg to state that the dinner is deferred until further orders.

Ainsworth & Boz wont come & press for delay. Well then though I know from the state of the bankers account at present that next week there wont probably be 5/ wherewith to buy a dinner — yet let them have their will. Something tells me that it will be long long before the banquet in question takes place — but it is their will. So be it. The greatest of all the names of Allah (Goethe says) is AMEN

Mind and be punctual at seven.

Yrs      W M Thackeray.

[69] O'Driscoll, for no apparent reason, omits this line and prints in its place, *March 10, 1857.* Following him, Ellis (*Ainsworth*, II, 194) assigns this letter and the one to Ainsworth above to that date, an impossible arrangement, since Thackeray lived on Jermyn Street only between December, 1843, and April, 1845.

270.                              TO HIS FAMILY
                         17-18 DECEMBER 1843

*Address:* M<sup>rs</sup> Carmichael Smyth | 81 Champs Elysées | Paris. *Postmarks:* 18
DE 1843, 20 DEC. 43 BOULOGNE. Hitherto unpublished.

                                              December 19.[70]
                                              27 Jermyn Street.

My dear ladies I have been looking out for the last 3 days for a
letter from Paris being anxious to know how all there are faring.
I write this from my bed a coach wheel having passed over my
head and cut it off but a surgeon was luckily at hand who set it right
again with sticking-plaster. This is the only personal news I have
to give, I think, unless you would like to know what I have had for
dinner every day since last week w<sup>h</sup> would make a very long sum,
or what I have been writing w<sup>h</sup> I would not do over again for twice
the money. I fear after all it will be New Year's day before I am
back for my hands are very full of business, and I can't comfortably
dispose of it until then — or indeed anyhow at all, for there is as
much as would take 2 months to do. But it is a comfort to think
that there is a decent income arranged for 1844 (please God my
health hold good) and actually a prospect of saving money at the
year's end. What a phoenix of a year 1845 will be if we see it!
These visions are so monstrous however, that I don't like to count
upon them as realities, and so we will wait to realize them till '45
comes.

I've nothing to say as usual for I don't leave this till 5 o'clock
and take a little trudge as far as Pall-Mall or possibly the Garrick
before dinner but the life I am sorry to say is a very jolly one —
plenty of work that is and plenty of fun. My eyes oblige me to live
moderately so that there are no excuses to do me harm. Here the
letter stopped yesterday: and yours is just come to hand — What I
admire in my dear Mamma's correspondence is that igstreme ingenuity at finding out ills to w<sup>h</sup> her darling is subject I have never

---

[70] A mistake for December 18, the day on which this letter was finished, as
the postmark shows.

been better in health than since I left home. I have had no headaches but in your poor old fancy. Now however and in spite of
your injunctions to the contrary, and since the last page was written,
I have got a swelled face — w^h will keep me to the house probably
for a day or two, w^h I shall employ in working at a long article for
the F.Q. R.[71] Shouldn't you like to come off post to see it? — the
worst is it wont wait for your coming, so you must make your mind
as easy as suckinstances will permit.

If you see M^rs Hankey tell her with my compliments that I have
done my very best with the lace, and placed it as I thought in much
better hands than Miss Hamerton's. Ask her too with the same
compliments where I shall leave what I can't sell of it? — If I had
been caught smuggling it a young Embassy man told me the other
day, I should have had an imprisonment and 300£ fine. The young
fellow insinuated that I was a fool for my pains. — and upon my
word I can't say I thinks he was very much in the wrong. But
knowing this I decline taking it back again.

As I could not go into the city with my swelled chop I have dispatched G. P's letter to Lubbocks: and won't forget the other
little commissions     I have begun with a story [72] w^h is to last
through the year in Fraser, and am to have my own way with the
worthy M^r Punch, whose pay is more than double of that I get
anywhere else. Dickens has just published a charming Christmas
book,[73] w^h I won't forget to bring with me. I have made much
friends with him and think your tirade against good dinners a
monstrous piece of superstition. Why not be merry when one can?
I was to have been merry tomorrow at the Harris's at my own
invite, b⟨ut⟩ am held back by my jor. The Waddell and Mary
Scott were at Kerwans [74] t'other day — Mary looking none the
better for her years — the Waddell magnificent in looks but as dull
an idiot as I ever met — She sings popular songs in an extremely

---

[71] Probably "New Accounts of Paris." See above, No. 264.

[72] *Barry Lyndon.*

[73] *A Christmas Carol,* reviewed by Thackeray in "A Box of Novels,"
*Fraser's Magazine,* February, 1844, pp. 153–169.

[74] A. V. Kirwan, who lived at 73 Gloucester Place and had offices at 9
Inner Temple Lane (*Royal Blue Book,* 1843).

small pipe, and I don't think I got any credit with her by begging
her to perform one of these ditties quicker.

God bless my dear Nanny I am glad to hear that she is good &
Baby good too — Upon my word I am quite as tired of this town as
you can be of my absence, and on New Years day please God I
may see you all again. This is to be a letter for you and the little
woman — I'm glad to hear G M is well again: and pray Heaven
bless all. W M T.

271.        ·   TO  RICHARD  BEDINGFIELD
                21  DECEMBER  1843

My text is taken from Bedingfield, *Cassell's Magazine*, II, 298–299.

R. C. 21 Decr., 1843.

My dear Bedingfield, —

I am sincerely sorry to hear of the accident which has befallen
Dr. Turner, and fear with you that, at his time of life, the consequences may be very doubtful. Your mother, please God, will be
able to bear up under this misfortune; and I trust, however it may
affect her domestic happiness, it will not at all injure her worldly
prospects.

I am only this moment come out after a five days' bout of illness
at my lodgings. I sent on Tuesday week last a very pressing note [75]
to Jerdan regarding the "Miser's Son," with a little notice which I
myself had written so as to save him trouble.

It was, I need not tell you a favourable one as the story deserved;
it has a great deal of talent of a great number of kinds, and many a
man has made a fortune with a tithe of the merit.

But in spite of this, Jerdan has not inserted my article. Have
you ever advertised in his paper or elsewhere? A laudatory paragraph here and there will do you no earthly good, unless the name
of your book is perpetually before the public. The best book I ever
wrote [76] I published with an unknown publisher, and we got off
two hundred and fifty copies of it, and this was after the success of

[75] See above, No. 267.
[76] *The Second Funeral of Napoleon*, published by Hugh Cunningham.

the Paris book, with some thirty pounds of advertisements, and hugely laudatory notices in a score of journals. Shakespeare himself would not get a hearing in Gray's Inn Lane.

Unless your publisher actually offers you money for a future work, I beg you to have nothing to do with him. Write short tales. Make a dash at all the magazines; and at one or two of them I can promise you, as I have said, not an acceptance of your articles, but a favourable hearing. It is, however, a bad trade at the best. The prizes in it are fewer and worse than in any other professional lottery; but I know it's useless damping a man who will be an author whether or no — men are doomed, as it were, to the calling.

Make up your mind to this, my dear fellow, that the "Miser's Son" will never succeed — not from want of merit, but from want of a publisher. Shut it up without delay, and turn to some work that will pay you. Eschew poetry above all (you've had too much of it), and read all the history you can. Don't mind this patriarchal tone from me. I'm old in the trade now, and have lived so much with all sorts of people in the world that I plume myself on my experience. Give my best love to your mother and aunt. I will call to-morrow to ask after their health, and that of your poor patient, and am always truly yours,

W. M. Thackeray.

I shall give you a notice in *Fraser* in the February number; [77] but I tell you it's no use.

272.        TO JOHN ALLEN
            DECEMBER 1843

Hitherto unpublished.

27 Jermyn St

My dear John Allen,

See what I have done. I have sent down your lectures on history to Edward Fitz in place of Hazlitts conversations [78] wh he left be-

[77] See "A Box of Novels."
[78] *Conversations of James Northcote, Esq., R. A.* (1830).

hind him. He has also left a watch in the same doubtful charge. I have made my arrangements to go away on Thursday and shan't have time before then to come and see you. Will you nobly call at Nickissons 215 Regent Street for Edward's watch and book and forgive me for sending away yours.

It's not my fault that I have not been to see you. Indeed I've been out every day. I wish you and your's a most merry Xmas and am always Yours upon my word & honour

W M T.

273.     TO PETER PURCELL
          25 DECEMBER 1843

My text is taken from an undated George D. Smith Catalogue.

Xmas Day, 1843.

My dear P. P.,

On this happy day I can't refrain from spending a penny to tender to you my respectful wishes. When, in my best clothes, I went to call on Mrs. Purcell in Portland Place and was informed by the Footboy that you were gone to Ireland, I felt more ashamed of myself than I have ever done any time these three weeks and thought "its Saxon return for Irish kindness and Hospitality." But you will please remember that I am a poor day-laborer in the vineyard and must work often when I would like to be taking my diversion — those last days of yours in London were just the busiest of all the month to me. I have had on this sacred day ELEVEN invitations to Dinner which I can't help thinking of with a sort of pride, and in the overflowing of my Bosom was anxious to write you a line by way of a shakehands for Xmas and the ensuing New Year, likewise to your Lady, your amiable Family, also to his Reverence and the rest of your party round the Halverstown Turkey this day. As an Agriculturist I would wish that the Humbug Crop should not be so plenteous in Ireland in 1844 as it has been in 1843 and with this have the honor to subscribe myself my dear Mr. Purcell's affectionate servant Emily Jenkinson.

274.                DIARY
## 1 JANUARY–9 DECEMBER 1844

Extracts published in *Biographical Introductions*, IV, xxxiv–xxxvi; V, xxxvi–xlii.

January 1: Came home after 2 months in England: in the midst of all sorts of jollity

2: Wrote Grant for Punch [1] — drawings. Articles Blessington — Bulwer. In the evening went to walk and see Stevens.

3: Wrote Hume's letter: Broun for P. dined in the evening with Fraser, and passed a great deal too jovial a night.

4: Read in a silly book called L'Empire a good story about the first K of Wurtemberg's wife: killed by her husband for adultery. 'Frederic William born in 1734 (?) married in 1780 the Princess Caroline of Brunswick Wolfenbuttel, who died the 27 September 1788.' For the rest of the story see. L'Empire ou 10 ans sous Napoleon par un Chambellan. Paris. Allardin 1836. V. 1. 220.[2] At home doing nothing all day.

5: Went to see Collignon. At home found the dear little wife wonderfully well. Pray God to keep her so and restore her love for me. Wrote a page of Fraser: on Irish novels.[3] Called at Aunt Ritchie's

6: Breakfast at Hankeys — No work — called on M. Bonnet & Heath about the Mysteres,[4] passed the evening at the Hamertons.

---

[1] "Leaves from the Lives of the Lords of Literature" (*Punch*, January 20, 1844, pp. 42–43). This parody of the writings of James Grant, whose *Paris and its People* Thackeray had recently reviewed (see above, No. 264), includes notices of the Countess of Blessington, Lord Brougham, Sir Thomas Broun, and Bulwer.

[2] "The Princess's Tragedy," which forms chapter 12 and two preceding chapters of *Barry Lyndon*, is based on the narrative of Princess Caroline's life and death in the Baron de la Mothe-Langon's *L'Empire*, I, 220–245. The only copy of this rare book known to me is in the Bibliothèque Nationale. A detailed account of Thackeray's use of his source is given in my unpublished Harvard doctoral dissertation, *Thackeray and France* (1940), pp. 238–241.

[3] See "A Box of Novels."

[4] Thackeray had been employed by a certain Giraldon (see below, No. 276) to translate Eugène Sue's *Mystères de Paris*, but he soon threw up this

[7]: Sunday another blank — dined at home with my wife very well. Unwell myself with irritation of the n. u.[5]

8: Wrote for Fraser. Lever. dined with T. Fraser [6] & spent the evening at Stevens's. too much drink.

9: At home all day repenting of yesterday. At night did h a dozen pages of translation of the Mystères.

10: Wrote for Fraser till 5. Lover. dined at Hankeys.

11: Wrote Fraser — dined at Biffi's alone, and went to see Arnal in L'Homme Blasé — [7] quite tired and weary with writing wh the evenings amusement did not cure

12: Spent all day idling with great profit. My wife at home. went to Corkrans [8] in the evening. 'We lived for a fortnight like people of 1000 a year & had 2£ to begin life.' Read Kenealy's Life of Maginn: [9] & Lever on Grant, & other Magazinery. Maginn a

---

job because he was not promptly paid. The translation was continued by other hands, however, and published by Chapman and Hall in weekly numbers during 1844 with illustrations made under the superintendence of Charles Heath. See *The New Sketch Book*, ed. Garnett, p. 310.

[5] See Appendix XXVIII.

[6] Thomas Fraser (d. 1869), the "laughing Tom" of "The Ballad of Bouillabaisse," was one of Thackeray's oldest Parisian friends. He was Paris correspondent of *The Morning Chronicle* from 1835 to 1855, when he became London secretary of the Hudson Bay Company.

[7] A comedy in two acts by Frédéric Auguste Duvert (1795–1876) and Augustin Théodore Lauzanne de Vaux-Roussel (1805–1877), first presented on November 18, 1843.

[8] Among Thackeray's closest friends in Paris were John Frazer Corkran (d. 1884), his wife, and their five children, who lived on the fifth floor of a large house near the Boulevard des Italiens. Corkran, a miscellaneous writer and Paris correspondent of *The Morning Herald*, was a genial, impractical, and eccentric Irishman. "People used to think he was very deaf, and would shout at him in order to make him hear," writes his daughter Henriette (*Celebrities and I*, p. 43); "but he was not deaf, only it was that he seldom listened, being in Dreamland. . . . As he was bald he wore a kind of wig, or rather a *toupet*, to conceal the nakedness of the top of his head. This *toupet* was generally on one side; my father, being extremely absent-minded, would push it, and push it, so that it often hung at the back of his neck in a disconsolate condition." Miss Corkran also records her impressions of Mrs. Carmichael-Smyth and of Thackeray himself (pp. 18–30 and 106–110).

[9] "Our Portrait Gallery. — No. XXXIV. William Maginn, LL. D." and "Paris and its People" in *The Dublin University Magazine*, January, 1844, pp. 72–111.

famous subject for moralizing     saw Giraldon about the Mystères. & Collignon

13: Wrote on Dickens Xmas Carol for Fraser     dined in town
and evening at Hamertons. Read Magazines &c

14: At home with sore throat. Wrote Lady Londonderry for
Punch [10]

15: Wrote Barry Lyndon for Fraser. dined with Lachevardiere
& others at the Rocher, a merry party, a costly dinner. I the sober-
est of the set for a wonder: and G P. in triumph at the effect of his
dose of Mercure on the sore throat of yesterday.

16: Wrote Barry Lyndon. Mem to read all the works of Titmarsh again in order to prevent repititions w$^h$ seem frequent.

17: Wrote Barry. beginning however to flag.

20: In these days got through the fag end of Chap IV of Barry
Lyndon with a great deal of dullness unwillingness & labor.

21: Wrote 'Mystères de Paris. Translation & puff the latter a
remarkable manifesto.

22: Idled all day — dined in town with Fraser     News from
Darley. Write something about his Cartoons ⟨. . .⟩[11]

23: Another idle day but well spent in walking to see Darley
⟨. . .⟩

24: Changing lodgings, & of course no work done: dinner with
Rodd & Fraser.

25: Wrote some of a nonsensical story out of Dumas's Othon
l'Archer [12] dined at home, my wife wonderfully well — to bed
very early: finding already a comfort in the independence perhaps
in the novelty of the lodgings.

26: And up for a wonder at 8 in consequence — Continued the

[10] "Lady L.'s Journal of a Visit to Foreign Courts," *Punch*, January 27,
pp. 52–54.

[11] This and some of the following entries were written in pencil and have
with the passage of time become so faint as to defy deciphering. Five words
are missing here, four lines in the next hiatus.

[12] Thackeray's burlesque of this slight medieval novel, published in 1840 by
Alexandre Dumas, was entitled "The Childe of Godesberg" when first offered
to Nickisson for *Fraser's Magazine*. It finally appeared as "A Legend of the
Rhine" in *George Cruikshank's Table-Book* for 1845. It will be recalled that
Thackeray passed a month in Godesberg in August and September, 1830.

story, and found my day's work comfortably done by 2 ½, all in consequence of the early rising. Dined at 4 and went to see 4 pieces at the Variétés. Bouffé [13] wonderful in l'Oncle Baptiste. Lafont admirably gentlemanlike & the evening very pleasant

27: A good day's work at the absurdity. Went for Isabella, dined at home, and in the evening at the Hamertons' very merry.

28: Wrote on the story, and to Wickoff [14] dined at the Ritchies.

29: Idle all day Went to Collingnon dined at Hankeys in the evening to Stevens.

30: More idleness — went with Hankey to see Fourreau — called on Mary & Fraser. dined at home; with my wife delightfully well.

February 1: In these days wrote letters for Hume and Wickoff. dined out on Wednesday; at home to day with my wife delightfully well.

2: Wrote all day for Punch (the next revolution) [15] dined at Osborne's, [16] and was amused and disgusted by the energy, good humour, roguery & vulgarity of Balfe. Began with Gaston. [17]

3: Continued the Punch article. dined at home and had a chat in the evening with the Hamertons.

4: All day at work on the Punch article dined at Hankey's.

---

[13] Hugues-Désiré-Marie Bouffé (1800–1888) and Pierre Lafont (1797–1873) were notable vaudeville actors of the day, the latter being particularly esteemed for his portrayals of young rakes and dandies. In addition to L'Oncle Baptiste (1842) by Émile Souvestre (1806–1854), the bill at the Théâtre des Variétés included La Vendetta, Le Chevalier de Guet, Marjolaine, and Chansonette (Moniteur universel).

[14] Henry Wikoff (c. 1813–1884), an American adventurer and writer who travelled widely in the United States and Europe. For Thackeray's business with him, see below, No. 275.

[15] "History of the Next French Revolution," Punch, February 24–April 20.

[16] George Alexander Osborne (1806–1893), a pianist and composer who was at this time supporting himself by giving music lessons. Mrs. Warrenne Blake (Memoirs of a Vanished Generation, London, 1909, p. 67) relates that it was at Osborne's own suggestion that Thackeray used his name in Vanity Fair. Michael William Balfe (1808–1870) is remembered chiefly for his opera, The Bohemian Girl (1843).

[17] I cannot explain this allusion.

5: At work till 3, and dispatched the Punch article, dined in town & saw Bouffe as M. Perrin.[18] Wrote to Forster

8: Passed these days idling. once to the play to see 4 pieces at the Palais Royal.[19] — At Collignons today —

17: Passed the whole of these days, with the exception of Wednesday & Thursday when I wrote the American letter, reading for B. L and writing with extreme difficulty a sheet. Dispatched it on Sunday with the Carmen Lilliense.[20]

10: Wrote on Barry Lyndon the Episode of the Candidate [21] and dined at a roaring party at Stevens's, where was plenty of pleasant nonsense.

20: Wrote a little, but interrupted by my wife went out and made 7 little calls.

21: Wrote all day Barry Lyndon — At 5 went out very tired and came back to bed still more tired at 9 ½ — I have been so idle all my life that continual labour annoys and excites me too much.

22: Wrote a couple of pages B L. but weary with headache: and passed the greater part of the day dawdling profitably at Hankeys. Read in that astonishingly corrupt book the Mémoires du Diable.[22] To remember the Demoiselles Anglaises.

23: Wrote a little Barry — read in Venedey's book,[23] went to see Mrs at Chaillot, dined at home and to bed early in the evening.

24: Wrote Barry. Saturday & Sunday — dined at Hankeys Sunday.

26: idling

---

[18] *Michel Perrin* at the Théâtre des Variétés.

[19] Where the following plays were presented on February 8: *Bonbonnière, Judith, Professeur de maintien, Les Deux ânes,* and *La Sœur de Jocrisse* (*Moniteur universel*).

[20] See above, No. 260.

[21] Barry's encounter with a candidate for holy orders in chapter 6 of *Barry Lyndon*.

[22] A novel published in 1837–1838 by Frédéric Soulié (1800–1847).

[23] *Irland* (1844) by Jacob Venedy (1805–1871), which Thackeray reviewed for *The Morning Chronicle* on March 16. This article has not previously been identified as his. Thackeray probably had some personal acquaintance with Venedy, a political exile who passed most of the years between 1835 and 1848 in Paris and frequented the Crowes' apartment.

27: Wrote Godesberg & drew.

28: Wrote Godesberg 2 pages & drew and dawdled

March 2: Wrote to Wykoff and left home and all dear ones there — six inside to Boulogne a pleasant party of singers to the opera &cc    Slept at the Hotel des Bains — it being too windy to cross on Sunday night.

4: ⟨. . .⟩[24]

5: ⟨. . .⟩

8: ⟨. . .⟩

9: ⟨. . .⟩

11: ⟨. . .⟩

14: Whites dinner

16: ⟨. . .⟩

29: Bradbury & Evans 4.

30: Serjeant Talfourd's dinner. 7. Garrick

May 1: Reeve's dinner. 16 Chester Sq$^{re}$ 7.

2: Kerwans dinner 7. Glocester Place

July 18: Formed a world of good resolves, as my custom is upon this day. Pray God I could keep them or some of them And do my duty by myself and my children! Came down to Brighton — and wrote Punch till dinner, afterwards to tea at my Aunt Thackeray's: and then made an abortive attempt to write Barry Lyndon. Read Peregrine Pickle in the coach — excellent for its liveliness and spirit and wonderful for its atrocious vulgarity.

19: At work on Barry Lyndon all day and wrote near ½ a sheet, dined and had tea with M$^{rs}$ Thackeray. No walking only work work before & after breakfast & dinner. Wrote a shake-hand letter to my Aunt Halliday and early to bed, where the bugs played the deuce with me.

20: Spent the chief part of the day riding about in a fly watching for the explosion of Captain Warner's machine. When we were all at dinner the machine exploded.[25] Wrote a little Who's M$^r$ Moss

---

[24] In this and the following hiatuses five, five, one, two, one, and one lines respectively are irrecoverable.

[25] See Thackeray's squib, "Captain Warner's Discovery," *Punch*, July 27, p. 53, here first identified as his. Nothing is known of "Who's M$^r$ Moss."

— dined with M^rs Thackeray and drunk tea with George Shakespear; whose selfishness is delightfully characteristic.

21: Left Brighton at 2 & ½; after writing 3 or 4 pages at an inn hard by the railroad. Brought away with me something like a fever w^h caused me to pass a hot uncomfortable night. Dined with the Hallidays.

22: Unwell all day with a sort of low fever. Read Smyth's Historic fancies,[26] and Warburton's Biography.[27]

23: Left London at 1 ½ for Dover, and passed the night there at the Ship Walked on the parade. Wrote for Punch — the beginning of the tour of the fat Contributor.[28] Read the Jest Book in the railway — a good subject for an article.

24: Off at 7 by the 'Dover' packet for Ostend A very pleasant passage of 7 hours ½. Hotel des Bains — a charming evening on the Dyke with a beautiful sunset — Capt. Vivian & M^r Harding. Some good instances of English selfishness. The hat near the window — 'Why was I such a d— fool as ever to leave England?'

25: Leaving Ostend at 6, arrived after a hot journey at 4 at Chaudfontaine; and found my dear little ones, and my mother — all well thank God. Anny, not improved in looks, but wonderfully intelligent and affectionate.[29] Harriet too amazingly advanced. It

[26] Thackeray reviewed *Historic Fancies* (1844) by George Sidney Smythe (1818–1857), later (1855) seventh Viscount Strangford, in *The Morning Chronicle* of August 2, 1844. This article has not previously been identified as his.

[27] Presumably Eliot Warburton's "Episodes of Eastern Travel," which appeared in *The Dublin University Magazine* from October, 1843, to February, 1844. In November, 1844, these papers were published in a volume called *The Crescent and the Cross.*

[28] "Wanderings of Our Fat Contributor," *Punch*, August 3, pp. 61–62. Thackeray utilized his study of the *Jest Book* in "Lord William Lennox's Readings and Recitations from Joe Miller," *Punch*, August 10, p. 74. This *jeu d'esprit* has not previously been identified as Thackeray's.

[29] "I was then a little girl of seven years old," Lady Ritchie (*Biographical Introductions*, V, xxxiv-xxxv) writes of this summer's holiday, "and we were in Belgium, in an old country house, which our grandparents had hired for the summer. It was a pretty place, with a pretty name, Chaudfontaine, not very far from Liège. It was an Arcadian sort of country, with pleasant trees. There were streams and valleys, little chapels among the hills, to which we small pilgrims used to be taken, tugging up by stony, climbing ways. I can remember

was a comfort beyond measure to see them. Took a bath at night —
the baths delightfully soft & agreeable.

26: With the children all day and mother. Another bath: and
a rainy walk home at night with the glowworms to light. A coach
full of cigar-smokers passing A who was talking about glowworms
said 'Papa those men have glowworms in their mouths.

27–28: Read Balzacs Chouans in w.ᵸ a good novel is spoiled.
Drew & dawdled on Sunday evening a delightful walk about this
pretty valley. But the prettiest part of all was the cleverness and
vivacity of my dear Anny. It ought to be a comfort to me to find
how the children have been bred up to love their father. Anny
looked quite pretty in her broad hat and pink frock. Bathed Saturday. Wrote for Punch ³⁰ a little on Sunday.

29: In the morning with mother and all the children to Liége,
but the day was rainy, and the only pleasures we could have were
to look at the ships in the Passage Lemonnier. Bought Capefigues
Empire & Consulate and looked through the first volume. Wrote
for Punch at night.

30: Again to Liége alone, and walked about the town for a couple of hours — Coming home found a very good simple creature
of a pasteur with whom willy nilly I was obliged to pass the day.
He ate more than we four — amused the children by all sorts of
tricks bored G P and rather touched me by his extreme goodness
and simplicity. He has never felt he says the passion de la chair,
and entertained me with 100 histories of his preachings, his family
& his wonderful mare.

31: Kept at home all day by the rain. Read 'Aymé Verd' a
clever novel by some young hand imitated from Scott — a very

---

the long, straggling garden at the back of our villa, and the snapdragons and
lupins that skirted the garden beds. In front of the house, with its many green
shutters, was a courtyard, enclosed by green gates, where we used to breakfast,
and outside the gates a long terraced road by the dried-up river, where I used
to walk with my father, holding his hand. He would come for a day or two;
sometimes he stayed at the villa, sometimes at a little inn in the village, a
whitewashed place with trellises, where we would fetch him of a morning. He
never remained very long with us; he came and went very suddenly."

³⁰ Probably "Travelling Notes by Our Fat Contributor. The Sea," *Punch*,
August 10, pp. 66–67.

touching scene of an old Curé turned out of his house by the Huguenots, of a Huguenot preacher ditto. Walked to the Cottage in the evening, and got volumes of Capefigue to read.

August 1: With mother the chief part of the day: and in the evening walked with her to M^r Morritt's — through a charming landscape of wood and little mountains Read Capefigue. The children delightful. I lose a great deal of the best kind of happiness by being deprived of their affectionate artless society.

2: Came to Brussels by the 6 ½ train, not in till 12. Read Capefigue in the coach. Moreau's trial — his fine defense — the Emperor's claptrap of a coronation &c. Went for a passport to the E. M. and in the evening to the play to hear the barber of Seville. The actress with a pretty fresh voice sang a modern song in the music-lesson scene. It was greatly applauded and of course greatly inferior to the delightful old music.

3: Passed all the day idling at Brussels in vain endeavouring to bring myself to work. In the evening to the pretty new theatre: where the l^es armes de Richelieu,[31] and the Chevalier de S^t George were very pleasantly acted.

4: Came to Antwerp with the idea of going to England. Still unconquerably idle. The wind was too strong to make the passage pleasant and so the scheme was put off. Read Mems of Talleyrand, and Mems of un Homme d'État.[32]

5: From Antwerp to Ostend reading more of the Homme d'État by the way. The pleasures of a rainy evening at Ostend and an uncomfortable inn, wrote a little travels and to bed early.

6: Off from Ostend at 8 by the Princess Mary, and arrived at Dover at 1 after a dismal sick passage. Took the train at 3 to London and read Talleyrands memoirs by the way. Found a letter from Hume with 10£ only.

---

[31] A play (1839) by Jean François Alfred Bayard (1796–1853) and Philippe François Pinel Dumanoir (1806–1865). *Le Chevalier de Saint George* (1840) was adapted from a novel of Roger de Beauvoir (for whom, see below, No. 624) by the author and Anne Honoré Joseph Duveyrier (1787–1865), called Mélesville.

[32] Neither of these books can be identified from Thackeray's notations of their titles.

7: Wrote Humes letter, dined at Lords and had a long walk with FitzGerald [33] in the park talking about his prospects w^h are sad enough. Saw Morton & walked with him to the house where he was to dine.

8: Breakfast at the Reform — dawdled there over Walpole. Lunched walked and dawdled farther with Morton, with whose young Cambridge cousin I dined — These boys are intolerable. But it would be good to study them. I recalled many of the flippancies and opinions of my own 22. Read a little in Daubigné's Memoirs [34] — exceedingly amusing & characteristic. Paid at the L. L [35] and looked about there. In the evening to Forster — smoke & sherry & water

9. Dinner Parkes 7.[36] But as usual feverish symptoms in the morning. Cant I for Heaven's sake be moderate? Drew for Punch — breakfasted with Warburton where was a very pleasant M^r Glyn [37] with stories about the war in Spain. At dinner in the evening heard more good stories about Cave the Mine-Speculator. More dawdling to see Evans, & Alfred Tennyson full of complaints.

10: Wrote and drew for Punch [38] the greater part of the day: and made improvement in the wood-drawing. Dined with Mahony at a chophouse. in the evening to Stone's and to bed early.

11: Disraeli's [39] dinner. 7 ¼ Read for B. L. all the morning at the Club — then walked, a pleasant dinner at Disraelis.

[33] Edward Marlborough FitzGerald, who was born in Dublin in 1802, matriculated at Trinity College, Cambridge, in 1825 but did not take a degree. He supported himself by journalism in London for many years before leaving England to avoid imprisonment for debt. See below, No. 343.

[34] The *Mémoires of* Théodore Agrippa d'Aubigné (1552–1630).

[35] The London Library.

[36] Joseph Parkes (1796–1865), liberal politician and parliamentary solicitor.

[37] Henry Glyn, the Captain Strong of *Pendennis*. See below, No. 1061.

[38] Probably the second part of "Travelling Notes of Our Fat Contributor. The Sea," *Punch*, August 17, pp. 83–84.

[39] Thackeray had only a slight acquaintance with Disraeli, though the two men must have met frequently in the middle eighteen-forties. The satirical tone of Thackeray's reviews of *Coningsby* (in *The Morning Chronicle* of May 13 and *The Pictorial Times* of May 25, 1844) and of *Sybil* (in *The Morning Chronicle* of May 13, 1845) can hardly have been pleasant to

12: Colburns dinner 6 ½  Read dawdled all day — cant bring myself to work.  To Bouverie S[t] and afterwards to dine at Colburns — where old Lady Morgan fished for compliments and got no sport.

13: Pichot called in the morning to breakfast afterwards to see the Club and the Drawing of the Art Union prizes.  Wrote a song for P.[40]  Gave P a dinner in the evening at the R. & late to bed.

14: Boxall's [41] dinner 6 ½  At home all day drawing and dawdling with B. L. lying like a night-mare on my mind.  Dined with Boxall; in the evening to M[rs] Twiss's music. a pleasant party — and pretty women.

15: Dinner to Lemon & Evans. — it was a great deal too good and w[d] have been better for ½ the good things w[h] M[r] Soyer [42] supplied in his anxiety to please Punch.

17: Three all but idle days: with Evans to day about the foreign trip.

---

Disraeli, who was mortally offended by Thackeray's burlesque of his fiction in *Novels by Eminent Hands*.  John Hollingshead (*London Chronicle*, March 25, 1899) writes: "In 1862 I was walking through the International Exhibition with [Thackeray], when we came across Benjamin Disraeli.  They saw each other, but showed no signs of recognition.  'He has never spoken to me,' said Thackeray, voluntarily, 'since I wrote the short parody of "Coningsby" ("Codlingsby") in "Punch".' "  Disraeli took a belated revenge seventeen years after Thackeray's death by putting him into *Endymion* as St. Barbe.  This caricature, which admirers of Thackeray who had come to know him only after *Vanity Fair* found more puzzling than offensive, is a romancer's fancy deriving from Disraeli's scanty and maliciously distorted recollections of Thackeray in the years before he became famous.

It should be noted that the identification of *The Morning Chronicle's* review of *Sybil* as Thackeray's is based on a fragment of a letter (which I have not traced) from Thackeray to Colburn of May 8, 1845, printed in a Sotheby catalogue of June 25, 1923: "Is Sybil ready?  Send me a copy, I will review it for the Chronicle."

[40] I have not identified this song.

[41] William Boxall (1800–1879), later (1867) knighted, the portrait painter. Mrs. Twiss was the wife of Horace Twiss (1787–1849), the politician and wit.

[42] Alexis Benoît Soyer (1809–1858), the famous chef of the Reform Club. Thackeray reviewed his *Gastronomic Regenerator* (1846), in a hitherto unidentified article for *The Morning Chronicle* of July 4, 1846, and put him into *Pendennis* as Mirobolante.

18: Wrote for Punch letter to Louis Philippe [43] went to Putney to dinner with C. Villiers.[44] The case of the cab a curious instance of character.

19: Wrote all day Barry Lyndon — dined with Bevan at the Reform Club where I met Emerson Tennent [45] and had much talk about a trip to the East.[46]

20: In the City again to arrange about the Eastern trip — wrote a little Barry Lyndon — & dined with Quin at a party where FitzGerald was in wonderful cue: but I was too much flustered myself thinking about the great voyage to enjoy the fun much. Ordered traps &c in the city to the amt of 15£.

21: Wrote Barry — made farewell arrangements. dined with Bevan at the G and took leave of the good fellows there. Left behind at Lubbocks a balance 95£

22: The last glimpse I had was of old Jo Gwilt's [47] grey head in Abingdon St reading the Times — came on to Southampton writing for Punch the whole way, & finished my article just as we got in. Went on board The Lady Mary Wood and was introduced to my fellow-passengers — The first evening very pleasant and beautifully calm. Left Southampton at 3 ¼: and may God prosper all and all we leave behind.

23: The second day of the voyage passed very pleasant & calm, eating & drinking all day — playing chess & smoking; at 6 we came off Ushant & into the bay of Biscay where though it was wonderfully calm considering yet

---

[43] "To the Napoleon of Peace," *Punch*, August 24, p. 90.

[44] Charles Pelham Villiers (1802–1898), grandson of the first Earl of Clarendon and younger brother of the fourth Earl, who was M. P. for Wolverhampton from 1835 to 1898.

[45] James Emerson Tennent (1804–1869), later (1845) knighted and (1867) created a Baronet, a well-known politician and miscellaneous writer. He was at this time M. P. for Belfast and Secretary to the India Board. He served as Civil Secretary to the Colonial Government of Ceylon from 1845 to 1850 and as Secretary to the Board of Trade from 1852 to 1867.

[46] See the preface to *Notes of a Journey from Cornhill to Grand Cairo* (*Works*, V, 587–588). The rest of this diary consists chiefly of brief memoranda for that narrative.

[47] An architect and archeologist (1784–1863) with whom Thackeray was friendly for many years.

24: I was laid up all Saturday — & this evening diversified with bugs, w.ʰ sent me up on deck to see a noble moon setting.

25: All well in the morning: & prayers under the awning. At dinner had Champagne in honor of the day & drank the Captains [48] health — came into Vigo in the evening & had a merry queer ½ hour there.

28: Anchored at night in Cadiz Had a pleasant 2 hours walk in Cadiz — the cleanest and liveliest of towns — 6 French war steamers were lying in there, and 1 with Joinville's [49] flag on the foremast.

29: Arrived at Gibralter after a pleasant run from Cadiz the straits exceedingly picturesque — and all quite sorry to leave the little ship — Went to the Clubhouse Hotel, where a fellow-traveller M.ʳ Robertson good-naturedly gave me up his bed & musquito curtains.

30: Was spent in dawdling through the hot lively town & in the afternoon in writing. Jews and midshipmen at a dirty dinner — the evening spent with M.ʳ Cresswell & Costello. dull but agreeable.

31: Left Gibraltar at 2 by our new boat the Tagus — very handsome — delightful run along the Spanish coast — The Rock of Gib[raltar] admirable in all its bearings — at night very damp & steaming hot. The bugs played frightful pranks with my eyes.

September 2: Fine weather & decent enjoyment of life — Passed Algiers rising very stately from the sea — & skirted by long dismal lines of African shores with here & there a fire smoking in the mountains & a lonely settlement every now & then. The table afforded a shelter from the bugs of the berth. Fell asleep over my work.

3: Made a little attempt on Barry Lyndon. & wrote a couple of pages in the cabin at night but was interrupted by the horrible bug-bites, and began to grow pretty considerably disgusted with my condition.

4: All attempts at dining very fruitless. Basins in requisition,

[48] Captain Samuel Lewis of the *Iberia*, to whom Thackeray's *Notes of a Journey from Cornhill to Grand Cairo* is dedicated.
[49] François d'Orléans (1818–1900), Prince de Joinville, the third son of Louis Philippe, Admiral of a fleet sent to bombard Mogador.

wind hard ahead, que diable allait il faire dans cette galère? [50]
Writing or thinking impossible — dawdled over Hajji Baba.[51]

5: Arrived at Malta at 12 — on shore to the inn drove to the
Governor's garden, and had great comfort in a large bugless bed;
and a dinner unaccompanied by nausea —

6: Off again for Athens — the sea rough enough to make all
nature uncomfortable — rather calmer towards night, when M[r]
Smith amused us all with his memorable query about the Jew Read
Eothen,[52] a clever book of Cambridge extraction.

7: Two days of fine weather but excessive discomfort. Just well
enough not to be sick.

9: A beautiful morning to enter the harbour of the Piræus On
shore by 9 o'clock, and passed the day leisurely in looking through
the town, the temple of Jupiter &c. making here & there a sketch
or two. Mem. The bed & musquito Curtain — the palace & Sentry
box.

10: Up early to the Acropolis, and after further sketching &
strolling in the town, was right glad to get back to the ship in the
evening to my bed on the table.

11: A charming cool calm day, the vessel skirting along all day
by innumerable blue hills and islands, & the only complaint that of
a little cold. Wrote a very little.

12: Was wakened at 5 to see the sun rise in Smyrna Gulph. Saw
the wonderful bazaars on shore — camels for the first time. the
Arabian nights alive — thought it impossible to see too much of
them — & was glad to get away in an hour. Drew a little.

13: Off the coast of Troy in the morning: and passed the day
pleasantly in listening to a whistling Berliner who amused us with
his music — In the evening a general concert to w[h] some good-
natured Oxford lads contributed their share. Punch & health-
drinking concluded the voyage. Drew and wrote a little.

14: Arrived in a fog w[h] prevented us from seeing the beauties of

[50] Molière, *Les Fourberies de Scapin*, II, vii.
[51] *The Adventures of Hajji Baba of Ispahan* (1824) by James Justinian
Morier (1780?–1849).
[52] See above, No. 62, April 29.

Constantinople — Walked after breakfast from Pera to Horn & saw the bazars Slave market &c.

15: Went to draw with Bill but his illness put a stop to the sketching, I was too stupified all day by the atrocious bugbites of the preceding night to be good for much, to bed at 8 & recovered myself by a tolerably sound sleep —

16: Wrote a little for Punch — then drew. Went on board the old Tagus, & took a delightful row down the most beautiful waters in the world.

17: Wrote a little and drew for Punch in the morning. In the afternoon to the Seraglio Gardens, Kitchen, review, white eunuchs. Driven away while making a sketch of the gate, and drew the Mosque of S! Sophia, dined at a Greek eating house, on a board. Tipsy Armenians singing about — queer boys to wait. Old gardener drunk wine.

18: Wrote Punch the whole day — drew for it & finished 4 letters of the F. C.[53] Took a walk to the burial ground of Pira — very picturesque. and again at work at night.

19: To the Tagus & Iberia, afterwards to the bazars and bought dresses for the ladies, & a dressing gown & trowsers. Drew a little but no writing —

20: About in a boat to the burying Morgue up the river drew but no work done. Saw the Sultan go to the Mosque of Tophana — Eunuchs, women, negroes, petitions, bad gunning, seedy look of the Sultan —

21: Paid a last visit to the Bazars & Slave-Market, and came off by the Iberia in the evening, leaving Constantinople looking more beautiful than ever. All sorts of Jews, Turks, filth, and oddity on board.

22: Tried to write Barry Lyndon.

23: And completed about 12 pages after a hard uncomfortable day's work. Just in time to dispatch by the Tagus as she left Smyrna

---

[53] By this time Thackeray had probably completed "Travelling Notes" and the first two papers of "Punch in the East." The first appeared in *Punch* between November 30 and December 14, 1844; the two first installments of the second appeared January 11 and January 18, 1845.

at 4 o'clock. Poor Sotheby looking the picture of death on the ladder of the Ship.

24: On shore at Smyrna & made the round of the bazaars, a sketch or 2 in the town; took a bath quite inferior to Constantinople: & in the evening off again for Rhodes. The Poles came on board & the French priest.

25: At sea off Mitylene — Cos. Patmos.

26: It looked beautiful from the shore as we anchored there, but is a ruin within except the fortifications w.<sup>h</sup> are in good order, & some of the ornaments & sculptures of the Knights' houses w.<sup>h</sup> are still in good preservation. The Jewish quarter horrible.

27: In the early morning through the beautiful bay of Glaucus to Telmessus or Makri to see tombs & a magnificent landscape. Remember the palm trees theatre with its beautiful outlook on the bay camels oleanders Another set of ruins at Antiphilos was visited in the evening but I did not go on shore.

28: A white squall in the morning dire consternation among the Jews & infidels — off Cyprus all day: and considerable qualmishness among all on board.

30: at Beyrout, landed, & a merry party in the evening there with the Tyne's people.

October 1: Could not get into Acre, and lay to at Caiffa.

2: Arrived at Jaffa and landed. English & Russian Consul. Governor bazaars & town at night. pipe outside the walls.

3: Made the journey from Jaffa to Jerusalem: by Ramle[h] setting off at 4 in the morning — Escort. Jereed play. plains, Armenian breakfast black shepherds, blue women wells & vast yellow flats; rocky country like waterfalls petrified. Abou Gosh — darkness into Jerusalem vineyards in above territory.

4: All day at home except a visit to Tennents at the G.<sup>k</sup> Convent, wrote a very little.

5: Wrote all the morning — Walked to M.<sup>t</sup> Olives, sketched along the way

6: to Church — the Service very well celebrated & affecting, drew in the afternoon —

7: Rode to Bethlehem — the most picturesque place I have seen here — breakfast at Gk Convent — row about horses —

8: Wrote in the morning — at noon walked out with M<sup>r</sup> Veitch Miriams Well — the tombs — & Siloam

9: At home dawdling — at the Sepulcher — the Latin Convent, to the Bishops teaparty.

10: Dined with Cornet Young, & to M<sup>r</sup> Veitch's at night.

11: In a beautiful sunrise quitted Jerusalem, and made quite pleasantly and without ennui or fatigue the journey to Ramleh, where we slept at the Greek Convent.

12: Arrived at Jaffa from Ramleh, after a ride through the dark and on board at 7 o'clock.

13: A calm but vessel pitching enough to make us all uncomfortable saw Alexandria at sunset but too late to get into the port.

14: Arrived at Alexandria and was hospitably received by M<sup>r</sup> Ryland there & found a letter from home, and good news of my dear dear little ones.

15: Left Alexandria, and sailed on the Mahmoodieh canal to Atfeh where we entered the Nile at sunset;

16: Landed at Boulac at 2 ½, & came to Alexandria to the Hotel d'Orient — to see Lewis.[54]

17: Through the bazaars — sketched & dined with Lewis — (the mad people at night. The leader of the Hag. Ibrahim Pasha [55] the Indians.

18: To the Citadel & Mosque of Hassan — the Hag place — the play — the old fellow with his plucked cock — tombs, howling women, no work done all these days — but sketching a little and wonderment everywhere.

19: To the pyramids, & 3 cheers for Punch on the top.

20: The Janissary late, to the tomb of the Caliphs the slave-market very striking — Arnaoots — devils. Desert.

21: To the gardens of Shonbras, and dined with Lewis in the evening — met the Friths at the Inn, & had a warm greeting of the kind old woman.

[54] See above, No. 86.
[55] The Egyptian general (1789–1848).

22: On board the Little 'Cairo' for Alexandria — reached Atfeh at night, and made ourselves comfortable on the tugged boat.

23: At Alexandria by 3, and off at 12 again for Malta in the old Iberia.

24: Sick all day though the weather fine, read the Prairie [56] — it is much better than the Scott novels I have read on board

25: At sea. No better  Found a waistcoat comfortable

26: At sea.

27: Arrived in the 2 Harbour at Malta at 12 ½  Just 4 days from Alexandria. Came into quarantine at Malta.

28: The first day of quarantine passed pleasantly enough with plenty of space, air and quite enough freedom. The Iberians visited us, & brought us the sad news of poor old Burtonshaw's illness — it terminated in his death this night. I had him round the waist only yesterday walking with him up & down the Ship. Sent off letters home to Paris & London. Wrote a little Journal at night.

29: We attended poor old Burtonshaws burial to day in the Quarantine ground behind the plague-hospital. Wrote ever so little Barry Lyndon.

30: Scribbled drawings all day.

31: Wrote Barry Lyndon.

November 1: Wrote Barry — but slowly & with great difficulty

2: Wrote Barry, with no more success than yesterday.

3: Finished Barry after great throes late at night.

4: Wrote 3 papers for Punch [57] — at work all day & too much for a wonder.

5: Wrote Athens for Punch

8: On this day did scarcely anything but write & design the characters for Mrs Perkins' ball

12: Came out of Quarantine, very weary of an imprisonment wh I had hoped to put to much greater profit. Dr Sankey took me to club Library &c, and after dawdling a fortnight in prison it was pleasant to do the same at liberty.

[56] By James Fenimore Cooper, published in 1827.

[57] Papers III to V of "Punch in the East," the first of which deals with Athens, published in *Punch* between January 25 and February 8, 1845.

13: Impossible to write at the Inn — too much noise clatter & discomfort — read Magarinn and Antar [58] instead of going to the races w.<sup>h</sup> all the world attended.

14: Dined at Sir Cecil Bishopp's [59] — News of poor Woolley's death arrived — perhaps the 3.<sup>d</sup> of our luckless expedition

15: Left Malta by the Iberia on Friday evening — writing a line of ceremonious consolation to D.<sup>r</sup> Sankey about poor Woolley.

16: And after a beautiful passage skirting Sicily through the straits of Messina by Stromboli came into Naples Bay on

17: Sunday evening at 6 — seeing the most magnificent sea landscape in the world lighted up by a sunset such as we dont see in England in August.

18: On shore at Naples — and took up our quarters at the Hotel du Globe — Went to Portici & Herculaneum after the botherations of the landing were concluded. In the evening to the Opera and fell asleep.

19: On shore at Nap Saw a couple of rooms at the Museum, and drove to the Grotto of Posilippa — always with the cauchemars of women.

20: To Pompei — where the women spoiled all — by their infernal vulgarity and insolence.

25: Left Naples glad to quit it and made an uncomfortable journey of 34 hours through Capua & Ceprana

26: to Rome w.<sup>h</sup> we reached at night.

December 9: In these days I've been advancing slowly with the Tour but pretty regularly in the afternoon walking with Brotherton about the town: and spending the night smoking with the Artist banditti.[60]

---

[58] Possibly *Antar, a Bedoueen Romance* (1820), a partial translation of the long Arabic *Romance of Antar*.

[59] The Rev. Sir Cecil Augustus Bisshopp (1821–1849), ninth Baronet.

[60] "Of the great men who visited Rome during this winter," Samuel Bevan writes of 1845–1846 in *Sand and Canvas*, London, 1849 (pp. 336–337), "M. A. Titmarsh was among the most popular. Himself an artist, he dropped down among us on his way from Cairo, no one knowing when he came or how he went away. Installed in a quiet bed-room at Franz's, in the Condotti, he appeared to amuse himself, like Asmodeus, with peering into the studios of his

275.                         TO HENRY WIKOFF
                           28 JANUARY 1844

Hitherto unpublished. *Endorsed* (by Thackeray): Copy of letter to M͞r
Wykoff. Long's Hotel. London.

                                    81 Champs Elysées. 28 Jan͞y 1844.
My dear Sir
   I have been exceedingly busy since your departure, and was unluckily out in my time calculation by a day — I ought to have
communicated with you earlier
   I must decline to sign the agreement you sent me. As I take your
word for the payment of the articles you must please to take mine
for supplying them, and I hope I shall not disappoint you. Your
agreement would bind me to remain in Paris when I might have a
mind to go to London or the Continent (whence European articles
might be equally well written) and I cannot sacrifice my liberty for
108 £ per annum.
   But I can promise to give you according to the agreement a couple of foreign letters and articles monthly with Paris & France *for
headquarters* — and also not to engage with any American paper
while writing for yours.[61] If this suffices please to write me a line
by return of post saying that you will instantly on your arrival at
New York forward a couple of months of salary to be paid to my
order by your bankers here and make arrangements with them that
I shall receive monthly payments in future; on receipt of your
letter I will send back by the same day's post a letter and article for
your paper, to be followed by 2 more by the Havre packet. You

---

countrymen, and while he rummaged over their dusty portfolios, or critically
scanned the pictures on the wall, would unconsciously read their secret
thoughts, and penetrate, as it were, the arcana of their pockets, without allowing them to imagine that he intended aught save a mere friendly visit. Many,
however, were the poor devils who managed to push through the winter on
the strength of the timely fillip administered by Titmarsh."
   [61] I have not been able to identify Wikoff's newspaper. It would appear
from Thackeray's account book for this year (see Appendix X) that he wrote
only three American letters, one in January and two in February.

will get my 2 months' correspondence by the time I get my 2 months
pay & we can then go on *au pair*. Your bankers afterwards can pay
my articles as I write them, but you & they must take my word for
their contents.

I am a bad man of business, and only settle with you as I would
with any other publisher. If I dont hear from you I shall conclude
the negociation at an end. Truly yrs W M Thackeray.

I reserve of course to myself the liberty of reproducing my articles if I think fit out of America —

276.                TO M. GIRALDON
                   2 FEBRUARY 1844

Extract published, *Biographical Introductions*, V, xxi. *Endorsed* (by Thackeray): Copy of letter to M. Giraldon.

                                    2 Feb. 1844.
                                    68 Champs Elysées. —

Sir

On giving you my MS I gave it with the express stipulation that
unless an immediate payment was made for it: it was not to be used:
& you promised me specifically that in sending the manuscript to
M⸢r⸣ Heath [62] you would acquaint him with that condition on my
part. The MS *has* been used: the proofs come back with many compliments, but I cannot pay my tradesmen with these; & must beg
to state what I before said that I will do nothing without my fee.

As soon as this sum is paid I will be glad to make the necessary
corrections to the proofs, and to continue the Translation — at the
rate of 4£ per sheet of Delloy's edition, not of the English w⸢h⸣ is
made to contain twice as much matter.

I return you the proofs though they have been printed against
my express conditions, and M⸢r⸣ Heath's letter, acknowledging that
if the work did not go on still I was to be paid? As soon as *I am* paid
I shall be very happy to proceed, and am Sir

                                    Y⸢rs⸣

M. Giraldon

[62] See above, No. 274, January 6.

277.        TO WILLIAM HARRISON AINSWORTH
4 FEBRUARY 1844

*Postmark:* FE 4 1844. Hitherto unpublished.

My dear Ainsworth

I would have come with the greatest pleasure but Gwilt has engaged me. How are you and the ladies and the young daughters?
I will come out one very early day to shake you by the hand

Yours        W M T.

278.        TO GEORGE WILLIAM NICKISSON
6 FEBRUARY 1844

*Address:* Mʳ Nickisson | 215 Regent Street | London | Angleterre. *Postmarks:*
PARIS 6 FEVR. 44, 8 FE 1844. Hitherto unpublished.

81 Champs Elysées. 6 Febr.

Dear Nickisson. Thanks for the money. The enclosed is a rob-
bery from the French — a burlesque of a serious romance — and
has good fun.[63] It only goes for volume 1 to p. 13. There will be
3 volumes. It is easily done as the story is before me, and I have
more now ready. As soon as I see part 2 of Lyndon I will fall to
work, and hope to send you 3 sheets of it this month as I'm now
quite free till the end of the month. We are all well, and I have
been working like a Trojan.

Yours        W M T.

In the *Journal des Debats* of to day Tuesday is a letter from
Fanny Ellsler at Milan saying that Wykoffs articles, are fraudulent
and unauthorized got up for the purpose of turning her to ridicule,
and false in detail.[64]

Send proofs.

[63] See above, No. 274, January 25.
[64] Mlle. Elssler renewed her complaint in *The Times,* but without avail.
Nickisson printed the fourth and last of Wikoff's articles in *Fraser's Magazine*
for March (pp. 274–190), together with the Chevalier's assurance that
"Mademoiselle Fanny Elssler gave me, a year since, a full and unqualified
assent to publish her travels, and she has never withdrawn that assent" (p. 275).

279.    TO CHAPMAN AND HALL
23 FEBRUARY 1844

*Address:* Mess.ʳˢ Chapman & Hall | 186 Strand | London | Angleterre. *Post-marks:* PARIS 24 FEVR. 44, 27 FE 1844. Hitherto unpublished.

My dear Sirs

I hope the Strand stands pretty well where it did, that the enter-prizing publishers of certain popular works and reviews are flourish-ing in health wealth and virtue, & that their amiable ladies have no reason to be dissatisfied with their husbands.

My present communication is to propose *three* articles for the F. Q. R.⁶⁵

1 on La Vie d'Artiste par Paul Smith a pseudonym of a clever French writer, wʰ will give an opportunity for a discussion on French art in general.

2. Irland. Von J. Venedey. just published.

3    L'Inde Anglaise. par le Comte de Warren

Three more brilliant subjects the human imagination can hardly I should think conceive.

I shant be able to begin with them before the 1ˢᵗ of the month having my hands full until that time; but should be glad to have a couple of sheets kept for me if you can afford me so much room. I am meanwhile working hard to get a head with a story in Fraser: wʰ has not made the least hit as yet but wʰ I trust will touch the public in another number or two.

Would not now be a good time to gather together, in one vast broad sheet all the puffs concerning Titmarsh's Ireland and see whether the public will not take off the few remaining copies of that work? I see by Venedey's book that an unlucky speech of mine viz that 'every man in Ireland looked like a rogue' has been carried

---

⁶⁵ Thackeray reviewed only one of these books, *L'Inde anglaise en 1843*. His article, which has not previously been identified, appeared in *The Foreign Quarterly Review* for April (pp. 213–229) under the running head, "Prob-lematic Invasion of British India." For Venedey's *Irland*, see above, No. 274, February 23.

about in that country, and that the remark has not made a favorable impression.

Can't you send me to any other country to travel? The dullness of this town is immeasurable and I am getting thinner and thinner every day. Ask somebody to write me a letter with a little news of dear old Cockneyland. I have not had a single line from any man, since I left London I think about twenty four years since. I propose to come and spend the money for the above named articles in your village. I wish they were done! —

Yours ever faithfully<br>W M Thackeray

81 Champs Élysées
I think it is the 23 February —
Who in Heavens name wrote the extraordinary article on the C$^{te}$ de la Garde in the Jan number? [66] M$^{rs}$ Gore I presume — It was quite unfit for a Quarterly, containing jokes & slang only good for a Magazine spirt.

280.        TO BRADBURY AND EVANS
26 FEBRUARY 1844

Hitherto unpublished. My text is taken from a transcript supplied by Mrs. Fuller.

My dear Sir[s],

I am glad that the Revolution [67] is approved of: and thank you for the remittance. My Bankers are Lubbocks, you say you have paid Coutts by the way. In case of mistake the above scrap [68] will effect the transfer.

I wish I could get an enterprising Publisher to reproduce my

[66] "The Congress of Vienna," which was published in *The Foreign Quarterly Review* for January (pp. 347–370).
[67] See above, No. 274, February 2.
[68] A draft (never used) which reads: "26th. February, 1844.

Pay Sir John Lubbock & Co. Twenty-Five Pounds.<br>£25. 0. 0.        W. M. Thackeray.<br>Messrs. Coutts."

stories. The last set containing Yellowplush are out of print I am told: having all been sold off at a low price. 6/s I think in the place of a guinea. And as I have got a public now I should be glad to bring out a good stout book full of tales, reprints from France, literary articles, etc. with illustrations by myself, outline etchings for the most part ⟨. . .⟩ [69]

or will you bring me to London and put me at the head of a slashing brilliant, gentlemanlike, sixpenny, aristocratic, literary paper? containing each week good reviews of a book or two, not notices; good novels in series: good theatrical articles, etc. a paper that — should not look for a large but a gentlemanlike circulation: and have a decided air of white kid gloves. I have begged and implored my friends Chapman and Hall on the subject. I am sure it would succeed. Have the papers signed and by good men, Buller, Carlyle, Forster, Milnes, [Fitz]Gerald, and a University man or two. I would take the Fine Arts, light literature and the theatre under my charge with the dinner giving (all except *me* paying part) and I know no man in Europe who would handle ⟨it better⟩.

Having confided to you a few chapters of my forthcoming work on the next French Revolution — you are bound in justice to print my words fairly — and I protest in the most solemn manner against several liberties which have been taken with my text.[70] What is a historian without accuracy? A mere romancer and I hold such a creature in the utmost contempt.

In the first place there were not a *hundred* and twenty-four forts round Paris but twenty-four, as will be shown in the subsequent chapters of my work.

Secondly I never called H. M. Louis Philippe a Prince among Sovereigns which is absurd: but in reference to His Majesty's great age named him a PRIAM among Sovereigns — a Classical allusion to his late Majesty the Eminent King of Troy.

---

[69] Part of the letter has here been cut away.

[70] It is some indication of the carelessness with which Thackeray's text has been treated that none of these errors has been corrected in the many reprints of "The History of the French Revolution."

Third. The two paragraphs beginning with the words 'Charen-
ton the great lunatic asylum' and ending 'the Government alarm'
should be inserted after ⟨. . .⟩ [71]

281.                    TO MRS. THACKERAY
                       11 MARCH 1844

*Address:* M^rs Thackeray | at M^rs Carmichael Smyth's | 81 Champs Elysées |
Paris. *Postmark:* 11 MR 1844. Hitherto unpublished.

My dearest little woman. After running away from you so suddenly last week, I have been waiting to get some news to give you
before I should write my letters of apology. But I have never been
able very well to make you understand the necessity of getting
money, w^h you seem to think grows naturally in the pockets, and so
it's no use to tell you why I came away; because it was quite requisite
that I should be in London to look after my money-matters w^h were
going on very badly in my absence.

They are not very much better yet but in a fair way of mending.
I think I see a couple of good posts [72] worth 300£ a year each before
me, w^h if I get, my income can easily be brought up to 800£ enough
to spend and save too. But I shan't write about these places until I
get them w^h really is very likely — one is at the Morning Chronicle
where my friends Doyle & Crowe are working anxiously in my favor. If I get it: I shall take a house, bring you to London, and the
young women soon after please God — but we must wait a while
and see.

I have not seen any of our friends as yet; but have been chiefly
busy with my friends the booksellers &c — and I have been greatly
annoyed at losing the friendship of a man for whom I had a very
warm regard — Harry Lorrequer by name, who instead of being

[71] Though the rest of the letter has been cut away, it may be surmised that
Thackeray's sentence continued: "the paragraph ending 'your countersign,
Valmy.'" See *Works*, VI, 235–237.
[72] For Thackeray's connection with *The Morning Chronicle* between 1844
and 1848, see Appendix XII. The other prospective post was probably
with *The Examiner*.

delighted as I expected he would have been by an article of mine on his works, has broken off with me in a fury, and vows that I have treated him most basely & cruelly.[73] On the other hand Boz writes that my notice of him [74] has touched him to the quick encouraged him and done him good — and I don't know what more. But they are hard people to deal with these literary men and who knows some day in noting a future work of his I may fall into the same disgrace as with poor Lever now.

Upon my word I think this quarrel with Lever is all I have to say since I came to London. The first week here is passed always in a constant whirl of nothing-doing, and it is only after a little pause that one has leisure to settle down. I shall wait for that and for the end of the week to write you something more satisfactory then. This is only to hope all is well, and to say the same of myself. God bless all of you.

What a shame it is that after a week's absence I should have no more to say than this! — But so it is — unless I told you how sick I was in the steamer, and how everybody else wanted the basin and how Mꝛ Lumley [75] the Director of the Opera shared a spittoon with me and ended by putting down my name on his free list for the opera — theres nothing interesting that I know of.

I saw Dan O'Connell yesterday at the Reform Club, all the world is mad about him here and I find myself in a minority of one regarding him and his conduct. The old rogue gave me a fierce look at wʰ I felt as if my heart was coming into my mouth — for he has no love for Titmarsh as I am told — indeed that author has offended people of every party in Ireland, and would be massacred were he to return thither.

I am just come in from another walk, wʰ I took in order to get some news to fill this page — Well I have seen more booksellers we have talked more scandal about the trade wʰ is no more interesting to you than the history of Nebuchadnezzar. Du Pre the singer

[73] See *Memoranda*, Charles Lever.
[74] See above, No. 270.
[75] Benjamin Lumley (1811–1875), manager of Her Majesty's Theatre from 1842 to 1852 and from 1856 to 1858.

has made a great success,[76] and the walls are placarded with bills about him w[h] would cover the side of a house. I saw old Coram Street the other day, and slunk through it with a heart ache — indeed my disposition is such that when I am in one place I long invariably for another, and I think now about the little room in the Champs Elysées as the most delightful little retreat in the world. Meanwhile I am lodged in my old apartments 27 Jermyn Street where they are very good to me. I have 3 rooms, the use of a footman, a Surgeon [77] below to purge physic sweat bleed &c. and all for the small charge of 25/ per week. Old Fitz has written to say that he will come soon to London: [78] but I shant live with him, he makes me too idle. I have not seen any of my favorite ladies: and have been only invited 5 times to dinner in the course of the week, w[h] is a sad falling off from last season. When I said I was quite well it is not true. I have the grippe like all the rest of the world: for w[h] I take medicine — none. wine a pint per day beer, o. sleep plenty, and am getting on very well under this clever treatment other people are dosing themselves to distraction and fare no better — I kept this little bit for a word for Anny but there is no time now to say anything but God bless her and Baby: and honest little Charley and all. I hope to hear you had good news from India by this mail w[h] has brought me no money from Hume as I expected, but 5£ in the shape of some fun w[h] I want to make of Lord Ellenborough's dispatch for Punch.[79]

I embrace you
W M T.

27 Jermyn Street: 11 March. 1844.

[76] As Arnold in Rossini's *Guillaume Tell* at Drury Lane (*Times*, March 11).
[77] John C. Chappell, surgeon, 27 Jermyn Street (*Royal Blue Book*, 1846).
[78] "I am still indignant at this nasty place London," FitzGerald wrote (*Letters and Literary Remains*, ed. Wright, I, 186) on April 11. "Thackeray, whom I came up to see, went off to Brighton the night after I arrived, and has not re-appeared: but I must wait some time longer for him."
[79] This squib does not appear to have been written.

282.        TO HENRY COLBURN
13 APRIL 1844

*Postmark:* April 15, 1844. My text is taken from Bernard Halliday's catalogue 194 (1935), where the postmark is also recorded.

Dear Sir,

The title alone of the enclosed wonderful paper [80] ought to make the N. M. use many hundred copies,

truly yrs

W. M. Thackeray,

27 Jermyn St., Saturday

283.        TO RICHARD BEDINGFIELD
13 MAY 1844

Hitherto unpublished.

R. C. Monday. 13 May.

My dear Bedingfield

I am living at Richmond for a few days very busy with some work I have on hand — pardon me for not having answered your note sooner, and for not coming to see you as I have been intending. Your note took a load off my mind: I see you are a good fellow, and can bear a hard word as well as a kind one. But I had a qualm in my mind respecting certain expressions ('bombastical and absurd' to wit) w.ʰ were used to characterize a certain novel.[81] They looked so ugly when I saw them in print after two months that I didn't venture to show my face in Montague Street for fear of being called over the coals. I got angry on reading 'The Miser's Son' at some reflections on Thomas Carlyle made by a young author — I

[80] "The Partie Fine," *New Monthly Magazine*, May, 1844, pp. 22–28.
[81] Thackeray had written (*Works*, XIII, 414): "The 'Miser's Son' . . . is evidently the work of a very young hand. . . . The writer aims . . . at sentiment and thoughtfulness, and writes sometimes wisely, sometimes poetically, and often (must it be said?) bombastically and absurdly."

shouldn't have allowed the words to stand had I seen a proof, but men in our trade write as fast as they speak unadvisedly sometimes. I will pick a crow with you some day, if you like, about some 'fine writing' in your novel: w.<sup>h</sup> moved my bile — while other parts struck me as exceedingly clever poetical and thoughtful.

I'm afraid you won't find my father & mother when you go to Paris. Their present address is 81 Champs Élysées: but I have just [received] a letter proclaiming a sudden move of the family to Belgium, Germany, Switzerland and I don't know where. They move on the 1.<sup>st</sup> of June: my father's health being the cause of the migration. I purpose D. V. to bring my wife and children to London directly: when I can get a house: and get money to get into the house: for both of w.<sup>h</sup> objects I am engaged at this moment in looking. I am at work on 20 different things and so flurried and bothered all day that I can't make visits as I ought to do.

I am sorry to hear that your Grandfather continues in so poor a state: and fear with you that at his age little hope can be entertained of amelioration.

Have you a mind to come out to Richmond and eat a plain dinner there with me? I am at the Rose Cottage Hotel and if you will come out on Friday or Saturday shall gladly offer you mutton-chops. Let me have a line directed there if it is worth your while to go such a distance for a tête à tête — The country is beautiful and I shall dine on either day at six — Friday for preference.

With best regards to your Mother, I am always dear Bedingfield faithfully yrs

W M Thackeray

284.            TO HENRY COLBURN
                    15 MAY 1844

*Postmark:* May 15, 1844. My text is taken from Bernard Halliday's catalogue 194 (1935), where the postmark is also given.

Dear Sir,

Here is a very little article [82] but in revenge I think a very good one.

                    Yours faithfully,
                    W. M. T.


285.        TO MRS. CARMICHAEL-SMYTH
                    1 JUNE 1844

*Address:* M^rs Carmichael-Smyth | Poste Restante | Chaudefontaine près Liège | Belgique. *Postmarks:* 1 JU 1844, LIEGE 5 JUIN. Extracts published in *Biographical Introductions*, V, xxxiii.

My dearest Mammy. If your Sunshine is as bright and warm at Chaudfontaine to day as it is here in a dingy court in Whitefriars you have all a pleasant welcome to your new abode — It is but a day's run over to join you, and I hope to do so before the month is out: but I have some awful work on hand w^h presses severely this month: — the debt of that unlucky pamphlet [83] to wipe off in the greater part — Fraser & the Chronicle and the mighty Punch above all w^l tie me here for many days to come — I can take my papers out to Richmond but not farther being obliged to be in constant communication with the people here.

[82] "Arabella; or, The Moral of the 'Partie Fine,' " *New Monthly Magazine*, June, 1844, pp. 169–172.

[83] Nothing is known of this pamphlet. Among Thackeray's recent contributions to *Punch* had been "Academy Exhibition" (May 11, p. 200), of which FitzGerald wrote to Frederick Tennyson: "I see in Punch a humorous catalogue of supposed pictures; Prince Albert's favourite spaniel and boot-jack, the Queen's Macaw with a Muffin, etc., by Landseer, etc., in which I recognize Thackeray's fancy. He is in full vigour and play and pay in London, writing in a dozen reviews, and a score of newspapers: and while health lasts he sails before the wind." (*Letters and Literary Remains*, ed. Wright, I, 191)

I have written to my wife to say I shall have her over and mean to keep my promise — I've had fifty answers to an advertisement in the Times — the one I like best being a proposal at *three* guineas per month at a lady's school — the best written I mean, and looking the best without reference to price at all. Were I to close with it I would have a lodging in the neighbourhood and a bed room in London — and pass my time as much as possible with the poor little Soul.

I dont know after all and though I never write what I've got to say — it seems to me there's no time for anything here — The day occupied with nothings that must be done — and a fresh labor for almost every day — This is not very conducive to fame, nor to money somehow though it ought to be, and there's no reason why with regular labor I shouldn't make near upon 1200 — BUT somehow it doesn't go beyond 65 or 70 a month — and in that occasional failures. The Chronicle is I believe as safe as if I had an engagement — if compliments can serve a man they are to be had in plenty — and a great deal of small flattery at tea and dinner-parties such as the specimen I sent you. Haven't I been saying exactly the same thing in every one of my short letters? — Well Ive nothing newer nor more interesting —

The papers cost twopence a piece now to Belgium and it seems as if I couldn't afford a shilling a week for those who are keeping my children for nothing — But I'll send over some scrubby remittance directly my month's accounts are paid in — till when what is called 'the balance' at the Bankers is in such a state that a very few guineas' weight would move it.

You have missed the delight of young Bedingfield at Paris whom I regaled with eel-pies and roast ducks at Richmond the other day — he is going to see some relative of his, and is not near such a bad fellow nor such an ass as he looks — If he could see a man or two in place of the old women he lives with, there would be a chance for him. Poor M^rs F. Thackeray [84] is here with her daughter — and a couple of adopted young ladies who help out her income — We

---

[84] Mrs. Francis Thackeray. Mary Augusta Thackeray, *Genealogy* (64), was her only daughter.

all went to the play last night — The 2nd time I think since I have been in London. If the theatre was a bore at least it was pleasant to see the young ladies' delight — and it comes across one as a remorse that all that time at Paris I never took Anny — God bless her — I want a sight of the pair of them very much — but when? it must be in private before I go and fetch Isabella — You'll see by the Seal where this is written — after a breakfast with 4 members of parliament — then a day's work at the Emperor of Russia [85] about whose visit all the towns agog. God bless all prays WMT.

286.           TO MRS. CARMICHAEL-SMYTH
               AND ANNE THACKERAY
               11 JUNE 1844

*Address:* Mrs Carmichael-Smyth | Chaudfontaine | près Liège | Belgique. *Postmarks:* 11 JU 1844, LIEGE 13 JUIN 1844. The note to Anne Thackeray is published in *Thackeray and his Daughter*, pp. 16–17.

27 Jermyn St June 11. 1844.

My dearest Mammy. Your welcome little letter was somehow four days on the road. It must have been a comfort to you to get your journey to a close and land all the passengers safely out of your ark. When shall I be able to visit it? in not many days I hope, though business grows upon me so thick, that it is very hard to get out of town But what I wd like to manage would be somewhere at the end of the month to pay you and the dear little girls a visit, then to go on to Paris for my wife, and bring her back to a house here wh I have found and where she will please God be very comfortable. It is at Twickenham an honest half-pay Captain [86] with a kind wife, 2 accomplished grown up daughters & some young ones, a big house — She is to have 3 little rooms and a maid to herself, and I to be free to live there for 2 days in the week — the whole to cost 150£. and the people seem so honest, well-bred and kind that I

[85] This labor was presumably for *The Morning Chronicle*, but there is nothing about the Emperor's visit in that paper which shows any trace of Thackeray's hand.
[86] Captain Alexander and his family.

dont think I can do better than give the poor little woman into their charge. It is just the place I should have looked for for her — and I like it so much that I don't think I shall try your Bakewell [87] plan. I think that's all the news — there's no use writing about my professional business w.ʰ is very incessant though paltry — I dont do above 20£ a month for the Chronicle instead of 40 — but it is my own fault — the fact is I cant write the politics and the literary part is badly paid. M.ʳ Punch is the great card: and I have made some great hits there. Also I'm engaged to write a Life of Talleyrand [88] in one small volume for w.ʰ Im to have two hundred guineas. It will be a great coup if I can do this and not touch the money: but have it at Christmas for my little girls. God bless them. I am yearning to see them with hair or without. As for writing to Anny its a difficult matter. Something always takes place similar to what used to happen when I wrote the first letter to you from school after the holidays — than w.ʰ sort of sentiment I doubt if there is anything more useless and foolish in the world. But it will do my heart good to see you all again, and if I can manage to do a quantity of work and get 10 days leave of absence from the 25.ᵗʰ or so: please God I will come, and so send love to all from my dearest Mammys affte son.

My dearest Nanny. Thank you for all your little letters. I am always made glad by the sight of them. and by hearing from Granny that you are well and good. I shall come and see you very soon, and you must tell me in your next letter if you & Baby want anything that I can bring. Mamma I hope will soon come & live with me in England, at a very pretty village called Twickenham which is by the river Thames. There are beautiful walks there meadows and trees and handsome houses in parks and gardens. How I should like to walk there with my dearest little girls. God bless them prays

Papa.

---

[87] When Thackeray brought his wife to England late in 1845, he entrusted her after all to Mrs. Bakewell, who took care of her during the rest of his life.

[88] Thackeray read widely for this volume, which Chapman and Hall duly announced for publication, but other projects intervened, and it was never written.

287. ## TO CHARLOTTE RITCHIE
### 12 JUNE 1844

*Address:* Miss Ritchie | 11 Rue d'Angoulême | Paris. *Postmarks:* 12 JU 1844, 14 JUIN 44 BOULOGNE. Hitherto unpublished.

12 June. 1844.

My dear Charlotte. Your letter has given me the greatest comfort. Ever since my mother wrote to me of her intention of travelling, I have been on the look out for some place for my poor little wife: and have succeeded I think in finding one at last. There is an old half pay Captain living at Twickenham with a large house, and a large kind family who consents to receive my wife and me — or so much of me as will be good for her, and possible for myself. I hope to pass 2 or 3 days a week with her: being very busy indeed in London employed upon a multiplicity of jobs in the literary way. M^rs Thackeray has just gone away, very sad I thought and dispirited — it was the first time I had seen her since her widowhood, and I have a cowardly horror of listening to those sad stories. I have seen the Dicks twice I think, & George Shakespear as many times — we have besides exchanged cards genteelly. London is so very big that people with the best will towards one another don't meet more than thrice a year, and everybody has a perfect good will for and a perfect neglect of his neighbour. I was in hopes I should have had the children when my mother made her move; but she fairly said it would break her heart to part with them & I know they are better with her than with me. All your goodness to. my wife makes me very gratefu⟨l. I⟩ don't think she will be happier here than at Paris, but I shall to be able to see her.

At the beginning of next month I shall try and come for her. Will you kindly notify to D^r Puzin that I intend to remove her: perhaps your father will kindly pay for me 225 francs to the Doctor for w^h there is a draft on my banker here in London. God bless you all — And give my love to the Hamertons for their kindness to my poor little invalid.

Always dear Charlotte affectionately yrs
W M T.

If my wife writes will you see it directed?

288.          TO CHAPMAN AND HALL
                    16 JULY 1844

Published in the *Bookmart*, III (1885), 146–147.

                              Reform Club. 16 July. 1844.
My dear Sirs

   I will engage to write the volume 'the life of Talleyrand, and to have the MS. in your hands by the 1 December — health permitting. and will sign an agreement to that effect if you will have the goodness to prepare one.

                 Very faithfully yrs dear Sirs
                      W M Thackeray
Messr$^s$ Chapman & Hall.


289.          TO CHAPMAN AND HALL
                    19 JULY 1844

*Address:* Mess$^{rs}$ Chapman & Hall | 186 Strand. *Postmark:* BRIGHTON JY 19 1844. Hitherto unpublished.

                 Most Private.
                 Albion Hotel. Brighton
                    Friday.
My dear Sirs.

   Have you a copy left of that amusing work the Irish Sketch Book? If so — do send it to M$^{rs}$ Halliday 9 Porchester Place. Oxford Square from me tomorrow.

   When I tell you that she is my dear aunt just come from India, that she came out to my father there, who married boarded & sumptuously treated her, that she has 1000 a year, and *I am her nearest relation* — You will, dear Sirs, see the propriety of sending her the work of a nephew who is

                 Your most humble Serv$^t$
                   M. A. Titmarsh.

290.    TO MRS. CARMICHAEL-SMYTH
5 AUGUST 1844

*Address:* M^rs Carmichael-Smyth. | Chaufontaine | près Liége. *Postmarks:*
OSTENDE 6 AOUT 1844, LIEGE 6 AOUT 1844. Published in part,
*Biographical Introductions*, V, xxxv.

Ostend. Monday. October [89]

My dearest Mammy. This is to say that I must go across the
water — for I could not find even a history of England at Brussels,
and for the sake of my story and Hume's letter it is much [the]
best that I should be on the Spot — I only made my mind up at
10 this morning, for it was hard to leave, and when ½ the train
went off to Chaufontaine from Malines as I came to this place, I
felt as happy as I used to be at Larkbeare with the dreadful Defiance
coach coming over the hill.[90] But I must go and do my duty that's
the end of it, and when it's over I shall come back to you — in a
week or so, when I shall be free for the month. I did no good at
Brussels, while I staid but reading enormously for Talleyrand's
Life — it seems a month since I was with you: [I] find the loneliness anything but jolly — but if I can do my work quickly I will
come jumping back again.

That is all I have to say except to wish you and my dear little
ones — I don't know what to wish them better than to be with
you — And though I am quite melancholy at parting with them,
let me tell you that will not prevent me from eating my dinner w^h
is just going to be served. I cross tomorrow morning & shall be in
time to send off my India letter in good style. The *Pope's Nuncio*
is to have my bed-room tomorrow — think of my being the warming pan to his Holiness's Lieutenant.

Open any letters for me, & take the money out — or no: keep
the letters till I write again.

[89] A mistake for Monday, August 5, as the postmark shows.
[90] Thackeray had intended to be gone only for the day. This letter was sent
to explain his failure to return. "I remember my grandmother's exclamation
of disappointment," writes Lady Ritchie (*Biographical Introductions*, V, xxxv),
"as she tore it open."

291.        TO GEORGE WILLIAM NICKISSON
                    20 AUGUST 1844

Hitherto unpublished.

                                                20 August. 1844.
My dear Nickisson

The most wonderful thing has happened. I am going to Egypt & everywhere on Thursday — but not before I send you Barry Lyndon complete for this month. I shall take the necessary books with me to complete it during the voyage and you shan't be left at fault.

Will you send me 25 *sovereigns* tomorrow Wednesday — that will ab!. make up our account inclusive of next month. Im so busy that I dont know where to turn, but am yrs

                            W M T.


292.        TO MRS. CARMICHAEL-SMYTH
                    21–22 AUGUST 1844

*Address:* M!ˢ Carmichael Smyth. | Chaufontaine. Liége | Belgique. *Postmarks:* LONDON 22 AUG 1844, LIEGE 25 AOUT 1844. Extract published in *Biographical Introductions*, V, xxxv-xxxvi.

                                Wednesday Ev.ᵍ 21 August.

My dearest Mammy — I am going to write to you the great news: but my heart fails me as I send it, and I wish it weren't true. I have just (only yesterday) had an offer to go passage free by the Oriental Company to Lisbon, Cadiz, Gibraltar, Tangier, Athens Constantinople, Jericho, Smyrna Syria Jerusalem in 10 weeks and I thought the chance so great that Ive accepted — its very hard for I intended to come placidly across the water on Saturday to see my dear little people, and I'm sure I shall be miserable for the main part of this grand voyage. But it offers such a chance as I may never get again — a book of course is ordered and go I do, tomorrow — I shall be able to answer the Malta question from the place itself, but now coming from Egypt they tell me the Quarantine is as long as usual. Think of tossing in the Bay of Biscay, and the stewards and the basin! I hardly believe in it myself yet — The offer was made to me on Monday night only and accepted yesterday — I go with M<sup>r</sup> J. Emerson Tennant to the care of the British Consul Alexandria, we shall find there the mails of September and October by both of w<sup>h</sup> please write putting my initials only at the outside of the letter — I dont a bit like it and am as uncomfortable as possible at this writing — perhaps because I have been up since 4 scribing as well as I could for Fraser. So farewell to Chaufontaine, w<sup>h</sup> now I have lost it. I find the most beautiful place in the world and everything there the most delightful. If G. P. will put my name to the 25£ bill he has hereby my authority (the practice is perfectly customary Bradbury & Evans the senders tell me), and it will serve to pay the expenses of the children back to Paris where please God I will meet them in November. I'm to write a book for 200£ for C & H. on the East first, or that Cockney part w<sup>h</sup> I shall see — then to do Talleyrand. Lubbock will pay per Delenert Puzin's allowance for the poor wife in my absence — Charlotte Ritchie has just sent me an odd *hopeless* letter of her's. I'll keep the scrap for board ship tomorrow. We leave London at 11. Southampton at 3 in the packet for the bay of Biscay O.[91] Tennant is to introduce me to all the personages. We are to see every thing & I'll send my dear mother the very last news from Palestine.

Southampton Thursday 22. On board the Lady Mary Wood — a fine ship, comfortable cabin — and quiet weather. God bless all behind, and give us a merry meeting at Xmas.

W M T.

[91] See "The Bay of Biscay," a popular song by Andrew Cherry (1762–1812), the music by John Davy, first introduced in the operatic sketch, *Spanish Dollars; or, The Priest of the Parish,* 1805 [1806].

293.                    CHAPMAN AND HALL
                         31 AUGUST 1844

*Address:* Mess.ʳˢ Chapman & Hall | 186 Strand | London | Per Lady Mary
Wood — August 31. *Postmark:* 9 SP 1844. Hitherto unpublished.

                                        Gibraltar. August 31.
My dear Sirs

There is not 1 word of news to be had here to make a letter for
the F. Q. R. All my news is about heat musquitoes and the 1000
inconveniences of this filthy place      The greatest of all the inconveniences is the being obliged to be off — We have just warning
that the Tagus is to be off immediately & I've only time for this
hasty scrawl.

If you want a high literary treat read the enclosed [92] before sealing it & sending it p. p. to my mother. You will see what exquisite
benevolence guides the pen of Titmarsh.

Shake all hands in England. Tell those who would travel that
they may go farther and fare much worse than in the blessed
neighbourhood of the Strand      It seems 1000 years since I set
off — And now for Malta Athens & Constantinople.

                            Yrs ever
                            W M T.


294.                    TO MRS. CARMICHAEL-SMYTH
                         31 AUGUST 1844

*Address:* M.ʳˢ Carmichael Smyth. | Chaufontaine. Liege | Belgique. *Post-
marks:* 9 SP 1844, LIEGE 11 SEPT. 1844. Hitherto unpublished.

                                        Gibraltar August 31.
My dearest Mammy. Our barque is on the sea [93] — and we
have received the most sudden sailing orders wʰ obliges me to keep

────────────

[92] The next letter and the manuscript sent with it.
[93] See Byron's "To Tom Moore." Dick Swiveller had recently given renewed currency to the stanza from which this line is drawn by his brilliant
adaptation of it in chapter 8 of *The Old Curiosity Shop*.

Lisbon & Cadiz for the next packet [94] — We are off for Malta, whence I'll write again. The quarantine is resolute at 21 days. I have written to the little woman 10 hurried lines. You too write to her & explain what sent me off in such a hurry. I enjoy myself very much all things considering (viz bugs musquitoes &c) and please God shall pass Xmas with you and my dear little girls. I

[94] With this letter Thackeray sent nearly all of chapter 3 of *Notes of a Journey from Cornhill to Grand Cairo.* For the most part the manuscript differs little from the printed text, but two excised sentences at the end of the third paragraph are worth recording: "I wonder is there any single good feeling that war inspires, and are not the very best of the qualities elicited by it, coarse brutal savage of a low order of intelligence? It is one of the few trades where a blockhead may be a hero." The manuscript concludes with two paragraphs describing Thackeray's landing at Lisbon, which would have appeared, had they been printed, at the beginning of chapter 2:

"As for the countries w^h we have seen beside that small moveable island called the Lady Mary Wood — they have been so numerous that description thereof is vain. A man who has seen Trafalgar Bay & Trafalgar Square in the same week may well confess to a bewilderment of ideas, and admit that it is difficult for him to remember or describe or understand more than a very very small part of what he saw. After that queer peep into Spain we had at Vigo, we were enabled to get rather a longer view of Lisbon. The city looked delightful as we entered the river at night, passed the huge ships that were lying there, saw fort & lighthouse, convent & palace, church & tower, long rows of fair tall houses, tall hills streaked with verdure long lines of quays reflected in the water, & swarms of small craft lying on it. We cast anchor between Lisbon & a small town on the opposite shore, where the shore was illuminated and crowds of little black figures seen gathered together, Rockets were seen blazing up in the sky and dying there, and immense Catherine wheels were whizzing round & round at an hour considerable past midnight. This Vauxhall festivity as we were informed was in honor of the image of a saint, many of w^h statues of holy personages are carried upon religious circuits at this time of year, and are received with this sort of festivity at each station. A very few hours afterwards a most tremendous row & thumping on board with a prodigious clamour of voices in unknown language woke up everybody with the first dawn — and we were rowed to Lisbon before 7 o'clock.

"Even when we landed the place did not at first seem to disappoint strange eyes — The customs house was very fine bustling & pleasantly planted with trees, Black horse Square peopled with sauntering Gallegos, accompanied by many large dogs (though they had sent back a poor little Italian greyhound of our company not much bigger than a rat) and ornamented in the center with a great swaggering statue of a plumed prince in bronze in a fine & stately place from w^h tall streets branched off, of houses of many stories looking very clean & white."

wish Anny were here — she would see & understand quite as much
as the best travellers.  God bless her & all

W M T.

I'm quite well as usual.  Keep the letters.

295.          TO MRS. CARMICHAEL-SMYTH
                   17 SEPTEMBER 1844

*Address:* M⟨rs⟩ Carmichael Smyth. | 81 Champs Elysées. | *Paris. Readdressed
to:* Chaufontaine | près Liege | Belgique. *Postmarks:* CONSTANTINOPLE
17 SEPT 44, PARIS 1 OCT. 44, LIEGE 3 OCT 1844. Hitherto unpublished. *Endorsed* (by Thackeray): M. Thackeray prie Monsieur Valin de
garder cette lettre pour Mme. Smyth ou dans le cas que Mme. Smyth ne
revienne à Paris de la lui expedier à son addresse — .

17 September — Pera.

My dearest Mammy     This scrap {must be for you and the
little woman}.  Ive written to her     It leaves me as usual in
perfect good health: but most wofully puzzled as to proceedings
and where to go next — For I have got Punch & Barry Lyndon
hanging round my neck, and so much to do and to see that I hardly
know where to turn.  For the first fortnight there was scarce anything to see; then comes such a heap of sights all at once as should
take a man 2 months to visit properly, and I dont know how long to
describe.  As for this it is the most beautiful place in the world —
So odd and beautiful that sometimes I think I couldn't do better
than make my journey end here, have no end of Turks to sit for
their likenesses in the little terrace by my rooms and devote myself
to drawing and easy meditation and writing.  But then there is the
Holy Land and Egypt to see, and the sight is to last one for life,
and to occupy only a month in the seeing — I don't know what to
do or how it will turn.  If I get my Sheet of Barry & 4 letters to
Punch done by Saturday I shall go the Syrian expedition — if not
stop here.  So please send 2 letters, 1 to Vienna poste R⟨estante⟩ 1
to Malta ditto — to tell me that please God, all are well.  I can't
stand the bay of Biscay in Nov⟨r⟩ ⟨and⟩ shall come back by Naples
&c. if I come that way  if not from here to Venice or Trieste.  Malta
will be 3 weeks quarantine — but that will be good for the purpose

of writing — Now mind and write both the letters and give me the news of you and my dear little ones. I went to buy them some little slippers in the bazaar yesterday such a wonderful place! The Arabian Nights come to life — The bugs have been routed out after 2 nights' torture. In the steamer I slept snugly on the table and so disappointed the brutes: they are the only drawbacks to a tourist's pleasure here; as for Athens you'll read how sulky I w⟨as about them⟩ & their disgusting behaviour. We have a pleasant good-natured party all things considered ⟨. . .⟩ [95] tenants impossible to get on with — the dullest kindest Irish people are aboard as all ⟨. . .⟩ little ch⟨. . .⟩ all the way — at night especially looking at th⟨. . .⟩ Great Bear, and the Milky way w^h is not difficult — and ⟨. . .⟩ and longitude — and have got together some ideas I thi⟨. . .⟩ remember better. The first sight of the camels a⟨. . .⟩ a month's sea sickness — also to hear the voices of the women behind the lattices at the Sultan's palace — likewise to see the slave-market — where you can buy a tolerably ugly and healthy negress for 20£. I reckon these & the peep of Spain at Vigo as the most startling incidents of this little cockney voyage. But I begin to be alarmed whether I shall be able to make anything like a book of it: in w^h case the 2 months expense will go for nothing. I shall send a line to Chaufontaine. and pray God bless you all, and bring me back as well as I am now.

W M T.

296.            TO MRS. THACKERAY
            17 SEPTEMBER 1844

*Address:* M^rs Thackeray | chez M. le Docteur Puzin | Rue des Batailles. Chaillot | Paris. *Postmark:* CONSTANTINOPLE 17 SEPT. 44. Printed in *Unpublished Letters by W. M. Thackeray,* ed. Shorter, pp. 4, 11–14, 18, where the drawings are reproduced in facsimile.

Constantinople. 17 September.

My dearest little woman Who ever thought I should live to write you a letter from Constantinople! — here it is by all the Gods

[95] This and the following hiatuses are respectively of about three, six, two, ten, twelve, thirteen, and fifteen words.

and I am sitting on a terrace under a tent at Pera, and looking out upon the actual gardens of the Seraglio across the blue Bosphorus yonder!

That is the Seraglio point if you look well you will see a minaret — above among the Cypresses is a great burying ground — Yonder mountains are the hills of Princess Islands, and beyond them Olympus — I believe Troy lies out there too — we passed the coast three days ago — a very ugly flat one no more picturesque than the entrance of the Thames.

Before that we passed the day at Smyrna — where I saw the most wonderful bazaars with the most astonishing Turks sitting and smoking in their dingy little shops — I saw the camels coming stalking along with their great splay feet and jangling bells — I saw the Caravan just arrived from Persia — and smoked a cheboque — no a narghilch under the Cypress and acacia trees close by the Caravan bridge — a negro boy brought me sherbet, and sat down and played for me on a rebeck.

Before that I saw Athens, and the hill of the Acropolis, and the ruined temples of Jupiter and Theseus; they are magnificent & mouldy and of the colour of rotten Stilton cheese. Athens is filthy beggarly racketty lousy buggy full of dogs donkeys and other vermin — a beggarly place with the most noble hills round about it.

Before Athens we saw Algiers rising up the hill, and before that Malta, where all the nations of the earth seem gathered together a royal stately old town. Palm trees grow there and prickly pears

and the musquitoes bite like fury — before Malta
we were at Gibralter and from that I wrote my dearest little woman a little bit of a letter.

Yesterday I was in the bazaars at Constantinople
and was thinking of buying you by way of a present
a little black slave girl — they are to be had for 10£ — but would
you like a pair of papooshes better or a beautiful veil or
Yackmack such as the Turkish ladies
wear? You can only see their noses and
eyes as they shuffle past in their 'yellow
slippers, and I was warned off from a
shop for looking at one too curiously She
was a delectable creature — her eyelids
painted and the tips of her fingers stained
with dirty red — that fellow behind is one
of the Eunuchs of the Sultan — only too
handsome — We saw some of these beasts
sunning themselves yesterday before the
palace w^h they inhabit from our caique
on the Bosphorus. Then I could describe
to you a Turkish bath I took — how I was sweated and shampooed
and kneaded by a great grinning Turk, as bad as you used to be at
Chateau Boppart.[96] But the paper is done, and the post is going
away and I have to write to mother, and so only say God bless my
dearest wife, and goodbye.

W M T.

297.          TO MRS. CARMICHAEL-SMYTH
                   SEPTEMBER 17, 1844

*Address:* M^rs Carmichael Smyth. | Chaufontaine. Liège | Belgique. | Viâ
Marseilles et France. *Postmarks:* CONSTANTINOPLE 17 SEPT. 44,
LIEGE 3 OCT. 1844. Hitherto unpublished.

Constantinople: 17 Sep^r 1844.

My dearest Mammy. I calculate that you ought to be at Paris by
the time the Marseilles mail reaches: and have sent a letter to 81

---

[96] See above, No. 207, and *Works,* V, 639–642.

to say I'm quite well, at Constantinople — delighted with all I see, and perplexed beyond measure with all I have to do. I've written to Isabella by the same mail, but theres no news in either letter — only to beg you to write 2 letters one to Malta, one to Vienna poste restante. I dont know at this minute whether I shall take the Syrian trip or whether I shant go hence to Venice — All will depend on the quantity of work I can get done between this and Saturday when the Syrian vessel (the Iberia) sails. If I come by Malta I shall make quarantine there I havent the courage to do the 12 days in November; & perhaps want an excuse to take one peep at Italy — We shall be there I believe on the 25 October. Write to say all are well — and God bless you every one [97]

W M T.

298.          TO CHARLOTTE RITCHIE
              23-28 OCTOBER 1844

*Address:* Miss Ritchie | 13 Rue d'Angoulême. Champs Élysées. | a Paris via Marseilles. *Postmarks:* MALTA OC. 28 1844, 3 NOV. 44 MARSEILLE. Published in part, *Ritchies in India*, p. 153.

Alexandria. 23 October 1844.

My dear Charlotte. Your letter has just reached me as we are on the point of sailing after the end of all the pleasures of the voyage, and indeed it was a most welcome one. My wife's letter I think is far the best and most reasonable she has written yet: and it is almost equally gratifying to find that she continues to be happy and pleased with her home away from us all — I shall get a sight of you all at Paris please God at about Xmas, when the little book shall be written containing the particulars of this eventful voyage. Yesterday at Cairo I met a little Attorney an old Schoolfellow of mine, whom I enjoined to give all the briefs possible to William; & he spoke in very respectful terms of that judicial authority as did several other Calcutta people who were at Cairo on their way out or home. There is no news of the Carmichaels coming home just

[97] As Tiny Tim says in "Stave Three" of *A Christmas Carol.*

yet: he has only leave they tell me to come as far as Calcutta, as yet. If you know where my people are will you let them have the last news of my well-doing? — After Jerusalem, Cairo, and the bugs this is no small good fortune many of our party have had touches of fever and delirium — but thank God as yet I have not had a greater ill than sea-sickness — and oh! I don't like to think of 20 days and the Bay of Biscay in November!

God bless you my dear Charlotte, and thank you all again and again for your kindness to my little wife. I must pack up my letter, and carry it ashore. I shall not be long after it, please God, in honest Christian parts. Yours ever affectionately

W M Thackeray

Malta. 28 October. Going to Italy after 15 days quarantine. Please a line poste restante Naples. — Can't pay postage.

299.          TO CHAPMAN AND HALL
10 JANUARY 1845

*Address:* Mess^rs Chapman & Hall | 186 Strand | London. *Postmark:* JA 24 1845. Hitherto unpublished.

Hotel d' Allemagne. Rome
January 10. 1845.

My dear Sirs

Although I looked 35 days running at the Post Office until I was sick and ashamed of applying the beasts would not give me your letters because they were supposed to be for M^r Jackeray instead of Thackeray, and I have only just got the letters — the money was quite safe at Tortoni's, where the clerks had declined to have anything to do with my bills, and where as soon as they found them covered they invited me to a ball — but I was too much enraged & disgusted to accept the invitation, and shan't be happy now until I am away from Rome.

I hope the Eastern Book will be successful — it is all but done — and seems to me to be — never mind what. I will go tooth and nail at Talleyrand directly I reach England, nay perhaps before at

Paris where my family now are — they might have spared me much pain and uneasiness if they had known their own intentions better, & not have determined me on this unlucky trip. For the last 3 weeks my annoyance has been so great at receiving no letters that I've done nothing — and it's only now the letters *are* come that I feel what a rage I have been in really. It seems such a shame to have kept a poor fellow pining & hoping, and I cant pardon them the bitterness of my feelings as I turned away day after day from the dd dd-dd-ddd-ddd post office. It is quite wonderful how I began cursing when your letters were given me, instead of being thankful for getting them at last — indeed they were very kind and I am much obliged to you for them. How I long to see the Strand again. It seems to me when I once get to London I shall never be a stranger & wanderer any more. Meanwhile I shake you both spirtually by the hand and am always sincerely yrs

**W M T.**

Dickens is to be here directly [1] but I shant see him. Remembrances to all specially Forster whose mourning I deplore.

300.          TO MRS. CARMICHAEL-SMYTH
              6 FEBRUARY 1845

*Address:* M^rs Carmichael Smyth. | 4 Avenue S^te Marie. Fbg du Roule | Paris. *Postmarks:* LIVORNO 6 FE, 13 FEVR. 45 PONT-DE-BOIS. Hitherto unpublished.

Leghorn. 6 Feb. 1845.

My dearest Mammy I am so far on my way home to you: after hearing not a syllable from you for 3 months. I have been at Florence 15 days where Lady Doyly [2] was very kind, and where the pictures delighted me: — for the last 4 days here, & be hanged to

[1] Dickens arrived in Rome on January 30, 1845. Forster's younger brother, Christopher, had died late in 1844.
[2] Lady Elizabeth Jane D'Oyly (d. 1875) was the second wife of Sir Charles D'Oyly (1781–1845), a distinguished Indian civilian and amateur artist. Among his productions are the illustrations to *The European in India* (1813) by Thomas Williamson and F. W. Blagdon.

them waiting for the Marseilles steamer w<sup>h</sup> has never come in: though the weather until to day when it blows a storm has been delightfully calm & fine. Well, how glad I shall be to see all the faces again! — Isabella's pension is not paid for this month: will you pay it till my arrival when I'll refund — I mustnt stay long with you when I come: but I hadn't the heart to take the German road and forego seeing the dear little things & their Granny.[3] Charles & Mary I suppose are with you and you have no doubt a new grandchild ere this — salute it for me. I have not seen Italy as I threatened, scarcely anything; the delay of the letters &c putting everything out of sorts. I hurry off this scrap from the Consul's office a good fellow [4] very kind to me, and hospitable in the dismallest town in Italy. Pisa the finest I think. The Cathedral beats S<sup>t</sup> Peter's hollow — the Venus de Medici is a humbug — I've only one minute we're going to dinner and as the Ship won't come I think you'll like to know that I'm well and hearty. Pray God all with you are so. It is awful not to have heard for such a time: and without M<sup>rs</sup> Shawe's news I should have been crazy. God bless you — Your affte W M T.

[3] Thackeray's homecoming is described by Lady Ritchie: "he arrived in the evening, and he kissed me; but my little sister cried because he had grown a moustache during his absence, and she thought he was another papa. Then he folded a newspaper and kissed her through it, and next morning when he came down he had shaved off his moustache, and she flung her arms round his neck, and knew him quite well." (*Biographical Introductions*, V, xlii)

[4] Alexander Macbean had been British Consul at Leghorn since November 28, 1843 (*Foreign Office List*, 1859).

301.                     TO HENRY VIZETELLY [5]
                             MARCH? 1845

My text is taken from Vizetelly's *Glances Back through Seventy Years*, I, 282.

Why doesn't the P. T. pay up? [6] Rate Keys for not sending on
my cheque. I have more than half a mind to post the holder of
Queen Vic.'s patent as a defaulter at the top of Cheops' Pyramid
for the information of future gadders about. The vigilant old
centuries, which look down so inquisitively, would have blinked
their weary eyes at the exposure.


302.                 TO MRS. CARMICHAEL-SMYTH
                          28 MARCH 1845


*Address:* Mʳˢ Carmichael Smyth | 4 Avenue Sᵗᵉ Marie | Faubourg du Roule |
Paris. *Postmarks:* 28 MR 1845, 30 MARS 45 BOULOGNE. Hitherto unpublished.

                                     27 Jermyn Sᵗ March 28.
My dearest Mammy Doesn't it seem a sin and a shame that I
should have neglected to write? last week I wrote 3/4 of a letter
and carried it about intending to finish every day until I lost or
mislaid it among 10000 other papers. It was in a bad humour too
so you are none the worse for the loss. I executed all the commissions, have Rothneys receipt on the book, put Mʳˢ O Gorman's
letter in the Po called on Hicks but he would not see me being
busy, & promised to write but has not written — Whats the use of

     [5] Vizetelly (1820–1894) was a publisher and wood engraver who made
Thackeray's acquaintance in 1843 and saw him frequently, though chiefly in
the way of business, during the next twenty years. His recollections of this
association are scattered through the two volumes of *Glances Back through
Seventy Years*. It was not until late in his life that Vizetelly began the work
for which he is remembered today, his publication of the first English translations of Zola's novels. This task was carried out despite a jail sentence (in
1888) and intense public hostility.
     [6] Thackeray had not yet received payment for a review of *Coningsby* which
was published in *The Pictorial Times* on May 25, 1844. While he was in the
East, a Mr. Keys had replaced Vizetelly as the magazine's publisher.

my entering into a correspondence with him? it will only cost
Charles money. I have been now near 3 weeks doing the Examiner [7] it takes a deal more time than I bargained for, and I don't
do it as well as many a worse man w$^d$ but I shall stay on for it helps
me in various ways to get news knowledge of a certain sort, means
of pleasantry for Punch, matter to talk of to India &c — so the
upshot is that I shall stay unless Fonblanque finds out what I suspect he may that he can get his work better done elsewhere. I have
been to dine twice or thrice with the Hallidays and found him a
jovial sensible and kind hearted old cock. He says there was a
difference between you and my aunt relative to a story you have
told me about M$^{rs}$ H's neglect of my aunt Maria [8] in her last illness. Halliday says the first news they had of her being in Calcutta, was conveyed in the news of her death and that he attended
her funeral — So out of a small matter enmities grow or coolnesses
w$^h$ are perhaps worse than hatreds as more difficult to repair. I am
in treaty for a suite of rooms in S$^t$ James's Street [9] looking down
Pall Mall — for 30£ a year on the 4 floor — and I have been looking at scores of houses and longing to take one — and the rest. But
until you settle I can't settle  Shall we ever do so?  If I had my wife
w$^d$ she have a penny worth more of happiness? I have been to the
good old Waddell Scotts & to the Crowes and no where else
scarcely — my time being occupied nearly all day with writing and

----

[7] Thackeray was associated with *The Examiner* for four months, but little
of his work is identifiable. For the most part the magazine's book reviews were
written by Forster, and Thackeray's tasks were very humble. He glances back
at this part of his career in describing Philip's services to *The Pall Mall
Gazette:* "on Tuesday of every week . . . it was this modest sub-editor's
duty to begin snipping and pasting paragraphs for the ensuing Saturday's issue.
He cut down the parliamentary speeches, giving due favouritism to the
orators of the *Pall Mall Gazette* party, and meagre outlines of their opponent's
discourses. If the leading public men on the side of the *Pall Mall Gazette* gave
entertainments, you may be sure they were duly chronicled in the fashionable
intelligence; if one of their party wrote a book it was pretty sure to get praise
from the critic. I am speaking of simple old days, you understand." (*Works,*
XI, 486)

[8] Mrs. Knox, Mrs. Carmichael-Smyth's sister.

[9] Thackeray lived at 88 St. James's Street from April, 1845, until June,
1846.

scissoring, after w$^h$ paying visits becomes a dreary duty — I go out as usual 6 times a week to dinner: but am pretty moderate and have adhered firmly to my resolution against brandy & water. Do you know what I am thinking of all the time I am writing to my dear old Mammy, and ought to be thinking of home and the dear little ones? no such thing — I am thinking of an article I must write to day about the President's message,[10] of a Review I must make to night of a new book of the Examiner's printers and the confusion we are in for too much copy. I recollect last year my letters used to be always in this hurried turbid style, and contained nothing but change-ringing of my perplexities. The Spring is come it is as warm as May — there I was trying to get off them with commencing a description of Spring, but it won't do & back they come again — The Talleyrand is put off sine die. The Eastern book just going into hand, and I have taken Eyre Crowe to help me in the illustrations, and in another w$^h$ is projected and of prodigious importance. This is the scheme by w$^h$ I expect to make a great deal of money it is to be called — but never mind what until it is ready meanwhile I must go away to work. This is not a letter only a scrap to say God bless all, and that I am quite well, — Let me hear of the little woman is she quieter? let the children go often, pay a coach if it rains — And so good bye to my dearest old mother.

W M T.

303.          TO THOMAS LONGMAN
6 APRIL 1845

Published in part by Melville, *Thackeray*, I, 138. My text is taken from a transcript supplied by Mrs. Fuller.

Reform Club,<br>Sunday, 6 April.

My dear Sir,

I hardly know what subjects to point out as suited to my capacity — light matters connected with Art, humorous reviews, critiques of

[10] "Polk's First Address," which appeared in *The Examiner* on March 29. The only review in this issue of *The Examiner* concerns Mrs. A. Marsh's

novels — French subjects, memoirs, poetry, history from Louis
XV. downwards and of an earlier period — that of Froissart and
Monstrelet. German light literature and poetry — though of these
I know but little beyond what I learned in a years residence in the
Country fourteen years ago: finally subjects relating to society in
general where a writer may be allowed to display the humourous
*ego*, or a victim is to be gently immolated. But I am better able to
follow than to lead and should hope to give satisfaction in my small
way.[11]

Very faithfully yours Dear Sir,<br>W. M. Thackeray.

To T. Longman, Esq.,
　　Paternoster Row.

### 304.　　TO GEORGE WILLIAM NICKISSON
#### 21 APRIL 1845

*Address:* G. W. Nickisson Esq? | 215 Regent St. *Postmark:* AP 21 1845.
Hitherto unpublished.

Monday April 21, 1845

My dear Nickisson

Remember that the Exhibition review[12] is booked for your
faithful

Titmarsh.

Between ourselves I believe I am in a career of most wonderful
money-getting.

---

*Mount Sorel; or the Heiress of the De Veres.* Neither of these contributions
has previously been identified as Thackeray's.

[11] For the further correspondence that eventually resulted in Thackeray's
single contribution to *The Edinburgh Review,* see below, No. 312.

[12] "Picture Gossip: In a Letter from Michael Angelo Titmarsh," *Fraser's
Magazine,* June, 1845, pp. 713–724. On June 12 of this year FitzGerald
wrote to Frederick Tennyson: "If you want to know something of the Exhibition . . . read Fraser's Magazine for this month; there Thackeray has a
paper on the matter, full of fun. I met Stone in the street the other day; he
took me by the button, and told me in perfect sincerity, and with increasing
warmth, how, though he loved old Thackeray, yet these yearly out-speakings

305.     TO RICHARD BEDINGFIELD
1 JUNE 1845

My text is taken from Bedingfield, *Cassell's Magazine*, II, 298.

88, St. James's Street.
Sunday, June 1.

My dear Bedingfield, —

I was very sorry not to see you the other day when you called, but I wasn't in fit state to receive anybody, labouring under a violent attack of bilious sickness, for which the only fit company was a basin. Luckily, my illnesses don't last long nor come very often.

I have read both your stories, and here you see they come back — that is cold encouragement to a man with a great deal of merit and imagination. I think they contain a great deal of good stuff, but I'm sure they are *not saleable* — that is the point. They are done in an old-fashioned manner, I think, and you could no more sell them than a tailor could a coat of 1830, or a milliner a bonnet which might have been quite the rage in the last reign.

It's not the merits of the thing I fall foul of — though I should like to quarrel with a little *fine writing* here and there — but only the question of trade. It is not because a story is bad or an author a fool that either should not be popular nowadays, as you and I know, who see many donkeys crowned with laurels, while certain clever

---

of his sorely tried him; not on account of himself (Stone), but on account of some of his friends, Charles Landseer, Maclise, etc. Stone worked himself up to such a pitch under the pressure of forced calmness that he at last said Thackeray would get himself horse-whipped one day by one of these infuriated Apelleses. At this I, who had partly agreed with Stone that ridicule, though true, needs not always to be spoken, began to laugh: and told him two could play at that game. These painters cling together, and bolster each other up, to such a degree, that they really have persuaded themselves that any one who ventures to laugh at one of their drawings, exhibited publickly for the express purpose of criticism, insults the whole corps. In the mean while old Thackeray laughs at all this; and goes on in his own way; writing hard for half a dozen Reviews and Newspapers all the morning; dining, drinking, and talking of a night; managing to preserve a fresh colour and perpetual flow of spirits under a wear-and-tear of thinking and feeding that would have knocked up any other man I know two years ago, at least." (*Letters and Literary Remains*, ed. Wright, I, 222–223)

fellows of our acquaintance fight vainly for a maintenance or a reputation. I can suit the magazines (but I can't hit the public, be hanged to them), and, from my knowledge of the former, I should say you will *never* get a good sale for commodities like these. Quiet, sentimental novelets won't do nowadays, I'm sure. Think of the high-seasoned dishes the British public has been feeding on for the last 30 years, and you'll agree with me that they won't go back to such simple fare as you give them in "The Blind Lover." All I can say, my dear fellow, is Try again. In reality, your system may be the right one and mine the wrong, but I'm sure I'm right as to *the state of the market.*

Ever yours,

W. M. T.

306.              TO CHARLOTTE RITCHIE
                    9–11 JUNE 1845 [13]

*Postmark:* 11 JU 1845. Published in part by Mrs. Warre-Cornish, *Family Letters,* pp. 25–26.

88 S.<sup>t</sup> James's St. Wednesday.

My dear Charlotte. Your welcome letter ought to have been answered long since but I was in a perplexity about the poor little woman and whether or not to tell her that the children had been here to see me. I fear lest she should be offended at hearing that they were come without her. About poor Brodie their former nurse we have been in the same perplexity: she is so prodigiously fond of the children that to see them for an hour w.<sup>d</sup> give her more pain than pleasure, and we have not had the heart to send to her. What a catalogue of domestic sentimentalities, isn't it? One more piece of sentiment and I'm done — our poor old John has gone the way of all flesh: and has left a scolding wife for a better world doubtless. I should have had black-edged paper at least to communicate such melancholy tidings.

[13] This letter was begun on Anny's birthday, Monday, June 9, and finished the following Wednesday.

I have just left the young ladies putting on smart frocks to go out to dinner, with my fellow traveller Emerson Tennent and his family — This is Anny's birthday. I wonder whether her mother will remember it. Her father didn't: and poor Nanny wouldn't say a word but kept her secret, until my mother remembered it. We have been engaged in a round of pleasures — They come and breakfast with me in the mornings, and we went to the Colosseum and the Zoological, and on Sunday we caught cold at Westminster Abbey: and then we went to the Bedingfields' (delicious rencontre!) and to a number of other friends old and new — the evening generally ends by both the children falling asleep in the carriage, and they are borne up like a pair of bundles to the bedroom. I have not seen the Langslows yet.[14] I only got Mʳ Langslow's card the day

[14] The background of the sad dilemma in which the Langslows at this time found themselves is set forth with judicial impartiality in a letter of January 23, 1844, from William Ritchie to his fiancée, Augusta Trimmer: "you have doubtless heard me or my sisters speak of an aunt we have at Ceylon, Mrs. Langslow, and to whom we are all most deeply attached. She is a being gifted with rare talents, infinite taste and wit, the most generous and kindest heart, but alas! with a sensibility so keen and exquisite as to have grown, from constant indulgence of it, quite morbid and Utopian. Her husband was a judge at Ceylon, an excellent lawyer, a clever man and an accomplished gentleman; but, strangely enough, he shared his wife's warm, chivalrous temperament, and they mutually stimulated each other in their wildly romantic principles, till they bordered upon Quixotism. In the rich, they everywhere saw oppression and insolence — in the poor, worth and excellence fettered by misery and degradation; and first in England, then in Malta, where he was Attorney-General, and lastly at Ceylon, where he was a judge, he has ever waged a crusade against his superiors in office, the governor of the land in which he lived, with motives, it is true, of the most expanded philanthropy, but too often, I fear, without adequate grounds for his indignation and under the influence of a distorted judgment. — The government of Ceylon have at last, after fierce contest, determined on suspending him from his office as judge — an event for which I have trembled ever since I came out [to India], and which is most distressing, as he is in bad health and has scarce any other means of support. There are, of course, two different stories told by the different parties of the island — the favourers of government declare that his opposition on all occasions has been most factious, and that, however able as a lawyer, his violence unfits him entirely for a judge. The liberal party, on the other hand, hold him up as a martyr to his principles and to his avowed determination to do equal justice between the native and the Englishman — and not to bow or tremble before the little greatness of the government — and they ascribe also

before my mother arrived, and have been too busy ever since to call. But M⸢ Jaffray has arranged a meeting for us next week. The Dicks have once presented their compliments, and requested the pleasure of M⸢ W⸢m⸣ Thackeray's company to dinner. It is queerly practised — Hospitality in this town. Old M⸢r⸣ Halliday understands it better however; and I go whenever I have a free day and ask for a share of his dinner — He is a very well informed shrewd kindly old man. My mother and M⸢rs⸣ Halliday have met. I'm very glad that the old feud is concluded but I think my mother is rather disappointed that my aunt did not give the children a gold watch apiece or a diamond-necklace or show some other token of the immensity of her admiration for them.

Wednesday.

The Chinese Exhibition and the Tower have been the points of attraction since the above sentence was written: and the evening passed off with a splendid festival at Capt⸢n⸣ Bechers, where the Bedingfield family were present. You should have seen Miss Turner skipping into the back drawing room, and as it were dancing to the music performed there! Time has not thinned poor M⸢rs⸣ Bedingfields hair in the least, and has given her son a pair of whiskers w⸢h⸣ protrude from his chin, and give him an appearance

---

to private enmity and cabal his removal. There is truth no doubt on both sides, and, for all I can hear, I think he has been dealt with arbitrarily and spitefully; but, as his best friend, I cannot conceal from myself that he has brought it upon his own head, by placing himself in a position where, as a judge, he should never have been — that is, at the mercy of the government, who, if he had acted with prudence, could never have injured him, however desirous of doing so. The natives of Colombo seem to be unanimous in his favour; a piece of plate is to be given him, and most numerously signed petitions to the Government at home have been forwarded on behalf of his restoration. But I fear the hope to be placed on them is but frail — and it is most melancholy to see a man with many noble qualities, sacrificing his all, £1,200 a year, for mistaken principles (perhaps, I should say, a mistaken application of *true* principle in consequence of distorted views)." (*Ritchies in India*, pp. 127–128) The remainder of Langslow's life was spent in England, where he endeavored fruitlessly to obtain redress for his grievances. See *In the privy council. Petition from R. Langslow late judge of district court of Colombo* (1847). It seems likely that certain traits of old Sedley after his ruin are drawn from Langslow.

that I wont take upon myself to characterize in writing. As usual:
the young ladies were falling asleep by the time the days pleasure
sight-seeing was over. So we put them to bed instead of taking
them to the family dinner party.

To day is the last day of the fete. At 12 o'clock one of the most
splendid one-horse flys that London can produce is to waft us to
Richmond where we shall see the deer in the park, and have sylla-
bubs for tea no doubt. And then comes tomorrow: and the dear
little souls and the kind mother disappear in the distance — and I
am left to my bachelor life again. If I did not know how much
better a guardian they have in her than myself, they never should
leave me — and it would be much better for me too. My Aunt
Halliday has just sent me the poor little wife's crazy letter, w^h is
consoling at any rate inasmuch as it shows she's happy. I'm delighted that you have resolved *not* to part with Jane: and should
have written to beg and implore you not, had I dared or thought
my advice worth giving. Good God! suppose she *did* marry a
member of Council [15] and have a house in Hyde Park Gardens,
what would that profit? — To exchange her mother's happiness
for a carriage and 3 footmen (possibly only 2) in Berlin-gloves and
powder, is a poor bargain after all. My dear old Aunt has lost
enough already — ⟨. . .⟩ [16]

307.        TO MRS. CARMICHAEL-SMYTH
                    JUNE 1845 [17]

Published in part by Mrs. Warre-Cornish, *Family Letters*, pp. 27–28.

My dearest Mammy  Your letter of Saturday arrived here on
Wednesday morning — doesn't it seem impudent to say I have had
no time to answer it till now? — but somehow the day has passed
and the postmans bell stopped ringing and it wasn't done. What a
picture you give of the place! — I wish September were come and

[15] The Council of the East India Company, not the Privy Council.
[16] The final lines of this letter have been cut away.
[17] This is Thackeray's first letter to his mother after she returned to Paris
with his children on June 12.

you were back at Paris: I will come then please God for 10 days
but shan't be able to move until then except from Saturday till
Tuesday — how well that w^d have done for Dieppe and back: but
it can't be helped. I wish you had never come that's the truth — for
I fancied myself perfectly happy until then — now I see the difference: and what a deal of the best sort of happiness it is God's will
that I should lose. White-bait dinners are all very well but —
hang the buts — it is those we are always sighing after. Well, let
us be thankful that those eels have such an admirable brown sauce
and that the champagne is iced to a nicety: a man can't have everything. There is no fun in writing this though — the paper gets dim
before my eyes and it is the scene of parting over again — Don't
fancy that I'm unhappy though: it's only the abstract pathos of the
thing that moves me. I never could bear to think of children parted
from their parents somehow without a tendency to blubbering: and
am as weak to this day upon the point, as I used to be at school. In
the meanwhile it will be a consolation to you to know that this
tender hearted being is cruelly hungry, and in 20 minutes from this
time will be on his way to a jollyfication. God bless all.

W M T.

I went to call on Lady Smyth yesterday: and found the lovely
creature reclining on her sofa in her dressing room. with her hair
in a crop. We talked polite literature in a most polite way, and Jim
expressed his opinion about the merits of Bulwer — It was all I
could do once or twice to prevent laughing — at the abstract absurdity — I am grinning over it now quite cheerfully after crying over
the abstract pathos — I daren't trust myself with *that* again though,
and tear off the half sheet

308.        TO WILLIAM HARRISON AINSWORTH
30 JUNE 1845

Published in part, Ellis, *Ainsworth*, II, 117–118.

Monday. June 30
My dear Ainsworth

I'm glad I wrote the 3ᵈ letter. Its the only one wʰ has produced
a satisfactory reply. Of course I'll come to dinner on Sunday: and
we are just as good friends as ever. Wasn't it much better to complain and explain? I think so — and the injured honor of *Titmarsh*
is now satisfied.[18]

I hadnt got your note and its enclosure when I wrote. Your
terms are prodigiously good — and if I can see the material for a
funny story you shall have it.[19] That for wʰ Colburn paid in advance; and wʰ he would not trust into the authors hands until he
got his money back will run to 30 possibly to 100 pages: and is too
long for you.[20]

---

[18] The cause of this quarrel is not known. Ellis, wishing to present Ainsworth as the offended party, substitutes *imperial house* for *injured honor* in
his text and refers to the resulting fabrication as Thackeray's "penitential
letter"!

[19] Ainsworth had recently become proprietor of *The New Monthly Magazine*, formerly the property of Colburn. Thackeray's "The Chest of Cigars"
appeared in the July number, his "Bob Robinson's First Love" in the August
number.

[20] This passage is explained by a fragment of a letter of May 8, 1845, from
Thackeray to Colburn (printed in Sotheby's catalogue of June 25, 1923):
"Will you send me the beginning of the Story I sent you wh. is gone clean out
of my mind, and also the commencement of a novel wh. I gave into your
hands?" The "Story," about which Ainsworth had evidently inquired, must
have been *Mrs. Perkins's Ball*, which Thackeray had begun as early as November 8, 1844. "A Legend of the Rhine," the only other tale of medium length
that he had on hand, was already being published in *George Cruikshank's
Table-Book*. The "commencement of a novel" was a draft of the early pages
of *Vanity Fair*, for which Thackeray at last found a publisher in the firm of
Bradbury and Evans. Vizetelly (*Glances Back through Seventy Years*, I, 284)
relates that Thackeray received "fifty guineas per part [for his novel], including the two sheets of letterpress, a couple of etchings, and the initials at the
commencement of the chapters. He reckoned the text, I remember, at no

There's one thing I regret very much too — and must be told to you now in making a clean breast of it — a certain paragraph in the next *Punch* relating to a certain advertisement about contributors 'not only of talent *but of rank*' [21]     This moved my wrath; and has been hardly handled — This was before our meeting & explanation — I always must think it a very objectionable advertisement — but shouldn't have lifted my hand to smite my friend; had explanation come earlier. So that now *you* must be called upon to play the part of forgiver in w^h I'm sure you will shine.

Ever yours my dear fellow<br>W M Thackeray —

309.      TO CHAPMAN AND HALL
JULY? 1845

*Address:* Mes^rs Chapman & Hall. | 186 Strand. Hitherto unpublished.

Dears Sirs

Could you try and get for me (to look at with the greatest care) — the Holy City & Bartlett's Jerusalem? [22] I want to fill up one or two blanks in my chapter.

My boy will fetch them whenever you send him.

Yrs ever<br>W. M. T.

---

more than five-and-twenty shillings a page, the two etchings at six guineas each, while as for the few initials at the beginning of the chapters, he threw these in."

[21] "Immense Opportunity," *Punch*, July 5, 1845.

[22] *Walks about the City and Environs of Jerusalem* (1844) by William Henry Bartlett (1809–1854).

310.          TO MRS. CARMICHAEL-SMYTH
7 JULY 1845

*Address:* M^rs Carmichael Smyth. | Luc sur Mer | Calvados. | France. *Post-marks:* 7 JY 1845, LA DELIVRANDE 10 JUIL. 45. Hitherto unpublished.

7 July.

My dearest Mammy

I write just a line to say I am well. I have written 2 letters on the other subject: & tore them up — it is best not stirring it. At least for the present. There are 100 things for and against all plans at present: and I will not consent to make you miserable by separating the children from you. When we can get G. P's affairs clear will be time to speak. Morris is ill. I sent down to him and hoped to have had a consultation with him ere this. You can't do without my Grandmother. Her living with me w^d cost 200 a year extra — that is to say a house servants &c wouldnt be less than 450£ a year — and I should get no benefit. Dont you see why I dont write? — Ive begun a dozen notes in this way — and flung them down mastered by the eternal perplexity. The Londoners are going out of town — the dinner parties become scarce. I still have my hands full of work: and am about to make more money than I do. Poor Langslow is in a peck of troubles: [23] and I believe quite destitute — I have nothing to tell you: only to pray God bless the children and you, and my dear old G P who has stood so nobly by them.

W M T.

[23] See above, No. 306.

311.      TO EDWARD CHAPMAN
9 JULY 1845

Hitherto unpublished.

88 S<u>t</u> James S<u>t</u>
July 9, 1845.

Dear Sir

I send back with thanks the 55£ you were good enough to lend me the other day —

I have been thinking over the bargain regarding the Eastern Book, and think you are rather hard upon me. The trip was a very expensive one. I was offered my own terms elsewhere — and I assure you undertook the book for you with the full conviction that it would be paid at the price of the other volume on w<u>h</u> I am engaged for you — viz two hundred guineas. I shall rely on your justice confidently however

Always yours
W M Thackeray.

312.     TO PROFESSOR MACVEY NAPIER [24]
16 JULY 1845

Published in part, *Selection from the Correspondence of the late Macvey Napier*, ed. Macvey Napier (London, 1879), pp. 498–499. My text is taken from a transcript supplied by Mrs. Fuller.

88, St. James's Street,
16 July, 1845.

Dear Sir,

I am glad to comply with your request that I should address you personally and thank you for the letters which you have written to Mr. Longman regarding my contributions to the Edinburgh Review.[25]

---

[24] Napier (1776–1847) was editor of *The Edinburgh Review* from 1829 till his death and of the seventh edition of *The Encyclopaedia Britannica*.
[25] See above, No. 303. "Will you tell me — confidently [*sic*], of course —,"

Eugene Sue has written a very great number of novels, beginning with maritime novels in the Satanic style so to speak: full of crime and murder of every description. He met in his early works with no very great success: he gave up the indecencies of language and astonished the world with "Mathilde" three years since, which had the singular quality among French novels of containing no improprieties of expression. In my mind it is one of the most immoral books in the world. "The Mysteries of Paris" followed with still greater success, and the same extreme cleverness of construction and the same sham virtue. It has been sold by tens of thousands in London in various shapes, in American editions, and illustrated English translations. The book just translated is of an old performance; it is called "Latréaumont" [26] in the French original.

To go through a course of Sue's writings would require I should think more than a short article and the subject has been much dealt with in minor periodicals here.

The "Glances at Life" [27] is a very kindly and agreeable little book by a Cockney philosopher. Could it be coupled in an article with N. P. Willis's Dashes at Life which Messrs. Longman now advertize?

A pleasant short paper might be written, I fancy, commenting upon the humours of the fair. Should the subject meet with your approval perhaps you will give me notice and state what space the Review can afford.

Should you not approve, I will look through Lady Hester Stanhope [28] and hope to be able to treat it to your satisfaction.

---

Napier had written to Hayward on April 12, "whether you know anything of a Mr. Thackeray, about whom Longman has written me, thinking he would be a good hand for light articles? He says (Longman) that this Mr. Thackeray is one of the best writers in *Punch*. One requires to be very much on one's guard in engaging with mere strangers. In a Journal like the *Edinbro'*, it is always of importance to keep up in respect of names." (*A Selection from the Correspondence of Abraham Hayward, from 1834 to 1884, with an Account of his Early Life*, ed. H. E. Carlisle, 2 vols., London, 1886, I, 106)

[26] Published in 1838.

[27] Cornelius Webbe's *Glances at Life: in City and Suburb* was printed in 1836; a second series appeared in 1845.

[28] *Memoirs of the Lady Hester Stanhope* (1845) by Charles Lewis Meryon (1783–1877).

I am bringing out a little book about the Mediteranean myself which I hope shortly to have the pleasure of sending you.

Dear Sir,

Your very obdt. Servt.

W. M. Thackeray.

313.                    TO ?

21 JULY 1845 [29]

My text is taken from an American Art Association catalogue, March 25, 1920.

88 St. James's St.

Monday 21 July

Dear Sir.

I am much flattered by your note. Will Thursday at 11 be a convenient hour? Or Friday or Saturday at the same time.

I have very little opportunity for criticism on the Fine Arts at present; but shall gladly avail myself of your kind offer.

Your very obedient servt.

W. M. Thackeray.

Be good enough to say when I shall call for you.

314.        TO MRS. CARMICHAEL-SMYTH

26 JULY 1845

*Address:* M^rs Carmichael-Smyth | Luc sur Mer | Calvados | France. *Post-marks:* 26 JY 1845, 28 JUIL. 40 BOULOGNE. Published in part, *Bio-graphical Introductions,* V, xlii-xliii; VI, xviii-xix.

Saturday.

My dearest Mammy. I have no more to say than usual. I am busy with scores of little jobs comme à l'ordinaire. The Examiner and I have parted company in the best humour possible: for it took more time than I could afford to give for four sovereigns: and I was much too clever a fellow to do it well; making omissions blunders &c w^h an honest plodding clerk w^d never have fallen into. So

---

[29] Thackeray was living at 88 St. James's Street on July 21 only in 1845.

that chain is off my leg: but there are plenty of other little ones binding me: I have only just found time to finish my book, and am here at an Inn at Chelsea for that purpose: looking out on the river and working away tant bien que mal. But I am gravelled with Jerusalem, not wishing to offend the public by a needless exhibition of heterodoxy: nor daring to be a hypocrite. I have been reading lots of books — Old Testament: Church Histories: Travels and advance but slowly in the labour. I find there was a sect in the early Church who denounced the Old Testament: and get into such a rage myself when reading all that murder and crime w$^h$ the name of the Almighty is blasphemously made to Sanction: that I don't dare to trust myself to write, and put off my work from day to day. When I get the book out of hand, please God I shall see the dear dear little and big faces again — I have fond visions of double cottages in the Hammersmith or Hampstead districts, where we could be all together, and yet each independent: what a blessing it would be to have a home once more. My position — you see I've nothing to say but about myself — appears to be very good — and my reputation in my profession of the best sort after the great guns     The admirers of M$^r$ Titmarsh are a small clique but a good and increasing one if I may gather from the daily offers that are made me: and the increased sums bid for my writings — Enough of this     You know or at least I hope I don't puff myself with vanity: but try & consider my chances fairly like those of an indifferent party.

Dont be alarmed about the Stockbroker — What harm can anything do me? I have but my skin — & my speculations have been mere bagatelles. I have lost 12£ and won about 40 — They don't occupy me at all. My poor little woman wrote me the craziest letter lately, and from Aunt Becher's notes I gather that she has been very unwell with head-attacks. Alexanders [30] family are with her now — God bless the kind soul. What a number of generations of ours' has she been kind to! And God bless my dear Mother and little ones, and all with you and near you: prays

W M T.

[30] Captain Alexander Becher.

315.      TO MRS. CARMICHAEL-SMYTH
2 AUGUST 1845

*Address:* M<sup>rs</sup> Carmichael-Smyth. | Luc sur Mer | Calvados | France. *Post-marks:* 2 AU 1845, LA DELIVRANDE 5 AOUT 45. Hitherto unpublished.

My dearest Mammy. I'm sure your advice is quite right — I'm not going to preach heterodoxy: I cant be hypocritical however, w<sup>h</sup> surely is a much greater sin against God. We don't know what orthodoxy is indeed. Your orthodoxy is not your neighbour's — Your opinion is personal to you as much as your eyes or your nose or the tone of your voice. Objects in nature make quite a different impression upon you to what they do upon any other individual. Why be unhappy then about the state of another's opinion? It is to doubt of God to doubt of his mercy to another. It is awful presumption I think for any Bishop, Priest layman or laywoman to say I have the true Faith: I am right: Wo betide all who disagree with me. What right have you then to think of being unhappy about the state of my opinions? What right have you to say that I am without God because I can't believe that God ordered Abraham to kill Isaac or that he ordered the bears to eat the little children who laughed at Elisha for being bald. You don't believe it yourself. You fancy you do: you search out explanations to reconcile these awful things to your mind — the Belief is gone, directly the explanation is necessary. What did the Saviour mean by searching the Scriptures? — that a man was to read them to the best of his own reason or to take his neighbours? What did he do himself by the Old Testament — he repealed it. He said that it was not the Jews alone that the Almighty Father would bless: but that God was God of all the world: that you should *not* take an eye for an eye &c but that you should love one another — Wasn't that a truth that you should do as you would be done by before the Saviour said it, as well as afterwards? Was revenge an ordinance of God in the reign of Julius Caesar, and not in that of Augustus? And yet the Jews said that their law of revenge was from God. It couldn't have been. It was not right. It was solemnly repealed by the

Saviour who said *It* has been said &c. but *I* say so & so. In saying so he himself denies that those words were as divine Authority — and the Jews murdered him for questioning their exclusive claims to divine favor: for propounding another law to that w$^h$ they had been taught to believe came to them from Jehovah especially, for setting up himself against their God — Why do I love the Saviour? (I love and adore the Blessed Character so much that I don't like to speak of it, and know myself to be such a rascal that I don't dare) — Because He is all Goodness Truth Purity — I dislike the Old Testament because it is the very contrary: because it contains no Gentleness no Humility no forgiveness — nothing but exclusiveness and pride curses and arrogance — Fancy Lot, fancy Ezekiel remonstrating with God! Fancy the Divine name used as the slaughter of the Cannanites was going on — Using the very same name, acting on the very same law the descendants of Joshua murdered the Christ. How were they to know that he was the Messiah? by his miracles? — numberless people according to the Hebrew books performed miracles: by his doctrines? It was the very contrary of that w$^h$ they had been taught to consider as Divine — and how could God change? — his very appearance was contrary to their belief, — that is to their interpretation of Scripture. You can't be the Messiah, they might say — The prophets tell us expressly that he is to be a King, and that Judah is to be exalted by him over all the earth — they literally interpreted the Bible, and crucified the Blessed Speaker of Truth and Love and Humility. I can't help applying as I read — I can't help seeing that two and two make an inevitable consequence of four — why is my dear old Mother to weep and be unhappy because my conclusions & her's don't tally? If you had been born a Catholic — you know what a good one you would have been: and then you would have been wretched if I had any doubts about the martyrdom of Polycarp or the Invention of the Holy Cross — and there are thousands of anxious mothers so deploring the errors of their sceptical children — But the Great Intelligence shines far far above all mothers and all sons — the Truth Absolute is God — And it seems to me hence almost blasphemous: that any blind prejudiced sinful mortal being should dare to be unhappy about the belief of another; should dare to say Lo I am right and my brothers must go to damnation — I Know God and my brother doesn't. And now I'll stop scolding my dearest old Mother about that favorite propensity of hers to be miserable. God bless all.

W M T.

316.     TO WILLIAM FREDERICK POLLOCK
AUGUST 1845

Hitherto unpublished.

88 S! James's S! Thursday.

My dear Pollock.

I want to write you a line about my unfortunate relative Langslow whose condition quite frightens me. The Chief Baron [31] he says has promised to take his case in hand; and I do hope and implore that something may be done for him. Lord Lyttelton [32] he says asked him 'Was he prepared to take duty if the Gov! called upon him?' on w! he Langslow hesitated and said he was not — this unfortunate declaration may serve to put the poor fellow's affairs in a worse case than ever; and may be urged to your father should he be making any application in Langslow's favor.

Will you kindly tell him that the meaning of the refusal I take to be this — He can't afford an outfit. He is utterly impoverished:

[31] Sir Jonathan Frederick Pollock (1783–1870), later (1866) first Baronet, one of the closest friends of Thackeray's later life. Pollock was educated at St. Paul's School and Trinity College, Cambridge, where he received his B. A. and M. A. degrees in 1806 and 1809. Called to the bar in the latter year, he soon built up an extensive practice. From 1831 to 1844 he was M. P. for Huntingdon, serving as Attorney-General in 1834–1835 and from 1841 to 1844. He presided over the Court of Exchequer as Lord Chief Baron from 1844 till his retirement in 1866 to his seat of Hatton in Middlesex. He was twice married. By his first wife he had seven sons and five daughters; by his second, the former Sarah Langslow, four sons and eight daughters.

[32] George William, fourth Baron Lyttleton (1817–1876), who had for some time interested himself in colonial questions, acted as Undersecretary for the Colonies from January to July, 1846. Thackeray knew him through Brookfield, who had been his tutor in 1834.

in so bad & desperate a condition, that upon my word I believe unless he gets some relief in spite of himself, *the man will lose his senses.* I write to you, I dont know why: except that I am so pained to see his condition that I take any the slightest chance to get him a helping hand: and beseech you to ask Sir Frederick Pollock to extend it. Perhaps he does not know how wretchedly poor Langslow is: how proud: and now really almost crazy by want hopelessness & sense of wrong — If the argument ad misericordiam can be used: for God's sake use it.

Yours dear Pollock<br>W M Thackeray.

317. TO CHARLOTTE RITCHIE<br>AUGUST 1845 [33]

Published in part by Mrs. Warre-Cornish, *Family Letters*, pp. 32–33.

My dear Charlotte. I've only time as usual for a line — as usual to thank you all for your kindness to my poor little woman. Give the man you wrote about anything you like — Also please find for me if the little woman wants anything &c. Here's 2 months pay for her in advance till *October* 9. Please remember this for me and in D[r] Puzin's receipt for he might somehow forget.

So Augusta has sailed to her Villiam [34] — Happy rogue! Every body who comes from Calcutta brings the best accounts of him and his popularity and his talents and his prosperity. The old Cambridge men I meet continually ask how is Gentleman Ritchie? I hope he'll be as rich as Follett,[35] though I'm sure he'll never be so stingy. Poor M[r] Langslow comes to me of a morning and talks of

[33] This letter was written shortly before August 9.
[34] Augusta Trimmer had recently sailed for Calcutta to join William Ritchie, whom she married on December 4 (*Ritchies in India*, p. 160).
[35] Sir William Webb Follett (1798–1845), the famous Tory lawyer, was Solicitor-General in 1834–1835 and 1841 and Attorney-General in 1844. "He was unfortunately parsimonious and too eager to accumulate a fortune," we learn from the *Dictionary of National Biography*, "and fell a victim to his application to professional work. . . . His personal property was sworn at 160,000£."

his own case and the Baron de Bode. The Hallidays I see from time to time very gay & jolly and kind. I've not been able to see them much of late though; on account of the business in the morning and the engagements at night. But the season's over now thank God: and I shall get a little quiet and leisure. I have been bothering my brain for a fortnight over a chapter about Jerusalem: w.ʰ contained some unorthodox remarks: but my dear old Mother has written me a letter so full of terror and expostulation, and dread of future consequences for my awful heresy that I have to cancel [36] it and begin afresh — Good bye dear Charlotte — What a comfort you & yours have been to me! That what I think every day.

Your affectionate<br>W M T.

318.                    TO MRS. THACKERAY
                        9 AUGUST 1845 [37]

Hitherto unpublished. My text is taken from a transcript supplied by Mrs. Fuller.

Pall Mall. 9 August

My dearest little woman. My news are of the usual sort. There's nothing to say: too much to do: too much dining and pleasuring: not enough quiet and reading. Scribble scribble in the morning, hob and nob in the evening — that has been my life during the Season. But the Queen has just this minute prorogued Parliament, the Season is over, and everybody is going away to leave me the town in quiet.

Who do you think is just come? no less a person than your brother Arthur. He was in London for a week, and dined with me continually. He is greatly improved, has never had a weeks illness in India, and altogether as manly good-natured and honest a fellow as I have seen for a long time. He is very anxious about his sister

---

[36] The nature of this cancelled chapter may be judged from Thackeray's letter of August 2.

[37] The prorogation of parliament occurred on August 9 in 1845 (*Annual Register*).

Isabella. Do you remember his coming to see you in bed just after Baby was born, and my dear little woman looking so happy and pretty? O for those days. I'm getting weary of being alone, and want some other companions besides those over the bottle.

Arthur is gone to his Aunts in Ireland: and promises to go to Paris afterwards and pay you a visit. Then he will go to see your Mother in Italy or wherever she is. As I suspected that amiable woman has been writing to her Sons in India accounts of my cruel treatment of you.

I had a letter from Anny the other day. 'Papa' she says, 'I am very unhappy I dont know y.' She is the true daughter of Mr. Yellowplush isn't she?

Bess Hamerton is come, and has brought me accounts of my dear little woman. So you have been magnetized by old Madame Dildie, and the magnetizing has done you good. Amen. Go on — Get well and strong and come and live in a pretty cottage I have my i on.

When the little ones come back in September, I hope not to be far off but to come over for a fortnight and hug you all. God bless you prays

W M T.

319.                    TO ANNE THACKERAY
                        AUGUST 1845 [38]

*Address:* Miss Thackeray. Hitherto unpublished.

What have I got to tell my dearest Anny? Uncle Arthur is come from India and will soon go to Paris to see Mamma. And in four or five weeks more I hope I shall see her there too, and my dearest little girls. As soon as I have finished my book and some other business I will come — How I should like to see both of you in the water! — The mignonette and Verbena Granny gave me are just dead. I used to look at them and long for my dearest little girls. God bless them prays Papa.

[38] This note was written shortly after Thackeray's letter of August 9, in which Arthur Shawe's arrival from India is first announced.

320.          TO MRS. CARMICHAEL-SMYTH
                    25 AUGUST 1845

*Address:* M^rs Carmichael Smyth. | Luc sur Mer | Calvados | France. *Post-marks:* 25 AU 1845, LA DÉLIVRANDE 28 AOUT 45. Hitherto unpublished.

My dearest Mammy. I write a hurried line on my way to some place in the country — I don't know where exactly Tunbridge Wells or Brighton — I take with me young Villiam [39] and a bag of books. I have been fool enough to sprain my ankle w^h is not bad but bothers me considerably. Arnica has done it monstrous good. I have sent 20£ to Delenerts for G. P. I didn't know how to get it to him at Caen, and intend to stop at this mysterious place in the country as long as ever I can bear it: long enough I hope to finish several things I have on hand, and to clear the way for coming to see you all next month or in October. This I think is all there is to say at these presents. The kind Ritchies give me continual accounts of the little woman, and my Aunt Langslow wrote me a note the other day (enclosing one from Charlotte) w^h, M^rs Langslow's, was as crazy as poor Isabella's I think. God bless all prays

                                        W M T.

321.          TO MRS. CARMICHAEL-SMYTH
                    7 SEPTEMBER 1845

*Address:* M^rs Carmichael Smyth. | 81 Champs Élysées | Paris. *Postmark:* BRIGHTON SE 8 1845. Extracts published in *Biographical Introductions*, V, xliii.

                              4 Grand Parade Brighton. Sunday.
My dearest Mammy. My inkstand is gone down to be washed and I begin pencilling until it's return. The weather here is delicious the place agrees with me excellently I have comfortable lodgings and young William (in a dark pepper & salt livery) makes an admirable good servant I find plenty of acquaintances: and work

[39] Thackeray's servant.

all day — My ancle is all but well. Only if ever I walk it begins to
swell. I don't know how I came to slip — I was walking soberly
under the colonnade in the Haymarket, when I felt it go from
under me without any rhyme or reason, and that is all I can tell
about it. Meanwhile the book doesn't get on — that remonstrance
of yours caused me to cancel a chapter: and since then my engagements have been so incessant that I've never been able to get back
to work on it. I hope to clear them however in 4 or 5 days, and
then to get to work and the book finished to come to you. I wish I
had a house and all of you here. It is the merriest place. There
are no trees to be sure: but the Sun is not too hot; and the sea looks
almost as blue as the Mediterranean. The Steamer going daily to
Dieppe tempts one hugely: but I am obliged to be within reach of
London: having incessant small business to transact there & with a
multiplicity of small labours publishers &c. I have just sent off an
article to the Edinburgh: but I rather expect to see it come back on
my hands: for the Editor though a learned man and Editor of the
Encyclopaedia Britannica as well is evidently a dull personage: and
two to one won't relish what I've sent him. What about the dearest
little Minny? I hope it's only thin she is: not unwell. I'd give a
guinea to hear her little voice — every now and then among the
crowds of children here of course I'm reminded of her and Anny:
and grow sentimental God bless them. Lettsom at Paris went to
see my wife. He says she was perfectly collected and reasonable
asked him about America, and suggested subjects of conversation:
but her letters to me are still entirely rambling and desperately
foolish. For the first 2 or 3 days after my arrival here I knew
nobody for a wonder. Now however the town is filling with plenty
of London friends. Yesterday I saw Mrs FitzGerald arrive in great
state — four in hand an army of flunkies and ladies' maids — and
piles of mysterious imperials — There's a prospect of good dinners!
The old woman's compliments are however overpowering to me:
and to hear how the toadies who surround her compliment *her* is a
good moral lesson. Ainsworth is here in a grand house doing
nothing. His pretty girl is come out again into the world but not
cured. The poor child's intellect is evidently gone, and she is only

not an idiot. God bless all. My wrist is quite tired with scribbling
for the pen hasn't left it all day.

Write to London. I don't know when I shall go though: in ten
days probably. I have plenty to keep me till then.

W M T.

322.　　　TO PROFESSOR MACVEY NAPIER
　　　SEPTEMBER 1845

Hitherto unpublished. My text is taken from a transcript supplied by Mrs.
Fuller.

88, St. James's Street,<br>Tuesday.

My dear Sir,

I am very much pleased and flattered by your kind opinion of
the Willisian article.[40] On reading it over I agree with you quite
that it would have been better for a little farther explanation between the critic and the reader: but it is very hard to insert it now.
I propose to alter a sentence at page 3, which does not do much: but
it serves perhaps to prepare the reader for Willis, in the character
of Sly [41] or Bottom introduced to splendors quite unknown to him.

"A Republican visiting an aristocratic Country for the first
time" [42] are his own words in the preface. He has written Pencil-
lings by the way and a half score of other books, with a great deal of
cleverness, almost of genius in them strange to say, but I think it is
fair to take him at his own word.

The extract about freexistence [43] is put forward by him with
perfect solemnity — of course I don't suppose he believes it but it is
fair to take him at his own word here too.

[40] Thackeray's review of Dashes at Life, which appeared in The Edinburgh
Review, October, 1845, pp. 470–480. For the alteration mentioned below,
see p. 471.

[41] See the Induction to The Taming of the Shrew and A Midsummer
Night's Dream, III, i.

[42] Willis wrote "monarchical country." Thackeray quotes this phrase twice,
pp. 471 and 480.

[43] See pp. 476–480.

We have it in black and white and he writes in the first person.

I am told by men who know him here: that some of the adventures did *almost* happen. Some old women did actually fall in love with him: he positively made a great *fureur* once in a certain English Society and he has now garbled his amours and republished them. The Baroness R. is a famous literary old lady who used to kiss and hug him — not Lady Morgan, "Lady Rachel" (a woman whom he describes as kissing him and declaring her love for him) very likely did so: as she did the same thing to a friend of mine in whose company Willis once bragged of this lady's favors etc., etc. The stories have a sort of truth, a pennyworth say to an intolerable deal of fiction,[44] and I should think that certain persons here and a great number in America will relish a joke at poor N. P's. expense.

Most faithfully yours my dear Sir,

W. M. Thackeray.

323.       TO PROFESSOR MACVEY NAPIER
16 OCTOBER 1845

Published in part, *Correspondence of Macvey Napier*, ed. Napier, p. 499. My text is taken from a transcript supplied by Mrs. Fuller.

88, St. James's Street,
October 16.

My dear Sir,

I have just received and acknowledge with many thanks your bankers' bill for 21£: from them or from you I shall always be delighted to receive communications of this nature. From your liberal payment I can't but conclude that you reward me not only for laboring but for being mutilated in your service. I assure you I suffered cruelly by the amputation which you were obliged to inflict upon my poor dear paper. I mourn still, as what father can help doing for his children? For several lovely jokes and promising facetiae which were born and might have lived but for your scissors urged by ruthless necessity. I trust however there are many more

---

[44] "O monstrous! but one half-pennyworth of bread to this intolerable deal of sack!" (*I Henry IV*, II, iv, 591–592)

which the future may bring forth; and which will meet with more favor in your eyes.

I thought Defoe [45] excellent (recognizing the hand of course immediately); it is the only article in the Review I have read for somehow Messrs. Longman haven't sent me a copy.

I quite agree with your friends, who say Willis' was too leniently used, O to think of my pet passages gone for ever.

Very faithfully yours dear Sir<br>W. M. Thackeray.

## 324.        TO MRS. CARMICHAEL-SMYTH
### 18 OCTOBER 1845

*Address:* M^rs Carmichael Smyth | 81 Champs Élysées | Paris. *Postmark:* 18 OC 1845. Hitherto unpublished.

2 Foxley Place. Camberwell New Road.

My dearest Mammy. M^rs Gloyne has very good naturedly proposed to go and fetch me my wife, and we have arranged that she is to leave this on Tuesday ev^g or Wednesday morning    She will be with you then in Paris on Friday or Thursday and can set off so as to be in Boulogne on Monday where I will be in waiting to bring the pair over — Good God why not all come to England. Tell G P every man who knows how to survey is eagerly engaged by the railroads at five to ten guineas a day.[46] It is a fact indeed: and I know such lots of railroad directors, that he might almost be sure to get employment    I will give you all a house at Richmond if you come    I saw a pretty furnished one there for the winter m^os for a guinea a week. God bless all

W M T.

[45] The article following Thackeray's in the October number of *The Edinburgh Review*.

[46] The winter of 1845–1846 witnessed the climax of the feverish outburst of speculation known as the railway mania, in which Thackeray, like nearly every other owner of railroad shares, lost what money he had invested. His "Diary of C. Jeames de la Pluche, Esq." (*Punch*, December 6, 1845–February 7, 1846) is the chief literary record of the boom.

I shall ⟨send⟩ M⟨rs⟩ Gloyne at all events unless I sh⟨d⟩ hear before Tuesday that my wife is already on the way.

I'll send a letter to Puzin by M⟨rs⟩ G. short & alluding to nothing

325.        TO MRS. CARMICHAEL-SMYTH
28 NOVEMBER 1845

*Address:* M⟨rs⟩ Carmichael Smyth | 81 Champs Élysées | Paris. *Postmarks:* 28 NO 1845, 30 NOV. 45 BOULOGNE. Extract published, *Biographical Introductions,* V, xxxii-xxxiii.

My dearest Mammy. I have been so awfully busy for the last 4 days that Ive never had a quarter of an hour before post time to send you a certificate of health. I thrive with the work thank God: and plunge about from one thing to another with an activity surprising in one of my age size and corpulence. The Chronicle articles are very well liked — they relieve the dullness of the estimable paper. We are all agog about the adhesion of Lord John and Lord Morpeth to the Corn Laws [47] — Peel is to go out they say, and Whigs resume sway — What a lickspittle of a country it is, where a couple of Lords who have held aloof from the Corn-law battle calmly step in at the end of it, head the party and take all the prize-money. What a fine fellow Cobden is — His speech in to days paper is a model of oratory I think — so manly clear and upright. Shall I be able to come and see you at Christmas? I hope *not:* for if I dont come it will be for a very good reason, and to put some money in my purse.[48] This is the place to earn it. Ah what would I give to — but never mind talking. Heres a note for Anny — it took me about two hours: during the whole of w⟨h⟩ time I was blubbering — But they are best with you: nothing could replace you — no lady the best to be had for money.

Your letter is just come in — It is a story of a Cock as well as a

---

[47] Lord John Russell announced his conversion to free trade in a manifesto dated November 22 and printed in *The Times* on November 27. He was supported by George Howard (1802–1864), styled Viscount Morpeth, later (1848) seventh Earl of Carlisle.

[48] *Othello,* Act I, Scene iii.

Bull I'm sure. The thing is impossible. I have sent the letter to Jeames White: who will look to it. The little woman is wonderfully well, and I am very glad you gave me the caution. What a fool to say I gave presents! But M<sup>rs</sup> Bakewell is to all seeming an excellent worthy woman. The difference in the poor little woman's appearance is remarkable now that she has some one to look after her and keep her clean. She has been on a visit to M<sup>rs</sup> Nasmythe and indulges herself in excursions in a fly — My visits please her exceedingly. God bless her so I go almost every other day. My railroad matters are very bad: but I have bought the share and am holding in hopes of better times. Atkinson Mary's friend was the unlucky fellow who let me in to the loss: — it was against all calculations, and more knowing hands than I have suffered desperately. I shall soon please God be able to clear my little losings. But the till has been swept quite clean. Dont however fancy I am pressed I can get as much as I want any day — My credit is wonderful among the booksellers and I have only to ask and have      God bless all.

W M T.

326.                FROM THOMAS FRASER
                    7 DECEMBER 1845

Hitherto unpublished.

9 Boulevard des Capucins<br>7 December 1845

My dear Thackeray

You have got the character of being very good natured and I am going to put that quality, if you possess it to the test, by asking you to assist me in getting some information for a man of whose name you probably never heard in the whole course of your life.

General Pepe [49] a Neapolitan general of high rank who commanded Murats army, and who saw a great deal of service during the Peninsular and Italian campaigns is about to publish his memoirs and is anxious that they should appear simultaneously in

---

[49] Guglielmo Pepe (1783–1855).

Italian, French & English.[50] The memoirs are written, & I have
seen the table of contents. They certainly promise well, being full
of incidents connected with the events which occurred at Naples in
Nelson's time, accounts of the events during the Peninsular war
where General Pepe commanded a French brigade, the insurrection
in Naples in 1820 of which the general was the concocter & leader
&c &c and I have no doubt but they would take well with the
English public. Do you think Chapman & Hall, with whom I believe you are in connexion, would be inclined to treat for such a
work? General Pepe applied to Colburn who at once agreed to
publish it going half profits, but that plan would not suit the General who would prefer a fixed sum.

If Chapman & Hall were inclined to entertain the affair the
whole or a portion of the MS. could be sent over for their inspection.

Will you have the kindness to enquire into this. You will be
doing me a great favour.

I saw your *people* a few days ago. They gave a very pleasant
party at the Maison Vallin. Your little girls were as merry as
crickets and appear in excellent health.

A prompt enquiry about Pepe's affair will greatly oblige me.
Believe me always

very sincerely yrs

Thomas Fraser.


327.                    TO  EDWARD  CHAPMAN
                       DECEMBER  ?  1845 [51]

Hitherto unpublished.

Dear Sir

Before the book goes to press it must be written I have been so
harassed by work the last fortnight that I have not been able to

---

[50] The *Memoirs of General Pepe* were published by Bentley in 1846. An
Italian edition appeared in the same year and a French edition a year later.

[51] This letter was probably written not long before December 22, when
Thackeray had apparently finished work on *Notes of a Journey from Cornhill
to Grand Cairo*. See below, No. 328.

write the Egyptian chapter. However it is all plain sailing and I set to work to day —

I will make up a Frontispiece for the book in a day or two. The gentleman who came from you respecting the Perkins woodblocks was good enough to say he w^d breakfast here on Monday and begin his labours. But I have not had time yet. Will you kindly with my compliments beg him to put off our meeting for a few days until I can be ready for him.[52]

Faithfully yours<br>W M Thackeray.

328.       TO EDWARD CHAPMAN<br>
             22 DECEMBER 1845

Hitherto unpublished.

22 Dec^r

My dear Sir

My servant brings with him, the dedication & preface & title to the Cornhill & Cairo w^h he will carry on to the Printers if you desire.

The enclosed letter is from my friend M^r Fraser Paris Coresp^t of the Morning Chronicle: relating to the memoirs of General Pépé a famous Neapolitan liberal of bygone times, who has a mind to publish his memoirs. As Napoleon came to the Prince Regent of England when in misfortune so Pepe comes to the threshold of Chapman & Hall.

One more favour; — would the accompanying story answer for your novel series or for the Edinburgh Tales? It is by the lady who wrote the popular series about Talleyrand in the N. M. Magazine [53] Would you kindly look at it in her behalf and mine.

Yours ever faithfully<br>W M Thackeray.

[52] The publication of *Mrs. Perkins's Ball* was delayed until the Christmas season of 1846.

[53] The articles on "The Late Prince Talleyrand" which were published in *The New Monthly Magazine* between January, 1844, and April, 1845, appear to have been the work of Thackeray's friend Mrs. Colmache.

329.               TO MRS. PROCTER?
                   27 DECEMBER 1845

Hitherto unpublished.

27 December —

I saw the little ones at M^r Macready's last night, and charged
them with a blessing for their parents.  Let that parting benediction
be now repeated in writing

it will soothe the bitterness of the adieu — may it be remembered
in the loneliness of absence!

Titmarsh goes back to the home of his children, the abode of his
blood-kindred — glad to press once more to his heart those beings
to whom Nature has given the warmest place there, but sorry —
ah how sorry!  to leave friends whose cordiality has bound him as
fondly as even the ties of relationship, whose smiling hospitality

has lit up his life with a thousand glad emotions; whose kindness as
it has made his heart glad hitherto, shall henceforth in absence
people it with sweet memories — Yes let the Future lower or
brighten as it will — the Past is ours! The treasure of grateful
spirits and friendly souls — over the Past Fate has no controul. It
is ours' as long as we merit to possess it — as long as we are not
callous to friendship, or forgetful of benefits — Ah let us be cautious
of the inestimable gift, and guard it better than we have done other
grosser and more substantial favours of fortune!

Farewell — my brain reels my eyes are full — I have only
courage left to write that I am ever

Your Anna Maria

330.        TO MRS. CARMICHAEL-SMYTH
30 DECEMBER 1845

*Address:* Mʳˢ Carmichael Smyth | 81 Champs Élysées | Paris. *Postmarks:* 30
DE 1845, 1 JANV. 46 BOULOGNE. Published in part, *Thackeray and his
Daughter*, pp. 19–20.

My dearest Mammy I had intended to set off for a weeks pleasuring with you to day and have come in upon the New Year's day
dinner: but I went a day behind hand in my work and as I see there
is no chance of being with you shall wait till Saturday & cross by a
Brighton or Southampton Boat — It is blowing a tempest here to
day too and I'm not sorry for the 3 days' delay. My dearest
Nanny's letter set me longing so to see all that I must come though
its not worth the while — though the pain of parting is much
greater than the pleasure of meeting — at least to my ill-regulated
mind. The house has slipped through my fingers and all I have
got is 2 servants to keep & nothing for them to do. A place however I will have and I'll have it big enough for every one of you so
that there shall be no reason why you should not see me. G. P is
as free of encumbrances as I am now. Tell him with my love I have
plenty of money to pay the bill when it comes; and we will chalk it
off the score for the babbies' board.

I have written I don't know how much letters to him & to
Charles on the horrible dispute between them. However I had best
perhaps not stick in my oar except in so far as concerns myself —
Here is my version of the unfair payments that have been made to
me — Of course I shall be bound to pay back Charles his 450 [54] —
What a time the debt comes upon one be hanged to it when the
exchequer is just emptied! But I'm not afraid of it — and dont like
to startle you by telling you what a big income I shall have next
year — Enough to clear my other encumbrancies and pay 1/2 the
450 besides please God. I didn't send the enclosed to Chas because
I dont know what G P means to do or sufft.$^{ly}$ the nature of the claims
made: what I dread is future litigation into w$^h$ Will [55] as sure as
fate will push us. But more of this when we meet this day week
please God

Tell my dear little Nanny I have got some books for her and
some pictures for Minny my heart is with them all day and with
my dearest old Mother.

In one of Anny's letters she wrote we have got a black *nuss* not
puss I thought it was a natural Yellowplushism — and was in
truth very much disgusted at the idea of the nigger bonne. God
bless all: and give you and me & my dear old G P a happy new
year.

331.                 TO ANNE THACKERAY
                    30 DECEMBER 1845

*Address:* Miss Thackeray | 81 Champs Élysées | Paris. Published in *Bio-
graphical Introductions*, VI, xxii.

                                        Dec$^r$ 30, 1845

My dearest Nanny

Your letter has made me and Mamma very happy, and very sad
too that we are away from our dearest little girls. But I for one
shall see you before very long, I hope in a week from this day, &

[54] Thackeray had repaid to the Carmichaels only £50 of the £500 that he
borrowed from Mary in 1841.
[55] William Henry Carmichael-Smyth (d. 1846) of the Bengal Civil Service,
Major Carmichael-Smyth's brother.

only write now to wish you a happy new Year. On Christmas day I dined with Mamma and she was very well and happy, only she grew very grave when we talked about you; and there were tears in her eyes the meaning of which I knew quite well. How glad I am that it is a black *puss* & not a black *nuss* you have got! I thought you did not know how to spell nurse & had spelt it en-you-double-ess. But I see the spelling gets better as the letters grow longer: they cannot be too long for me. Laura [56] must be a very good natured girl. I hope my dear Nanny is so too — not merely to her schoolmistress and friends but to everybody: — to her servants and her nurses. I would sooner have you gentle and humble-minded than ever so clever. Who was born on Christmas day? Somebody who was so great that all the world worships him; and so good that all the world loves him; and so gentle & humble that he never spoke an unkind word. But I hope my Nanny is proud with no one. And there is a little sermon, and a great deal of love and affection from Papa. May God send my dearest children many happy new years.

I wonder who will kiss Minny for me?

332.     TO GEORGE PRYME
DECEMBER 1845? [57]

Hitherto unpublished.

88 S<sup>t</sup> James's S<sup>t</sup> Wednesday

My dear M<sup>r</sup> Pryme

I am engaged to dine with my wife on Thursday; and as it is the only free day I have this week I must not disappoint her. But those little parties are over very early: and if you will allow me to come in the evening and pay my respects to M<sup>r</sup> Pryme I shall be very glad indeed.

Very faithfully yours
W M Thackeray.

[56] Laura Colmache, daughter of Mrs. Colmache, who figures in *Chapters*, pp. 44 and 153.
[57] This note was perhaps written to Pryme not long before Thackeray dined with him on December 26, 1845. See below, Appendix XI.

### 333.     TO WILLIAM HARRISON AINSWORTH
1845? [58]

Facsimile published in Adrian Joline's *Meditations of an Autograph Collector* (New York and London, 1902), after p. 66.

> 88 St. James's St
> Monday

My dear Ainsworth.

Will you give me your name at the G [59] for Thursday at 6, and come and dine with me there? I want to ask 3 or 4 of the littery purfession.

> Yrs always
> W M T.

Answer here


### 334.     TO MAJOR CARMICHAEL-SMYTH
JANUARY? 1846 [1]

Hitherto unpublished.

My dear Father. Accompanying this is a state-manifesto of w.h I keep a copy, and w.h I should like to send to Charles. Were anything to happen to you, Will [2] would push him into law: — and whatever you leave would be swallowed up by the lawyers amongst them.

Whatever you have I don't know — I don't as I needn't tell you, want a shilling of it: but it will be a great thing to have the question settled — Give Charles his dividend in God's name. Shut up the Paris house, and come over and live with me. It will be a saving to all of us: give me a home w.h I am weary of being without: and

[58] Thackeray had rooms at 88 St. James's Street only between April, 1845, and June, 1846.

[59] The Garrick Club.

[1] This letter was written shortly after Thackeray's letter to his mother of December 30, 1845.

[2] William Henry Carmichael-Smyth.

give the greatest happiness I am sure to my dearest Mother; whose happiness I know you look to beyond anything else in the world.

I have lost the Chester Street house. *Lubbocks refused to answer to my respectability:* though I wrote to them saying (what was under the mark) that my engagements would bring me 1200£ this year, and begging them to do me this kindness. It was not polite but Im glad of it. We will have a bigger house in some cheap unfashionable quarter.

After I have paid off the 200£ w^h I owe (the money 250£ was pressed upon me and I wish to God the lender had left it alone: for I should never have lost it) — I must get to work to pay off Charles or Mary her 450£. Three years will please God pay off the 2 sums: if I have a steady home to go to — My position is now to all appearances so good, that I may calculate on laying by at least 500 next year. I am engaged to write a monthly story at 60£ a number — I have besides 700£ between Punch & the Chronicle: though I dont calculate on the latter beyond the year as I am a very weak & poor politician only good for outside articles and occasional jeux d'esprit — The 400 may subside possibly into 2 or 300 but you see there will be enough and to spare.

335.            TO MRS. PROCTER
                JANUARY? 1846

Hitherto unpublished. My text is taken from a transcript given Lady Ritchie by George Murray Smith.

My dear Mrs Procter,

I have just received the enclosed billet from the man who is pensioned while starves a knowles.[3] At dinner to-day I will tell you how I came to knock at your door yesterday: and am meanwhile scribbling scribbling for the dear life — this is scribbling paper and

---

[3] It was thought by some that the £200 pension which Tennyson was granted on October 15, 1845, should have gone to the veteran playwright, James Sheridan Knowles. Among Knowles's partisans was Bulwer-Lytton, who attacked "School-Miss Alfred" for the effeminacy of his poetry in the second part of *The New Timon*, published January 12, 1846. Bulwer-Lytton con-

not the beautiful gilt edged which ought to be used by the hurried,

Titmarsh.

### 336.    TO WILLIAM CHARLES MACREADY
### 6 FEBRUARY 1846

Hitherto unpublished.

88 S<sup>t</sup> James's S<sup>t</sup>  Friday.

My dear Sir

White has been here just now in rather a wild tone of dejection about the play.[4] He says you think my dictum of *'safe'* an unsatisfactory kind of praise, and are doubtful whether you should go to the boards and peril his future reputation upon The King of the Commons & a slender success.

What I meant by 'safe' is the best word to be applied to a play I think: safe of a real agreeable — of course I dont know how permanent — success. The play seems to me to be better than the Lady of Lyons with the exception of the admirable climax of the latter — always pleasing, tender, jovial — interesting in a word. The main character a capital hearty *rôle* to go to the public with. I have brought away the most pleasant impression of it. What more is requisite? A work of supreme genius? {Who is the dramatist to write one?} I don't think this is or pretends to be one but it pleases exceedingly though it does not astonish: and, I take it, this is as

---

cludes his poem by charging his own muse to remain faithful to the Spartan standards of the eighteenth century,

Tho' Theban taste the Saxon's purse controuls,<br/>
And pensions Tennyson, while starves a Knowles.

Tennyson's scarifying reply "The New Timon, and the Poets," is reprinted in Lounsbury's *Tennyson*, pp. 526–527. Thackeray reviewed *The New Timon* in *The Morning Chronicle*, April 21, 1846, p. 5. This article has not previously been identified as his.

[4] Macready had received *The King of the Commons* from the Rev. James White on December 31, 1845. On February 5, 1846, he read it to a party of friends including Thackeray, and on the following day received this "Note from Thackeray, sticking up for White's play" (*Diaries*, ed. Toynbee, II, 317, 321). *The King of the Commons* was performed on May 20 with considerable success.

valuable a quality as any in a play. I speak here the truth the whole truth & nothing but the truth — But then who am I to be a critic?

Very faithfully yours

W M Thackeray.

337.        TO EDWARD FitzGERALD
FEBRUARY? 1846 [5]

Published in part, *Thackeray and Edward Fitzgerald*, ed. Shorter, pp. 13–14.

* * *

o such beastliness! It will be a lesson to me against pastry cooks for ever. Gurlyle has called twice upon me and I've returned the visit once in rather a haughty & patronizing way. Some good-natured friend told me something good natured he had said w[h] did not suit my humour [6] — Ive resigned at the Morning Chronicle: but am otherwise well doing. Why do I fill this letter with Is? — Tell me your Is dear old fellow. Nickisson & Blackwood both decline poor Morton's paper: and we shall have to put our hands in our pockets for poor honest Elizabeth. I have had more than one pensioner myself & expences innumerable but am good for a month £3.6.8.

---

[5] This letter seems to have been written between the appearance of *Notes of a Journey from Cornhill to Grand Cairo* in mid-January, 1846, and the publication of Thackeray's book review, "Carus's Travels in England," in *The Morning Chronicle* of March 16. This was his first literary article for the paper after his three reviews of Christmas books were printed on December 25, 26, and 31, 1845, though he may possibly have contributed political leaders in the interval. See Appendix XII.

[6] This story is told by Charles Gavan Duffy, reporting an interview with Carlyle in the summer of 1849: "I inquired if he saw much of Thackeray. No, he said, not latterly. Thackeray was much enraged with him because, after he made a book of travels for the P. & O. Company, who had invited him to go on a voyage to Africa in one of their steamers, he (Carlyle) had compared the transaction to the practice of a blind fiddler going to and fro on a penny ferry-boat in Scotland, and playing tunes to the passengers for halfpence. Charles Buller told Thackeray; and when he complained, it was necessary to inform him frankly that it was undoubtedly his opinion that, out of respect for himself and his profession, a man like Thackeray ought not to have gone fiddling for halfpence or otherwise, in any steamboat under the sky." (*Conversations with Carlyle*, pp. 76–77) See *Works*, VI, 112–114.

The last 2 months I have had poor young Coventry Patmore, thrown on the world, his father bolted,[7] he

\*   \*   \*

Lettsom is here like a good fellow. We went the other night to the Butlers' Club he has discovered      There was only one butler but he was very rich. I wish you could have heard him describe his residence with a family in Paris in the year when Munseer Dulong was shot by Marshal Bogo.[8] Bewjawd says I I think's the way of pronouncing the name. 'I *think* you'll find it Bogo' says he with a solemnity w$^h$ I can't describe: but it gratifies me to find that I described the place very accurately [9] before having seen it. Good Heavens how I'm astonished at the length of this. It is like one of Morton's letters for size. I am going to Brighton for 3 days holiday. God bless you my dear old friend — It does me good to shake you by the hand sometimes and think of hundreds & hundreds of years ago.

W M T.

338.        TO MRS. CARMICHAEL-SMYTH
            16 FEBRUARY 1846

*Address:* M$^{rs}$ Carmichael-Smyth | 81 Champs Élysées | Paris. *Postmarks:* BRIGHTON FE 16 1846, 18 FEVR. 46 BOULOGNE. Published in part, *Biographical Introductions*, V, xliii.

Monday.

My dearest Mammy. I have just got my foot in the stirrup to be off to Brighton for 2 or 3 days quiet & meditation: and have not

[7] Peter George Patmore and his wife departed precipitately from England late in 1845 after the failure of a wild speculation in railway shares. Their sons George and Coventry (1823–1896), the poet, whom they left behind, were reduced without warning from comfort to penury. Thackeray appears to have met Coventry at the Procters'.

[8] Thomas Robert Bugeaud de la Piconnerie (1784–1849), Marshal of France, killed François Charles Dulong in a duel on January 29, 1834.

[9] Thackeray mentions, but does not describe, the "Butlers' Club" at the "Wheel of Fortune" public-house in the final installment of "The Diary of C. Jeames de la Pluche, Esq.," which appeared in *Punch* on February 7, 1846, *Works*, III, 423.

a word to say even to fill this 1/2 sheet. Haven't I gorged you with flummery from the newspapers? [10] They are all mighty polite except one fellow (a friend of mine) who calls me a heartless & self-sufficient Cockney, w.ʰ I bear with entire good-humour. The book is not only praised but also sells very well. They have already got rid of 1000 more than the Irish book sold altogether — I have been house-hunting like a maniac. What do you say to a beautiful house and farm of seven acres at 3 miles from London? — Cocks hens paddocks gardens &c. This can be had for 200£ a year — a perfect country domain. I am making a failure at the Chronicle all my articles miss fire: except the literary ones. I shall be kicked out at the end of the year. I have been to dine with great people — Lord Melbourne [11] to whit — and I have met other genteel characters. I have but to keep a Brougham and be a man of the world during the season. But I am sick & tired of the world & of people of fashion & no fashion: and am in a most restless & misanthropic state.

Brighton. There was no use continuing my imaginary grievances. A little fresh air down here does one a power of good: only as the

[10] Representative reviews of *Notes of a Journey from Cornhill to Grand Cairo* will be found in *The Athenaeum*, January 24, pp. 89–91, and January 31, pp. 118–120; in *Fraser's Magazine*, January, pp. 85–96; in *The New Monthly Magazine*, February, pp. 240–243; and in *The Spectator*, January 24, 1846, pp. 88–89.

[11] "I met Lord Melbourne at dinner to-day," wrote Mrs. Caroline Norton to Antonio Panizzi in November, 1845, "and mentioned to him having seen you and Mr. Thackeray. He begged me to write for him, to ask you if you would dine with him on Monday, and Mr. Thackeray also. He has asked the Duff Gordons and Mr. Fonblanque for that day. Will you let me know as soon as convenient, and will you, who are an old friend of Lord Melbourne's, explain anything that may seem odd or blunt in this mode of inviting without introduction, though indeed he persists very obstinately that Mr. Thackeray is a clergyman, with whom he is, or ought to be, acquainted. I said I did not think it clerical to write about the Bishop of Bullochesmithy, and that I did not think Mr. Thackeray was a clergyman at all; but this is not of importance in comparison of his coming to dinner at half-past seven, punctual, on Monday." (Jane Gray Perkins, *The Life of the Honourable Mrs. Norton*, New York, 1909, p. 196) Lord Melbourne had no doubt confused Thackeray with one of his many clerical relatives. The Bishop of Bullocksmithy turns up often in Thackeray's books; see, for example, *Works*, VI, 344.

deuce will have it there are dinner-givers here too: whose hospitalities undo the service of the fresh air. More puffs of the book have
taken place. I shall continue to send you no more of these bulletins:
but let us offer up prayers for a second edition. I have brought
down here poor Blanchards Life and Works to make a notice of: [12]
the misfortune is that the works are of a very small-beer and
amiable kind: unsusceptible of much praise: hence the tone in w^h
the Critic speaks of them must seem forced & cold.

I'm in alarm about M^rs Colmache's paper.[13] I had it put up to
bring to Ainsworth and — forgot it. I told my servant where it
was & to post it — & it has never come. I hope it is not lost through
this fatal blundering.

God bless you all. I begin to be afraid lest dissatisfied as I am
without a home; I shall be equally restless when I get one: but I
want above all things to try.

Ever my dear old Mothers      Affte W M T.


339.      TO MRS. CARMICHAEL-SMYTH
6 MARCH 1846

*Address:* M^rs Carmichael-Smyth | 81 Champs Élysées | Paris. *Postmark:*
8 MR 1846. Hitherto unpublished.

Friday.

My dearest Mammy. I have had a letter begun these 4 days
and carried about in my pocket till it grew crumpled and past sending. It said nothing however. There are never any news. One
day's hurry and turmoil resembles the next, and with a great pother
I do wonderfully little. The consideration of these subjects always
makes me glum: that's why my letters to you are so dismal. And it
doesn't make me much happier to get yours', w^h give me fits of
homesickness. The M^rs is very well indeed and lively and tolerably
sensible: one of her letters to Anny begins very well indeed but it

[12] "A Brother of the Press on the History of a Literary Man," *Fraser's
Magazine*, March, 1846, pp. 332–342.
[13] See above, No. 328.

rambles off at the end to the Queen of Spain and the King of Hanover in unintelligible inanity — Aunt Becher sent me your letter; and a request for Titmarsh [14] w.h I sent her: and now comes an offer to pay from the good old soul. Also I have had a packet from Luc [15] — all the correspondence — with an appeal to my sense of justice and a request from Mary that I should read it. I don't think I shall, and have not yet read one line of it or answered her — I don't see what good I could do, or how it is possible to make friends now. The chronicle & I must part or I must cut down half the salary. They are most provokingly friendly all the time, and insist that I should neither resign nor disgorge — but how can one but act honorably by people who are so good-natured? Heighho I wish and I wish and I wish every day that you w(ere) here and I had a home w.h I should neglect when I had it. It is the nature of the beau to be dissatisfied.

My gaieties have had a considerable lull. I don't like or trust the new acquaintances, and shabby fashionable people. The women are abominably free and easy, and inspire one with involuntary doubts, that it is not all talk with them. M.rs Brookfield is my beau-ideal. I have been in love with her these four years — not so as to endanger peace or appetite but she always seems to me to speak and do and think as a woman should. You should have seen the three Camberwell ladies the other day, my wife M.rs Gloyne and M.rs Bakewell — one mending the right hand breeches pocket another the left the third a hole in my coat-tail! Such a Paris among these three Venuses. Nothing though can be more kind honest and goodnatured, and the Bakewell especially is a treasure I rather dread the husband though: and don't know how our evenings will pass in his company. Did you read Sir Henry Harding's [16] letter about the battle of Ferozeshah and he and 'dear little Arthur' [17]

[14] *Notes of a Journey from Cornhill to Grand Cairo.*

[15] Luc sur Mer, where Colonel and Mrs. Carmichael were staying.

[16] Sir Henry Hardinge (1785–1856), later (May 2, 1846) first Viscount Hardinge of Lahore, was Governor-General of India from 1844 to 1848 and made his administration notable by a campaign against the Sikhs.

[17] Major Arthur Somerset (b. 1816) was the older son of Lord Fitzroy Somerset (1788–1855), youngest son of the fifth Duke of Beaufort and as

standing in front of their line to prevent the men from firing? It is the prettiest story in the world of chivalry, and little Arthur's mother must be the happiest & proudest woman in England. I saw Lord Fitzroy Somerset walking in S.^t James's Park — with 2 girls in black, and absolutely crying. He had just quarreled with his son about a marriage before receiving the news of the poor fellow's death, in that tremendous carnage. It is quite curious to see how many *new suits* of black clothes there appear to be about Harley S.^t and in the Indian district. I am going to day to dine with the Prinseps and all the Pattle girls. [18] — By Jove I feel a hundred years old.

My dearest little Nanny's letter was capital. God bless both of them. By hook or by crook they must and shall come here soon: and all of you my dearest old Mother. My free mornings are past in house-hunting. I must light upon one before long.

Tell M.^rs Colmache with my best regards that her article will in all probability appear next month: but Ainsworth (with whom I made it a personal matter) is very full and though he would like occasional articles, can't take a regular series — indeed he has no space for them & does not even write himself    How I wish we had money to stock the 6 acre farm G P to manage & the girls to run about in it! God bless all. G. M must come to England & get well

340.          TO MRS. CARMICHAEL-SMYTH
                    MARCH 1846

Hitherto unpublished.

My dearest Mammy. You get on these rare occasions when I write at all, the fag-end of my day, when I am quite weary of the

first Baron Raglan (1852) commander of the English army in the Crimean War. Major Somerset had quarreled with his father over his marriage on July 8, 1845, to Emilie Louise, daughter of the Baron de Baumbach of Hesse. He was mortally wounded in the battle of Ferozeshah on December 21 and died four days later. This episode appears to have suggested to Thackeray George Osborne's quarrel with his father over his marriage to Amelia, shortly before his death at Waterloo.          [18] See above, No. 62, note 23.

sight of a pen and my hand aches with scribbling. That is why the letters have such a dismal tone I think. Its near 5 o'clock and it has been all day work work. & yesterday & 2 days before & tomorrow & so on. What a martyr I am to be sure! I shouldn't have written to day but for the money. I believe it is your money too that I send: for in the last 3 months I have been paying off old advances from publishers to enable me to meet that abominable Railroad Smash, and don't like to appear too greedy or needy with them. 'The Novel without a hero' [19] begins to come out on the first of May. I have done nothing to it since I came back, being pestered with innumerable small jobs and — not forced to it — that is the fact. I can't do anything now without force, and feel quite capable of carrying three or four packs more on my back. I spend my spare hours still house-hunting I have not the least fear of not myself getting on well — only of not being a good father of a family without a wife. I wouldn't break your heart and my children's for the sake of seeing them an hour a day. Unless I liked a Governess I couldn't live with her and if I did — O fie. The flesh is very weak, le coeur sent toujours le besoin d'aimer. What a mercy it is that I've kept clear hitherto — The dear little woman is extremely well at times. We have been to the play in a private box and she enjoys herself in her little way. I dine there when I can tomorrow and Thursday last. Only after a day's work it is poor holiday making.

Was it poor Barwell's death the 3ᵈ you speak of? That of Macleod the Captain of the Great Liverpool shocked me a great deal: and that awful principle of mistaken honor.[20] Who are Christians in the world? Priests and Aristocracy have killed the spirit of Christianity I think: the one by inventing curses, the other honor.

[19] *Vanity Fair.*
[20] The *Great Liverpool*, a steam ship of the Peninsular and Oriental Steam Navigation Company plying between Southampton and Alexandria, was wrecked on the coast of Galicia near Corunna on February 24, 1846. Though all on board but three were saved and Captain Macleod was acquitted of blame — the disaster being attributed to a variation of the current caused by the prevailing wind — he afterwards committed suicide. (*Annual Register,* 1846, pp. 36–37)

What a moral sentiment! I get painfully moral every day and find myself talking so much and practising so little that I'm very very much afraid my dearest Mammy that your dearly beloved Son is only a — I'm quite sure it is wrong of you to be so awfully proud of certain people as you evidently are. Who is humble? My dear old G P is a humble man I think. I wish you were all seated at my humble board: eating humble pie for I'm very hungry & tired. I have been poring over the life of David Hume all day: the most amiable & honest of heathens: his life is excellently selfish and good-humoured & correct and he went out of the world quite unconcerned and with a grin on his face, entering into Eternity as if he were stepping into a Court ball. I have written a little article about the book [21] w.<sup>h</sup> is a very heavy one: and it is remaining *undigested* upon me — a great nuisance — And tomorrow I must go plunge into something else. Now I must go and dress and take a little walk and then — O the beefsteaks won't I punish them. It is a pleasure to dine alone as I shall do, and think of you and my dear dear little women

W M T.

341.                    TO MRS. PROCTER
                    24 APRIL 1846

Hitherto unpublished. My text is taken from a transcript given Lady Ritchie by George Murray Smith.

88, St James Street,
24 April.

My dear Mrs Procter,

It is most provoking that all your good intentions fail regarding me. I have got the toothache very bad, and am engaged on the 6th too. Let me be consoled by hearing that you at any rate are happy and are free of the ojous influenza,

Yours ever, dear Mrs Procter,
W. M. Thackeray.

[21] Thackeray's review of *The Life and Correspondence of David Hume*

I have often thought since how entirely natural unaffected and agreeable one of your guests made himself the last time I dined with you. I don't mean me, nor Colson.[22]


342.                    TO MRS. PROCTER
                       26 APRIL 1846

Hitherto unpublished. My text is taken from a transcript given Lady Ritchie by George Murray Smith.

88, St James Street,
Sunday, April 26, 1846.

Mr William Thackeray will have very much pleasure in dining with Mr and Mrs Procter on Sunday the 8th of May. He hopes to hear that Mrs Procter's indisposition has ceased and that she is restored to that drawing-room of which woman is ever the most *elegant ornament* in the opinion of Mr William Thackeray.

But Mr William Thackeray had much rather not go to the Dentist's, as his tooth is a favourite still, although it has given him such pain. And how often (Mr William Thackeray remarks) are we loth to part from those whom long attachment has bound to us, although their conduct is only a source of affliction to us, and we know them to be rotten at the core!

That Mrs Procter has often experienced the truth of this observation Mr William Thackeray is quite sure, and oh, how earnestly Mr William Thackeray prays that a lady so amiable as Mrs Procter, may never be called upon by Fate, by toothache, by the conduct of friends, or the ingratitude of her numerous children, to say "Alas! Mr William Thackeray's remark was only (as usual) too correct!

---

(1846) by John Hill Burton (1809–1881) appeared in *The Morning Chronicle* on March 23. It has not previously been identified as his.

[22] Possibly Jasint Colson, 26 Store Street, Bedford Square (*Royal Blue Book*, 1846).

## 343. TO EDWARD MARLBOROUGH FITZGERALD
### 30 APRIL 1846

Hitherto unpublished.

88 S.$^{t}$ James's S.$^{t}$ 30 April. 1846.

Dear FitzGerald

Let me entreat that we may meet no more upon the subject of your present most unhappy position. My counsel to you I repeat w.$^{h}$ is to quit the Country: you have no other course.

Reflect that by remaining here you can do no good. Going to prison will not discharge your great or small debts. One of the bitterest of all the bitter mortifications you have to endure, will be thus leaving the servants & poor tradesmen with their claims unsatisfied.[23] If you could pay them by staying I would say stay.

As for the children and your desire to have them with you — reflect for their own welfare w.$^{h}$ is the better lot for them to be with their mother or with you? Think how you have neglected them & how admirably & tenderly she has cared for them. To separate them from her would be the greatest crime of all. She has a right to keep them, & *to take any steps to keep them.* Think of the details being published of the cause w.$^{h}$ has led her to demand a separation — that you brought your mistress into your house — that you introduced your daughter to your mistress — the long story of passion, ill-treatment, neglect on your part. The ⟨other⟩ dispute is quite a trifle compared to this one, w.$^{h}$ w.$^{d}$ ruin you past hope. Go away in God's name & work & humble ⟨yourself⟩ and amend. Try & be worthy of your wife & children when you come back to claim them. Depend upon it that tender & affectionate creature who has pardoned you so much without repentance on your part, will not be hard-hearted when you amend. But prove it. You are bound to do this as clearly as any other criminal

If you choose to go to any cheap town abroad I will give you means — a pound a week say for the next 6 months — to exist upon.

[23] This is a theme on which Thackeray enlarges in *Vanity Fair*. See particularly chapters 36 and 37.

During that time you can write enough to keep you [an]other 6 months. Send me over your papers & I will try & dispose of them here. I will give you 5£ to go away & 5£ to the poor washerwoman. God knows I don't write in any proud spirit. May Heaven pardon the sins of both of us.

I must beg you not to call upon me — I have told you why I myself have avoided you. Ever since I heard that fatal story about poor Isabella I could not find it in me to show a confidence w$^h$ existed no more. Nor in spite of your denials can I resist King-lake's testimony against you. I dont mean as regards the injury past. I wish to God I could say not guilty.

As soon as you are ready to move Send me word & you shall have the little viaticum. Farewell & believe me

Sincerely yours<br>W M T.

## 344.          TO WILLIAM CHARLES MACREADY? [24]<br>JUNE 1846

Hitherto unpublished.

13 Young S$^t$<br>Kensington.  Wednesday

My dear Sir.

We feed Ibrahim Pasha on Friday here: [25] or I sh$^d$ have had the greatest pleasure.

Your note went to another member of this club Martin Thackeray my name is Villiam like that of a well known dramatic author and artist.

Most sincerely yours<br>W M Thackeray.

[24] If it is assumed that this note is to Macready, the otherwise pointless allusion to "a well known dramatic . . . artist" in the second paragraph is explained.

[25] Thackeray describes the banquet for Ibrahim Pasha given at the Reform Club late in June in his article on Soyer's *Gastronomic Regenerator*. See above, No. 274, August 15, 1844.

345.        TO MRS. CARMICHAEL-SMYTH
              2 JULY 1846

*Address:* Mrs Carmichael-Smyth | 81 Champs Élysées | Paris. *Postmarks:*
PAID 3 JU 1846. Published in part, *Thackeray and his Daughter*, pp. 21–22.

13 Young St Kensington. July 2.

My dearest Mammy. GP. writes me word that you are unwell
and that a change of air w{d} do you good: What such a good change
as to come here with the little ones, and GM for whom there is a
capital room: and GP. who says he w{d} be nervous about coming —
but who has no more cause to be frightened than I. Who is to
attack him? His only creditor the railroad is broken up and gone
the deuce knows where — Whenever the Gas Company ask for
their 5/ in the pound they shall have it; but it is my impression the
matter is quite out of their mind and that they will never apply
unless bothered to do so. I do beg pray implore and entreat him
to come — I know you won't be happy without him with that ingenious knack you have of making yourself uncomfortable: and I
hope & pray in God that we shall all be able to live together and
that I may not be deprived of my mother & my children. There are
2 capital bed-rooms & a little sitting room for you & GP — a
famous bed room for G. M. on the first floor — 2 rooms for the
children on second very airy & comfortable; a couple of rooms big
enough for Servants, & 2 little ones quite large enough for me —
There's a good study for me down stairs & a dining room & drawing room, and a little court yard or garden and a little green house:
and Kensington Gardens at the gate, and omnibuses every 2
minutes What can mortal want more? [26] — If I ask my friends I

---

[26] Thackeray made his home at 13 Young Street from June, 1846, till May,
1854. "It was not till late in the autumn that we came to live with my father
at Kensington," writes Lady Ritchie (*Biographical Introductions*, I, xxvii–
xxviii). "It was a dark wintry evening. The fires were lighted, the servants
were engaged, Eliza — what family would be complete without its Eliza? —
was in waiting to show us our rooms. He was away; he had not expected us so
early. We saw the drawing-room, the empty study; there was the feeling of
London — London smelt of tobacco, we thought; we stared out through the

can ask them to my own quarters — We may all be independent &
together — What will your eating & drinking cost? — not 60£ for
the two — Let GM contribute what she likes — and how much
does an whole establishment stand us in?  500£ a year will go a
very great way to keep it: I'm sure.  At all events I ask it as a favor
that the Experiment should be tried: and am sure that we shall all
be the happier & better for it.  I'm not ready for you yet: but hope
in a fortnight to be prepared — I have been opening the trunks to
day  Full of the lumbering useless old books; and woful relics of
old days — In one of them I find a power of old shirts of mine
from India; and sheets napkins & napkins and table cloths very
welcome.  All the wooden beds I have confiscated without exception and will have nothing but iron — Not knowing who's box is
who's I came on one I take to be Grandmamma's — a venerable
repository of old workboxes &c, I have shut it down & shall consign
it solemnly to her room —

God bless my dearest little women.  It will be a comfort to me
to see them and I look to Kensington Gardens, & to breakfasting

---

uncurtained windows at the dark garden behind; and then climbing the stairs,
we looked in at his bedroom door, and came to our own rooms above it. There
were pictures ready hung on the walls of the schoolroom, and of the adjoining
fire-lit nursery — the Thorwaldsen prints, Hunt's delightful sleepy boy
yawning at us over the chimney-piece, all of which he had caused to be put
up; and the picture of himself as a child he had hung up with his own hands,
Eliza told us.

"Once more, after his first happy married years, my father had a home and a
family — if a house, two young children, three servants, and a little black cat
can be called a family.

"My grandmother, who had brought us over to England, returned to her
husband in Paris; but her mother, an old lady wrapped in Indian shawls,
presently came to live with us, and divided her time between Kensington and
the Champs Elysées until 1848, when she died at Paris. We did not see very
much of our great-grandmother; she rarely spoke, and was almost always in
her room; but though my father was very busy, and often away from home,
we seemed to live with him, and were indeed with him constantly — in the
early mornings, and when he was drawing, and on Sundays especially, and on
holidays when the work was finished. We often went for little expeditions
together, which he liked. He was well and strong, and able both to work and
to enjoy life to the full."

For Lady Ritchie's further memories of Young Street, see *Chapters*, pp.
73–102.

together; and to many a happy day please God. Their mother is
so well and calm, that when they are of an age suff.! she will be
quite well able too to come back to us — and I cant be sufficiently
thankful for that famous old M.ʳ Bakewell's admirable care of her.
Gloyne too has been as good as good can be —

I pity Mary poor soul and her renewed misfortune & disappointment. Will you ever come together again I wonder?

I find the greatest comfort and enjoyment in the quiet of this
place after the racket of S.! James's S.! I am going to quit the
Chronicle very likely but if I do it will be for something better.
God bless my dearest mother

W M T.

346.              TO JANE SHAWE
                  JULY 1846

*Address:* Miss Ja⟨ne Shawe⟩ ²⁷ | Casino d⟨  ⟩ | presso Li⟨vorno⟩ | I⟨talia⟩.
*Postmarks:* Camberwell, LIVORNO 23 1846. Published in *Thackeray and
his Daughter*, pp. 22–23.

*    *    *

What shall I tell you about my dear little girls? I see as little of
them as you do almost. I have just taken a house big enough for
the whole family: but I cannot get Major Smyth to come to England, and so I lose my mother and my children too for some time
at least. It would break her heart to part with them: and I can't
bear that she should be alone and separated from us all. Here is
the last report just come from Paris about Anny. "I assure you
Nanny wants a firmer hand than mine. She fights every inch of
her way — if it's only to wash her face or put on her stockings she
will not do it without an argument — She is so clever: so selfish: so
generous: so tender-hearted yet so careless of giving pain." — I am
afraid very much she is going to be a man of genius: I would far
sooner have had her an amiable & affectionate woman — But little
Minny will be that, please God. — and the Sisters love each other
admirably. As for me I am child-sick, and when I see in Kensing-

---

²⁷ The first half of this letter (and with it most of the address) has been lost.

ton Gardens or my friends' houses a pair of little girls at all resembling my own, become quite maudlin over them.

In my trade I am getting on very well: and doing everything
but saving money. Good bye my dear Jane, and remember that I
am always as in old times affectionately yours

W M Thackeray

347.                    TO JOHN FORSTER
                        18 JULY 1846

Hitherto unpublished.

13 Young St Kensington<br>July 18. 1846.

My dear Forster.

What time will the Richmond business occur? — on Wednesday
isn't it? — I only remember it just this minute, after accepting an
invitation from Sir F. Pollock, wh I shouldn't like to miss —
When will you come and see my new domain? — on Tuesday at
6 o'clock? I owe Collinson [28] a dinner & have asked him: and offer
you a share of mutton-chop.

What a wonderful manifesto in the Times this morning! [29] —
what a deplorable consternation in my camp! —

Yours<br>W M T.

[28] Henry Collinson, 46 Inner Temple Hall Staircase (*Royal Blue Book*,
1846), who was called to the bar on November 20, 1846 (*Law List*, 1858).

[29] A pompous leader in *The Times* of July 18 defended Lord John Russell's
coalition cabinet and ridiculed the contention that a ministry must have a
mouthpiece among the London newspapers, asserting that it is shameful to see
"any member of the British press reduced to the subjection which that implies." This blast was directed against *The Morning Chronicle*, a Whig
journal often employed for government pronouncements, the editorial policy of
which was opposed to the inclusion of Tories in Russell's cabinet.

348.          TO MRS. CARMICHAEL-SMYTH
                    18 JULY 1846

Hitherto unpublished.

I must send my dearest Mammy two words I know in consideration of the anniversary; though I don't see why such ought to be
kept, or that any of us have any particular occasion for pride or
thankfulness at my being five and thirty. Sackcloth and ashes
would be the best wear for this kind of holiday and all sorts of
sorrow and humiliation for sins follies shortcomings. — money and
talents wasted and the long chapter of faults and errors. . . Well,
I am thankful though for the blessing of my dearest old Mother's
affection: & that my children should have found parents when God
deprived them of their own. What a happiness it will be to see you
next month — as for going to Dieppe — that must rest with you —
it will not be a penniworth more convenient for me than Paris.
My house is very comfortable and I like the quiet and the walk into
town and the homely air it has. Jim [30] dined with me 2 or 3 days
ago & some others. The flower of the flock is young Doddington
the handsomest and finest young fellow I almost ever saw —

I have but a line to send to say God bless all: and most of all on
this day my best and dearest Mother.

                                        W M T.

349.               TO MRS. CARLYLE
                    25 JULY 1846?

My text is taken from *New Letters and Memorials of Jane Welsh Carlyle*, ed.
Sir James Crichton-Brown (London, 1903), II, 24.

                                        July 25

My Dear Mrs. Carlyle — For God's sake stop Mme. Bölte. I
have governidges calling at all hours with High Dutch accents and

[30] Sir James Carmichael and James Doddington Carmichael-Smyth (1820–
1893), Major Carmichael-Smyth's nephews.

reams of testimonials. One today, one yesterday and a letter the day before, and on going to dine at Punch, by Heavens! there was a letter from a German lady on my plate. And I don't want a Gerwoman; and all our plans are uncertain. Farewell.

Your truly etached,

W. M. T.

350.        TO MRS. CARMICHAEL-SMYTH
6 AUGUST 1846

Published in part, *Biographical Introductions*, I, xxvi-xxvii.

13 Young S! Kensington
August 6. 1846.

My dearest Mammy I am beginning to count the days now till you come: and have got the rooms ready in the rough, all but a couple of bedsteads & a few etceteras w!! however will fall into their places in a day or two. As usual I am full of business and racket — working every day, and yet not advancing somehow, and poor too — although every body gives me credit for making a fortune — say 800£ a year that's about it till the novel begins — and there's not much to be saved out of that. I like Kensington very much indeed: walk in and out too sometimes: and have health and much more work and leisure too. Arthur Shawe has been with me and left me — the kindest creature: but the slowest coach in the world. The poor little woman gets no better, and plays the nastiest pranks more frequently than ever. Now that old Bakewell is come back domestic storms too seem to ravage the household: and Gloyne meditates going away. But I don't see what place can possibly suit her: and as my wife likes her and has been very kindly tended by her, I have offered a little bonus of 10£ a year to her to stay. Of course with the approbation of the heads of the family.

My Aunt Halliday has sent me a farewell letter and a store of mango-pickles and chutney — she is gone to Boulogne, where also will be the Lows [31] & the Dicks and the Irvings — quite a Shakespear Colony.[32] M<sup>rs</sup> Irving is charming.

All the London gaieties are over. I've dined 3 days running at my own expense strange to say, and enjoyed that relaxation amazingly — Old Dwarkanauth [33] went off in the tremendous thunderstorm of Saturday. The last claps killed him.

Shan't you bring a servant with the children? or shall I hire some? I say *some* because my woman, my man's wife is great with &c — very sick and likely to be laid up though the affair wont take place for 4 months. But they are so honest and excellent a couple, and so cheap, that I haven't it in my heart to change them —

I have been more busy in the Chronicle lately but having got the habit of the daily news dont send you the dearer paper. Most likely you'll see the best of the articles in Galignani and of course will put down all the good ones to me.

And now love to all and O ye Gods how glad I shall be to see all the faces old & young. Next week I will send the needful: and then and always am my dearest old Mothers

W M T.

Should you like a day Governess for the children while they are here? There will be a nice school room for them overhead.

[31] Major John Low (1788–1880), *Genealogy* (82), and his wife, the former Augusta Ludlow Shakespear, *Genealogy* (81), whom he had married in 1829. From 1831 to 1842 Low was British Resident at the Court of Lucknow. After some years in England, he returned to India in 1847 and was Resident successively at Ajmeer and Hyderabad. From 1853 to 1858 he was Military Member of Council at Calcutta. He then retired to his estate of Clatto at Cupar in the county of Fife, receiving the Grand Cross of the Star of India. He later was made a K. C. B. (1862) and a Lieutenant-General. See *Memorials*, pp. 311–313.

[32] Mrs. Dick and Mrs. Irvine were Mrs. Low's sisters.

[33] The Baboo Dwarkanauth Tagore died on August 1 at St. George's Hotel, London, aged fifty-one. He was a member of a wealthy and distinguished Hindoo family in Calcutta, where he had many European friends, and was making his second visit to England. (*Annual Register*, 1846, pp. 272–274)

351.                    DIARY
              11–18 AUGUST 1846

Extract published in *Biographical Introductions*, VI, xxi.

August 11.

No criminal informations ag^st the Press have taken place since Atty General Copley [34] — Pollock made a speech in the H of C, w^h was cheered by Peel and says henceforth that mode is impossible.

Read in Hume Vol VIII Quakers — a woman swore she died & was brought to life by one — in Moore, & books of Irish history — wrote about it for M. C. [35] — read in noble old Montaigne.

Old M^r Conyers has joined Brookes's that he may have the pleasure of blackballing Peel when proposed there.

W. August 12 —

Fifty years ago Rogers went to dine with Charles Fox Sheridan & Talleyrand at Hackney where Fox had a natural son born deaf & dumb — coming away after dinner T said to R. We have dined with the most eloquent man in the world, and his only talk has been on his fingers:

Guillemard of Gower S^t used to know T very well. 'T is not a brilliant man in conversation' G told Kenyon: he is very taciturn: says one thing a night w^h he thinks of well before hand & w^h you never forget.

Kenyon has information about Talleyrand in America.

Procter told us about Hazlitt being in love with Nancy Walker. about whom he wrote the Liber Amoris. He was quite wild about her and talked of his passion to everybody. One day he met Basil Montagu's son: seized upon him and in a walk of many miles told the story to him. Montagu left him near Haydon's. Haydon was not at home: but his man & model was. Hazlitt unbosomed himself to the model. By God Sir says he I couldn't help it so I told him.

---

[34] Sir John Singleton Copley (1772–1863), who as first Baron Lyndhurst (1827) was three times Lord Chancellor.

[35] "Moore's History of Ireland," *Morning Chronicle*, August 20, 1846. This review has not previously been identified as Thackeray's.

He then went to look for lodgings; and the woman of the house remarking his care-worn appearance asked the cause of it — By God Sir he said she seemed a kind soul and so I told *her*! Hazlitt was distracted about the woman who was not without a certain grace.

W. J. Fox [36] for a long time had a platonic attachment to Miss Flower. She wrote to his dictation: tended his Reverence when ill in bed: was all in all to him and his wife the mother of his 3 children nothing. The poor woman bore this for a long time very meekly but at last broke out and rebuked her husband who like a philosopher sent her about her business. Miss Flower now came to live with him and has remained for a long time — but meanwhile Mꭈ Fox has become a great man, a league orator with thoughts of Parliament, having long flung the Reverend aux orties, & now desirous to live as respectably as may be.

Miss Flower is dismissed as Mꭅˢ Fox was and is dying of a broken heart at Brighton.

In order to be near Fox the Flowers had come to live in the same street. After his rupture with Stella it wᵈ appear his Reverence took up his abode with Vanessa altogether. And one night coming home in the omnibus where he fell asleep the driver who knew his guest quite well but not his family differences drew up and rang and set him down — at his own door. Drive on says Fox jumping in again — as poor Mꭅˢ Fox sate waiting & hoping at the window . . . — Are you any better you who fling stones?

Read in Montaigne. Keate's Pelew Islands and the pretty story of Lee Boo [37] etched an unsuccessful steel plate: and wrote on the

[36] William Johnson Fox (1786–1864), after a successful early career as a Unitarian minister in Fareham and elsewhere, secured a church in London and became editor of *The Monthly Repository*. Forming an intimacy with Eliza Flower, who directed the musical services in his chapel and wrote for his periodical, he separated about 1834 from his wife. In the early eighteen-forties he contributed to *The Morning Chronicle*, and in 1846 he was one of the strongest writers for the newly-founded *Daily News*. He abandoned the church and journalism for politics in later life, serving as M. P. for Oldham from 1847 to 1863. Both he and Miss Flower were close friends of Browning.
[37] George Keate (1729–1797) tells this story in chapters 21, 22, and 27 of his *Account of the Pelew Islands* (London, 1788). Lee Boo was a son of the

MRS. BROOKFIELD, THACKERAY, AND ELIZABETH BARRETT IN 1845

*From a sketch by Thackeray*

Moore article. pretty dinner at Kenyon's.[38] asked Procter, him & Browning [39] to Garrick on Wednesday next.

Thursday. 13. Etched a plate: wrote Moore's H of Ireland; dined with my wife who was very well: and heard or saw nothing remarkable except Sir Chas Napiers's [40] astonishing old hat. He was very anxious Punch sh^d abuse his new steamer Sidon

As we came home from our water-party on Saturday: many instances of Bacchic fury occurred. Young Bradbury [41] was rolling about on the box of the fly, so helplessly bespattering himself — Evans by his side — but only cheerfully drunk. I took home Leigh who had been utterly stupid & speechless for several hours past, & had to conduct him 4 miles nearly beyond my own door to Bedford S^t Old Wrackham's compromise was amusing. The good natured old gentleman felt rather ashamed that I should go all the way alone with our tipsy friend: so on getting out of the coach he gave me *five shillings* as his part of the fare.

The river-excursion w^d make a good chapter in Paul de Kock. Champagne began the instant we got on board: & the ladies sang songs one against another — A Scotch lady [42] in especial sang some very sweet & simple ditties; Her M^rs a B [43] tried to écraser with

King of the Pelew Islands who at his father's desire accompanied certain sailors shipwrecked there in 1783 when they returned to England. His simplicity, friendliness, and handsome appearance, which corresponded exactly with the qualities expected at the time of a "noble savage," made him a general favorite until his death by smallpox not long after he reached London. He was attended in his last illness by Dr. James Carmichael-Smyth, the Major's father, at whose London residence Thackeray may as a boy have heard of Keate's book and Lee Boo's history.

[38] John Kenyon (1784–1856), a wealthy amateur of letters who was the friend of many of the great literary figures of his time.

[39] The drawing facing page 246 testifies that Thackeray knew Elizabeth Barrett as well as Robert Browning before they eloped on September 12, 1846. He did not become intimate with them, however, until the winter of 1853–1854.        [40] Admiral Sir Charles Napier (1786–1860).

[41] Henry Bradbury (1831–1860), the oldest son of William Bradbury.

[42] The wife of Robert Chambers (1802–1871), the Scotch author and publisher.

[43] The wife of Gilbert Abbott à Beckett (1811–1856), a London journalist, long a writer for *Punch*, who served during the last seven years of his life as a metropolitan police magistrate.

'Charlie Charlie' performed with the most approved shrieks and roulades. I made my court to M̲ʳˢ à B by saying 'What a sweet voice M̲ʳˢ Chambers has got.'

Forster was prodigious in his banter and talk to the ladies perfectly confounding them with the power & splendor of his oratory. Jerrold [44] chirped and laughed & made laugh with all his might, and little Evans had his hat knocked off.

Had a very pleasant stroll on Monday on Wimbledon Common with Procter Forster & Leigh Hunt. Hunt as usual in great force; his wan good humoured face encircled with a great clean shirt-collar, and a sort of holiday dress put on to receive us.

Passing by Horne Tooke's [45] house we talked about Pitt deserted on his death-bed like William the Conqueror — and Tookes friends Burdett & orator Thelwall. 'Thelwall I knew', Hunt said, he was a practitioner of oratory and believed in it.' But I won't put down the bad puns the good fellow made at a most comfortable dinner at the Rose & Crown J Jouster served by a neat-handed little waitress who blushed hugely when she told us there were stewed eels & roast ducks for dinner. All was very good, too good — the champagne & claret just for all the world like London wine.

The common was noble and the air and the green country delightfully fresh — The day quite a holiday.

Next day Tuesday I went with my wife to Camberwell Fair — But I saw nothing funny or pleasant: only a great collection of ginger-bread booths and people swinging in merry-go-rounds. So

[44] Thackeray first knew Douglas William Jerrold (1803–1857) in Paris during 1835 and 1836 when the two used to meet of an evening in the rooms of John Barnett on the Rue d'Amboise. In these conversations the idea of *Punch* was first conceived (Athol Mayhew, *A Jorum of 'Punch,'* London, 1895, pp. 20–25), and after the founding of that magazine in 1841 Thackeray saw Jerrold frequently at the weekly dinners of its staff. Their want of sympathy for each other, which plainly appears in Thackeray's letters, is discussed in Spielmann's *History of "Punch,"* pp. 74 and 311–312. Thackeray had a real admiration for Jerrold's work, however, as is shown by his review (hitherto unidentified) of *Mrs. Caudle's Curtain Lectures* in *The Morning Chronicle* of December 26, 1845.

[45] John Horne Tooke (1736–1812), politician and philologist; John Thelwall (1764–1834), reformer and lecturer on elocution; Sir Francis Burdett (1770–1844), politician.

we hired a cab & drove up beautiful Norwood Hill to Beulah Spa — There wasn't a soul in those charming gardens. Tents down, ponds seedy, roses moulting troubadours fled.

## 352. TO HENRY VIZETELLY
### 13 SEPTEMBER 1846

My text is taken from Vizetelly's *Glances back through Seventy Years*, I, 283.

Dear Sir, — I return the drawings after making a few alterations in them. Present Mr. Titmarsh's compliments to your talented young man, and say M. A. T. would take it as a favour if he would kindly confine his improvements to the Mulligans' and Mrs. Perkins's other guests' extremities. In your young gentleman's otherwise praiseworthy corrections of my vile drawing, a certain *je ne sais quoi*, which I flatter myself exists in the original sketches, seems to have given him the slip, and I have tried in vain to recapture it. Somehow I prefer my own Nuremburg dolls to Mr. Thwaits's [46] super-fine wax models. — Yours,

W. M. T.

Sept. 13.

## 353. TO HORACE SMITH
### 21 SEPTEMBER 1846

My text is taken from *Biographical Introductions*, VI, xxxii–xxxiii.

My dear Mr. Smith, — I write to own the criticism in *The Chronicle* to-day.[47] The best of your poems, instead of making me laugh, has had the other effect, and the notice is written in rather a dolorous strain. Do you consider this an insult? All the best comic stuff so affects me, — Sancho, Falstaff, even Fielding in 'Amelia.'

[46] A young etcher in Vizetelly's employ, who had a hand in the frontispiece to *Notes of a Journey from Cornhill to Grand Cairo* as well as the illustrations to *Mrs. Perkins's Ball*.

[47] "Horace Smith's *Poetical Works*," *Morning Chronicle*, September 21, 1846, p. 6.

'Fanny's Ghost' is the sweetest, most charming lyric. I know why it is so beautiful. I recollect reading some of the verses in 'Gaieties and Gravities' [48] eighteen years ago, and in imitation of them, and after the manner of the Greeks, began a classical drama, 'Ariadne in Naxos,' [49] which would do for Punch if I could find it. I take a short cut [50] to say I am most sincerely, dear Mr. Smith, yours,

W. M. T.

With compliments to Miss Smith in a postscript!

### 354.   FROM MAJOR CARMICHAEL-SMYTH TO MRS. CARMICHAEL-SMYTH SEPTEMBER? 1846 [51]

My text is taken from *Thackeray and his Daughter*, pp. 26–27.

Paris

Annie is now of an age when she can receive a great deal of useful information with much advantage, and she has a mind thirsting for knowledge. William should have a very respectable female to look after the children when he cannot be with them, and he should also devote as much time as he can spare to their instruction.

I had just written so far when I received a letter from Mrs. Collemache, and she tells me Bess [52] is preparing to go to England, and will probably be with you before the end of this month. So we may consider this matter as settled for the present.

Give the children many kisses from their old Grandpapa, who will often regret the loss of their merry faces. God bless you, dearest, and with kind love to William.

I am ever your most affectionate

Henry Carmichael-Smyth.

[48] Smith's *Gaieties and Gravities* were published in three volumes in 1825.
[49] See *Works*, II, 306–307.
[50] These words are written in Thackeray's slanting hand.
[51] Mrs. Fuller dates this letter April, 1847, but it seems probable that it was written shortly after Mrs. Carmichael-Smyth brought Thackeray's children to London.
[52] Miss Hamerton.

355.     TO SIR JAMES EMERSON TENNENT
              1–3 OCTOBER 1846

*Address:* Sir James Tennent | &c &c &c. | Colombo Ceylon. *Postmark:* 3 OC
1846. Hitherto unpublished.

13 Young S$^t$ Kensington.

My dear Tennent I own to a great trepidation on opening your
letter: almost as great as when I heard from L$^d$ Lyttleton that he
had made a dispatch of my private letter to him; [53] of w$^h$ he did
not inform me until some days after the despatch (take it with an i
or an e) had left London. I know L$^d$ Lyttleton a little, belong to a
Cambridge society with him, am very intimate with a very intimate
friend of his and wrote him a *private letter* with such contents as
couldn't be intended for public i's. He made it into a state document suo periculo and to my wonder — but when the deed was
done and couldn't be helped I was not in truth grieved at it — and
pictured you aux abois beating the Governor — But upon my word
I had no notion of implicating you; and am indeed heartily glad
that you have met my *bévue* with such kindness & good humour.

My opinion is that 'Langslow was victimized by the Colonial
Aristocracy' — but our fight isn't over yet, and I swear we will
have him righted (At this moment 3 little boys are climbing into
my garden from the next, and I remember them in a dream a long
time ago & writing this very sentence about Langslow in this very
room and summer evening to you — but this is a digression). He
was sent away without knowing the charges against him or having
an opportunity of defence: and the Privy Council has just rein-
stated reimbursed rather a man turned out at Newfoundland under
similar circumstances. The days of military governors are over:
dem 'um. O that the Whigs would appoint you: but will they? I
believe whilst there's a Russell or Grey unprovided for they will
not. They are more infernal aristocrats and more noble and audacious jobbers than the Tories — or Peel whatdyecallems. When
Peel went out Punch went over to him with the rest of the well-
thinking part of the nation. What a pity he's such a dem Humbug.

[53] I have not traced this letter. For its subject, see above, No. 316.

All this twaddle is the best I have to say — My life is passed in monotonous quill-driving in joke-spinning, in overeating myself in the season, in family duty now. I have got a capital big house at Kensington for 65£ and my mother & children with me whom Lady Tennent (and give my love to her) received so kindly — I am doing well, but lost 500£ in the sanguinary railroads and have not paid all off yet. But there is a good income being made — £12 or 1500 next year I should think or perhaps more.

I never have been able to get within the guard of the Chronicle — they don't bring me into their confidence and a letter w^h Arthur Buller wrote me might as well have been addressed to the Reform Club Porter for any interest I have. He is a dear good fellow. Charles I see once or twice a year and he is always the kindest of men: — but when a man is a Whig one can't *aborder* him on terms of equality. He becomes something Divine and above you — all the Whigs are: so I have not been to see the Jidge Advocate: [54] our Ben Aws. Forster is the greatest man I know. Great and Beneficent like a Superior Power — He is the Chief of the Daily News [55] and conducts it with great ability I think and whenever anybody is in a scrape we all fly to him for refuge. He is omniscient and works miracles. The other day I went in to surprise him at dinner — he and another gent were dining: they had begun with 2 platefulls of mulgatawney s⟨oup⟩ & says I I'll have no soup. But the Ineffable said HENRY BRING SOUP — and there was soup — and my basin was bigger than the other basins. He had some Champagne very good for 5/ a bottle on trial. This is very good said the Great One — actually as good as my own —

 (w^h as everybody knows is excellent) How much do you pay for your Champagne? some one asked. HENRY how much do I pay for my Champagne? said the Supreme One — (knowing full well, but willing to try Henry's faith) 'Alf a guinea a bottle said Henry with great

---

[54] Charles Buller had become Judge Advocate General earlier in the year.

[55] A post he held in succession to Dickens from February 9, 1846, till the following October.

gravity. And perhaps its true but the miracle of the soup I cant explain. His bath is a miracle too — he gets into it every morning he so stout and the bath not much bigger than a Biddy (excuse the expression). We are going to have him in a statue at Madame Tussauds.

What nonsense & stuff is this I write? I have no better. Dickens, Lever & Ainsworth are in Switzerland. Dear old Stanfield the last time I saw him was in a glory of exultation at the newly erected Cheedle (Catholic) Church. But I think Romanism begins to be drawn rather milder; and the Poop of Room that Scarlick Harlock is not perwhirting so many as fommly. I saw Bill Bivin yesterday in the Temple in white kid gloves w$^h$ made a sunshine in that seedy place. Davy Roberts makes merry at his usual sober pace. Kind George Young has not forgotten me in spite of my not going to see him all the year and asked me to Ryde: but I couldnt as usual. Indeed I am I believe a small lion now. And you will have heard of good kind old James Hartley's loss of his plain honest wife. What after 10 children to die in childbed? — The good fellow is broken-hearted I am told, and haven't the courage to go & see.

I think I have no more to say. I have had this in my pocket for 2 days, and well nigh forgot it but that somebody just this minute spoke of Forster. Farewell my dear Tennent Ask Arthur Buller to kiss Ea [56] for me — not that I ever did, but I should like to from your description. Be appy. Keep up your spirts aginst disappintments: and if you cannot reign as Governor, be beloved & esteemed as Secretary [57] — Yours ever

### W M T.

[56] Tennent's daughter Eleanor.
[57] See above, Au. 19. No. 274.

356.        TO GEORGE WILLIAM NICKISSON
              3 OCTOBER 1846

My text is taken from *The Athenæum* (1887), I, 736.

October 3, 1846.

My dear Nickisson, — I beg you 10000 pardons for not answering your note. I quite forgot it, that's the truth, until it reproached me yesterday. Will you pay a special attention to the accompanying paper by young Patmore the poet — he is himself a most deserving and clever young fellow who will be a genius some day; and his paper is so odd, humourous and amusing that I hope you will secure it and its author as a future contributor.

Yours ever

W. M. T.

I hope the sea-air will do you and Mrs. Nickisson and Master Nickisson all the good which such good people deserve. If you will use this for next month I promise you an article (D.V.). The fact is that young Mr. Patmore wants help at this present juncture.

357.            TO MRS. PROCTER
             25 NOVEMBER 1846? [58]

Hitherto unpublished. My text is taken from a transcript given Lady Ritchie by George Murray Smith.

13, Young Street,<br>Kensington Square.<br>Wednesday 25th.

My dear Mrs Procter,

I only got your kind note late last night, and have myself a distinguished party at home to-day comprising that very K—— who somebody wished should shoot me. Could somebody! I should

[58] The place of this letter in the Procter sequence points to 1846. During the months that followed Thackeray's removal to Young Street in that year, Wednesday came on the twenty-fifth only in November.

have been delighted else to dine with you, but K and I will drink your health and rush into each others arms afterwards. Indeed never was anybody so utterly mistaken as Somebody was regarding my feelings towards the K in question. Only I know that nothing will convince Somebody: not protests: nor explanations of any kind: and I must bear up against misconceptions like other martyrs in this world: and content myself by feeling convinced of the angelic purity and honesty of the feelings of my own bosom.

Yours, dear Mrs Procter,

William Makepeace Thackeray.

## 358.          TO MRS. CARMICHAEL-SMYTH
### 4 DECEMBER 1846

*Address:* M<sup>rs</sup> Carmichael Smyth | 17 Rue des Vignes. Chaillot | Paris. *Postmark:* 4 DE 1846. Published in part, *Thackeray and his Daughter*, pp. 25–26.

Friday. Dec<sup>r</sup> 4. 1846.

My dearest Mammy. I have been meditating a line to you day after day: but there are points we don't like to talk about though we think of them always: You know how it pains me to think of my dearest mother being unhappy; Anny read me your letter the other day: it brought back all sorts of early early times, and induced an irresistible burst of tears on my part. at w<sup>h</sup> the Child looked astonished. Her eyes were quite dry. They don't care: not even for you. They'll have to complain some day of the same indifference in your Grand-grandchildren. Now they are with me I am getting so fond of them that I can understand the pangs of the dear old mother who loses them: and who by instinct is 100 times fonder of them than ever a man could be. But it is best that they should be away from you: — at least that they should be away either from you or me. There can't be two first principles in a house. We should secretly be jealous of one another: or I should resign the parental place altogether to you, and be a bachelor still. Whereas now God Almighty grant I may be a father to my children. Continual thoughts of them chase I don't know how many wickednesses out of my mind: Their society makes many of my old amusements seem trivial & shameful. What bounties are there of Providence in the very instincts w$^h$ God gives us — To talk about such things though is wrong I think and engenders pride. But think about them and be humble.

Only I write so far to give my dearest old Mother a consolation in her bereavement. Remember the children are in their natural place: with their nearest friend working their natural influence: getting and giving the good let us hope, w$^h$ the Divine Benevolence appointed to result from the union between parents & children. May I hold fast by it I pray to God our Father.

And how thankful this makes me to you & my dear old G P, who have kept the children for me and watched them so nobly & tenderly — Kind and affectionate hearts, dear & steadfast friends, for this I thank and bless you as the father of my children.

Good bye dearest old Mother. Venables is coming to dine here on Tuesday — my old schoolfellow you know who spoiled my profile.[59] Should you like to come?

W M T.

359. TO MRS. PRYME<br>12 DECEMBER 1846 [60]

Hitherto unpublished.

13 Young S$^t$ Saturday 12 Dec

My dear M$^{rs}$ Pryme     I will come with the greatest pleasure.

Most sincerely yours<br>W M Thackeray

[59] See above, No. 7.
[60] During the years that Thackeray lived at 13 Young Street December 12 fell on a Saturday only in 1846.

ANNE AND HARRIET THACKERAY

*From a sketch by Thackeray*

HARRIET THACKERAY READING "NICHOLAS NICKLEBY"

*From a sketch by Thackeray*

360.                 TO JOHN FORSTER
                    22 DECEMBER 1846

Hitherto unpublished. My text is taken from a transcript supplied by Mrs. Fuller.

13 Young Street, Kensington.
Tuesday, December 22nd, 1846.

My dear Forster. It is against my principle to thank you for the very kind, pretty, friendly notice of "Mrs. Perkins".[61] She's doing very well as you will be glad to hear; and I've sent over the Xaminer to my mother whose opinion of the critic I leave you to imagine.

Ever yours
W. M. Thackeray.

361.          TO MRS. CARMICHAEL-SMYTH
                    23 DECEMBER 1846

*Address:* M[rs] Carmichael Smyth | 2 Rue de Ponthieu | à Paris. *Postmarks:* 23 DE 1846, 25 DEC. 46 BOULOGNE. Published in part, *Thackeray and his Daughter*, p. 27.

My dearest Mammy  A line just to wish you — though I know it's a humbug — a merry Xmas. Next year please God you shall have such a one really, and your old eyes will be gladdened by the sight of the children — They are meanwhile doing the greatest good to their Father. that must be the poor dear old Mother's only consolation — G M just walks in & says that she has put by 300£ for you to come to you when she dies — as you may be pressed now about the furniture will you have 50 or 100 now?  That is her message. And mayn't I contribute some trifle?  Buy something that is pretty & useful and let me pay ever so little.  I shall begin refunding your 200 next year & hope to pay off Sampayo [62] this.  I

---

[61] In *The Examiner*, December 19, 1846, pp. 804–805.
[62] I cannot explain this debt.

have paid 250 besides of railway debts this year — and then — and then Mary's 450£ — It seems a long way on to solvency doesn't it? — But my prospects are very much improved and Vanity Fair may make me — The thought thereof makes me very humble & frightened: not elated. God Almighty keep me to my duty.

We are going to have roast beef and a Xmas party tomorrow: and to dine with the Crowes at Hampsted on Xmas. Eugenie [63] is here  I have asked 2 bachelors tomorrow with an i to her. What a shame it is that no man marries such a fine young generous creature. Bess is great in the household affairs and the best & briskest of all managers. She manages the children admirably: she gives me too good dinners that is her only fault — Mrs Perkins is a great success — the greatest I have had — very nearly as great as Dickens.[64] that is Perkins 500 Dickens 25000 only that difference!  but we are selling out our edition very fast near 1500 are gone out of 2000 already — and this is a great success for the likes of me.

God bless you my dearest old mother & G P.  When you get this anny and her old sinner of a father will be at Church praying heartily for us all.

W M T.

362.            TO EDWARD CHAPMAN
                        1846 [65]

Hitherto unpublished.

                                13 Young St Kensington
My dear Sir

I will dine with you tomorrow with much pleasure, and am glad to hear that at last I am to have the fortune of a second edition.[66]

Our bargain for the first was made upon the notion that it was a half guinea book on the same terms as the Irish book — I certainly

---

[63] Eugenie Crowe. See *Memoranda*.

[64] Whose Christmas book this year was *The Battle of Life*.

[65] This note appears to have been written not long after Thackeray settled in Young Street.

[66] Of *Notes of a Journey from Cornhill to Grand Cairo*.

ought to have my share of the 1400 odd shillings w.<sup>h</sup> the book has brought in and suggest accordingly that division. The book would have sold some hundreds more but for the extra price put upon it: and it is surely not fair that I should be the loser.

But I was always a bad hand at accounts and put myself honestly into your hands as men of business to deal fairly with me. We will ask Forster tomorrow whether or no I am right in my claim to the 1400 sixpences.

Faithfully yrs<br>W M Thackeray

363.     TO FREDERICK J. GOLDSMITH <sup>67</sup>
1846

My text is taken from *The Bookworm*, V, 333.

> 13, Young S.<sup>t</sup>., Kensington Square, the house with the bow windows on the left right hand side near the Kings Arms, Kensington Palace Gate, Thursday Evg.

My dear Frederick, I hope you have not forgotten your engagement to me for tomorrow 1/4 to 7 o'clock. An omnibus from Picadilly will drop you at the entrance of Young St. and my maid shall walk home with you and a lanthorn in the evening.

Your affte. Aunt,<br>W. M. Thackeray

[*Sketch*]

<sup>67</sup> Goldsmith, whom Thackeray had befriended as a boy (see above, No. 73), entered the service of the East India Company at an early age and was dispatched hastily to the East when his superiors discovered that he had surreptitiously published a tragedy in five acts. He returned to England in 1846 and encountered Thackeray quite by chance at a dinner party. The following morning he received this note. (*Athenæum*, 1891, p. 474)

364.                    TO MRS. PROCTER
                              1846?

Hitherto unpublished. My text is taken from a transcript given Lady Ritchie
by George Murray Smith.

                              13, Young Street,
                                 Kensington.
                                 Wednesday.
Madam,

   You heap coals of fire on my head. I can't come. But, ah! it was
kind of you to ask me. May I come after dinner? Will I ever say
an unkyind word of Harley Street again? If I do I am a villain as
well as,

                    Your most faithful,
                        S — B.
                       [*Sketch*]

   It will comfort Procter's heart to know I have raised £10 for my
poor client.


365.                   TO MRS. PROCTER
                            1846? [68]

Hitherto unpublished. My text is taken from a transcript given Lady Ritchie
by George Murray Smith.

My dear Mrs Procter,

   I told you a story yesterday. I asked John, my domestic, whether
Mr Dickens had called, and behold he did come with Miss

---

[68] Thackeray reviewed *The Babes in the Woods*, a crude poem of unknown
authorship written in ballad metre, in "On Some Illustrated Children's Books"
(*Fraser's Magazine*, April, 1846). This note was perhaps written later in the
year, after Thackeray had moved to Young Street.

Hogarth [69] on his arm: and Forster followed presently adventuring by himself. So I'm glad of this and that I told you a fib.

Yours always,

**W. M. T.**

I have got the babbies in the wood packed up for you but am too shabby to pay a porter, and wait till the Printer's Devil comes.

## 366.  TO WILLIAM EDMONDSTOUNE AYTOUN [1]
### 2 JANUARY 1847

My text is taken from Sir Theodore Martin's *Memoir of William Edmondstoune Aytoun* (Edinburgh and London, n. d.), pp. 131–133.

13 Young Street, Kensington,
Jan. 2, 1847.

My dear Aytoun,

I hope The Maclosky received the Mulligan present.[2] I ought to have written before, answering your kind, hearty letter, but business, you know, and weariness of quill-driving after business hours, &c. I don't write to anybody, that's the fact, unless I want something of them, and perhaps that's the case at this present.

I think I have never had any ambition hitherto, or cared what the world thought my work, good or bad; but now the truth forces itself upon me, if the world will once take to admiring Titmarsh, all his guineas will be multiplied by 10. Guineas are good. I have got children, only 10 years more to the fore, say, &c.; now is the time, my lad, to make your A when the sun at length has begun to shine.

Well, I think if I can make a push at the present minute — if my friends will shout, Titmarsh for ever! hurrah for, &c., &c., I may go up with a run to a pretty fair place in my trade and be allowed to appear before the public as among the first fiddles. But

[69] Georgina Hogarth (d. 1917), Dickens's sister-in-law.
[1] Aytoun (1813–1865), the Edinburgh lawyer and poet, well known for *The Bon Gualtier Ballads* (1845), which he wrote with Theodore Martin.
[2] *Mrs. Perkins's Ball*, in which the Mulligan of Ballymulligan figures prominently.

my tunes must be heard in the streets, and organs must grind them.
Ha! Now do you read me?

Why don't 'Blackwood' give me an article? Because he refused
the best story I ever wrote? ³ Colburn refused the present "Novel
without a Hero", and if any man at Blackwood's or Colburn's, and
if any man since — fiddle-de-dee. Upon my word and honour, I
never said so much about myself before: but I know this, if I had
the command of 'Blackwood', and a humoristical person like Titmarsh should come up and labour hard and honestly (please God)
for 10 years, I would give him a hand. Now try, like a man, re-
volving these things in your soul, and see if you can't help me. . . .
And if I can but save a little money, by the Lord! I'll try and
keep it.

Some day when less selfish I will write to you about other matters
than the present ego. The dining season has begun in London
already, I am sorry to say, and the Christmas feeding is frightfully
severe. . . . I have my children with me, and am mighty happy
in that paternal character — preside over legs of mutton comfortably — go to church at early morning and like it — pay rates and
taxes, &c., &c. Between this line and the above, a man has brought
me the 'Times' on "The Battle of Life" to read.⁴ Appy Dickens!
But I love Pickwick and Crummles too well to abuse this great
man. Aliquando bonus. And you, young man, coming up in the
world full of fight, take counsel from a venerable and peaceable
old gladiator who has stripped for many battles. Gad, sir, this
caution is a very good sign. Do you remember how complimentary
Scott and Goethe were? I like the patriarchal air of some people.
Have you ever any snow in Scotland?

(Here follows an admirable drawing of a dustman singing beside his cart, with snow deep in the street).

As I was walking in just now I met this fellow singing "I dreamt

³ *The Great Hoggarty Diamond*, according to Sir Theodore Martin
(*Memoir of Aytoun*, p. 132). For Colburn's refusal of *Vanity Fair*, see above,
No. 308.

⁴ A very severe review of *The Battle of Life* appeared in *The Times* of
January 2. For Crummles, see chapters 22–25, 29, 30, and 48 of *Nicholas
Nickleby*.

that I dwelt in marble halls" [5] driving a dust-cart. I burst out laughing, and so did he. He is as good as Leech's boy in the last 'Punch'. How good Leech is, and what a genuine humour! And Hans Christian Andersen,[6] have you read him? I am wild about him, having only just discovered that delightful delicate fanciful creature. Goodbye, my dear Aytoun. I wish you a merry Christmas, and to honest Johnny Blackwood.[7] Thank him for the Magazine. I shall enjoy it in bed to-morrow morning, when I've left orders *not* to be called for church.

Yours ever,<br>W. M. T.

367.        TO MRS. CAROLINE NORTON<br>5 JANUARY 1847

Hitherto unpublished.

Kensington. January 5. 1847.

Dear M[rs] Norton  The beautiful little book[8] arrived yesterday at last to the delight of my daughters. But how can their Papa serve it? Had it come a fortnight sooner when I was making an article in Fraser about Xmas books it might have received notice — though perhaps it's best not. When I wish to be particularly kind grateful & laudatory my blessings are sure to go wrong, and I find myself abusing at the persons I like best, or falling foul of somebody else instead of praising them. Instead of praising the Drawing Room Scrap book for instance, I find I have made remarks on the Editor's

[5] By Michael Balfe. "The last 'Punch' " is ambiguous, but Thackeray probably refers to "The Rising Generation" in the issue of December 26, p. 264.

[6] The Danish poet and story-teller (1805–1875), the first part of the first series of whose fairy tales was published in 1835, and who was famous throughout Europe by 1845 when the third part appeared.

[7] John Blackwood (1818–1879) was Thackeray's closest friend in this famous publishing family. The two men met in London, where Blackwood had offices between 1840 and 1845, and after he returned to Edinburgh in the latter year to edit *Blackwood's Magazine*, he had several opportunities to entertain Thackeray during the latter's visits to Scotland.

[8] This is *Aunt Carry's Ballads for Children* (1847).

buttons, on her personal appearance of the w͟h to speak favorably seems on my part to be a *balourdise* and impertinence — but I couldn't help it — and finally abusing Sir Wedwardgeorgeearle-lyttonbulwerlyttonbart for calling you the daughter of a beam with a large B.[9]

Now, I have no place left either for praising or railing I am no longer a writer in the Chronicle but author on my own account (please order Vanity Fair of all booksellers) — and if I admired Aunt Carry's ballads ever so (and I dont until tomorrow, for I've not had the time to read them yet) I dont know where I could proclaim my feelings — I will hope however to find some channel for these gushing sentiments w͟h swell at present in the heart of Yours, dear M͟rs Norton, most faithfully.

W M Thackeray.

Lady Duff Gordon [10] is very polite to me and so is Sir A.     Kinglake gave the finest banquet the season has produced

---

[9] Thackeray's article, "A Grumble about the *Christmas Books*," appeared in *Fraser's Magazine*, January, 1847, 111–126. In this he reviews *Fisher's Drawing-Room Scrap-Book* by the Hon. Mrs. Norton (pp. 122–125). The book contained two portraits of Mrs Norton, together with some verses by Bulwer, on which Thackeray's comment is: "Sir Bulmer [*sic*] calls her a radiant Stranger — a spirit of the Star, and a daughter of the Beam, with a large B. . . . Let us hope that the statement is erroneous, and the pedigree not also correct. . . . Come, come, Sir Bulmer. . . . Isn't a woman good enough for you that inherits Sheridan's genius and sweet Cecilia's eyes and voice, but you must assume an inspired air, and declare she is a stray angel? In the picture of the lady, she has a black velvet band around her forehead, and buttons on her dress. Fancy an angel in buttons!"

[10] The former Lucy Austin (1821–1869), writer and hostess, who had married Sir Alexander Duff-Gordon (1811–1872), third Baronet, in 1840.

in w^h the ladies were provided with bouquets & glasses most noble to see. Hayward [11] said somebody had no tact: and your humble servant did as is above depicted — I hope that fashion of the big glasses will expand every day — as for the nosegays — but I can't do fashionable intelligence. I hope you have nursed your patient [12] into good health and that you will permit me to come & see you when you return to London.

368.          TO MRS. PROCTER
              JANUARY 1847 [13]

Published in *Biographical Introductions*, I, xxiii. My text is taken from a transcript given Lady Ritchie by George Murray Smith.

The little girls are glad and free, to wait upon the Misses P. You ask my children as I see, to come to dinner and to tea, but why the deuce you don't ask me, that is a point I cannot see.

369.          FROM EDWARD FrrzGERALD
              JANUARY 1847

Hitherto unpublished.

My dear old Thackeray

I have intended to write to you 20 times since my return from London.[14] First, I meant to tell you how it was I did not go to y^r house as I have agreed to do one Sunday; we were to have dined & gone to Gurlyles: but I was so stupified with cold I thought the best thing was to go to bed. And next day I left London. By this

[11] Abraham Hayward (1801–1884), barrister and magazine writer, who was one of the arbiters of literary society in London. In later years Thackeray often visited his chambers in the Temple and dined with him at the Athenæum Club.

[12] No doubt Mrs. Norton's son Fletcher (1829–1859), a delicate boy who was frequently ill.

[13] This note was written a few days before Thackeray's letter to Mrs. Procter of January 15, 1847.

[14] As he had planned (*Letters and Literary Remains*, ed. Wright, I, 242), FitzGerald came to London for the Christmas season of 1846.

time my apology comes rather late: for doubtless you have forgot the occasion of it.

Secondly I wanted to tell you I have (shall have by the 10th) £5 for that poor Elizabeth [15] if you think this a proper season to give it her in — Have you heard of Morton? — I read in some paper that you Punches have been caricaturing the Irish distresses — which I hope is not true. The Times does what it can to prevent people giving privately — as if there were any danger of their doing so too much! I cannot believe the Times's is good Political Economy; good Charity I am sure it is not. What they say of Ireland may as well be said of the poor in England; let the Government do all — a very comfortable doctrine; but I thought it had become almost exploded.

What a wretched affair is the Battle of Life — scarce even the few good touches that generally redeem Dickens — I see yr Perkins greatly extolled in Spectator & Athenaeum [16] — Dickens' last Dombey has a very fine account of the over-cramming Educator's system; [17] worth whole volumes of Essays on the subject if Bigotry would believe that laughs may tell truth. The boy who talks Greek in his sleep seems to me terrible as Macbeth —

I, in company with many people here, have got an influenza that makes me now feel as if I had walked 40 miles & then been beaten for my pains. On Friday I am going to assist at a rent-dinner — no tenants of mine or my Father — but of an old Squire's who persists in thinking I can talk to entertain the farmers.

Pray put the Honorable Julia into Punch; she is fair game. I doubt [if] Lord Lindsay becomes troublesome. Remember [me] to all your's I know little & great & believe me yr's ever,

Edward FitzGerald.

[15] See above, No. 337.

[16] *Mrs. Perkins's Ball* is praised in *The Athenæum* of December 19, 1846 (pp. 1290–1291) and in *The Spectator* of the same date (p. 1218).

[17] In chapter 12, published in number IV of *Dombey and Son* for January. Tozer, the boy whom FitzGerald mentions, talks scraps of Greek and Latin in his sleep, "which, in the silence of the night, had an inexpressibly wicked and guilty effect." Of the next number (chapters 14 to 16) George Hodder tells the following story in *Memoirs of my Time* (London, 1870, p. 277): "Putting

370. TO WILLIAM EDMONDSTOUNE AYTOUN
11 JANUARY 1847

My text is taken from Martin's *Memoir of Aytoun*, pp. 134–135.

13 Young Street, Kensington, Monday Night.
Jan. 13,[18] 1847.

My dear Aytoun, —

The copy of Mrs. Perkins which was sent by the Mulligan to the other chieftain has met with a mishap. It travelled to Edinburgh in the portmanteau of a friend of mine, who arrived at ten o'clock at night and started for Inverness the next morning at six. Mrs. P. went with him. He forgot her at Inverness and came back to London whither Mrs. Perkins was sent after him at a cost of 4s.10d. for carriage. She is not worth that money either for you or me to pay and waits in my room till you come to town in spring.

I have been thinking of the other matter on which I unbusmd myself to you and withdraw my former letter. Puffs are good and the testimony of good men; but I don't think these will make a success for a man and he ought to stand as the public chooses to put him. I will try please God to do my best and the money will come perhaps some day! Meanwhile a man so lucky as myself has no reason to complain. So let all puffing alone, though as you know I am glad if I can have and deserve your private good opinion. The women like 'Vanity Fair', I find very much, and the publishers are quite in good spirits regarding that venture.

This is all I have to say — in the solitude of midnight — with a quiet cigar and the weakest gin-and-water in the world ruminating over a child's ball from which I have just come, having gone as chaperon to my little girls. One of them had her hair plaited in

---

No. 5 of 'Dombey and Son' in his pocket, [Thackeray] hastened down to Mr. Punch's printing-office, and entering the editor's room, where I chanced to be the only person present except Mr. Mark Lemon himself, he dashed it on to the table with startling vehemence, and exclaimed, 'There's no writing against such power as this — one has no chance! Read that chapter describing young Paul's death: it is unsurpassed — it is stupendous!' "

[18] A mistake, apparently, for Monday, January 11.

two tails, the other had ringlets [*sketch of the two children*] and the most fascinating bows of blue ribbon. It was very merry and likewise sentimental. We went in a fly quite genteel, and, law! what a comfort it was when it was over!

Adyou. —

Yours sincerely,

W. M. Thackeray.

371.          TO GEORGE HODDER [19]
11 JANUARY 1847

Published in George Hodder's *Memories of my Time* (London, 1870), p. 243.

13 Young S! Kensington. January 11.

Dear Hodder. I thank you very much for your note and am very glad that my little book [20] has given you pleasure. I hope the future works of the same author will please you, and indeed am quite anxious to have as many people as may be of your opinion. It is not my intention to return to Constantinople at present and when there I hope I shall be more moral than in former days, and shall have no desire to fling the handkerchief to any members whatsoever of His Highness's seraglio.[21]

Truly yrs

W M Thackeray.

[19] A Grub Street hack (d. 1870) who served as Thackeray's amanuensis while he was writing *The Four Georges* in 1855 and as manager for a series of these lectures delivered in 1857. Hodder made good use of his opportunities for observation, and the impressions of Thackeray recorded in *Memories of my Time*, though diffuse, have real value.

[20] *Notes of a Journey from Cornhill to Grand Cairo.*

[21] See *Works*, V, 643–645.

372.                    TO MRS. PROCTER
                      15 JANUARY 1847

Hitherto unpublished. My text is taken from a transcript given Lady Ritchie
by George Murray Smith.

                                        Friday. 15 January.
Dear Mrs Procter,
    The sashes are the prettiest of ribbons — an appy and grateful
father wears them round his art. I can't help thinking how extraordinarily good and kind every one was to my little girls at your
house. My views of human nature are beginning to change entirely, and I find myself getting fond of new good and kind
people every day. The Lumleys Acton Warburton Pauncefoot [22]
(is his name so?) and all those dear kind pretty virtuous young
ladies. In fact I am growing a benevolent humbug. But,
                            Always truly yours,
                              W. M. Thackeray.


373.                   TO MRS. BROOKFIELD
                      15 JANUARY 1847

Facsimile in *Collection of Letters*, p. 51.

                13 Young Sᵗ Kensington. January 15. 1847.
    My dear Mʳˢ Brookfield  Please to remember that your husband
and you are engaged on Monday to your obedient Servant
                        W M Thackeray
            Author of 'The Death Shriek' 'Passion flowers'
                      and other poems

[22] I.e., the family of Benjamin Lumley, Thomas Acton Warburton, and
Julian Pauncefote (1828–1902), later (1889) first Baron Pauncefote, Envoy
Extraordinary to the United States (1889–1893) and Ambassador (1893–
1902). Warburton (d. 1894) was a brother of Eliott Warburton.

374.            TO ALBANY FONBLANQUE
                27 JANUARY 1847

*Address:* A. Fonblanque Esq^re | Connaught Square. *Postmark:* JA 27 1847.
Published in part, *Biographical Introductions*, VI, xxvii–xxviii.

My dear Fonblanque.

A great qualm has just come over me, about our conversation this
morning. I am going to do a series of novels by the most popular
authors for Punch [23] and Bulwer's is actually done, the blocks
designed and the Story in progress it is George Barnwell He

will quote Plato speak in Big Phrases, and let out his Nunkys old
&c — numbers of others are to follow Cooper, James, Dickens,
Lever &c. but they will all be good natured — and I cant afford to
give up my plan. It is my bread indeed for next year.

I am bound to tell you this (How the deuce did I forget it in
our talk this morning?) lest you should be putting your hospitable

[23] *Punch's Prize Novelists,* later called *Novels by Eminent Hands,* which began on April 3 with the first part of "George de Barnwell. By E. L. B. L. B. B.
L. L. B. B. B. L. L. L." The parody of Dickens was never written.

intentions into execution, and after having had my legs sub iisdem trabibus [24] with Bulwer I sh^d seem to betray him — I can't leave him out of the caricatures — all that I promise is to be friendly and meek in spirit.

Very faithfully yours

W M Thackeray —

What I said about M^r Hallam's [25] intentions regarding me was told me as a *secret*. So if you are good enough to ask any of the Committee to canvass for me — his name must not appear. [26]

## 375.     TO THE REV. WILLIAM BROOKFIELD
### 3 FEBRUARY 1847

Hitherto unpublished. My text is taken from a transcript supplied by Mrs. Fuller and from the *Goodyear Catalogue*, lot 320. *Endorsed:* Feb. 3, 1847, Rec'd at Southampton. W. H. B.

Under the confessional seal in the railway. [27]

My dear old Reverence,

I think from some words you let drop about 30 miles off, about my insanity yesterday, explanation is necessary on my part.

Without the ether I should never have broken out as I did about a certain personage (we are just come to a station) but in the etherial or natural state, my opinion is the same. I think the personage you know what. Her innocence, looks, angelical sweetness

---

[24] Horace, *Odes*, III, ii, 27–28. See Thackeray's translation of this poem in "A Pictorial Rhapsody" (*Works*, XIII, 331).

[25] Thackeray had met Henry Hallam (1777–1859), who was much esteemed in Whig society as the author of three monumental historical works, through his favorite niece, Mrs. Brookfield. They continued to see each other frequently until 1851, though they were never intimate.

[26] No doubt Hallam wished to have Thackeray elected to the Athenæum, of which both he and Fonblanque were members. Thackeray was not admitted to this club until 1851.

[27] Thackeray wrote this letter on his way home to London from Southampton, where he had seen the Brookfields at the home of their friends, the Fanshawes (see below, No. 376). It would appear that he gave voice to the unguarded language for which he apologizes while under the influence of ether, probably administered by Dr. Bullar, a Southampton physician who experimented with anesthetics (see below, No. 543).

and kindness charm and ravish me to the highest degree; and every now and then in contemplating them I burst out into uncouth raptures. They are not the least dangerous — it is a sort of artistical delight (a spiritual sensuality so to speak) — other beautiful objects in Nature so affect me, children, landscapes, harmonies of colour, music, etc. Little Minny and the Person most of all. By my soul I think my love for the one is as pure as my love for the other — and believe I never had a bad thought for either. If I had, could I shake you by the hand, or have for you a sincere and generous regard? My dear old fellow, you and God Almighty may know all my thoughts about your wife; — I'm not ashamed of one of them — since the days of the dear old twopenny tart dinner [28] till now.

The misfortune is in incautious speaking about her. Such a person ought not to be praised in public and in my fits of enthusiasm I cannot refrain. I shall try to correct this, and beg your pardon for it. Indeed I didn't intend that the Joseph the carpenter simile should go to her ears; and write you now under the seal of confession. My breast is so clean that you will have no difficulty I think in giving me absolution.

'Evins! Here is Wimbledon Station. Well, I have opened my bowels to you. Indeed there has not been much secret before; and I've always admired the generous spirit in which you have witnessed my queer raptures. If I had envy, or what you call passion, or a wicked thought . . . I should have cut you long ago, and never could have had the rascality to say as I do now that I'm yours sincerely and affectionately,

W. M. T.

[28] Mrs. Brookfield tells this story in *Collection of Letters* (p. 176): "When, soon after our marriage, Mr. Brookfield introduced his early college friend Mr. Thackeray, to me, he brought him one day unexpectedly to dine with us. There was, fortunately, a good plain dinner, but I was young and shy enough to feel embarassed because we had no sweets, and I privately sent my maid to the nearest confectioner's to buy a dish of tartlets, which I thought would give a finish to our simple meal. When they were placed before me, I timidly offered our guest a small one, saying, 'Will you have a tartlet, Mr. Thackeray?' 'I will, but I'll have a two-penny one, if you please,' he answered, so beamingly, that we all laughed, and my shyness disappeared."

376.      TO THE REV. JOHN ALLEN
18 FEBRUARY 1847

Hitherto unpublished.

13 Young S$^t$ Kensington Sq$^{re}$
February 18. 1847.

My dear old John Allen.

I was smoking a pipe last night at Brookfield's, and he put into my hand your note about the Pauper & Prison Schools [29] — I know it must have hurt you more to write it than even him to receive it.

My first consolation to him was 'Well, John Allen is right, you're *not* a fit man, I sh$^d$ think, for such a plan' — Brookfield said 'I've such a perfect confidence in Allen's honesty & goodness that I can't be angry at anything he says: but &c —— You understand the but — w$^h$ did not express any single bad feeling but a great deal of sadness & humiliation. 'Our sins find us out' [30] — says he. I suppose Allen judges of me by his recollections of me fifteen years ago — I shan't show the letter to my wife he said after a pause — and we pretended to talk about something else —

I wonder whether you *are* judging of him from fifteen years ago? my dear fellow: if you are I think you do him a great wrong — and sh$^d$ be set to know him better — If he had not been a just and generous heart, I dont think he would have taken your letter as he did — Few men of your standing & profession would be indifferent to a reproof from you — on parade as it were — and w$^d$ not be severely wounded at thinking you refused them your confidence. Well, at least he acted a good and humble Christian part, in the way in w$^h$ he bore your public rebuke of him. He seemed to me to suffer very keenly and to bear it very generously — I was much affected when he said 'Our sins find us out'.

Perhaps I am not a fair man to judge of him: for I have received from him the greatest obligations and benefits: and have for him

[29] Brookfield had applied for an Inspectorship of Schools, and Allen, one of the original Inspectors, had been consulted concerning his appointment.
[30] *Numbers*, 32, 23.

and his wife (who is a sort of angel in my eyes) the most cordial & tender feelings — I meet numbers of men who are sceptics about him — I have seen him more than any one. I have been constantly with him for hours during the last 2 years — any child might have listened to our multiplied conversations — for w$^h$ I assure you, and for the good they have done me, I have occasion to thank God Almighty — to whom I am grateful for his friendship, as one of the greatest benefits ever awarded to me. I dont say that I have found a faultless man — but if he had been a hypocrite I should have caught him tripping all this time — and that I never did — but have always found him just earnest humble and bent on doing his duty. The good he has done me, there is no need to brag about — I dont mean the 100£ w$^h$ he brought me last year when I was in a strait through some railway folly — but of another sort —

I often fancy this good fellow may get into disgrace with his superior officers by the fact of his intimacy with such a reprobate as me — smoking pipes at midnight with a caricaturist a writer in Punch &c &c — Somebody asked him the other day how much he got for contributing to that periodical? — Who knows but his Chiefs doubt about him as some of his comrades do —

Now it is not Punch that has perverted Brookfield; but Brookfield has converted Punch! & that's something to have done in these days. Two years ago I used only to make a passive opposition agst the Anti-church and Bishop sneers — last year I made an active one (Jerrold & I had a sort of war & I came off conqueror) [31] and it was

---

[31] From this letter and that of February 24, Thackeray's controversy with Jerrold can be conjecturally reconstructed. In his first paper "On Clerical Snobs," which appeared in Punch on May 16, 1846, Thackeray reproves those journalists who let slip no opportunity to attack the clergy. He argues that most Victorian parsons live useful, selfless, and honorable lives. And he concludes: "But what is this? Instead of 'showing up' the parsons, are we indulging in maudlin praises of that monstrous black-coated race? O saintly Francis [Thackeray], lying at rest under the turf; O Jimmy [White], and Johnny [Allen], and Willy [Brookfield], friends of my youth! O noble and dear old Elias [Thackeray]! how should he who knows you not respect you and your calling? May this pen never write a pennyworth again, if it ever casts ridicule upon either!" (Works, VI, 342) Jerrold, who had been very fierce against the church in the columns of Punch, thought that Thackeray's reproof was directed

THE REV. WILLIAM BROOKFIELD AT THE AGE OF FORTY

*From a painting by Samuel Laurence*

through his influence — It's something to stop half a million of people from jeering at the Church every week — No cry is more popular. At this minute we might be turning the Bishop of London into such scorn & ridicule upon perfectly just grounds too, and to the delight of the public. It's William Brookfield who stopped it, & you may tell the Bench so and I wish you would — by his kindness, his tenderness, his honest pious life.

You see this long letter is more about me than about Brookfield — but it's the only test I have to try him by: and as he is on his promotion, and you are incredulous I think about him, I think I ought to tell you the good that I know of him.

Of course he knows nothing about this letter — only it seemed to me my duty to write it — and not to copy it.

Yours my dear old friend<br>W M Thackeray.

How are all your little ones and M<sup>rs</sup> Allen? Do you know of a very good governess & perfect lady to command my house and children?

## 377.     FROM MRS. BROOKFIELD
### 18 FEBRUARY 1847

Published in *Mrs. Brookfield*, pp. 206–207. My text is taken from the *Howe Proofs*.

Southampton, Feby 18th

My dear Mr. Thackeray,

As I hope to be at home tomorrow it seems hardly worth while to write any more than just a few lines to thank you for yr. letter [32]

---

specifically at him. The upshot of the argument that followed, one of many between the two men over the *Punch* dinner table, was that Jerrold agreed henceforth to moderate his anti-clericalism.

[32] I have not traced this letter. That Thackeray had been forgiven when he wrote it is obvious from the tenor of a note sent by Brookfield to his wife on February 15: "Thackwack came in at 9 last night, and we conversed till small hours. . . . Little Fanshawe, you may assure her, was spoken of as she would have liked if listening through the keyhole. You alone came in for the un-

which amused us extremely & for which Mrs. Fanshawe also was much obliged & desires her best thanks & respects or regards. Totty [33] could not get ready soon enough to come with me, so that at all events you will not expect her till next week — & further particulars I may be empowered to enter into when I see you. — It was entirely out of my power to answer yr. kind letter yesterday, tho' I tried hard to do so, & made several beginnings. You rose grander & more awful in the majesty of yr. authorship each time I made the feeble attempt to write a few unpretending words in answer to yr. letter, & it is only the fear of appearing rude & ungrateful which has mastered my trepidation today. — The ancient doctors are still alive & have been experimenting on me with hot air & sulphur baths satisfactorily, setting me up to brave the airs of Pulteney [34] again. —

Bishop Oaks on an ambling Palfry rides by in innocent self-contentment.

You left a great blank behind you — not to be filled up at all.

Believe me, Yours most sincerely,

J. O. Brookfield

I beg yr. pardon for crossing. Will you give my love to the two children.

---

measured tempest of our abuse." (*Mrs. Brookfield*, I, 205) Mrs. Brookfield was staying with Mrs. Fanshawe, wife of the Rev. Charles S. Fanshawe, who had become Perpetual Curate of Holy Trinity Church, Southampton, in 1837.

[33] The Fanshawes' daughter, whom Thackeray had invited to spend a few days at 13 Young Street with Anne and Harriet.

[34] The Brookfields lived at 23 Great Pulteney Street from early in 1844 until May, 1847 (*Mrs. Brookfield*, I, 136 and 211–212).

378.            TO THE REV. JOHN ALLEN
                22 FEBRUARY 1847

Hitherto unpublished.

Kensington Monday.
22 Feb. 1847

My dear Allen.

One word more on Brookfield's business — with whom on your own showing I think you have dealt very hardly — very unluckily I should say — for who w^d ever suppose you guilty of wilful injustice to anybody?

But your verdict of 'levity & looseness of talk' — damning charges agst a clergyman on his promotion — is delivered upon recollections of 15 years back — upon 2 sermons you've heard since, and 2 occasions of meeting him in society subsequently.

We'll admit the Cambridge levity. But was the temptation nothing? Consider the kindly social jovial temperament of the man, son of a rigid dissenting Attorney, free for the first time — courted by young men of the highest class — in quite a new society joining in amusements in w^h nobody about him took shame — intoxicated with the freedom, and the fine company of the place — and only the more inclined to enter into its gaieties from its contrast with the gloom & narrowness of his own home — He doesn't make any debts that I know of: when his College Course is done he becomes private tutor: he is beloved by his pupil [35] to this present day. His tutoring over he takes orders and is beloved by his people at Southampton in a manner quite curious to witness. I saw him there the other day. It was a sort of fête in the town. The very levity w^h shocks you, charms & wins others — a warm sympathy, a most kindly heart, a generous humour, an honest life make him numberless friends, and give him many opportunities of doing good, w^h he wouldn't have had but for this levity & looseness of talk w^h John Allen condemns — I think you have cruelly wronged him —

[35] Lord Lyttleton. For these details of Brookfield's early life, see *Memoranda*.

That he was quite unfit for the post proposed for him I believe with you — but charges of levity & looseness damn a man for any other — They are not proven either — they come from a private suspicion in your mind if I may judge from my own — for I had the same suspicions — only removed by several years of the closest friendship and intimacy in w.ʰ I've learned to appreciate his generous and affectionate heart and thoroughly to believe in his Xtian sincerity.

His poor wife — who has heard of the business after all — writes me a letter just now — urging me 'to urge on W.ᵐ the propriety of getting some testimonials from his intimate friends, his rectors &c — not with a view to future promotion but to set himself right' — I am just going to see her to say I think he ought to do no such thing. He is quite too high placed: and should hold his peace.

But I dont think his friends should: and I as one of them and loving both him & you, think you ought to go down to D.ʳ Shuttleworth [36] & say 'My verdict has been so & so — but those who know Brookfield a thousand times better than I do deny my opinion altogether — and say he's a good parson a good Christian, a good man — ' And I'll agitate this wherever I can: and I know you my dear old John Allen so well that I am sure there's no man in the world w.ᵈ be more happy than yourself to find that you have been in the wrong.

Yours, my dear Allen affectionately
    W M Thackeray.

I have written to Reeve of the Council Office to speak to Shuttleworth: my object is to show you're in the wrong and to get as many people as possible to show it too.

---

[36] James Phillips Kay-Shuttleworth (1804–1877), M.D., later (1850) first Baronet, founder of the English system of popular education. From 1839 to 1849 he served as secretary to the committee of the Privy Council that administered the funds granted for education by the House of Commons.

379.        TO HENRY REEVE
22 FEBRUARY 1847

Hitherto unpublished. *Endorsed:* 23. Feb. 1847 | M.ʳ Thackeray on Brook-fields | appl.

13 Young S.ᵗ Kensington. Monday. Feb 22. 1847.
My dear Reeve.

John Allen, the School-Inspector a friend of mine (about whose motives and personal character there can be no more question than about Pascal's or Vincent de Paul's) has been talking with D.ʳ Kay Shuttleworth regarding Brookfield: and has charged him with 'levity & a loose life.' The loose life & levity apply to 15 years ago, when both were lads at Cambridge: and Brookfield living with the gay young men there. You know he is a man of great humour, kindliness, & social popular qualities. Coming up to college a humble man he was very much courted by the greatest people there. and indeed doesn't disguise the fact that his life in those days was a light & worldly one.

But 'levity & loose talk' are cruel charges to remember I think & to make against the hard-working parson of 36; beloved wherever he has been; respected by every body he has had to deal with; cheerful, upright, laborious; living most honorably on a small income. I saw him the other day at Southampton, where he was curate — There was a sort of fête when he arrived: and I joked with him, about his going through the town blessing the people like Sir Roger de Coverley.[37] Men don't get this sort of esteem & affection nowadays for nothing. The very 'levity' w.ʰ Allen doesn't like, the geniality & humour w.ʰ in a worldly man went wrong possibly — come to be useful to the good kind hearted generous parson, and awaken good in others w.ʰ perfectly spotless people w.ᵈ never know how to create. I can answer for it in my own case. I have known & loved Allen for years but he never acted upon me — and I do believe I have reason to thank God Almighty that I have been

---

[37] See *The Spectator*, numbers 106 and 107.

so intimate with Brookfield as I have for the last 3 years — more than anybody else probably.

Now do go to D^r Shuttleworth & say from a man who has been in the most close and intimate relations with Brookfield — a worldly man if you like, passing nights in his company that I have got the very greatest benefit from it, that in hours & hours (in the meeting of 2 men let me say of great powers of humour) — no talk has passed that a child might not hear: that with the greatest heartiness & kindliness he never does forget his calling: that I never saw a man less of a hypocrite (and with some penetration in such a long intimacy as our's I'm sure I should have found him out) and that what John Allen calls levity in him I do believe ought to be interpreted quite otherwise as a humourous generous affectionate frankness — quite as good qualities in a working parson as the utmost asceticism could be.

> Yours dear Reeve most sincerely
> W M Thackeray.

380.          TO HENRY REEVE
          23 FEBRUARY 1847

*Hitherto unpublished. Endorsed:* 1847.

13 Young Street Kensington Tuesday 23 Feb

My dear Reeve

One note written yesterday to the public man Reeve lies before me. 'Tis addressed to the Privy Council and as the Stamp is already on the document I care not to alter its destination.

I can't come on the 4^th — that is I have got an hydraulic disorganization, w^h compels me to give up going out for a little — & can only dine at home at Clubs or where refuge is at hand with the instantaneous p-t de Ch-mbre. By this post 4 invitations are respectfully declined.

But why not come and dine here *in boy* as the French say — It w^d be a charity to me and you know I could &c whenever I had a mind. You can have your claret & my mutton. Do you know my Persicos odi [38] the very point alluded to by you.

### Michael Angelo to his Cook

| | |
|---|---|
| Dear Lucy you know what my wish is | Persicos odi |
|  I hate all your Frenchified fuss. | Puer apparatus |
| Your silly entrées and made dishes | Displicent nexæ |
|  Were never intended for us. | Philyra coronæ |
| No footman in lace & in ruffles | Mitte sectari |
|  Need dangle behind my arm-chair | Rosa quo locorum |
| And never mind seeking for truffles | Sera moretur |
|  Although they be ever so rare | |
| | |
| But a plain leg of mutton my Lucy | Simplici MYRTo |
|  I prythee get ready at three | Nihil adlabores |
| Have it tender & smoking & juicy | Sedulus curo |
|  And what better meat can there be? | Neque te ministrum |
| And when it has feasted the master | Dedecet myrtus |
|  'Twill amply provide for the maid | Neque me sub arta |
| Meanwhile I will smoke my Canaster | Vite bibentem |
|  And tipple my ale in the shade. | |

381.
### TO MARK LEMON
### 24 FEBRUARY 1847

Hitherto unpublished.

Feb. 24. 1847. Kensington.

My dear Lemon

 That concluding benedictory paragraph in the Snobs [39] I hope wont be construed in any unpleasant way by any other laborer on the paper. I mean of course I hope Jerrold won't fancy that I

---

[38] Horace, *Odes*, I, xxxviii. Thackeray's "imitation" was first published in "Memorials of Gormandising," *Fraser's Magazine*, June, 1841.

[39] "To laugh at [Snobs] is *Mr. Punch's* business. May he laugh honestly, hit no foul blow, and tell the truth when at his very broadest grin — never forgetting that if Fun is good, Truth is still better, and Love best of all." (*Works*, VI, 464)

reflect on him now as he did in the Parson-Snob Controversy.[40] I think his opinions are wrong on many points, but I'm sure he believes them honestly, and I don't think that he or any man *has* hit a foul blow in Punch.

What I mean applies to my own case & that of all of us — who set up as Satirical-Moralists — and having such a vast multitude of readers whom we not only amuse but teach. And indeed, a solemn prayer to God Almighty was in my thoughts that we may never forget truth & Justice and kindness as the great ends of our profession. There's something of the same strain in Vanity Fair.[41] A few years ago I should have sneered at the idea of setting up as a teacher at all, and perhaps at this pompous and pious way of talking about a few papers of jokes in Punch — but I have got to believe in the business, and in many other things since then. And our profession seems to me to be as serious as the Parson's own. Please God we'll be honest & kind was what I meant and all I meant. I swear nothing more.

Yours dear Lemon faithfully<br>W M T.

## 382.  TO THE REV. ALEXANDER JOHN SCOTT [42]
### 25 FEBRUARY 1847

*Address:* Rev^d A. J. Scott | 40 Glocester Crescent | Regents Park. *Postmark:* FE 26. Hitherto unpublished. *Endorsed:* M^r Thackeray | 1847.

Kensington Thursday.

My dear Scott I will come with pleasure more so as I recognize the hand of the North British Reviewer     I thought it was you certainly, and was going to write and ask. Praise in the right place is

---

[40] See above, No. 376.

[41] The last paragraph of chapter 8 (*Works*, I, 70–72), first of the four chapters that make up the number for March.

[42] Scott (1805–1866) was a Presbyterian minister who became in November, 1848, Professor of English Language and Literature at University College, London. In later years Thackeray visited him in Manchester, where he was first Principal of Owens College from 1851 to 1857.

awfully sweet: and when you touch my humanity you stap my vitals.[43] Indeed the business of grinning seems to me to grow every day graver & graver; and I begin to hope we are a sort of parsons. May God Almighty give us heart to be humble & speak the truth. See Punch of this day in w$^h$ the Snob intimates this in a benedictory farewell address. To be sure it is rather fulsome in fellows of our sort. I mean mine not your's — worldly men — stained with all sorts of dissoluteness — to set up as popular teachers: but the Pons Asinorum is true even though Jack Ketch or Silenus enunciates it. I dont know why I preach this sermon to you, only that the matter is lying on my mind, and I am much touched by your good opinion

Sincerely yours

W M Thackeray.

## 383. TO GEORGE WILLIAM NICKISSON
### 1 MARCH 1847

Hitherto unpublished. My text is taken from a transcript supplied by Mr. J. L. Stokes.

Young S$^t$

13 Kensington Sq$^r$ March 1. 1847.

My dear Nickisson

I was attracted to the Charterhouse Article in the Magazine, and amazed by a certain paragraph [44] — from Wesley to Titmarsh is a very great break in the school-annals, and the latter was a very bad scholar, who bitterly regrets his place of education. But it was very

---

[43] A phrase used frequently by Lord Foppington in Sheridan's *A Trip to Scarborough* (1777).

[44] "Another celebrated Carthusian was John Wesley, whose eventful and important life is the subject of one of Southey's finest biographies; and with this eminent name our recollection of the celebrated scholars of this house would seem to terminate. Future historians will include our friend Mr. Thackeray among the ornaments of the Chartreux; and justly too, though he has only begun of late to give his talents fair play, and assume the position in our literature unquestionably his due." (Peter Cunningham, "Chronicles of Charter House," *Fraser's Magazine*, March, 1847, pp. 345–346)

kind & well-meant of Cunningham I suppose to say such handsome things. I wonder whether they are true. Please God I'll be honest & not puffed up by this sort of laudation. Such compliments make me awfully grave, instead of being elated & joyful; — only they deserve acknowledgment of course w^h please hereby to receive.

I think the chief good I got out of Charterhouse was to learn to hate bullying & tyranny and to love kind hearted simple children. And I hope my own get the benefit of that sad experience I had there, and so escape rough words & brutal treatment — It's lucky the paper is no bigger, or you might be served with a homily. Thank you for the good-will, and believe me dear Nickisson

Yours sincerely<br>W M Thackeray.

384.              TO HENRY BRADBURY
                    13 MARCH 1847

*Address:* H. R. Bradbury Esq^re | Whitefriars.  Hitherto unpublished.

13 Young S^t Kensington<br>Saturday 13 March

Dear Bradbury Junior

I shall be very happy indeed to contribute a sketch [45] — but as for the few lines I can't promise for I am a costive poet.

Faithfully yours<br>W M Thackeray

385.              TO BESS HAMERTON
                    16 MARCH 1847

Hitherto unpublished.

My dear Bess. I know you will be grieved but I hope not angry at this letter w^h I think it is fair to write to you. After all your care & kindness it seems very ungrateful to say to you "Dont stay with us any more*" but it w^d be worse not to speak openly my mind

[45] Possibly to *Punch's Pocket Book* for 1848.

now it is made up. You have not got the affection of the children. They are afraid of you: & though I know you have done your utmost & your best by them & by me — yet, right or wrong, I think the little girls won't give you their confidence, & that its best we sh^d part. I have thought as much for some time past: & the notion, now confirmed, has produced a reserve on my part, w^h I daresay you have remarked in me, & w^h has been very painful to me.

My Gmother knows nothing of my feelings. I have given it always in your favor in your differences with her. I have checked Anny twice or thrice when about to make complaints: I have just now had some talk with her and see from what she says & feels that were you to live ten years together, the ideas of both of you are so different, you could never be cordial. What remains for me, dear Bess, with this conviction on my mind, but to speak it to you openly?

The subject is so painful to me that I have thought it better to write than to speak of it & shall not enter into it with the children. Will you kindly also not mention it to them. They know quite well the high opinion I have of you & the regard & confidence w^h you merit from me.

Yours dear Bess sincerely & gratefully<br>W M T.

*I dont mean now, or a month hence or 2 months hence, but when you go to Ireland.

## 386. TO MRS. CARMICHAEL-SMYTH
### 16 MARCH 1847

*Address:* M^rs Carmichael-Smyth. | 2 Rue de Ponthieu | Paris. *Postmarks:* 16 MR 1847, 18 MARS 47 BOULOGNE. Hitherto unpublished.

My dearest Mammy Will be thunderstruck at this manifesto [46] but it is quite necessary. Anny & Bess do not go on well together. The child is the woman's superior in every respect: and subject to a vulgar worrying discipline w^h makes her unhappy. She has once or twice shown a disposition to complain w^h I have checked: but she

[46] A copy of the preceding letter to Miss Hamerton.

has opened her heart to me to day & the above document has gone up to Bess's room — She's not an English lady — that's the fact. I sit entirely dumb & stupefied before her — I order my breakfast in my own room & fly in utter despair. The commonplaces in that enormous brogue kill me: and she falls to worrying Nanny as soon as I go out. And so we part. Mind, I've the utmost respect & regard for her honesty and active discharge of duty as far as she knows it: but this is not the woman to rule such a delicate soul as my dearest Nanny's. What a noble creature she is thank God. May I love her and be her friend more & more. As for Minny who can help loving her?

Well, I have been to GM: & begged her as a personal favor to stop with me for some months: to w^h the old Soul gladly consents: so that you will have no fear of her during Charles's visit to Paris, unless indeed her mind sh^d alter now she has made the promise, & she sh^d incline from that very reason to break away.

I am in treaty for a Paragon-Governess to all accounts — a Miss Drury — clergyman's daughter — all her relations gentlefolks — a miracle of sweet temper & gentleness and beloved by every body — not pretty & 27. I've not seen her yet: but she is to come up from Staffordshire on trial presently. Should she not suit, why, we must try a sort of Nursery Governess-maid and companion, and send the children to M^rs Dance's [47] friends the Miss Hares — I met them at M^rs Dances the other day, kind & seemingly simple good ladies. The children went to a dancing-match there one day & were pleased & Minny not frightened. But I would prefer the paragon, & that Anny should have somebody to attach herself to. I ought to be more with them — but how? It is work work, think think all day. Men of my sort I suppose can do no otherwise — I am always thinking of No IV or No V.[48] &c — All things go very well in that

[47] Mrs. Dance (d. 1854) was the former Mrs. Ralph Ingilby, widow since 1831 of the younger brother of Sir Henry Ingilby, first Baronet. She had four children by her first marriage: Charles Henry (1827–1894), Ralph Mitford (1829–1857), Harriet Jane (m. 1856), and Mary Lipscomb Ingilby. She married Charles Dance (1794–1863), the dramatist, in 1840.

[48] Number IV of *Vanity Fair* for April (chapters 12 to 14) and number V for May (chapters 15 to 18).

respect — In the summer P.G. I shall send over the little ones to
see their Granny, if she has room for them. They both yearn after
you — dear Souls — and you — But I know it is best they should
remain with their father. God mend his sins, and make him do his
duty. Last Sunday was March 14 — my dear little Jane died on
that day — Anny & I went to Church in the morning: and I'm
thinking of having a home-church every morning. All this writing
is very virtuous isn't it? O God purify us and make clean our
hearts.

Now that GM is to stay: Mʳˢ Gloyne may tell her about the
Bayonne business it would have been cruel I think only to mention
it the day before she went away You have my say, dearest old
Mother & now back to work work work. God bless you and my dear
old GP.

W M T.

There's a letter from Butterworth Baily [49] no longer in the
direction conveying the official damper to poor Madame Delder's
hopes. When Bess goes I wonder wᵈ Aunt Ritchie let Charlotte
come to me for 2 or 3 months?

387.        TO MRS. CARMICHAEL-SMYTH
6 APRIL 1847

*Address:* Mʳˢ Carmichael Smyth | 2 Rue Ponthieu Champs Élysées | Paris.
*Postmark:* 8 AVRIL 47 BOULOGNE. Hitherto unpublished.

April 6. 1847.

My dearest Mammy. The Gloyne banishment has cost me a
valuable day's work. I decide right against you: and shall use my
influence (if I use it all) with Mʳˢ G to stay rather than go. My
Grandmother ought to have people she likes within reach. She is
very lonely and feeble, and in my belief so near her last days, that
any morning I may have to send you a black seal. As for what the

[49] William Butterworth Bayley (1782–1860), who ended his four-year term
as a director of the East India Company's Civil Service earlier in 1847 (*Post
Office London Directory*, 1847, p. 55).

world says or M$^{rs}$ Gloyne says or what not I don't care a straw.
I won't have her in the house on any account. But let her hang
about; and come & see and comfort the poor old Soul from time to
time. As for me and poor Gloyne fiddlededee — The fact is you
ought to have taken my Grandmother away with you: as I saw
most clearly at the time: but how could I add fresh troubles &
perplexities to that poor heart secretly half-breaking with parting
from the children? God bless them. Every day I understand better
what your pang must have been at parting with them — They are a
noble pair. They do me so much good that I won't brag of it.
There is something angelical in Minny's sweetness: and I have
almost as much veneration for Anny's brains as you have for
your own prodigy of a son. God Almighty guard & prosper us
all.

Well, the Governess has come — not such a paragon as I expected — but ladylike, timid, kind and unaffected seemingly —
They have begun their lessons today in the school room — They
dine at 3, GM likes her dinner then. When I dine at home therefore w$^h$ is much oftener now than last year, I shall banquet alone
or with a friend. and have the little ones for dessert. — Anny is
employed in taking Miss Drury's measure — I mean morally. She
will be the Governess's mistress I expect — Miss D is not ill-look-
ing, but of such a countenance & complexion as don't render her
dangerous. Thank God for that — Her people are good — clergymen fellows of colleges & so forth — and at any rate she's a lady.
Poor dear Bess used to raise my gorge with her coarseness, and
rebukes of the children for being vulgar — She tell my little
princesses they were vulgar! I shant move any more in the business.
I never said or did a rude thing to her; although you all give it
against me. I persist that the proper thing in life is to call a poker
a poker — Good God what was I to do when of her own accord she
offered to stop the rest of the year with me? — Well. She was
a most kind honest & worthy woman — Peace go with her: but I
want a lady to be with my children.

If Gloyne goes my Grandmother says she'll go too. Not that
she can or will. But she will be uncomfortable: and no comfort

ought to be taken from her. I don't think you know how near the end is — And so no more —

I have said my say to G that I dont think she ought to go and henceforth hold my tongue on the business — God bless my dearest old Mammy & GP. Here are more perplexities for you to debate — And all this time I ought to be at my work, yearning my bread. Goodbye

W M T.

388.      TO MRS. CARMICHAEL-SMYTH
15 APRIL 1847

*Address:* M$^{rs}$ Carmichael Smyth | 2 Rue Ponthieu. Champs Élysées | Paris.
*Postmarks:* 15 AP 1847, 17 AVRIL 47 BOULOGNE. Hitherto unpublished.

My dearest Mammy I have lost stolen or mislaid a little note for you w$^h$ ought to have gone 2 days ago to tell you not to be looking out quite so soon for what must happen before very many months or years though. The old lady is pretty cheerful orders the dinners: seems very fond of me: bullies Anny: and I think is as happy with us as may be — Quin told me of course that she was breaking up w$^h$ was not much news, but did not say anything about Cancer — I am in a state of distraction with No V — I lost a whole week last week with our domestic perplexities, doubts about G M, comings & goings of M$^{rs}$ Gloyne &c — and must fly the house I see to get quiet. M$^{rs}$ Gloyne is gone — and the old lady quite resigned to her departure — I am therefore content — for M$^{rs}$ G was a very awkward customer in my house — being neither a servant nor a lady. Poor woman. I fear I have treated her with haughtiness and repent of that unchristianism. Arthur Shawe is gone back to his wife at last — Poor Langslow so poor as to be obliged to borrow money for the expenses of his wife's illness & funeral [50] — My little women are delightful. The Governess just the thing — and I feel easy in my mind that I shan't fall in love with her — I cant write — I'm thinking of V.

God bless you
W M T.

[50] Mrs. Langslow died on April 8, 1847 (*Memorials*, p. 510).

389.   TO THE REV. ALEXANDER JOHN SCOTT
20 APRIL 1847

*Address:* A. J. Scott Esq[re] | 40 Glocester Crescent | Regents Park. *Postmark:*
AP 20 1847. Hitherto unpublished.

Young S[t] Tuesday.

My dear Scott

I grieve to say I am going to dine at 2 places tomorrow — at the
Temple & afterwards in a politer quarter — and can't with the best
will in the world propose myself for a 3[d] dinner.

Dinner no 2 does not take place till 8 o'clock so that I shall be
too late to make a bow to M[rs] Scott in the evening; but I will remember your Wednesdays and will not fail to ask soon for a cup
of tea.

Yours dear Scott sincerely
W M Thackeray.

390.        TO EDWARD CHAPMAN
29 MAY 1847

Hitherto unpublished.

May 29. 1847.

My dear Sir

Coming home last night I found a lawyers letter from an Irish
Railroad of w[h] I've the good luck to be a registered proprietor,[51]
and of w[h] the shares w[h] I sold for some twopenny premium have
been thrown back on my hands. I have to pay 150£ between today
& Monday —

Can I realize on the 2nd Edition of M[rs] Perkins? I am horribly
pressed or I should not think of dunning you; but please to consider the necessity of the case, & see what can be done for me.

Yours
W M Thackeray.

[51] See above, No. 314.

391.     TO MRS. CARMICHAEL-SMYTH
29 MAY 1847

*Address:* M^rs Carmichael Smyth. | 2 Rue de Ponthieu | Champs Élysées | Paris.
*Postmarks:* 29 MY 1847, 31 MAI 47 BOULOGNE. Published in part, *Biographical Introductions*, I, xxxiii.

My dearest Mammy What has happened since I wrote a year ago? The same story of everyday work work gobble gobble scuffling through the day with business and a sort of pleasure w^h becomes a business, till bed-time — and no prospect of more than temporary quiet. I have just got my months work done (all but one days work more and I ought to be about that now) — and with Tuesday the next month begins, & the next work &c — was ever such martyrdom! on the best of victuals to be sure — But I suppose there is no use in a man thinking about what he does in this world, what he is capable of doing & knowing is the thing: and when we go hence into A Somewhere where there will be time and quiet sufficient doubtless, who knows what a deal of good may be found in us yet? What a thing it will be to be made good & wise. You see I am always thinking about Vanity Fair. Everything is very flat and dull — Nobody cares about O'Connell being dead [52] for instance any more than for Queen Anne — and upon this subject, and upon human greatness in general — (here an article for Punch comes into my head that might be made apropos of O'C's demise) — I don't see that I am called on to write letters to you.

Well, yesterday was my dear little Minny's birthday, and we had a day of heat and idleness at Hampstead Court,[53] finished with a cold-collation at M^rs Barber's at Twickenham, where all the ladies assembled were excellently kind to the children. They behaved like fine little queens as they are, full of grace and fine manners I think. The pictures did not charm them over much, but General Macleods [54] palace of Moorshedabad, with a little hawab, palan-

[52] Daniel O'Connell died in Genoa on May 15. The projected *Punch* article was apparently not written.     [53] Where the Crowes lived.
[54] Lieutenant-General Duncan Macleod (1780–1856), the designer of this Indian palace.

keens elephants bearers &c 2 inches high delighted them hugely, and so did the labyrinth and the Chestnut trees in fair bloom, and the gardens all over green & sunshine. We all went to bed very tired and sober at 10 o'clock. M$^{rs}$ Parker coming to console G M in our absence — She is weakly, and of course moving surely downwards, but in pretty good spirits, and pleased with her little household occupations, fidgetting the servants quite unrestrained & ringing the bells with unbounded liberty. Miss Drury is very good & sensible — and I like her because she seems to understand & appreciate our dear Anny's great noble heart & genius. She'll be a young woman directly, and please God a she-friend to me. The night before seeing King Lear was to be performed [55] I took her & M$^{rs}$ Brookfield and Eugenie and Miss Drury — we all found the play a bore and Anny shut her ears when old Lear began cursing his children. We are the most superstitious people in England — It is almost blasphemy to say a play of Shakespeare is bad. I can't help it if I think so — and there are other pieces of bookolatry too w$^h$ make me rebel. I can't bring myself to read the savage curses and cut-throat imprecations in the Psalms for instance — w$^h$ come alongside of passages of the utmost beauty & piety. The prayer-saying of a morning is a very good thing though I trust. &c &c Amen that it may prove so —

I am very sorry indeed to hear from M$^{rs}$ Auber, how you have let domestic circumstances worry you and of my dear old mothers secret sorrows and yearnings and vain tears. What a character for Vanity Fair that poor woman is whom you are so passionately longing after. How mad people are. I mean incapable from perversity and insane egotism, of seeing the right. Mary never could I think. Well perhaps I'm as mad as she. I'm told she writes very affectionately to my G. M: and I daresay doesn't know that it is a lie, and never doubts but that she is one of the finest hearted creatures in the world. Would GP. like to try Boulogne for a few weeks — As GM has been here for 8 or 9 months at free quarters, she might

[55] Macready appeared in *Lear* on May 26 at the Princess's Theatre (*Diaries*, ed. Toynbee, II, 367).

afford a house — or I will if need be, though my debts are unpaid still — and seem endless.

And so having said nothing, I come to Good bye and God bless my dearest Mammy & G P. I am as well as any mortal man almost (I have dined at home all the week) and am now going to dress in my best for a genteel party at Mʳ Chas Bullers. God bless you

W M T.

## 392.    TO WILLIAM HARRISON AINSWORTH
### 1 JUNE 1847

Published in part by Ellis, *Ainsworth*, II, 44–45.

13 Young Sᵗ Kensington Sqʳᵉ<br>June 1.

My dear Ainsworth.

I was sorry not to find you at home yesterday: when I came to see those pretty young ladies once more if I could; and to tell you how it was the Mulligan didn't come to your ball.[56]

I had entered it for the 20ᵗʰ by some blunder into my ledger, and was quite prepared on that night as bear witness Mʳˢ Talfourd with whom I dined — From her I learned just as I was setting off that all was over, and from everybody else that it was one of the handsomest parties ever seen. Not being a dancing or even a supping man now the loss of the good things doesn't very much affect me: but I should have liked to have shaken hands with old friends to whom I beg to be very kindly remembered.

Yours dear Ainsworth truly<br>W M Thackeray.

[56] Ellis (*Ainsworth*, II, 44) writes that this ball "was given at Kensal Manor House to celebrate the coming out of Miss Blanche Ainsworth — the youngest daughter — about 1847." Thackeray's allusion to the Mulligan (of *Mrs. Perkins's Ball*) also points to 1847.

393.            TO JOHN MURRAY
                  3 JUNE 1847

My text is taken from George Paston [Emily Morse Symonds], *At John Murray's* (London, 1932), p. 71, where the date is given.

I ought to have thanked you sooner for the last number of the *Quarterly*, in which someone was pleased to make favourable mention of my name.[57] I show my gratitude now that I have a favour to ask. Three of the heroes of a story I am writing are going to be present this very next number [58] at the battle of Waterloo, whereof you announce a new history by Mr. Gleig.[59] If the book is ready (and only awaiting the 18th for publication) would you kindly let me have a copy? Titmarsh at Waterloo will be a very remarkable and brilliant performance, doubtless. Yours, dear Sir, very much obliged,

                                    W. M. Thackeray

394.    FROM JOHN FORSTER TO THACKERAY
                  9 JUNE 1847

Hitherto unpublished.

                              58, Lincoln Inn Fields
                              June 9. 1847

Dear Thackeray

You must be quite aware that I am entitled to ask from you some explanation of the reasons which induced you to behave to me with such marked discourtesy last night. Dickens is kind enough to offer to see you for this purpose, and to convey this note to you.

                              Very truly yrs
                                    John Forster

W M Thackeray Esq

[57] There is a passing reference to "the joyous Titmarsh" in *The Quarterly Review* for June, 1847, p. 90.
[58] The battle was deferred till the last chapter (32) of number IX for September.
[59] *The Story of the Battle of Waterloo* by George Robert Gleig (1796–1888).

395.                    TO JOHN FORSTER
                        9 JUNE 1847

*Address:* J. Forster Esq^re | Favored by Sir A. Duff-Gordon. Hitherto unpub-
lished. Original owned by the Comte de Suzannet. A copy in Thackeray's
hand is owned by Mrs. Fuller.

                              June 9. 1847.
                              13 Young S^t Kensington Sq^e
Sir
   The explanation of my conduct last night lies in words used by
yourself many weeks ago when you were pleased to inform a mutual acquaintance that I was 'as false as hell.'
   It certainly would have been [an] act of treachery on my part to
shake the hand of a gentleman who had formed such an opinion of
me: and I dont see, under the circumstances, how I could have acted
otherwise than I did.
   I am Sir. your very obedient servant
                        W M Thackeray.
J. Forster Esq^re


396.   FROM JOHN FORSTER TO THACKERAY
                   9 JUNE 1847

Hitherto unpublished.

                              58, Lincoln Inn Fields
                              June 9. 1847
Sir
   Your letter, coupled with the information which Sir Alexander
Duff-Gordon empowers Mr Dickens to add to it — I mean, of
course, the disclosure of the name of your informant — puts me in
possession of your reasons for your last night's demeanour towards
me. For this, I have to thank you.
   In reference to the alleged language used in conversation with

Mr Taylor,[60] I desire, very earnestly, to say that I have no recollection whatever of using the expression, or anything like the expression, you quote. But I cannot say that I did not use it. I am quite sure, in any case, that in conveying to you any portion of a very private conversation which passed in my own chambers — and in which, if the expression were ever used, all that went before and followed after was I presume, from its effect upon you, omitted — Mr Taylor broke his plighted word to me, and committed a gross breach of confidence.

Whether a similar proceeding on the part of any other man who may have held any conversation with you of which *I* was the subject, at a time when we were in habits of the friendliest communication — or whether any report made to me, long ago, of the private pleasantries of your pen and pencil with me for their theme [61] — may have more than once afforded me an opportunity, not embraced, of acting with just discourtesy towards you — is a question which I leave to your own remembrance.

I am Sir,

Your very obedient servant

John Forster

W. M. Thackeray Esq[e]

[60] Tom Taylor (1817–1880), the son of a Durham brewer, matriculated at Trinity College, Cambridge, in 1837, received his B.A. and M.A. degrees in 1840 and 1843, and came up to London in 1844. Though he was called to the bar in 1846 and had chambers at 10 Crown Office Row, where Thackeray put up his nameplate for several years, he devoted himself chiefly to journalism. He was a prolific dramatist, a reporter for *The Morning Chronicle* and *The Daily News*, and a writer for *Punch* from 1844 until his death.

[61] The report was perhaps made by Dickens. In the Widener Collection of the Harvard College Library there is the following undated note from Dickens to Jerdan: "When you come here tomorrow, will you put that caricature of Thackeray's relative to Forster and Bulwer, in your pocket? I wish to have an opportunity of glancing at it for an instant — alone of course — and you promised me you would shew it to me." For examples of Thackeray's caricatures of Forster, see above, No. 355, and below, No. 1680.

## 397. FROM CHARLES DICKENS TO JOHN FORSTER
## 9 JUNE 1847

My text is taken from *The Letters of Charles Dickens*, ed. Dexter, II, 28–29.

Athenæum
Wednesday night, Ninth June 1847

My Dear Forster, — I saw Gordon just now (1/2 p. 9) and in handing him your letter, said what you wished. He read it, attentively, and said he presumed there was an end of the matter. Did I think Thackeray had anything more to do? I said, no. That I had considered that an end of it, and had said so much to you. He then observed that Thackeray was coming at eleven o'clock, and he would give it to him, and so close the business.

I said that as far as Thackeray was concerned, and separating my remark from you, or your affair, I should tell him, if he were there, that I thought these things arose in his jesting much too lightly between what was true and what was false, and what he owed to both, and not being sufficiently steady to the former. Gordon said he quite assented to this. I added that I was bound to say beyond this, that in reference to his Imitations in Punch [62] (out of which, as I understood from you, the conversation with Mr. Taylor had arisen), I had a strong opinion of my own: and that it was that they did no honor to literature or literary men, and should be left to very inferior and miserable hands: which I desired Thackeray to know. Gordon quite assented to this, also, and said that your letter did you, in his opinion, great credit, that it was full of good sense and manly dealing, and that he had read it with great satisfaction. I told him, with reference to that paragraph of retort on Thackeray, that as I had reason to know its force better than you did even, [63] I had not objected to it, but had felt it ought to be there, and I told him (as I never told you, though I had my reason 7 or 8 years ago) why.

[62] *Novels by Eminent Hands.*
[63] For a caricature of Dickens by Thackeray, which was presumably not unique, see below, No. 1680.

Gordon said, towards the close of our interview, that he hoped this w^d have no unpleasant bearings on Mr. Taylor, who, he was sure, had merely spoken in jest. I said that I understood you had been, during my absence from England, in habits of intimacy and familiarity, and that I denied a man's right to jest, after that fashion. I said, moreover, that I could not oppose your sending a copy of that letter to Mr. Taylor, if you were so inclined, though I should object to your addressing him on the subject in any other form. Gordon replied that he thought your desire would be a reasonable one, if you *did* desire to send him that copy.

Beyond this, I described your real conversation with Mr. Taylor, as you described it to me, and Gordon said, more than once, that he thought Thackeray altogether wrong in the sort of behaviour he had adopted towards you at Procter's, and that he had better have taken you aside, and told you his offence.

I have omitted nothing of the purport of our conversation, — which I detail here, of course, only for you. Nothing could possibly be more frank, sensible, or gentlemanly in the best sense, than Gordon's behaviour through the whole affair. There did not appear to be the smallest difference of opinion between himself and me. — Always affectionately.

## 398.   FROM JOHN FORSTER TO TOM TAYLOR
### 10 JUNE 1847

Hitherto unpublished. My text is taken from a transcript (supplied by the Comte de Suzannet, who owns the original) of a memorandum concerning the "false as hell" quarrel drawn up by Forster. Original of the note not traced.

58 Lincoln's Inn Fields. June 10 1847.

Dear Taylor,

I have no feeling but one of deep regret in sending you the correspondence [64] which you will find copied on the opposite page of this letter. Few things could have given me greater pain, or could have been more unexpected by me, than such an interruption of

[64] The letters exchanged by Forster and Thackeray on June 9.

that familiar intimacy with you, in which I have always had sincere pleasure.

Believe me

J. F.

399.                    TO CHARLES DICKENS
                        11 JUNE 1847

*Address:* Charles Dickens Esq^re | 1 Chester Place. | Regents Park. Hitherto unpublished. Original owned by the Comte de Suzannet. Mrs. Fuller owns a first draft of this letter, which does not differ materially from the Comte de Suzannet's manuscript.

13 Young S^t Kensington. June 11. 1847.

My dear Dickens  One word more, & in the interest of peace only about the matter between Forster & myself.  I am concerned that Taylor should be brought into trouble, through my means, with a man who has been friendly to him, and for whom he feels and expresses a sincere regard.  The unlucky 'false as hell' I took to be a reflexion on my private honor & character, and though the charge was so vague that I could not notice it specially, I had nothing for it but to cut the man who had made it.

The conversation during w^h this accusation was made I heard nothing about: but I confess that I have a light on it now, and can understand how a man of Forsters emphatic way of talking (I wish to speak of this without any discourtesy), chafed by ridicule, should have uttered the words w^h formed the subject of my difference with him —[65] He consigned me to Hell for making caricatures of him: roasting me as I own & I'm sorry for it, to have done him.  If this interpretation is right, the charge of treachery vanishes: the Hell is perfectly harmless: and my conduct of the other night quite uncalled for.

Taylor should not have let the words slip, but that was all his fault.  And as I fell into error by hearing only one unfortunate

---

[65] In his first draft Thackeray began the next sentence: "And as we have all heard him adjure the Divinity many times" — , then crossed these words out, and continued as above.

phrase of a conversation, so Forster can't know all the good that Taylor has said of him, and I assure you the latter has always been his very constant & steady friend. His character has always been safe in Taylor's hands; his talents, good-nature, services, &c constantly and warmly acknowledged. If he had broken more confidence this dispute would never have occurred. He never thought the words were serious: it was only I who persisted in considering them so. As indeed I could do no otherwise — and with that conviction, how was I to shake a man's hand? I sh^d have been a knave if I had.

And the affair seems to me to stand thus. Forster ought not to have used the words: Taylor ought not to have told them: and I ought not to have taken them up. And I for my part am sorry I did: and I beg you to use your good offices to prevent any breach between Forster & Taylor.

Yours my dear Dickens sincerely<br>W M Thackeray —

## 400.    FROM SIR ALEXANDER DUFF-GORDON
## TO CHARLES DICKENS
### 11 JUNE 1847

Hitherto unpublished. My text is taken from a transcript of the Forster Memorandum supplied by the Comte de Suzannet.

My Dear Dickens,

Although I told Thackeray that in my opinion the correspondence should cease, still as Thackeray's letter to you can do nothing but good I have relaxed with Thackeray to send it.

It would be absurd that Tom Taylor and Forster should no longer be friends because Thackeray, for once in his life, took things too seriously.

Yours truly<br>A D Gordon

## 401.   FROM TOM TAYLOR TO JOHN FORSTER
## 11 JUNE 1847

Hitherto unpublished. My text is taken from a transcript of the Forster Memorandum supplied by the Comte de Suzannet.

Friday, June 11th 1847.

My Dear Forster,

I do not write with any expectation or wish to exonerate myself from blame in this most disagreeable affair. I only wish to set you right on matters of fact, which affect the inferences you must draw as to the real nature of my communication to Thackeray of what you said.

If I had repeated the conversation, to which you allude, I should have been justly chargeable with "breach of confidence". What I really did, however imprudent and mischievous, by no means amounts to this.

The conversation did not take place on the occasion you mentioned in your second letter. It was, as I said last night, some time before, when proceeding together to dine at Macready's that you expressed the opinion in question of Thackeray. You may perhaps, on the time being recalled to you, recollect this and also how I received it. I laughed excessively, believing that you were speaking under the influence of some momentary resentment, and struck only by the extravagance of your phrase. Soon after I expressed to Thackeray (I do not remember how the subject was started) my astonishment at the feeling which existed between you, and then it was that forgetting the obvious duty of passing over in silence what was said confidentially however hastily, (indeed the more hastily the more confidentially), I repeated the unlucky expression, remarking on its vehemence laughingly, and in fact expecting that it would produce no more effect on Thackeray than it did on me when used by you. I forgot that it was personal to him and not to me. He was galled by it, and I at the time expressed my regret at having been foolish enough to repeat it. These are the facts. I have committed an act of great imprudence, folly, and mischievousness. But

I have committed it without any intention of making mischief, or deliberate violation of implied, still less of plighted, secrecy.

I am sincerely sorry for what has occurred and mean to make the only use I can of it — as a lesson for the future.

Of course the occurrence must shake your confidence in me. This I am prepared for and regret very sincerely. But my greatest pain arises from this, not that I have acted foolishly and thoughtlessly, not that I have got myself into a scrape, and two of my friends into a quarrel, but that I have inflicted upon you the shock which follows the first implanting of distrust in one in whom you have felt confidence.

Time alone can prove whether or not I am capable of profiting enough by the lesson of this unhappy affair to merit the same trust as you have hitherto placed in me.

Frankly and honestly I tender my remorseful apologies for what I have done. I have certainly wronged you, not so much as you think now, but quite enough to account for any bitterness of feeling you may have towards me. I feel self-reproach — not of the kind I should feel if I had broken my word, or acted treacherously with malice aforethought, but of that kind which the fool may be supposed to feel when he finds that the arrows which he scatters have struck one who has treated him with kindness and merited only kindness in return.

I write this at length rather to ease my own mind than to satisfy or appease yours. I am not at all anxious to exonerate myself from blame, but only that the blame may be as fairly apportioned to the offence as possible.

With a renewal of my regret

Believe me

Yours most sincerely

Tom Taylor

P. S. I shall be glad to hear that the complexion of the affair is altered by my recalling to you the occasion on which the words were used. Your letter I did not see till my return from Macready's last night or I should not have mentioned the subject then.

Should I not also write to Dickens and to Gordon (or will you write to the former?) clearing myself of the imputation of "breach of confidence" which you lay me under, and which I am quite and do readily excuse you for attributing to me,[66] but which I cannot allow to continue unanswered, either to you or to them.

402.      FROM JOHN FORSTER TO
CHARLES DICKENS
12 JUNE 1847

Hitherto unpublished. My text is taken from a transcript of the Forster Memorandum supplied by the Comte de Suzannet.

58 Lincoln's Inn Fields. June 12 1847.

My Dear Dickens,

I return you Thackeray's note. Like you, I cannot but respect the spirit of it, and feel that it is generously and frankly written. He sums up the three mistakes, quite truly; and I should but ill recognize his doing so, if I hesitated to acknowledge mine, and to say that I am very sorry for it. Pray make what use of this letter you think best. I wrote to Taylor this morning, as we agreed last night; I am more than ever glad that there was no word of reproach in my note.

J. F.

403.    FROM JOHN FORSTER TO TOM TAYLOR
12 JUNE 1847

Hitherto unpublished. My text is taken from a transcript of the Forster Memorandum supplied by the Comte de Suzannet.

58 Lincoln's Inn Fields. June 12 1847.

My Dear Taylor,

Without entering into any discussion of the distinction you desire to point out — or thinking it necessary to do so —, I cannot hesi-

---

[66] So in the original, the Comte de Suzannet notes.

tate, after reading your letter of yesterday, to acquit you truly of anything but indiscretion, in regard to this late matter. Pray understand that I do so without reserve. I have communicated this to Dickens, and give you liberty to use the present note as you please.

J. F.

404.                    TO MRS. MACREADY
                       15 JUNE 1847

My text is taken from an undated George D. Smith catalogue.

13 Young St., Kensington, June 15.

I am sure, considering circumstances, you and Mr. Macready will give me some other day but the 21st for Greenwich. Dickens has just written begging me to dine with him and meet Forster, and make up Quarrels and be Friends. I had asked Sir A. Gordon and Lady Gordon who had promised to meet you: but he too is implicated in the Reconciliation Dinner. Any day from the 23rd to the 28th I am quite free and beg you to select one of these for our meeting.

William Makepeace Thackeray.

405.        TO THE REV. WILLIAM BROOKFIELD
                       15? JUNE 1847

Published in *Collection of Letters*, p. 5.

My dear W    There will be no dinner at Greenwich on Monday — Dickens has chosen that day for a reconciliation banquet between Forster & me.

Is Madam gone [67] and is she better? My heart follows her respectfully to Devonshire, and the dismal scenes of my youth.

[67] The Brookfields had given up their residence in Great Pulteney Street. Mrs. Brookfield spent the next few months with relatives in the country, first in Southampton and later in Bristol. Brookfield established himself in the cellars of St. Luke's Church in Soho, of which he was curate.

I am being brought to bed of my seventh darling [68] with inexpressible throes: and dine out every day till Juice knows when.

I'll come to you on Sunday night if you like — though, stop. Why shouldnt you after church come & sleep out here in the country?

Yours —  Jos: Osborne.

406.   TO ARTHUR SHAWE
21 JUNE 1847

Hitherto unpublished.

13 Young S$^t$ Kensington. 21 June.

My dear Arthur I may as well surprize you by answering your uncles [69] queries with that celerity with w$^h$ you know bad news always travels. A very funny Hungarian novel might do & a history of Hungary from the Magyar not from the German w$^h$ is as common here as ditch-water. But the times are the worst ever known for every kind of literature, and nobody will think of buying such a pig in the poke as M$^r$ Shawe offers. He must first do the books & *then* its 5 chances to 1, that he sells them. It is best that the truth sh$^d$ be told unpalateable though it be in this instance. I have had many such applications to answer of late & all most unfavorably to beginners — a very good fellow among others an ex-officer of Hungarian hussars & known too in literature.

We are all moighty well here, and I am working my brains all day & my — chest all night as usual — The great people I know would make your eyes wink. I wish it were the end of the season & a little quiet could be had. Vanity Fair does decently well, but I've not paid my debts yet and here the 21 I've not sent a word in of No VII.

I hear very alarming accounts of poor Jane's state of mind. M$^{rs}$ Spencer told M$^{rs}$ Gloyne that she was fairly out of her mind, but what to believe from such an informant as your — never mind whom

---

[68] For July, chapters 23 to 25.
[69] Colonel Shawe, whom Arthur Shawe was visiting in Ireland.

— The life the poor girl leads must be so infernal that I shouldn't be surprized at any fatal ending of it. The children get on very well with their governess a nice sober hearty jolly ladylike person — with whom there's no danger of falling in love, w^h is a great mussy. M^rs Brookfield still keeps possession of this ♥ , but this romantic passion doesn't disturb my sleep or my happytight for wittles. M^rs Bakewell was here t'other day: with good accounts of the poor little woman. She doesn't want to see me or the children. I intend to go & look at her out of a cab. She is quite happy & perfectly quiet. How I wish her Mother would take a turn at paying the Quarters bills. Thank God however for health and means of defraying them.

Give my affectionate regards to M^rs Arthur: & good old Aunt Mary. D^r Thackeray of Chester [70] has just sent me a pressing invitation & a prodigious long yarn about arboriculture — fancy applying to me about it! Good bye my dear old fellow. Kiss Corselles for me, and any pretty girl you may select. I dont see so much of Sawbones of late — though we are the best of friends. I wish I had you here for No VIII of V. F. when the Battle of Waterloo must positively come off.[71]

Ajew. Affectionately yours<br>
W M T.

It is all bosh about Pardoe [72] getting the 900. Nobody gets such sums.

[70] Dr. William Makepeace Thackeray (1770–1849), *Genealogy* (30), was educated at Rugby and at Cambridge, where he received an M.B. degree in 1794 and an M.D. degree in 1800. He practised during the whole of his mature life in Chester. See *Memorials*, pp. 89–96.

[71] See above, No. 393.

[72] See above, No. 226.

### 407.    TO THE REV. WILLIAM BROOKFIELD
### JUNE? 1847 [73]

Published in *Collection of Letters*, pp. 6–7.

My dear old B.       Can you come & dine on Thursday at 6. I shall be at home — no party — nothing — only me. And about your nightcap? Why not come out for a day or two? Though the rooms are very comfortable in the Church-vaults.

Farewell ever your Louisa.

and Madam? is she well? &c.

### 408.               TO LEIGH HUNT
### JUNE? 1847

*Address:* Leigh Hunt Esq^re | &c &c &c.  Published by Mr. Wilson, *Boston Transcript*, July 31, 1920.

My dear Hunt.

It never rains but it pours. The Amateurs give you a benefit.[74] Gov^t gives you a pension and Titmarsh sends you his famous work.[75] I have been wanting to bring it any day this fortnight but have been ceaselessly busy since I saw you.

Congratulations on your pension will come as a matter of course. I dont offer any but believe me

Yours dear Hunt most sincerely<br>W M Thackeray

[73] This letter appears to have been written shortly after Brookfield went to live in the cellars of St. Luke's Church.

[74] It was stated in *The Athenæum* for June 12 (p. 624) that certain "literary amateurs" planned to provide for Leigh Hunt, whose needs the government had not seen fit to supply, by a series of theatrical performances. On June 26 the same journal announced (p. 679) that Hunt had been granted a pension of £200. The amateurs, headed by Dickens (*Letters*, ed. Dexter, II, 30–35), realizing that Hunt would no longer need the large sum they had intended to secure for him, cancelled their London engagements and gave only the two performances they had scheduled in Manchester and Liverpool on July 26 and 28.

[75] *Mrs. Perkins's Ball.*

409. TO MRS. CARMICHAEL-SMYTH
2 JULY 1847

*Address:* M⁽ʳˢ⁾ Carmichael Smyth | 2 Rue de Ponthieu. Champs Élysées | Paris.
*Postmarks:* 2 JY 1847, 4 JUIL. 47 BOULOGNE. Published in part, *Biographical Introductions*, I, xxxii, xxxiv, xxxvi; IX, xlvii–xlviii.

My dearest Mammy. I have had 4 copies of L'Illustration sent to me by friends indignant at the owdacious piracy.[76] It won't do me any harm, and besides I believe there is no remedy, were it ever so injurious. And this isn't the only evil out of the book — O Gorman Mahon [77] swears he is the particular Mulligan and that he will kill & eat me whenever we meet. There are 4 other Mulligans in London though not so warlike: but I am sorry about O'Gorman whose salt I have eaten, and whom I didn't know when I invented Mulligan first. So Bess has gone away more indignant than ever the Crowes tell me, and though every body gives it against me, I vow I can't see that I have done her any earthly wrong. There are no end of quarrels in this wicked Vanity Fair, and my feet are perpetually in hot water.

Jerrold hates me, Ainsworth hates me, Dickens mistrusts me, Forster says I am false as hell,[78] and Bulwer curses me — he is the only one who has any reason — yes the others have a good one too as times go. I was the most popular man in the craft until within ab⁽ᵗ⁾ 12 months — and behold I've begun to succeed. It makes me very sad at heart though, this envy and meanness — in the great sages & teachers of the world. Am I envious and mean too I wonder? These fellows think so I know. Amen. God knows only. I

---

[76] It appears that *L'Illustration* reprinted *Mrs. Perkins's Ball*, but *Vanity Fair* did not escape piracy. In chapter 36 Thackeray entreats "the public newspapers which are in the habit of extracting portions of the various periodical works now published, *not* to reprint the following exact narrative and calculations [of how to live on nothing a year]" (*Works*, I, 348).

[77] Charles James Patrick Mahon (1800–1891), known as "the O'Gorman Mahon," a formidable adventurer and politician, described in the *Dictionary of National Biography* as "one of the last of the old race of dare-devil Irish gentlemen." He is supposed to have fought thirteen duels during his life.

[78] See above, No. 395.

scarcely understand any motive for any action of my own or anybody else's —

Of course you are quite right about Vanity Fair and Amelia being
selfish — it is mentioned in this very number.[79] My object is not to
make a perfect character or anything like it. Dont you see how
odious all the people are in the book (with exception of Dobbin) —
behind whom all there lies a dark moral I hope. What I want is
to make a set of people living without God in the world [80] (only
that is a cant phrase) greedy pompous mean perfectly self-satisfied
for the most part and at ease about their superior virtue. Dobbin &
poor Briggs are the only 2 people with real humility as yet.
Amelia's is to come, when her scoundrel of a husband is well dead
with a ball in his odious bowels; when she has had sufferings, a
child, and a religion [81]— But she has at present a quality above
most people whizz: LOVE — by w.[h] she shall be saved. Save me,
save me too O my God and Father, cleanse my heart and teach me
my duty.

I wasn't going to write in this way when I began. But these
thoughts pursue me plentifully. Will they ever come to a good
end? I should doubt God who gave them if I doubted that.

Why I dont write to you more is partly because I am ashamed.
What good to tell you what I have for dinner? it's always the same.
The people talk the same things: I guttle down a great quantity of
Champagne & Claret and laugh a great deal. But I haven't the face
to put down the transactions on paper. They make one blush to
think of them. I tell G M of the Lords I meet — it delights the
old lady hugely. I have never met above 3 men who were not
sneaks G P is one, I am not sorry to say: though I am sure I don't
show it in my behavior, except in little trivial instances to be re-

---

[79] VII for July, chapters 23 to 25. For the passage to which Thackeray refers, see *Works*, I, 225–226.

[80] *Ephesians*, 2, 12. Compare the celebrated paragraph in Newman's *Apo-
logia pro Vita Sua* (ed. Wilfrid Ward, Oxford, 1913, pp. 334–335), which
turns upon the same phrase.

[81] Amelia's husband dies in chapter 32 (number IX), her child is born in
chapter 35 (X), and her severest sufferings occur in chapters 46 and 50 (XIII
and XIV).

marked by psychologists. The other day poor old M.ʳ FitzGerald [82]
came out & fainted on the stairs at a party from heat and age and
exhaustion — You should have seen what care we took of him
getting him off to his carriage &c. But if he was cared for, how
much more was M.ʳˢ Fitz looked after? She was quite unconscious
in the great room listening to Alboni,[83] & covered all over with
diamonds & rouge — the attention every body paid her was something quite curious. The way in w.ʰ we spared her feelings, and got
her into somebody else's carriage was the last Vanity Fair benevolence I have seen since ever so long — since the night before almost.
It's always going on. I pick up bits here and there, and keep my
eyes pretty open, and am just as great a humbug as my neighbours
— God help us. Who is conscious? Is poor Mary conscious? She
fancies herself endowed with every virtue. I sicken as I see her
hand-writing — That sacrament is awful. Why couldn't she go &
fetch it? She must order God to come to her. Follies so tremendous performed under the Eyes of the Divine Wisdom I think only
elevate (so to speak) one's notion of the latter — as one feels after
looking into a microscope, how infinite littleness even is.

I am glad you have got M.ʳˢ Huyshe to comfort your old heart.
I saw Wentworth's tomb-stone [84] over the boys' gallery, at Harrow
the other day: and took a walk with him on Tallaton Common —
as the parson preached the foolishest sermon — It's a long time
back — A great gap of sinful wasted life lies between — But it has
been followed all through by the love of my dearest old mother.

As soon as the 3 Punch men who are gone to Paris for a holiday
return, I will try & run over to Boulogne and take a house for w.ʰ

[82] FitzGerald's father had no position except as the husband of Mrs. Fitz-
Gerald, who was independently wealthy. He was engaged upon a disastrous
coal-mining venture, by which he fondly hoped to recoup his broken fortunes,
but which went bankrupt not long before his death in March, 1852. "I do not
think I told you my Father was dead;" wrote his son (*Letters and Literary
Remains*, ed. Wright, II, 4) to Frederick Tennyson, "like poor old Sedley in
Thackeray's Vanity Fair, all his Coal schemes at an end. He died in March,
after an illness of three weeks, saying 'that engine works well' (meaning one of
his Colliery steam engines) as he lay in the stupor of Death."

[83] Marietta Alboni (1826–1894), the famous contralto.

[84] See above, No. 9.

I shan't mind paying, as the old lady won't. But all she saves will be for you, and I am rather glad that some dear relations of mine should have their minds at ease, and know that I am not making any very serious drain on the purse of the poor old soul.

Miss Drury continues to be a very jolly honest young lady I think and the children are still tolerable. Towards the end of the month I get so nervous that I don't speak to anybody scarcely, and once actually got up in the middle of the night and came down & wrote in my night-shimee: but that don't happen often, and I own I had had a nap after dinner that day. The publishers are quite contented — and now I must get to work. God bless my dearest old Mammy and G P: and send us a good meeting at Boulogne.

W M T.

### 410.    TO CHARLES WENTWORTH DILKE [85]
#### JULY 1847

Hitherto unpublished.

*    *    *

Morton is a very good German I should say — I have not heard him talk but I have heard him read and understand perfectly. He has 100 accomplishments and deals in ever so many languages

*    *    *

Did you see that adv⁺ about Vanity Fair in the Athenæum? [86] by Jove it is the greatest comp⁺ I ever had in my life.

*    *    *

[85] Charles Wentworth Dilke (1789–1864), editor of *The Athenæum* from 1830 to 1846 and manager of *The Daily News* from 1846 to 1849.

[86] The advertisements for the first six numbers of Thackeray's novel in *The Athenæum* follow the same pattern: "VANITY FAIR. — Pen and Pencil Sketches of English Society. No. VI. By W. M. THACKERAY (Titmarsh). With numerous illustrations. Price 1*s*." (May 29, p. 581) In *The Athenæum* for July 3 (p. 720), however, Bradbury and Evans found it worth their while to insert a much more elaborate notice:

"NEW WORK BY MICHAEL ANGELO TITMARSH<br>This day is published, price 1*s*. with numerous Illustrations on<br>Steel and Wood, Part VII. of

411.            FROM MRS. PROCTER TO
                ABRAHAM HAYWARD
                23 JULY 1847

Published in *A Selection from the Correspondence of Abraham Hayward* (New York, 1887), I, 121–122.

13, Upper Harley Street,
July 23, 1847.

My dear Sir,

I send you "Vanity Fair", and I have, as you wished, marked some parts of it.[87] Not perhaps the best, but the most suitable for extracts, as it appears to me. The one quality for which I think Mr. Thackeray deserves the highest praise is the total absence of affectation. He relies, and wisely, upon his own power of describing and interesting the reader in what is simple and true. Like Goldsmith and Sterne he does not elaborate or insist too much upon any feeling, but trusts to our understanding and sympathy.

> "Some natural sorrow, grief, or pain,
>     That has been and may be again."

The characters are neither devils nor angels, but living, breathing people.[88] They neither appear through a trapdoor, nor change their

---

VANITY FAIR:
PEN AND PENCIL SKETCHES OF ENGLISH SOCIETY.
By W. M. THACKERAY
Author of 'Mrs. Perkins's Ball', &c.

'Everything is simple, natural and unaffected. Common sense sits smiling on the top of every page.' — *Morning Chronicle.*

'If Mr. Thackeray were to die to-morrow, his name would be transmitted down to posterity by his "Vanity Fair". He is the Fielding of the nineteenth century.' — *Sun.*"

[87] It will be seen from the notes which follow that Hayward leant heavily on Mrs. Procter's suggestions in his essay on "Thackeray's Writings" (*Edinburgh Review*, January, 1848, pp. 46–67). He seems also to have been guided by her in his choice of extracts for quotation. See below, No. 436.

[88] "The great charm of [*Vanity Fair*] is its entire freedom from mannerism and affectation both in style and sentiment . . . [Thackeray] never exhausts, elaborates, or insists too much upon anything. . . . His effects are uniformly

father and mother in the third volume. One feels well acquainted with all his characters, although they have no pet phrase or peculiar expression, and except in the case of Dobbin's lisp they have no distinguishing habit, or manner of speaking. He has also permitted us to have a story without one of those character-servants who talk as no servant ever did, or would be permitted to talk. Amelia Sedley is charming: she is not an angel, only a good, true, kindhearted girl, who loves an idle, selfish man much better than he deserves (a habit we women are rather given to): —

> "A creature not too bright or good
> For human nature's daily food,
> For transient sorrows, simple wiles,
> Praise, blame, love, kisses, tears and smiles." [89]

His people are neither above or below one's sympathy, he treats of feelings common to all classes and to all times. And I feel it a great relief, that he has no wish to prove or disprove anything. I rejoice to read again a good old-fashioned love story. He has avoided the two extremes in which so many of our popular writers delight; he allows that a gentleman may have a kind heart, and does not confine all virtue to St. Giles's; neither does he make out that all beauty and intelligence are to be found in Belgravia alone. [90]

---

the effects of sound wholesome legitimate art; and we need hardly add that we are never harrowed up with physical horrors of the Eugene Sue school in his writings, or that there are no melodramatic villains to be found in them. One touch of nature makes the whole world kin, and here are touches of nature by the dozen." (p. 50) The lines Mrs. Procter quotes are from Wordsworth's "The Solitary Reaper."

[89] "Amelia is a gentle, amiable, sweet-tempered girl, who cannot be better described than in the oft-quoted lines of Wordsworth — " (p. 54); there follows Mrs. Procter's citation from "She was a Phantom of Delight."

[90] "There are good people of quality as well as bad in his pages, — pretty much as we find them in the world; and the work is certainly not written with the view of proving the want of re-organisation in society, nor indeed of proving any thing else, which to us is a great relief. . . . Mr. Thackeray has kept his science and political economy (if he has any) for some other emergency, and given us a plain old-fashioned love-story, which any genuine novel reader of the old school may honestly, plentifully, and conscientiously cry over." (pp. 52–53)

He seems to me to excel in the pathetic parts: the scene between old Sedley and his wife (p. 152),[91] some short passages about Amelia, are expressed with the delicacy of a woman. I send you also "Chronicle of a Drum", which seems to me very striking. I have not ventured to mark it, and indeed I feel it rather absurd my having attempted to point out what appeared to me merits in *Vanity Fair*, to one so much better able both to appreciate and praise them.

Yours faithfully,<br>A. B. Procter.

412.     TO THE REV. WILLIAM BROOKFIELD
AUGUST? 1847

Published in *Collection of Letters*, p. 6.

La Dimanche.

Monsieur l'Abbé

De retour de Gravesend J'ai trouvé chez moi un billet de M. Crowe qui m'invite à diner demain a 6 heures précises a Ampstead.

En même temps M. Crowe m'a envoyé une lettre pour vous — ne vous trouvant pas à votre ancien logement (ou l'addresse de l'horrible bouge [92] ou vous démeurez actuellement est heureusement ignorée) — Force fut a M. Crowe de s'addresser à moi — à moi qui connois l'ignoble caveau que vous occupez indignement — sous les dalles humides d'une église déserte dans le voisinage fétide de fourmillans Irlandais.

Cette lettre Monsieur dont Je parle — cette lettre — Je l'ai laissée à la maison. Demain il sera trop tard de vous faire part de l'aimable invitation de notre ami commun.

Je remplis enfin mon devoir envers M. Crowe en vous faisant

[91] In chapter 18 (*Works*, I, 160–162).

[92] On August 26 Brookfield wrote to his wife from "L'horrible bouge," his rooms in the cellars of St. Luke's Church: "The Godfather to whom my present abode is indebted for the above designation sits beside me — brewing Vanity — in a dreadful fright lest the month of Sept. should arrive before No. next. I encountered him in Piccadilly on his way to my subterranean Palace." (*Mrs. Brookfield*, I, 242)

savoir les intentions hospitalières à votre égard. Et je vous quitte Monsieur en vous donnant les assurances réiterées de ma haute consideration —

Chevalier de Titmarsh

J'offre a Madame l'Abbesse mes hommages respectueux.

413.  TO MRS. PROCTER<br>27? AUGUST 1847 [93]

Hitherto unpublished. My text is taken from a transcript given Lady Ritchie by George Murray Smith.

Kensington.<br>Friday.

My dear Mrs Procter,

I will come on Sunday with the greatest delight. But do not make a dinner if you please. You know how retiring are the habits, and what of all others is the favourite society of

E.L.B.L. BB. LL. BBLBL. BL & BB.[94]

Pray forgive my not writing yesterday. Indeed I was so busy scribble scribbling all day till dinner time that I forgot all but Amelia and the Battle of Waterloo.

---

[93] Amelia and the Battle of Waterloo are the subjects of chapter 32 of *Vanity Fair*, which concludes part IX of the novel, published at the end of August. Thackeray's numbers were rarely finished more than a day or two before his deadline. It seems probable, therefore, that this note was written on August 27, the last Friday in the month.

[94] The supply of names apportioned at christening to Edward George Earle Lytton Bulwer was considered by most of his contemporaries to be more than ample. There was consequently a good deal of joking at his expense when on February 10, 1844, he assumed by royal license the additional surname of Lytton. See above, No. 374.

414.                    TO ABRAHAM HAYWARD
                          5 SEPTEMBER 1847

Hitherto unpublished.

                                13 Young S.ᵗ Kensington September 5.

My dear Hayward   Thank you very much for writing and for
your good opinion.  I found an opportunity of getting a holiday
abroad just after I had last heard from you, and rushed away at a
moments warning quite forgetting that catalogue raisonné of Titmarsh's works w.ʰ I had promised to you.[95]  I tried to make it — but
to tell you the truth I couldn't — it was too severe a task for my
sheep-facedness, and I couldn't sit down and contemplate and describe my own merits —  They are in the hands of honest critics;
and though I dont profess to write for posterity and have a much
greater value for pudding yet I don't mind saying that especially
of latter years (for I look upon the first efforts as jokes, and school-
boy exercises as it were) I have done my best to work as an artist
telling the truth, and morbidly perhaps, eschewing humbug.  And
as for the future who knows? —  People will read a novel or two or
a few ballads of mine I daresay, when we are
I saw M.ʳˢ Norton & Lady Harriet Dorsay[96]
in a churchyard at Laeken — where George
Osborne is buried.  I am glad you are waiting for I hope that V. F
improves.

                            Very faithfully yours dear Hayward
                                W M Thackeray.


      F. Tennyson[97] a friend of mine living at Leghorn wrote over to
ask, if any of us knew a most delightful amusing Irishman, the

      [95] Mrs. Procter's letter of July 23 was no doubt written to make good
Thackeray's forgotten promise.
      [96] The former Lady Harriet Gardiner (1812–1869), step-daughter of Lady
Blessington and wife of Count D'Orsay.  Lady D'Orsay's dubious career after
leaving her husband in 1831 is described in Mr. Michael Sadleir's *Blessington-
D'Orsay* (London, 1933), pp. 180–181.  She married the Hon. Charles
Spencer Cowper shortly after D'Orsay's death in 1852.
      [97] Frederick Tennyson (1807–1898), the older brother of the poet, lived in

friend of Canning, George IV, Bulwer, the Duke of Wellington, who had mixed in all the society & politics of England for the last 20 years and who was the nephew of — Lord FitzGerald. Who can this be? [98]

415.                    TO MISS KER [99]
                        SEPTEMBER 1847

*Address:* Miss Ker | 40 Gloster Crescent | Regents Park.  Hitherto unpublished.
*Endorsed:* Sep! 1847.

My dear Miss Ker —

I have broken the confidence of private life and opened a letter addressed to 'Miss Thackeray' w^h arrived during the absence from town of that young lady.

I wish she & Minny were here to accept your kind invitation to come and celebrate their little friends birthday, but they are at Paris with my mother, and I am alone in this dismal Kensington.

                    very faithfully yours
                    W M Thackeray.

416.              TO MRS. CARMICHAEL-SMYTH
                        21 OCTOBER 1847

*Address:* M^rs Carmichael Smyth | Rue de Ponthieu. 2. | Champs Élysées | Paris.
*Postmark:* 21 OC 1847.  Extract published in *Biographical Introductions,* I, xxxiv.

                                        21 October.

My dearest Mammy   I am just back from Brighton where I found kind friends fresh air and a little renovation of health & spirits — God forgive me if I have wronged you my dearest old Mother: the wrong has made two of us very miserable — and pray

---

Italy from 1839 to 1859. Thackeray had known him at Cambridge and kept in touch with him through FitzGerald, his most faithful correspondent.

[98] Probably Edward Marlborough FitzGerald.

[99] Miss Ker was the governess of the Rev. Alexander Scott's children.

God the first difference may be the last & only one between me & my dearest Mother. GP's letters were far from harsh they were admirable in kindness & gentleness — only of course supposing me to be entirely in the wrong: and pointing out very guardedly the grief w$^h$ I was inflicting on you — I met John Henry Forrest at Brighton — it pleased me to hear the affectionateness with w$^h$ he spoke of my dear old G P. How to find a Governess is now the puzzle — if Charlotte Ritchie w$^d$ but come over for a little while! The housekeeping expences are a trifle — It is the constant drain elsewhere. I repeatedly asked Miss D to get everything the children wanted — and didn't leave her any money for I thought G M. would advance anything required — It wasn't much to expect from her — considering she paid 0 except the piano — & the shirts — & about 10£ of coals I think — but I really didn't know the little ones wanted anything.

As for a Governess — I dont intend her to go into society & to appear among my friends only as little as possible — I'll wrap her up in precautions. I'll keep myself safe & clear in conscience regarding her — and now I must go to work. It seems never to end. The last numbers of V F [100] you'll like the best I think. It does everything but sell; and appears really immensely to increase my reputation if not my income.

God bless you and G P & G M & my dearest little women

W M T.

417.        TO WILLIAM SMITH WILLIAMS [101]
                   23 OCTOBER 1847

Published in part by Thomas J. Wise and J. Alexander Symington, *The Brontës: their Lives, Friendships & Correspondence* (Oxford, 1932), II, 149.

                                    13 Young S$^t$ Kensington. October 23.
My dear Sir

I wish you had not sent me Jane Eyre. It interested me so much that I have lost (or won if you like) a whole day in reading it at

---

[100] Numbers IX and X for September and October, chapters 30 to 35.
[101] Though Williams (1800–1875) left no original writing of value, he per-

the busiest period, with the printers I know waiting for copy. Who the author can be I can't guess — if a woman she knows her language better than most ladies do, or has had a 'classical' education. It is a fine book though — the man & woman capital — the style very generous and upright so to speak. I thought it was Kinglake for some time. The plot of the story is one with w$^h$ I am familiar.[102] Some of the love passages made me cry — to the astonishment of John who came in with the coals. S$^t$ John the Missionary is a failure I think but a good failure there are parts excellent I dont know why I tell you this but that I have been exceedingly moved & pleased by Jane Eyre. It is a womans writing, but whose? Give my respects and thanks to the author — whose novel is the first English one (& the French are only romances now) that I've been able to read for many a day.

Very truly yours my dear Sir<br>
W M Thackeray —

---

formed useful services to literature as a publisher's adviser. In his youth he had known Keats, Hazlitt, and Leigh Hunt, and after George Smith employed him in 1845 as literary assistant to the firm of Smith, Elder, and Company, he became acquainted with most of the great Victorian writers. He gave Charlotte Brontë the first significant encouragement she received as a writer, and he was instrumental in persuading Smith to publish *Jane Eyre*.

[102] Charlotte Brontë expressed the pleasure that Thackeray's praise gave her in a letter to Williams of October 28. "The plot of 'Jane Eyre' may be a hackneyed one," she writes (Wise and Symington, *The Brontës*, II, 150). "Mr Thackeray remarks that it is familiar to him. But having read comparatively few novels I never chanced to meet with it, and I thought it original." Thackeray's phrasing is ambiguous, but it seems likely that he refers, not to a literary parallel, but to the similarity between his own history and certain parts of *Jane Eyre*. See below, No. 440.

418.    TO JAMES JUSTINIAN MORIER
25 OCTOBER 1847

Hitherto unpublished.

13 Young S.ᵗ Kensington
25 October. 1847.

My dear M.ʳ Morier

I went out of town to Brighton the day after I saw you having previously put up the enclosed packet w.ʰ I wanted to lay at Hajji Baba's feet [103] as thus

I found it still on my mantel piece on my return — having grown dingy during my absence —

Your old friend Horace Smith was very hospitable to me feeding me with cakes from Mutton's and all sorts of good things. He

[103] See above, No. 274, September 4.

spoke kindly of you behind your back — a benevolent & eccentric old man.

I wish to account for not having sooner availed myself of the permission you were good enough to give me that I might come & see. To day is my first free day, & I have (by the V.D) this minute done no XI [104] of Vanity Fair

Faithfully yours my dear Sir

W M Thackeray.

### 419.      TO EDWARD CHAPMAN
### OCTOBER? 1847

*Address:* E. Chapman Esq^re | 186 Strand. Hitherto unpublished.

My dear Sir

Will you send copies of the Irish Sketchbook & Cornhill to A. Hayward Esq^r Kings B^h Walk. he is the Edinburgh Reviewer — I'm to be done in the Quarterly too so who knows what reputation is in store for

M A Titmarsh

### 420.      TO MRS. CARMICHAEL-SMYTH
### 2 NOVEMBER 1847

*Address:* M^rs Carmichael-Smyth | 2 Rue de Ponthieu. | Champs Élysées | Paris.
*Postmarks:* 2 NO 1847, 4 NOV. 47 BOULOGNE. Hitherto unpublished.

Nov^r 2. 1847.

My dearest Mother I have just engaged with a very nice plain kind-looking governess — about 28, with 6 or 7 brothers & sisters living at Richmond with their Pa & Ma — an ex captain in the army — good virtuous tender sort of people seemingly — those with whom I once talked of placing Isabella indeed. And Miss Alexander [105] is to come as soon as I like, and do for me — Shall I

[104] Chapters 36 to 38 for November.
[105] A daughter of Captain Alexander.

send her over to you to bring the children back? — She has friends
at Paris who would receive her — but this would cost 7 or 8£ w^h
may as well be spared if there can be found any feasible way of
transport for the little women. I'm so glad I thought of these people — they are to all outward [appearance] thoroughly respectable
— and the mother of the family a tender grey-haired long-suffering
looking woman, with something that reminds me of my dearest old
Mother — whom I have caused to suffer of late.[106] God help us —
w^h has had I wonder the greater pain of the 2? This business has
made me feel ten years older — and you dearest old Soul? —

I am come into town after a ride to Richmond (you must know
I have bought a horse & ride 2 or 3 hours every day with great enjoyment to myself & good to my health) for Kensington is so awfully lonely — and White gives me a dinner at the Club His poor
little Lily is I fear sinking into consumption [107] a hideous constant
doubt hanging over him and his dear good wife — They have been
my comfort in the times of my troubles.

And what do you think of Brookfield offering to go halves in
housekeeping with me? M^{rs} B managing the children — loving her
as I do — mong Dieu what a temptation it was! but you see the
upshot. That *would* be dangerous, and so I keep off —

Write me and say how things are to be managed about the children. And with love to all God bless my dearest old Mother.

W M T.

[106] See above, No. 416.
[107] Lily White died some weeks before May 4, 1848, when Dickens (*Letters*,
ed. Dexter, II, 85–86) wrote White a note of condolence on her death.

421.     TO THE REV. WILLIAM BROOKFIELD
NOVEMBER 1847 [108]

Published in *Collection of Letters*, pp. 8–9.

My dear WHB     I daresay you are disgusted at my not coming to the bouge [109] on Sunday night but there was a good reason: wʰ may be explained if required hereafter. And I had made up my account for some days at Southampton [110] hoping to start this day but there is another good reason for staying at home. The poor old GMother's will burial &c. detaining me in town — Did you see her death in the papers? [111]

Why I write now is to beg and implore and entreat that you and Mʳˢ B will come and take those 3 nice little rooms here and stop with me until you have found other lodgment. It will be the very greatest comfort and kindness to me and I shall take it quite hangry

 if you don't come. Will you come on Saturday now? The good things you shall have for dinner are quite incredible. I have got a box of preserved apricots from Fortnum & Mason's wʰ alone ought to make any lady happy — and two shall be put under my lady's pillow every night. Now do come — and farewell — My barb is at the postern. I have had him clipped and his effect in the Park is quite tremenjus.

[108] Brookfield wrote to his wife on November 3, 1847: "This morning has produced no adventures, save that after Litany I behoved to push on to Kensington and found Thack. droring for his new Annual which is to be called 'Our Street.' He has engaged a Governess — a young person from Richmond. He invites us to go there for two or three weeks. What think you? *i.e.*, after Governidge and babes are arrived." (*Mrs. Brookfield*, I, 250–251) The present letter, reinforcing Thackeray's verbal invitation, was apparently written after Sunday, November 6, and before the following Saturday. The Brookfields did not accept Thackeray's offer.

[109] See above, No. 372.

[110] Where Mrs. Brookfield was staying.

[111] "DIED On the 1st inst., at Paris, Harriet, widow of Col. E. W. Butler, of the Bengal Artillery" (*Times*, November 6).

422.                  TO ARTHUR SHAWE
                      15 NOVEMBER 1847

Extract published in *Biographical Introductions*, I, xxii–xxiii.

                              13 Young S: Kensington.

My dear Arthur   I wish I had any news worth the telling —
The poor little woman is as usual having had a smart fit of cholera
or something similar from w? however she rallied speedily. The
children are still with my mother at Paris, between whom & me
still goes on the first dispute we have ever had in our lives — about
the governess question: on w? I intend to have my own way.

The good old G Mother has departed this life a fortnight to day
— leaving but a very small modicum behind her: w? little please
God shall not be befooled away like the former part of our family
fortune — she went out insensibly almost: and my dear old
Nanny [112] remained with her G Mother through the last scenes,
and comforted her. Is not your Mother in Paris? Somebody told
me so I think — I wish she would show some sign of recognition of
poor Isabella's claims upon her, that the formality of enmity might
be given up — I mean it is hard to be at war with any mortal — So
your regiment is coming back and you are hard run for money —
if men will marry you know what comes — It is always the same
tale with me always earning always paying never having. I have
had to send over 50£ for the old G Mother's funeral expenses &c
— the poor old Governor at the other side of the water having no
money, & the bankers here refusing to advance even to bury her.

I'm very sorry indeed to hear of my sister-in-law's ill health —
What a catalogue of dreary complaints & condolences I am writing!
— Nothing but death quarrels money & ill-ness. Ah Vanitas Vanitatum.[113] I grow as melancholy as an owl, & daily more vexatious
of spirit.

I have bought a hoss and ride in the Park with great elegance.

[112] Lady Ritchie has written above these words: "Minny was the good girl
not I     A R."
[113] See Thackeray's poem of this name (*Works*, XIII, 100–02). Other
echoes of *Ecclesiastes* will be noted elsewhere in the letter.

Strange to say, not knowing a horse from a cow everybody says I have got a most wonderful bargain, a splendid stepper &c. One of my prettiest and amiablest female friends M$^{rs}$ Henry Bayley [114] has just fallen at Brighton where the F.C used to ride with her, and broken her nose — the dearest little nose in the world. She is an Indian Civil Servants wife, her usband knowing Merrick. I must & will write to him. I have a letter before me now written to him this time last year but so gloomy that I didn't send it: and I don't think I will send this.

M$^{rs}$ Bayley sent me a bottle of chutney — I wish you could have seen her face when I told her that I was very much obliged to her & had rubbed it into my hair. But all is Vanity after all. Good bye my dear old fellow. And believe me

Yours afftly<br>W M T.

423.

TO RICHARD BEDINGFIELD
23 NOVEMBER 1847

My text is taken from Bedingfield's "Thackeray," *Cassell's Magazine*, II, 299, where the date is given.

My dear Bedingfield, —

I beg your pardon for not writing sooner. I would have come to you to-morrow with pleasure, but I am engaged to dine with Mr. Macready.[115]

You saw, I daresay, in the papers the death of the old g. mother at Paris. The children are not back yet, but always coming, and I hope my troubles in this respect are over.

Don't be displeased at my not reviewing you. By Jove, I have not time to do 1/2 what I ought to do, and have books upon books on my table at this minute — all the works of private friends who want a criticism.

Yours distractedly,<br>W. M. T.

[114] See above, No. 62, April 11.
[115] Macready noted in his *Diaries* (ed. Toynbee, II, 378) on November 23:

424.                          TO MRS. BROOKFIELD
                             DECEMBER 1847? [116]

My text is taken from *Thackeray in the United States*, II, 119.

My dear Young Lady, — I send you two bottles for this evening's drinking, by that little Harriet whose appearance may or
may not please you, but who is willing, good-natured, honest, and
disposed to do her best. She does not in the least know for what
purpose (except to act as a mere bottle holder) she waits to-night
upon the wife of the Rev'd Francis Whitestock. Ever my dear
young lady yours,

                              Ambrose Ignatius Goddard.

Mrs. Brookfield, with 2 Bottles Mumsy My deary.


425.                          TO EDWARD CHAPMAN
                             28 DECEMBER 1847

Hitherto unpublished.

                                                  28 Dec[r] 1847

My dear Chapman

Will you send me the remaining 60£ by the bearer if you please.
Indeed I'm very sorry for everybody's delays and misfortunes.

                              Yours

                              W. M. T.

---

"Berlioz, M. Barnet, Benedict, Tom Taylor, Thomson, Thackeray, Hardwick,
Mason, Jerdan, Elliotson, Mahlenfeldt came to dinner."

[116] "The Curate's Walk," in which Brookfield appears as the Rev. Francis
Whitestock, was published in *Punch* between November 27 and December 4,
1847. It seems likely that this note was written during that period or a little
later.

426.        TO MAJOR COMPTON [117]
                28 DECEMBER 1847

Hitherto unpublished.

13 Young S! Kensington. 28 Dec
Omnibus from Picadilly drops you at the head
of the street.

My dear Compton

I want awfully to see you — and to night if poss — I have a chapter about Madras in V F [118] and dont want to make any blunders.

For Evn's sake try & come up to me here.  Take cabs — anything.
I shall dine at 4 o'clock if you will eat a hasty morsel with my
children & their distracted parent who is so late with his months
work as to be almost out of his mind.

Yours ever
W M Thackeray

427.        TO ABRAHAM HAYWARD
                29 DECEMBER 1847

Hitherto unpublished.

29 Dec.ʳ 1847
On my way from the Printing
Office.

My dear Hayward

My head is only this minute above water and out of the months
whirlpool of work — I thought I was going down in it once or
twice and should never come up again and your article in the R. [119]
blazed out so cheerfully as to make me almost frantic all the while.

[117] The commander of the Forty-eighth Native Infantry in India, according
to a note on the original.
[118] Chapter 43, the first of the four chapters that make up part XIII of *Vanity
Fair* for January, 1848.
[119] See above, No. 411.

To be wrecked and so near port — the people hailing you from in shore — everybody crying out 'Hurray Titmarsh' and down you go just as you have hold of the pier — I mean that after reading the Review the day before Xmas I got into such a panic lest I shouldn't finish my work that I didn't dare write and thank you, before the number was out. What shall I say about it? about the article I mean? but that it has pleased me and all my friends that it will be as useful to me as you wished it should and that it is most friendly pleasant & kindly. Everybody is talking to me and congratulating me about it. I have met 2 fellows this day with E. R's under their arms, who came up and shook hands as if some great good luck had happened to me — And so it has (There are 20 men talking here as I write and you must please to excuse the incoherency) — But indeed my dear Hayward I am very cordially thankful and obliged to you.

Yours always faithfully
W M Thackeray.

428.        TO RICHARD BEDINGFIELD
1847? [120]

My text is taken from Bedingfield, *Cassell's Magazine*, II, 298.

Kensington, Tuesday.

My dear Bedingfield, —

I shall have great pleasure in coming to you on Monday evening; but not the ladies, thank you. My grandmother is too old to go out, and Miss Hammerton stops to take care of her. I don't know if you got the orders. I spoke about them on Saturday, and will write a reminder to Mr. Lemon to-day.

Truly yours,
W. M. Thackeray.

[120] This and the two following notes were written between December, 1846, and March, 1847, when Bess Hamerton was living at 13 Young Street.

429.          TO RICHARD BEDINGFIELD
1847?

My text is taken from Bedingfield, *Cassell's Magazine*, II, 298.

My dear Bedingfield, —

I am much vexed that you lost your ticket yesterday by my blunder. I sent a messenger with it to No. 17, like an ass, and he returned, of course, not finding you. I will get you others soon, however, and am always yours,

W. M. T.

430.          TO RICHARD BEDINGFIELD
1847?

My text is taken from Bedingfield, *Cassell's Magazine*, II, 298.

Kensington, Sunday.

My dear Bedingfield, —

A horrid remembrance comes over me, as I am madly plunging through my work, that you wrote to me for theatre tickets, and sent me an invitation to an evening party. My dear fellow, I beg your pardon! I've lost the letters, or they lie hidden in the enormous heaps. They came when I was writing for life and death. I forgot to send to Lemon. I'll write to him to-night: and beg you to make my excuses to Mrs. Marston, and I regret very much that I am engaged to dinner on Monday, or I should have had the pleasure of coming to her party. I know this is rude. But what can I do? — do my work, to be sure, and go at it again this moment.

Ever yours,

W. M. T.

431.        TO MRS. CARMICHAEL-SMYTH
1847? [121]

Hitherto unpublished.

My dearest Mammy. It was because Jones said the oss had need
of great and constant exercise, that I thought on days when he
wasn't wanted at home, Burgess might turn a penny out of him for
himself by driving him on a 2 or 3 hours job but I know how
dangerous this kind of liberty is, and begin to think it was utterly
green of me to propose it — It was of course not with a notion of
my letting out the horse for hire Evns forbid. He had best remain
at home when not wanted & take his chance

I will send your wonderful story to Chapman & to Smith & Elder
who will send it back again. It may be from an angels pen and I
doubt if you will get a publisher to bring it out except at the author's
charges. As for getting money by it it is a vain hope — and to
suppose it will succeed because it will do people good — is as green
almost as my horse-dealings. The publishers don't care a straw for
a friend of mine, but for what will put money in their pockets —
and consider, will your tale cover an outlay of 60 or 70£ and give
them a return for their risk and trouble? say 100£ of a half crown
book sold at 1/6$^d$ to the trade, costing 6$^d$ let us say to produce they
would require to sell 2000 to pay £100 — & how many books do
you think sell 2000? not one in as many 100.

To day has been too bitter cold to go out, and I have passed it as
I best might over books and magazines & so forth — Ate a big
dinner with a good appetite, and slept excellent well. Am taking
bark and like it very much indeed. Feel very well — my pulse a
little quicker again but no sort of indication of fever.

God bless all    W M T.

[121] This letter appears to have been written not long after Thackeray bought
his first riding horse late in 1847. See above, No. 421.

432.          TO MRS. FITzGERALD
1847? [122]

*Address:* M<sup>rs</sup> or Miss FitzGerald | 26 Park Lane.  Hitherto unpublished.

My dear M<sup>rs</sup> FitzGerald
    If you have done with Jane Hair a lady wants it please.
                    ever sincerely yours
                    W M Thackeray


433.          TO LEIGH HUNT
1847 [123]

Hitherto unpublished.

Brookfield (a parson) and Thackeray (a buffoon) are going to dine together at the latter's house tomorrow at seven o'clock.  They propose to Hunt (a pensioner) to partake of their humble food.  viz

A  Les macheturnips
B  Les pommes de terre au naturel
C  La sauce aux capres
D  La bread-sauce.

---

[122] See above, No. 417.
[123] Hunt's pension was announced in June, 1847 (see above, No. 407), and this note was probably written during the next few months.

434.                        TO MRS. PROCTER
                                1847? [124]

Hitherto unpublished. My text is taken from a transcript given Lady Ritchie by George Murray Smith.

If you please Mum I will come to dinner but not in the morning please Mum — for this month Mum I am later than ever Mum if you please.

Your most obedient servant,<br>[Sketch]

P. S. If you please Mum has Miss P. had any more dreams about a *serting person*? He *hopes so* and that they will come *trew*.


435.                        TO LEIGH HUNT
                            3 JANUARY 1848

Published in *The Cornhill Magazine*.

13 Young S.<br>January 3. 1847.[1]

My dear Hunt

I have not only not had time to thank you for the Jar of Honey: but I have not even tasted any of it; nor of Tennyson's Medley — having been so consumedly occupied with business, and with Jollification subsequently in these latter days  We have had supper parties singing parties dinner-parties headaches rather in the morning &c — but the week must not pass over without saying Hail to Leigh Hunt.

Last week we were to have met at the Procters but I forgot & you were ill — Can we meet any where this week? For instance tomor-

---

[124] The place of this letter in the Procter sequence points to 1847.

[1] A mistake for 1848. Hunt's *A Jar of Honey from Mount Hybla* is advertised as "now ready" in *The Athenæum* for December 18, 1847, and Tennyson's *The Princess. A Medley* is reviewed in the same journal on January 1, 1848.

row at 5 there will be 2 woodcocks presented by M^r^ J. O'Connell: and you shall have a bit or not as you like: and with or without an answer.

My dear Hunt I wish you an H. N. Y.

Yours ever

W M Thackeray.

## 436. TO MRS. CARMICHAEL-SMYTH 7 JANUARY 1848

Extracts published in *Biographical Introductions*, IX, xlix–l.

January 7. 1848.

My dearest Mammy. I see to my dismay on looking over the bankers acct that you have not drawn the money to meet Abels bill as I expected, and so that I shall have 60£ instead of 35 to pay this month — please if you can only draw for 35 giving me a little more time for the remainder: for on going to the publishers to draw my money tother day I was met with a smiling reference to some old books by w^h^ it appeared I had overdrawn them 120£ 2 years ago — about w^h^ fatal circumstance I was quite ignorant, and of course it renders me so much the poorer. Dont mind if you are pledged however in any way, for I can borrow plenty. But it seems as if saving is a doomed impossibility — There is always something: Just now I have the pleasure of a railroad suit [2] hanging over me: w^h^ I believe is begun. — o what a turmoil it is — under w^h^ I live laugh and grow fat however. There is no use denying the matter or blinking it now. I am become a sort of great man in my way — all but at the top of the tree: indeed there if the truth were known and having a great fight up there with Dickens. I get such a deal of praise wherever I go that it is rather wearisome to hear. I don't think my head is a bit turned please God: for I've always got my own opinion, and when men and newspapers say Our Street is the finest &c. I know a devilish deal better, and don't disguise the truth

[2] See above, No. 324.

either — This London world is full of a parcel of good-natured tom-fools and directly one begins to cry O all the rest say prodigious. The Quarterly is paying me compliments [3] as well as the Edinburgh the Quarterly that never gave a lift to a struggling man yet or patronized anybody but a dandy lord or a man of made reputation. As a puff the Edinburgh is famous: as a criticism utterly drivelling: the man who wrote it has no more idea of humour than I have of Algebra. — and even one or two good passages w$^h$ I was surprized at his selecting turn out to have been marked for him by M$^{rs}$ Procter [4] — who has twice his brains as a judge of sentimental works — As for victuals and drink they are only too plenty: and I know such a power of Lords as w$^d$ make some folks envy — 'He has succeeded in society, little Hayward says who after great pains has worked himself into a number of great houses — his manners are brusque but they like him' — He seems and the great people too perhaps rather surprised that I am [a] gentleman — they dont know who I had for my father & mother and that there are 2 old people living in Paris on 200 a year, as grand folks as ever they were. I have never seen finer gentlefolks than you two — or prouder — as I told my dearest old Mother once before. Well it does one good travelling about amongst all these people and watching their ways. Something turns up daily. Even the rides on the little cob fructify and I see a deal of sights from his Punchy back — Tell Mary that I may be seen riding any day with 3 Lords: it will please that candid unenvious spirit. Heighho. God help us and pardon us jealousy and meanness pride and low ambition — Here's a deal of selfish talk — I have been idle and very much the better for it during all the week, having been awfully behindhand and worked with no XIII. The book doesn't pay yet with all its unquestionable success.

The poor little wife seems gradually sinking lower I think. The

---

[3] A writer in *The Quarterly Review* of January, 1848 (p. 296), remarks of Thackeray's *Irish Sketch Book*: "though somewhat disfigured by the flippancies of his assumed character of the Cockney *Titmarsh* — [it] exhibits a great deal of keen and judicious observation, with a happy power of delineating both scenery and character, and gives in his lively manner (*ridentum dicere verum quid vetat?*) one of the best pictures we have seen (though it be but a sketch) of the natural features and social conditions of Ireland."

[4] See above, No. 411.

governess is very good very honest very eager to do her duty very gawky not by any means wise, or fit to guide Anny's mind. But she can teach her geography and music and what they call history and hemming &c — and my dear old Nan goes on thinking for herself, and no small beer of herself — I am obliged to snub her continually, with delight at what she says all the time. They are noble children. Thank God. And the governess — a nuisance. By the by here is a letter from Bess w$^h$ came in a blank cover to me: and w$^h$ I will pay 10$^d$ for if you like. To night is the Crowe's flare up at Hampstead. 15/ for a fly — to see such a set of people dancing. My poor dear Eugénie has lost her beauty wofully: her nose has bulged out with the influenza & her complexion is going — I wish she could get a husband though, that kind honest soul. I always fall in love with M$^{rs}$ Brookfield when I see her — though I suspect she is rather too like Amelia: [5] and there are 3 or 4 more very nice indeed — with whom that Adonis of a Titmarsh is very much smitten — The little Ingleby sang here on New Years Night and looked like an angel. It is worth a guinea to watch the mother and the artificial innocence of the 2 daughters, dear girls, they grow younger & younger every year. Next night it was a Miss Elliot daughter of the Commodore who was really natural and sang in every European language and almost as well as Grisi and the next night it was somebody else — It would be better if he saw the children somebody will say — well I saw them yesterday till 7, and tonight shall have them till bed time — and haven't I refused Lord Holland [6] himself on Sunday to dine with them? Unheard of parental tenderness!

God bless my dearest old Mother & G P.

[5] On October 7, 1847, Mrs. Brookfield had complained to Harry Hallam: "Mr. Thackeray has now got a 2nd Amelia, Lady Jane Sheepshanks. I wish he had made Amelia more exciting especially as the remark is he has thought of me in her character. And on the plan of 2 negatives making one affirmative, I suppose I may take the 2 dull ones of the book to make one Mrs. B. You know he told William that though Amelia was not a copy of me he should not have conceived the character if he had not known me — and though she has the right amount of antiphlegm and affectionateness she is really an uncommonly dull and a selfish character, and very apathetic to the only person who cares for her, the quaint Capt. Dobbin." (*Mrs. Brookfield*, I, 247–248) See below, No. 483.

[6] Henry Edward Fox (1802–1859), fourth Baron Holland.

437.        FROM CHARLES DICKENS
                9 JANUARY 1848

Extracts published by Lady Ritchie, *From the Porch* (New York, 1913), pp.
33–34. My text is taken from a transcript supplied by Mrs. Fuller.

Devonshire Terrace,
Sunday Ninth January 1848.

My dear Thackeray,

I need not tell you that I have been delighted — and cut tender,
as it were to the very heart — by your generous letter.[7] You would
never have written it if you had not known how truly and heartily
I should feel it. I will only say the spirit in which I read it, was
worthy of the spirit in which you wrote it, and that I think there is
nothing in the world or out of it to which I am so sensitive as the
least mark of such a manly and gallant regard.

I *do* sometimes please myself with thinking that my success has
opened the way for good writers. And of this, I am quite sure now,
and hope I shall be when I die — that in all my social doings I am
mindful of this honour and dignity and always try to do something
towards the quiet assertion of their right place. I am always possessed with the hope of leaving the position of literary men in England, something better and more independent than I found it.

There's a wild and egotistical fancy for you! See what it is to get
into my confidence so thoroughly!

It is curious, about Punch, that I was so strongly impressed by
the absurdity and injustice of my being left out of those imitations,[8]
that I several times said at home here I would write to you and
urge the merits of the case. But I never made up my mind to do so,
for I feared you might misunderstand me.

I will tell you now, candidly, that I did not admire the design —
but I think it is a great pity to take advantage of the means our
calling gives us with such accursed readiness, of at all depreciating

[7] The contents of this letter, which I have been unable to trace, may be surmised from Dickens's reply.
[8] *Novels by Eminent Hands.* See above, No. 374.

or vulgarizing each other — but this seems to me to be one of the main reasons why we are generally more divided among ourselves than artists who have not those means at their command — and that I thought your power thrown away on that series, however happily executed. So now I have made a clean breast too, and have nothing more to confess but that I am saving up the perusal of Vanity Fair until I shall have done Dombey and that I cried most bitterly over your affecting picture of that cock-boat manned by babies,[9] and shall never forget it.

Kate says that whomsoever you bring on the 26th. will be warmly welcomed. We don't go in for grandeur on the occasion, and I am bent on a prodigious country dance at about the small hours.

Believe me my dear fellow I am very proud of your letter and very happy in its receipt. If I were to pursue the subject, I should come out in a style that would be full of all sorts of faults not insincerity. You have given me a new reason (if I wanted any) for interest in all you do, and for gratification in your progress afterwards: and though I did not write about Harness [10] with the least grain of ill humour, I think of him now as if he had done me a great service in occasioning me to write at all.

Affectionately yours,

Charles Dickens.

[9] In "The Curate's Walk" (*Works*, VI, 548).

[10] The Rev. William Harness (1790–1869) had gone to Harrow with Byron and was the intimate friend of Wordsworth, Southey, and Miss Mitford. He had published an eight-volume edition of Shakespeare's *Works* in 1825. In 1848 he was Perpetual Curate of Knightsbridge district, supervising the construction of the church of All Saints, of which he was Perpetual Curate from 1849 until his death.

438.                        TO MRS. JAMES [11]
                           11 JANUARY 1848

*Address:* M^rs James. Published by Mr. Wilson, *Boston Transcript,* July 31, 1920.

                                             January 11. 1848
Madam

In calling at your house under the pretext of enquiring for my stick I beg totally to deny the truth of every single word that I said yesterday, and to point out the cruelty the unkyindness the injustice of your own criticisms on the works of a celebrated author.

To attack a man defenceless, confiding, under your own roof: to plunge daggers into him while he sate open-bosomed at your drawing room table — ah Madam what conduck is this! *You* a bishops daughter, M^rs Jeames! Down with the bench I say that ever bore such cruelty.

Pray do you suppose that you are a better critic than the Times Mam? I should like to know are you or the leading journal of Europe the best judge on littery matters? *You* find fault while the Times praises [12] — *You* cry fy at the *very passidge* w^h the Thunderer hisself admits to be an honor to *humannaty*! Do you think after that I care for the opinions of a lawyer in very *modrit pracktus* and of a lady who's a going to live in Curzon Street? I treat

---

[11] The former Maria Otter (d. 1891), daughter of the Bishop of Chichester, who had married William Milbourne James (1807–1881), later (1869) knighted, in 1846. James was one of the ablest barristers of his time. He became Vice Chancellor of the Duchy of Lancaster and a Q. C. in 1853 and Vice Chancellor of the Court of Chancery in 1869. From 1870 till his death he was Lord Justice of Appeal and a member of the Privy Council.

[12] Mrs. James took exception to "the picture . . . of 'the lady whom nobody knows,' living in a state of unequivocal splendour but equivocal respectability, alike despised and envied by her virtuous and detestable neighbours, walking with an air that shows pride of beauty and shame of position," a portrait which seemed to the reviewer of *Our Street* in *The Times* (January 11) "a finer trait of humanity in a few — very few lines — than many which more laborious artists would require pages to exhibit."

both as they *deserve* and I am waiting on my horse at the door and *will just thank you to send me down my stick.*

Your obeajnt serv!

The bearer is below and wants his stick.[13]

439.      TO MRS. EDWARD MARLBOROUGH
FɪᴛᴢGERALD
18 JANUARY 1848 [14]

Hitherto unpublished.

13 Young S! Kensington Sq!ᵉ
Wednesday Night.

My dear Mʳˢ Fitzgerald

I have just seen Dʳ Quin & he says he thinks you would let me come & see you. I have wanted to do so many & many a time: my fear was that the recollection of past days so painful to you,[15] and the false reports you have had of me might render my visit unwelcome. God knows I never tried to do you a wrong: & that I always had the warmest & truest regard for you: but I was not called upon to right myself until you thought proper to hear me.

On the very last day when we talked together, I saw that there was some wrong impression on your part, (wʰ your kind heart only let you hint) but how could I answer hints; and was it not better to let myself seem in the wrong, at the cost of any good feeling that you might have had towards me, than to occasion differences in your family, wʰ (I thought then) were still reconcileable? I knew nothing about your family circumstances. I could not guess or surmise your misery. Upon my word & honour I thought that you apart from money-affairs (about wʰ I was also entirely in the dark) were

[13] This sentence is written on the envelope.

[14] In his note of Monday, January 31, to Mrs. FitzGerald, Thackeray apologizes for his failure to take advantage of an invitation to call he had received a week before. It is therefore reasonable to assign this letter, which procured him his invitation, to Wednesday, January 18.

[15] See above, No. 343.

happy. You were a hypocrite too — for w^h indeed I love & honor you. I told you at the beginning, that it was you I regarded & not your husband: I never told him otherwise — but enfin, why continue? If you will let me come to see you I will tell you more if you wish it: or tell you nothing but that I am from first to last sincerely & affectionately yours.

W M Thackeray

You mayn't value or you may be angry at what I say — Indeed & indeed I so heartily sympathize with your unhappiness, that I can't but speak my mind now I have a chance — & tell you that I never was guilty of any intentional wrong towards you or your children. May God bless you all.

## 440.    TO WILLIAM SMITH WILLIAMS
### JANUARY 1848

My text is taken from E. Baumer Williams' "Extracts from some Unpublished Letters of Charlotte Brontë," *Macmillan's Magazine*, LXIV (1891), 123.

13 Young Street,<br>Kensington.

My dear Mr. Williams,

I am quite vexed that by some blundering of mine I should have delayed answering Currer Bell's enormous compliment so long.[16]

---

[16] The second edition of *Jane Eyre*, published shortly before January 22, 1848, is dedicated to Thackeray. "There is a man in our own days," Miss Brontë writes in her preface, "whose words are not framed to tickle delicate ears: who, to my thinking, comes before the great ones of society, much as the son of Imlah came before the throned Kings of Judah and Israel; and who speaks truth as deep, with a power as prophet-like and as vital — a mien as dauntless and as daring. Is the satirist of 'Vanity Fair' admired in high places? I cannot tell; but I think if some of those amongst whom he hurls the Greek fire of his sarcasm, and over whom he flashes the levin-brand of his denunciation, were to heed his warnings in time — they or their seed might yet escape a fatal Ramoth-Gilead.

"Why have I alluded to this man? I have alluded to him, reader, because I think I see in him an intellect profounder and more unique than his contemporaries have yet recognized; because I regard him as the first social regenerator of the day — as the very master of that working corps who would restore to

I didn't know what to say in reply; it quite flustered and upset me. Is it true, I wonder? I'm — But a truce to egotism. Thank you for your kindness in sending me the volumes, and (indirectly) for the greatest compliment I have ever received in my life.

Faithfully yours,

W. M. Thackeray.

---

rectitude the warped system of things; because I think no commentator on his writings has yet found the comparison that suits him, the terms which rightly characterize his talent. They say he is like Fielding: they talk of his wit, humour, comic powers. He resembles Fielding as an eagle does a vulture: Fielding could stoop on carrion, but Thackeray never does. His wit is bright, his humour attractive, but both bear the same relation, to his serious genius that the mere lambent sheet-lightning playing under the edge of the summer-cloud, does to the electric death-spark hid in its womb. Finally; I have alluded to Mr. Thackeray, because to him — if he will accept the tribute of a total stranger — I have dedicated this second edition of 'JANE EYRE'."

With his note to Williams Thackeray enclosed a letter to Miss Brontë, which has not been preserved. Its contents are reflected, however, in Miss Brontë's letter to Williams of January 28. Thackeray was duly grateful, but he did not conceal from Miss Brontë that her compliment was not altogether happy. "It appears," she writes (Wise and Symington, *The Brontës*, II, 183), "that his private position is in some points similar to that I have ascribed to Mr. Rochester, that thence arose a report that 'Jane Eyre' had been written by a governess in his family, and that the dedication coming now has confirmed everybody in the surmise."

This scandal received wider circulation through a paragraph in the irresponsible essay on *Vanity Fair, Jane Eyre*, and the *Report for 1847 of the Governesses' Benevolent Institution* — a sufficiently malicious concatenation of titles — that Elizabeth Rigby (1809–1893), later (1849) Lady Eastlake, wrote for *The Quarterly Review* (December, 1848, pp. 153–185): ". . . various rumours, more or less romantic, have been current in Mayfair, the metropolis of gossip, as to the authorship [of *Jane Eyre*]. For example, Jane Eyre is sentimentally assumed to have proceeded from the pen of Mr. Thackeray's governess, whom he had himself chosen as his model of Becky, and who, in mingled love and revenge, personified him in return as Mr. Rochester. In this case, it is evident that the author of 'Vanity Fair', whose own pencil makes him greyhaired, has had the best of it, though his children may have had the worst, having, at all events, succeeded in hitting that vulnerable point in the Becky bosom, which it is our firm belief no man born of woman, from her Soho to her Ostend days, had ever so much as grazed. To this ingenious rumour the coincidence of the second edition of Jane Eyre being dedicated to Mr. Thackeray has probably given rise." (pp. 174–175) As late as October, 1850, Thackeray was still going out of his way to contradict this slander (see below, No. 721), which is occasionally to be met with in one version or another today.

441.                    TO MRS. PROCTER
                       JANUARY? 1848 [17]

Hitherto unpublished. My text is taken from a transcript given Lady Ritchie by George Murray Smith.

My dear Mrs Procter,

I have been wanting many days to come and see you especially when Jane Eyre came out. I thought you would like it better than anybody, but old Mrs Taylor [18] said she had never read the book, and so I repressed my little movement of vanity and sent it (I mean J. E.) to her instead of bringing it to you.

I can't make any appointment this week being in the midst of operations just now, and strange to say very late with my work. [19] And about the chicken pox which rages in my house is it not dangerous to bring it into the bosom of a family?

I am very sorry indeed that you write of being unwell and — the rest. Why?

— Wrote a week ago. I've been hoping and hoping to see you ever since but 1000 obstacles intervene and I hear now that Miss Adelaide (I wish to be respectful) has the C. P.

Did I bring it when I came the other day? My Anny has been very unwell with it: and I am in the thick of my monthly misery.

                                        But ever yours,
                                          W. M. T.


[17] This note was written shortly after the publication of the second edition of *Jane Eyre*.
[18] Possibly Mrs. Thomas Taylor (1784–1858), the widowed mother of Thackeray's friend, Tom Taylor.
[19] Part XIV of *Vanity Fair* for February, chapters 47 to 50.

442.              TO FRANCIS FLADGATE [20]
                     JANUARY 1848 [21]

Hitherto unpublished.

My dear Fladgate. With that kind of feeling wh one has heard
of [22] — (the donkey between 2 bundles
of hay) I'm obliged to put my case before you.

[20] Fladgate (1799–1892), a barrister of independent means who as a young
man had known Keats, was one of the closest friends of Thackeray's later life.
He was much seen at the Garrick Club, of which he was long the oldest member. Barham (*Garrick Club*, p. 30) describes him as "One of the most polished gentlemen and good-natured persons I ever met."

[21] This note was written shortly before Ainsworth's birthday, February 4,
1848, when *The Lancashire Witches* was appearing serially in *The Sunday
Times*. Since February 4 came on a Friday this year, we may no doubt suppose
that Ainsworth's dinner was held the following day.

[22] Thackeray wrote *feeling with wh one has heard of*.

On the 1st Saturday after my arrival in town I made a solemn
engagement to dine with Ainsworth on his *Birthday* — and it is the
very Saturday I am engaged to you — Don't be angry with me for
not coming to you, but how can I to both? [23]

        Farewell, distractedly yours W M T.

P. S. There is one thing I forgot. Have you ordered

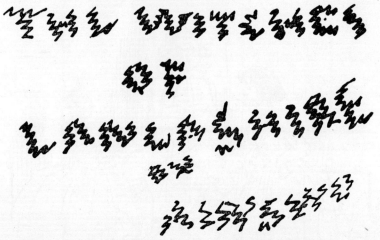

I thought I was drunk when I saw the placards in the street

---

[23] In the large drawing at the head of this letter Thackeray has depicted
himself as Macheath in *The Beggar's Opera* (II, xiii), saying to Ainsworth and
Fladgate, his Polly and Lucy:

        How happy could I be with either,
          Were t'other dear charmer away!

443.                        TO MISS WEDDERBURN [24]
                            26 JANUARY 1848

*Address:* Miss Wedderburn | 7 Chesham Place.  Hitherto unpublished.

                                                    26 Jan.ʸ

Dear Madam

   In speaking about me to my friend Higgins [25] last night you made
use of language so extraordinary that I am bound as a gentleman to
notice it — you said, it appears, that I was — that you thought —
that you preferred my — in a word — some prodigious opinions
were uttered by you of wʰ though I don't believe a word, I cant help
owning that they pleased my vanity hugely.

   As the Printers devil is good enough to call on me this morning,
and is passing on his return to Fleet Street very near your door, I
send for your inspection my friend Doyles capital book of carica-
toons,[26] and the Painted Almanack a charming book in my idea.

   Inside the Cartoon book are 2 or 3 drawings by Mʳ Titmarsh wʰ
are very dismal in point of execution but have I think some expression.

   Should you be at home, the boy also can show you 2 or 3 blocks*
on their way to the engravers, who will cut away the little expression wʰ the faces at present wear.  In one Becky is going into dinner:
in another poor Amelia is sitting on the cold stones in Russell Square
looking up at a house where — but for the rest see No XIV.

   Yours dear Miss Wedderburn most faithfully

                                    W M Thackeray.

*wʰ please to return to him instanter

   [24] Miss Wedderburn was living at this time with the family of Edward How-
ley Palmer at 7 Chesham Place (*Royal Blue Books*, 1846 and 1851).
   [25] See *Memoranda.*
   [26] *Selections from the Rejected Cartoons*, finished at the same time as *Our
Street*, as a note from Doyle to Leech in the copy of the former in the Widener
Collection of the Harvard College Library attests.

444.                    TO MARK LEMON
                       28 JANUARY 1848

Hitherto unpublished.

                                                        Friday
                            My dear Lemon
                                I lost all yesterday owing to the
                            headache after Dickens's ball.[27] And
                            yet I didn't debauch. Ask Leech whom
                            I refused to join in an unholy project
                            of topping up with segars and brandy-
                            anwater. I cant be ready till tomorrow
                            at 12 though for I have the last 1/2
                            sheet of V. F to finish today.
                                               Yours ever
                                               W M T.

445.                    TO MRS. EDWARD MARLBOROUGH
                            FɪᴛᴢGERALD
                            31 JANUARY 1848

*Address:* Mʳˢ FitzGerald | 12 Pelham Crescent | Brompton. *Postmark:* JA 31
1848. Hitherto unpublished.

                                    13 Young Sᵗ Kensington.
                                    Monday Jan 31.

My dear Mʳˢ FitzGerald
    I know what you have been thinking the past week — but indeed
it is not so — At the end of the month I always have a life-&-death
struggle to get out my number of Vanity Fair — I am always engaged for a week before hand    My life is passed in dining and
pennyalining I have only 1 free day this week and that I must give

    [27] Which was given on Wednesday, January 26. See above, No. 437.

to the children. Pray dont think I am neglectful — and let me come to see an old kind friend one day next week.

Ever faithfully yours<br>W M Thackeray.

446.       TO LEIGH HUNT<br>
            FEBRUARY 1848

*Address:* Leigh Hunt Esq^re | &c &c &c. Hitherto unpublished.

My dear Monsieur Hunt

I should like you to tell me if there isn't a little delicate fiddle-playing in the last chapter of the present No XIV.

Yours without any particular motive<br>W M T.

I am going to dine at home at 5 tomorrow quite quiet with only one friend — the entertainment concluding at 9.

447.       TO GRAHAM WILLMORE<br>
           4 FEBRUARY 1848 [28]

Hitherto unpublished.

Kensington Feb 4.

Dear Sir

I am much obliged to you for your pamphlet and the note with w^h you have been good enough to accompany it. It gives me great pleasure to think that any writing of mine sh^d afford matter for thought or approval to men devoted to graver pursuits than my own. I have read the pamphlet with much pleasure: having had some doubts about the Institution w^h you defend and whether it was not too cumbrous and complicated for times w^h change and ad-

---

[28] The tenor of the last paragraph points to 1848. Thackeray was in Paris on February 4, 1849, and Willmore's *Is Trial by Jury Worth Keeping* had reached a third edition by 1850.

348    TO GRAHAM WILLMORE    1848

vance so rapidly as ours — There was no such thing as a Press when
the Jury was invented — a really free press is scarcely 20 years old
with us — I don't know how far the use of that engine will go, or
serve to supersede the other great popular safeguard — What you
say about the odium brought on country magistrates by giving them
increased powers of summary convictions is very weighty I think:
their administration is odious enough already. And yet (I don't
know anything about the subject and only speak from feeling) will
the people be contented much longer do you think with that juris-
diction of individuals set over them not because they are learned in
the law, but because they have a county status as parsons squires and
what not? Mayn't the railroad system enable an expert judicial
officer to superintend 20 times as much country, as a county magistrate now has in charge?

But the great beauty of the jury system I think has been that the
jury has covered the judge. All Europe is covered over with corrupt judges I believe, and their office continually exposed to bribery,
or to doubt at any rate, w$^h$ is as bad. It is from this that the 12 men
have defended our bench, and kept it from stain. And in times
when one may look for any conceivable change almost & political
convulsion brought on whether by popular outbreak or patrician
conservatism & resistance I hope the judges will never lose their 12
pawns, or their honor may be trampled down, in the struggle. I am
dear Sir

Your very faithful Servt<br>W M Thackeray

Graham Willmore Esq$^r$

448.    TO MRS. CARMICHAEL-SMITH
4 FEBRUARY 1848 [29]

*Address:* Mrs Carmichael Smyth | 2 Rue Ponthieu | Champs Élysées | Paris.
*Postmarks:* 5 FE 1848, 6 FEVR. 48 BOULOGNE. Hitherto unpublished.

My dearest Mother I have had the enclosed [30] in my pocket for days, shrinking from sending to you, because I knew that I must make you unhappy. But there is no help for it. The children are quite well. Anny's toe greatly better. The nail can't be kept on for almost all of it is gone, and the new one formed: the swelling subsided, the pain diminished: everything going on as well as may be. I am perfectly content with Mr Merriman: [31] and decline sending for other doctors. Ah my mother do be tranquil: do believe that the children are well happy and well cared for. Why, with my belief, it would be a crime on my part, to send for Quin. I could no more make such a promise than I could say Mahomet was Prophet — I lay down the pen and think & think about you as I do many a time in the day and night — I didn't sleep one wink that night the pencil writing was written. 'There she is, I say to myself, her young taken from her, yearning after them, unhappy — 'He won't write to me: he won't have the doctors I put faith in, I who brought the children up, what does he know?' — Dearest Mother I must do my duty in the midst of all this. I must act by my own conscience, not yours. The rest is in the hands of †

I wrote to Hicks by this evenings post begging him to make arrangements for acting on the Will immediately. I send you 1/2 of what I've got. I can get plenty more. God bless you.

[29] See the next letter.
[30] No doubt the "pencil writing" referred to below, which has not been preserved.
[31] The surgeon John Jones Merriman (1800–1881), who with his brother Dr. James Nathaniel Merriman held the appointment of apothecary extraordinary to Her Majesty. He lived at 12 and 13 Young Street (*Post Office London Directory*, 1847).

449.      TO MRS. RITCHIE
5 FEBRUARY 1848

Hitherto unpublished.

Kensington. Feb 5. 1848.

My dear Aunt

You have very good right to complain of some nephews and nieces of your's who might put a pen to paper occasionally, and gratify an old aunt who sits in the country by her fireside lonely and without news — that is you may scold all except your nephew Titmarsh whose pen is so occupied in providing for the butcher the baker the candlestick-maker that he has very little time for his friends and relatives. Do you know I have not written to my mother for 3 weeks till yesterday, and then I was obliged to send her a scolding      My dear old Mother is always tormenting herself about the children, and their illnesses      You must know they have had the chicken pox — Anny rather badly: also she had a sore toe w$^h$ has troubled her: and her poor Granny is so alarmed about these things that she writes me over the most dismal letters, telling me what to do, entreating me to employ her doctor, not mine &c — I am obliged to say no to these prayers: and also to be compelled to give annoyance to such a gentle and loving creature. Now both these young ladies are quite well and seated in my room in my arm chairs reading.

Their Governess has gone to pass the day with her family it being her sisters birthday. and we three are presently going out for a days holiday likewise — they to pass the day with some friends and I to take 4 little boys to the play. I like taking children to the play — their laughing makes me laugh if the play does not.

So Constantia has found a nice young man, has she? Amen. She is a nice young lass and I hope she will be happy. I should like a wife myself very much: but keep myself occupied by falling in love with twenty women at a time. You must know I am become quite a Lion now, and live with all sorts of great people: but their flattery has not turned my head as yet, please God, and my reign as a fashionable literary man will very soon be over: and somebody else will be favorite in my stead.

The Bedingfields have got the snuggest little cottage in the world everything neat trim spick & span and apple pie. It w^d do your heart good to see. So Charles sent you some wine — do you want anything else my dear Aunt? do tell me if you do: for indeed I would have no greater pleasure in life than in contributing in any way to your comfort. God bless you.

[For a fragment of a letter to Mrs. Brookfield, 25? February, 1848, see letter 1, Appendix XXVI]

450.     TO MRS. IRVINE
FEBRUARY 1848 [32]

My text is taken from a facsimile in *Unpublished Letters by W. M. Thackeray,* ed. Shorter, pp. 15–17.

Helas, madame et cousine, je suis engagé a diner à Newgate demain avec les Chérifs de Londres — nous irons voir les prisonniers les treadmills et les jolis petits condamnes qu'on va pendre.

Apres je vais dans plusieurs soirées élegantes (Surtout chez cette dame, Miladi Gordon, que votre mari aime tant). Ainsi je ne serai de retour à Kensington qu'a minuit, bien trop tard pour venir frap-

---

[32] This note was written at about the same time as Thackeray's letter of February 5 to Mrs. Ritchie, in which he remarks that his daughters have recovered from the chicken-pox.

per a votre petite porte si tranquille de votre Cottage si calme où tout ce grand et petit monde sera couché.

Mes demoiselles sont guéries maintenant de leur chicken pock — Elles envoient mille salutations d'amitie à la colonie de Littl' Olland Ouse.[33]

Adieu Madame et chère cousine votre affectionné
Chevalier de Titmarsh.

451.                    TO MARK LEMON
                       18 FEBRUARY 1848

Hitherto unpublished.

My dear Lemon

I will be ready the 1st thing tomorrow morning — with a letter to my dear Ray [34] about J O'Connell & the Irish.*

I suppose you keep open for Lord J's financial statement to night.[35]  5 per cent income tax ought to provoke a howl from Punch —

The bishops row about the Sovereign Pontiff might be jocular.

I am by some accident a little in arrears with V. F.[36]

Yours ever
W M T.

* The 2 cuts sent yesterday are for this

[33] Where the Irvines were living.
[34] "Mr. Punch for Repeal," *Punch*, February 26.
[35] Lord John Russell, Prime Minister and First Lord of the Treasury, read his financial statement in the House of Commons on February 18. It is the subject of several squibs in *Punch* for February 26. The clerical bickering that attended the appointment of a new Archbishop of Canterbury is dealt with in the same issue under the heading "Liberality of Rumour."
[36] Thackeray was at work on number XV, chapters 51 to 53, the last of which includes the famous scene in which Rawdon Crawley discovers his wife with Lord Steyne. "When we congratulated him, many years ago," writes James Hannay (*Brief Memoir of the Late Mr. Thackeray*, Edinburgh, 1864, pp. 20–21), "on the touch in *Vanity Fair* in which Becky 'admires' her husband when he is giving Lord Steyne the chastisement which ruins *her* for life, 'Well,' he said, — 'when I wrote the sentence, I slapped my fist on the table, and said '*that* is a touch of genius!' "

Hélas, madame et cousine, je suis engagé
a diner à Newgate demain avec les Chérifs
de Londres — nous irons voir les prisonniers
les treadmills et les jolis petits condamnés
qu'on va pendre

Après je vais dans plusieurs soirées élégantes

THACKERAY'S LETTER TO MRS. IRVINE OF FEBRUARY, 1848

(surtout chez cette dame, Mladi Gordon, que votre
mari aime tant) — Ainsi je ne serai de retour
à Kensington qu'à minuit, bien trop tard
pour venir frapper a votre petite porte si franc
.ville de votre Cottage si calme où tout ce

grand et petit monde

sera couché.

Mes demoiselles sont guéries maintenant
de leur chickenpock — Elles envoient mille
salutations d'amitié à la colonie de

Litl' Olland Ous.
　　　　　Adieu Madame et chère Cousine
　　　Votre affectionné
　　　　　　Chevalier de Titmarsh.

THACKERAY'S LETTER TO MRS. IRVINE OF FEBRUARY, 1848

452.     TO GEORGE HENRY LEWES [37]
6 MARCH 1848

Hitherto unpublished. *Endorsed:* Thackeray to G. H. Lewes.

13 Young S[t] Kensington.
6 March. 1848

My dear Sir

I have just read your notice in the Chronicle [38] (I conclude it is
a friend who has penned it) and am much affected by the friendliness of the sympathy, and by the kindness of the reproof of the critic.

That passage w[h] you quote bears very hardly upon the poor alderman certainly: but I don't mean that the man deprived of turtle
would as a consequence steal bread: only that he in the possession of
luxuries and riding through life respectably in a gig, should be very
chary of despising poor Lazarus on foot, & look very humbly and
leniently upon the faults of his less fortunate brethren — If Becky
had had 5000 a year I have no doubt in my mind that she would

---

[37] Lewes (1817–1878), who lived with George Eliot from 1854 until his
death, was one of Thackeray's strongest partisans among the younger generation
of London writers.

[38] An article ostensibly on *The Book of Snobs* which develops into a general
survey of Thackeray's work. Though Lewes deals chiefly in praise, he finds
reason for protest in Thackeray's books. He complains that the world is not so
corrupt as Thackeray would have us believe; "in *Vanity Fair*, his greatest work,
how little there is to love! The people are all scamps, scoundrels, or humbugs."
Lewes takes particular exception to a "detestable passage" in chapter 41 of the
novel (*Works*, I, 407–408), "wherein after allowing Becky, with dramatic
propriety, to sophisticate with herself to the effect that it is only her poverty
which makes her vicious, [Thackeray] adds from himself this remark: — 'And
who knows but Rebecca was right in her speculations — and that it was only a
question of money and fortune which made the difference between her and an
honest woman? If you take temptations into account, who is to say that he is
better than his neighbour? A comfortable career of prosperity, if it does not
make people honest, at least keeps them so. An alderman coming from a turtle
feast will not step out of his carriage to steal a leg of mutton; *but put him to
starve, and see if he will not purloin a loaf.*' Was it carelessness, or deep misanthropy, distorting an otherwise clear judgment, which allowed such a remark
to fall? What, in the face of starving thousands, men who literally die for
want of bread, yet who prefer death to stealing, shall it be said that honesty is
only the virtue of abundance!" (*Morning Chronicle*, March 6)

have been respectable; increased her fortune advanced her family
in the world: laid up treasures for herself in the shape of 3 per cents,
social position, reputation &c — like Louis Philippe let us say, or
like many a person highly & comfortably placed in the world not
guilty of many wrongs of commission, satisfied with himself, never
doubting of his merit, and decorously angry at the errors of less
lucky men. What satire is so awful as Lead us not into temptation?
What is the gospel and life of our Lord (excuse me for mentioning
it) but a tremendous Protest against pride and self-righteousness?
God forgive us all, I pray, and deliver us from evil.

I am quite aware of the dismal roguery w^h goes all through the
Vanity Fair story — and God forbid that the world should be like
it altogether: though I fear it is more like it than we like to own.
But my object is to make every body engaged, engaged in the pursuit of Vanity and I must carry my story through in this dreary
minor key, with only occasional hints here & there of better things
— of better things w^h it does not become me to preach.

I never scarcely write letters to critics and beg you to excuse me
for sending you this. It is only because I have just laid down the
paper, and am much moved by the sincere goodwill of my critic.

very faithfully yours<br>W M Thackeray.

453.                    TO ANDREW DOYLE? [39]
                       7 MARCH 1848

Hitherto unpublished.

13 Young S^t Kensington Sq^e<br>March 7. 1848

My dear Sir

Will you kindly forward the enclosed to my critic in the Chronicle of yesterday. I need not tell you how very much gratified I am
to have my writings so spoken of.

Yours very much obliged<br>W M Thackeray

[39] Editor of *The Morning Chronicle* from 1843 to 1848.

454.      TO FREDERICK GOLDSMITH
8 MARCH 1848? [40]

Hitherto unpublished.

Kensington Wednesday.

My dear Goldsmith.

Though I had as clean forgotten the invitation (not I mean the invitation for that I remembered perfectly, but thought in the festive exhilaration of the wine-cup we only spoke of invitations in general) — though I say I had forgotten yet I will come with pleasure at 6 1/2 to the O. C.

Yours ever

W M T.

455.      TO MRS. CARMICHAEL-SMYTH
10 MARCH 1848

*Address:* M$^{rs}$ Carmichael Smyth. | 2 Rue de Ponthieu | Champs Élysées | Paris.
*Postmarks:* 10 MR 1848, 11 MARS 48 BOULOGNE. Hitherto unpublished.

All my dearest old mothers praises alarm me, and everybody else's indeed: They are so very undeserved as I fancy. I dont remember now what there was that makes you so pleased in my last note [41] except God save the republic, w$^{h}$ is a manifest truth for some time at least — I mean to be fulfilled at some time. But I don't believe in communism socialism or Louis Blanc [42] — I have been reading his Organisation du Travail lately w$^{h}$ points out the evils of our present system most clearly, but proposes a remedy so absurd

[40] Thackeray dined with Goldsmith on Saturday, March 11, 1848. It is quite possible that this note was written the previous Wednesday.

[41] This letter, which was written shortly after the establishment of the second French Republic on February 24, has not been preserved.

[42] Blanc (1813–1882), the radical politician and man-of-letters, had published *De l'Organisation du travail* in 1840. He left France in the autumn of 1848 to avoid arrest and lived for many years thereafter in London, where Thackeray was his good friend.

and detestable as it seems to me that the worst tyranny w^d be more acceptable feasible and conducive to the general happiness. I cant find the end of the question between property and labour. We want something almost equal to a Divine Person to settle it. I mean if there is ever to be an elucidation of the mystery it is to be solved by a preacher of such novelty and authority, as will awaken and convince mankind — but O how and when? — the question of poverty is that of death disease winter or any other natural phenomenon. I dont know how either is to stop. Universal suffrage as the French are going to practise it seems to me a monstrous tyranny more intolerable than Nicholas or the Austrians. It breaks machines it drives out and breaks faith with two thousand honest English workmen, it sets the pavions to cry out for eight francs a day in lieu of four; the weavers to ask twelve hours pay for ten hour labour &c. I dont know any government so reckless brutal and suicidal as such a one would be if persisting long — for who on earth supposes that capitalists can afford to give up eighteen per cent of profit and go on with these works? that they make eighteen per cent profit? — Why we know very well that with all the pain degradation pinching starving of the present manufacturing system the manufacturers barely keep their heads above water, that when they do make profits the profit that they get from the labour of each individual is so infinitesimally small that to compare it to the difference between 12 & 10 is absurd: that in agriculture with famine wages and the utmost screwing of laborers the utmost rate of profit may be said to be 3 1/2 per cent — Why a rise takes place in wages, and the whole social machine goes under water — every body is ruined. Nobody is benefitted — that surplus of 3 or 4 per cent w^h the people battle for when got is nothing among them — unless a miracle comes, and a new God that can divide that small fish among so many. Well, who know? — Why not? — When one reads of those maniacal Irishmen calling upon Government to relieve them or else — or else they will repeal [43] — what can one do but turn away sickening at the folly of both cries. How can repeal teach them to dig & spin better? Suppose Paddy had in fee simple the land for w^h he pays

[43] See "Mr. Punch for Repeal," *Punch*, February 26.

or owes to his landlord, who would be better at the end of a few score of years?  One goes round in a perpetual circle of grief pain starvation, there seems no way out, and the end of a violent revolution w$^d$ be that everybody would be at his neighbour's throat and a hundred times more miserable than now.  I think 40000£ is too much for a Bishop, but I think he should have very large and even splendid allowances.  I am certain that wealth is good for the poor: and feel pretty sure that any change in the division of it, would only end in some such similar and seemingly partial scheme as that w$^h$ at present revolts us — To cry out against selfishness is very well — but it is the great motive of all the world.  Our means of happiness are selfish our love selfish (it pleases us to attach to somebody) we labor love are lazy for ourselves and as we see out of our own eyes — We never should get children but for ardent selfishness: we — Here comes in at this minute G. P's prodigious letter! — It is the best thing I ever heard in my life this X purposes.  Why we are as quiet here as ever — the disturbers of the public peace of London were not 300 penniless pickpockets.  We won't have an armed or violent revolution here, please God — and if we do every man of orderly feelings and peaceful notions in the country would be on the Gov$^t$ side.  Republicans and all.  I am for a social republic not communism — My dear old parents.  You will say I am a sad luke warm reformer after this.  No.  God bless you both.  I think the collision of poverty agst property is begun in France, but not here as yet.  And my dear little ones are as safe at Kensington D. V. as in any corner of this habitable globe — I say Goodbye I am going to ride out and dine at Addiscombe — it will be queer to see the old place — The children are splendid: they are gone to dine at Harris's with his 2 little grand children.

God bless you

W M T.

456.                    TO ABRAHAM HAYWARD
                           10 MARCH 1848

Hitherto unpublished.

My dear Hayward

I ought to have written before to thank you — not for your good
opinion because that has nothing to do with thanks — but for your
good nature in thinking of writing — and I am very glad indeed
you like XV. What a wonder it is that the story does not succeed in
spite of all the praise of the world and the critics — I cant understand how it is it does not sell more.

I have a good thing to tell you w$^h$ is worth at least the pains of
reading a note      My step father writes me this minute from Paris.
He is in the greatest state of alarm about the riots w$^h$ are taking
place in this country believes that a bloody revolution is imminent
here and begs that I should send the children over to Paris to him
for protection!

:This is the greatest thing I have heard yet come out of the Revolution.

                         Salut et Fraternité
                              W M T.

457.                         DIARY
                        10-15 MARCH 1848

Hitherto unpublished.

Friday. March 10

We went in a party from Bouverie Street [44] to taste port wine in
the City and dine on beef steaks there. The beefsteaks were admirable served in the back parlor of a dirty little inn opposite the
Excise Office, famous for steaks. The tipsy Scotch landlord had a
face like one of them. The people in various boxes about were roar-

      [44] Bradbury and Evans, the publishers of *Punch*, had offices at 11 Bouverie
Street.

ing with jokes & fun; except one young fellow who sate over a glass of ale & a pipe reading a French novel under a greasy sky light. You could see piles of emptied bottles overhead.

At the wine merchants we saw piles more. 6000 & 5000 in a line. We moralized upon the state of men's own cellars, where one is proud of showing a little heap of 4 or 5 dozen. Then we had Punch at Toms [45] a stifling and filthy place of resort. All the entertainment was quite odd & foreign the beef-steak house, the wine cellars, the smoking-place; and we gave ourselves dandyfied West End airs no doubt: Snobs all.

After Tom's we went to see the horse-riders at Drury Lane; [46] where I was astonished by the grace and perfection of equitation of Mad[lle] Caroline. an English rider performed too showing a great deal of coarse agility as a sailor an Irishman a Scotchman &c — but the curious p[t] was the difference in the style of the artists & the absence of grace in the English professor.

Dorsay L[d] Chesterfield [47] L[d] Granville and D[r] Quin were in a stage box & invited me in very good humouredly. They were all delighted with the performance and encouraged the rideresses as they passed. Indeed it was much pleasanter to see the fellows jumping standing 1 2 3 on each other vaulting & tumbling &c than to hear the best comedy at least for the time. In the midst of all her surprizing jumps and caracoles Mademoiselle Caroline had always her eyes on Milor, and took her last jump giving a Parthian glance at him.

L[d] Granville has scratched his nose in the exercise of his profession as master of the Buckhounds he scarred it in going through a bullfinch. Baring Wall [48] says a little bird has bitten Lord Gran-

---

[45] Tom's Coffee House, Cowper's Court, Cornhill (*Post Office London Directory*, 1847).

[46] "THEATRE ROYAL, DRURY LANE. CIRQUE NATIONAL DE PARIS. THIS EVENING a variety of EQUESTRIAN PERFORMANCES by the entire Troupe. To conclude with THE FRENCH HUSSARS by Mdlles. Mathilde, Brilloff, Virginie, Florentine, Emmelina, Ducos, Amaglia, &c. Doors open at half-past 7 o'clock to commence at 8." (*Times*, March 10)

[47] George Stanhope (1805–1866), sixth Earl of Chesterfield; Granville George Leveson-Gower (1815–1891), second Earl of Granville.

[48] Charles Baring Wall (1795–1853), an M. P. from 1819 till his death.

villes nose. All these great persons were perfectly good humoured easy & unaffected — enjoying the sport before them with the utmost simplicity & childish good humour.

At supper for the early beefsteak left us hungry at 11 o'clock — we went to Offley's — for the first time on my part during these 12 years. The place was quite deserted: only Bardolph of Brazennose sitting there solitary drinking and drunk. Leech recognized him from the acc.[t] in P.[49]

Leech was sulky. Quin is a humbug and quack says he. I know it. I said I knew Q to be a very kind and good natured and serviceable man: and cited things in his favor. L: still angry says — Quin is, compared to a regular physician what Dorsay is compared to a regular gentleman!

I wonder what he and Lemon were talking about: when I left the pit and went into the genteel box? — 'That d— lickspittle Thackeray' &c — it was all evident: and yet I didn't kiss anybody's tails at all.

Friday passed the morning in a headache, and in reading K. Arthur by Bulwer, and in drawing a little. Louis Philippe measured by Moses. At 3 o'clock rode to Croydon,[50] taking a wrong turning at Kensington and losing time in the Clapham direction.

---

[49] "A Night's Pleasure," *Punch*, January 8–February 19, 1848. See *Works*, VI, 576–582.

[50] On his way to Addiscombe, where he had been invited by his friend Frederick Goldsmith, an orderly officer. "My impression is," Goldsmith writes (*Athenæum*, 1891, p. 474), "that he did not long remain *incognito*, and that there was a certain slight unsteadiness evinced by the cadets, who must have recognized him when he accompanied me to chapel in the evening. But one circumstance in connexion with the visit to Addiscombe recalls itself distinctly to my mind. He expressed a wish to see some of the rooms in the Governor's house — or mansion, as it was usually styled. One, a bed-room, he entered and examined with curious interest. Suddenly he said something in a low voice which caused me to turn towards him. I observed that he was much affected and made a hurried movement to the door. An explanation of the incident was soon afforded. The elder Mrs. Thackeray had, by a second marriage, become the wife of Major Carmichael Smyth, a distinguished officer of engineers, who had been for some time Governor of Addiscombe College. Her son William, when quite a youth, had resided with her and his stepfather at the last-named institution, and now chanced to be revisiting the familiar locality. Coming

All the country for miles round is covered by opulent little villas completed or in course of completion — came out on the Brixton road by a bran new church with a campanile and cross imported from the 10ᵗʰ century. The villas dont slacken until you get to Streatham, where I saw the well-remembered church, trees Inn & schools on the common. All sorts of recollections of my youth came back to me: dark and sad and painful with my dear good mother as a gentle angel interposing between me and misery — . Railroads and new buildings have cut through the old Addiscombe lane — numbers of new buildings have sprung round the house it has been spoilt & painted white. I went to see our old quarters: wʰ were shown us by Sir E Stannus [51] the present Governor — the chairs in the drawing-room were still ours, and I recognized what I am sure was my mothers bed — it made me feel very queer — My old room is the Generals dressing room — how well I remember the cawing of the rooks there of a morning! they were still talking away in the wilderness wʰ is quite unaltered.[52]

Dined with the orderly officers and after Chapel went to see old Mother Dodd at the hospital [53] a vulgar old harridan flattering & lying: but she was kind to me as a child: and I gave her a sovereign.

Rode back to town on Saturday & wrote for Punch: dined at the Oriental Club with Goldsmid and went to the Eagle Tavern [54] & the Albert saloon. The latter was quite a remarkable sight, the play & the audience =ly so. A couple of aristocratic seducers carry off bright eyed Emma & her companion they are followed by a couple of tars and combats hornpipes &c fill up the piece: but it was tre-

---

into his mother's sleeping apartment, he had recognized the old-fashioned bedstead; and there were possibly portraits or other objects which helped to intensify the vividness of the retrospect."

[51] Colonel Sir Ephraïm G. Stannus, Lieutenant-Governor of Addiscombe from 1834 till his death in 1850 (Vibart, *Addiscombe*, pp. 104 and 190).

[52] It will be observed that these paragraphs foreshadow the central situation of the first six chapters of *Esmond*, the loneliness of Harry's unhappy boyhood and its alleviation by the maternal love of Lady Castlewood. Here, indeed, are the very rooks that haunt Castlewood Hall in Thackeray's novel.

[53] Thackeray wrote *hospitable*.

[54] Otherwise known as the Grecian Saloon (see above, No. 62, June 2). Both it and the Albert Saloon were in Hoxton.

mendous to see the audience: and the boys in the gallery We were in the stalls. They cost 3$^d$

Sunday at home all day. Morgan John [55] & Glyn dined, wrote for M.C.[56] M. J. told of Father Tom Maguire, who was famous for keeping greyhounds. I give them names of one syllable Father Tom said, aisy to be called after them. such as Port and Clart: and thim names!

Monday. Rode with Leech and came back wet through with the rain. Both of us fell in love with the charming Jane Ingleby. At dinner at Lady Blessingtons [57] Prince Louis, who looks like a courier — Lds Chesterfield Elphinstone [58] Strangford and Madame Laffitte (Charles) — she chattered all dinner time in a curious semifashionable slang She had bare shoulders w$^h$ looked however chiffonie like her crumpled tawdry white satin dress. She laughed at the failures of the Paris bankers her own husband included — and she tried to sell Lord Chesterfield a bargain of a bracelet but the good natured nobleman would not bite. The Miss Powers [59] were very kind pleasant witty and *good* as I thought. My Lady exceedingly gracious. Dorsay always frank & pleasant; showed us his special constables wrist-badge and truncheon: and took us in custody in the way the police manage it — You must go under this singular grip Lord Strangford & I were walked about the room like a pair of babies.

Major Davidoff of the Russian Guard spoke about the Emperor

[55] Morgan John O'Connell (1811–1875), one of Thackeray's closest friends in middle and later life. He was educated at Trinity College, Dublin, receiving his B. A. degree in 1833, and became a student at Gray's Inn the same year. From 1835 to 1852 he represented Kerry in parliament. He later succeeded to the Coppinger estates in Cork. Daniel O'Connell was his uncle.

[56] I have not succeeded in identifying this article, which was presumably a political leader.

[57] Marguerite Power (1789–1849), Countess of Blessington, the mistress of Gore House, with whom Thackeray formed a warm friendship in the last two years of her life. Prince Louis, of course, was the future Napoléon III.

[58] John Buller-Fullerton-Elphinstone (1807–1860), thirteenth Baron Elphinstone; Percy Smythe (1780–1855), sixth Viscount Strangford.

[59] Marguerite and Ellen, daughters of Robert Power, Lady Blessington's brother. Thackeray's favorite was Marguerite, who assisted her aunt in editing *The Keepsake*.

of whom L^d Strangford told stories respecting his courage & accession — the last story was about Rubini. Rubini asked the Emperor for a uniform and decoration as singer at the Imperial Chapel.[60] The Emperor gave him the *medal* of S^t Ann not the cross, mind, Davidoff laid great stress upon this, and then the great potentate and a confidential General set to work and invented a uniform for the singer, embroidered all over with fiddles trumpets and orchestral ornaments to suit his profession. There is a sort of humour in this.

A picture of the K of Hanover [61] was in the room sent to Dorsay by that sovereign. L^d Strangford said the King was the most popular monarch in Europe and I'm most popular amongst my clergy G— d— my eyes. the king said.

At M^rs Foxs [62] on Tuesday this story was trumped by C. Villiers who said that at King Ernests first accession Major Fancourt was his secretary & it was the Kings delight to ask the great Hanoverian nobles to dinner, and bawl out abuse of every one of them to Fancourt at the other end of the table. All his guests understood English as well as he did, and were obliged to look as if they comprehended nothing.

Let me put down here a story told me by Sir George Aston: of the first gentleman in Europe: when he was P. R and staying at Brighton Sir George Aston was on a visit at the Pavillion, and Gillrays Duke of Norfolk [63] was invited from Arundel. A conspiracy was arranged to make the old nobleman drunk: the Duke of Clarence [64] bustled round the table at each toast and saw that the buttler filled every man's glass — The old Duke though infirm & aware of the plot laid agst him determined not to flinch and drank with the strongest and youngest there, seeing many under the table. At last

---

[60] Nicholas I (1796–1855) had called Rubini to St. Petersburg in 1843.

[61] King Ernest Augustus of Hanover (1771–1851), fifth son of George III.

[62] Mrs. George Lane Fox, a well known London hostess.

[63] Charles Howard (1746–1815), eleventh Duke of Norfolk. Thackeray used the story which follows in his lecture on George IV (*Works*, VII, 698–699).

[64] William Henry, Duke of Clarence (1765–1837), afterwards (1831) William IV.

the First Gentleman proposed bumpers of pale brandy w<sup>h</sup> was brought in great glasses. Jocky of Norfolk stood up drank off his — and then called for his carriage and said he would go home to Arundel. He was pressed in vain to stay as he had promised: he said no: intimated his anger at the trick put upon him and insisted upon his departure.

But by the time the chariot and four famous black horses had arrived, the old man was quite drunk and tumbling about. When put into his carriage he could not sit up even but sank down from the cushions, still hiccupping out that he would go home to Arundel

The greatest gentleman in Europe ordered a servant to go to each side of the carriage — one to hold up the Duke's head the other his Grace's legs w<sup>h</sup> were helpless dangling out at the open doors, and bade the coachman drive for 1/2 an hour up & down the gravel walks, by w<sup>h</sup> time Norfolk was perfectly done and was put to bed fancying that he was in his room at Arundel.

Present at M<sup>rs</sup> Fox's Luttrell,[65] L<sup>d</sup> Lincoln, de Mauley & Milnes & C. Villiers who is always capitally humourous & sardonic: good old M<sup>r</sup> Luttrell laughed & fell asleep alternately.

M<sup>rs</sup> Fox said the mob on the day of the Trafalgar Sq<sup>r</sup> riot stopped Lady Hoggs [66] bran new blue carriage and insulted her for an Aristocrat. Lady Hogg was never so much pleased in her life.

Wrote an article on the Kennington meeting for M. C.[67] after dinner at home with my dearest little women whose sweetness and artless kindness is O how different from Vanity Fair talk. I tried in vain to convince the fine folks at M<sup>rs</sup> Fox's that revolution was upon us: that we were wicked in our scorn of the people. They all thought there was poverty & discomfort to be sure, but that they were pretty good in themselves; that powder & liveries were very decent & proper though certainly absurd — the footmen themselves would

[65] Henry Luttrell (1765?–1851), the poet and wit; Henry Pelham-Clinton (1811–1864), styled Lord Lincoln, later (1851) fifth Duke of Newcastle; William Ponsonby (1787–1855), first Baron de Mauley.

[66] Lady Mary Hogg (d. 1874), wife of Sir James Hogg, who had been created a Baronet in 1846.

[67] "Meeting on Kennington Common," *Morning Chronicle*, March 14, 1848. This article has not previously been identified as Thackeray's.

not give them up C.V. said — Why, the gladiators at Rome were proud of their profession, & their masters saw nothing wicked in it. I suppose Article II in the M C. appeared Wednesday 15.[68] wont be as much liked as Art. I.

458.        TO EDWARD FrtzGERALD
            MARCH–MAY 1848 [69]

Published in part, *Biographical Introductions*, I, xxxiv–xxxv.

My dear old Yedward  It is not true what Gurlyle has written to you about my having become a tremenjuous lion &c — [70] too grand to &c — but what is true is that a feller who is writing all day for money gets sick of pens and paper when his work is over, and I go on dawdling and thinking of writing and months pass away. All that about being a Lion is nonsense. I cant eat more dinners than I used last year and dine at home with my dear little women three times a week: but 2 or 3 great people ask me to their houses: and Vanity Fair does everything but pay. I am glad if you like it. I don't care a dem if some other people do or dont: and always try to keep that damper against flattery. 'What does it matter whether

---

[68] "Chartist Meeting," *Morning Chronicle*, March 15, 1848. This article has not previously been identified as Thackeray's.

[69] Thackeray appears to have begun this letter in the middle of March and finished it early in May.

[70] This letter of Carlyle's has not been preserved, but he presumably told FitzGerald, as he did Charles Gavan Duffy (*Conversations with Carlyle*, p. 76) the following year, that "Thackeray . . . was essentially a man of grim, silent, stern nature, but lately he had circulated among fashionable people, dining out every day, and he covered this native disposition with a varnish of smooth, smiling complacency, not at all pleasant to contemplate. The course he had got into since he had taken to cultivate dinner-eating in fashionable houses was not salutary discipline for work of any sort, one might surmise." FitzGerald wrote to Frederick Tennyson on May 4: ". . . Thackeray is progressing greatly in his line: he publishes a Novel in numbers — Vanity Fair — which began dull, I thought: but gets better every number, and has some very fine things indeed in it. He is become a great man I am told: goes to Holland House, and Devonshire House: and for some reason or other, will not write a word to me. But I am sure this is not because he is asked to Holland House." (*Letters and Literary Remains*, ed. Wright, I, 271)

this man who is an ass likes your book or not' I have had the Edinburgh Review about me and upon my word haven't read it or so much as opened my copy. I looked at it at the Club but not through and — this modesty is furiously egotistical.

This was wrote I dont know how long ago: but my mind was unequal to the gigantic effort of filling a whole 1/2 sheet and I think another No. of V. F [71] has been written since 'I penned the above lines' — as the novelists say.

I caught a glimpse of the old Frau Mutter [72] riding alone in the Park a few weeks ago: and looking very melancholy I've not had the courage to call. but I have seen both Ainsworth and Albert Smith.[73] The latter is a good kind creature, though Heaven has written Snob undisguisedly on his mean keen good-natured intelligent face. As for Ainsworth he is more hairy than ever. He  begins to sprout at his under lip now and curls all over really its not unlike him. He was at dinner where I was yesterday, and made an observation about Harvey sauce O with such emphasis and solemnity. I burst out laughing but Jack Shepherd didn't know at what.

A letter from the young Madrileno of the Calle de las Caritas [74] arrived yesterday he says 'Not a word from Fitz.

Your namesake [75] they say has been stabbed in the *bas ventre* at Civita Vecchia. I am afraid he is recovering. The world does not contain a greater villain.

Gurlyle is immensely grand and savage now. He has a Cromwellian letter against the Irish in this weeks Examiner [76] I declare it seems like insanity almost his contempt for all mankind, and the way in w^h he shirks from the argument when called upon to préciser his own remedies for the state of things. Last Sunday I saw Jeames Spending walking in the Park with some children and a lady from

[71] Number XVI for April, chapters 54 to 56.
[72] Mrs. FitzGerald.
[73] Albert Richard Smith (1816–1860), the novelist, magazine writer, and lecturer.
[74] Saville Morton, at this time Madrid correspondent of a London journal.
[75] Edward Marlborough FitzGerald.
[76] "Repeal of the Union," *Examiner*, April 29.

the country I am one of the swells there. I have got a cob w$^h$ is the admiration of all — strong handsome goodnatured fast and never tired. You shall have a ride behind me if you come to London. Why dont you? I am going to give a party on the 9$^{th}$ May. M$^{rs}$ Dickens & Miss Hogarth made me give it. And I am in a great funk. I have not got a shilling Isn't it wonderful? I make a great deal of money and it goes pouring and pouring out in a frightful volubility.

My little women are delightful. They are drawing at my work table at this minute: and they act upon me after the world like soda water. God bless em. I have a Governess for them an excellent woman but a great ass. Leech drew a caricature the other day of a little boy & Guardsman, under w$^h$ was a dialogue with 'Little boy *loq*. Isn't Boyloq a French author? asked the Governess. But I dont like to part with her she is so kind and thoroughly good.

I have got a black niece [77] staying with me: daughter of a natural sister of mine. She was never in Europe before & wrote to my mother the other day as her 'dear Grandmamma' Fancy the astonishment of that dear majestic old woman!

This letter has been delayed and delayed until I fancied it would never go — Nevertheless I am always yours, and like you almost as much as I did 20 years ago. God bless you my dear old fellow

W M T.

[77] The daughter of Thackeray's illegitimate half-sister, Mrs. Blechynden. See *Memoranda*, Major and Mrs. Carmichael-Smyth.

459.        TO CHARLES ROWLAND DICKEN
                    30 MARCH 1848

Facsimile in *The Dickensian*, XVII (1921), 80.

March 30.

My dear Dicken [78]

I'm very sorry I am engaged on Saturday, and as for little Crawley now that Lord Steyne & he have quarrelled [79] who cares what happens to the little beggar? Pitch into him he has got no friends.

I forget how the block was made.

Yours ever

W M T.

460.        TO DR. CARPENTER [80]
                    30 MARCH 1848

Hitherto unpublished. My text is taken from a transcript supplied by Mrs. Fuller.

Kensington,
March 30th., 1848.

Dear Dr. Carpenter,

I would come with the greatest pleasure but that I am bound by a most special engagement to my little girls for Tuesday, when we

[78] Thackeray wrote *Dickens*, a mistake which led the editors of *The Dickensian* into excusable confusion. Actually the letter was sent to Dicken (1801–1873), reader and librarian to Charterhouse in Thackeray's time and for many years afterwards, who had written: "Come and dine, and look up old friends and young, and see how 'Georgy Osborne' is getting on" (D. D., *National Review*, XIII, 800).

[79] As they do in the last chapter (53) of the March, 1848, number of *Vanity Fair*.

[80] William Benjamin Carpenter (1813–1885), M. D., a distinguished physician and scientist.

are going to the play. And I go out so much that I cannot afford to disappoint them and myself of this nice pleasure. With best regards to Mrs. Carpenter, believe me,

Very faithfully yours,<br>W. M. Thackeray.

461.       FROM CHARLES DICKENS
30 MARCH 1848

Hitherto unpublished.

Devonshire Terrace<br>Thirtieth March 1848.

My Dear Thackeray.

I purpose holding a solemn dinner here on Tuesday the 11$^{th}$ of April, to celebrate the conclusion of a certain immortal book.[81] Hour, half past six. It couldn't be done without you. Therefore, book it cher citoyen! —

Ever Faithfully Yours<br>Charles Dickens

W. M. Thackeray Esquire.

462.       TO LADY MOLESWORTH
2 APRIL 1848

My text is taken from a facsimile in Caroline Shipman's "Some Treasures of the Daly Library," *The Critic*, XXXVI (1900), 217–219.

Kensington, April 2, 1849.[82]

Dear Lady Molesworth,

Solomon in all his glory, I am sure, never had such a waistcoat as I shall have the honour of sporting at your party on Sunday 16. I imagine myself already attired in the brocade (see the next page): I will try, however, and not lose my head with vanity, or fancy all

---

[81] *Dombey and Son.*

[82] A mistake for the revolutionary year 1848, as is shown by the content of the letter and by the fact that April 16 fell on a Sunday in that year but not in 1849.

the ladies in love with me if they had such a garment. It is before me now: and almost too splendid to ⟨. . .⟩[83] (Madame having been slain at the threshold) I will put on the waistcoat and say, "Citizens! respect the citizeness who gives of her riches! Before you touch the hem of her garment strike through the waistcoat of Titmarsh! See — they are of the same piece!" and the citizens will cheer you, and your beautiful house and furniture will be safe. As for me, I will wear your colours as long — as long as they will hold together, and I am told there is enough for 2 waistcoats for a slim man like

Your very much obliged

463.          TO JOHN FORSTER
          14 APRIL 1848

Extract published in Forster's *Life and Times of Oliver Goldsmith* (London, 1854), II, 467. My text is taken from a transcript supplied by Mrs. Fuller.

Good Friday. Kensington.

My dear Forster,

I would not write to thank you for Goldsmith,[84] until I had finished reading him and although I wanted to write a life of him myself (after Fielding which has long been a favourite biographical project of mine) — what can I say, but that your book is delightful? I have read it with the greatest interest and pleasure, got a capital notion of Goldsmith out of it, and quite sympathise with your love for the dear simple kindly creature. I was in his chambers in Brick Court [85] the other day. Davidson [86] has them now, they were Sergt. Murphy's — the bedroom is a closet without any light in it. It quite pains me to think of the kind old fellow dying off there. There is

[83] Several lines have here been torn from the letter.
[84] *The Life and Adventures of Oliver Goldsmith*, advertised as "Now Ready" in *The Athenæum* of April 15, 1848, p. 379.
[85] On the second floor at 2 Brick Court.
[86] Henry Davison (1805?–1860), knighted in 1856, one of Thackeray's oldest friends. He was educated at Trinity College, Oxford, where he took his B. A. and M. A. degrees in 1829 and 1834, and in the latter year was admitted to the bar by the Inner Temple. In 1857 he went out to Madras as Puisne Judge of the Supreme Court. He became Chief Justice in 1859, the year in which Thackeray dedicated *The Virginians* to him.

DRAWING IN THACKERAY'S LETTER OF APRIL 2, 1848

some good carved work in the room: and one can fancy him with General Oglethorpe and the other Topham Beauclerc, wasn't it? and the fellow coming in with the screw of tea and sugar.[87] What a fine picture Leslie would make of it. That crowd of hangers on and lazy good humour, how thoroughly Irish it is. Maginn used always to have a half dozen of tipsy fellows in his train, to whom he gave money and clothes, (by credit at the tailors) which they used to pawn. How prettily Horneck comes in, and lights up the story with a little smile of sentiment. I think both of them must have been in love with him.

> "And as the hare whom hounds and horns pursue,
> *Pants to the place* from which at first she flew." [88]

What an exquisite simile it is! What language! What is it that brings tears to one's eyes in reading the lines? I passed two rainy days at Glengariff in Ireland,[89] reading the Animated Nature with delight and surprize. What a charming simplicity and sweetness: what a dear old humourist! I have just come to his death the fact is — and I give you my word, I am quite affected by it. He is our personal friend. I'm sure I have a perfect notion of his individuality — his eyes, the quiver of his mouth, and his voice and brogue. I'm certain he had a *plaintive* look, not the heroic one which Reynolds tried to give him.[90] How delightful is the love they all bore him and what pleasant courteous stately figures they are in the picture.

You see this is an interjectional commentary. I am delighted in a word with the book (except the first book which I don't think is full enough of the subject, and has too didactic and auctorial an air) and write off in a hurry to say how very much obliged to you I am for your gift.

Yours my dear Forster, most sincerely

W. M. Thackeray.

[87] Forster tells this story in *The Life and Adventures of Oliver Goldsmith*, pp. 492–494.
[88] Quoted inexactly from *The Deserted Village*, ll. 93–94.
[89] In early August, 1842.
[90] In the famous painting at the National Gallery.

464.                TO MRS. CARMICHAEL-SMYTH
                            14 APRIL 1848

*Address:* M<sup>rs</sup> Carmichael Smyth | Rue de Ponthieu 2. | Champs Élysées | Paris.
*Postmarks:* 15 AVRIL 48 BOULOGNE, PARIS 15 AVRIL 48. Hitherto unpublished.

April 14.

Dearest Mother I know what you have been saying this many
⟨wee⟩ks how many weeks? past — You dont know how many days
pass ⟨whe⟩n I cant write: not but that I might with management &
by instalments, but the perpetual printer's devil takes so much out
of a man: and what have I to say? — but that I wish to God you
could make it convenient to come to England: and that I cant help
feeling that you are {unkind} — you see what I mean.

I didn't move in the Ashurst business <sup>91</sup> because I thought when
G P. bought the furniture &c — he as it were burned the ships &
would not leave France — I have written now again: offering on
my part to pay, and saying that the proposal came solely from me
and without Major Smyth's concurrence — but now that there are
⟨for⟩eign disturbances, who knows whether the people will be likely
⟨to⟩ come to such good terms? — Let us hope they will.

I have the pleasure of paying 70£ for a railroad next week and
100 in a year more — so much money flung down the sea owing to
the fatal folly of that abominable rail-road-mania year.

There didn't seem to me any hurry about the 94£ remaining of
Gms legacy to you. I have paid you 91£ of it and sent Aunt Becher
10£ the other day; the good old creature said she w<sup>d</sup> not use the
check but I have written to her be⟨see⟩ching her to do so.

When I hear from Ashurst, I will pay the sum of money for the
release of the outlawry: and invest say 50£ stock of the remainder
— the money is in your name & G P's — so you must draw your
dividends whenever it seems best to you. I have n⟨othing⟩ to do
with the house either, of w<sup>h</sup> you are the possessor of the mor⟨t⟩gage
— and was only executor of 94£ of w<sup>h</sup> I have paid 101.

<sup>91</sup> See above, No. 164.

My own expences are something very severe — and with debts keep me always paying & poor. I have paid away a very great deal this year: and everybody supposes that I am rich, & will cry out when I die poor. By jupiter, I dont know, personally ⟨how I⟩ could save for some time at least — until my dear old Nanny is b⟨ig⟩ enough to take the household rudder and keep things down — I can't do with less than 3 servants: the man is out on errands 1/2 the day running backwards & forwards to printing offices — indispensable. Poor M^rs Onslow is a dreadful bore — and the children dont like her  Alexander is another bore: but admirable in many points keeping the children to their work unceasingly always kind & ⟨goo⟩d-humoured with all their factiousness and bent on doing her duty — only she is no more a fit match for Anny's brains, than John is for mine — I think from a hint of M^rs Crowe's that Miss Kellar is disengaged: she seemed to me to have brains and her German and French were very good or ought to be — This one speaks French ⟨v⟩ery decently for an Englishwoman.

I am writing a little for the Chronicle [92] and getting good pay always thinking, plunging about, thinking as usual — And am clearly a roaring lion in the genteel world. The Duke of Devonshire [93] called on me the other day if you please, and I am going to

[92] I have not succeeded in identifying these articles, which are probably political leaders.

[93] William George Spencer Cavendish (1790–1858), sixth Duke of Devonshire, a great Whig magnate whose properties brought an annual income of £180,750 in 1883 (Bateman, *Great Landowners*, p. 130). He is described by the ninth Duke of Argyll (*Passages from the Past*, 2 vols., London, 1907, I, 76) as "the model of the old English noble of his time. Very tall, very benignant, full of poetic spirit, delighting in doing good, full of schemes for the improvement of the people on his immense property, and generous almost to a fault." Thackeray's acquaintance with the Duke, who was a patron of literature and an original member of the Roxburghe Club, had begun a few weeks earlier. He wrote to Lady Castlereagh on Friday, April 7 (in a fragment from a letter printed in Sotheby's catalogue of March 26–27, 1934): "I was very much disappointed at not being able to wait upon you and Milor on Wednesday night; but I received a very kind message from the D—ke of D—re, who begged Mrs. Norton to take me to his house; and she ordered me to be in waiting at 10 o'clock, and took me (she sitting bodkin in her own brougham, and indeed there are very few more beautiful bodkins in the world) — and I was obliged to wait until she left the party. But such is man, and amidst all the splendors

his house to night. I don't care a straw for the great people I find: only knowing them makes me a little more impatient of the airs of the ⟨sm⟩all great. I am in love with my old flames: but there's no danger with any of them. Poor M^rs Brookfield is ill on a sofa repeatedly: & I have no less than 3 others Eugénie, Virginia Pattle & Miss Perry [94] — a new one. Its a queer life: but my dearest little children comfort me inexpressibly and I always love my dearest old Mother    God bless you & G P.

Yours affte    W M T.

465.                TO RICHARD DOYLE
                    29 APRIL 1848

*Address:* R. Doyle Esq^re | 17 Cambridge Terrace. *Postmark:* AP 29 1848. Hitherto unpublished.

Sir

A man must be very idle who has time to copy such rubbish as the above.

My impression is that Lady Granville's [95] swarries commence *after* the 1 May. whizz: the 8^th & following days

---

of that assembly where there were flowers piled up as high as haystacks and ices both cream and water — such I say is man that I longed to be elsewhere or at least to be like a little bird at two places at once."

[94] See *Memoranda*, Mrs. Elliot and Kate Perry.

[95] Lady Marie Louise Granville (1812–1860), wife of the fifth Earl, well known as a Whig hostess.

But I shall be in the world to night and hear what is the real state of the case.

Ever your attached<br>Sydney Morgan.

466.     TO THE DUKE OF DEVONSHIRE
1 MAY 1848

My text is taken from S. Arthur Strong's "The Kindest-hearted of the Great," *Longman's Magazine*, XXXI (1898), 314–316.

Kensington: May 1, 1848.

My Lord Duke, — Mrs. Rawdon Crawley, whom I saw last week, and whom I informed of your Grace's desire to have her portrait, was good enough to permit me to copy a little drawing made of her "in happier days," she said with a sigh, by Smee, the Royal Academician.

Mrs. Crawley now lives in a small but very pretty little house in Belgravia, and is conspicuous for her numerous charities, which always get into the newspapers, and her unaffected piety. Many of the most exalted and spotless of her own sex visit her, and are of opinion that she is a *most injured woman*. There is no *sort of truth* in the stories regarding Mrs. Crawley and the late Lord Steyne. The licentious character of that nobleman alone gave rise to reports from which, alas! the most spotless life and reputation cannot always defend themselves. The present Sir Rawdon Crawley (who succeeded his late uncle, Sir Pitt, 1832; Sir Pitt died on the passing of the Reform Bill) does not see his mother, and his undutifulness is a cause of the deepest grief to that admirable lady. "If it were not for *higher things*," she says, how could she have borne up against the world's calumny, a wicked husband's cruelty and falseness, and the thanklessness (sharper than a serpent's tooth) of an adored child? [96] But she has been preserved, mercifully preserved, to bear

[96] *King Lear*, I, ii, 311–312. Lady Kicklebury's pleasant variation on these lines will be remembered: "Shakespeare was very right in stating how much sharper than a thankless tooth it is to have a serpent child" (*Works*, IX, 207).

all these griefs, and awaits her reward *elsewhere*. The italics are Mrs. Crawley's own.

She took the style and title of Lady Crawley for some time after Sir Pitt's death in 1832; but it turned out that Colonel Crawley, Governor of Coventry Island, had died of fever three months before his brother, whereupon Mrs. Rawdon was obliged to lay down the title which she had prematurely assumed.

The late Jos. Sedley, Esq., of the Bengal Civil Service, left her two lakhs of rupees, on the interest of which the widow lives in the practices of piety and benevolence before mentioned. She has lost what little good looks she once possessed, and wears false hair and teeth (the latter give her rather a ghastly look when she smiles), and — for a pious woman — is the best-crinolined lady in Knightsbridge district.

Colonel and Mrs. W. Dobbin live in Hampshire, near Sir R. Crawley; Lady Jane was godmother to their little girl, and the ladies are exceedingly attached to each other. The Colonel's *History of the Punjaub* is looked for with much anxiety in some circles.

Captain and Lt.-Colonel G. Sedley-Osborne (he wishes, he says, to be distinguished from some other branches of the Osborne family, and is descended by the mother's side from Sir Charles Sedley) is, I need not say, well, for I saw him in a most richly embroidered cambric pink shirt with diamond studs, bowing to your Grace at the last party at Devonshire House. He is in Parliament; but the property left him by his Grandfather has, I hear, been a good deal overrated.

He was very sweet upon Miss Crawley, Sir Pitt's daughter, who married her cousin, the present Baronet, and a good deal cut up when he was refused. He is not, however, a man to be permanently cast down by sentimental disappointments. His chief cause of annoyance at the present moment is that he is growing bald, but his whiskers are still without a gray hair and the finest in London.

I think these are the latest particulars relating to a number of persons about whom your Grace was good enough to express some interest. I am very glad to be enabled to give this information, and am —

Your Grace's very much obliged servant,

W. M. Thackeray.

P.S. — Lady O'Dowd is at O'Dowdstown arming. She has just sent in a letter of adhesion to the Lord-Lieutenant, which has been acknowledged by his Excellency's private secretary, Mr. Corry Connellan. Miss Glorvina O'Dowd is thinking of coming up to the Castle to marry the last-named gentleman.

P. S. 2. — The India mail just arrived announces the utter ruin of the Union Bank of Calcutta, in which all Mrs. Crawley's money was. Will Fate never cease to persecute that suffering saint?

467.     TO MR. AND MRS. HENRY COLE? [97]
2 MAY 1848

Hitherto unpublished.

13 Young S$^t$ Kensington
ye 2 May 1848

M$^r$ Thackeray regrets that a previous ingaygement for Saturday May 14 will prevent him from having ye Honour of dining with Lord and Lady Great Grimsby

Please have copied and engraved. W M T.

468.     TO JOHN LEYCESTER ADOLPHUS
11 MAY 1848

My text is taken from Maggs' catalogue number 652 (1937), where the last two pages of this letter are given in facsimile.

May 11

I feel very much annoyed and repentant this morning, when I think of that mad performance of last night, and the words that I

[97] The compiler of the *Lambert Catalogue* (II, 64) gives the Coles as the recipients of this note without revealing the source of his information.

used in reply to yours.[98] 'Outrageous' is a deuced hard epithet to apply to a gentleman's language, and I quite blush now when I think of it.

I was frightened out of all propriety by the compliments w^h you paid me: and am so unused to speaking that I lose myself entirely, plunge about wildly catching at words, and trying to keep above water. I suppose this nervousness would go off with practice; but in the meanwhile I beseech you to believe that I am not a reasonable being while under the panic of speaking and that I never would have used such a phrase, had I been in my senses —

I wonder whether what you said about Vanity Fair is correct — (regarding the drawings I know you are wrong, for they are tenth or twentieth rate performances having a meaning perhaps but a ludicrous badness of execution —) but about the writing? — The publishers are at this minute several hundred pounds out of pocket by me, that I know for certain — and I try to keep down any elation w^h my friends' praises may cause to me, by keeping this fact steadily before my eyes.

Excuse me for boring you with a long note: but I wish to ask pardon for what (as I see them with a slight headache this morning) appear to have been very absurd and ungrateful words.

Faithfully yours my dear Sir<br>W M Thackeray.

[98] At the annual dinner of the Royal Literary Fund on May 10 it fell to Adolphus (1795–1862), barrister and author of the well-known *Letters to Richard Heber* (1821) demonstrating (before the veil of anonymity was lifted) that Scott wrote the Waverley novels, to propose the toast of " 'THE NOVEL-ISTS OF GREAT BRITAIN,' connected with the name of one of the most distinguished of our day, MR. THACKERAY." He described Thackeray's work as "brilliant, and . . . provokingly graceful and adroit," concluding with a compliment to the "congenial labours of his pencil." Thackeray responded in part: "I have been called upon to make a speech in reply to what I must call, the most astounding and most undeserved laudation (cheers). Having a liking for caricature myself, . . . I must not complain of the sort of brilliancy of colour with which MR. ADOLPHUS has chosen to depict a portrait which I cannot recognize (cheers and laughter). Whereas it may be supposed; and yet — but really — to use a *novel* expression, I feel myself totally at a loss to answer the compliments he has paid me; and I am utterly at a stand still (renewed cheers and laughter)." (*Report of the Anniversary of the Royal Literary Fund*, London, 1848, pp. 27–29)

469.        TO MRS. CARMICHAEL-SMYTH
                15–16 MAY 1848

*Address:* M$^{rs}$ Carmichael Smyth | 2 Rue de Ponthieu. Champs Élysées. | Paris.
*Postmarks:* 16 MAY 1848, 17 MAI 48 BOULOGNE. Published in part,
*Biographical Introductions,* I, xxxv–xxxvi.

My dearest Mother I can't tell why Ashurst has not answered
in the Gas business [99] — his clerk wrote promising that M$^r$ Ashurst
w$^d$ write next week: next week passed & a day or two more and I
wrote again; but have had no reply to this letter: tomorrow I will
write again. In the meantime nobody on earth w$^d$ stir in the matter
if we did not move it: and G P might pay a visit to London of any
length without fear. Anny is always wishing for you. Alexander
has not brains enough to get a strong hold upon her heart and she
must have a good deal of solitude. Not that this is harmful for her
with her particular bent and strong critical faculty; she will learn
for herself more than most people can teach. Pray God she may
always continue to be, as she is now, generous and loving and just.

We three have had a long walk in the Park and by the Serpentine
after dinner to day: a beautiful day and sight. Yesterday I had a
letter from a lady who has just lost a little child and who ends her
letter 'if anything can console his father it will be this heavenly
weather'. — And yet the woman feels very acutely the loss of the
child.

Last Sunday we were at Eton and Windsor it was almost too
much pleasure though for one day — the weather furiously bright,
the landscape beautiful. We dined at an Eton boarding house for
boys — They had excellent fish meat puddings and beer and a glass
of wine. The hall in w$^h$ we dined was Gothic and hung round with
banners helmets and quaint devices. The little fellows have the
snuggest little studies and a most gentlemanlike look. I shall go
down again and get it up for a novel probably.[100] We were locked

---

[99] See above No. 164.
[100] Thackeray no doubt brought away from Eton the idea for *Dr. Birch and
his Young Friends,* his Christmas book for 1848, though when he came to write
that story, he drew upon Charterhouse rather than Eton for the details of his
setting.

into S$^t$ Georges Chapel at Windsor w$^h$ caused me to be too late for a dinner to w$^h$ I was engaged at the house of a certain old M$^r$ Bandinel where John Henry Forrest and his wife were staying. He is a real good fellow that John Henry, frank straight forward and well-mannered, worth 10 of Jim [101] who was at dinner too and whose brains have dwindled away to zero almost. It is a pity to see how his wife has changed in a year from being a pretty young woman to being a fatigued plain middle-aged person.

I am afraid my dear M$^{rs}$ Brookfield will die. She sinks and sinks and gets gradually worse. She lies on a sofa now and the Doctor says she must confine herself to a floor of the house. She will go to bed presently, and then — Amen. It will be better for her — She never says a word but I know the cause of a great part of her malady well enough — a husband whom she has loved with the most fanatical fondness and who — and who is my friend too — a good fellow upright generous kind to all the world except her.

I went to see poor dear old M$^{rs}$ Buller at Richmond the other day. She is gone quite into the state of old womanhood. Her false teeth looked ghastly in her mouth and her chestnut wig over her wrinkled old forehead. Dear old haggard eyes how beautiful they were, even in my time — and how kind & affectionate she has always been to me. O Thackeray she said what a hardship it is to live to be old — and then she added with a sigh I have one hope left and that is — *blue pill and cod-liver oil*. It was tremendous the satire. Old Buller was dying down stairs: the lamp of life just flickering out. He has been a good honest and kindly man — And M$^{rs}$ Buller told me with tears in her eyes what a comfort her sons had been to her. Charles with his worldly indifferent manner never forgets his duty — He has been largely assisting his father and mother for the last 2 years: when Arthur came home wanting money Charles gave him all his savings: he never brags about his goodness, but goes laughing through the world, indifferent, honest and to be depended on. I was glad to hear that good story about him.

There has come over a very nice letter from the childrens Uncle

[101] Sir James Carmichael.

Merrick: but as for M^rs Shawe I have told Jane that we are two. I can't mend that broken pot. It is done and over: and I cant ask my children to love or respect that woman.

The party [102] went off à merveille — We had saddle of mutton and fowls and the poor old plated goods out. The lions did not come: but the good-natured people did: and everything passed off very comfortably little Jingleby M^rs Dance's daughter singing charmingly and Virginia [103] looking divine. Anny & Minny & Alexander had fled the premises previously — What a mercy it is too to have got rid of my niece!

Next day at the Literary Fund I made as I am told an excellent funny speech. It is very curious I was in such a panic that I didn't know what I said & dont know now. And this I think is my Chronicle of Vanity Fair. I finish it D. V. next month how glad I shall be: for I dislike everybody in the book except Dob: & poor Amelia.

Monday. I am in the midst of my work and have only time to say God bless my dear old Mother & G P.

470.     TO MRS. CARMICHAEL-SMYTH
5 JUNE 1848

*Address:* M^rs Carmichael Smyth | Rue de Ponthieu. 2. | Champs Élysées. Paris.
*Postmarks:* 5 JU 1848, 9 JUIN 48 BOULOGNE. Hitherto unpublished.

Monday June 5.

My dearest Mammy We are wondering why we don't hear from you, and Minny that she had no letter on her birthday. Is our dear G P better? Robert [104] showed me a letter from David [105] w^h mentioned that he was ill. I was thinking of setting off to you: but — but the Printers devil was waiting down stairs for cop⟨y. He⟩ always is hanging about the premises. I never can see 3 days clear before

[102] On May 9. See above, No. 458.
[103] Virginia Pattle. For Thackeray's niece, see above, No. 458.
[104] Major Carmichael-Smyth's younger brother, Robert Stewart Carmichael-Smyth.
[105] Probably Robert's orphan nephew, David Freemantle Carmichael-Smyth (b. 1836).

me, or I should have been with my dearest old Mother before this — She has many a time thought it hard I am sure that I didn't come: but what laws has necessity? I have been no where only once or twice for a day into the country with the children & back at night — But all the country wont show a healthier girl than Anny, & Minny is wonderfully improved strengthened & fattened.

Ashurst answered last week about the Gas people they will take 5/in the £ on the 114£ that is to say 30£ will settle the whole affair, and I am expecting every day money w^h will enable me to pay that. I dont want to draw upon your fund: but try to hold that as untouchable: so that there may be 500£ for you, & the Albion S^t house at any rate. I have had very severe drains on me since last Michaelmas — railroad call — a horse — &c — and these keep me pretty poor — Sampayo my old creditor to whom I paid 50 in Feb has sent to me for his last 50 and thats what keeps the 30 unpaid — but it is as good as paid — £300 of debts of one sort or another have been paid out of my earnings of the last 6 months thank God — no wonder that my balance is low. But I am to have 100£ for the reprint of the Hoggarty Diamond, perhaps to day, (but I don't like to dun) and that will pay Gas & Sampayo — Now, I owe another 100 for being called to the Bar 5 friends volunteered to lend it to me think of that! — There's always something, isn't there? Well, I am to have 1000 a year for my next story and with Punch & what not can do very like 700 or 750 more it is a good income; but when shall I have fairly turned the corner? —

And now my dearest old Mother when will you come to us? This month I have a double number to do, and shall be awfully busy: and when the book is done I want a month of utter idleness somewhere     You come and command in Kensington whilst I take that. Poor Alexander must go: she is not clever enough for Anny — though a most excellent affectionate dutiful woman. My dear old girl. She is as wise as an old man. In 3 years she will be a charming companion to me: and fill up a part of a great vacuum w^h exists inside me — Little Tizzy [106] the little girl whom M^rs Buller adopted has just refused one of the cleverest and best young gentle-

[106] Theresa Reviss.  See *Memoranda*.

men I ever met in my life with a fortune of 5000£ a year — such a
match as there is hardly in England — One can't, I mean, account
for the tastes of young girls. And I tremble lest my dear Nanny
should take it into her head to fall in love with a dull fellow, as
some people ⟨I⟩ know have done. The dear old Buller was snuffed
out very calmly: [107] after a very noble upright generous life. I went
to see the widow who has always been very fond of me — and wrote
her a letter w^h she said consoled her more than any she had. She
bears up very well, but is most heartily a widow and loves and
cherishes her husbands memory. She is going to live with Charles.
Arthur and his pretty nice amiable milksop Amelia sort of wife go
to India next month. We are going to Elkington's to buy plate and
vanities to day    He brought her and their 2 pretty children on
Saturday night to Kensington and we 3 went to Jenny Lind in the
Lucia: [108] I think we all fell asleep during the ballet: in w^h I dont
see the least charm any more. One or 2 people have found out how
careless the last no [109] of V.F is, but the cue is to admire it and consider the author a prodigy. O you donkies!

I have just seen Evans he can not give me an answer about the
H. D [110] for 2 or 3 days but will tell me — indeed you may consider
the matter as done and come as soon as you like to us all. May God
bless my dearest old Mother & G P. I must go away and look to
the beautiful spoons and forks and pomps and vanities of this wicked
world. But God — I mean that I have many serious thoughts and
will try & not be vain of praise, and humbly to say & remember the
truth.

[107] "DEATHS . . . May 17 — At Richmond, aged 73, Charles Buller,
esq." (*Annual Register*, 1848).
[108] Donizetti's *Lucia da Lammermoor* was given at Her Majesty's Theatre
on Saturday, June 3, with Jenny Lind as Lucia (*Times*).
[109] XVIII, chapters 61–63.
[110] Bradbury and Evans did not republish *The Great Hoggarty Diamond*
until 1849. Thackeray's preface to this edition is dated January 25.

471.                      TO MISS SMITH [111]
                            6 JUNE 1848

My text is taken from a facsimile in the Grolier Club's *Catalogue of an Exhibition Commemorating the Hundredth Anniversary of the Birth of William Makepeace Thackeray*, New York, 1912, p. 71.

                              13 Young S.t Kensington.
                              June 6. 1848.

Ah, dear Miss Smith! I shall be outatown on Sunday the 18.th: and I never dine out on that day because it is the Hannawussary of the death of my dear friend Captain George Osborne of the —th regiment.[112]

                              Yours always
                              W M T.


[For a letter to Mrs. Elliot and Kate Perry, 30 June, 1848, see letter 2, Appendix XXVI.]


472.                      TO MRS. PROCTER
                            JUNE 1848

Hitherto unpublished. My text is taken from a transcript given Lady Ritchie by George Murray Smith.

Yes, dear Madam, I shall come with sincere pleasure, and ah! can I be angry that Mr Lumley should choose *you* for Secretary? (Tres joli) Why did I not come on Friday is a question which I would rather not answer, the chief Baron [113] kept me talking till near 12 o'clock when I thought it would be too late: and so as it was pouring with rain I went to Mrs Brunel's.[114] Ask the Miss

---

[111] One of the daughters of Horace Smith — Eliza, Rosalind, and Laura —, which, it is impossible to say, for Thackeray knew all three well. See Lady Ritchie's *Blackstick Papers*, pp. 114–129.

[112] See chapter 32 of *Vanity Fair*.

[113] Sir Frederick Pollock, Lord Chief Baron of the Exchequer.

[114] The wife (m. 1836) of Isambard Kingdom Brunel (1806–1859), the civil engineer.

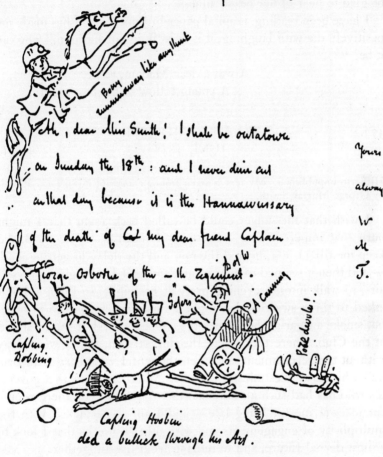

13 Young St. Kensington.
June 6. 1848.

Oh, dear Miss Smith! I shall be out a town
on Sunday the 18th: and I never dine out
on that day because it is the Hanniwersary
of the death of Cot my dear friend Captain
George Osborne of the —th Regiment.

Capting Dobbing

Capting Hooben
ded a bullick through his Art.

Yours
always
W
M
T.

THACKERAY'S LETTER OF 6 JUNE, 1848

Huttons if I didn't. There was a little governess there who did for me completely. She is prettier than Virginia [115] she has a sweeter nose than Miss Hutton — I mean the [*Sketch*] one not the [*Sketch*] one, — she is lovelier than Amelia herself: and I am sure you will be glad to hear of her beautifulness.

I have been reading a capital paper in Punch which has made me positively die with laughing, it is by a "Lady of Fashion," who can it be? [116]

Always, dear Madam, respectfully yours,
A young fellow of the best society.

473.        TO MRS. PROCTER
JUNE 1848

Hitherto unpublished. My text is taken from a transcript given Lady Ritchie by George Murray Smith.

I wish that messenger could be called back again that I might burn that imperent note — but what I mean is — The C. B. did keep me till 11 3/4, he and the rain and the delay in getting a cab — and then it seemed to me too late, and as if I were giving myself airs, to walk into an evening party at midnight: so though I was asked to three swarries that night I thought I would go to none, but smoke a cigar at the Club and so to bed. Well, it was so stupid at the Club, where there were the dullest men, that I went away without the refreshment, and then thought I would try Mrs Brunels which is at Westminster close by. And there I saw that governess who has had such an effect on this Art: and even there people cut jokes at me for being late — and I am so perplexed with the multiplicity of engagements and with other concerns that I look to a most dismal future, and to retiring from life altogether.

[115] Virginia Pattle.
[116] Thackeray's "Yesterday; a Tale of the Polish Ball. By a Lady of Fashion," was published in *Punch* on June 10, 1848.

THACKERAY IN 1848

From a sketch by Count D'Orsay

474.          TO MRS. PROCTER
             JUNE? 1848 [117]

Hitherto unpublished. My text is taken from a transcript given Lady Ritchie
by George Murray Smith.

                     This evening.
                 After they are gone to bed.

My dear Mrs Procter,

I wish (for various reasons) to let you know what happened when
I came home three quarters of an hour ago.

"Papa, (says Anny) they've been to fetch that sketch Count Dorsay made of you. I think it's uglier than you are."

Minny says: "I don't think you're ugly at all.

Now wasn't it hard to come away from Harley Street to this sort
of tea?

                Your obedient servant,

475.              TO ?
            JUNE 1848? [118]

Hitherto unpublished.

Madam

Because I had just come home from Brighton and thought I
ought to stay at home with my family I had to incur the following
conversation [*here a hand points to the opposite page; see page 388*]

Now wouldn't it have been much nicer to have gone to Richmond
with Dicky Doyle?

               Respectfully yours.

[117] Count D'Orsay's sketch of Thackeray is dated June 16, 1848. It is reproduced above, facing page 386.

[118] It is not unlikely that this note was written at about the same time as the
one to Mrs. Procter preceding it. The joke in each case is the same, though
Thackeray has varied the details somewhat.

Little Darling. Papa. Tommy has just made a drawing of you.
But I think its uglier than you are.

Tommy.  O no it's not.

476.                  TO HENRY VIZETELLY
                        JUNE? 1848 [119]

My text is taken from Vizetelly's *Glances back through Seventy Years*, I, 286.

Young Street, Thursday.

Dear H. V. — I have discovered Cham [120] in Salisbury Square —
in what I fancy was Pamela-Richardson's old house,[121] and he is to
breakfast in Young Street on Sunday. Please be of the party, as
there are only you and your brother whom de Noé knows over here
that I can ask to meet him. The hour, eleven, will admit of the
devout attending early matins. I have asked Higgins, T. T.,[122]
Dickey D., and Leech, but neither Mark nor Jerrold. Young
Douglas, if asked, would most likely not come, but if he did, he'd
take especial care that his own effulgence should obscure all lesser
lights, Cham's included. —

                                      Yours,
                                      W. M. Thackeray.


477.                  TO MRS. BROOKFIELD
                        JUNE 1848

Hitherto unpublished.

Dear Mʳˢ Brookfield

Count Dorsay came to dinner on Friday, splendid in a large blue
coat and an immense flower in his button gracious and good natured

[119] See the next letter.
[120] Amédée de Noé (1819–1879), the caricaturist. He was called "Cham"
(Ham) because he was the second son of the Comte de Noé (Noah). Vizetelly
describes this breakfast, which lasted until four in the afternoon, in *Glances back
through Seventy Years*, I, 286–288.
[121] Samuel Richardson wrote *Pamela* (1740–1741) at 11 Salisbury Court,
which by Thackeray's time had come to be known as Salisbury Square (Wheat-
ley [and Cunningham], *London*, III, 202).
[122] Tom Taylor, Dickey Doyle (after whose name Thackeray sketched a
small bird), and Mark Lemon.

beyond measure. Jacob Omnium Morris of the Times,[123] and K Macaulay [124] with my little French friend [125] formed the party — The little Frenchman remarked how the 2 latter were incessantly watching the great Dorsay during dinner. He drank wine with both of them, and pronounced Morris to be one of the handsomest men he had ever seen. So he is, beautiful, with an expression of melancholy tenderness in his large brown eyes, and a tone of voice that's quite heart-breaking — A little German governess said about him the other day — Il n'est pas permis d'avoir d'aussi beaux yeux que ca. *es ist polizey-verboten* — Dorsay charmed the young fellow with kindness.

He speaks the queerest English in the world and the most singular French. He doesn't speak French any more that is but a splendid jargon. He pleases I think by his unbounded good humour and generous sympathy with everybody. It was a comfort to see him eat roast-beef such a quantity of it! He likes it just as well as the best of great dinners. He says it is the best and what is better.

He read us a letter from a spirituel friend at Paris describing the scene — very brilliant lively and sparkling and false. By some strange coincidence the Times correspondent of yesterday had a passage in his contribution word for word the same as that w$^h$ Dorsay read us. So these great folks are in relation with the Times are they? Lady Blessington read me a letter from the same place, from Madame Guiccioli now Madame de Boissy [126] — the compliments w$^d$ have staggered any weak person. They were stunning tremendous — Do women write often to each other in this way? I wonder.

[123] Mowbray Morris (1819–1874), manager of *The Times* from 1847 to 1873. George Richmond's portrait of Morris is reproduced in *The History of the Times, 1841–1884* (London, 1939), opposite p. 64.

[124] Kenneth Macaulay (1815–1867), a prominent London barrister, later a Q. C. (1850) and M. P. for Cambridge (1857–1865).

[125] Amédée de Noé.

[126] The former Teresa Gamba (c. 1800–1873), daughter of Count Ruggiero Gamba of Rome, who had been Byron's mistress between 1819 and 1823, when she was married to the sexagenarian Count Guiccioli. She had recently remarried, her second choice being Hilaire Rouillé, Marquis de Boissy. In his *Literary Life and Correspondence of the Countess of Blessington*, 2 vols. (New York, 1855), II, 34–36, Richard Robert Madden prints what appears to be

478.          TO MRS. BROOKFIELD
              JUNE 1848 [127]

Published in *Collection of Letters*, p. 136.

My dear —

Will you I mean Mꝛ Brookfield like to come to Mꝛˢ Sartoris's swoary to night there will be very pretty music. And yesterday when I met her I said I wanted her very much to go and sing to a sick lady of my acquaintance & she said she would with the greatest pleasure in the world and I think it would be right if Mꝛ Brookfield should call upon her, and I am disengaged on Wednesday next either for evening or dinner and Mꝛˢ Sartoris's number is 99 Eaton Place and I am your very obdt Servt

                                   W M Thackeray.

479.          TO MRS. BROOKFIELD
              22? JUNE 1848

Hitherto unpublished.

Dear Madam

On examining Mꝛˢ Sartoris this evening, I am happy to tell you that lady was by no means impressed with the notion wʰ you have yourself regarding your own mental condition. She describes your behaviour as sane, your conversation as agreeable, and makes no

---

the letter that Thackeray describes. It is dated June 20, 1848, and begins: "Votre lettre et les nouvelles que m'ont apporté de vous mes amies les Sampieri, m'ont fait un bien grand plaisir. Vous les avez comblés de ces politesses dont personne ne connait autant que vous le secret enchanteur, car personne ne possède plus que vous tant ce qui en fait le charme, le cœur, la grace, l'esprit. Enfin ils emportent avec eux votre souvenir, et le souvenir de *tout ce* et *de tous ceux* qui vous entourent, comme la réalization de ce qu'ils ne croyaient peut-être qu'un idéal." The letter to Count D'Orsay mentioned above is evidently that from the Marquis de Boissy to M. Bastide, Minister of Foreign Affairs, published in *L'Assemblée nationale* of June 20, a copy of which was sent to Lady Blessington along with the Marquise de Boissy's letter. It also is printed by Madden (II, 36–38).

[127] See the next letter.

allusion whatever to the little circumstance w.<sup>h</sup> has caused you disquiet.[128] Ah Madam! I promise you *I* would never tell if — if I could sing like M.<sup>rs</sup> Sartoris.

This is written between the dinner and the Concert — I thought I would take the earliest opportunity to let you know that you are not considered as a person that whose intellect is in the least degree disordered, and that I am

Your most obedient Servt.

Horatio Hyle Chapman.

480.           TO MRS. CARMICHAEL-SMYTH
29 JUNE 1848

*Address:* M.<sup>rs</sup> Carmichael Smyth | Rue Ponthieu 2 | Champs Élysées | Paris. *Postmarks:* 29 JU 1848, 30 JUIN 48 BOULOGNE. Published in part, *Biographical Introductions*, I, xxxvi–xxxvii.

28 June.[129]

My dearest old Mammy. Vanity Fair is this instant done [130] and I have been worked so hard that I can hardly hold a pen and say God bless my dearest old Mother. I had not time even to listen to

---

[128] Mrs. Brookfield wrote to her husband on June 22: "Mrs. Sartoris did come yesterday and after a few preliminaries proposed to sing to me; took off her bonnet and poured forth in German, Italian, and English. I felt it was so very good-natured of her, as she came alone and there was only my stupid lout of a self to hear her, language seemed inadequate to express due gratitude and in my really genuine admiration for all artists, it seemed to me the right thing to kiss her hand. She took it with a smile as if she had *expected* it, squeezed my hand, hoped I would let her come again, left Mr. Sartoris's card for you and disappeared, leaving me in a cold sweat (to be coarse) as to whether the kiss of the hand might not have been *un peu trop fort.*" (*Mrs. Brookfield*, II, 268–269)

[129] A mistake for June 29, when *The Rivals* was given at Drury Lane. There was no performance of Sheridan's comedy the previous evening.

[130] Of "Before the Curtain," presumably the last part of *Vanity Fair* in the order of composition, Eyre Crowe (*Thackeray's Haunts and Homes*, pp. 55–56) tells the following story: "It occurred in June, 1848, one day when Thackeray came at lunch-time to my father's Hampstead house. Torrens McCullagh, happening to be one of the party, said across the table to Thackeray, 'Well, I see you are going to shut up your puppets in their box!' His immediate reply was, 'Yes; and, with your permission, I'll work up that simile.'"

the awful cannonading in your town: [131] Thank God you are going to leave it. Here are the children come in a fly to fetch me, we are going to have a little holiday and see the Rivals to night. The bore is that the Governess must come too, and instead of being with them, I must endure her. I am very much pleased to have done — very melancholy and beat, and humble in mind I hope praying to — not to feel elation &c for I get so much praise that I want keeping down — And I want to send one line just to kiss my dearest old Mother. and G P.

481.                      TO MRS. PROCTER
                          29 JUNE 1848

Hitherto unpublished. My text is taken from a transcript given Lady Ritchie by George Murray Smith.

My dear Mrs Procter,

Engaged on Sunday: have been for past ten days, in such a state of work and excitement as have put me in a fever. Don't you see I am so nervous I can hardly write. Just come away from printing office, and waiting for little girls to go a pleasuring somewhere, then to see the Rivals this evening — if that Governess would but have taken the broad hint I gave her and have gone home for the night but not she: and instead of having the children's company in private box, must sit back and see this stupid young lady.

Is Procter here? There is a bachelor dinner knocked up yesterday at my house tomorrow at 7 1/2. Roast beef etc. R. S. V. P. Here's the slip of the dedication just put in my hands, you see it is very simple.[132] I should have liked to put down you too but suppose mustn't say of a lady that I am affectionately yours,

                                        W. M. T.

[131] The Parisian insurrection of June 23 to 26, which was accompanied by bloody street fighting.
[132] "To B. W. Procter this story is affectionately dedicated" (*Works*, I, xli).

482.                 TO MRS. PROCTER
                     30 JUNE 1848

Hitherto unpublished. My text is taken from a transcript given Lady Ritchie
by George Murray Smith.

Mon dieu. Mon dieu, I quite forgot. But I have been like a
raving maniac all the week — finishing

                     [*Sketch*]

V. F. I got done in one way or another last night, and took the
children to the play.

We are going to Mrs Macready's to-night, are you? Pray forgive
me and believe me,

            Yours, in spite of all my irregularities,
                     W. M. T.

483.                 TO MRS. BROOKFIELD
                     30 JUNE 1848

*Address:* Mrs Brookfield | 15 Portman St. Published in *Collection of Letters*,
p. 23.

My dear Mrs Brookfield

Now that it is over and irremediable I am thinking with a sort of
horror of a bad joke in the last number of V.F. wh may perhaps
annoy somebody whom I wouldn't wish to displease. Amelia is
represented as having a lady's maid and the lady's maid's name is
Payne [133] — I laughed when I wrote it and thought it was good
fun: but now who knows whether you & Payne & everybody won't
be angry, and in fine I am in a great tremor.

The only way will be for you, I fear, to change Payne's name to
her Christian one. Pray dont be angry if you are: and forgive me
if I've offended — You know you are only a piece of Amelia — My
Mother is another half: my poor little wife *y est pour beaucoup* and
I am yours most sincerely

                     W M Thackeray.

I hope you will write to say that you forgive me.

[133] In chapter 67 (*Works*, I, 663).

484.        FROM MRS. BROOKFIELD
              1 JULY 1848

Hitherto unpublished.

My dear M.<sup>r</sup> Thackeray,

I was much amused by your little note, tho' I was relieved to find, when I read the V. F. that Payne was no portrait & only having the name in common, may I think fairly pass as a mere coincidence sh.<sup>d</sup> it ever transpire that the two maids have that communion together — I am very glad you have made such a brilliant wind up, it was altogether delightful except Amelia herself who provokes one to a degree which makes one rejoice with real malice at her child's being preferred to her at last, — wh: I sincerely hope was *really* the case, & not a mere fancy of her own — another thing I quite disapproved of in Amelia was her greeting to Dobbin at Ostend — *having written*, I think was quite enough for her to do — she ought to have been far too much ashamed of her previous brutality even to go out to meet him — & he sh.<sup>d</sup> have found her in an agony of remorse on her knees in her own room — with George only sent to meet him. Will you forgive these remarks from wh: I could not refrain & please to thank Annie with my love for her kind present of the most splendid Brobdignag Strawberries wh: I was going to write to thank her for, but thought I w.<sup>d</sup> merge it in this to you, as writing is rather uphill work lying down — Miss Procter was here yesterday, they seem much pleased with the dedication I hope it will quite blot out all remembrance of the Evening Party lack of invitation.

                       Believe me,
                         Ever yours sincerely
                         Jane O. Brookfield

15 Portman St   Sat.<sup>y</sup>

485.                    TO WILLIAM JOYCE
                          JULY 1848? [134]

Hitherto unpublished.

                                        Kensington. Thursday.

My dear M[r] Joyce

Did anybody tell you that we are going to give M[r] Bradbury a
dinner at Greenwich on Saturday. Trafalgar. 5.30 and that we hope
very much for the pleasure of your company — I mean the P P &
especially

                              Yours ever
                              W M Thackeray


486.                    TO MRS. BROOKFIELD
                          10 JULY 1848

Published in *Collection of Letters*, pp. 126–127.

My dear Madam

On calling on our mutual friend M[rs] Procter yesterday she was
polite enough to offer me a seat in her box at Drury Lane Theatre
this evening, when *Her Majesty* honors the play-house with a visit
for the benefit of M[r] Macready.[135] Shakspeare is always amusing
and I am told the aspect of the Beefeaters at the Royal box is very
*imposing*.

I mentioned to M[rs] Procter that I had myself witnessed many
entertainments of this nature and did not very much desire to be
present: but intimated to her that I had a friend who I believed
was most anxious to witness M[r] Macready's performance in the
*august presence* of the Sovereign.

[134] William Joyce was an engraver on wood of 11 Bolt Court, Fleet Street
(*Post Office London Directory*, 1847). According to a note on the original,
the dinner to which he is invited was given by Thackeray and the "Punch
People" to celebrate the completion of *Vanity Fair*.
[135] Macready's farewell performance before leaving for America was given at
Drury Lane on July 10, 1848. He appeared in *Henry VIII*, and his audience
included Queen Victoria and Prince Albert.

I mentioned the name of your husband, and found that *she had already* with her usual politeness dispatched a card to that gentleman. Whom I shall therefore have the happiness of meeting this evening.

But, perhaps you are aware, that *a chosen few* are admitted *behind the scenes* of the Theatre, where when the Curtain rises, they appear *behind the performers,* and with loyal hearts join in the National Anthem at the very feet of their Queen. My reverend friend has an elegant voice — perhaps he would like to lift it up in a chorus, w.ʰ though performed in the *Temple of Thespis,* I cannot but consider to be in the nature of a *hymn.* I send therefore a ticket of w.ʰ I beg his polite acceptance, and am dear Madam

With the utmost respect

Your very faithful Servt  W M Thackeray.

I was a little late for the magnificent entertainment of my *titled friends* Sir William & Lady Molesworth on Saturday, and indeed the first course had been removed when I made my appearance.

The banquet was sumptuous in the extreme, & the company of the most select order — I had the happiness of sitting next to Clarence Bulbul Esq.ᵉ [136] M. P. and opposite was the Most Noble the Marquess of Steyne — Fancy my happiness in the company of persons so *distinguished*.

A delightful concert followed the dinner and the whole concluded with a Sumptuous supper: nor did the party separate until a late hour.

487.                    TO MRS. PROCTER
JULY 1848

Hitherto unpublished. My text is taken from a transcript given Lady Ritchie by George Murray Smith.

1848.

Remember Tuesday 18th, 7 1/2. It is fate. I have asked no end of people. It is really my birthday. Who will come? You and two

---

[136] See *Works*, IX, 57–58.

young ladies or you two and one, let me know on account of the festive preparations.

If Miss Adelaide goes to dine with Mrs Brookfield tomorrow, perhaps she will tell her how much pleased I am I asked to dine there on Friday. She said Mr Brookfield dines out. By Jupiter it's too much. I met Mrs Princess in the Park whose husband dines out too: but she will take me in. I am done — off — hurray — good bye.

488.          TO FREDERICK J. GOLDSMITH
                         JULY 1848

My text is taken from Goldsmith, *Athenæum*, 1891, p. 474.

Captain Swankey
Mr. Thackeray, 13, Young Street, Kensington Square
A drum. Tuesday, July 18.

489.          TO MR. AND MRS. SARTORIS
                         JULY 1848

Facsimile in *Thackeray in the United States*, I, 363.

M⁣ʳ Thackeray requests the pleasure of Mʳ & Mʳˢ Sartoris's company to a little drum on Tuesday July 18.

490.                TO EDWARD CHAPMAN
                      18 JULY 1848

Hitherto unpublished.

                                    Kensington July 18. 1848.

Dear Chapman

I think of making my move at the beginning of next week and passing some time at Spa or Aix la Chapelle but as usual want some money before I go.

If you could give me 50£ in advance now of the Kickleburys abroad [137] you would very much oblige me. I want it now to pay a debt not of mine, and for w^h I have the funds at the bankers — but these funds cannot be touched until certain formalities are complied with w^h require a few weeks time — and I should like if possible to settle the business to day, of all days in the year.*

                              Very faithfully yours
                              W M Thackeray.

* The fact is it is a claim against my old step-father the only one ags^t the old gentleman: and this is my birthday and I sh^d like to clear it off and be able to write to my mother to that effect: but this is private.

491.             WILLIAM HENRY ASHURST
                      18 JULY 1848

My text is taken from Lewis Melville's *The Thackeray Country* (London, 1911), pp. 118–119.

                              13 Young Street, Kensington,
                              July 18, 1848.

My dear Sir, —

Times have been bad with me, and I have not been able until now to spare the sum necessary for the Gas Company and Major Smyth. I have now £30 at your orders, for which I send a cheque.

[137] See below, No. 517.

Will you kindly acknowledge it, and send me the receipt of the Gas Company.

Very faithfully yours,

Dear Sir,

W. M. Thackeray.

492.        TO MRS. CARMICHAEL-SMYTH
                    18 JULY 1848

*Address:* M^rs Carmichael Smyth | 2 Rue Ponthieu. Champs Élysées | Paris.
*Postmarks:* 20 JY 1848, 21 JUIL 48 BOULOGNE. Hitherto unpublished.

My dearest Mammy I send you a line as by duty bound yours having just come in — I am in the midst of a tea and dinner party — apropos of the finale of V.F. — the volume comes out to day. It has sold 1000 already: and I was coaxed or worried into a small festival. Lady Pollock is to be my mistress of the house, and the silver dishes are out once again with tea for no less than 50 persons — no Lords: and yet few of my old acquaintances — The children are at Richmond where Anny has already taken Captain Alexanders measurement, and I saw them 2 days ago. There's a letter from her for you containing nothing, and also one from Madame de Baurel [138] w^h she begs me to forward. I'm not pleased with this lady. If she wanted she might have come here: but she works at me rather than to me, and indeed I can do nothing for her.

Yesterday I was at the Procters' and signed the will — there is another informality and delay — the will has been witnessed incorrectly it will be necessary for one of the witnesses to make a declaration in the presence of the English Consul and I was about to write a letter to M^r Harrison [139] of Cambridge Square to ask for Bess's address. I will now write however to the Procters to send the will over, to Miss Hamerton at Paris, and the negotiation will D V. be complete.

[138] A *protégée* of Mrs. Carmichael-Smyth.
[139] Charles Harrison, 7 Cambridge Square and 19 Bedford Row (*Post Office London Directory*, 1847).

As for the bygone question [140] Amen. I am as innocent as a baby. Anny dislikes her and complains of her. She was no more — never mind, let the stick drop where it fell. I am not going to pick it up.

I have sent off the needful to Ashurst to day — 30£: w^h I must take out of the balance left by GM of 94: when that is available — and that little job being done now: my dear old GP is no longer a Robin Hood. God bless him, and my dearest old Mother.

I shall try and go for a fortnight to Spa when I can arrange matters so as to get myself free. And if I like it perhaps I'll stop for six weeks there: and compose that book [141] w^h is coming out. May God Almighty keep me honest and keep pride and vanity down. In spite of himself a man gets worldly and ambitious in this great place: with every body courting & flattering. I am frightened at it and my own infernal pride and arrogance*— There's the poney come I'll go & take a ride and think about my mother and my dear little women: God bless them all.

* What I mean is that all of a sudden I am a great man. I am ashamed of it: but yet I cant help seeing it — being elated by it trying to keep it down — &c.

### 493.     TO WILLIAM CHARLES MACREADY
#### 21 JULY 1848

Published by Dr. Rosenbach, *Catalogue of the Books and Manuscripts of Harry Elkins Widener* (Philadelphia, 1918), II, 250. *Endorsed:* Thackeray with "Vanity Fair" July 22, 48.

July 21.

My dear Macready

On Monday I am really engaged. I was going to send my slave this morning with the accompanying volume w^h I hope may serve to amuse an hour or two whilst you are crossing the ingens aequor.[142]

Always yours dear Macready

W M Thackeray.

[140] See above, No. 386.
[141] *Pendennis.*
[142] Horace, *Odes*, I, vii, 32.

494.                TO MRS. PROCTER
                    25 JULY 1848

Hitherto unpublished. My text is taken from a transcript given Lady Ritchie
by George Murray Smith.

                                        Fountain Hotel,
                                        Canterbury.
                                        July 25, 1848.

My dear Mrs Procter,

I don't know whether I am sorry that I shall not be able to eat
your Haunch of Venison tomorrow (in the first place Brookfield
said the neck was rather too highly preserved two days ago — is it
two days or more?) I am not sorry or glad: I don't care about anything: about going away, or staying, or anybody: — not even about
— never mind what. But that pipe is smoked out and broken. Well,
I came here yesterday on a sudden letter from my brother-in-law
which reached me as I was lying in bed conning the map and seeing
whither [143] I should go for my holiday. Our regiment marches
from Canterbury to Edinburgh say. In on Wednesday, come and
go with us, see the leave taking here, the march through London to
the railroad, the halt at Derby Inn. I thought it sounded like very
good fun: and so it would be if I had the courage to go through
with it. But I'm too old. I went to his room at barracks last night
and enjoyed the conversation of several lieutenants and captains.
They told old Joe Miller of an immoral tendency and I find I can't
bear it. I will pursue my old wheel and cross to Ostend tomorrow,
to Spa, and so forth.

And yet it's a pity. My brother-in-law (who is interupting this
with appropriate remarks,) has just told me a story about his servant Sweeny, and a white and blue livery he has bought of a Jew for
this carroty-headed Irish rapparee which is wonderful to listen to:
so were some of the stories descriptive of military manner last night.
The life of the young men of the old fellows who associate with the
young men and vie with them in the narration of Millerian tales of

[143] The transcript reads *whether*.

barracks, regimental fights and drunkenness are curious to hear: and I would go on but for a sense of shame. I'm too old to hear these poor fellows' tipsy jokes. London seems a thousand miles off already and yesterday ever so many years ago. I did not call to take leave, not liking such adieux. When I come back I shall hope to take my dear little women to some place by the sea side. I saw them on Sunday, and we had a merry day at Richmond and Hampton Court and Forster was uncommonly kind pleasant and genuinely good natured. By the way, that puts me in mind, did you see the Spectator? [144] If we put on our cocked-hats on account of the Examiner article,[145] that of the Spectator caused us to remove a part of our dress and submit to a whipping. I don't care for the praise or for the blame or for anything. Yes I do. I care for kind friends who are always good and cordial to me. Will you write to me at Spa? Good bye.

W. M. T.

495.                TO MRS. BROOKFIELD
                      26–28 JULY 1848

Published in part, *Collection of Letters*, pp. 9–15. The passage between daggers was overscored by Mrs. Brookfield.

Brussells Friday.

I have just had a dreadful omen. Somebody gave me a paper knife with a mother of pearl blade and a beautiful silver-handle — Anny recognized it in a minute lying upon my dressing table with a 'Here's M^rs Soandso's butter-knife' I suppose she cant have seen

---

[144] In *The Spectator* of July 22 (pp. 709–710) there appeared a severe review of *Vanity Fair* by Robert Stephen Rintoul (1787–1858), the magazine's editor from 1828 until his death. Like most contemporary critics he protests against Thackeray's preoccupation with the seamy side of life. He goes on to argue that since this preoccupation implies "a want of imagination and large comprehension of life," *Vanity Fair* cannot be regarded as "a fiction of high art."

[145] Forster's review of *Vanity Fair* was published in *The Examiner* of July 22 (pp. 468–470). See below, No. 503.

it above twice, but that child remembers everything — Well this morning, being fairly on my travels, & having the butter-knife in my desk I thought I would begin to cut open a book I had bought — The moment I tried — never having as yet had occasion to use it the blade broke away from the beautiful handle.

What does this portend? It is now There is a blade and there is a hilt:

but they refuse to act together. Something is going to happen I am sure.

† I took leave of my family on Sunday after a day in the rain at Hampton Court — & my daughters didn't seem much to care, though they have already discovered the emptiness of Captain Alexander and gave me to understand that they are tired of living with him.† Forster was dining with Mr Chapman the publisher where we passed the day. His Article in the Examiner did not please me so much as his genuine good nature in insisting upon walking with Anny at night and holding an umbrella over her through the pouring rain. Did you read the Spectator's sarcastic notice of V.F. I dont think it is just but I think Rintoul is a very honest man, and rather inclined to deal severely with his private friends, lest he shd fall in to the other extreme — to be sure he keeps out of it (I mean the other extreme) very well.

I passed Monday night & part of Tuesday in the artless society of some officers of the 21st or Royal Scots Fusiliers in Garrison at Canterbury. We went to a barrack room where we drank about — out of a silver cup & a glass — I heard such stale old foul garrison stories. I recognized among the stories many old friends of my youth, very pleasant to meet when one was eighteen, but of whom one is rather shy now — Not so these officers however they tell each other the stalest and wickedest old Jo Millers: the jolly grey headed old Majors have no reverence for the beardless ensigns nor vice versâ. I heard of the Father & son in the other regiment in garrison at Canterbury, the Slashers if you please being carried up drunk to bed the night before. Fancy what a life — Some of ours I dont mean yours Maam but I mean mine & others are not much better though more civilized.

We went to see the Wizard Jacobs at the theatre. He came up in the midst of the entertainment and spoke across the box to the young officers. He knows them in private life. They think him a good fellow. He came up & asked them confidentially if they didn't like a trick he had just performed. 'Neat little thing isnt it the great Jacobs said — brought it over from Paris.' They go to his entertainment every night. Fancy what a career of pleasure.

A wholesome young Squire with a large brown face and a short waistcoat came up to us and said Sorry youre goin Ive sent up to  barricks a great lot o' rabbuts — they were of no use those rabbuts, the 21st was to march the next day. I saw the men walking about on the last day taking leave of their sweethearts (who will probably be consoled by the Slashers) I was carried off by my brother in law through the rain to see a great sight — the regimental soup tureens and dish covers before they were put away. 'Feel THAT' says he, 'William just feel the weight of that' I was called upon twice to try the weight of that soup dish and expressed the very highest gratification at being admitted to that privilege. Poor simple young fellows and old youngsters! I felt ashamed of myself for spying out their follies: and fled from them and came off to Dover.

It was pouring with rain all day, and I had no opportunity of putting anything into the beautiful new Sketch-books. I passed an hour in the Cathedral wʰ seemed all beautiful to me — the fifteenth century part, the thirteenth century part and the crypt above all: wʰ they say is older than the Conquest. The most charming harmonious powerful combination of shafts and arches — beautiful wʰ ever way you saw them developed like a fine music or the figures in a kaleidoscope rolling out mysteriously. A beautiful foundation for a beautiful building I thought how some peoples towering intellects and splendid cultivated geniuses rise up on simple beautiful foundations hidden out of sight — or how this might be a good simile if I knew of any very good and wise man just now. But I don't know of many do you?

Part of the crypt was given up to French Calvinists, and texts from the French Bible of some later sect are still painted on the pillars surrounded with French ornaments: looking very queer and out of place. So for the matter of that do we look queer and out of place in that grand soaring artificial building. We may put a shovel-hat on the pinnacle of the steeple, as Omar did a crescent on the peak of the Church at Jerusalem — but it doesn't belong to us — I mean according to the fitness of things. We ought to go to Church in a very strong elegant beautifully neat room. Crosiers and banners, incense and gim-cracks, grand processions of priests and monks (with an Inquisition in the distance, and Lies, Avarice tyranny, torture, all sorts of horrible and unnatural oppressions & falsehoods kept out of sight) — such a place as this ought to belong to the old religion. How somebody of my acquaintance would like to walk into a beautiful carved confessional, or go and kiss the Rood or the pavement of Abecketts shrine. Fancy the Church quite full, the altar lined with pontifical gentlemen bobbing up and down, the dear little boys in white and red flinging about the incense pots, the music roaring out from the organ, all the monks & clergy in their stalls, and the Archbishop on his throne — O how fine! And then think of † our Lord speaking quite simply to simple Syrian people, a child or two may be at his knees, as he taught them that Love was the truth. Ah, as one thinks of it — how grand that figure looks and how small all the rest — But I daresay I am getting out of my depth.

I came on hither yesterday, having passed the day previous at Dover where it rained incessantly, and where I only had the courage to write the first sentence of this letter — being utterly cast down and more under the influence of blue devil than I ever remember before but a fine bright sky at five o'clock in the morning and a jolly brisk breeze, and the ship cutting through the water at 15 miles an hour restored cheerfulness to this wearied sperrit, and enabled it to partake freely of beefsteak aux pommes-de-terre at Ostend, after an hour of wᶠ amusement it was time to take the train

and come on to Brussels — The country is delightfully well cultivated — all along the line you pass by the most cheerful landscapes
with old cities gardens cornfields and rustic labor.

At the table d'hôte I sate next a French gentleman and his —
lady. She first sent away the bread — She then said *Mais mon ami
ce potage est abominable* then she took a piece of pudding on her
fork not to eat but to smell — after w̶ʰ she sent it away. Experience
told me it was a little Grisette giving herself airs. So I complimented the waiter on the bread, recommended the soup to a man,
and took two portions of the pudding under her nose. Then we
went (I found a companion and ardent admirer in the person of a
Manchester Merchant) to the play to see Déjazet in Gentil Bernard [146] — of w̶ʰ piece I shall say nothing but that I think it was the
wickedest I ever saw and one of the pleasantest — adorably funny
& naughty. As the part (Gentil Bernard is a prodigious rake) is
acted by a woman, the reality is taken from it and one can bear to
listen but such a little rake, such charming impudence, such little
songs, such little dresses! She looked as mignon as a China image,
and danced fought sang and capered in a way that w̶ᵈ have set Walpole mad could he have seen her.

And now writing has made me hungry and if you please I will
go and breakfast — at a Café with lots of newspapers and garçons
bawling out 'Volla Msieur how pleasant to think of) The Manchester admirer goes to London to day and will take this — If you want
any more please send me word Poste Restante at Spa.

I am going to day to the Hotel de la Terrasse where Becky used
to live, and shall pass by Captain Osbornes lodgings where I recollect meeting him and his little wife who has married again somebody told me: but it is always the way with these grandes passions.
M̶ʳˢ Dobbins or some such name she is now: always an overrated
woman I thought — How curious it is! I believe perfectly in all
those people & feel quite an interest in the Inn in w̶ʰ they lived.

Goodbye my dear gentleman & lady and let me hear the latter
is getting well.

                          W M T

[146] *Gentil-Bernard, ou l'Art d'aimer* (1846), a vaudeville by Philippe Du-

496.        TO MRS. CARMICHAEL-SMYTH
                26–29 JULY 1848

*Address:* M^rs Carmichael Smyth | 2 Rue Ponthieu. Champs Élysées | Paris.
*Postmarks:* BRUXELLES 29 JUIL. 1848, 30 JUIL. 48 VAL^NES· Published
in part, *Biographical Introductions*, IX, 1.

Dover — Brussells Saturday.

I am only so far on my journey, dearest Mother, though I left
London on Monday for Canterbury very irresolute whether I
should go to Edinburgh with Arthur Shawe's regiment the 21^st w^h
was to march yesterday from Canterbury for the modern Awthens
or cross the water. The former plan proposed by Arthur seemed to
offer some novelty and amusement, & the humours of a military
society and movement I thought might carry me through a few
days very well: but 2 or 3 hours in barracks with the young men
dispelled that idea very quickly. They told filthy old military Joe
Millers, and told me how they had got drunk with the Slashers the
night before, the Colonel of the Slashers boxing the ears of his son
the Lieutenant the Lieutenant having a match at Billingsgate with
him and being carried drunk to bed by the sentry who left the gate
in order to accommodate the young fellow. All this had I had the
courage to go through with it & follow the regiment through from
Canterbury barracks where the band of the Slashers would play
them out to Derby and Edinburgh, might have been a good sight
enough and useful on some future day: but I couldn't come up to
the point. I was too old to listen to the stories of these poor young
fellows and ashamed to spy out their actions, w^h are no better nor
worse than those of other wild good-natured young men at college
and elsewhere: but a sort of modesty said no, and so I left honest
Arthur and the Fusileers to their own simple devices and follies:
and came on to Dover where I had a long dismal rainy day utterly
to myself and the blue devils — that is to an extreme languor melancholy and unwillingness to work. V. F being over it is as if the
back bone of your stays were out.

---

manoir and Louis-François Nicolaie (1811–1879), called Clairville. The title
rôle was one of Mlle. Déjazet's best known parts.

A fine fresh breeze and sunshine dispelled the blue devils at five o'clock on Wednesday morning, and we came across to Ostend without basins, and since I have passed a couple of days sauntering about Brussells and going to the play with great pleasure and profit. To day if I get some letters for w$^h$ I am waiting I shall go off to Spa, uncertain whither else, but I feel quite a different man for the 2 days, & that the water is already flowing into the basin again. What an egotistical life the artists is. I wonder whether other people are always thinking of themselves as we are. One comfort here is that not a soul knows anything about Titmarsh the Great and that personage is taken no more notice of than a tall ungainly man deserves to be. It is pleasant to go about and see the people happy in the Cafés, the second rate dandies in the promenades, the actresses capering and singing at the theatre: & to think theres no printer's devil waiting no dinner for the evening. I went to see Dejazet the night before last in the most delightful absurd wicked little comedy in w$^h$ she acted with the grace and archness of a little demon. There was the strangest mixture of the frightening & the ludicrous in the piece. It could only be written and admired in a society in the last stage of corruption, as our's is. I feel persuaded that there is an awful time coming for all of us. What a good martyr you would make and what a fat worldly cowardly one I should be! And yet though with a great deal of trembling puffing & hesitation I think I would have the tooth out after all.

I sent you the Examiner Mary takes in the Spectator I suppose and you'll see that. It has taken down my breeches and whipped me soundly. I dont care 2$^d$: but I think how vexed Mary will be: and that annoys me. O this world of envy and injustice.

I have got a German governess for the children. I have a very good character with her from M$^{rs}$ Benedict [147] the Composers wife with whom she has lived these 3 years. She speaks French not well: and is gawky & plain, but M$^{rs}$ B says she is very affectionate to and much loved by the children — that is the great point. Alexander was very stupid but she did her duty excellently Minny was very

---

[147] The former Adèle Jean (d. 1851), wife of Julius Benedict (1804–1885), later (1871) knighted, the composer and conductor.

much attached to her and Anny suffered her very dutifully. She is awfully clever that child ⟨. . .⟩[148]

God bless my dearest mother. I'll go pack up my portmanteau & to breakfast          W M T.

497.                    TO MRS. BROOKFIELD
                           JULY?  1848

Hitherto unpublished.

Dear M^rs Brookfield     I dont send this that is the other paper,[149] on account of the compliments to W M T, that is I hope I don't, but it seems a very clever kind funny letter, and may perhaps call up a smile on a sofa that ⟨. . .⟩[150] please send me back the note. You see what the writer says about the difference between talking and writing — how I should like to write. If I might, I think I could.

We had a dinner with the young guardsmen of the ⟨. . .⟩[151] from its dullness, the dullness of the Blues on guard quite distinct from the dullness of the Guards.  There was a pretty little boy of 17 lost in aiguillettes epaulets & scarlet quite silent during dinner — the nicest little fellow when he came to take his uniform off and smoke, 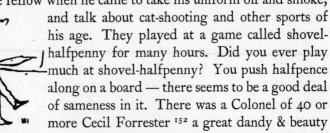 and talk about cat-shooting and other sports of his age. They played at a game called shovel-halfpenny for many hours.  Did you ever play much at shovel-halfpenny?  You push halfpence along on a board — there seems to be a good deal of sameness in it.  There was a Colonel of 40 or more Cecil Forrester [152] a great dandy & beauty still he does not look 25, and is O so delightfully vacuous and good-

[148] Four or five lines have here been torn from the letter.

[149] Possibly *The Examiner*, in which there was a generally favorable review of *Vanity Fair* by Forster. See below, No. 503.

[150] Eight lines have here been cut from the letter.

[151] Eight lines have here been cut from the letter.

[152] George Cecil Weld Forester (1807–1886), later (1874) third Baron Forester and a General in the army.

natured. But I perceive I am only giving you notes of a scene, w<u>h</u> is passing very clearly in my own mind, but w<u>h</u> you cant be called upon to understand — never having been at a mess, never having heard of shovel halfpenny perhaps — and of what a number of things besides w<u>h</u> these young fellows talked of!

I am sitting in my own room in solitude trying as hard as I can to think about Pendennis. I have been trying it ever so many mornings of late. But instead of Pen, ah Mon Dieu how one sits and thinks of all sorts of other things. Yours always

W M T.

498.    TO MRS. BROOKFIELD
1-5 AUGUST 1848

*Address:* M<u>rs</u> Brookfield | M<u>rs</u> Powell | Loughton | Essex. *Postmarks:* SPA 5 AOUT 1848, AU 7 1848. Published in part, *Collection of Letters,* pp. 15–22.

Hotel des Pays Bas Spa.
August 1-5.

My dear friend, whoever you may be who receive these lines, for unless I receive a letter from the person whom I privately mean, I shall send them post-paid to somebody else — I have the pleasure to inform you that on yesterday the 30<u>th</u> at 7 a.m. I left Brussells with w<u>h</u> I was much pleased and not a little tired, and arrived quite safe per railroad and diligence at the watering-place of Spa. I slept a great deal in the coach, having bought a book at Brussells to amuse me, and having for companions three clergymen (of the deplorable Romish faith) with large idolatrous three-cornered hats, who read their breviaries all the time I was awake, and I have no doubt gave utterance to their damnable Popish opinions when the *Stranger's ears were closed*: and lucky for the priests that I was so situated; for, speaking their language a great deal better than they do themselves, being not only image-worshippers but Belgians whose jargon is as abominable as their superstition, I would have engaged them in a controversy in w<u>h</u> I daresay they would have been utterly confounded by one who had the 39 articles of truth on his side. Their hats could hardly get out of the coach door when they quitted the carriage, and one of them when he took off his to make a parting salute to the company, quite extinguished a little passenger.

We arrived at Spa at two o'clock, and being driven on the top of the diligence to two of the principal hotels, they would not take me in as I had only a little portmanteau, or at least only would offer me a servant's bed room. These miserable miscreants did not see by my appearance that I was not a flunkey but on the contrary a great and popular author and I intend to have two fine pictures painted when I return to England of the Landlord of the Hotel de l'Orange refusing a bedchamber to the celebrated Titmarsh and of the Proprietor of the Hotel d'York offering Jeames a second floor back closet! Poor misguided people! It was on the 30th July 1848.

The first thing I did after *at length* securing a *handsome* apartment at the Hotel de Paybaw: was to survey the town and partake of a glass of water at the Pouhon Well, where the late Peter the Great Imperator of the Borussians appears also to have drunk, so that two great men at least have refreshed themselves at that fountain. I was next conducted to the baths, where a splendid concert of wind & stringed instruments was performed under my window; and many hundreds of gentlefolks of all nations were congregated in the public walk no doubt to celebrate my arrival. They are so polite however at this place of elegant ease that they did not take the least notice of the Illustrious Stranger, but allowed him to walk about quite unmolested and (to all appearance) unremarked. I went to the table d'hote with perfect affability and just like an ordinary person — an *ordinary* person at a table *d'hote*, mark the pleasantry. If that joke does not make your sides ache what my dear friend can move you?

We had a number of good things — fifteen or sixteen too many I should say. I was myself obliged to give in at about the twenty fifth dish; but there was a Flemish lady next to me, a fair blue eyed being, who carried on long after the English author's meal was concluded, and who said at dinner to day (when she beat me by at least treble the amount of victuals) — that she was languid and tired all day, and an invalid so weak and delicate that she could not walk. No wonder thought an observer of human nature who saw her eating a second supply of lobster salad w^h she introduced with her knife — no wonder, my blue eyed female, that you are ill, when you take such a preposterous quantity of nourishment: but as the waters of this place are eminently ferruginous, I presume that she used the knife in question for the purpose of taking steel with her dinner. The subject I feel is growing painful and we will if you please turn to more delicate themes.

I retired to my apartment at seven, with the same book w^h I had purchased, and w^h set me into a sound sleep until 10, when it was time to go to rest. At eight I was up and stirring: at 8/20 I was climbing the brow of a little mountain w^h overlooks this pretty town, and whence from among firs and oaks, I could look down upon the spires of the Church and the roofs of the Redoute and the principal & inferior buildings, and the vast plains & hills beyond topped in many places with pine woods and covered with green crops and yellow corn. Had I a friend to walk hand in hand with him or her on these quiet hills the promenade methinks might be pleasant. I thought of many such as I paced among the rocks and shrubberies. Breakfast succeeded that solitary but healthy reverie, when Coffee and eggs were served to the Victim of Sentiment.

Sketch-book in hand the individual last alluded to set forth in quest of objects suitable for his pencil. But it is more respectful to Nature to look at her and gaze with pleasure rather than to sit down with pert assurance and begin to take her portrait. A man who persists in sketching is like one who insists on singing during the performance of an opera. What business has *he* to be trying his stupid voice? He is not there to imitate but to admire to the best of his power. Thrice the rain came down and drove me away from my foolish endeavours as I was making the most abominable caricatures of pretty quaint cottages shaded by huge ancient trees.

In the evening was a fine music at the Redoute: w^h being concluded those who had a mind were free to repair to a magnificent neighboring saloon superbly lighted, where a great number of persons were assembled amusing themselves round two tables covered with green cloth and ornamented with a great deal of money.

They were engaged at a game w.ʰ seems very simple — One side of the table is marked red & the other black: and you have but to decide w.ʰ of the red or the black you prefer, and if the colour you choose is turned up on the cards w.ʰ a gentleman deals, another gentleman opposite to him gives you five francs or a napoleon or whatever sum of money you have thought fit to bet upon your favorite colour.

But if your colour loses then he takes your Napoleon — This he did I am sorry to say to me twice and as I thought this was enough I came home and wrote a letter full of nonsense to     My dear M.ʳˢ Brookfield

You see how nearly you were missing this delightful letter for upon my word I had packed it up small and was going to send it off in a rage to Somebody else this very day — to a young lady whom some people think overrated very likely, or to some deserving person, when o gioja o felicita (I dont know whether that is the way to spell gioja but rather pique myself on the j) when O bonheur suprême, the waiter enters my room at 10 o'clock this morning just as I had finished writing page 7 of PENDENNIS and brings me the Times newspaper and a beautiful thick two and four penny letter in a fine large hand. I eagerly seized — the newspaper (Ha! Ha! I had somebody there!), and was quickly absorbed in its contents. The news from Ireland is of great interest and importance & we may indeed return thanks that the deplorable revolution and rebellion w.ʰ everybody anticipated in that country has been averted in so singular, I may say unprecedented a manner. How pitiful is the Figure cut by M.ʳ Smith OBrien,¹⁵³ and indeed by Popery altogether! &c &c. One day has passed away here, very like its defunct predecessor. I have not lost any more money at the odious gambling table but go and watch the players there with a great deal of in-

¹⁵³ William Smith O'Brien (1803–1864), the Irish politician, one of whose exploits Thackeray had recently celebrated in "The Battle of Limerick" (*Works*, XIII, 182–185).

terest. There are ladies playing, young & pretty ones too: one is
very like a lady I used to know a curates wife in a street off Gold-
en Square — whatdyoucallit street where the piano forte maker
lives [154] — and I daresay this person is puzzled why I always go
and stare at her so. She has her whole soul in the pastime: puts out
her five franc pieces in the most timid way, and watches them disappear under the croupier's rake with eyes so uncommonly sad and
tender that I feel inclined to go up to her and say 'Madam you are
exceedingly like a lady a curates wife whom I once knew in England
and as I take an interest in you I wish you would get out of this
place as quick as you can, and take your beautiful eyes off the black
and red? But I suppose it would be thought rude if I were to make
any such statement and — ah! what do I remember? there's no use
in sending off this letter to day; this is Friday and it cannot be delivered on Sunday in a Protestant metropolis — There was no use
in hurrying home from Lady — never mind it's only an Irish
baronets wife who tries to disguise her Limerick brogue but the
fact is she has an exceedingly pretty daughter — I say there was
no use in hurrying home so as to get this off by the post.

Yesterday, I did not know a soul in this place: but got in the
course of the day a neat note from a lady who had had the delight
of an introduction to me at D-v-nsh-re House — and who proposed
tea in the most flattering manner. Now I know a French Duke and
Duchess and at least six of the most genteel persons in Spa: and
some of us are going out riding in a few minutes the rain having
cleared off, the sky being bright, and the surrounding hills and
woods looking uncommonly green & tempting. . . . [*A pause of
2 hours is supposed to have taken place since the above was written:
a gentleman enters as from horseback into the room No 32 of the
Hotel des Pays Bas looking onto the Fountain in the GRAND place.
He divests himself of a part of his dress w.h has been spattered with
mud during an arduous but delightful ride over commons, roads,
woods nay mountains. He curls his hair in the most killing manner:*

[154] John Broadwood & Sons, pianoforte makers, 32 and 33 Great Pulteney
Street, near Golden Square (*Post Office London Directory*, 1847). See above,
No. 376.

*and prepares to go out to dinner The purple shadows are falling over the grand place, and the roofs of the houses looking westward are in a flame. The clock of the old church strikes six. 'tis the appointed hour. He gives one last glance at the looking glass and his last thought is for — ..see page 4 the last 3 words.*[155]

The dinner was exceedingly stupid. I very nearly fell asleep by the side of the lady of the house. It was all over by 9 o'clock 1/2 an hour before Payne came to fetch you to bed and I went to the gambling house and lost two Napoleons more. May this be a warning to all dissipated middle-aged persons. I have just got 2 new novels from the libery by M$^r$ Fielding. The one is Amelia the most delightful portrait of a woman that surely ever was painted; the other is Joseph Andrews w$^h$ gives me no particular pleasure for it is both coarse and careless, and the author makes an absurd brag of his twopenny learning upon w$^h$ he values himself evidently more than upon the best of his own qualities. Good night. You see I am writing to you as if I was talking. It is but 10 o'clock, and yet it seems quite time here to go to bed. I dont believe John Pauls ingenious statement. I dont intend to be the best of husbands. I have got a letter from Anny so clever humourous & wise that it is fit to be printed in a book. As for Miss Jingleby I admire her pretty face & manners more than her singing w$^h$ is very nice and just what a lady's sh$^d$ be; but I believe my heart is not engaged in that quarter. Why, there is 6 times as much writing in my letter as in yours. You ought to send me ever so many pages, if bargains were equal between the male & faymale but they never are.

There is a Prince here who is seventy two years of age and wears frills to his trowsers.

What if I were to pay my bill and go off this minute to the Rhine? It will be better to see that than these genteel dandies here — I don't care about the beauties of the Rhine any more; but it is always pleasant and friendly — There is no reason why I should not sleep at Bonn tonight — looking out on the Rhine — opposite Drachenfels — that is the best way of travelling surely, never to know where you are going, until the moment and Fate say Go. Who

---

[155] Which are: *dear M$^{rs}$ Brookfield.*

knows, by setting off at 12 o'clock, something may happen to alter
the whole course of my life? Perhaps I may meet with some beautiful creature who +++ but then it is such a bore packing up those
shirts.

I wonder whether anybody will write to me Post Restante at
Hombourg near Frankfort on the Mayne: and if you would kindly
send a line to Anny at Captain Alexander's Montpelier Row
Twickenham telling her to write to me there and not at Brussells,
you would add Madam to the many obligations you have already
conferred on your most faithful Serv$^t$　　　W M Thackeray

I have made a dreadful dumpy little letter but an envelope w$^d$
cost 1/2$^d$ more.

I do not like to say anything disrespectful of Dover as you are
going there but it seemed awfully stupid. May I come & see you
as I pass through? a line at the Ship for me w$^d$n't fail to bring me.

499.　　　　TO MRS. CARMICHAEL-SMYTH
　　　　　　4 AUGUST 1848

*Address:* M$^{rs}$ Carmichael Smyth | 2 Rue Ponthieu. Champs Élysées | Paris.
*Postmarks:* SPA 4 AOUT, 6 AOUT 1848 VAL$^{NES}$. Published in part, *Biographical Introductions,* II, xxxiii–xxxv.

My dearest Mother　Your letter did not reach me till yesterday
Thursday morning, although it must have been delayed a day in
the Post Office by the stupid old Post master here who is too old
to do anything but talk about his business — And so it w$^d$ have been
quite too late to send to M$^r$ Archibald who will bring you nothing
from us but the bottle of divine pomatum w$^h$ I trust will do good to
my dear old G P. I don't think the visit to Paris can be made out
though for the children. The governess whom I have engaged has
no home or friends in London except M$^{rs}$ Benedict and her house,
w$^h$ during the absence of M$^{rs}$ Benedict in the country, and until my
return, Miss What dyoucallum (I don't know her name) is to
occupy. At my return I had proposed that the children & I and the
Governess should go for a few weeks to the sea somewhere: where
I could work upon Pendennis w$^h$ is the name of the new book. In

October you will be at Brighton please God, when you can see us all continually. It will be much more convenient to defer our meeting till then. The remains of poor old G Ms legacy will float you and the furniture over. I wonder will you take a house with three extra rooms so that we could stow into it on coming down? I sh$^d$ think for 60£ a year one might easily find such a one, and I can afford or the deuce is in it to pay the extra part for the sake of the accommodation — You might for 60 have the upper part of a house and the use of a cook for the wittles: as for the dignity I dont believe it matters a pinch of snuff. Tom Carlyle lives in perfect dignity in a little 40 house at Chelsea with a snuffy Scotch maid to open the door, and the best company in England ringing at it. It is only the second and third chop great folks who care about Show — and — Why don't you live with a maid yourself? I think I hear somebody saying. Well I can't. I want a man to be going my own messages w$^h$ occupy him pretty well — There must be a cook and a woman about the children. That horse is the best doctor I get in London. In fine there are 100 good reasons for a lazy liberal not extravagant but costly way of life.

The blue devils walked away after a very few days of rest and idleness, and the cheerful solitude and indolence of this pretty gay tranquil place have done me the greatest good in the world. I opened my fire yesterday with the first chapter of Pendennis, and have had another good spell this morning before breakfast: such a good one as authorized 2 mutton chops along with my coffee. The walks and rides about are charming and the country has a sweet peaceful friendly look, that I'm sure I shall remember with pleasure a long time hence. Chaufontaine [156] looked very sad & bankrupt as we passed it on Sunday. They have got a Sunday service here in an extinct gambling house: and a clerical professor to perform whom you have to pay just like any other showman who comes. I shall go next Sunday. I did not know anybody until yesterday, when some fine folks to whom I had been introduced at the Duke of Devonshire's & whom I had quite forgotten made up to me: and introduced me to other fine people. There is a clique of them here:

[156] See above, p. 145, note 29.

and in knowing one you know all. Hence follow rides visits walks tea-parties tittle-tattle & watering-place gossip. There will be too much of it I suspect and I will be off in a day or two: and when gone I am sure I shall think of this as one of the pleasantest places possible, though while here I have yawned a good deal and not known what to do with myself many an hour. It is different now that I am able to write again: but that was impossible for some days after leaving London.

The steel water gives almost everybody a headache here. I always wake with a little one though I go to bed early and very sober. I go to the gambling shop and watch the people at play with a good deal of interest. The eagerness & feverishness of the women is very curious. There is one old fellow a scoundrel making his daughter play for him she is growing quite hot and feverish at it: so much so that I would like to pull his ears — Sometimes I have a shy myself but without any passion, and I dont lose or win 20 francs. There is a poor devil in the Hotel here who has a favorite scheme about wh he was bragging to me three nights ago, and with wh he was enabled to win two hundred francs a day — A few years ago I should have believed him & I daresay tried to join in the speculation but I don't any more, and told him very kindly that he could not fail to blow up before long. Yesterday I saw him leaning against a pillar in the gambling room with the saddest hang dog look. The blow up had taken place. He could afford to lose 24 times running — but he lost 25 times. It was all over. He wont be able to pay his Inn-bill.

I have got the most stunning letter from Anny. It is quite marvellous for its cleverness and humour: as it is charming for its affection. Thank God Almighty for it. They have requested white frocks 'for a certain day' as Miss Anny calls it: viz that of Miss A's marriage. It will not be very long after that please God that I shall descend upon Twickenham, and whisk off my ladies to the sea somewhere.

And now I will pack up these 2 scraps of paper and carry them off to the Post. Give my love to my kind old Aunts for me. Always my dearest mothers affte W M T.

500.       TO LADY BLESSINGTON
20 AUGUST 1848

Hitherto unpublished.

20 August.

Dear Lady Blessington.

Thank you for your good opinion about V. F: and for many
many kind intentions in my behalf. I should have liked of all things
to have gone to the private view of Stowe:[157] such sights suit the
gloomy temper of my soul and besides are good for my purposes
as a tradesman and Satirist — but I was away at Spa, Hombourg,
Cologne and only came back last night to find O such a quantity
of letters! amongst w$^h$ your's the very first that I opened and *almost*
the most flattering of all. But there is another w$^h$ says — well I
don't know what it doesn't say: — it is from the mysterious author
of Jane Eyre, and would make me blush if anything could.[158]

I am going to fetch my daughters from Twickenham and to
transport my household to Brighton for 6 weeks in w$^h$ time, please
fate, I will do the first numbers of PENDENNIS — Vanity Fair
is doing very well commercially I'm happy to say at last. They
have sold 1500 of the volumes w$^h$ is very well in these times of
revolution and dismay.

You know that I promised your Ladyship a little story,[159] w$^h$ I

[157] Stowe Park, Buckinghamshire, the country seat of Richard Plantagenet
Temple-Nugent-Brydges-Chandos-Grenville (1797–1861), second Duke of
Buckingham. Within ten years of his accession in 1839 the Duke had con-
trived to ruin himself "by a system of accumulating estates purchased with
borrowed money, and by excessive expenditure." His landed property was sold
by his creditors, and between August and October, 1848, everything in his
mansion at Stowe was disposed of in a forty-day sale. (G. E. C., *Complete Peerage*, ed. Gibbs and others, II, 409) This excursion to Stowe must have stirred
ominous forebodings in Lady Blessington's mind. See below, No. 584.

[158] Thackeray did not preserve this letter. Its contents were no doubt very
similar to the paragraph on Thackeray in Charlotte Brontë's letter to Williams
of August 14. See Wise and Symington, *The Brontës*, II, 244.

[159] For *The Keepsake* of 1849, which Lady Blessington edited. Thackeray's
contribution, "An Interesting Event" (reprinted in *Stray Papers*, ed. Melville,
pp. 259–265), appears to be the tale he had from Higgins, for it concludes

heard from Higgins once and thought straightway to put into print.
Well, I've forgotten the main part of the little story, and the wretch
won't tell it me again: saying that it will annoy a worthy couple,
violate the sanctity of private life &c &c. — I must cast about then
for another little subject: or see if I can drag back into memory
again those fugitive incidents in Higgins's tale, and use it in spite
of him. It is nothing in the least harmful to any mortal soul —
only a tale about a silver teapot.

I saw the King and the Vicar of the Empire,[160] and all sorts of
sights at Cologne & Spa and Hombourg. and O for shame! I lost
5£ at the horrid rouge et noir & roulette. But I intend to make it
pay me in my Xmas book w^h is to be called Lady Kicklebury abroad.

But why do I write all this? intending as I do to try and pay a
visit to Gore House this evening and shake hands with kind people
who have been kind to me — whilst my back was turned too — that
is the rarity of it — no it isn't. The world is a much kinder and
better world than some bilious-covered satirists have painted it —
I must give up the yellow cover I think and come out in a fresher
tone — and now I can say no more but that I am yours most faithfully up in a corner [161]

W M Thackeray

501.     TO THE REV. WILLIAM BROOKFIELD
21 AUGUST 1848

*Address:* Rev^d W. H. B. Published in *Collection of Letters,* p. 22.

21 August.  Home.

My dear old B. I am just come back, and execute my first vow
w^h was to tell you on landing that there is a certain bath near Min-

with the rueful determination of a disgruntled godfather to buy a "silver mug
or papboat" for the infant whose birth the story chronicles.

[160] Friedrich Wilhelm IV of Prussia (1795–1861), who had come to the
throne in 1840. After the outbreak of the revolution of 1848, he championed
a united Germany on the pattern of the medieval Holy Roman Empire.

[161] Thackeray's signature is crowded into the extreme corner of the final
page of this letter.

den and 6 hours from Cologne by the railway (so that people may
go all the way at their ease) where all sorts of complaints — including of course yours all and several are to be cured — The bath
is Rehda, Station Rehda. Dᴿ Sutro [162] of the London German Hospital knows all about it. I met an acquaintance just come thence (a
Mʳˢ Bracebridge and her marri) who told me of it. People are
ground young there — a young physician has just been cured of far-
gone tubercles in the lungs; maladies of languor, rheumatisms, liver-
complaints all sort of wonders are performed there, especially
female wonders — Y not take Madam there: go drink, bathe, and
be cured? Y not go there as well as any where else this summer
season? Y not come up and see this German Doctor, or ask Bullar
to write to him? Do my dear old fellow; and I will vow a candle
to honest Horne's [163] chapel if you are cured. Did the Vienna beer
in wʰ I drank your health not do you any good? God bless you my
dear Brookfield and believe that I'm always affectionately yours

W M T

502.          TO MRS. BROOKFIELD
31 AUGUST 1848

*Address:* Mʳˢ Brookfield | 15 Portman Sᵗ | Portman Sqʳᵉ. *Postmark:* AU 31
1848. Hitherto unpublished.

Thursday.

Madam

If you put a letter in the post this very night addressed to W M
Thackeray Esqʳ 13 Young Sᵗ Kensington and stating that you are
disengaged tomorrow evening and will be able to receive that
gentleman — your communication will be attended to (at 1/2 past
6) & nothing extra required

Your well wisher
Octaviophilus.

[162] Dr. Sigismund Sutro, 3 Great Marlborough Street (*Royal Blue Book,*
1846).
[163] The Rev. Thomas Hartwell Horne, incumbent of St. Edmund the King
and Martyr on Lombard Street (*Post Office London Directory,* 1847).

503.            TO ROBERT BELL[164]
                3 SEPTEMBER 1848

My text is taken from *The Times*, July 17, 1911, p. 8.

                                Sunday, Septr. 3rd
My dear Bell

Although I have made a rule to myself never to thank critics yet
I like to break it continually, and especially in the present instance
for what I hope is the excellent article in Fraser. [165] It seems to
me very just in most points as regards the author: some he questions
as usual — If I had put in more fresh air as you call it my object
would have been defeated — It is to indicate, in cheerful terms,
that we are for the most part an abominably foolish and selfish
people "desperately wicked" and all eager after vanities. Everybody is you see in that book, — for instance if I had made Amelia
a higher order of woman there would have been no vanity in Dobbins falling in love with her, whereas the impression at present is
that he is a fool for his pains that he has married a silly little thing
and in fact has found out his error rather a sweet and tender one
however, *quia multum amavit* I want to leave everybody dissatisfied and unhappy at the end of the story — we ought all to be
with our own and all other stories. Good God dont I see (in that
may-be cracked and warped looking glass in which I am always

[164] Bell (1800–1867), a journalist and miscellaneous writer whose most
memorable enterprise was an annotated edition of the English poets in twenty-
four volumes (1854–1857). He was long a close friend of Thackeray, near
whom he was buried (at his own desire) in Kensal Green Cemetery.
[165] Bell writes in his generally admiring review (*Fraser's Magazine*, September, 1848, pp. 320–323): "Over-good people will be apt to shudder at a story
so full of petty vices and grovelling passions. They will be afraid to trust it in
the hands of young ladies and gentlemen, lest the unredeemed wickedness of its
pictures should corrupt their morals, and send them into the world shut up in
a crust of selfishness and suspicion." "The people who fill up the motley scenes
of *Vanity Fair*, with two or three exceptions, are as vicious and odious as a clever
condensation of the vilest qualities can make them. . . . And poor Amelia goes
but a short way to purify the foul atmosphere." But on the whole he justifies
Thackeray as a moralist who portrays vices for "the benefit of mankind."

looking) my own weaknesses wickednesses lusts follies shortcomings? in company let us hope with better qualities about which
we will pretermit discourse. We must lift up our voices about these
and howl to a congregation of fools: so much at least has been my
endeavour. You have all of you taken my misanthropy to task —
I wish I could myself: but take the world by a certain standard (you
know what I mean) and who dares talk of having any virtue at all?
For instance Forster says After a scene with Blifil, the air is cleared
by a laugh of Tom Jones [166] — Why Tom Jones in my holding is
as big a rogue as Blifil. Before God he is — I mean the man is selfish
according to his nature as Blifil according to his. In fact I've a
strong impression that we are most of us not fit for — never mind.

Pathos I hold should be very occasional indeed in humourous
works and indicated rather than expressed or expressed very rarely.
In the passage where Amelia is represented as trying to separate
herself from the boy — She goes upstairs and leaves him with his
aunt 'as that poor Lady Jane Grey tried the axe that was to separate her slender life' [167] I say that is a fine image whoever wrote
it (& I came on it quite by surprize in a review the other day) that
is greatly pathetic I think: it leaves you to make your own sad pictures — We shouldn't do much more than that I think in comic

---

[166] Though Forster calls *Vanity Fair* "one of the most original works of real
genius that has of late been given to the world," he devotes a good part of his
article in *The Examiner* to what he terms Thackeray's "grave defect": "If
Thackeray falls short of Fielding, much of whose peculiar power and more of
whose manner he has inherited or studiously acquired, it is because an equal
amount of large cordiality has not raised him entirely above the region of sneering, into that of simple uncontaminated human affection. . . . It cannot be
denied that it is in those characters where great natural talents and energy are
combined with unredeemed depravity that the author puts forth his full powers,
and that in the management and contemplation of them he seems absolutely to
revel. . . . We feel that the atmosphere of the work is overloaded with these
exhalations of human folly and wickedness. We gasp for a more liberal alterna-
tion of refreshing breezes of unsophisticated honesty. Fielding, after he has
administered a sufficient dose of Blifil's choke-damp, purifies the air by a hearty
laugh from Tom Jones. But the stifling ingredients are administered by Mr.
Thackeray to excess, without the necessary relief." (*Examiner*, July 22, 1848,
p. 468)
[167] Chapter 50 (*Works*, I, 484).

books — In a story written in the pathetic key it would be different
& then the comedy perhaps should be occasional. Some day — but
a truce to egotistical twaddle. It seems to me such a time ago that
V F was written that one may talk of it as of some body elses performance. My dear Bell I am very thankful for your friendliness
& pleased to have your good opinion.

Faithfully yours

W. M. Thackeray.

504.               TO MRS. BROOKFIELD
                   5 SEPTEMBER 1848 [168]

Published in part in *The Orphan of Pimlico* . . . *by William Makepeace
Thackeray* (London, 1876).

New York.   September 5, 1848.

Dear Madam

It seems to me a long time since I had the honour of seeing you.
I should be glad to have some account of your health. We made a
beautiful voyage of 13 & 1/2 days, and reached this fine city yesterday — the entrance of the bay is beautiful, the magnificent woods of
the Susquehannah stretch down to the shore, & from Hoboken
Lighthouse to Vancouvers Island the bay presents one brilliant
blaze of natural & commercial loveliness — Hearing that Titmarsh
was on board the steamer the Lord Mayor and Aldermen of New
York came down to receive us, and the batteries on Long Island
fired a salute. General Jackson called at my hotel (the Astor
house) I found him a kind old man though he has a wooden leg and
takes a great deal of snuff. Broadway has certainly disappointed
me — it is nothing to be compared to our own dear Holborn Hill.
But the beautiful range of the Alleyghanny mountains w[h] I see from
my windows, and the roar of the Niagara Cataract w[h] empties itself
out of the Mississippi into the Oregon Territory, have an effect,
w[h] your fine eye for the picturesque and keen sense of the Beautiful
& the Natural would I am sure lead you to appreciate — The oysters

[168] The story behind this letter, if there was one, has not been recorded.

here are much larger than ours: and the canvass-backed ducks are reckoned, and indeed are, a delicacy — The house where Washington is born is still shown; but the General I am informed is dead much regretted. The clergy here is both numerous and respected and the Archbishop of New York is a most venerable and delightful prelate, whose sermons are however a little long. The ladies are without exception the — but here the first gong sounds for dinner and the black slave who waits on me comes up & says 'Massa! Hab only five minutes for dinnah! Make haste, git no pumpkin-pie else,' so unwillingly I am obliged to break off my note and to subscribe myself

My dear Madam
Your very faithful Serv<sup>t</sup>
W M Thackeray

What I really mean is that I should like very much to come on Friday or Saturday if W is at home.

505.          TO LADY BLESSINGTON
SEPTEMBER 1848

*Address:* The Countess of Blessington. Hitherto unpublished.

I send my lady a little sketch w<sup>h</sup> I hope will be suitable for the pages of the Keepsake. [169] If there is one phrase in it w<sup>h</sup> may call a blush upon any cheek, (and perhaps there is) I will be very happy to expunge the same and replace it or amend it. I saw Jacob Omnium at Brighton on Saturday, he was in a sad confusion of ideas, he said he couldn't write a little paper: it is awfully difficult to him. All Brighton is in an uproar about the Pie. I mean the pie I *didn't* bring to Burnham Beeches. M<sup>rs</sup> Mutton took it to Horace Smith, and wanted my address in London: w<sup>h</sup> Horace refused to give — the pie was hawked about for sale at a reduced price: and finally purchased by a friend of mine, who made it a present to another friend who invited a party to meet it who ate it and found

[169] See above, No. 500.

it execrable — The grouse & the partridges had quarrelled, and would have disagreed with us too if we had come in contact with them — I mean that they were in a highly unwholesome state, and we shouldn't have liked them — So we lost nothing by not having the pie, I am not a humbug, (as some young ladies [170] insisted) witnesses can be brought to show that the pie was ordered made eaten &c — By the way what a fine day this w^d be for a picnic — so fine that I am going to take my daughters to Gravesend or Erith: and eat shrimps fresh out of the river.

But now comes the real and important part of this note — *There will be a place vacant in the Post Office soon* that of Assistant Secretary at present held by M^r James Campbell. What a place for a man of letters! I think if Lord Clanricarde [171] would give it to me I would satisfy my employers, and that my profession would be pleased by hearing of the appointment of one of us. I wonder might I write to him, or is there any kind person who would advocate my cause?

Always dear Lady Blessington your very much obliged<br>W M Thackeray.

506.               TO LADY BLESSINGTON
                      SEPTEMBER 1848

*Hitherto unpublished.*

Dear Lady Blessington

You are very good and kind. I have written a letter to Lord Clanricarde who can but say no: but there is no harm at least in letting every body know that I am anxious to get employment, and no Gov^t would do itself harm by giving it to men of our profession.

Why havent I been to Gore House? Because I have been to Brighton for the sea air and because when in London there has been

---

[170] The Miss Powers.

[171] Ulick John de Burgh (1802–1874), fourteenth Earl and first Marquess of Clanricarde, Postmaster-General from 1846 to 1852.

a sick friend [172] of mine (and I don't mind owning that She is the most &c &c &c) who has taken some of my evenings, and my daughters & Pendennis some others.

Here I find is a page of the interesting event w^h I have let slip —I send it to your Ladyship; and I dont care a fig what those young ladies think of

Your very much misunderstood

W M Thackeray.

What a pie I will order if I get the Post Office Place!


507.          TO MRS. PROCTER
              13 SEPTEMBER 1848

Hitherto unpublished. My text is taken from a transcript given Lady Ritchie by George Murray Smith.

Kensington,
13, September, 1848.

My dear Mrs Procter,

I know what your opinion has been for some days past: but I am obliged to bear up against the unkind unjust cruel sentiments of many of my fellow creatures: and bow down gently to my persecutors. How do you know, I should like to know, whether I have not had my portmanteau packed and ready to start for Dover twice and what circumstances have intervened to prevent me? Once I went to Brighton for two days and departed swearing to go back again, but it is always the same difficulty. A seaside lodging in the present state of my finances is impossible. I have got a pile of bills before me now that by heaven are perfectly ludicrous, I have paid heaps since I came back. I have a leg of mutton and live at the rate of a coach and six. I don't know how it is — the old story which I am always grumbling to you about, but the seaside trip is finished that is quite clear: and I can't think of transporting this extravagant household out of the parish. My mother is coming soon, thank Heaven, to take the command over me, and I shall be

[172] Mrs. Brookfield.

solvent some day let us hope. I think it is impossible for literary men to write natural letters any more: I was just going to say something, but thinks I in future ages when this letter comes to be seen, they will say he was in embarrassed circumstances, he was reckless and laughed at his prodigality, he was etc.

I have before me beside the bills four notes requesting advances of money. Ha. Ha! Isn't it enough to make one wild?

Two nights ago good-natured Forster asked the children to dinner and took us to the play: [173] where I bored myself and slept a great deal. Brookfield and the other children were however perfectly happy with Paul Pry and the Wreck ashore, in which my beloved Miss Woolgan did not look her best I thought. No body does look so any more. At Brighton Virginia [174] was on the sofa lovely, interesting and unwell. I did not care two-pence. Here is somebody else on the sofa here looking uncommonly pretty too and with eyes just as bright as those which have rolled round me for the last six years. [175] Well, it's all over. I wish I could get into the coach this minute and come and talk to you about it. But it is *all* done for. She never cared 2 1/2d for me — and my heart is a wacuum. But I go and see her and have a kind tender fraternal or paternal regard and that sort of thing — but the rest is all gone. Why, we used to admire the Scottish chiefs once and cry over Thaddeus of Warsaw.[176] Fond follies of youth!

Tomorrow it will be eight years since my poor dear little wife jumped into the great calm sunshiny sea off the Isle of Wight: [177] and she has been dead or worse ever since. Good God what a year of pain and hope the first one was and bitter bitter tears — that's all over too. Love, hope, infernal pain and disappointment. All I remember is that some people were very kind to me. You among the first, my dear good friends.

[173] At the Haymarket Theatre, where the bill on September 11 included *Paul Pry* by John Poole, and *The Wreck Ashore* (1830) and *Shocking Events* (1838), both by John Baldwin Buckstone.
[174] Miss Pattle.
[175] Mrs. Brookfield, whom Thackeray first met in 1842. See *Memoranda*.
[176] Novels by Jane Porter (1776–1850), published in 1803 and 1810. Compare *Works*, XII, 377.      [177] See above, No. 187.

Among the four letters is one from a man who used to give me very good dinners twelve years ago and whom Fate has pursued since. He recalls the old times, and then fires off a salvo of compliments, introduces his own mishaps, and proposes a little loan of *deux ou trois livres sterlings*, he doesn't say two or three pounds but puts it in French: and concludes with *scusatemi* (in a clerk-like Lombard Street hand) and 'sincerely and devotedly yours'. So and so. Isn't it pitiful? I will shut up this note and go and have a walk with the little people.

Always yours affectionately,

W. M. T.

508.                    TO JANE SHAWE
                     19 SEPTEMBER 1848

Published in part, *Thackeray and his Daughter*, pp. 29–30.

Kensington 19 Sep.ʳ 1848.

My dear Jane

I write a line just to shake you by the hand and wish you a happy voyage to your brother. I ought to write and thank him too for he wrote me the kindest letter about his nieces, and you will be able to give him a good report of them thank God. If ever I make a decent drawing of the little women he shall have it: but I hope he will judge for himself in England before long, and to see him here, where those who have been good to my poor little wife and children are always welcome. Won't you write to us and tell us that you are well and happy? I hope you will be so, dear Jane, and after the grief of parting with your Mother for a little, enjoy a grand voyage and a sight of new countries and people. I wish I had the journey before me, and could see the place where I was born again.

It is about this time eight years that the Jupiter came into Cork with our poor little woman ⟨. . .⟩ [178] on board — My dear, I can't

[178] One word is here irrecoverably overscored.

forget how tenderly you always loved her: and look over often in my mind that gap of time since she has been dead to us all and see that dear artless sweet creature who charmed us both so. What a whirl of life I've seen since then, but never her better I think: whose reason it pleased God to destroy before her body: and who cares for none of us now. Nest ce pas mourir tous les jours — dont you recollect her singing and her sweet sweet voice? She goes to Epsom tomorrow when you sail for India. Go, stay, die, prosper, she doesn't care. Amen  Her anxious little soul would have been alarmed at my prosperities such as they are. She was always afraid of people flattering me: and I get a deal of that sort of meat nowadays — Here comes Anny with a pair of letters of w$^h$ Minny's is the best: and Annys by no means overburthened with affection, but sincerity is the next best thing — the child has a very warm heart and w$^d$ love you if she knew you — She says at the end Give my love to Uncle Charles [179] — and I say so too — Give my love to him with all my heart. I wish him and you a good voyage. We have had a difference, I know how it began — but I hardly know what it is — And I remember that he and Mary were once very kindly and warmly disposed towards me and helped me & mine at the time of our greatest need. So give him my love and Farewell dear Jane

509.        TO LADY BLESSINGTON
                25? SEPTEMBER 1848

Hitherto unpublished.

                           **Monday Night.**

Dear Lady Blessington

    Lord Clanricarde wrote me to day a similar letter to that w$^h$ you have kindly sent me: and I sent my servant off express to Sandgate with a rejoinder w$^h$ might help I thought in my favour. But I don't think we shall *order the pie yet*. Nor indeed does it

[179] Charles Carmichael, who had gone out to India to repair his broken fortunes.

much matter for a year or two. I have got the bat in my hands and, please God, have strength for a good long innings. Time and work will however bowl out the best player: and it is then that a refuge will be welcome and a comfortable shelter and refreshment under the tents — under the *Marquee* I was going to say upon my word & honour, but I remembered it was a pun.

The great point however is as you kindly say to put myself forward as a candidate for this thing or that. Whether I win or lose now is of little consequence — but what *does* please me is the ready friendliness with w.ʰ you have backed, and Lord Clanricarde has received, my petition.

Always yours, dear Lady Blessington, sincerely
W M Thackeray.

I thought I might possibly get a second answer from Monseigneur tomorrow and waited until then before I wrote to you. Indeed I think I sh.ᵈ be sorry at this minute to give up my old vagabond way of life, and my honest friend Pendennis though he is not born yet.

510.     TO LADY BLESSINGTON
1 OCTOBER 1848

Hitherto unpublished.

1 October. Kensington.
Dear Lady Blessington. Fate has decided against us and we are not to have the pie. Another man has got it and deserves it too. But what matters? Cant I make a pie of my own? Let me begin Pendennis this instant and cram it with beef pigeons hard eggs & the most delicious pepper and spice — We will make it very good — much better than that one we had at Burnham Beeches w.ʰ was fade and stale.[180]

I got a very kind note from Lord Clanricarde last night announcing our fate; and that there is nothing in his department w.ʰ

[180] See above, No. 505.

can ever suit me. [181] Amen. I was coming to pay my devoirs to
your Ladyship, but was too unwell for a wonder — A dinner at the
Oriental of six curries had quite done me up — it was not pickled
salmon this time. For shame that a man near 40 years old a father
and a moralist by trade should have to make such humiliating confessions.

If you please, I should like the Subeditor of the Keepsake [182] to
be informed that the little story is by M<sup>r</sup> Titmarsh not by M<sup>r</sup>
Thackeray: though the latter's name may figure in the bill of fare
I mean in the table of contents (you see this letter is all about
eating.)

And I assure you, and ought perhaps to be ashamed of that too,
that I feel relieved at the turn affairs took in the Post Office case.
Fancy being told 'You shall go to Aldersgate St every day of your
life. No more liberty no more rambles & sauntering: but be a
slave until death do you claim' — it isn't such a tempting thing
after all. See the fable of the Fox and the Grapes as recounted
by Æsop: and believe me faithfully yours

W M Thackeray

[181] Trollope, who was at this time a clerk in the Post Office, writes: "In 1848
there fell a vacancy in the situation of Assistant-Secretary at the General Post-
Office, and Lord Clanricarde either offered it to [Thackeray] or promised to
give it to him. The Postmaster-General had the disposal of the place, but was
not altogether free from control in the matter. When he made known his purpose at the Post-Office, he was met by an assurance from the officer next under
him [the Secretary, Lt.-Col. William Leader Maberly] that the thing could not
be done. The services were wanted of a man who had had experience in the
Post-Office; and, moreover, it was necessary that the feelings of other gentlemen
should be consulted. Men who have been serving in an office many years do
not like to see even a man of genius put over their heads. In fact, the office
would have been up in arms at such an injustice. Lord Clanricarde, who in a
matter of patronage was not scrupulous, was still a good-natured man and
amenable. He attempted to befriend his friend till he found that it was impossible, and then, with the best grace in the world, accepted the official nomi-
nee that was offered to him." (*Thackeray*, pp. 33–34)

[182] Marguerite Power.

511.        TO JOSEPH CUNDALL[183]
4 OCTOBER 1848

Hitherto unpublished.

13 Young S! Kensington.   October 4
Dear M! Cundall

My friend M! Marvy [184] tells me that he is in negotiation with
you regarding some plates, and wishes a word from me of introduction. I think the specimen of the Constable admirable, the
project a novel & good one, & the artist is an intimate friend of
mine for whom I have the very greatest esteem & regard. Anything
w! you can do in his behalf will greatly oblige

Yours very truly
W M Thackeray —

512.        TO MRS. BROOKFIELD
4 OCTOBER 1848

*Address:* M!ˢ Brookfield | Clevedon Court. Clevedon | Somerset. *Postmark:*
BRISTOL OC 5 1848. Published in *Collection of Letters,* pp. 27–28, from
which the text of the postscript is taken. Original of the first three paragraphs
in the Morgan Library.

Wednesday morning.   October 4
Dear M!ˢ Brookfield   If you would write me a line to say that
you made a good journey and were pretty well, to Sir Thomas
Cullums [185] Hardwick Bury S! Edmunds — you would confer indeed a favor on yours respectfully.

William dined here last night & was pretty cheerful        As I
passed by Portman S! after you were gone, just to take a look up at

[183] A bookseller, with offices at 12 Old Bond Street (*Post Office London Directory,* 1847).
[184] Marvy passed the winter of 1848–1849 with Thackeray at 13 Young
Street. For his book, see *Memoranda.*
[185] The Rev. Sir Thomas Cullum (1777–1855), eighth Baronet, Rector of
Knoddishall, Suffolk.

the windows, the usual boy started forward to take the horse — I laughed a sad laugh — I didn't want nobody to take the horse. It is a long time since you were away

The cab is at the door to take me to the railroad Mʳˢ Procter was very kind and Adelaide sympathized with me. I have just opened my desk There are all the papers I had at Spa — Pendennis unread since, & your letter. ¹⁸⁶ Good bye dear Mʳˢ Brookfield.

Always yours

W M T.

*L'homme propose.* Since this was wrote the author went to the railroad, found that he arrived a minute too late, and that there were no trains for 4 1/2 hours. So I came back into town and saw the publishers, who begged and implored me so, not to go out pleasuring, &c., that I am going to Brighton instead of Bury. I looked in the map, I was thinking of coming to Weston-Super-Mare, — only it seemed such a hint.

513.                    TO MRS. BROOKFIELD
                    7–9 OCTOBER 1848

Published in part, *Collection of Letters*, pp. 64–66.

Brighton. Saturday — Monday.

Thank you for your letter dear Mʳˢ Brookfield it made this gay place look twice as gay yesterday when I got it — Last night when I had come home to work, 2 men spied a light in my room & came in and began smoking — they talked about racing and the odds all the time, one of them I am happy to say is a Lord, & the other a Brighton buck — when they were gone (& indeed I listened to them with a great deal of pleasure for I like to hear people of all sorts) at midnight & in the quiet I read your letter over again, and one from Miss Anny and from my dear old Mother who is to come on the 12ᵗʰ and whose heart is yearning for her children — I must be at home to receive her and some days ten or so at least to make

---

¹⁸⁶ See above, No. 498.

her comfortable, so, with many thanks for M⟨rs⟩ Elton's invitation [187]
I must decline it for the present if you please. You may be sure I
went the very first thing to Virginia and her sisters,[188] who were
very kind to me and I think are very fond of me, and their talk
and V's beauty consoled me for my heart was very sore, and I was
ill and out of spirits. A change, a fine air, a wonderful sunshine and
moonlight, and a great spectacle of happy people perpetually rolling
by has done me all the good in the world and then one of the Miss
Smiths told me a story w⟨h⟩ is the very thing for the beginning of
Pendennis, w⟨h⟩ is actually begun and in progress — This is a comical beginning rather; the other, w⟨h⟩ I did not like, was sentimental;
and will yet come in very well after the startling comical business
has been played off. — [189] See how beautifully I have put stops to

[187] The former Rhoda Susan Willis (d. 1873), who had married Arthur
Hallam Elton (1818–1883), later (1853) seventh Baronet, in 1841. Mrs.
Elton had invited Thackeray to Clevedon Court in Somersetshire, a few miles
from Bristol, where she and her husband lived with the latter's father, Sir
Charles Abraham Elton (1778–1853), sixth Baronet. Thackeray was greatly
taken with Clevedon Court, which he visited later in the month, and patterned
Castlewood Hall in *Esmond* after it. Some of the drawings that he made dur-
ing his stay have been privately printed in a brochure called *William Makepeace
Thackeray at Clevedon Court* (Bristol, n. d.).

[188] The Pattles.

[189] Thackeray wrote a few pages of *Pendennis* at Spa on August 3 and 4 and
then put the novel aside for more than two months. He set to work again upon
hearing the following story from Miss Eliza Smith, who afterwards repeated it
to Lady Ritchie (*Blackstick Papers*, pp. 127–128): "It concerned a family
living in Brighton, somewhere near Kemp Town. There was a somewhat
autocratic father and a romantic young son who had lost his heart to the housemaid and determined to marry her. The father made the young man give his
word of honour that he would not marry clandestinely, and then having dismissed him rang the bell for the butler. To the butler this Major Pendennis
said, 'Morgan' (or whatever his name was), 'I wish you to retire from my
service, but I will give you £200 in bank-notes if you will marry the housemaid
before twelve o'clock to-morrow.' The butler said, 'Certainly, sir,' and the
young man next morning was told of that which had occurred. As far as I
remember a melancholy and sensational event immediately followed; for the
poor young fellow was so overwhelmed that he rushed out and distractedly blew
his brains out on the Downs behind the house, and the butler meanwhile,
having changed his £200, sent a message to say that he had omitted to mention
that he had a wife already, and that this would doubtless invalidate the ceremony he had just gone through with the housemaid."

the last sentence; and crossed the i's & dotted the t's! It was written 4 hours ago before dinner; before Jullien's concert, before a walk by the sea shore — I have been thinking what a number of ladies, and gentlemen too, live like you just now — in a smart papered room with rats gnawing behind the Wainscot. Be hanged to the rats! but they are a sort of company. You must have a poker ready, and if the rats come out, bang, beat them on the head. This is an allegory. Why, it would work up into a little moral poem, if you chose to write it. Jullien [190] was splendid in his white waist-coat, and played famous easy music, w.h anybody may comprehend & like. There was a delightful cornet-à-piston (mark the ` on the a) — the fact is I am thinking about something else all the while. and very tired & weary — But I thought I would like to say good night to you: and what news shall I give you just for the last? Well then, Miss Virginia is gone away: not to come back while I am here. Good night, Mam if you please.

Madam I did not think about you one bit all yesterday, being entirely occupied with my 2 new friends M.rs Pendennis & her son M.r Arthur Pendennis. I got up very early again this morning and was with them for more than two hours before breakfast. He is a very good natured generous young fellow and I begin to like him considerably. I wonder whether he is interesting to me from selfish reasons and because I fancy we resemble each other in many points, [191] & whether I can get the public to like him too? We had

[190] Louis George Antoine Jules Jullien (1812–1860), the best known of Victorian concert masters.

[191] Lucy Baxter (*American Family*, pp. 5–6) reports the following conversation at her parents' home in New York during the winter of 1852–1853: "After dinner Mr. Thackeray often sat chatting while my sister was dressing for a ball to which he himself might be going. It was on one of these occasions that, turning over the leaves of 'Pendennis' as it lay on the table beside him, he said, smiling, from time to time:

" 'Yes, it is very like — it is certainly very like.'

" 'Like whom, Mr. Thackeray?' said my mother.

" 'Oh, like me, to be sure; Pendennis is very like me.'

" 'Surely not,' objected my mother, 'for Pendennis was so weak!'

" 'Ah, well, Mrs. Baxter,' he said, with a shrug of his great shoulders and a comical look, 'your humble servant is not very strong.' "

the most magnificent Sunshiny Sunday: and I passed the evening
very rationally with Mʳ Fonblanque, and Mʳ Sheil ¹⁹² — a great
orator of whom perhaps you have heard, at present lying here
afflicted with gout and with such an Irish wife.  Never was a truer
saying than that those people are foreigners — They have neither
English notions, manners, nor morals — I mean what is right &
natural to them is absurd and unreasonable to us.  It was as good
as Mʳˢ O'Dowd to hear Mʳˢ Sheil interrupt her Richard, and give
her opinions on the state of Ireland to those 2 great hard-headed
keen accomplished men of the world.  Richard listened to her
foolishness with admirable forbearance & good-humour — I'm
afraid I dont respect your sex enough though. — Yes I do when
they are occupied with loving & sentiment rather than with other
business of life.

I had a mind to send you a Weekly Paper, containing con-
temptuous remarks regarding an author of your acquaintance.  I
don't know who this critic is but he always has a shot at me once
a month, & I bet a guinea he is an Irishman.

So we have got the Cholera.  Are you looking out for a visit?
Did you try the Stethoscope?  and after listening at your chest did
it say that your lungs were sore? — A gentleman ⟨. . .⟩ ¹⁹³

514.                   TO MRS. BROOKFIELD
                       14 OCTOBER 1848

*Address:* Mʳˢ Brookfield | 15 Portman St.  Published in part, *Collection of
Letters*, pp. 23–25.

                   13 Young Sᵗ Kensington.   Saturday.
My dear lady Brookfield.

I wrote you a letter 3 nights ago in the French language, describing my disappointment at not having received any news of you
— Those wʰ I had from Mʳˢ Turpin ¹⁹⁴ (who had had a letter

---

¹⁹² Richard Lalor Sheil (1791–1851), who had married the heiress Mrs.
Anastasia Power in 1830.
¹⁹³ The concluding pages of this letter have not been preserved.
¹⁹⁴ Mrs. Turpin and Mrs. Payne were Mrs. Brookfield's maids.

from M<sup>rs</sup> Payne) were not good, and it would have been a pleasure to your humble Servant to have had a line.     Mr. Villiam dined with the children good naturedly on Sunday when I was yet away at Brighton. My parents are not come yet the old gentleman having had an attack of illness to w<sup>h</sup> he is subject, but they promise to be with me on Tuesday, that is, some day next week I hope. I virtuously refuse 3 invitations by this days post and keep myself in readiness to pass the first 2 or 3 evenings on my Papas lap — That night I wrote to you the French letter, I wrote one to Miss Brandauer the Governess warning her off — I didnt send either — I've a great mind to send your's though its rather funny, though I daresay with plenty of mistakes [195] — and written by quite a different man to the English man who is yours respectfully. A language I'm sure would change a man: so does a hand-writing I am sure if I wrote to you in this hand [196] and adopted it for a continuance my disposition & sentiments would alter and all my views of life — I tried to copy (not now but the other day) a letter Miss Procter showed me from her Uncle in a commercial hand and found myself after 3 pages quite an honest regular stupid commercial man. Such is sensibility — and the mimetic faculty in some singularly organized beings — How many people are you? You are M<sup>r</sup> Packmans M<sup>rs</sup> B and M<sup>r</sup> Jackson's [197] M<sup>rs</sup> B and ah you are my M<sup>rs</sup> B (You know you are, now) and quite different to us all, and you are your sisters M<sup>rs</sup> B and Miss Wynne's — and you make gentle fun of us all round to your own private B, and offer us up to make him sport You see I am making you out to be an Ogre's wife and poor William the Ogre to whom you serve us up cooked for dinner — Well stick a knife into me, here is my busam. I wont cry out — you poor Ogre's wife — I know you are good natured and soft hearted au fond.

[195] This letter has not been preserved.

[196] This sentence is written thus far in a large slanting hand; the rest of the letter is in Thackeray's customary upright hand.

[197] The Rev. John Jackson (1811–1885), at this time Rector of St. James's, Piccadilly and later Bishop of Lincoln (1853–1868) and Bishop of London (1868–1885); Charlotte Williams Wynn (1807–1869), the friend of Carlyle and Maurice.

I have been rereading the Hoggarty Diamond this morning —
upon my word and honour if it does not make you cry I shall have
a mean opinion of you. It was written at a time of great affliction, [198]
when my heart was very soft and humble. Amen. Ich habe auch
viel geliebt — and after all I see on reading over my books, that
the woman I have been perpetually describing is not you nor my
mother but that poor little wife of mine, who now does not care
$2^d$ for anything but her dinner and her glass of porter. [199]

How do you like your's? Why shouldn't I set off this instant
to the G.W. Station, and come and shake hands and ask your
family for some dinner? — I should like it very much — Well. I
am looking out of [the] window to see if the˙ rain will stop or give
me an excuse for not going to Hatton to the Chief Baron — I wont
go. Thats a comfort.

I am writing to $W^m$. to ask him to come and dine tomorrow —
we will drink your health if he comes. I should like to take another
sheet and go on tittle tattling: it drops off almost as fast as talking,
I fancy you lying on the sofa and the boy outside walking up & down
the hoss — but I wont. Tomorrow is Sunday. Good bye dear lady:
and believe me yours in the most friendly manner.

W M T.

[198] *The Great Hoggarty Diamond* was published from September to December, 1841, in *Fraser's Magazine*. It was written during the previous spring
and summer.

[199] Compare chapter 47 of *Vanity Fair* in which Thackeray describes the
madness of Lord George Gaunt: ". . . the brilliant dandy diplomatist of the
Congress of Vienna . . . forgot . . . wife, children, love, ambition, vanity.
But he remembered his dinner-hour, and used to cry if his wine-and-water was
not strong enough." (*Works*, I, 459)

515.    TO THE REV. WILLIAM BROOKFIELD
              18? OCTOBER 1848 [200]

Published in *Collection of Letters*, pp. 28–30.

> Refawrum.

My dear Reverence. I take up the pen to congratulate you on the lovely weather w^h must (with the company of those to whom you are attached) render your stay at Clevedon so delightful. It snowed here this morning: since w^h there has been a fog succeeded by a drizzly rain. I have passed the day reading & trying to alter Pendennis w^h is without any manner of doubt awfully stupid — the very best passages w^h pleased the author only last week, looking hideously dull by the dull fog of this day. I pray I pray that it may be the weather: will you say something for it at Church next Sunday. My old parents arrived last night. It was quite a sight to see the poor old Mother with the children. And Bradbury the printer coming to dun me for Pendennis this morning, I slunk away from home where working is an utter impossibility and have been operating on it here. The real truth is now, that there is 1/2 an hour before dinner: and I dont know what to do unless I write you a Screed to pass away the time. There are secret & selfish motives in the most seemingly generous actions of men.

Tother day I went to Harley Street and saw the most beautiful pair of embroidered slippers worked for a lady, at whose feet I &c — and I begin more and more to think Adelaide Procter an uncommonly nice dear good girl. Old Dilke of the Athenæum vows that Procter & his wife between them wrote Jane Eyre and when I protest ignorance says 'Pooh you know who wrote it. You are the deepest rogue in England &c — I wonder whether it can be true? It is just possible and then what a singular circumstance is the x fire of the two dedications. [201] O, mong Jew, but I wish

---

[200] The Carmichael-Smyths planned to arrive on Tuesday, October 17 (see above, No. 514); this letter was probably written the following day.

[201] See above, No. 440 and No. 481.

Pendennis were better. As if I had not enough to do I have begun
to blaze away in the Chronicle again [202] — it is an awful bribe that
5 guineas an article — After I saw you on Sunday I did actually
come back straight on the omnibus. I have been to the Cyder
Cellars since again to hear the man sing about going to be hanged.[203]
I have had a headache afterwards. I have drawn. I have written
— I have distracted my mind with healthy labour. Now wasn't this

[202] Thackeray continued to write for *The Morning Chronicle* until after
November 28 (see below, Nos. 527 and 528), but I have identified none of
his contributions during these weeks.

[203] The following account of Ross of the Cider Cellars and his song of "Sam
Hall," introduced into chapter 30 of *Pendennis* as Mr. Hodgen and "The Body
Snatcher," is taken from David Masson's *Memories of London in the Forties*
(pp. 153–155): "The evening is pretty far advanced; and the supping groups
at the crowded tables, grey heads and literary celebrities among them, have
composed themselves in a lull following previous songs, for the appearance of
the great Ross. He makes his appearance at last, in a kind of raised box or
pulpit in one corner of the room; — a strange gruesome figure, in ragged
clothes, with a battered old hat on his head, his face stained and grimed to
represent a chimney-sweep's, and a piece of short black pipe in his mouth.
Removing his pipe, and looking round with a dull, brutal scowl or glare, he
begins, as if half in soliloquy, half in address to an imaginary audience, his
slow chaunt of the condemned felon, whose last night in prison has come, and
who is to be hanged next morning: —

> " 'My name it is Sam Hall,
>        Chimney-sweep,
>        Chimney-sweep:
> My name it is Sam Hall,
>        Chimney-sweep.
> My name it is Sam Hall;
> I've robbed both great and small;
> And now I pays for all:
>        *Damn your eyes!*'

"Some three or four stanzas follow, in which the poor semi-bestial, illiterate,
and religionless wretch, in the same slow chaunt, as if to a psalm-tune, antici-
pates the incidents of the coming morning; — the arrival of the sheriffs, the
arrival of the hangman, the drive to Tyburn; each stanza, however heart-
broken, ending with the one ghastly apostrophe which is the sole figure of
speech that life-long custom has provided for his soul's relief. Thus: —

> " 'And the parson he will come,
>        He will come,
>        He will come:
> And the parson he will come,

## Mr. Pips his Diary.

SATURDAY, March 10th, 1849.—To Drury Lane this evening, to see the Horsemanship, which did divert me mightily; but had rather it had been at Astley's. After that, to Supper at the Cider Cellars in Maiden Lane, wherein was much Company, great and small, and did call for Kidneys and Stout, then a small glass of *Aqua-vitæ* and water, and thereto a Cigar. While we supped, the Singers did entertain us with Glees and comical Ditties; but oh, to hear with how little wit the young sparks about town are tickled! But the thing that did most take me was to see and hear one ROSS sing the song of SAM HALL the chimney-sweep, going to be hanged: for he had begrimed his muzzle to look unshaven, and in rusty black clothes, with a battered old Hat on his crown and a short Pipe in his mouth, did sit upon the platform, leaning over the back of a chair: so making believe that he was on his way to Tyburn. And then he did sing to a dismal Psalm-tune, how that his name was SAM HALL, and that he had been a great Thief, and was now about to pay for

all with his life; and thereupon he swore an Oath, which did make me somewhat laugh, though divers laughed at it. Then, in so many verses, how his Master had badly taught him and now he must hang for it, how he should ride up Holborn Hill in a Cart, and the Sheriffs would come and preach to him, and after them would come the Hangman; and at the end of each verse he did repeat his Oath. Last of all, how that he should go up to the Gallows; and desired the Prayers of his Audience, and ended by cursing them all round. Methinks it had been a Sermon to a Rogue to hear him, and I wish it may have done good to some of the Company. Yet was his cursing very horrible, albeit to not a few it seemed a high Joke; but I do doubt that they understood the song. After SAM HALL, to pay for my Supper, which cost me 2s. 2d., besides 4d. to the Waiter; and then home in a Cab, being late, and I fearing to anger my Wife, which cost me 2s. more; but I grudged not the money, having been much diverted, and so to bed.

MANNERS·AND·CVSTOMS·OF·Yᵉ·ENGLYSHE·IN·1849.    Nᵒ I.

A·CYDERE·CELLARE·DVRYNG·A·COMYCK·SONGE.

### ANOTHER BANKRUPT PIER.

WE regret to perceive that a cruel attempt has been made to drag no less a member of the Pierage than the Herne Bay Pier into the Court of Bankruptcy. The noble defaulter gallantly excused himself on the ground of his not being a trader, and thus the *dolce far niente*, or fact of there being "nothing doing," has at last proved beneficial to his interests. We are glad that the Herne Bay Pier has been spared this ignominy, for it would have been shameful to break him up into dividends, shiver his old timbers, and melt down his old iron into something like a farthing in the pound, at a time when its prospects are beginning to brighten.

It may be said of Herne Bay, as of many others of a retiring and secluded nature, that it has only to be known to be admired; and we must confess, that since we have become better acquainted with Herne Bay, we have been much struck by its quiet unobtrusive attractions, which make any one glad to see it again, who has once paid it a visit. We trust the noble Pier will be able to keep its head above water; and we have little doubt of such a result, for the number of its friends increases every year; and we hope to see its coffers filled with something better than water, which, when they have been under repair, has too often flowed into them.

### AN OXFORD BONFIRE.

OXFORD is "flaring up" again with a vengeance. The following paragraph is extracted from the *Morning Post:*—

"SUPPRESSION OF HETERODOXY IN OXFORD.—We are informed that a work, recently published by MR. FROUDE, M.A., Fellow of Exeter College, entitled *The Nemesis of Truth*, was a few days since publicly burned by the authorities in the College Hall."

We have never read MR. FROUDE's book. Possibly it may be a very bad one. If so, the learned authorities had better have left it alone. Or, at least, to have publicly refuted it would have been wiser than to have publicly burned it. The blaze of such fires is conspicuous. Oxford ought to know that candles thus lighted are sometimes not easily put out. Really, the University ought to be ashamed of this remarkably mediæval proceeding. It is fortunate for MR. FROUDE that Oxford can only burn books. Had it the unlimited power of fire and faggot, we are afraid that "FROUDE's Remains" would at present be a heap of cinders.

Printed by William Bradbury, of No. 13, Upper Woburn Place, in the Parish of St Pancras, and Frederick Mullett Evans of No. 7, Church Row, Stoke Newington, both in the County of Middlesex, Printers, at their Office in Lombard Street, in the Precinct of Whitefriars, in the City of London, and Published by them at No. 85, Fleet Street, in the Parish of St. Bride, in the City of London.—SATURDAY, MARCH 17th, 1849.

"A CYDERE CELLARE DURYING A COMYCK SONGE"

*From* Punch, *March 17, 1849*

much better than plodding about with you in heavy boots amidst fields and woods?

But, unless you come back, and as soon as my work is done I think a day or two might be pleasantly spent in your society, if the house of Clevedon admits of holding any more. [204] Does Harry Hallam go out with dog & gun? I should like to come & see him

shoot, and in fact get up field sports through him and others  Do you remark all that elaborate shading the shot &c? — all that has been done to while away the time until dinner's ready: and upon my conscience I believe it is very near come — Yes it is 6 1/2.

> He will come.
> And the parson he will come,
> And he'll look so blasted glum;
> And he'll talk of Kingdom Come:
>         *Damn his eyes!*'

"The last stanza of all will be addition enough: —

> " 'And now I goes upstairs,
>         To the drop,
>         To the drop:
> And now I goes upstairs,
>         To the drop;
> And now I goes upstairs,
> There's a hend to all my cares:
> So you'll tip me all your prayers:
>         *Damn your eyes!*' "

[204] Thackeray was at Clevedon Court by Wednesday, October 26, and he remained there until the following Monday.

If M^{rs} Parr ²⁰⁵ is at Clevedon present the respects of Mephis-
topheles as also to any other persons with whom I am acquainted
in your numerous and agreeable family circle.


516.        TO WILLIAMS AND NORGATE? ²⁰⁶
                24 OCTOBER 1848

Hitherto unpublished.

                            13 Young S^t Kensington Sq^r
                                24 October 1848.

Gentlemen

I have received your cheque and the obliging letter from M^r
Tauchnitz both of w^h I acknowledge with thanks.

Mess^{rs} Bradbury & Evans will send you proofs of my little story
'The Great Hoggarty Diamond' w^h I shall be glad to see published
by M^r Tauchnitz, and shall trust to him for the terms.

My story of Pendennis now commences, ²⁰⁷ I hope it will turn
out as well as its predecessor —

                    Very faithfully your Servt
                    W M Thackeray —


517.        TO EDWARD CHAPMAN
                25 OCTOBER 1848

Hitherto unpublished.

                        Clevedon Court. Clevedon Somerset.
                        Wednesday
                        I leave on Saturday this place for
                        Oxford.

My dear Chapman.

The events abroad ²⁰⁸ make Lady Kickleburys Tour much too
serious — We must have Doctor Birch and his young friends or

---

²⁰⁵ Julia Elizabeth Elton (d. 1881), Mrs. Brookfield's oldest sister, had married Thomas Clements Parr (1804?–1863), a wealthy barrister, in 1836.
²⁰⁶ Baron Tauchnitz's British agents. See below, No. 801.
²⁰⁷ Number I for November, chapters 1 to 3.
²⁰⁸ The revolutions in Germany that followed the French Revolution of February, 1848.

some such title — I am drawing & French master in the school & will make some fun of it.

I have brought a lot of blocks into the country to do them: but I believe that the soft point would be the thing after all, with the aid of my friend Marvy.

At any rate I pray you to send a steel-plate big enough for 4 of the drawings to M^r Marvy 16. Berners St. I am sure we shall do them better than the wood — I could do 4 of a day easily, & he would have them bitten in no time — They could be transferred to the lithographic stone myriads could be printed &c.

But hark I hear the bell w^h calls to lunch.

and am yours ever

W M Thackeray.

I have some doz designs of D^r Birchs done, [209] & think them good odd & new.

[For a fragment of a letter to Mrs. Brookfield, October, 1848, see letter 3, Appendix XXVI.]

518.　　　　　　TO MRS. BROOKFIELD
　　　　　　　　　1 NOVEMBER 1848

Published in part, *Collection of Letters*, pp. 31–33.

Dear M^rs Brookfield. I was at Oxford [210] by the time your dinner was over, and found eight or nine jovial gentlemen in black feasting in the common-room, and drinking Port wine solemnly. I found there my friend whom I mistook for the man of the train and they are indeed very much alike, and I emused the society by telling them of the event w^h had just occurred — We had a great sitting of Port wine, and I daresay the evening was pleasant enough

I was thinking of the last 4 or 5 days — I think I've never

[209] Mrs. Brookfield appears to have served as the model for Thackeray's drawings of Miss Raby in *Dr. Birch and his Young Friends*.

[210] Where he was invited by his friend Charles Neate, for whom see below, No. 531.

known any happier ones: and intend to love that dear old Clevedon for all the days of my life — They gave me a bed in college, such a bed, I could not sleep: but I hope you did well after that long journey and all those blunders and delays and agitations — Yester-  day (for this is 7 1/2 o'clock in the morning would you believe it?) a party of us drove in an Oxford cart to Blenheim: where we saw some noble pictures — a portrait by Raphael — one of the great Raphaels of the world (look this is College paper with beautiful lines already made) a series of magnificent Rubens, — one of w^h representing himself walking in a garden with M^rs Rubens and the Babby, did one good to look at and remember, and some very questionable Titians indeed (I mean on the score of authenticity not of morals though the sub- jects are taken from the loves of those extraordinary Gods & Goddesses mentioned in Lempriere's Dictionary) and we walked in the Park with much profit surveying the great copper-coloured trees, and the glum old bridge and pillar and Rosamonds Well, and the queer grand ugly but magnificent house — a piece of splen- did barbarism, yet grand and imposing somehow, like a chief raddled over with war-paint and attired with careful hideousness — well I cant make out the simile on paper though it is in my own mind pretty clear. What you would have liked best was the Chapel dedicated to God & the Duke of Marlborough — the monu- ment to the latter occupies the whole place almost so that the Former is quite secondary. O what comes! — It was the Scout who brought me your letter, and I am very much obliged to you for it, and very sorry indeed to hear that you have been ill and in pain. Shall I set off this instant and come to Portman S^t? — it is only about 2 1/2 hours off. No — you wouldn't let me in. I will  come on Friday. I was afraid the Journey would agitate you. That was what I was thinking of as I was lying in the Oxford man's bed awake. After Blenheim I went to Magdalen Chapel to a High Mass there — O Cherubim and Seraphim, how you would like it! The Chapel is the most sumptuous edifice carved & frittered

MRS. BROOKFIELD AT THE AGE OF THIRTY
*From a painting by George Richmond*

all over with the richest stone work like the lace of a lady's boudoir — the windows are filled with pictures of the Saints painted in a grey colour real Catholic Saints male & female I mean so that I wondered how they got there: and this makes a sort of rich twilight in the Church, w^h is lighted up by a multitude of wax candles in gold sconces: and you say your prayers in carved stalls wadded with velvet cushions. They have a full chorus of boys some two dozen I should think; who sing quite ravishingly. It is a sort of perfection of sensuous gratification: Childrens voices charm me so that they set all my sensibilities into a quiver — do they you? I am sure they do. These pretty brats with sweet innocent faces and white robes sang quite celestially, no not celestially — for I don't believe it is devotion at all: but a high delight out of w^h one comes not im- purified I hope: but with a thankful pleased gentle frame of mind. I suppose I have a great faculty of enjoyment — At Clevedon I had gratification in looking at trees landscapes effects of shine and shadow &c — w^h made that dear old inspector who walked with me wonder — well, there can be no harm in these I'm sure — What a shame it is to go on bragging about what is after all sheer roaring good health for the most part — O my dear lady that you could be well — And now I'm going to breakfast. Gby I have been lionizing the town ever since, and am come home quite tired I have break- fasted here lunched at X^t Church seen Merton and All Souls with Norman Macdonald [211] where there is a beautiful library and a boar's head in the kitchen over w^h it was good to see Normans eyes gloating: and it being All Saints day am going to Chapel here: where they have also a very good music I am told. Are you better Mam? I hope you are. On Friday I hope to have the pleasure to see you: and am till then and even till Saturday yours

W M T.

[211] Norman Hilton Macdonald (1807?–1857), Fellow of All Souls College, Oxford, from 1827 until his death.

519.                    TO MRS. PROCTER
                       1 NOVEMBER 1848

Hitherto unpublished. My text is taken from a transcript given Lady Ritchie
by George Murray Smith.

                                        St John's College,
                                           Oxford.
                                        Nov. 1, 1848.

My dear Mrs Procter,

Well, it is wonderful what a clever young person Miss Procter
is: for I have written you a long letter in four tight little pages
and it's before me now, but I am going to pop it into the fire and
not into the post: for it seems to me flippant and annoying. Are
you better? I hope so indeed. I come to town on Friday too with
Punch (which is getting perfectly odious to me) and next day hope
to come and see how Harley Street looks — cheerful I trust. I
have been lionizing all day, and am working in the dark, just
before Chapel time — but I have mentioned all this in the other
letter which I don't send.

Also I said how happy I had been at Clevedon, and what a dear
place it was and what kind people, and there was a sketch of the
place, — well, you shall have the sketch taken out of the letter —
(he cuts the drawing out of the other letters and burns the rest).
There now, isn't it handsome? — and there's my picture on the
other side too — which do you think is the prettiest? It is really
pitch dark, and I only write one word to show that I had not forgotten the Upper Arley Street in the midst of my wanderings and
pleasures.

Be well by Saturday, and believe me always yours and Miss
Adelaide's (what a clever girl she is)

                                        W. M. T.
                       [sketch]

520.       TO MRS. BROOKFIELD
NOVEMBER 1848 [212]

Published in part, *Collection of Letters*, pp. 7–8. The words between daggers were overscored by Mrs. Brookfield.

Madam       Although I am certainly committing a breach of confidence I venture to offer my friend up to you [213] because you have considerable humour and I think will possibly laugh at him. You know you yourself often hand over some folks to some other folks: and deserve to be treated as you treat others.

The cirkimstance arose out of a letter w^h H sent me containing prodigious compliments I answered that these praises (from all quarters) frightened me rather than elated me, and sent him a drawing for a lady's album with a caution not to ask for any more. Hence the reply. Ah Madam how much richer truth is than fiction, and how great that phrase about the inner circles is!

I write from the place from w^h I heard your little voice last night, I mean this morning, at who knows how much oclock? I wonder whether you will laugh as much as I do: my Papa in the next room must think me insane. But I'm not, and am of Madam the serviteur and frère affectionné

**W M T.**

[212] Mrs. Brookfield (*Collection of Letters*, p. 7) assigns this letter to 1847. That it belongs rather to 1848 is evident not only from its intimate tone but also from Thackeray's reference to Major Carmichael-Smyth, who was staying with him in London in November, 1848, but not in 1847.

[213] Thackeray's letter is written on the third and fourth pages of the following note:

Temple    Nov 5

My dear Thackeray

A thousand thanks — It will do admirably, & I will not trouble you again in the same manner. Don't get nervous, or think about criticism, or trouble yourself about the opinions of friends. You have completely beaten Dickens out of the inner circle already.

I dine at Gore House today — Look in if you can —
Ever Yours<br>A. Hayward.

Tell (if you please) your cousin Arry that it is Miss Justice
† Wightman † and not Miss Justice † Wigram † who is attached
to me, [214] so that he need be under no alarm. Miss W is a dear
pretty clever creature and when we are united I will send you a
large piece of cake.


521.          TO ROBERT STEPHEN RINTOUL
                    6 NOVEMBER 1848

*Address:* S. Rintoul, Esq. | Wellington St. | Strand. *Postmark:* NO. 6 1848.
Hitherto unpublished.

                                        Monday. 6 Nov.ʳ
My dear Rintoul.

I was thinking this morning in bed, I wonder whether the Spectator has said anything about Pendennis? [215] I wonder whether
he likes it or whether he doesn't? Whether I have no imagination
or whether he is wrong? Either is possible — But one thing is
quite certain that he'll speak honestly whever way he thinks.

Then I remembered how on my return from Brighton I found
2 invitations to eat Scotch venison with you, and that the venison
was eaten several days before I knew of it, or was come back: and
lest you should have made any assault upon the author, and before
I read the Spectator (wh I am going now to Jacob Omnium's to
do) I thought it my duty though rather late in the day to be sure,
to thank you & your Son for the invitation

                              Always yours sincerely
                              W M Thackeray


[214] Miss Wightman was the daughter of Sir William Wightman (1784–
1863), Judge of the Queen's Bench from 1841 until his death; Miss Wigram
of Sir James Wigram (1793–1866), Vice-Chancellor from 1841 to 1850.
[215] Rintoul's impression of the first number of *Pendennis* was decidedly favorable. He felt that it was even more promising than the early chapters of
*Vanity Fair.* (*Spectator*, November 4, p. 1070)

522.          TO MRS. BROOKFIELD
              9 NOVEMBER 1848

Hitherto unpublished.  My text is taken from a transcript made by Mrs. Fuller.

Dear Madam, If you please have I left my pocket book on
your drawing-room table?  I should be glad to receive it if so: as
it contains some MS w.<sup>h</sup> I want.  It is a nice purple little book with
a gilt clasp — given me by one who — but away with recollections.
I have been walking with her to day and she is — ruined.  I mean
the bank in India is broke, and I fear My dear good kind Mrs.
P. [216] has lost a great deal of money. *She* wouldn't be angry if I
called her a good f-ll-w.

Should you like to see me lampooned in a novel? [217]  I found

---

[216] Mrs. Procter.
[217] In chapter 22 of Lever's *Roland Cashel*, which first appeared in number
VII of that novel, published for November, 1848, there is to be found the following caricature of Thackeray: "Mr. Elias Howle was one of a peculiar class,
which this age, so fertile in inventions, has engendered — a publisher's man-
of-all-work, ready for everything, from statistics to satire, and equally prepared
to expound prophecy or write squibs for *Punch*. . . . Mr. Howle . . . was
the creator of that new school of travel which, writing expressly for London
readers, refers everything to the standard of 'town'; and whether it be a trait
of Icelandic life, or some remnant of old-world existence in the far East, all
must be brought for trial to the bar of 'Seven Dials,' or stand to plead in the
dock of Pall Mall or Piccadilly.  Whatever errors or misconceptions he might
fall into respecting his subjects, he made none regarding his readers.  He knew
them by heart — their leanings, their weakness, and their prejudices; and how
pleasantly could he flatter their town-bred self-sufficiency — how slyly insinuate
their vast superiority over all other citizens, insidiously assuring them that the
Thames at Richmond was infinitely finer than the Rhine or the Danube, and
that a trip to Margate was richer in repayal than a visit to the Bosphorus!
Ireland was . . . a splendid field for his peculiar talents. . . . 'this inspired
Cockney' determined . . . not to counsel nor console, not to lament over nor
bewail our varied mass of errors and misfortunes, but to laugh at us.  To hunt
out as many incongruities — many real enough, some fictitious — as he could
find; to unveil all that he could discover of social anomaly; and, without any
reference to, or any knowledge of, the people, to bring them up for judgment
before his less volatile and more happily circumstanced countrymen, certain of
the verdict he sought for — a hearty laugh.  His mission was to make 'Punch'
out of Ireland, and no one was more capable for the office.
"A word of Mr. Howle in the flesh, and we have done.  He was large and

one on my return home last night with a notice from a dimgood-
natured friend — in w.ʰ Harry Lorrequer has paid me off for jokes
upon him. He is very savage and evidently hurt. This is rather
good coming 2 days after the announcement in the Chronicle that
I was a "Satirist without an enemy" ? [218] I'll send that to Lever I
think. Well, it only made me laugh.

Why do I give a shilling to a messenger to carry this when there
is plenty of time before dinner to go with my own message? I am
now going to meet the Spectator, [219] a lawyer of repute and the
Journal des Débats at dinner here, and afterwards to — to Mrs.
Lane Fox's

I remain dear Sir or Madam

Yours always<br>W M T.

523.          TO MRS. BROOKFIELD
              NOVEMBER 1848

Hitherto unpublished. Mrs. Fuller's transcript of this letter, the original of
which is in French, is not accessible, but she has supplied me with the translation printed below.

Your little letter, madame, has given me such pleasure. When
I came in, long after midnight, I found a good many letters. I

---

heavily built, but neither muscular nor athletic; his frame and all his gestures
indicated weakness and uncertainty. His head was capacious, but not remarkable for what phrenologists call moral development, while the sinister expression
of his eyes — half submissive, half satirical — suggested doubts of his sincerity.
There was nothing honest about him but his mouth; this was large, full, thick-
lipped, and sensual — the mouth of one who loved to dine well, and yet feel
that his agreeability was an ample receipt in full for the best entertainment that
ever graced Blackwall or the 'Freres'." (*Novels of Charles Lever*, ed. by his
Daughter, 37 vols., London, 1897–99, XIV, 264–265)

[218] The brief notice of the first number of *Pendennis* in *The Morning
Chronicle* of November 7, 1848, concludes with the words: "We scarcely feel
it is necessary to wish this popular *censor morum* — this 'satirist without an
enemy' — success. We feel that he has the power to command it."

[219] The journalists were Robert Stephen Rintoul and John Lemoinne. The
lawyer is not easy to identify, for Thackeray had many well-known legal friends.

waited till I was in bed. Then I began reading them, and when I came to the last I saw, Oh joy! that it was from you. Why do a few words written by you give me such pleasure? The unexpected note lightened my solitude, as did a certain dear voice one evening at Clevedon. Oh! how happy I was there! I shall always love that delightful place.

Because you have been so kind, because I have enjoyed a quiet peaceful night, and woke to joy, I said to myself this morning, 'Why not go past her window, and call out Good Day? But will my lady know who it is who is riding past her window?'

As your little notes do me so much good, try and write oftener to me, madame. You are so kind — surely you won't refuse a drop of water (to one who dwells in the desert)? I wonder if you remember the day we talked of death. I thought of myself as damned, and of you as an angel full of pity. Surely you will be able to make your way to me (wherever I may be) and give me one of your sweet smiles? I long for you to give me your blessing, my angel. When you look at me, when you think of me, I am in paradise.

My mother, dear good woman that she is, loves you. We talked of you a long time this morning. Oh, why are you always ailing, while we, who deserve nothing, are always well.

We talked of you so often on Saturday. I fell into a panic; I feared you were far more ill than you are, thank God (Yes, thank God, my dear suffering friend). I spent a fearful day, full of wretched anxiety. And then, in the evening, I came to see you. Oh, how relieved I felt to see you happy, smiling, with your husband close to you. You were good to me. You always are, excepting when you feel I'm not to be trusted.

I went to see dear old FitzGerald yesterday. I have cared for him tenderly and with a noble affection for twenty years. When we first became friends I had not learnt to love a woman.

Shall I send you this letter? I've carried it about in my pocket (for a long time). It was there when I came to see you on Saturday; now and again I read it over and add a few lines. I feel when I write that I am talking to you. I can say anything on paper.

I long to tell someone, anyone, that I love you. Why shouldn't I tell you, or William? My heart is so full, and why should I feel ashamed of what is on my part a tender pure friendship? I am proud of my feeling for you. And you, dear lady, do trust me.

524.        TO DAVID ROBERTS
            14 NOVEMBER 1848

Hitherto unpublished.

                                        13 Young S$^t$ Kensington. Nov. 14
My dear Roberts

A French artist-engraver [220] one of the very best creatures I ever knew of that or any nation has just found a job here to do w$^h$ will keep him honorably during the next 18 months of his countrys misrule. He has engaged to supply 20 sketch-engravings (etching aquatint soft-point &c mixed) of so many landscapes and I want to know will you let him do one from you? I thought if he might copy that one in the G Smoking room (that & Stanfields to whom I write too) they w$^d$ be good subjects and help him famously on. Creswick [221] has given him his choice of many quite delighted with a Constable w$^h$ he has done. And if you can aid in this good work without detriment to yourself my dear Roberts you will very much oblige

                            Yours most sincerely
                            W M Thackeray.

[220] Louis Marvy.
[221] Thomas Creswick (1811–1869), the landscape painter.

525.            TO EDWARD CHAPMAN
                  22 NOVEMBER 1848

Hitherto unpublished.

Nov.͏ʳ 22.

Dear Chapman

The Elias Howle affair [222] will make a good Author's Misery for Punch — It didn't annoy me a bit farther than to think that a man who was once very kind to me and I believe fond of me, should have committed himself so far. To make remarks about my person, the honesty or dishonesty of my appearance can't injure me — I have pushed the caricaturing of myself almost to affectation — but it wont profit Lever to gibbet a rival in that way. 'Snooks in the Holy land' [223] is quite fair that is to say my sort of writing carried to the absurd — that is what I was trying to do in those parodies in Punch one of w.ʰ [224] I suppose has got me the Howle rejoinder —

And so let us give his old sowl
A howl
For twas he got the noggin to rowl.

I suppose that's the meaning — and thought already in another number of Roland Cashel I detected a shot against myself.

I cant make it a condition of my liking for a man that I should like his books or praise them not liking them. I never could bring myself to consider Lever seriously as an author, but thought him one of the most charming and agreeable men I ever met in my life. I know for my part that a man may like my writing or not, and I don't care a straw, at least I think not.

Out of those Punch parodies I left his bad French w.ʰ is one of

[222] See above, No. 522. The "Author's Misery" inspired by Lever's attack is "Mr. Tims and a Good-natured Friend," *Punch*, December 2, 1848 (*Works*, VI, 747).
[223] Lever introduces Howle as "the author of *Snooks in the Holy Land*, the wittiest thing of the day" (*Novels of Charles Lever*, XIV, 266), a fling at *Notes of a Journey from Cornhill to Grand Cairo*.
[224] "Phil Fogarty. A Tale of the Fighting Onety-Oneth. By Harry Rollicker," *Punch*, August 7–21, 1847. For the song, see *Works*, VI, 491.

the great points a caricaturist would not fail to seize — in fact it was with the gloves I was sparring    I am very sorry he has taken them off. If caricaturing with the pencil is, as I hold it, quite fair, why not that with the pen? Lever has a right to by far the greater part of his attack on me — all but the sheer personality of w.ʰ I am sorry and annoyed to hear a man use, as one would be if a gentleman in public suddenly used bad language. It is not the person assailed but the assailant one feels for. Somebody should tell him that such behaviour will hurt him without in the least injuring me.

If he has had his fire and is content — I wonder whether he will be able to understand that it is not out of fear of future castigation that I am ready to shake hands with him? Fancy a literary war in w.ʰ a man descends to describing odious personal peculiarities in his rival! What I think you might do is to warn him at least to stop — Why, he doesnt write English let alone French and German — and you as my publisher my friend and a gentleman are not called upon to have your house made the office for publishing this dreary personality. Make fun of my books, my style, my public works — but of me a gentleman — O for shame.

Ever yours dear Chapman<br>W M T.

526.    TO ARTHUR HUGH CLOUGH [225]
24 NOVEMBER 1848

*Address:* A. Clough Esq.ᵉ Hitherto unpublished.

13 Young S.ᵗ Kensington<br>26 Nov.ʳ

My dear M.ʳ Clough. I have been reading the Bothy [226] all the morning and am charmed with it. I have never been there

---

[225] Arthur Hugh Clough (1819–1861), whose religious scruples had caused him in October to give up the Fellowship at Oriel which he had held since 1842.

[226] Clough had just published *The Bothie of Tober-Na-Vuolich*, under its original title, *The Bothie of Toper-na-Fuosich: A Long-Vacation Pastoral.*

but I think it must be like Scotland — Scotland hexametrically laid out that is (Ive only got this sheet of paper & you see have been making exercises on it)* and it seems to me to give one the proper Idyllic feeling wʰ is 1/2 sensual & 1/2 spiritual I take it — serene beauty awakening pleasant meditation — what is it? — Your description of the Sky & the landscape — and that figure of the young fellow bathing shapely with shining limbs and the blue blue sky for a background — are delightful to me — I can imagine to myself the Goddess of bathing in a sort of shimmer under the water — Was it as clear as Rosamond's Well? [227] — I have been going over some of the same ground (of youth) in this present number of Pendennis: wʰ I fear will be considered rather warm by the puritans: but I think you'll understand it — that is if you care for such trivialities, or take the trouble to look under the stream of the story.

I must tell you that I was very much pleased indeed by your sending me the book, and dont mind owning that I took a great liking to you. When you come to London I hope you will come and see me. Mʳˢ Pendennis is living with me (She is my mother) and I have a couple of little girls whom you shall hear read if you like.

I owe Neate [228] a letter about his Dialogues but the fact is — that I have only last night finished my work and lazing in bed this morning Your poem arrived in wʰ I read as far as the Goddess of Bathing, and thought I would write off at once at a heat.

Faithfully yours

W M Thackeray.

* [Here appears, written in a minute hand: "This is not fair really now, for it is wrote with a magnifying glass. But *this* is with the naked i." ]

[227] "Fair Rosamond's Well" is in the grounds of Blenheim Castle, and figures romantically in Scott's *Woodstock*, chap. xviii, where Alice Lee goes to fetch a pitcher of water from "a spring, supposed to be peculiarly pure." Cf. *The Bothie*, canto iii.

[228] Neate (1806–1879) was educated at the Collège Bourbon in Paris, where Sainte-Beuve was his schoolfellow, and at Lincoln College, Oxford. He passed the rest of his life as a Fellow of Oriel College, serving as Drummond Professor

527.                TO LADY CASTLEREAGH [229]
                    28 NOVEMBER 1848

Hitherto unpublished.

Kensington. Nov. 28

Dear Lady Castlereagh. Surely it is time to answer the kindest letter from the kindest lady. I have been waiting day after day hoping to see my work so clear before me that I might say yes to your cordial offer of hospitality — but it seems to grow upon me, and I am tied here by 100 petty little obligations to printers engravers artists publishers & the like. Sometimes I have a mind to leave the fire with all the irons in it and fly altogether. But what will those anxious folks who come with little accounts at Xmas say? I must try & meet them with an honest countenance and a pocket full of money.

I'm sure that you and Lord Castlereagh will be glad to hear that the latter is increasing and multiplying considerably, and that M^r Pendennis makes me much richer than M^r Vanity Fair. And if I don't see your Ladyship I hope there's no offence in telling you

---

of Political Economy from 1857 to 1862. His interests were varied, for he was a barrister, a well-known steeple-chase rider, a good classical scholar, and a master of spoken and written French. When he was unseated for bribery (as Thackeray thought, unfairly) after being elected to parliament for Oxford in March, 1857, Thackeray stood in his place at a second election the following July (see Appendix XVIII). Neate was M. P. for Oxford from 1863 to 1868. He published *Dialogues des Morts: Guizot et Louis Blanc* at Oxford in 1848.

[229] Thackeray was for many years the intimate friend of the former Lady Elizabeth Frances Jocelyn (1813–1884), daughter of the third Earl of Roden and widow of the sixth Viscount Powerscourt, and of her second husband Frederick William Robert Stewart (1805–1872), styled Viscount Castlereagh, later (1854) fourth Marquess of Londonderry. Lord Castlereagh, a nephew of the famous Regency statesman, was one of the wealthiest noblemen in the United Kingdom, for the Londonderry estates realized an annual rent-roll of £100,118 in 1883 (Bateman, *Great Landowners*, p. 277). Most of his Irish property was in County Down, of which he was M. P. from 1826 to 1852 and Lord Lieutenant from 1845 to 1864. His death, it is stated in *The Times* (November 27, 1872), followed a "long seclusion, in consequence of mental illness." Lady Castlereagh became a Roman Catholic in 1855.

that I think about you very many times: that though you may be
ever so far off you can't prevent me from bearing your face in
mind; and that you and Castlereagh's great kindness & friendliness
makes me sincerely grateful. If I say too much about it I beg your
pardon: but I dont know for my part why we should hide honest
feelings, & cover up under a mask of sarcasm what is a great deal
better I mean peace & good will. If any man has reason to turn
good natured surely it is this present scribe, As I was writing to
Hayward the other day [230] the marks of kindness & sympathy I get
are so great now as to frighten rather than elate me — What are
we told to do when men praise us most: and isn't that the time
when a man should be most on his guard? — I shan't apologize for
writing in this tone — we have talked it here in London I think —
how curious men are! — this is not apologizing but apologizing for
apologizing — Brisons la dessus. What do you think of the world
now and where are we and at the beginning of what? — I should
like to have a nights talk about it with you & Milor over the fire
until when it came to bedtime we'd be terrified to take our candles.
Well I don't despair of knocking up at that once savage porter at
Powerscourt [231] and seeing him smile — How well I recollect the
place; the Dargle and a walk I had there with *one* of the truth-
telling men that I met in Ireland — Why will they pull the longbow so prodigiously?

Lady Ashburton [232] has sent me invitations as kind as yours. I
wrote to say that I had 3 books to launch & make the pictures for,
2 papers to write in constantly, [233] an Irish Railway call to meet,
my parents staying with me (I will be proud to show your ladyship a mother that I have, & to ask whether among all the Duchesses
& Empresses of this life there are many much finer ladies) — and
a sprained ankle — Lady A. believed all but the sprained ankle
that she said was a fib — why? — Why should one tell lies? I had

[230] I have not traced this letter.
[231] The Castlereaghs' country seat near Wicklow, which Thackeray had visited in September, 1842. See *Works*, V, 486–488.
[232] See *Memoranda*.
[233] The books were *Pendennis*, *Dr. Birch and his Young Friends*, and *The
Book of Snobs*; the papers, *Punch* and *The Morning Chronicle*.

much rather not have a sprain — it was the longbow that put me
in mind of this. Excuse this rambling: but I am writing dead beat
after a long day's labour—and as in the summer you may remember
I thought to myself after such another day, how pleasant it would
be just to see a certain friendly face, even so — at post time with
sheets of drawings & writings just turned off, I thought I would
like to say a word of acknowledgment and write my thanks & remembrances to Lady Castlereagh,

always most faithfully yours

W M Thackeray.

528.        FROM MRS. BROOKFIELD
        28 NOVEMBER 1848 [234]

Hitherto unpublished.

Tuesday Morng.

My dear Mʳ Thackeray,

  Will you send word how your foot is today — I am afraid it
was giving you a great deal of pain yesterday & I should be glad
to hear what the Surgeon said of it, but a message will do if it
should tire you to write — Why did you leave that odious Roland
Cashel behind you? I can hardly resist savagely tearing it up tho'
this wᵈ not make much difference to Mʳ Lever. I liked what you
said of his attack & should like him to see your letter to Mʳ Chapman — only that he is evidently too ungentlemanly himself to
understand an *opposite* character — it is underating yʳ French correspondent [235] to speak of Lever's as "un portrait assez fidèle" —
wᵈ you like a few notes added from a friend upon that point? I

---

[234] Mrs. Brookfield's letter was apparently written the Tuesday after Thackeray's letter to Chapman of Wednesday, November 22.

[235] Probably Philarète Chasles, for whom Thackeray had recently written a
short sketch of his early life (see below, No. 565). The manuscript of this
brief autobiography has not survived, but its gist is preserved in the opening
pages of Chasles's "Le Roman de Mœurs en Angleterre. La Foire aux
Vanités," *Revue des Deux Mondes*, February 15–March 1, 1849, pp. 537–
571 and 721–759.

never knew so much of y$^r$ history before & thank you for letting me read it — I thought it very affecting — I wonder if it always came naturally to you to relate things in that simple kind of way or whether it has been acquired — it is very touching when it is used in describing real misfortunes which other people are generally inclined to dress up — I hope to see you soon with y$^r$ foot quite well — & will you oblige me by burning Roland Cashel — I would not add what I was going to say  Goodbye — Ever yours

J. O. B.

529.                TO MRS. BROOKFIELD
                   29 NOVEMBER 1848

Published in *Collection of Letters*, pp. 33–34.

My dear lady  I am very much pained and shocked at the news brought at dinner to day that poor dear Charles Buller is gone. [236] Good God think about the poor Mother surviving and what an anguish that must be!  If I were to die I can't bear to think of my Mother living beyond me, as I daresay she will: but isn't it an awful awful sudden summons?  There go wit fame friendship ambition high repute. Ah aimons nous bien, it seems to me that is the only thing we can carry away. When we go let us have some who love us wherever we are. I send you this little line as I tell you & W$^m$ most things.  Good night.

[236] Thackeray commemorates the death of Charles Buller on November 29, 1848, in the "Epilogue" to *Dr. Birch and his Young Friends*:

> Who knows the inscrutable design?
> Blessed be He who took and gave:
> Why should your mother, Charles, not mine,
> Be weeping at her darling's grave?

530.                    TO MRS. BROOKFIELD
                       DECEMBER 1848? [237]

Published in part, *Collection of Letters*, pp. 125–126.

As I am waiting to see M^rs Buller I find an old review, with an advertisement in it containing a great part of an article I wrote about Fielding in 1840, in the Times. [238] Perhaps Madam will like to see it and M^r Williams.

My wife was just sickening at that moment. I wrote it at Margate where I had taken her and used to walk out 3 miles to a little bowling green and write there in an arbour — coming home and wondering what was the melancholy oppressing the poor little woman. The Times gave me 5 guineas for the article. I recollect I thought it rather shabby pay. and 12 days after it appeared in the paper, my poor little wife's malady showed itself by an attempt at suicide.

How queer it is to be carried back all of a sudden to that time, and all that belonged to it — and read this article over. Doesn't the apology for Fielding read like an apology for somebody else too? God help us. What a deal of cares and pleasures and struggles and happiness I have had since that day in the little sunshiny arbour where with scarcely any money in my pocket, & a crazy wife, and 2 little children (Minny was a baby 2 months old) I was writing this notice about Fielding. Grief, Love, Fame if you like — I have had no little of all since then — (I dont mean to take the Fame for more than it's worth, or brag about it with any peculiar elation) ⟨. . .⟩[239]

---

[237] It seems likely that this letter was written shortly after Charles Buller's death. Mrs. Buller died on March 13, 1849.

[238] "Fielding's Works," *The Times*, September 2, 1840; reprinted in *Stray Papers*, ed. Melville, pp. 103–112.

[239] The concluding pages of this letter have not been preserved.

531.       **TO CHARLES NEATE**
            7 DECEMBER 1848

Hitherto unpublished.

Kensington. Dec<sup>r</sup> 7. 1848.

Ce cher Neate se fache contre moi. Il croit que je l'oublie, que je le neglige — Eh bien, non Monsieur, voyez cet envelope sale — la superscription a été écrite depuis dix jours au moins, il contenoit une lettre longue drôle curieuse absurde passionnée — lettre que j'ai brulée, comme je brule beaucoup d'autres maintenant — ou je parle de souffrances que j'ai — d'horribles peines de coeur qui sans cesse me poursuivent. D'autres ont passé par la. Souffrons et taisons nous. Du courage Spartiate! — Si le rénard que tu as volé te ronge le sein — tiens le et ne parle pas. [240]

Voila que je récommence — c'est la troisieme lettre je vous assure que je vous fais — peut etre dois je bruler celle-ci encor. Pourquoi parler? Cest que je ne puis guère penser à autre chose, et ne puis parler que de ce qui me passe par le coeur. J'étois a moitié fou a Oxford. [241] Vous etiez tous si bons pour moi et cependant rien ne ne m'allait — Avec Clough sur le banc du *trap* sedebat atra Cura [242]

Je causais avec elle, tandis que vous autres me faisoient — bah. J'ai une horrible nouvelle a vous annoncer vos dialogues [243] mon ami et bien je les ai *perdus!* parole d'honneur. En quittant Oxford j'ai tâche de lire dans le petit livre     Je l'ai trouvé et brillant et spirituel et bien écrit — mais je n'ai pu continuer — Je pensais à autre chose vous dis je — J'y pense nuit et jour.

Votre lettre m'a beaucoup touché, je ne scais pourquoi — l'impression reste encor — ainsi qu'une grande amitié que je sens pour cet admirable Clough si bon et si tendre dont le poeme [244] m'a

---

[240] See Plutarch's life of Lycurgus (*Plutarch's Lives. The Translation Called Dryden's*, corrected and revised by Arthur Hugh Clough, 5 vols., London, 1859, I, 108), which Thackeray appears to have read in a French translation.

[241] See above, No. 519.

[242] Horace, *Odes*, III, i, 40.

[243] *Dialogues des Morts: Guizot et Louis Blanc*, which Neate had published at Oxford earlier in the year.     [244] *The Bothie of Toper-na-Fuosich.*

charmé, je lui avais déja écrit quand votre lettre est arrivée. Quel frais et délicieux poète, quel tresor d'homme cela doit etre! — Je veux le revoir, Bien mais bien des fois j'ai pensé a lui.

Ayez du courage, et renvoyez moi les Dialogues. Je n'écris pas le Francais par principes (vous le verrez bien vous qui connoisser la langue)     Je l'écris par coeur voyons si le votre vous dit de parler dans cette langue. A la fin du mois je vous lirai — quand j'aurai fini mes travaux.

Ah — tandis que je cause avec vous je pense a une autre — Elle ne m'aime pas. Elle me plaint. Adieu — Brulez ma lettre, vraiment je ne puis bruler d'avantage —

On me dit que les boys ont eu un debate a l'Union sur les Writings of Titmarsh — et qu'on l'a trouvé auteur moral. J'aurai voté le contraire moi — Je vous salue —

Yours

W M Thackeray.

## 532.      TO THE COUNT D'ORSAY
### DECEMBER 1848

My text is taken from a facsimile in Broadley's *Chats on Autographs*, p. 221.

My dear Count     This note has just come to hand, and You see I take the freedom with you of speaking the truth. I dont like this announcement [245] at all. Our Saviour & the Count Dorsay ought not to appear in those big letters. It somehow looks as if you and our Lord were on a par, and put forth as equal attractions by the publisher. Dont mind my saying this, for I'm sure this sort of announcement (merely on account of the unfortunate typography) is likely to shock many honest folks.

Yours always faithfully

W M Thackeray

[245] See the handbill reproduced on the opposite page.

HEAVEN AND EARTH SHALL PASS AWAY:
BUT MY WORDS SHALL NOT PASS AWAY.

THESE WORDS OF **OUR SAVIOUR** AS RECORDED IN

ST. LUKE'S GOSPEL, CH. XXI. S3, SUGGESTED TO

## THE COUNT D'ORSAY

a Picture, which in its high intellectual character, and the simplicity
of its conception, has excited an extraordinary sensation. It would
be difficult to describe in adequate terms the emotions which have
been elicited by the contemplation of this work.

Mr. LANE (who has executed the Engraving in lithography)
was so impressed by the elevation and the manifold graces of the
design, that he entered upon his work with a zeal which the
Publisher hopes will be evident on examination of the result.

## THE ORIGINAL PICTURE,

WITH THE

### LITHOGRAPHIC STONE

(PREVIOUS TO THE PROCESS OF PRINTING),

will be privately exhibited at the Gallery of Mr. Hogarth, 5 Haymarket,
on Saturday next, December 9th, when the favour of your Company is
requested, between the hours of 10 and 3.

Haymarket, December 7.

HANDBILL FOR A PAINTING BY
COUNT D'ORSAY

My dear Coriat — This note has just come to hand,
and You see I take the freedom with you of speaking the truth.

I don't like this announcement at all. Our Saviour at the Court Dressy
ought not to appear in those big letters. It somehow looks as if you
and our Lord were on a par, and put forth as equal attractions
by the publisher. I don't mind my saying this - for I'm sure this sort
of announcement in bil (carrying) an account of the unfortunate typography,
is likely to shock many honest folks.

Yours always faithfully
W M Thackeray

THACKERAY'S COMMENT ON THE HANDBILL

533.　　　　TO LADY BLESSINGTON
　　　　　　　12 DECEMBER 1848

Hitherto unpublished.

Dear Lady Blessington

I write under sad circumstances and put myself upon your known generosity. When I myself last week fixed Tuesday as the day so long delayed for feasting upon the famous Oeufs à l'Espartero [246] — I forgot that it was the 12 December — a day sacred to all old Charterhouse men who meet at the old school and dine together afterwards making each other speeches suitable to the occasion. To day is to be a grand field day, Peel is to be in the chair at the dinner, the Archbishop of C [247] preaches: everybody will be there.

May I break my promise to you and go? I think I shall be glad if you won't let me off: but that I ought to ask — for you understand what an effect upon the sale of Pendennis may be produced by a complimentary speech, replied to in an appropriate manner by M$^r$ Titmarsh, and heard by 3 or 400 gentlemen of all callings and professions in life who will naturally be interested in their man.

 Now Madam the scale is in your (but what a fool I am to attempt to draw it) — I humbly ask your Ladyship is [it] to be Charterhouse or is it to be Oeufs à l'Espartero?

One word saying 'Go' or 'Come here' will decide my fate. I shall be happy w$^h$ ever way it be.

　　　　　Always faithfully yours dear Lady Blessington
　　　　　　　　　W M Thackeray

[246] A dish named for Baldomero Espartero (1792–1879), the progressivist general who defended the Spanish monarchy against Carlist insurrections.
[247] John Bird Sumner (1780–1862), who had become primate earlier in the year, was a governor of Charterhouse.

534.                    TO EDWARD CHAPMAN
                           DECEMBER 1848

*Address:* E. Chapman Esq^re | 186 Strand. Hitherto unpublished.

Two plates [248] are wanting the little school room & the Hamper
for Briggs — they must go in.

I have marked the plates to face the pages.

Immediate.  Want answer. [249]

535.                    TO EDWARD CHAPMAN
                           DECEMBER 1848

Hitherto unpublished.

Ingrate! here is your book.  I kept it back a day because I was
engaged on the ballad w^h ends it [250] — and w^h — but ask Forster
ask posterity what they think of it.

Send me the plates with the copy set up in pages.  The frontispiece is the boy drawing the caricature.

536.        TO THE REV. WILLIAM BROOKFIELD
                       DECEMBER 1848? [251]

Published in *Collection of Letters*, p. 129.

M^r Inspector

M^r Kenyon having called upon me to fix a day when you may
have the honor of meeting me at his house; I have propoſed
Christmas Eve — and am, with compliments to the geehrte Frau
Schulinspektorinn,

                                         Yours
                                      W M T.

[248] To *Dr. Birch and his Young Friends*, published for Christmas, 1848.
[249] The last three words are written on the envelope.
[250] "The End of the Play."
[251] Brookfield received his appointment as Inspector of Schools in February,
1848.  It seems likely that this note was written shortly before the following
Christmas.

537.         TO MRS. BROOKFIELD
             18 DECEMBER 1848

*Address:* M<sup>rs</sup> Brookfield. Hitherto unpublished.

Dear Lady, I think it is better to go to work than to be galli-
vanting this fine morning. So I send you as compagnon de voyage
Dickens's book [252] w<sup>h</sup> I found last night. I shall be at the Old Club,
Brighton. God bless you

W M T.

Yes besides I send you a curiosity the brouillon of the ballad
wrote through that night of 13-14 Dec<sup>r</sup>
1848
I've *not* sent the pome. [253]

538.        FROM MRS. BROOKFIELD
             18 DECEMBER 1848

Hitherto unpublished.

15 Portman St.<br>2 Prospect Place Southampton

My dear M<sup>r</sup> Thackeray,

Your book was a most welcome surprise with the little note, &
thank you for sending it — I had just time to read the book thro'
on the journey — & here it is beguiling old M<sup>r</sup> Bullar's sick bed
this Eveg — as he is not able to appear below at present. William
stopped for Inspections at Winchester & on arriving here after me
was so horrified by the want of a dressing room that he has taken
a bed at M<sup>r</sup> Fanshawe's — whose mild face was bent upon me at
dinner here today — one fits soon in to the old niche to which one
had been accustomed anywhere — but a periodical yearly visit anywhere, such as we pay here — brings with it many melancholy

---

[252] *The Haunted Man.*
[253] This sentence is written on the envelope.

thoughts & supposing each person would quietly take off their mask & show all that was passing in their minds perhaps the congratulatory speeches of one's not being the least changed might be in abeyance on both sides — Here however, there always appear to be fewer changes than anywhere else, & I feel almost a hypocrite myself while I fancy they are so frank — D.ʳ Joseph ²⁵⁴ has been dwelling on his favorite theory of the one duty for all of us "Self annihilation & in this he includes everything that can give us pleasure — especially the cultivation of the affections," as being all self indulgence & not high enough to take up our thoughts, I am so much hurried that you will hardly make out what I have already written — We were in a most bewildering confusion at starting today — Harry ²⁵⁵ with a split thumb-nail to take off his thoughts from the Norse lady — & W.ᵐ declaring he had no socks in his drawers to pack up — I brought away the key of the tea chest & also of the cellaret, which will appear a marked want of kindly forethought for our young friend  the ground floor incumbent tho' he came & gave a very kind goodbye — to whom I must write an apology with the keys, directly. Will you send me the Poem? — which you were going to put in to y.ʳ note this morning? — The usual enquiries of how I like Pendennis ²⁵⁶ have had to be replied to which it is peculiarly disagreeable to me to do — & I think I shall adopt an air of stolid dulness when any such questions are put to me & avoid the necessity of making commonplace compliments to what you have written, which if you overheard w.ᵈ be quite likely to provoke you to throw a book at my head, which I feel quite inclined to do to myself

Have you seen much of your friend Murphy ²⁵⁷ already? I hope you are already the better for Brighton & please to write &

²⁵⁴ Dr. Joseph Bullar.
²⁵⁵ Harry Hallam.
²⁵⁶ Number II for December, chapters 4 to 6.
²⁵⁷ Francis Stack Murphy (1810?–1860), barrister and M. P. for Cork from 1837 to 1853. He had studied under Thackeray's friend "Father Prout" at Clongoweswood College and saw Thackeray frequently at Evans's and the Garrick Club. See Yates, [His] Recollections and Experiences, 2 vols., London, 1884, II, 6.

say you are so — as soon as you will be so kind — Goodnight —
William is out or w^d send you his love, — but I send you mine
instead, & Believe me

Always your faithful sister Jane

539.                 TO MRS. BROOKFIELD
                     18 DECEMBER 1848

Extracts published by Dr. Rosenbach, *A Book Hunter's Holiday* (Boston,
1936), p. 21. My text is taken from a transcript supplied by Mrs. Fuller.

Monday night

As I went up to bed I thought about this time she's — as I got
up I remembered, about this time she's — [*sketch of a woman saying her prayers*] Amen. I didn't read Dickens,[258] only the first 20
pages, not having time. My mother did though and was very much
moved. She says there's something in it will affect you personally.
Mind my copy is only a loan: and you must give it back when we
meet next year. What shall I tell you that will please you? Well,
my dear pretty Virginia and Mrs. Prinsep are here at Brighton?
No — they are in London: and I here away, with nobody to console
me but positively the Miss Smiths — the Miss Smiths and the Sea!
Welcome welcome thou stormy whisperer! the talk of the eldest
Miss S. is almost as ceaseless. I have been out to buy [the] Haunted
Man for the younger one the pretty one who made me the purse
you know. Il est toujours galant ce scelerat de Titmarsh — I have
written 1 page of P-nd-nn-s, [259] but can't go on because it is very
near post time and I wish to know so very much whether some
friends of mine arrived safely at their destiny. What a good dear
fellow your brother [260] is. What a fine gentleman — I rank myself
among the spoonies. Soft-heartedness seems to me better than
anything better than stars and garters great intellect blazing wit &c.

I knew it [261] would come. Here it is at this very minute. Thank

---

[258] *The Haunted Man.*
[259] The latter part of Number III, chapters 7 to 10.
[260] Charles Elton.
[261] Mrs. Brookfield's letter of December 18.

you, ma soeur. Joseph Bullar may go annihilate himself: as monks
whip and starved fakirs cut their limbs off — but we won't. No
dear lady we will do better: we will love each other while we may
here and afterwards, if you go first you will kneel for me in heaven
and bring me there — if I, I swear the best thought I have is to
remember that I shall have your love surviving me and with a
constant tenderness blessing my memory. I can't all perish living
in your heart. That in itself is a sort of seal and assurance of
heaven. [262] Here is what I was writing to that poor Lady Ashburton
who asked for a letter from me [263] — only I can't but suppose to be
your present grief the more keenly, [264] for if I were to die tomorrow I think I should leave two women behind me in whose
hearts the tenderest remembrance of me wd. live as thank God it
deserves to do. Say that I die and live yet in the love of my sur-
vivors? isn't that a warrant of immortality almost? say that my
2 dearest friends precede me and enter into Gds futurity spotless
and angelical I feel that I have 2 advocates in Heaven and that my
love penetrates there as it were. It seems to me that Love proves
God. By love I believe and am saved. And I think misgivings
about future happiness or the intentions of the Divine Beneficence
towards us are no better than Blasphemy and that you might as
well say "Hate your neighbour, avenge the wrongs done you by
doing evil and inflicting pain on your part, as predicate the same
of the Almighty or dare to suppose that his Wisdom and Authority

[262] Compare with this passage the reflections of Harry Esmond when he is
reunited with Lady Castlewood (in the famous chapter, "The 29th December"): "Gracious God, who was he, weak and friendless creature, that such a
love should be poured out upon him? Not in vain — not in vain has he lived
— hard and thankless should he be to think so — that has such a treasure given
him. What is ambition compared to that, but selfish vanity? To be rich, to be
famous? What do these profit a year hence, when other names sound louder
than yours, when you lie hidden away under the ground, along with idle titles
engraven on your coffin? But only true love lives after you — follows your
memory with secret blessing — or precedes you, and intercedes for you. *Non
omnis moriar* — if dying, I yet live in a tender heart or two; nor am lost and
hopeless living, if a sainted departed soul still loves and prays for me." (*Works,*
VII, 195)
[263] Consoling her for the death of her intimate friend, Charles Buller.
[264] So reads Mrs. Fuller's transcript. I can suggest no reasonable emendation.

wd. think of revenging themselves by making meaner creatures miserable. If you have a perfect consciousness that you here on earth are ardently and fondly pursuing with your affection a friend, in invisible regions beautified, removed from the possibility of ill, taken up to the consummation of truth, and in the midst of that glory and perfection I say *loving you still* how quickly grief should pass away" — and here the paper stops — it was written just before I made the mark on this. You see what I was thinking about — about you always, whose attachment I assume as awarded to me: and that dear old woman with the solemn eyes at home, God bless the pair of you: and keep me straight and honest. This seems to me the consequence of all affection. When I think about you or my mother or my children (I ought to think more about those 2 dear little women) a natural Grace follows and I say God pardon me and make me pure.

Write to me again and again. Again and again I thank my dear William for his confidence in me. If I were to lose you I should despair and go wrong. And so Goodbye dear lady.

[*sketch of a woman kneeling*]

540.         TO JOHN DOUGLAS COOK [265]
              19 DECEMBER 1848

Hitherto unpublished.

Brighton.  Old Club.
Tuesday 19 Dec[r]

My dear Cook

I have come away from town neglecting to answer your hospitable proffer: but I must perforce decline it and all others this week w[h] I pass with my friend M[r] Arthur Pendennis here at Brighton.

Always faithfully yours
W M Thackeray.

[265] Cook (1811–1868) was editor of *The Morning Chronicle* from 1852 to 1855 and of *The Saturday Review* from 1855 to 1868.

541.                  TO EDWARD FɪᴛᴢGERALD
                        19 DECEMBER 1848

*Address:* Edward Fitz-Gerald Esqʳᵉ | 19 Charlotte Street | Rathbone Place
London. *Postmarks:* BRIGHTON 1848, DE 19 1848. Published in Thomas
Wright's *Life of Edward FitzGerald*, I, 224.

                    Brighton   Old Club.   Tuesday.
My dear old Cupid. I did not come to see thee for I was working day & night to finish that Xmas affair — and the few spare
hours I had went — R! never mind where. As soon as the book &
Punch & the plates for Pendennis were done and the very day when
somebody left town I came down to this Mirean Eboad — and am
directly very much better, I slept well, I have laughed already
twice this morning: I have begun Pendennis III: and have leisure
to think of my friend & wish he was here. Come, Eros! Come,
Boy-god of the twanging bow! Is not Venus thy mother here? —
thou shalt ride in her chariot and by thy side shall be if not Mars
at least Titmars.
    How these men of letters dash off these things! C'est étonnant
ma parole d'honneur, c'est étonnant.


542.                  TO MRS. BROOKFIELD
                      19–22 DECEMBER 1848

Published in part, *Collection of Letters*, pp. 34–37. The passages between
daggers have been overscored by Mrs. Brookfield.

Tuesday.
    Good night my dear Madam. Since I came home from dining
with Mʳ Morier I have been writing a letter to Mʳ T. Carlyle: [266]
and thinking about other things as well as the letter all the time.
And I have read over a letter I recᵈ to day, wʰ apologizes for everything, and whereof the tremulous author ceaselessly doubts & misgives — Who knows whether she is not converted by Joseph Bullar

[266] I have not traced this letter.

by this time? She is a sister of mine and her name is God bless her. Wednesday.

This is the night after. When I am alone I come back to you & think of you O so kindly. It is just 10 1/2 o'clock. I wonder what you are doing? 〈. . .〉 [267] I was at work until 7 o'clock not to very much purpose but executing with great labour & hardship the day's work. Then I went to dine with D.ʳ Hall the crack Doctor here, a literate man a traveller & otherwise a kind big wig. After dinner we went to [268] hear M.ʳ Sortain [269] lecture of whom you may perhaps have heard me speak as a great remarkable orator and preacher of the Lady Huntingdon Connexion [270] (the paper is so greasy that I am forced to try several pens and manners of hand-writing but none will do) — We had a fine lecture with brilliant Irish metaphors and outbursts of rhetoric addressed to an assembly of mechanics shopboys and young women who could not and per-haps had best not understand that flashy speaker. It was about the origin of nations he spoke — one of those big themes on w.ʰ a man may talk eternally and with a never-ending outpouring of words, and he talked magnificently about the Arabs for the most part, and tried to prove that because the Arabs acknowledge their descent from Ishmael or Esau, therefore the Old Testament History was true, but the Arabs may have had Esau for a father, & yet the bears may not have eaten up the little children for quizzing Elisha's bald head — and yet Joshua may not have received Divine orders to slaughter man woman & child; and yet — but never mind the horrid story of hatred murder bigotry and persecution. As I was writing to Carlyle last night (I haven't sent the letter as usual and shall not most likely) Saint Stephen was pelted to death by Old

[267] Mrs. Brookfield has here overscored some twenty words beyond recovery.

[268] The letter thus far and the postscript are in Thackeray's upright hand; the rest of the letter is in his slanting hand.

[269] The Rev. Joseph Sortain (1809–1860), Pastor of North Street Chapel in Brighton from 1832 until his death, and author of several historical novels.

[270] Selina Hastings (1707–1791), Countess of Huntingdon, was converted to Methodism early in her married life and had an important part in introduc-ing the faith in fashionable society. Her "connection," the Wesleyan term for a religious group, was still flourishing in Victorian times.

Testaments; & Our Lord was killed like a felon by the law w$^h$ he came to repeal.

I was thinking about Joseph Bullar's doctrine after I went to bed: founded on what I cant but think a blasphemous asceticism w$^h$ has obtained in the world ever so long: and w$^h$ is disposed to curse hate and undervalue the world altogether. Why should we? What we see here of this world is but an expression of God's will so to speak — a beautiful earth & sky and sea — beautiful affections and sorrows, wonderful changes and developments of creation, suns rising stars shining birds singing, clouds and shadows changing & fading, people loving each other smiling & crying  The multiplied phenomena of nature (multiplied in fact and fancy in art and science in every way that a man's intellect or education or imagination can be brought to bear) — and who is to say that we are to ignore all these or not value them and love them, because there is another unknown world yet to come? Why, that unknown future world is but a manifestation of God-Almightys Will and a development of Nature neither more nor less than this in w$^h$ we are; and an angel glorified or a sparrow on a gutter, are equally parts of his Creation. The light upon all the Saints in Heaven is just as much (and no more) Gods work, as the Sun w$^h$ shall shine tomorrow upon this infinitesimal speck of creation, and under w$^h$ I shall read, please God, a letter from my kindest Lady & friend. About my future state I dont know. I leave it in the disposal of the Awful Father: but for to day: I thank God that I can love you; and that you yonder (and others beside) are thinking of me with a tender regard; Hallelujah may be greater in degree than this, but not in kind: and countless ages of stars may be blazing infinitely: but you & I have a right to rejoice and believe in our little part, and to trust in to day as in tomorrow. God bless my dear Lady and her husband. I hope you are asleep now: and must go too for the candles are just winking out.

Thursday. I'm glad to see among the new inspectors in the Gazette in this mornings paper my old acquaintance Longueville Jones, [271] an excellent worthy lively accomplished fellow: whom I

---

[271] See above, No. 62, note 136. Before his marriage Jones was a Fellow, Lec-

like the better because he flung up Fellow-and-Tutorship at Cambridge in order to marry on nothing a year. We worked in Galignani's newspaper for 10 francs a day very cheerily 10 years ago: since when he has been a Schoolmaster, taken pupils or bid for them, and battled manfully with fortune. W^m will be sure to like him I think, he is so honest and cheerful. But I own I didn't much 'taste' M^rs J. Boo — what a gross man that must be who invented the expression.

I have sent off my letter to Lady Ashburton this morning: [272] ending with some pretty phrases about poor old CB.: whose fate affects me very much so much that I feel as if I was making my will & getting ready to march too — Well, Maam, I have as good a right to presentiments as you have: and to sickly fancies and despondencies But I should like to see before I die, and think of it daily more & more the commencement of J. C's Christianism in the world: where I am sure people may be made 100 times happier than by its present forms — Judaism, asceticism, Bullarism, I wonder will He come again and tell it us?

You are not hurt are you that I said so much about you? I ventured to write that if I died there was a woman who would tenderly deplore me? Non Soeur — The similarity of the cases w^d comfort I think that poor afflicted lady. It was easy to see what a deep regard there was between them. Though they were not of the sentimental sort like you & the buffoon your humble Servant and

---

turer, and Dean of Magdalene College, Cambridge. He subsequently settled in France for a time, opened a college in Manchester, and was, on December 16, 1848, appointed Inspector of Schools in Wales. He held this post until 1864.

[272] "I wonder if Lady Ashburton will write to you," Mrs. Brookfield speculated in her reply to Thackeray's letter; "I think she must have felt your letter very much, as so few would really understand her grief, and it is one of the most painful and absurd ways of the world to assume that one is in affliction for anyone who happens to have been related to us, while intimacies which must have a much deeper root from having been sought out for ourselves and made where real sympathy exists, — these are so soon to be forgotten, 'only a friend, no relation,' you hear said many times when the words should be reversed into 'only a relation!' Not but that I am very fond of my relations, but there must be exceptions." (*Mrs. Brookfield*, II, 272)

made a practice of condemning as maudlin sentiments w^h are not so — but on the contrary natural simple ennobling we are taught to be ashamed of our best feelings all our life. I don't want to blubber upon everybody's shoulder, but to have a good-will for all, & a strong very strong regard for a few w^h I shan't be ashamed to own to them — So I am sorry now that I cut out the 1 or 2 warm words If you are not only so and so to me but so and so*est* of all why sh^d I hide it? It is near upon 3 o'clock and I am getting rather anxious about the post from Southampton viâ London — why, if it doesn't come in you wont get any letter tomorrow.

— No. Nothing and I made so sure. Well. I'll try and go to work. Its only one more little drop. God bless you dear Lady.

By the way I may as well send this though to say that I shall be back in London on Saturday — where all favors will be thankfully received by

W M T.

No. I went to the post office and turned back. I must not write to Madam unless she does to me. Who knows what has happened? † ⟨. . .⟩ [273] W^m does not like too much writing. Well he has been ⟨. . .⟩ [274] generous to me.† You have been to Miss Ogle's [275] I hope. I had a company dinner at Horace Smith's — his Lord, his Baronet, Lady Morgan and a Dowager Countess to tea — But I came away early to write a little and to think about various things. As I sit here all day I have arranged the whole matter. † I am only to write occasionally to you ⟨. . .⟩ [276] dignified and quite proper. Good † night dear M^rs Brookfield, Ah it is too late. † ⟨. . .⟩ [277] nothing. W^h shall it be? Not the last, not the last.†

Friday. I have had a good mornings work: and at 2 o'clock — comes your letter [278] — dear friend. Thank you, what a coward

---

[273] Two words are here irrecoverably overscored.
[274] Two words are here irrecoverably overscored.
[275] A wealthy friend of the Brookfields.
[276] Two words are here irrecoverably overscored.
[277] About eight words are here irrecoverably overscored.
[278] Mrs. Brookfield's letter of December 21.

I was! I'll go out and walk and be happy for an hour. Its a grand frosty sunshine. Tomorrow m̃ early back to London & work all Sunday Xmas day Monday & Tuesday — dine out with the old folks on Thursday — must be at home New Year's day Monday. But who knows I may see you sometime in the week my d. d. s.

543.     FROM MRS. BROOKFIELD
21 DECEMBER 1848

My text is taken from *Mrs. Brookfield and her Circle*, pp. 273–274.

Southampton,
21 Dec.

My dear Mr. Thackeray,

It is so very cold and dismal to-day I don't feel as if I could write though I wish to thank you for your letter and the notes of the Ballad [279] — which I shall keep as a curiosity and perhaps

[279] No doubt the same verses that Thackeray decided at the last moment not to include in his first letter of December 18. They cannot be the lines beginning " 'Tis one o'clock, the boy from *Punch* is sitting in the passage here" (printed below, No. 662), as the authors of *Mrs. Brookfield* (II, 273) suggest, for this engaging doggerel was written on a morning in 1849, not "through the night of 13–14 Dec!". It is possible, however, that the evening of December 13 was made memorable by the episode recounted in a poem called "What Might Have Been," which I print below for the first time from a transcript supplied by Mrs. Fuller, and that Thackeray composed these lines during the night that followed:

> As we two slowly walked that night,
>     Silence fell on us, as of fear;
> I was afraid to face the light
>     Lest you should see that I loved you, dear.
>
> You drew my arm against your heart,
>     So close I could feel it beating near;
> You were brave enough for a lover's part —
>     You were so sure that I loved you, dear.
>
> Then you murmured a word or two,
>     And tenderly stooped your listening ear;

leave it, with all your letters as a legacy to Annie for her to work into your memoir according to her discretion 50 years hence.[280] Do you know that if you do not write in more commonplace style to me I shall be quite unable to answer you at all — I have just read your letter over again and thought how flat and dull all that I could say would be and how presumptuous I am to be writing anything by way of an answer, except to say I am grateful.

I saw that Dickens's was a presentation copy to you and will take care of it — there is a bit at the end about a little dead child which is very touching and perhaps was what your mother thought I should feel.

William is at the school to-day for the inspection — I meant to have gone, never having seen him *officially* employed, but I have

---

> For you thought that all you had to do
>     Was to hear me say that I loved you, dear.
>
> But, though your face was so close to mine
>     That you touched my cheek with your chestnut hair
> I wouldn't my lips to yours resign;
>     And yet I loved you — I loved you, dear.
>
> And all at once you were cold and pale,
>     Because you thought that I did not care;
> I cried a little behind my veil —
>     But that was because I loved you, dear.
>
> And so you thought 'twas a drop of rain
>     That splashed your hand?  But it was a tear;
> For then you said you'd never again
>     Ask me to say that I loved you, dear.
>
> Ah! I have suffered, and so have you;
>     And to-night, if you were but standing here,
> I'd make you an answer straight and true,
>     If you'd ask me again if I loved you, dear.

Some doubt is cast on the authenticity of "What Might Have Been" — which, in any event, one would willingly believe not to be by Thackeray — by the fact that the Berg Collection of the New York Public Library contains a copy of the poem in the hand of the forger whose activities are described in Appendix XXVII.  But it is entirely conceivable that the forger, who had access to much genuine Thackeray manuscript, made his transcription from an original in Thackeray's hand.

[280] Lady Ritchie's *Biographical Introductions* began to appear just fifty years later, but she made little use in them of Thackeray's letters to Mrs. Brookfield.

a return of pain and must not go out. William Bullar dosed me with *Chloroform* as a medicine and it is very soothing. Dr. Joseph has just been in with some of his theories as to all suffering coming upon us as a distinct punishment for a distinct and definite sin, which it is our duty to be seeking out — I told him I felt I must be horribly wicked to require so much discipline, but that if I had encouraged such a thought it would have driven me to despair. He said it was the best thing I could come to, as a transition state, all of us ought to go through the stage of despair before we could be fit for any real peace or comfort!

If I had time I would write all this over again as an entirely new letter — for my awe of you with which I began writing has quite disappeared and I don't mind a bit whether I have written idiotcy or sense — which is a great proof of my confidence in you.

Ever your friend,<br>Jane Brookfield.

[For a fragment of a letter to Mrs. Brookfield, 22 December, 1848, see letter 4, Appendix XXVI.]

544.      TO CHARLES NEATE
24 DECEMBER 1848

Hitherto unpublished.

13 Young S<sup>t</sup> Kensington.<br>Eve of the Nativity.

Sir

It is seldom that I sit down with less satisfaction than at the present moment to write a letter w<sup>h</sup> gives me great pleasure to address to you.

I read your pamphlet [281] only yesterday. I think it at once crabbed and good French. It has not the easy flow of another foreigner who sometimes writes in that language, nor his graceful gram-

---

[281] *Dialogues des Morts.* The other foreigner, of course, is Thackeray himself.

matical inaccuracies. It has fine thoughts — uncommon fine and generously & naturally expressed such as les Revolutions qui dormaient aux portes de tous les palais &c I dont think it leads to much but what does in this cul de sac of an existence? — I wonder whether I shall even read it again? I think not: but by Jove its very clever.

This is the 9<sup>th</sup> of 12 letters I am writing this evening worn out by my own labours but still willing to remember the kyindness of others. I wish you well If you choose to come & dine here on Tuesday there will be some pretty girls and you can have a bed.

As for remarks made by you on confidential communications of my own absurd boasts uttered and puerile braggadocio displayed they may be pardoned in one who lives in a College where he loses 1/2 his opportunities by going notoriously to sleep after dinner — If I am an ass as some hint I am

Sir my brother<br>Your fellow citizen<br>W M Thackeray

545.   TO EDWARD CHAPMAN
25 DECEMBER 1848

Hitherto unpublished.

Xmas day.   Reform Club.

Dear Chapman

Would it be too great a liberty to request a few copies of my book w<sup>h</sup> seems to have a pretty good success should be sent to the Author? My mother & children have seen it for some days past at a friend's house, but not at my own and I should be glad to be allowed to send it to one or 2 persons when the trade is supplied.

The D N says theyve not had one — an article spoiled. Is there one at the Weekly Chronicle? John Bull? Observer? J W. Folthorpe at Brighton said he had ordered copies and could not get them — Whitaker sent him one.

Please send one uncoloured
>J. H. Reynolds Esq. Newport I of Wight.
>Rev^d J^s White. Bonchurch I of Wight.

Coloured
>Hon^ble M^rs Herbert [282]
>>*Wilton. Salisbury.*
>Hon^ble M^rs Spring Rice [283]
>>*Hither Green. Lewisham.*
>Viscountess Castlereagh.
>>*Powers Court. Wicklow. Ireland.*
>M^rs *Carlyle.*
>M^rs *Dickens.*
>The Lady Ashburton
>>*The Grange. Alresford.*
>Lady Cullum
>>*Hardwick. Bury S^t Edmunds.*

They may go by post at 6^d apiece w^h I dont mind paying.


546.      TO EDWARD CHAPMAN
              25? DECEMBER 1848

*Address:* E. Chapman Esq^re | 186 Strand. Hitherto unpublished.

Dear Chapman

On 2^nd thoughts dont if you please send to Lady Castlereagh.

Your injured
**W M T.**

[282] The former Mary Elizabeth A'Court-Repington (1822–1911), a famous beauty who had married the statesman Sidney Herbert (1810–1861), later (1861) first Baron Herbert of Lea, in 1846.
[283] The former Ellen Mary Frere (d. 1869), who had married Stephen Edmond Spring-Rice (1814–1865), oldest son of the first Baron Monteagle, in 1839. Spring-Rice was Deputy-Chairman of the Board of Customs and a close friend of Brookfield, who went yachting every year with him.

547.                TO EDWARD CHAPMAN
                        DECEMBER 1848

Hitherto unpublished.

My dear Sir

I hope the book goes well for *foughs* see Britannia (the last sentence) 'Tator, Chronicle.

Might I have a few more copies? I should like very much to send 1 to Aytoun & Napier care of Longman & Blackwood.

Yours ever

W M T.


548.    TO THE REV. WILLIAM BROOKFIELD
                27 DECEMBER 1848

*Address:* Rev⁴ W. H. Brookfield. | at Miss Ogle's | Southampton. *Postmark:* KENSINGTON DE 27 1848. Hitherto unpublished.

My dear Vieux

I have not been able to go out to day being too busy at home: but hope to bring the key and the Sarmon on Friday, when, with my best compliments to the Miss Ogles, I shall have great pleasure in dining with them. We are all going to the play to night [284] that is they are: for I dont think I shall be able to go till late, having proceeded awfully slowly with Pen: since my return from Brighton. Farewell

Yours   W M T.

[284] Probably one of the Christmas pantomimes.

## 549.        TO JOHN KENYON
### 29 DECEMBER 1848 [285]

Hitherto unpublished.

Kensington. Friday.

Dear Kenyon

For Tuesday 16th (if naught intervene) I will be yours with pleasure, as indeed I am now — very sincerely and wishing you an HNY.

W M T.

## 550.        TO SAMUEL BEVAN
### DECEMBER? 1848 [286]

My text is taken from a facsimile in *The Autographic Mirror*, II (1864), 156.

Dear Bevan

I dont like the looks of the ballad at all in print but if you please prefer to have it in this way exactly. 'Be blowed' &c would never do in a printed ballad of

Yours very truly

W M Thackeray.

[285] Among possible years January 16 fell on a Tuesday only in 1849. This letter must therefore have been written on December 29, 1848, the Friday before New Year's day.

[286] Samuel Bevan's *Sand and Canvas*, in which "The Three Sailors" first appeared, was reviewed in *The Spectator* of January 20, 1849, pp. 64–65. Thackeray probably saw the proofs of his verses a few weeks earlier.

Thackeray told Dr. John Brown that the original of "Little Billee," as he sometimes called "The Three Sailors," was an "old French song which is still sung by Breton sailors" (Peddie, *Recollections of Dr. John Brown*, pp. 147–148). For the origin and dissemination of the narrative which, in one form or another, Thackeray used, see William J. Entwistle's *European Balladry* (Oxford, 1939), pp. 79 and 140. Professor Entwistle harshly reckons "The Three Sailors" as "a jocose ballad of the period of decadence, despite the respectability of its authorship."

The Three Sailors.

There were three sailors in Bristol city
Who took a boat and went to sea.

But first with beef and Captains biscuit
And pickled pork they loaded she.

There was guzzling Jack & gorging Jimmy
And the youngest he was little Billy.

Now very soon they were so greedy
They didn't have not one split pea.

Says guzzling Jack to gorging Jimmy
I am confounded hung—ery.

Says Gorging Jim to guzzling Jacky
We have no wittles so we must eat we.

Says Guzzling Jack to gorging Jimmy
O gorging Jim what a fool you be.

There's little Bill as is young & tender
We're old & tough so let's eat he.

O Bill we're going to kill and eat you
So undo the collar of your chemee.

When Bill he heard this information
He used his pocket handkerchee

O let me say my Catechism
As my poor Mammy taught to me.

Make haste make haste says guzzling Jacky
Whilst Jim pulled out his snickersnee.

So Bill went up the main-top-gallant mast
Where down he fell on his bended knee.

He scarce had said his Catechism
When up he jumped there's land I see

There's Jerusalem & Madagascar
And North & South Amerikey

Theres the British fleet a riding at Anchor
With Admiral Napier K C B

So when they came to the Admirals vessel
He hanged fat Jack and flogged Jimmy

But as for little Bill he made him
The Captain of a Seventy three.


551.      TO LADY BLESSINGTON
1848 [287]

*Address:* The Countess of Blessington. Published in part by the third Earl of Lytton, *The Life of Edward Bulwer* (London, 1913), I, 548.

Kensington. The morning after.

Dear Lady Blessington.

I whish to igsplain what I meant last night with regard to a certain antipathy to a certain great author. I have no sort of personal dislike (not that it matters much whether I have or not) to Sir E L B L on the contrary the only time I met him, at the immortial Ainsworth's years ago, I thought him very pleasant: and I know, from his conduct to my dear little Blanchard,[288] that he can be a most generous and delicate minded friend. BUT there are sentiments in his writing w^h always anger me, big words w^h make me furious, and a premeditated fine writing against w^h I cant help rebelling. My antipathy don't go any farther than this: and it is accompanied by a great deal of admiration.

I felt ashamed of myself when I came home and thought how needlessly I had spoken of this. What does it matter one way or

[287] This letter was almost certainly written in 1848 during the first months of Thackeray's friendship with Lady Blessington.
[288] For Bulwer-Lytton's services to Blanchard, see above, No. 93.

the other, and what cause had I to select Sir H Bulwer[289] of all men in the world for these odious confidences? It was very rude. I am always making rude speeches and apologizing for them, like a nuisance to society.

And now I remember how Sir B. Lytton spoke in a very different manner to a mutual friend about

Your very humble Serv[t]

W M Thackeray

552.          TO MRS. BROOKFIELD
1848

Published in *Collection of Letters*, pp. 137–138.

My dear sick lady. I send you one 2 3 4 5. 6. 7. mss. just to amuse you for 10 minutes. Anny's I am sure will: isn't it good? Her perillious passage and the wanting to see me? The letters are to ladies who bother one about the Bath and Washhouse Fête: and the verses[290] (marked 2) were written in a moment of depression — I wonder whether you'll like No 2.

[289] Henry Lytton Earle Bulwer (1801–1872), later (1871) first Baron Dalling and Bulwer, a distinguished diplomatist. He was the novelist's brother.
[290] Possibly the following lines, which Thackeray set down in the same notebook that contains his diary for March 10–15, 1848, printed above:

In the midst of all the joy as I behold it,
When I seek the recollections of long years,
When I labor & endeavor to behold it
Giving way to the infirmity of tears.

O my grey grey hairs
What a fool I seem
What a fitful dream
Which thy life declares.
How I wake all night
When the moon shines bright
With a ghastly light
On my grey grey hairs.

Though we may not say it
And the secret rests
In 2 sad breasts

Virginia wasn't at dinner after all yesterday: wasnt that a Judgment on somebody? She stopped to take care of a sick sister she has: but I made myself as happy as circumstances admitted and drank your health in a glass of M<sup>r</sup> Prinsep's excellent claret. — One cannot drink mere Port this weather —

When you have read all the little papers please put them back and send them by the Printers devil to their owner. It has just crossed my mind that you may think it very conceited my sending you notes to read addressed to grand ladies as if I was proud of my cleverness in writing them and of being in a state of correspondence with such grand persons: but I don't want to show off, only to try and give you ever so little amusement — and I don't choose to think about what other people choose to think about

Yours dear M<sup>rs</sup> Brookfield

W M Thackeray.

In silence folded
Yet we both obey it
And it throbs and smarts
And tears our hearts
But we never told it.
Though my lips are mute
And its signal flies
In a flash from my eyes
When your own behold it,
And reply unto it
With a glance of light
O beaming bright
Yet we never told it.

553.    TO THE REV. WILLIAM BROOKFIELD
1848? [291]

*Address:* Rev^d W. H. Brookfield | 15 Portman St. Published in *Collection of Letters*, p. 27.

My dear Vieux

When I came home last night I found a beautiful opera ticket for this evening. Jenny Lind — charming bally — box 72. I am going to dine at home with the children and shall go to the opera, and will leave your name down below.

Do come and we will sit we 2 and see the piece like 2 lords: and we can do the other part afterwards.

I present my respectful compliments to M^rs Brookfield and am

Yours —

If you can come to dinner. Theres a curry.

554.    TO THE REV. WILLIAM BROOKFIELD
1848?

Published in *Collection of Letters*, p. 137.

My dear Vieux

I have told the mouche to call for me at the Punch Office at 8 and to come round by Portman S^t fust. If you like you can come and we can go to a little play, a little something — to Hampstead even if you are up to it. If you'd like best to sit at home — I'd like to smoke a pipe with you. If you'd like best to sit at home alone: I can go about my own business. But don't mind choosing w^h way of the 3 you prefer: and bleave me

hallis yours

W M T.

[291] The Brookfields moved to Portman Street in April, 1848. Jenny Lind sang in London during both 1848 and 1849, but Mrs. Brookfield was an invalid (as she appears to have been when this note was written, for Thackeray does not include her in his invitation) only in 1848.

## 555.    TO THE REV. WILLIAM BROOKFIELD
### 1848?

Published in *Collection of Letters*, p. 54.

Will you send me 2 cigars per bearer, I am working with 3 pipe-smoking Frenchmen, and I cant smoke their abominations — And I hope M^me is pretty well after her triumphant debut last night.

## 556.    TO MRS. CROWE
### 1848? [292]

My text is taken from *Thackeray in the United States*, II, 116.

Madame, — Oi shall be igsthramely deloighted to accompanee me friend Mr. Titmarsh oither to the tay (or supper) intherteenment invoited by yur ginerousity, and if the lovely Miss Eujanee[293] will fut a polka wid the humblest of her sleeves she shall foind that me dancing has been maloigned in certain quarters by a miserable enemee of our beautiful and bloighted Oirland. I have the honor to remeen, your most obagient servt,

Mulligan.

[292] Since the Mulligan figures in *Our Street*, written for Christmas, 1847, it seems likely that this note is to be assigned to the London season of 1848.
[293] Eugenie Crowe.

557.        TO THE REV. WILLIAM HARNESS
                        1848? [294]

Hitherto unpublished.

My dear Harness

I have promised the young ones to dine with them, and the word
of a republican is always sacred

                        Yours fraternally
                        W M T.

P. S.  I am going to work tonight.


558.        TO GEORGE HENRY LEWES
                        1848? [295]

Hitherto unpublished.

                        Garrick. Wednesday.
My dear L.

The story is all absurd.  I am passing through town for an hour,
and except next Sunday don't know when I shall be here.  Give
this message with my regards to Hunt please — and my polight
respects to Madam.

                        Health & fraternity
                        W M T.


[294] This note appears to have been written not long after the Revolution of
February, 1848, in France.
[295] "Health & fraternity" points to the revolutionary year of 1848.

### 559.　TO ANTONIO PANIZZI
### 1848

Hitherto unpublished. My text is taken from a transcript supplied by Mr. Blatner, who owns the original.

My dear Panizzi

For the love you bear me I entreat you receive hospitably the bearer an exile an artist and my friend. M. Marvy wishes to be introduced to the first room of the British Museum, and to make studies and researches there wh. he will explain to those who are set in authority over the place. I recommend him to your kindness and assure you of my particular commendation —

Thackeray

### 560.　TO MARGUERITE POWER
### 1848?

Hitherto unpublished.

My dear Miss Power

I ate some cucumber yesterday at Gegrgrinnidge and have such a Headake and am besides Ingaged O Miss! How I wish it was to you!

Your respectful admirer,<br>Villiam Theckery

You see I have got such a headache that I actually forget how to spell my own name.

561.                    TO MRS. PROCTER
                           1848?

Hitherto unpublished. My text is taken from a transcript given Lady Ritchie
by George Murray Smith.

                          [sketch]
My dear Mrs Procter,

I quite forgot it was MONDAY — Monday is Punch day. I
was not there last week (being unwell) and next week I must
attend.

But we dine early: business is over by 8 1/2 or so: and if you
please I will come to tea, nice and early, leaving those vulgar Punch
creatures just as they begin to smoke.

V. F. is getting later and later — but I am still yours (with my
respectful compliments to a young lady[296] who has dreams.)

                          W. M. Thackeray.


562.                    TO MRS. BROOKFIELD
                        3 JANUARY 1849?

My text is taken from a facsimile in the *Goodyear Catalogue*, lot 320.

                            Jan 3.

My dear Lady  I like to write you a line to night to show you
how I was right about a point w.<sup>h</sup> has been long clear to me, who
can understand very well how any man who has been near you and
lived or travelled with you must end by what I arrived at years
ago, and cannot do otherwise than regard you. When H. Hallam
spoke as he did to night I'm sure he said what has been upon his
mind for many months, that he was angry at my constant visits
to you. But thank God I have never concealed the affection I have
for you — your husband knows it as well as you or I do, and I
think I have such a claim to the love of both of you as no relation-

---

[296] Adelaide Procter.

my dear Miss Power

I ate some Cucumber
yesterday at gregsrimridge
and have such a Headacke
and am besides Engaged
O Miss! How I wish it
was to you!.
Your respectful admirer
William Theckery

You see I have got such a headache that I actually forget how to spell my own name.

THACKERAY'S LETTER OF 1848 TO MARGUERITE POWER

A FAMILY PARTY AT CHESHAM PLACE, JANUARY 5, 1849

*From a sketch by Thackeray*

ship, however close, ought to question or supersede. If ever he asks the question I hope it will frankly be told him that I claim to be as one of your brothers, or the closest and dearest of your friends. As for William, I am bound to him by benefits by the most generous confidence and repeated proofs of friendship; and to you dear lady by an affection w$^h$ I hope wont finish with my life of w$^h$ you have formed for a long time past one of the greatest and I hope the purest pleasures. If I had a bad thought towards you I think I could not look my friend or you in the face, and I see no shame in owning that I love you. I have W$^{m's}$ permission, your's, that of my own heart and conscience for constantly, daily if I can, seeing you. Who has a right to forbid me my great happiness? If neither of those three, who else? God bless you and us all dear Sister and Friend. I like to say so. and declare how much and how entirely I regard you.

W M T.

[For fragments of a letter to Mrs. Brookfield, 31 January, 1849, see letter 5, Appendix XXVI.]

563.    TO MRS. BROOKFIELD
1–2 FEBRUARY 1849

Published in part, *Collection of Letters*, pp. 38–42.

Meurice's Hotel. Rivoli Street, Paris.

My dear lady. If you please I am come home very tired and sleepy from the Opera where my friend Jim Rothschild[1] gave me a place in his box. There was a grand ballet of w$^h$ I could not understand one word that is one pas for not a word was spoken, and I saw some celebrities in the place. The President, M. Lamartine[2] in a box near a handsome lady — M. Marrast in a box near

---

[1] James, Baron de Rothschild (1792–1868), head of the Parisian branch of the great banking house.

[2] Louis Napoléon had been elected President of the French Republic on December 20, 1848. The poet Lamartine was an unsuccessful candidate for

a handsome lady — there was one with a bouquet of lilies or some
sort of white flowers so enormous that it looked like a bouquet in
a pantomime w<sup>h</sup> was to turn into something & out of w<sup>h</sup> a beautiful
dancer was to spring. The house was crammed with well dressed
folks and is sumptuous and splendid beyond measure: but O think
of old Lamartine in a box by a handsome lady — not any harm in
the least that I know of, only that the most venerable and grizzle-
bearded statesman and philosophers find time from their business
and political quandaries, to come and sigh and ogle a little at the
side of ladies in boxes. I am undergoing the quarantine of family
dinners with the most angelic patience      Yesterday being the first
day it was an old friend<sup>3</sup> and leg of lamb. I graciously said to the old
friend Why the deuce wouldn't you let me go & dine at a Restaurant,
dont you suppose I have leg of lamb at home? To day with an
aunt of mine<sup>4</sup> where we had mock-turtle soup by heavens; and I
arranged with my other aunt for another dinner — I knew how it
would be — it must be: and there is my cousin to come off yet;
who says you must come and dine I have not a soul: but will give
you a good Indian dinner — I will make a paper in Punch about it
and exhale my griefs in print. I will tell you about my cousin when
I get home when I get to Portman Street that is and see ma bonne
petite soeur. Why didn't I stop and see her yesterday? What
brought me to this place? Well, I am glad I came. It will give
me a subject for at least 6 weeks in Punch:<sup>5</sup> of w<sup>h</sup> I was getting so
weary that I thought I must have done with it. Are you better for
a little country air? did you walk in that cheerful paddock, where
the cows are; and had you clothes enough to your bed? I shall go
to mine now after writing this witty page: for I have been writing

the post. Armand Marrast (1801–1852) was Mayor of Paris after the revolution of February, 1848.

<sup>3</sup> Tom Fraser. See "On Some Dinners at Paris," *Punch*, March 3, 1849
(*Works*, VI, 156–157).

<sup>4</sup> The two aunts were Mrs. Ritchie and Mrs Halliday; the cousin, Mrs.
Carmichael.

<sup>5</sup> In addition to "On Some Dinners at Paris," Thackeray's visit inspired
the following contributions to *Punch*: "Paris Revisited. By an Old Paris
Man," February 10; "The Ballad of Bouillabaisse," February 17; and "Two
or Three Theatres at Paris," February 24.

and spinning about all day; and am very tired and sleepy if you please. Bon soir Madame. I like to say Good night though just before jumping into the comfortable French bed. May you sleep in yours & GBY.

Saturday — Though there is no use in writing because there is no Post, but que voulez vous Madame? on aime à dire un petit bonjour a ses amies. I feel almost used to the place already and begin to be interested about the politics. Some say there is a revolution ready for to day[6] — the town is crammed with soldiers and one has a curious feeling of interest and excitement as in walking about on ice that's rather dangerous and may tumble in at any moment. I had 3 newspapers for my breakfast w.h my man (it is rather grand having a laquais de place and I cant do without him and invent all sorts of pretexts to employ him) bought for 5d of your money — The mild papers say we have escaped an immense danger a formidable plot has been crushed and Paris would have been in fire and fury but for the timely discovery — the Red Republicans say — Plot — no such thing — the infernal tyrants at the head of affairs wish to find a pretext for persecuting patriots and the good and the brave are shut up in dungeons — Plot or no plot? Which is it? I think I prefer to believe that there has been a direful conspiracy and that we have escaped a tremendous danger: it makes one feel brave somehow: and as if one had some merit in overthrowing this rascally conspiracy. I am going to the Chamber directly. The Secretary at the Embassy got me a ticket — the Embassy is wonderfully civil. Lord Normanby[7] is my dearest friend. He is going to take me to the President very likely to ask me to dinner. You would have thought I was an Earl I was received with so much of empressement by the Ambassador. I had not been in Paris 10 minutes before I met 10 people of my acquaintance Bess Hamerton among the very first — We shook hands. She has

[6] Louis Napoléon had forced the National Assembly to vote its own dissolution on January 29, a step that was expected to give rise to violent popular protest.

[7] Constantine Henry Phipps (1797–1863), first Marquess of Normanby, who was Ambassador at Paris from 1846 to 1852.

forgiven me[8] — poor old body. As for my cousin — O it was wonderful. You know she was bred up with me as my sister — We
have not met for 5 years on account of a coolness that is a great heat
resulting out of a dispute in w.ʰ I was called to be umpire, and
gave judgment against her & her husband — But we have met, it
is forgotten. How we did kiss and smack away at each other! But
what a lie it was! Poor soul she performed beautifully — What
William, not the least changed just the same as ever in spite of all
your fame — fame be hanged thought I (pardonnez moi le mot)
just the same simple creature — O what a hypocrite I felt! I like her
too: but she poor poor soul!— Well she did her comedy exceedingly
well — I could only say My dear you have grown older: that was
the only bit of truth that passed and she didn't like it. Quand vous
serez bien vieille[9] and I say to you, My dear you are grown old
(only I shan't say my dear but something much more distant and
respectful) I wonder whether you will like it? Now it is time to
go to the Chamber — but it was far pleasanter to sit and chatter
with Madame.

I have been to see a piece of a piece called The Mystères de
Londres[10] since the above — and most tremendous mysteries they
were indeed. It appears that there lived in London 3 or 4 years
ago a young Grandee of Spain and Count of the Empire the Marquis of Rio Santo an Irishman by birth who in order to free his
native country from the intolerable tyranny of England imagined
to organize an extraordinary conspiracy of the rogues & thieves of
the metropolis, with whom some of the principal merchants jewellers & physicians were concerned, who were to undermine and
destroy somehow the infamous British power. The merchants were
to forge & utter bank notes, the jewellers to sell sham diamonds to
the aristocracy and so ruin them, the physicians to murder suitable
persons by their artful prescriptions, and the whole realm being
plunged into anarchy by their manoeuvres, Ireland was to get its

[8] See above, No. 384.
[9] See below, No. 917.
[10] A melodrama adapted from the popular romance (1844) by Paul Féval
(1817–1887).

own in the midst of the squabble. This astonishing Marquis being elected Supreme Chief of a secret society called the Gentlemen of the Night had his spies and retainers among the very highest classes of society — The Police and the Magistrature were corrupted, the very Beefeaters of the Queen contaminated, and you saw the evidences of such a conspiracy as would make your eyes open with terror — Who knows Madam but perhaps some of the School-Inspectors themselves were bought over, and a Jesuistic C—K[11] an ambitious T—nl—ng an unscrupulous Br—kf—ld himself may have been seduced to mislead our youth and teach our very babes and sucklings a precocious perverseness? — This is getting to be so very like print that I shall copy it out very likely all but the Inspector part for a periodical with w.h I am connected,[12] Well, numbers of beautiful women were in love with the Marquis or otherwise subjugated by him, and the most lovely and innocent of all was employed to go Saint Jamess on a drawing room day and steal the diamonds of Lady Brompton the Mistress of His Grace Prince Dimitri Tolstoi the Russian Ambassador who had lent Lady B the diamonds to sport at S.t James's, before he sent them off to his Imperial Master the Emperor of Russia for whom the trifles in question were purchased. Lady Brompton came to court having her train held up by her jockey. Suzanne came to court her train likewise carried by her page — one or both of them were affidés of the Association of Gentlemen of the Night, the jockeys were changed and Lady Bromptons jewels absolutely taken off her neck — So great was the rage of His Grace Prince Dimitri Tolstoi that he threatened war should be declared by his Emperor unless the brilliants were restored. I dont know what supervened for exhausted nature would bear no more. But you should have seen the Court of S.t James — the Beefeaters, the Life Guards, the Heralds at Arms in their tabards of the sixteenth century and the ushers an-

[11] The Rev. F. C. Cook, appointed Inspector of Schools in 1844 (Frank Smith, *Life and Work of Sir James Kay-Shuttleworth*, London, 1923, p. 154), and the Rev. Edward Douglas Tinling (d. 1897), who had married Katherine Maria Elton (d. 1876), Mrs. Brookfield's sister.
[12] See "Two or Three Theatres at Paris" (*Works*, VI, 152–154).

nouncing the great folks as they went into the presence of the Sovereign—Lady Campbell—the Countess of Derby and the Archbishop
of Canterbury were announced — O such an archbishop! He had on
·a velvet Trencher-cap and a dress something like our real and vener-
ated prelates, and a rich curling wig, and he stopped and blessed the
people making crucificial signs on the stairs — The various lords
went into the chamber in red robes & long flowing wigs — the
wonder of the parody was that it was so like and yet so absurdly
unlike. O'Connell appeared saluted as 'Daniel' by the Count of
Rio Santo, and announcing that he himself though *brisé par la lutte*
with the oppressors of his country; yet strongly reprobated anything like violent measures on the part of M. de Rio Santo and
his fellow patriots — the band played Godsafe the Quin in the
most delightful absurd manner — The best of it is that these things
admirably as they tickled me are only one degree more absurd than
what they pretend to copy. The Archbishop had a wig only the
other day, though not quite such a wig as this. The Chiefs of the
police came in with oilskin-hats policemen's coats quite correct and
white tights and silk-stockings, w.ʰ made one laugh (so that the
people in the stalls next me didn't know what I was at) — but
the parody was in fine prodigious and will afford matter to no end
of penny a line speculation — Ah but all the same I wish I had had
a letter from my lady to day. I came home on purpose Madame
and why did you disappoint me? Aren't you well? Tell me how
you are if you please Madame & Soeur. I sit in my little snug
room and say God bless you and M.ʳ Williams, I will smoke a cigar
and think about circumstances. I wonder whether you read all I
write? Why here is near 4 pages of Pendennis: and that young
fellow was once absurdly attached to a lady who didn't read all he
wrote.[13] If you will send me a letter tomorrow I will read it over
three times. I have only this little scrap left to say my prayers in
w.ʰ are GBY & 3 more.

[13] See chapter 12 of *Pendennis* (*Works*, II, 113).

564.     TO MRS. RITCHIE
      2 FEBRUARY 1849 [14]

Hitherto unpublished.

My dear Aunt

A special dinner to w[h] I was engaged tomorrow has been put off as I found on my arrival at home last night, by a message from the President: and the party is deferred till Tuesday. There are to be some people present whom I am very anxious to see, and I hope M[r] Ritchie will let me off my rash promise and let me come to you some other day. I could not make heads or tails of the Ballet last night and instead of Madame R.[15] who is said to be a most agreeable woman found only her husband a most uninteresting Israelite.

Always afftly yours<br>W M T.

565.    TO W. RAYMOND SAMS
     4 FEBRUARY 1849? [16]

*Address:* W R Sams Esq[re]. Hitherto unpublished.

Dear Sams

I am your man. Where does J J [17] live? Give him the compts of 'le poète Thackeray.'

---

[14] The date of this note is fixed by Thackeray's reference to the incomprehensible ballet at the Opéra. See above, No. 563.

[15] Gertrude Henriette Sontag (1806?–1854), the famous soprano, had married an Italian diplomat named Count de Rossi in 1829 and retired from the stage in 1830. Having lost her fortune in the revolutionary disturbances of 1848, she was forced to return to the theatre. She made her first public appearance in London on July 7, 1850. Four years later she died of cholera during a singing tour in Mexico.

[16] See the next letter.

[17] Jules Gabriel Janin (1804–1874), the critic and man-of-letters. After the success of *L'Âne mort et la Femme guillotinée* (1829), a parody of the romantic tale of terror, he began his connection with the *Journal des Débats* which lasted for forty years. He published essays on Richardson and Sterne,

566.           TO MRS. BROOKFIELD
              4–5 FEBRUARY 1849

Published in part, *Collection of Letters*, pp. 74–78. The words between daggers were overscored by Mrs. Brookfield.

My dear lady, I have been to see a great character to day and another still greater yesterday. To days was Jules Janin, whose books you never read nor do I suppose you could very well. He is the critic of the Journal des Debats and has made his weekly feuilleton famous throughout Europe. He does not know a word of English but he translated Sterne and I think Clarissa Harlowe: one week having no theatres to describe in his feuilleton or no other subject handy, he described his own marriage w^h took place in fact that week and absolutely made a present of his sensations to all the European public — He has the most wonderful verve, humour, oddity, honesty, bonhommie: he was ill with the gout or recovering perhaps but bounced about the room gesticulating joking gasconading quoting Latin — pulling out his books w^h are very handsome, and tossing about his curling brown hair — a magnificent jolly intelligent face such as would suit Pan I should think a flood of humourous rich jovial talk — and now I have described this how are you to have the least idea of him? I daresay its not a bit like him. He recommended me to read Diderot w^h I have been reading in at his recommendation; and that is a remarkable sentimental Cynic too in his ways of thinking and sudden humours not unlike — not unlike M^r Bows of the Chatteris Theatre.[18] I can fancy Harry Pendennis and him seated on the bridge and talking of their mutual mishap — no Arthur Pendennis the boy's name is — I shall be forgetting my own next. But mind you my similes dont go any farther: and I hope you don't go for to fancy that you know any-

---

prefixed to translations of their work, but it does not appear — as Thackeray states in the next letter — that he claimed himself to be the translator. In 1841 he announced his marriage in a feuilleton entitled "Mariage du critique," but when Thackeray first met him, he was living in a bachelor apartment on the Rue de Vaugirard.

[18] See chapter 6 of *Pendennis*.

body like Miss Fotheringay You dont suppose that I think *you* have no heart do you? but theres many a woman who has none and about whom men go crazy — such was the other character I saw yesterday. We had a long talk: in w$^h$ she showed me her interior and I inspected it and left it in a state of wonderment w$^h$ I can't describe — This woman six years ago was my sister and we were generously fond of each other up to about 10 years since. She is kind frank open-handed not very refined: with a warm outpouring of language — and thinks herself the most feeling creature in the world. The way in w$^h$ she fascinates some people is quite extraordinary. She affected me by telling me of an old friend of ours in the country D$^r$ Portman's daughter[19] indeed who was a parson in our parts — who died of consumption the other day, after leading the purest and saintliest life and who after she had rec$^d$ the sacrament read over her friends letter and actually died with it on the bed. Her husband adores her — He is an old Cavalry Colonel of 60 and the poor fellow away now in India and yearning after her writes her yards & yards of the most tender submissive frantic letters — Five or six other men are crazy about her. She trotted them all out one after another before me last night — not humourously I mean or making fun of them, but complacently describing their adoration for her and acquiescing in their opinion of herself — Friends lovers husband she coaxes them all and no more cares for them than worthy Miss Fotheringay did. O Becky is a trifle to her: and I am sure I might draw her picture and she never w$^d$ know in the least that it was herself. I suppose I did not fall in love with her myself because we were brought up together — She was a very simple generous creature then —

Tuesday — Friends came in as I was writing last night — perhaps in time to stop my chattering But I am encore tout émerveillé de † ma cousine.† By all the Gods I never had the opportunity of inspecting such a naturalness and coquetry. — Not that I suppose there are not many such women. But I have only myself known one or two women intimately: and I daresay the novelty

[19] Possibly Harriet Huyshe, daughter of the Rev. Francis Huyshe.

would wear off if I knew more — I had the Revue des 2 Mondes[20] & the Journal des Debats to dinner, and what do you think by way of a delicate attention the Chef served us up? Mock-turtle soup again: and uncommonly good it was too. After dinner I went to a ball at the Prefecture of Police — the most splendid apartments I ever saw in my life, such lights pillars marble hangings carving and gilding. I'm sure King Belshazzar could not have been more magnificently lodged. There must have been fifteen hundred people: of whom I did not know one single soul. I am surprised that the people did not faint in the saloons w.h were like burning fiery furnaces, but there they were dancing and tripping away — ogling & flirting and I suppose not finding the place a bit inconveniently warm. The women were very queer looking bodies for the most part I thought, but the men dandies every one fierce and trim with curling little mustachios: I felt dimly that I was 3 inches taller than any body in the room, but I hope nobody took notice of me. There was a rush for ices at a footman who brought those refreshments w.h was perfectly terrific — They were scattered melting over the heads of the crowd as I ran out of it in a panic. There was an old British dowager with two daughters seated up against a wall, very dowdy & sad. Poor old body I wonder what she wanted there? and whether that was what she called pleasure?

I went to see W.ms old friend and mine Bowes — He has 40000 a year and palaces in the country, and here he is a manager of the Theatre of Varieties — and his talk was about actors and coulisses all the time of our interview — I wish it could be the last: but he has made me promise to dine with him and go I must to be killed by his melancholy gentlemanlikeness. I think that's all I did yesterday. Dear lady I am pained at your having been unwell — I thought you must have been when Saturday came without any letter. There wont be one today I bet twopence. I am going to a lecture at the Institute — a lecture on Burns by M. Chasles who is Professor of English literature. What a course of lionizing isn't it? But it must stop for isn't the month the shortest of months?

[20] Philarète Chasles and John Lemoinne.

I went to see my old haunts when I came to Paris thirteen years ago[21] and made believe to be a painter — just after I was ruined and before I fell in love and took to marriage & writing. It was a very jolly time. I was as poor as Job: and sketched away most abominably, but pretty contented: and we used to meet in each others little rooms and talk about Art and smoke pipes and drink bad brandy & water. That awful habit still remains; but where is Art that dear Mistress whom I loved though in a very indolent capricious manner but with a real sincerity? I see her far, very far off. I jilted her, I know it very well: but you see it was Fate ordained that marriage never should take place: and forced me to take on with another lady, two other ladies, three other ladies. I mean the Muse, and my wife, and &c — Well, you are very good to listen to all this egotistic prattle, chère soeur si douce et si bonne — I have no reason to be ashamed of my loves seeing that all three are quite lawful. Did you go to see my people yesterday? — Some day when his Reverence is away will you have the children? and not if you please be so vain as to fancy that you cant amuse them or that they will be bored in your house. They must & shall be fond of you if you please — Alfred's open mouth as he looked at the broken bottle and spilt wine must have been a grand picture of agony.[22]

I couldn't find the Lecture Room at the Institute so I went to the Louvre instead,[23] and took a feast with the statues and pictures. The Venus of Milo is the grandest figure of figures. The wave of the lines of the figure wherever seen fills my senses with pleasure. What is it that so charms and satisfies one in certain lines? O the man who atchieved that statue was a beautiful genius — I have

[21] Actually Thackeray has in mind his removal to France in 1834, fifteen years earlier.

[22] There appears to be no other record of Tennyson's mishap.

[23] In the catalogue of the *Collection de M. Alfred Bovet*, Paris, 1887 (pp. 432–433) a two-page letter that Thackeray wrote to Chasles on February 6 is described, the first page being reproduced in facsimile and the second in part translated:

"My dear M. Chasles.

"In that famous letter upon my table at home, I told you how it came to pass that the biography of Titmarsh reached you without any envelope    I

been sitting thinking of it these 10 minutes in a delightful sensuous rumination. The colours of the Titian pictures comfort one's eyes similarly and after these feasts w^h wouldn't please my lady very much I daresay, being I should think too earthy for you, I went and looked at a picture I usedn't to care much for in old days, an Angel saluting a Virgin & Child by Pietro of Cortona — a secret smiling angel with a lily in her hand looking so tender and gentle — I wished that instant to make a copy of it and do it beautifully w^h I can't, and present it to somebody on Lady day. — There now; just fancy it is done, and presented in a neat compliment and hung up in your room — a pretty piece dainty and devotional — I drove

had put it into one of the numbers of Pendennis surrounding the packet with

a bandeau, & open at each end so that it might be inspected at the Custom House. I rode down to Bossange's with it myself on horseback but as I pulled the packet out of my pocket to give to the gentleman who came out from the shop to speak to me (for naturally I couldn't ride into the Shop) behold the bandeau had come off, and I was obliged to give the papers loose to M^s Bossange Barthes Lowell, whom I have made much too tall in the picture. Thus it happened that my Confidences reached you open, and may have been read by all the shopboys for what I know, though they were only intended for you and me." "J'ai été à l'Institut hier à deux heures," the translation continues, "espérant vous y rencontrer à votre cours, mais le concierge n'a pu me dire où vous étiez, et un étudiant qui passait avec ses livres et sa barbe se mit à rire lorsque je lui adressai la même question, ce qui me rendit si honteux que je me précipitai vers le pont des Arts et me réfugiai au Louvre, où je me mis sous la protection de ma déesse la Vénus de Milo. J'espère vous visiter samedi et avoir le plaisir de faire la connaissance de madame Chasles." And, finally, a sentence of direct quotation: "I did not know one single soul in the Prefets ball, and the women were so badly dressed that I thought I was in England."

Chasles employed the autobiographical notes that Thackeray had entrusted to Barthès & Lowell, foreign booksellers, late Bossange & Co., 14 Great Marlborough Street (*Post Office London Directory*, 1847), in "Le Roman de moeurs en Angleterre. — *La Foire aux vanités*" (*Revue des deux mondes*, February–March, 1849, pp. 537–571 and 721–759), devoting three pages (538–540) to a sketch of his subject's life.

about with † my cousin † and wondered at her more and more. She is come to my dearest William now: though she doesn't care a phig for me: she told me astonishing things showed me a letter in wʰ every word was true and wʰ was a fib from beginning to end — a miracle of deception — flattered fondled coaxed — O she was worth coming to Paris for. † And my mother bred this woman that is the wonder.† Pray God to keep us simple. I have never looked at anything in my life wʰ has so amazed me — Why this is as good almost as if I had you to talk to. Let us go out and have another walk.

567.     TO MRS. BROOKFIELD
FEBRUARY 1849

Published in part, *Collection of Letters*, pp. 56–57. The words between daggers were overscored by Mrs. Brookfield.

Last night was a dinner at Spencer Cowper's[24] — the man who used to be called the fortunate youth some years back when 10 or perhaps 20000 a year were suddenly left him by a distant relative, and when he was without a guinea in the world. It was a Sybaritic repast in a magnificent apartment and we were all of us young voluptuaries of fashion. There were portraits of Louis Quatorze's ladies round the room (I was going to say salle a manger but room after all is as good a word) We sate in the comfortablest armchairs and valets went round every instant filling our glasses with the most exquisite liquors. The glasses were as big as at Kinglake's dinner[25] — Do you remember Kinglake's feast Ma'am? then we adjourned into wadded drawing rooms all over sofas and lighted with a hundred candles where smoking was practised and we en-

[24] Charles Spencer Cowper (1816–1879), third son of the fifth Earl Cowper. He later (1852) married Lady Harriet D'Orsay, Count D'Orsay's widow.
[25] See above, No. 367.

joyed a pleasant and lively conversation — carried on in the 2 languages of w.ʰ we young dogs are perfect masters. As I came away at midnight I saw Cowpers carriage-lamps blazing in the court yard, keeping watch until the fortunate youth should come out to pay a visit to some Becky no doubt. The young men were clever very frank and gentlemanlike, rather well read — quite as pleasant companions as one deserves to meet — and as for your humble servant, he saw a chapter or two of Pendennis in some of them.

I am going with † my cousin † to day to see Alexis the Somnambulist. She came in yesterday evening and talked to me for 2 hours before dinner. I astonished her by finding out her secrets by some of those hits que vous savez — Look, here is a bit of paper with a note to her actually commenced in reply to my dearest William[26] — but I couldn't get out my dearest † Mary † in return: and stopped at my, — but I like her better than I did — and begin to make allowances for a woman of great talents married to a stupid generous obstinate devoted heavy dragoon, thirty years her senior. My dear old mother with her imperial manner tried to take the command of both of them, and was always anxious to make them understand that I was the divinest creature in the world, whose shoe-strings neither of them were fit to tie — Hence bickerings hatreds secret jealousies and open revolt And I can fancy them both worked up to a pitch of hatred of me that my success in life must have rendered only more bitter.

But about Alexis — this wonder of wonders reads letters or tells you their contents and the names of their authors without ever thinking of opening the seal; and I want you very much if you please and instantly on receipt of this to send me a bit of your hair that I may have a consultation on it. Mind you I dont want it for myself — I pledge you my word I'll burn it or give you back

---

[26] The following fragment of a note is written at the bottom of the last page of this letter:
"My
   "I am just come home, to write until dinner-time: or I would come out to you — Will 12 tomorrow do, or shall I come to you at 4 or so? Al."

every single hair being too proud to steal what you don't think it is your duty to give (Indeed I am hurt with myself that I should have asked anything that you should have refused: & have miscalculated the sum as it were, that you owed me.) But do, if you please Mum, gratify my curiosity in this matter and consult the soothsayer regarding you. My cousin showed him letters and vows he is right in every particular. And as I shan't be very long here, I propose by return of post for that favour.

Are you going to dine at Lansdowne House on Saturday? The post has come in & brings me an invitation, and a letter from my Ma and my daughters but none from my sister. Are you ill again dear lady? — Dont be ill — God bless you — Good bye. I shall write again if you please but I shant be long before I come — dont be ill Im afraid you are You haven't been to Kensington. My love to Mʳ Williams. Farewell & write tomorrow.


568.                    TO MRS. JAMES
                      14 FEBRUARY 1849

Hitherto unpublished. [See reproduction facing page 509.]

Young Street Kensington Sqʳᵉ My dear Mʳˢ James I am very sorry indeed to hear that you have been ill and am on the other hand glad to think that you are once more restored to the duties of hospitality: I have been at Paris and am only come back just now and I should be so glad to dine with you on Thursday still if your project of a dinner party still holds good but if you have filled up your table please to let me know and to believe me my dear Mʳˢ James (without the slightest preparations or ruling of lines or any nonsense wʰ any man who really can use his pen would think unworthy of him) I say I beg you to believe that I am without any circumlocution most sincerely yours and of course Mʳ Wᵐ James's that popular but eccentric author & individual W M Thackeray Feb 14 1849.

569.                TO MRS. BROOKFIELD
                    12–13 MARCH 1849

*Address:* M^rs Brookfield | 15 Portman S^t | Portman Sq^re London. *Postmarks:*
CAMBRIDGE MR 13 1849, 13 MR 1849. Published in part, *Collection of
Letters,* pp. 117–120. The passages between daggers have been overscored by
Mrs. Brookfield.

Madam I have only had one opportunity of saying how do you
do to day, on the envelope of a letter w^h you will have received
from another and even more intimate friend[27] — This is to inform
you that I am so utterly and dreadfully miserable now he has just
gone off at near eleven o'clock to Norwich by the horrid mail, that
I think I can't bear this place beyond tomorrow and must come
home again. We had a very pleasant breakfast though at D^r
Mayne's[28] with 2 well-bred young gentlemen of the University[29]
and broiled fowls and mushrooms just as we remember them 200
years ago. † M^rs Mayne you will be sorry to hear does not look so
pretty mornings as when candlelight illumines her simple beauties
& is much inferior in this respect to 2 dear friends of mine[30] in
⟨. . .⟩[31] who always look neat & tidy at whatever hour (and I see
them constantly and at every hour in the day) † I see them. I have
had the meanness not to take a private room and write in con-

[27] Brookfield's letter of March 12, published in *Mrs. Brookfield,* p. 275.
Thackeray's salutation was the little drawing reproduced on the opposite page.
[28] Henry James Sumner Maine (1822–1888), the great jurist, who was
Regius Professor of Civil Law at Cambridge from 1847 to 1854. He and
Brookfield were fellow members of the Apostles' Club and friends of Harry
Hallam. He was knighted in 1871.
[29] Identified in Brookfield's letter as Julian Henry Charles Fane (1827–
1870), fourth son of the eleventh Earl of Westmorland; and William George
Granville Venables Vernon Harcourt (1827–1904), later (1873) knighted.
Fane published a volume of *Poems* in 1852 and had a distinguished career in
the diplomatic service. Harcourt wrote for *The Morning Chronicle* and *The
Saturday Review* and built up a large law practice before he became famous
as a Liberal statesman.
[30] Kate Perry and Mrs. Elliot. See *Memoranda.*
[31] Here one or two words are irrecoverably overscored.

THACKERAY BY HIMSELF

*Sketch made inside an envelope the Rev. W. H. Brookfield was addressing to his wife.*

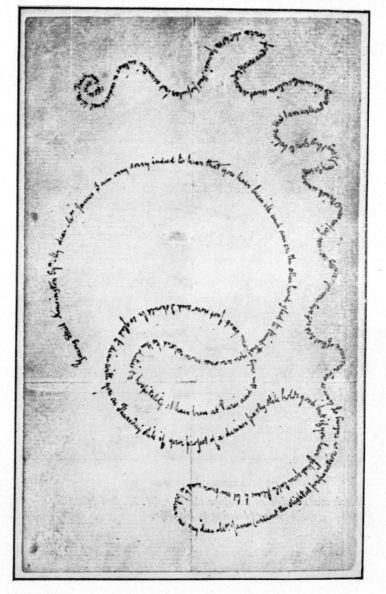

THACKERAY'S LETTER OF 14 FEBRUARY, 1849

sequence in the Coffee-Apartment in a great state of disquiet. Young
undergraduates are eating supper: Chattering is going on incessantly
I wonder whether Villiam is safe in the train, or will he come back
in 2 minutes too late for the conveyance? — Yes, here he comes
actually — No, it is only the waiter with a fresh supply of bitter
beer for the young gents. Well we brexfsted with M$^r$ & M$^{rs}$ Mayne
and I thought him a most kind gentle and loveable sort of man so
to speak, and liked her artlessness & simplicity (not that[32] (this is
the same horrid ink of last night w$^h$ will blot) not that she is to
be compared I say to Miss Elliot & M$^{rs}$ Perry) and then we went
to fetch walks over the ground forgotten — yet somehow well remembered     He says he is going to bring you down here and
that you will like it and be very happy — Mon Dieu Madame will
you be very happy if you know that I am entirely miserable? and if
you go away for another fortnight after Clevedon miserable I shall
be as I deserve to be. for if I dont see you I am unneasy: † and shall
find it ⟨. . .⟩ [33] to the ⟨. . .⟩ your being happy in the ⟨. . .⟩,† w$^h$ is
very selfish of me my sister & friend, but we are made so. † Why
should I ⟨. . .⟩ † Just now W$^m$ I was going to write V$^m$ but I knew
you wouldn't like it, said She is dining at Lady Monteagle's[34] so I
said Let us drink her health & we did in a mixture of ale & soda water
very good, there was a bagman asleep in the room — and we drank
your health & both of us said God bless her. I think this is the chief
part of my transactions during the day — In fact I know what is
the chief part of my transactions it lies in one letter of the Alfybick
and that letter is U — isn't that neat and clever? Dear kind lady
bear with my follies, and let time make me wiser.

I think I said we walked about in haunts once familiar, we went
to the Union where we read the papers then down to the river
where we saw the young fellows in the boats then amidst the college-

---

[32] There is a large inkspot on the manuscript here.

[33] In this and the following hiatuses there are respectively two, one, two, and
eight or nine words irrecoverably overscored.

[34] Lady Mary Anne Monteagle (1800–1889), second wife of the first
Baron (1790–1866), and step-mother of Stephen Spring-Rice.

groves, and cætera, & peeped into various courts & halls and were not unamused, but bitterly melancholious: though I must say W<sup>m</sup> complimented me on my healthy appearance and he for his part looked uncommonly well. I went then to see my relations — old D<sup>r</sup> Thackeray 75 years of age perfectly healthy handsome stupid & happy — who is not a bit changed in 20 years, nor is his wife strange to say. I told him he looked like my Grandfather[35] his Uncle, on w<sup>h</sup> he said 'Your Grandfather was by no means the handsomest of the Thackerays' and so I suppose he prides hisself on his personal beauty.

At 4 we went to dine with Don † Thompson † in Hall — where the thing to me most striking was the — if you please — the smell of the dinner exactly like what I remember aforetime — Savoury odours of youth borne across I dont know what storms and deserts struggles passions poverties hopes hopeless loves & useless loves of twenty years! — There is a sentiment suddenly worked out of a number of veal & mutton-joints and surprizes me just as much as it astonishes you — But the best (or worst) of being used to the pen is that one chatters with it as with the tongue to certain persons and all things blurt out for good or for bad. You know how to take the good parts generously & to forget the bad, dear kind lady. But we both agreed that Don Jeronimo † Thompson † & all the big wigs assembled and drinking Port round a horse shoe table in the combination room, were intolerably pompous & donnish, and that it is better to meet a gentleman or 2 than all these. Then we went to Jenny Linds Concert for w<sup>h</sup> a gentleman here gave us tickets: and at the end of the 1<sup>st</sup> Act we agreed to come away. It struck me as atrociously stupid — I was thinking of something else the whole time she was jugulating away, & oh I was so glad to get to the Inn and have a cigar and I wanted so to go away with M<sup>r</sup> Williams, for I feel entirely out of place in this town. This seems to me to be spoken all in a breath and has been written without a full stop      Does it not strike you as entirely frantic and queer? Well

I wish I wish I were back. I like to say Goodnight to my lady my lady my lady. Gby.

I receive this moment a charming letter — Insatiable woman. Won't you have too much pleasure tomorrow a child's party a tea party and — but O I must come come just to say good night to my soeur.

I am going out to breakfast to see some of the gallant young blades of the University and to night if I last until then to the Union to hear a debate — What a queer thing it is! I think W^m is a little disappointed that I have not been made enough a lion of: whereas my timid nature trembles before such honors: and my vanity would be to go through life as a gentleman — as a Major Pendennis you have hit it — I believe I never do think about my public character and certainly did not see the gyps waiters and undergraduates whispering in Hall as your Villiam did or thought he did. He was quite happy in some dreary rooms in College where I would have perished of ennui — thus are we constituted. An old hook nosed clergyman has just come into the Coffee room and is looking over my shoulder I think, he has put a stop to the sentence beginning 'thus are we &c'

Jenny Lind made 400£ by the Concert last night and has given 100 to the Hospital — this seems rather pompous sort of piety. It would be better to charge people less than 31/6^d for tickets, and omit the charity to the poor. But you see people are never satisfied (the hook nosed clergyman has just addressed a remark) — only I pitied my cousins the Miss Thackerays[36] last night who were longing to go, & couldn't because tickets for four or five of them in the second rows would have cost as many guineas; and their father couldn't afford any such sum.

I wonder whether I shall come back to London tomorrow and if I shall have another letter from anybody — No I think not she will be going to write then she will draw back and think one letter is enough — But this last is such a funny & kind one that I can live on it for 2 days pretty well. Adieu J'ai l'espoir de vous revoir

[36] Dr. Thackeray's children by his second marriage.

bientot — So Dashwood is spooney is he? I am glad you put the
M$^r$ before his name: and present my very best compliments to M$^{rs}$
Fanshawe    If you see M$^{rs}$ Elliot remember me to her most
kindly: and now to breakfast. G B Y

570.        TO DR. FREDERIC THACKERAY
                    14 MARCH 1849

*Address:* D$^r$ Thackeray | S$^t$ Andrews St | Cambridge. *Postmarks:* 14 MR
1849, CAMBRIDGE MR 15 1849. Hitherto unpublished.

                        13 Young S$^t$ Kensington Sq$^e$
                              March 14.
My dear Doctor Thackeray
    You will see by the date that it is all over. The young men
wouldn't talk to me, the Dons thought I had come to put them
into a book, everybody suspected me: and I felt myself so miserable, that I thought the best course was to fly    I rushed away
in a perfect panic by the 2 o'clock train, & didn't like to face you
before I came off, knowing that you & M$^{rs}$ Thackeray would be
bent upon feasting & entertaining me. But I am glad to have been
at Cambridge if only for the pleasure of shaking hands with you
and seeing you look so well.
                    Always faithfully yours dear D$^r$ Thackeray
                        **W M Thackeray**

571.                    TO THE REV. WILLIAM AND
                            MRS. BROOKFIELD
                            9 APRIL 1849 [37]

Published in part, *Collection of Letters*, pp. 43–45.

My dear persons.

After lying in bed until you had reached Clifton[38] exceeding
melancholy from want of sleep (induced by no romantic inward
feelings, but by other causes much more material and vulgar viz
late smoking &c of previous nights) shall I tell you what it was
dissipated my blue devils? As I was going towards London the
postman stopped me in the street & asked me if I w$^d$ take my letters?
w$^h$ he handed to me — One was an Opera box w$^h$ I sent off to M$^{rs}$
Maine for tomorrow and one was a letter from an Attorney de-
manding instantly 112£ for that abominable Irish railway:[39] and
in presence of this real calamity all the sentimental ones vanished
straight — I began to think how I must raise the money: how I
must go to work nor be shilly shallying any longer, and with this
real care staring me in the face I began to forget imaginary grievances & to think about going to work immediately & how for the
next 3 months I must screw & save in order to pay off the money.
And this is the way Mam that the grim duties of the world put the
soft feelings aside: we've no time to be listening to *their* little meek
petitions and tender home prattle, in presence of the imperative
Duty — who says 'Come Come, no more of this here — Get to
work Mister,' and so we go and join the working gang: behind w$^h$
Necessity marches cracking his whip — This metaphor has not been
worked out so completely as it might be: but it means that I am
resolved to go to work directly.

[37] The date of this letter is set by Thackeray's reference to the procession
before the Lord Mayor's annual Easter dinner. This event took place at the
Mansion House, the Sheriffs of Middlesex and their ladies attending, on April
9, 1849 (*Times*, April 10). Mrs. Brookfield no doubt received the letter in
Clifton on April 10, the date given in *Collection of Letters*, p. 43.

[38] The Brookfields visited the Parrs in Clifton before continuing to Clevedon
Court, some seventeen miles away.           [39] See above, No. 324.

So being determined on this I went off at once to the Star and Garter at Richmond and dined with those 2 nice women and their husbands, viz. the Strutts[40] & Romillys    We had every sort of luxury for dinner, and afterwards talked about Vanity Fair & Pendennis almost incessantly (though I declare I led away the conversation at least 10 times but they would come back) so that the evening was uncommonly pleasant. Once twice thrice, it came into my head I wonder what those people at Clifton are doing? I would give 2/6ᵈ to be with them, but in the meanwhile it must be confessed the Star & Garter is not bad: these ladies are handsome and good & clever & kind: that Solicitor General talks with great pleasantness — & so I came home in a fly with an old gentleman who knew Sir S. Romilly[41] and we talked of the dark end of that history of a very good & wise man — & how he adored his wife (it was her death wʰ caused his suicide) and how his son was equally attached to his own of whose affection for her husband my informer gave many pretty instances — This conversation brought me to Kensington, where after thinking about the 112£ a little and a little more about some friends of mine, whom I pray God to make happy I fell into a great big sleep — from wʰ I wake at this present 8 o'clock in the morning to say Bon Jour Madame.

Where do you think this is wrote from? from an attorneys office old Jewry. The Lord Mayor the Sheriffs their coaches and footmen in gold and silk stockings have just passed in a splendid procession through the mud and pouring rain — I have been to the bankers to see how much money I have got. I have got 120£ I owe 112£ — from 120 take 112 — leave 8 for the rest of the month — Isn't that pleasant? — Well, but I know how to raise some — the bankers say I may overdraw. Things isn't so bad.

But now (this is from the Garrick Club) now I say for the wonderful wonder of wonders — There is a chance for Mr Williams such as he little looked for. EMMA is free. The great

---

[40] Edward Strutt (1801–1880), later (1856) first Baron Belper, a well-known statesman; and Sir John Romilly (1802–1874), later (1866) first Baron Romilly, who became Solicitor-General in 1848. Mrs. Strutt (d. 1890) and Lady Romilly (d. 1856) were sisters of Thackeray's friend, Mrs. James.
[41] Sir Samuel Romilly (1757–1818), the law reformer, father of Sir John.

Catastrophe has happened last night she and her mother fled from the infamous Richards and took refuge at M<sup>rs</sup> Procter's — where they had Hadlid & Hagnis's beds who went and slept with M<sup>r</sup> & M<sup>rs</sup> Goldsmid[42] next door. M<sup>r</sup> & M<sup>rs</sup> P called at Kensington at 11 o'clock, and brought the news — Richards had treated his wife infimusly — Richards had assailed her with the most brutal language and outrages — that innocent woman Madame Gagiotti poor thing who meddled with nothing & remained all day in her own garret so as to give no trouble was flung out of the house by him indeed only stayed in order to protect his daughters life    The brute refused to allow the famous picture to be exhibited — in fact is a madman and a ruffian.

Procter & I went off to make peace and having heard Richards's story — I believe that he has been more wronged than they. The mother-in-law is at the bottom of all the mischief — It was she who made the girl marry Richards and the marriage made she declined leaving her daughter, in fact the poor devil who has a bad temper a foolish head an immense vanity has been victimised by the women; and I pity him a great deal more than them. O what a comedy it would make![43] but the separation I suppose is final and it will be best for both parties*

I wonder whether you will give me a luncheon on Thursday? I might stop for 2 hours on my way to Taunton, & make you my handshake. This would be very nice — I thought of writing to M<sup>rs</sup> Elton and offering myself but I should like first to have the approval of M<sup>r</sup> Williams, for after all I am not an indifferent person, but claim to rank as the aff<sup>te</sup> brother of both of you.

### W M T

* It will end no doubt in his having to pay a 4<sup>th</sup> of his income, for the pleasure of being a month married to her, and she will be an angelic martyr & x x

[42] The Procters lived at 13 Upper Harley Street; their neighbor at number 15 was Francis Henry Goldsmid (*Post Office London Directory*, 1847).

[43] Thackeray's comedy, *The Wolves and the Lamb*, has the same theme.

572.                      TO MRS. ELLIOT
                         18 APRIL 1849

My text is taken from a facsimile in *Collection of Letters*, p. 72.

                                        Kensington Wednesday
My dear M^rs Elliot

I was very much amused by your wicked little note w^h I received
at Taunton duly  I went afterwards to Exeter and then — o then!
I went on to Clifton where I spent nearly two days very agreeably
at the house of my friends M^r & M^rs Parr. M^rs P is a daughter
of Sir Charles Elton of Clevedon Court Bart. A very pleasing
person was staying at her house a M^rs Bloomfield or some such
name: her husband a clergyman & School Inspector very pleasant
too. Your amiable friends Lord & Lady Melgund[44] came back in
the train with yours ever

                         W M T

[44] William Hugh Elliot-Murray-Kynynmound (1814–1891), styled Lord
Melgund, later (1859) third Earl of Minto, who before succeeding to his
title represented various Scotch constituencies in parliament and wrote a book
on education in Scotland. In 1844 he married his cousin Emma Hislop
(1824–1882), only daughter of General Sir Thomas and Lady Hislop. Lady
Hislop was the former Emma Elliot (d. 1866), sister of Mrs. Elliot's husband
and daughter of Hugh Elliot (1752–1830), Governor of Madras and a
younger brother of the first Earl of Minto (1751–1814). The fortunes of
the Minto family were founded by the first Earl, who accumulated £245,000
while Governor-General of India between 1806 and 1813. In 1883 the
Minto estates were worth £15,860 annually (Bateman, *Great Landowners*,
p. 312).

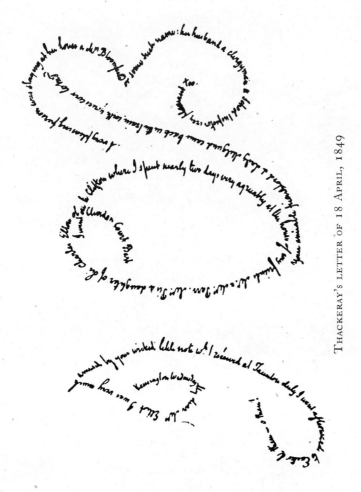

THACKERAY'S LETTER OF 18 APRIL, 1849

573.          TO MRS. PARR
              18 APRIL 1849

Hitherto unpublished.

              13 Young S! Kensington.   April 18.

Dear M!ˢ Parr

Look what it is to be a moral and instructive writer, and to be properly appreciated by persons of good character.[45] Think of me if you please on Saturday the 28ᵗʰ at a house where the wine is uncommonly good & plentiful, and where Virtue has got me the entrée — Well, I own, I am very much pleased indeed to have the good word of this good man.

And I'm glad to take this as a sort of pretext to write a line & thank you for your kindness. Those little holydays are very pleasant and sunshiny whatever the weather may be: but behold they are over; and I must put my nose to the grinding-stone and work all day.

I should have been very melancholy in the train but that I came up with a Lord & Lady who are friends of mine; and their elegant attentions diverted my sombre thoughts — To day I dine with the

---

[45] Thackeray's letter is written on the third and fourth pages of the following note from Sir Robert Inglis (1786–1855), an old Tory gentleman regarded as a pattern of courtesy and integrity, who was M. P. for Oxford from 1829 to 1854, President of the Literary Club, and an Antiquary of the Royal Academy:

               "Milton Bryan
                Woburn, Bed.
                 April 13. 1849

"My dear Sir

"I am very much gratified by your letter; & thank you for the kindness with which you have received mine.

"May we look forward to the pleasure of seeing you at dinner in Bedford Square on Saturday the 28 April at 1/4 before 7.

               "Believe me my dear Sir
                 faithfully yours
                  Robert H Inglis."

lovely widow of Siromfridévy[46] — Give my very best regards to
Velasquez and all other members of your family as far up as Papa:
and believe me, my dear Mʳˢ Parr

Always faithfully yours

W M Thackeray

574.                     TO MRS. JAMES
                     20 APRIL 1849 [47]

Hitherto unpublished.

Kensington. Friday.

My dear Mʳˢ James

   Aving promized to dine hout on Sattidy the 28ᵗʰ with Sir Robert
Arry Hinglish Bart M P. I must with regret refuge your polite
faviour for tomorrow and dine with Mʳ Punch on that day. But
has hour dinner is herly, I will with kind permishn look in in the
hevening and request the refreshmint of a *cuppatee*

Your very obedient Servᵗ

W M Thackeray

   P. S. I'm shaw my dear parince will like dining with you very
considerabble.

---

   [46] Lady Jane Davy (1780–1855), widow of the great scientist Sir Hum-
phry Davy (1778–1829), who at sixty-nine still took great pleasure in
London society.
   [47] For the date, see above, No. 573.

575.        TO JOHN BELL [48]
          20 APRIL 1849 [49]

*Address:* J. Bell Esq[re] | 1 Victoria Terrace | Marlbro' Road. Kensington.
Hitherto unpublished.

Kensington. Friday. 20 April

My dear Sir

You do me very much honour: and I already see myself in the Sculpture Room no 1556. Bust of a gentleman. I should have come to thank you yesterday but I stayed at home at work all day this being the struggling time of the month with

Yours very much obliged & gratified
W M Thackeray.

The Printers boy who bears this has with him some blocks of mine for Punch & Pendennis[50] — I somehow rather wish you would look at them, and see that there is some expression in them at least w[h] those villains of wood engravers cut out.

---

[48] John Bell (1811–1895), the sculptor. The projected bust does not appear to have been made.

[49] During the years that Thackeray was writing *Pendennis*, April 20 fell on Friday only in 1849.

[50] Number VII, chapters 21 to 23.

576.            FROM MRS. BROOKFIELD
                 23 APRIL 1849

My text is taken from *Mrs. Brookfield and her Circle*, pp. 280–281.

Clevedon Court,
23 April, 49.

Dear William Thackeray,

You gave such a hardworked picture of yourself when you
wrote last,[51] I wonder you could ask or wish to be written to when
you are so busy. I have just been seeing William off to London.
He had hoped to be here another week at least. I told him I should
be writing to you to-day, and he will try to see you one evening
if your numerous engagements don't interfere. Major T. and his
wife[52] come here to-day, with another brother officer, a very plain
Capt. B., who plays the flute and brings it with him. Rhoda[53] is
preparing for duets with him. He has never been here before, and
we are told to expect scars from small-pox and other personal
blemishes to weigh against his intrinsic worthiness. I am to leave
the state Green room and remove into the one which was yours,[54]
which I shall very much prefer, as Agnes[55] will be a protection to me
next door. I had a fright even with William in the house the first
night I came. Just as I had put out the candle and was getting
into bed, I felt the hand which one has dreaded all one's life,
clutching hold of my foot, of course it must have been mere fancy,
but I was so sure at the moment that it really was the hand that
I ran off with bare feet down to Arthur and Rhoda's rooms, and

---

[51] I have not traced this letter.

[52] There is further information about these persons in *Mrs. Brookfield*, pp.
282–283.

[53] The former Mrs. Rhoda Baird (d. 1873), who had married Arthur Hallam Elton (1818–1883), later (1853) seventh Baronet, in 1841.

[54] When Thackeray visited Clevedon Court in October, 1848.

[55] Mary Agnes Elton, the third daughter of Arthur Hallam Elton.

brought them both back armed with pokers, but nothing could be found and I had to look rather foolish the next morning at breakfast when daylight had sobered me into owning that I must have been mistaken, which I could not admit overnight . . . I have just been interrupted by a long visit from Lady Elton, and now it is post time.

Imagine Miss W—— being so touched by my saying I hoped she would come and see me in London, that she left the room and burst into tears, and begged Rhoda would explain her apparent coldness by the depth of gratitude she was inwardly feeling.

William talks of Saturday for our going to Cambridge so I suppose about Thursday week I shall come back. We shall get Pendennis down here, I shall expect to see a great deal of the Major in this No., as you would bring him out so completely *con amore.*

Yours,<br>J. O. B.

577.    TO THE REV. WILLIAM BROOKFIELD
APRIL 1849 [56]

Published in *Collection of Letters,* p. 58.

My dear Vieux

If you come home in any decent time I wish you would go off to poor M<sup>rs</sup> Crowe at Hampstead. A letter has just come from Eugenie, who describes the poor lady as low, wretched, and hysterical — She may drop. — Now a word or two of kindness from a black coat might make all the difference to her, and who so able to administer as your reverence? I am going out myself to laugh, talk and to the best of my ability soothe & cheer her: but the pro-

[56] This letter was written shortly before Thackeray and Brookfield went to Hampstead on Sunday, April 29. See below, No. 586.

fessional man is the best depend upon it: and I wish you would stretch a point in order to see her.

Yours till this evening

W M T

## 578.     TO THE REV. WILLIAM BROOKFIELD
### APRIL 1849 [57]

Hitherto unpublished.

Dearly beloved     If you are no⟨t engaged⟩ why not dine here? I've beal at Brightl ald very lear dul Peldellis     My parelts isl't yet cub.

Your wellwisher

W M T.

5 o'clock     We might go to the Procters to T.

[57] This letter was written shortly before April 27, when the Carmichael-Smyths arrived in London.

579.      **TO ADELAIDE PROCTER**
                     **APRIL 1849**

Hitherto unpublished.

My dear Miss Procter

My parents have just arrived from Paris and have presented their child with a new gold pen, I try it on this sheet Yours is the first name I have written with it and the first use I make of it is to declare with its aid that I am the most faithful of your servants

After reading over Captain Higginsons passionate appeal Emily sate for some moments in deep meditation. She did not love him

& yet she thought she ought to reward so much constancy. Her aunt M^rs Heavyside observed her in silence.

Don't you think that you ought to have some return for that beautiful pair of slippers? If you were to work a pair for me, and were to ask for a lock of my hair I'm sure I would give it you with your Mammas permission.

580.          TO MRS. BROOKFIELD
                  27 APRIL 1849

*Address:* M^rs Brookfield | Clevedon Court. Clevedon | near Bristol. *Postmarks:* AP 27 1849, BRISTOL AP 28 1849. Published in part, *Collection of Letters*, p. 128. The passages enclosed between daggers were overscored by Mrs. Brookfield.

We have been to Shoolbreds to buy a gown for Granny, we have been to Madame Victorine's to order new dresses for ourselves, we have been to call at M^rs Elliots M^rs Prinseps Lady Rothschilds[58] M^r H Hallams, M^rs James, M^rs Pollock, Lady Pollock — and the young women are gone home & I am igspecting M^r William to dine here. I've ordered such a nice dinner. We are to go to Sartorissa's afterwards. Will you go there next Friday?

[58] Thackeray had met Lady Louisa de Rothschild (1821–1910), wife of Sir Anthony de Rothschild (1810–1876), first Baronet, when he was travelling down the Rhine on his way back to England in August, 1848. "The . . . charm of our day's journey," wrote Lady Louisa (Lucy Cohen, *Lady de Rothschild and her Daughters, 1821–1931*, London, 1935, p. 34), "was Mr. Thackeray's presence. Strange enough, we made acquaintance directly and he remained with us the whole day. We talked of literature, drawings, Jews, of whom he has a bad opinion, politics, etc., and we parted very good friends — at least I fancy so. He seems a good and an honest man, with a kind heart, notwithstanding a large fund of satire. I like him better than his books." Lady de Rothschild's daughter Constance (1843–1931), later Lady Battersea, recalled that on this occasion Thackeray lifted her on his shoulder and walked up and down the deck, telling her fairy tales. Thackeray and Lady de Rothschild met frequently in society after their return to London, and when Thackeray gave his lectures on the English Humourists in 1851, his friend attended them faithfully, regarding each, not "as a lecture but as a conversation with Thackeray" (p. 35). Among the other members of the numerous Rothschild clan, Thackeray was particularly friendly with Baron Lionel de Rothschild.

I think I shall go somewhere on Sunday Monday & Tuesday I have no engagements for those 3 days, isn't it wonderful? But I will be magnanimous and not bother my dear lady's friends. I saw Harry Hallam he and the faithful Maine were reading hard. Maine wanted me to fix to go to his house on Friday 4 May — but I wouldn't. Harry was very pleasant jovial & gracious. He has been speaking well of me to the Elliots the artful dodger! He knew they would tell me again — What kind women they are. They say they had a very nice letter from you — I didn't have a nice letter from you — and as for your letter to my Mama w^h I read — O Mam how frightened you were when you wrote it — and what for were you in a fright? You have much more brains imagination wit than she — how conceited it is to be afraid then —

I saw my lovely VIRGINIA[59] to day — she looked rather yellow though, but was as kind & merry as ever. The children seemed to stare to hear me laugh & talk — I never do at home — I cant before those solemn old people — I think the dear old Mater Dolorosa[60] gloomifies me more than the old gentleman — I would die rather than make a joke to her. In fact . . . . . .

† This letter is of a piece with yours. There is a gêne somehow. ⟨. . .⟩[61] for a month ma soeur, come back and let me talk to you —.† Give my best regards to all the people at Clevedon, whom I like: † and ⟨. . .⟩ †

[59] Virginia Pattle.
[60] See below, App. XXVI, October, 1848.
[61] In this and the following hiatus there are respectively about nine and eleven words irrecoverably overscored.

581.                    TO MRS. JAMES
                        27 APRIL 1849

*Address:* M^rs James | 37 Gloster Place | Portman Sq^re. *Postmark:* AP 27 1849.
Hitherto unpublished.

                                    Kensington.  Thursday ev^g
My dear M^rs James

I have read the Ways & Means — and think it what shall I
say? — a masterpiece. It is the most admirable good sense — the
most brilliant argument, the most lucid statement — upon my
word I'm so delighted with it that I can't help breaking out into
this laudation; and expect the author of that pamphlet will take
I don't know what rank ere long as a statesman and a public
benefactor — Present my compliments to him — and remember
if you please that I'm one of the first: before all the world is
talking about him.

                        Always sincerely yours
                        W M Thackeray.


582.                    FROM MRS. BROOKFIELD
                        28 APRIL 1849

My text is taken from *Mrs. Brookfield and her Circle*, pp. 284–286.

                        Clevedon Court,
                            28th April, 1849.
What a shame that you should read my letter to your mother.
I thought it remarkably freely written and neatly expressed, and I
congratulated myself on your being away at the time and that I
could therefore be so easy — not that I care at all for being stupid
to you but I expect you to feel ashamed of me if I show any dulness
to people who already wonder (as you do yourself), "what there
is in me."

I am very glad that you are free again now and able to thread the

mazes of refined society without any distraction. You have plenty
to fill your letter with but how can I thrust a description of Cap.
B—— upon you in return? Yet there has been no better novelty
here than his arrival. I have been walking a good deal lately
with the T.'s, Arthur and B——, and the cousin to whom the
Captain gallantly dedicates himself when unappropriated by Mrs.
T., who is writing at the same table with me in all innocence while
I am dipping my pen in venom to run her down; she is so singularly well satisfied with herself that I don't feel much remorse.
Rhoda observed her the first day she arrived, scanning me all over
with a satirical expression, conveying her perfect acquaintance with
a bygone flirtation. However, I looked so harmless and so perfectly indifferent that she relented and came up to me in an olive
branch spirit, with a little speech about having heard so much of
me from her husband that she had *quite longed* to make my
acquaintance, and ever since she has been in her most condescending
mood towards me, but I can't respond, and feel sorry because the
husband evidently wishes me to praise the wife to him, and is
always leading the conversation towards her, but all I can bring
out is praise for her music, which is rather good. It is amusing to
see him wrapped up in his children and this lady, and to recollect
his extreme of politeness to me when I met him here before. I think
he is inclined to laugh sometimes himself when the former visit is
alluded to.

We walked to the sea yesterday, and I boldly went into the
library and ordered No. seven to be sent to me immediately on
its appearance down here, "We get it either the 1st or 2nd of the
month," they said, which seems very behindhand when we get it
in London on the 30th. I am glad you are to dine at the Royal
Academy, and is the Bust to be made? Rhoda has heard that
Virginia[62] has quite eclipsed Miss A. in the Duke of D——'s
admiration. As to Turpin's looking so handsome she is not at all
in favour with me and getting quite spoilt as a good servant. I
daresay in a new place she would come out quite briskly again, but

[62] Virginia Pattle.

I think we shall have to dismiss her. Now don't take her yourself, you would not like it. What an odd girl Adelaide Procter is, I should give her a little quiet set down some day if I were you, I think it would be friendly and do her good. Do you think me very spiteful to-day? I am afraid I have abused everybody I have mentioned, which seems ill-natured. I would not do it to any-one I did not know so well as I do you, and where it is not likely to do harm to anyone. Such dreadful pens with all my attempts at mending them, they won't write any cleaner, which I daresay revolts your sense of propriety, as you pique yourself so much on your own handwriting. I am glad William was to dine with you last night.[63] I have heard from him every day though he was so busy as hardly to have time for it, and Harry penned me a note which came with yours this morning, and another letter from Mrs. F. very kind as usual, but giving but a bad account of herself, and a prim, well-worded A. Bullar. Five letters, all so different I read them while I was dressing, William's and yours first, — and they made me so late I was obliged to breakfast upstairs.

I sang for two hours yesterday by myself in the schoolroom, fully believing that no one could hear me, when I came down and found they were all listening in the Hall which was unpleasant. Give my love to Anny and Minny, and thank you for being so kind as to write to me, but please do not feel *généd* any more. Good-bye.

583.                    TO MRS. BAYNE
                          MAY? 1849

*Address:* Mʳˢ Bayne | The Cottage | Wimbledon Common. Hitherto un-published.

                     13 Young Sᵗ Kensington.
                            Friday.

You are very kind indeed dear Mʳˢ Bayne to propose a holiday for the children: but Anny is at this time deeply engaged with

---

[63] This dinner is described in a letter of April 28 from Brookfield to his wife. It was held at the Garrick Club, and Clarkson Stanfield and Frank Fladgate were among those present. (*Mrs. Brookfield*, II, 283–284)

masters and examinations and I should not like to take her from them — When the Spring comes we will drive over to Wimbledon if you will kindly receive us & I will have a days sketching or idleness, and they a romp with your little ones. I have my mother with me now who is my comfort my housekeeper and governess in chief — If you ever come London-wards you will pass by our Street and I hope you will come and see her — Ever sincerely yours (& in the midst of such a worry of writing as will excuse me I hope for not having sooner answered)

W M Thackeray

584.     TO HENRY VIZETELLY
            MAY 1849

My text is taken from Vizetelly's *Glances Back through Seventy Years*, I, 350.

Your arrangement of the company at the Academy dinner is all wrong, Jupiter[64] notwithstanding. The plan I have roughly sketched out will show you where most of the big and little stars twinkled. It was a very cold and formal affair — almost as dull as my Lord Carlisle's late patronising spread given to certain well-known gents from Grub-street.[65]

W. M. T.

[64] *The Times*, from an article in which Vizetelly had prepared an engraving of the Royal Academy banquet of 1849 for *The Illustrated London News*.

[65] "I remember Thackeray's mentioning [Lord Carlisle's] having once invited a dozen literary men, including four or five of the 'Punch' set, to dinner, when to his lordship's evident chagrin the repast turned out a singularly dull affair. 'Of course,' said Thackeray, 'we all knew each others' pet stories, and all the dear old jokes, and this acted as a wet blanket upon us. No one would have thought of trotting out a good new story simply for one of his *confrères* to crib for his next magazine article. If Lord Carlisle had asked half-a-dozen literary men and half-a-dozen lords, we should in this case have fit audience found, and been able to amuse the quality at the trifling inconvenience of boring ourselves.' " (Vizetelly, *Glances Back through Seventy Years*, I, 293)

585.     TO FREDERICK MULLETT EVANS
3 MAY 1849 [66]

My text is taken from a transcript supplied by Mrs. Fuller.

Thursday, May 3,
My dear Evans,

I have taken the bowl *meo periculo*. It will cost B. and E. £25 one day, and I shall have engraved on it "From the publishers to the Author of Vanity Fair and Pendennis" with the dates of those remarkable works.

I hope one day you and Bradbury will come and hausel the bowl.

Yours always,
W. M. Thackeray.

586.     TO MRS. BROOKFIELD
4 MAY 1849

Published in part, *Collection of Letters*, pp. 67–69. The passages enclosed between daggers were overscored by Mrs. Brookfield.

My dear Sister. Has William written to you about our trip to Hampstead on Sunday? It was very pleasant — We went first to Saint Mark's Church, where I always thought you went but where the pugh-openers had never heard of such a person as M^rs JOB. and having heard a jolly & perfectly stupid sermon, walked over Primrose Hill to the Crowes: where his Reverence gave M^rs C. 1/2 an hour's private talk whilst I was talking under the blossomy apple-tree about newspapers to Monsieur Crowe and thinking ⟨. . .⟩[67] — but never mind me. Well, M^rs Crowe was delighted with W^m and his manner of discoorsing her: and indeed though I say it that shouldnt, from what he said afterwards and from what

[66] Among possible years May 3 fell on a Thursday only in 1849.
[67] Mrs. Brookfield has cut away four or five words here.

we have often talked over pipes in private that is a pious and kind soul, I mean his, and calculated to soothe & comfort, and appreciate and elevate so to speak out of despair many a soul that your more tremendous rigorous divines would leave on the way side, where Sin that robber had left them half kilt. I will have a Samaritan parson when I fall among thieves. You dear lady may send for an ascetic if you like for what is he to find wrong in *you*?

I have talked to my mother about her going to Paris with the children     She is very much pleased at the notion: and it wont be very lonely to me: for the fact is the present state of home society has become intolerable to me from no fault of anybody's but my own sort of oversensitiveness and impatience with people who have no sense of humour — and though I shall grumble and *poser* myself in a pathetic attitude selon mon ordinaire, I shant be very unhappy — This only applies in *this* case mind — not in never mind who's — so I shall be alone for some months at any rate and vow & swear I will save money — You see I go on writing on the Club paper because its no object & there's no blotting book.

Have you read Dickens?[68] — O it is charming. Bravo Dickens. It has some of his very prettiest touches — those inimitable Dickens touches w^h make such a great man of him. And the reading of the book has done another author a great deal of good. In the first place it pleases the other Author to see that Dickens who has long left off alluding to his the O A's works has been copying the O A, and greatly simplifying his style and foregoing the use of fine words. By this the public will be the gainer and David Copperfield will be improved by taking a lesson from Vanity Fair. Secondly, it has put me upon my mettle — for ah Madam all the mettle was out of me, and Ive been dreadfully & curiously cast down this month past — I say secondly it has put me on my mettle, and made me feel that I must do something that I have fame and name & family to support, † and that I won't go: mustn't go on talking or ⟨. . .⟩[69] my Sister ⟨. . .⟩ really dear William's kind

---

[68] The first number of *David Copperfield*, chapters 1 to 3.

[69] This and the following hiatuses are respectively of about two, four, and three words.

letter has brought ⟨. . .⟩ thank God.† But now write please and tell me what's the matter.

I have just come away from a dismal sight — Gore House full of Snobs looking at the furniture[70] — foul Jews, odious bombazeen women who drove up in mysterious flies w^h they had hired, the wretches, to be fine so as to come in state to a fashionable lounge — Brutes keeping their hats on in the kind old drawing-rooms — I longed to knock some of 'em off: and say Sir be civil in a lady's room — but I beg your pardon you're so fond of Lord Lyttleton. I forgot. There was one of the servants there not a powdered one but a butler a whatdyoucallit[71] — My heart melted towards him & I gave him a pound — Ah it was a strange sad picture of Wanaty Fair. My mind is all boiling up with it. Indeed it is in a queer state — † Indeed ⟨. . .⟩ [72] lady comes back. God bless her. ⟨. . .⟩ sister my friend — Come soon — Write sooner ⟨. . .⟩ † The day I had kept for you I have given away to the C.B.Pollock who has turtle but what is turtle compared to &c ? — (neat again this) And I shall go to dress tomorrow & no Sister Janey. I want you back so as to give Lady Castlereagh a dinner — she is very kind generous & compatissante. Come back comeback. I give my best remembrances to all at Clevedon Court.

## W M T.

[70] Lady Blessington's long career as a London hostess was terminated in April, 1849, when Count D'Orsay slipped away to France to avoid imprisonment for debt. She at once set about arranging for the sale of Gore House, and on May 4, three days before the auction began, the public was admitted to her mansion to inspect the "costly and elegant effects of the Rt. Honble the Countess of Blessington, retiring to the continent." (Sadleir, *Blessington-D'Orsay*, pp. 341–343)

[71] F. Avillon, Lady Blessington's valet, who wrote to her on May 8 from Gore House: "M. Thackeray est venu aussi, et avait les larmes aux yeux en partant. *C'est peut être la seule personne que j'ai vu réellement affecté en votre départ.*" (R. R. Madden, *The Literary Life and Correspondence of the Countess of Blessington*, I, 176)

[72] This and the following hiatuses are respectively of about five, four, and two words.

587.     TO THE REV. WILLIAM BROOKFIELD
### MAY 1849 [73]

Published in part, *Collection of Letters*, p. 54.

My dear Vieux

A long walk and stroll in Richmond Park yesterday; a blue followed by a black this morning have left me calmer — exhausted but melancholy. I shall dine at the Garrick at 7 o'clock or so and go to the Lyceum afterwards — Come into town if you get this in time and let us go. Or if not, write me a friendly word. I did not bother Madam with any further letter: but hope to gladn my eyes by a sight of her on Thursday, when I want to come and dress at your house previous to going to Lady Davy's —

Get David Copperfield: by Jingo it's beautiful — it beats the yellow chap of this month hollow —

Gby.
W M T.

588.      TO LADY BLESSINGTON
### 6 MAY 1849

*Address:* The Countess of Blessington. | Hotel de la Ville de Paris | Place de la Ville-Evêque | Paris. *Postmarks:* 7 MY 1849, 8 MAI 49 BOULOGNE. Hitherto unpublished.

Kensington. May 6.

Dear Lady Blessington

On the day I was starting into the country last month[74] (and upon an errand w^h didn't admit of any delay) I got Miss Power's note saying that you were going to Paris and kindly wanted to say Goodbye. I hate saying Goodbye to people who have been kind to me. Isn't it much better to say How do you do my lady?

---

[73] This note was written shortly after Thackeray's letter of May 4 to Mrs. Brookfield. The principal play at the Lyceum at this time was *The Husband of my Wife* (1849), a farce of unknown authorship.

[74] On April 14.

Are you well? Are you merry at Paris and snugly settled in the dear old place? — I've been once at Gore House since. *C'etoit nâvrant* — I won't talk to you about it — But I'm glad I went There was nobody there I knew but the maitre-d'hotel looking very sad — I should have liked to shake hands with him: so I gave him a suvering instead — I don't say this for a brag about my generosity only I liked it. As for the house, I beg to say Madam that is wasn't the beautiful ornaments and furnitures that made the house but the kind people in it — its nothing now you are gone; and I vow and declare my belief that you can talk just as pleasantly from a mahogany chair, as from one whereof the legs were covered with the most precious gold.

Well, because there are no rents from Ireland, shall there be no more Oeufs à l'Espartéro? When did we ever have a better dinner than on that day at Burnham beeches when the Herr Graf cooked the potatoes and I came from Brighton with the game pie containing 2 grouse 2 partridges 3 ostriches 2 cassowaries &c — only I forgot it.[75] Cannot a contented mind be happy with potatoes and a giggot? I bet 2$^d$ that in 6 months you will be more gay in Paris than at Kensington, & as for those young ladies, how nice it will be to make them wait upon us old folks (there's a galanterie) — and then they shall sit down afterwards to cold potatoes.

Every day I get more ashamed of my yellow cover & former misanthropical turn. The world is a great deal better than some satirists have painted it — and I am forced to say so when folks speak about you. What is there nobody going to say an unkind word about Lady Blessington? says I to myself — and indeed I've not heard one — Nothing but esteem for your kindness, nothing but sympathy and regard, and of course a little natural selfish regret that we sh$^d$ have lost a house where so many people were made so happy. The way in w$^h$ people speak about you does credit to the world as well as you — isn't it worth while almost to have a touch of mishap if it brings you as indeed it has brought you, such a deal of friendly sympathy?

[75] See above, No. 498.

I began a letter the day I had finished my number — but tore it up because it contained too much about myself — indeed I suppose we have all got our own bitter griefs — I have for my part and have been for the last month the glummest & most melancholy author who ever cracked a joke with a sad heart. My work shows my dullness I think — but on the other hand there is a fellow by the name of Dickens who is bringing out a rival publication and who has written beautifully. Bravo Dickens! Davy Copperfield has beautiful things in it — those sweet little inimitable bits w^h make one so fond of him. And let me tell your Ladyship that I think he has been reading a certain yellow-covered book and with advantage too: for he has simplified his style: kept out of the fine words and in fact is doing his best. I am glad of it. I hope it will put somebody on his mettle — somebody who has been careless of everything of late — but I wont go into the dolefuls — Ah, my lady who hasn't his share?

I believe the world goes on being very gay. I reel from dinner party to dinner-party — I wallow in turtle and swim in claret and Shampang — I would like a cozy dinner with you very much better if you please. Won't we go & dine at Restaurants and have a matelotte at Bercy, when I come to Paris? Bedad we will ladies: and I hope I'll come soon. But a railroad in your native country w^h Evn confound I mean the railroad has swept down violently upon me and almost carried me off my legs — I'm as poor as Job: but it's not that w^h makes me unhappy — It's — never mind what I say. One person has about as many crosses as another I suppose.

Goodbye dear Lady Blessington. Present my most respectful homages to the young ladies,[76] and inform Monsieur D'Orsay that I should like to have one of his great shakes of the hand. And believe me, ever faithfully yours

W M Thackeray

[76] The Miss Powers.

589.          FROM MRS. BROOKFIELD
                        MAY 1849 [77]

Hitherto unpublished.

I only write to say I am not ill thank you — & only put off
returning because I fancied W$^m$ wished me to have a little more
Country as he delayed going to Cambridge but I have arranged
to come on Saturday, so that I shall hope to see you again very
soon — I did not think it *at all* a dull N$^o$ & Rhoda said it was
the best & most amusing she had read — so that you have some
humble supporters — I don't like you to talk of being savage &
dismal — when you feel so I would not go out to parties if I were
you — for it will wear you out by & by if you go on acting 2 or
3 different characters at once — do you know I often feel afraid
of your making yourself quite ill with all the various excitements
of your present life — but I suppose it was always something of
the same kind — I can't fancy you ever going on without some
daily excitement — & I wish you could have a rest from everything
for a few weeks & try the effect of it — but as this is quite impossible
it is no use wishing it — I am glad they[78] are going to Paris — that
will take off one of y$^r$ parts for a time — that of the family man, —
& you will only have the author & the Major & the "satirist" & the
sentimentalist &c &c &c to keep up for the time they are away — for
the *pose* wh: you describe of the family man isolated from his
children will *fit in* to the other characters very well — & you need
not keep up your acquaintance with Indian affairs to discuss after
dinner with y$^r$ Father — I hope you don't think me very cool &
flippant — but I really do think you are *living too fast,* as the
phraze is. & I wish you could somehow contrive to lower the steam
— I thought Laura Bell had a dash of Anny in her which I liked —
& Pen's languor at home & spruceness at the Claverings is most
natural, & what all sisters have smarted under from their brothers
at home at the Pendennis age — Rhoda liked Capt: Short[79] the

---

[77] This is Mrs. Brookfield's reply to Thackeray's letter of May 4.
[78] Thackeray's family.                              [79] Captain Strong.

best in the book — I am writing in the midst of talking — the Youngs[80] are here — redolent of David Copperfield — which I haven't seen & am in no hurry for, tho' y$^r$ description of it is encouraging — I don't know that you are quite impartial in y$^r$ praises because you w$^d$ feel it a generous course to praise him up — altho' it is absurd to put him in the position of a rival to you — We have still a sick house here poor little Agnes seriously ill but better to-day —

Goodbye my dear brother W$^m$ — & excuse this hasty scrawl wh: W$^m$ always says is the regular form with which all my letters end, I am so glad he was of comfort to poor M$^{rs}$ Crowe

590.                          TO MARK LEMON
                              9 MAY 1849

Hitherto unpublished.

                                        Young S$^t$ Wednesday.

My dear Lemon

This news is very heart-breaking. Why here is M$^r$ Brown opening with a club,[81] his next is to be about a ball, a dinner a fashionable assembly & so forth; 'The manners & customs of the English' the great attraction of Punch[82] are on the self-same subjects: it appears to me you will cut the throats of those 2 series by your projected Extra number — but I can't commit suicide and slit my own artery: so that you must put the Fashionable part into the hands of another writer.

                              Always faithfully yours though
                              W M Thackeray

[80] Julian Young and his wife, close friends of the Eltons (*Mrs. Brookfield*, II, 296–297).

[81] The seventh of *Mr. Brown's Letters to a Young Man about Town* and the first part of "Mr. Brown the Elder takes Mr. Brown the Younger to a Club," *Punch*, May 12, 1849.

[82] Doyle's famous series of caricatures, illustrating Percival Leigh's *Mr. Pips his Diary*, which appeared in *Punch* from March 17 to December 29, 1849. The extra number against which Thackeray protests was not issued.

The Punch boy has just brought me a box from Edinburgh containing a silver statue of Punch and a compliment from 80 Edinenses[83] — with polite remarks about the Snob, Jeames &c —

591.          TO DR. JOHN BROWN [84]
                    11 MAY 1849

My text is taken from Dr. Brown and Henry H. Lancaster's "Thackeray,"
*North British Review*, XL (1864), 223–224.

13, Young Street, Kensington Square,
                    May 11, 1848.[85]

My dear Sir, — The arms and the man[86] arrived in safety yesterday, and I am glad to know the names of two of the eighty Edinburgh friends who have taken such a kind method of showing
their good-will towards me. If you are grati I am gratior. Such
tokens of regard & sympathy are very precious to a writer like
myself, who have some difficulty still in making people understand

---

[83] See the next letter.
[84] See *Memoranda*.
[85] A mistake for 1849, as the postscript of the preceding letter shows.
[86] "There happened to be placed in the window of an Edinburgh jeweller
a silver statuette of *Mr. Punch*, with his dress *en rigeur*, — his comfortable
and tidy paunch, with all its buttons; his hunch; his knee-breeches, with their
ties; his compact little legs, one foot a little forward; and the intrepid and
honest, kindly little fellow firmly set on his pins, with his customary look of
up to and good for anything. In his hand was his weapon, a pen; his skull was
an inkhorn, and his cap its lid. A passer-by — who had long been grateful to
our author, as to a dear unknown and enriching friend, for his writings in
*Fraser* and in *Punch*, and had longed for some way of reaching him, and
telling him how his work was relished and valued — bethought himself of
sending this inkstand to Mr. Thackeray. He went in, and asked its price.
'Ten guineas, sir.' He said to himself, 'There are many who feel as I do;
why shouldn't we send him up to him? I'll get eighty several half-crowns,
that will do it;' (he had ascertained that there would be a discount for ready
money). With the help of a friend, who says he awoke to Thackeray, and
divined his great future, when he came, one evening, in *Fraser* for May 1844,
on the word '*kinopium*' [in "Little Travels and Road-side Sketches;" see *Works*,
VI, 268], the half-crowns were soon forthcoming, and it is pleasant to remember, that in the 'octogint' are the names of Lord Jeffrey and Sir William
Hamilton, who gave their half-crowns with the heartiest good-will. A short

what you have been good enough to find out in Edinburgh that under the mask satirical there walks about a sentimental gentleman who means not unkindly to any mortal person. I can see exactly the same expression under the vizard of my little friend in silver, and hope some day to shake the whole octogint by the hand gratos & gratas, and thank them for their friendliness and regard. I think I had best say no more on the subject lest I should be tempted into some enthusiastic writing of w^h I am afraid. I assure you these tokens of what I can't help acknowledging as popularity — make me humble as well as grateful — and make me feel an almost awful sense of the responsibility w^h falls upon a man in such a station. Is it deserved or undeserved? Who is this that sets up to preach to mankind, and to laugh at many things w^h men reverence? I hope I may be able to tell the truth always, & to see it aright, according to the eyes w^h God Almighty gives me. And if, in the exercise of my calling, I get friends, and find encouragement and sympathy, I need not tell you how much I feel and am thankful for this sup-port. — Indeed I can't reply lightly upon this subject or feel otherwise than very grave when people begin to praise me as you do. Wishing you and my Edinburgh friends all health and hap-piness believe me my dear Sir most faithfully yours

W. M. Thackeray.

note was written telling the story. The little man in silver was duly packed, and sent with the following inscription round the base: —

GULIELMO MAKEPEACE THACKERAY.
ARMA VIRUMQUE
GRATI NECNON GRATÆ EDINENSES
LXXX
D.     D.     D."

(*North British Review*, XL, 117–118)

592.            TO THE REV. WILLIAM AND
                    MRS. BROOKFIELD
                    16 MAY 1849

Published in *Collection of Letters*, p. 120.

Wednesday. Midnight

I have made an awful smash at the Literary Fund,[87] and have tumbled into Evins knows where. — It was a tremendous exhibition of madness & imbecility. Good night. I hope you 2 are sound asleep, Why isn't there somebody that I could go & smoke a pipe to?

Bon Soir

But O! What a smash I have made! —
I am talking quite out loud to myself at the G[88] sentences I intended to have uttered: but they wouldnt come in time.

593.            TO MRS. BROOKFIELD
                    17–19 MAY 1849

Published in part, *Collection of Letters*, pp. 121–124.

My dear Turpin.[89]

After the fatal night of the Literary Fund disaster, when I came home to bed (breaking out into exglimations in the cab and letting off madly parts of the speech w.h wouldn't explode at the proper time) I found the house lighted up, and the poor old mother waiting to hear the result of the day — so I told her that I was utterly beaten & had made a fool of myself, upon w.h with a sort of cry she says 'No you didn't old man' — and it appears that she had been behind a pillar in the gallery all the time and heard the

[87] Thackeray's singularly incoherent speech at the Royal Literary Fund dinner on May 16, 1849, is printed in Melville's *William Makepeace Thackeray*, II, 68–70.
[88] The Garrick Club.
[89] The name of a maid of Mrs. Brookfield's.

speeches — and as for mine she thinks it was beautiful. — So you see if theres no pleasing everybody, yet some people are easily enough satisfied. The children came down in the morning and told me about my beautiful speech w^h Granny had heard. She got up early and told them the story about it you may be sure: *her* story, w^h is not the true one but like what womens stories are.

I have a faint glimmering notion of Sir Charles Hedges[90] having made his appearance somewhere in the middle of the speech, but of what was said I haven't the smallest idea. The discomfiture will make a good chapter for Pen. It is thus we make flêche de tout bois and I suppose every single circumstance w^h occurs to pain or please me henceforth, will go into print somehow or the other so take care if you please to be very well behaved and kind to me, or else you may come in for a savage chapter in the very next number.

As soon as I rallied from the abominable headache w^h the Free Masons tavern always gives, I went out to see some ladies who are quite like sisters to me,[91] they are so kind lively and cheerful. Old Lady Morley[92] was there and we had a jolly lunch, and afterwards one of these ladies told me by whom she sate at Lansdowne House, and what they talked about and how pleased she my friend was. She is a kind generous soul and I love her sincerely.

After the luncheon (this is wrote on Saturday, for all yesterday I was so busy from nine till five when my hoss was brought & I took a ride and it was too late for the post) I went to see Matthew[93] that friend of my youth whom I used to think 20 years ago the most fascinating accomplished witty and delightful of men — I found an old man in a room smelling of brandy & water at 5 o'clock at Islington, quite the same man that I remember only grown coarser and stale somehow, like a piece of goods that has been hanging up in a shop window. He has had 15 years of a vulgar wife, much solitude, very much brandy & water I should think, and

[90] In his Literary Fund speech Thackeray referred in passing to Sir Charles Hedges (d. 1714), Secretary of State in 1705 and 1706, when Addison was Under-Secretary.
[91] Mrs. Elliot and Miss Perry.
[92] The dowager Lady Morley (d. 1857), widow of the first Earl of Morley.
[93] See above, No. 49.

a depressing profession: for what can be more depressing than a long course of hypocrisy to a man of no small sense of humour? — It was a painful meeting We tried to talk unreservedly, and as I looked at his face I remembered the fellow I was so fond of — he asked me if I still consorted with any Cambridge men, and so I mentioned Kinglake and one Brookfield of whom I saw a good deal. He was surprized at this as he heard Brookfield was so violent a Puseyite as to be just on the point of going to Rome. He cant walk, having paralysis in his legs, but he preaches every Sunday he says, being hoisted into his pulpit before service, and waiting there whilst his curate reads down below. I think he has very likely repented: he spoke of his preaching seriously and without affectation: perhaps he has got to be sincere at last after a long dark lonely life. He showed me his daughter of 15, a prettyish girl with a shrewish face, and bad manners — the wife did not show — He must have been glad too when I went away and I daresay is more scornful about me than I about him — ⟨Fa⟩, I used to worship him for about 6 months — and now he points a moral and adorns a tale[94] such as it is in Pendennis. He lives in the D of Bedfords Park at Woburn, and wanted me to come down and see him, and go to the Abbey he said where the Duke w^d be so glad to have me[95] — but I declined this treat — O fie for shame. How proud we get! Poor old Harry Matthew, and this battered vulgar man was my idol of youth! My dear old FitzGerald is always right about men: and said from the first that this was a bad one and a sham. You see, some folks have a knack of setting up for themselves idols to worship — Dont be flying off in one of your fits of passion, I don't mean you.

Then I went to dine at Alfred Montgomerys[96] where were his

[94] Dr. Johnson, *The Vanity of Human Wishes*, l. 219.

[95] Matthew had been Rector of Eversholt in Bedfordshire, a preferment worth £480 annually, since 1843. The living was given him by Francis Russell (1788–1861), seventh Duke of Bedford, whose country seat of Woburn Abbey was two miles away.

[96] Montgomery was a dandy and man-about-town who lived at 63 Eaton Place and had offices in Somerset House, where he was a Commissioner of Inland Revenue (*Post Office London Directory*, 1847).

wife and sister. I dont think so much of the wife tho she is pretty and clever — but Beckyfied somehow and too much of a petite maitresse I suppose a deal of flattery has been poured into her ears, and numberless men have dangled round that pretty light little creature. The sister with her bright eyes was very nice though, and I passed an evening in great delectation till midnight drawing nonsense pictures for these ladies who have both plenty of relish for nonsense. I wish to the deuce I had somebody who liked it at home. Yesterday after working all day, & then going to the London Library to audit accounts doesn't that sound grand? and taking a ride, I came home to dinner, fell asleep as usual afterwards slep for 12 hours, and am now going to attack Monsieur Pendennis.

Here is the journal. Now Mum how have you been emused? Is Kings very fine, is Trinity better?[97] did you have a nice T at M^rs Maine's? When are you coming back? — Lord & Lady Castlereagh came here yesterday and I want you to come back so that I may give them an entertainment — for I told my lady that I wanted to show her that other lady mentioned in the Punch article as mending her husband's chest of drawers[98] — but I said waistcoat. Sir Bulwer Lytton called yesterday — To night I am going to the bar dinner, and shall probbbly make another speech — I dont mind about failing there so I shall do pretty well. I rode by Portman Street on Thursday — Please to write and let me know whether you'll dine on the 28^th or the 30^th or can give me both those days to choose from. And so God bless both on you.

---

[97] For the Brookfields' visit to Cambridge, see *Mrs. Brookfield*, II, 287.

[98] "Or will you please to step into Mrs. J.'s lodgings, who is waiting, and at work, until her husband comes home from chambers? She blushes and puts the work away on hearing the knock, but when she sees who the visitor is, she takes it with a smile from behind the sofa cushion, and behold, it is one of J.'s waistcoats, on which she is sewing buttons. She might have been a Countess blazing in diamonds had Fate so willed it, and the higher her station the more she would have adorned it. But she looks as charming while plying her needle as the great lady in the palace whose equal she is, in beauty, in goodness, in high-bred grace and simplicity: at least, I can't fancy her better, or any Peeress being more than her peer." ("Some More Words About Ladies," *Punch*, April 14, 1849; *Works*, VI, 619)

594.            TO LADY CASTLEREAGH
                  26 MAY 1849

My text is taken from Maggs's catalogue 522 (1929), where the first page is
reproduced in facsimile.

                          13, Young St., Saturday, 26 May
Dear Lady Castlereagh

I was so delighted by the sight of your card on my return home
some days ago that I vowed a vow to write you a letter of thanks
the moment my work was concluded for the month. It is this
moment over: and this is the fulfilment of the vow. But I am so
tired that I can't find anything proper or pretty to say only that
you are very kind w$^h$ I daresay you have heard, & that I feel very
much honoured. And now will your Ladyship be so good as to
fix a day for that little celebration w$^h$ you have promised to attend?
31, 1, 2, 6, are all free days in my calendar and I should humbly
suggest that the repast instead of tea should consist of leg of lamb
and salad. I cant show the Italian paragon[99] for those reasons
before stated, but there is a lady who was mentioned in my article
in Punch, w$^h$ you have read, who is a clergyman's not a lawyer's
wife as therin described, and whom I brag about a great deal. And
there are pretty girls at Kensington as well as in Belgravia, w$^h$
please tell with my compliments to Lord Castlereagh, and in fine
I am bent upon the lamb & the spinach.
                          W. M. Thackeray.


595.            TO ARTHUR SHAWE
                  27 MAY 1849

Published in part, *Thackeray and his Daughter*, pp. 30–31.

                          13 Young S$^t$ Kensington May 27.
My dear Shawe. This is your niece Harriet's (or Minny as we
call her) birthday — and as she was seated at the window yonder

[99] Mrs. Richards. See above, No. 571.

just now I made a drawing of her, and bethought me that you and Jane would be glad to hear about the children — Minny is 9. Anny will be 12 on the 9 June — and is a great sensible clever girl, with a very homely face, and a very good heart and a very good head and an uncommonly good opinion of herself as such clever people will sometimes have. Minny is very well for cleverness too as children go: and both have a great deal of spoiling and fondness from my mother, who supplies to them the place of their own — now nearly nine years removed from them. She is at Epsom very well, and I got a letter yesterday from M$^r$ Bakewell to say that she was quite happy and very much pleased at seeing the folks pass by to the Derby. So you see there are pretty good accounts of all this family, including your brother-in-law the writer of the present; who is become quite a lion within the last 2 years, dines with a lord almost every day, and is rather prosperous as times go. But though I am at the top of the tree in my business and making a good income now (near upon £2000 let us say) — yet it is only within the last few months that I have got to this point, and was abominably hit by an unfortunate railroad speculation of w$^h$ I have still not discharged the obligation — so that I am in debt ⟨. . .⟩[100] a glimpse of his regiment last year, and the young men — very fast g⟨. . .⟩[101] a week of that life would tire me pretty completely. He writes to me no⟨. . .⟩ to do for money that I can't afford to keep up correspondences, and ⟨. . .⟩ Shawe. I ought to have written to you to shake you by the hand and t⟨. . .⟩ poor wife & the girls. Can't you find amongst your Civilians, a goo⟨. . .⟩ bride-cake with a great deal of pleasure.

When you go to Calcutta I hope you will go & see my cousin Ritchie ⟨. . .⟩ also another very old & intimate friend Sir Arthur Buller — I often th⟨. . .⟩ the deuced cost w$^h$ is the difficulty in these matters: for what we call ⟨. . .⟩ papers half a dozen politicals appointed — one of them Edgeworth a ⟨. . .⟩ can never hope to make

---

[100] This letter is written on a single leaf, the bottom third of which has been lost. There is consequently a gap of about seven lines in the text at this point.

[101] About six words are missing here and in each of the hiatuses indicated below.

much more than I do now, and as m⟨. . .⟩ hand comes and pushes me out. I met Lord Hardinge at a public ⟨. . .⟩ liked very much I am told; and old Napier as I hear was immen⟨. . .⟩ Punch. I got an Arabic & Persian dictionary and astonished mysel⟨. . .⟩

Hyde Park is as brilliant and the Season as gay and splendid as ⟨. . .⟩ who seem all handsome — The leaves and verdure are of such a br⟨. . .⟩ to come and have a holyday in our's? — I must shut up my bu⟨. . .⟩ Church with my young ladies. They send their love to their Al⟨. . .⟩

596.                    TO DR. QUIN
                       MAY? 1849

Hitherto unpublished.

                              13 Young Sᵗ Kensington
My dear Quin
    Will you come out & see (in her bed laid up with sudden maladies) the mother of your friend
                        W M Thackeray.

A little way past Slater's the butchers, & the house with the bow-windows.

597.                    TO MRS. YORKE [102]
                       1 JUNE 1849

My text is taken from a facsimile in Gerald Fiennes's "Some Notes on Thackeray," *New Review*, X (1894), 502–503.

                       13 Young Sᵗ Kensington Sqʳᵉ June 1. 1849.
Dear Mʳˢ Yorke
    In the matter of the curacy I pen the following lines, and address them to you because of the softness of your sex, and in order

[102] The former Marian Emily Montgomery (d. 1895), who in 1830 had

to try and interest you unduly for a gentleman who is in want of just such a cure as M$^r$ Yorke seems to have vacant

M$^r$ Thomas one of the curates of S$^t$ James's, of High Church Principles, wants very much to be married. He has been engaged this ever so many years in the most romantic manner. He could be made every way happy by such an addition to his means. He can be perfectly recommended I don't know whether he is not going to write to M$^r$ Yorke. Mentioning the latters need the other day to my friend M$^r$ School inspector Brookfield, his wife overheard the conversation, and you must know it is she who is M$^r$ Thomas's patron or matron in the matter; and who interests herself in promoting not only the cause of the church w$^h$ she has very much at heart but a pretty little love affair, w$^h$ I think all good-natured persons like to forward. And as for me, I wish prosperity to both with all my heart. Always dear M$^{rs}$ Yorke yours very sincerely

W M Thackeray

598.          TO MRS. BROOKFIELD
                 8 JUNE 1849

Published in part, *Collection of Letters*, pp. 60–61.

My Dear Lady[103] (It was begun dear Sir to somebody of the other sex) I think Hit is just possible that M$^r$ W$^m$ on returning to day may like to have his wife to his self and that the appearance of my eternal countenance might be a bor. Hence I stay away. but I have some points of importance to wige.

M$^r$ Yorke is in town at 63 Eaton Place — Hadn't M$^r$ Thomas best call on him there instantly? He goes away tomorrow, and arrived yesterday when you 2 were also away. If you think fit to

married the Hon. and Rev. Grantham Munton Yorke (1809–1879), younger brother of the fourth Earl of Hardwicke. Yorke was Rector of St. Philip, Birmingham, from 1844 to 1874, Rural Dean of Birmingham from 1850 to 1875, and Dean of Worcester from 1874 till his death. He and his family were good friends of Thackeray for many years.

[103] The "L" of *Lady* is written over an "S".

write a note to M<sup>r</sup> T., the present messenger may carry the same —

And about tomorrow the birthday[104] of my now motherless daughter Miss Anny. Will you come out (being as I must consider you if you please, the children's aunt) at 2 or 3 o'clock or so and take innocent pleasures with them such as the Colosseum, and the Sological Gardens, and are you free so as to give them some dinner or tea in the evening? I dine out myself at 8 o'clock and should like them to share innocent pleasures with their relation — My mother writes from Fareham that the old Grand Aunt is better and will not depart probably yet awhile —

And now concerning Monday. You two must please remember that you are engaged to this house at 7 — I have written to remind the Scotts — to ask the Pollocks, and the Carlyles are coming.

And now with regard to this evening. I dine in Westbourne Terrace — then I must go to Marshalls[105] in Eaton Square, and then to M<sup>rs</sup> Sartoris — where I dont expect to see you: but if a gentleman of the name of W.H.B should have a mind to go: we might &c &c &c.

Madam I hope you have had a pleasant walk on Clapham's breezy common: and that you are pooty well. I myself was very quiet; went with the children to Hampstead and then to the opera and only one party — I am writing at the Reform Club until 4 o'clock when I have an ingaygement with o such a charming person — and tête à tête too — Well, it is with the dentist's arm chair.

But I should like to have the above queries satisfactrily answered, and am always Madam's

(                                    )

W M T.

---

[104] June 9.

[105] William Marshall (1796–1872) of 85 Eaton Square, a wealthy linen manufacturer of Leeds and Shrewsbury, who had been in parliament almost uninterruptedly since 1826.

599.                    TO MRS. PROCTER
                        8–9 JUNE 1849 [106]

Hitherto unpublished. My text is taken from a transcript given to Lady Ritchie by George Murray Smith.

Saturday M^d M^g [107]
June 9, 1849.

My dear Mrs Procter,

Ten minutes reflection in the cab as it brought me home has convinced me that I was very wrong in showing any anger I might feel much more in saying that I would never shake hands with Adelaide as long as I lived.[108] That is very absurd. I shall be very happy, whenever she is minded, to shake hands with Miss Procter. But I have made the attempt more than half a dozen times lately and it has been always met with so much reluctance on your daughter's part, that I am tired on mine of making any more efforts at showing my good will; and can afford no further advances when they are met with so very little cordiality.

Of course I have perceived for some time past that I have done something which has displeased both of you — something doubtless connected with the dispute between Mrs Richards and her husband, but what, upon my honour, I cannot tell in the least: nor indeed am I disposed to ask. The difference between one and the other could be of little importance to me: it seems to me that my opinion regarding them is pretty much the same as your own. I wish that I had never heard of either or that they had not interfered with a friendship of many years which has brought me a great deal of pleasure and kindness.

But though you and your daughter may be convinced that I have acted somehow unworthily or in a manner not meeting your approbation, yet I can't afford to go into the controversy, or right

---

[106] This letter was begun on Friday, June 8, as the reference to Mr. Marshall's reception shows, and finished the following morning.

[107] The transcript reads "M^d M^d "

[108] The origin of this quarrel, which had been in the offing for some time (see above, No. 582), is obscure.

myself or defend myself if any need of defence there be. If you make my conduct a cause of quarrel or coldness, then I must leave it — I am not disposed to change it or to explain it or to apologize for it: and as I vow that I don't know in the least what it is that has angered you, I must also say that I never intend to inquire.

And so Good-night, my dear old friend. You will understand I hope that it was not too much wine which caused me to be angry an hour since, but the repetition of a behaviour which I have borne with a great deal of good humour for many weeks past, and which I must decline any longer to endure.

If I for my part said anything to-night which was discourteous, I ask your pardon. I was exceedingly pained and excited, but not by wine. A man of my age and I hope character has no right to the reception which my friend's daughter has chosen to give me, and I am sorry that I have received it from any member from whom I have hitherto had so much hospitality and affection.

If this note should appear in the morning to be at all inspired by the excitement of which you spoke I will burn it, but I suspect it will not turn out so, and is only the expression of what has been annoying me considerably for some time.

Always truly yours, dear Mrs Procter,

W. M. Thackeray.

P. S. Here is the morning and a beautiful sunshine. I think there may have been a little too much wine in the case last night, that is that a claret-cup of which I had two large glasses at Mr Marshall's may have caused me if not to feel at least to speak more violently than I ought as a gentleman to do. For, however annoyed I might feel, that a young lady the daughter of old friends, should so treat me — I was very wrong to show that my feelings or my honour were wounded, and of course should have exhibited no vehemence of words or manner which might be remarked by others or painful to you. I beg your pardon and Miss Procter's and Procter's for this, and must now get to my work.

7 o'clock.

600.         TO MRS. PROCTER
            14 JUNE 1849

Hitherto unpublished. My text is taken from a transcript given Lady Ritchie by George Murray Smith.

June 14, 1849.

My dear Mrs Procter,

Yes, but I hope you will ask me before then, now I am alone in this world. The children went to-day, Minny giving me a fine fright previously by hiding herself in the closet, and leaving[109] me to imagine that the little rogue had gone out into the street and lost herself there. The old aunt was better after being just at the very brink of the grave, nay someway down into it, but came up again for a little time — the Doctor says she may last for a month or a year yet or go at any moment, my parents will stay with her sometime: possibly till the end of all things. This good old lady was a mother to my mother in her youth.

If I had seen you alone for two minutes the other day, I should have told you a little bit of what I feel about your letter. Dear Mrs Procter, it makes me very grateful and happy to think that I have your friendship. Adelaide also wrote to say that she on her part had fancied I was very cold and constrained and so I was but — but we have all been playing at cross purposes.

God bless you.
Ever sincerely your friend,
W. M. T.

[109] The transcript reads *bading*.

601.                    TO MRS. BROOKFIELD
                          JUNE 1849? [110]

Hitherto unpublished.

My dear lady Although I was, on ossback, twice close by your
door this morning, and very hungry having had no breakfast and
worked a good bit, yet I had the virtue to resist coming in, and
asking you for lunch, w^h act of self-denial please place to my credit.

I am going to a ball at 27 Cavendish Squar this evening thence
to Sir W. Molesworth's concert, and I'm not asked out to dinner
anywhere. I'm going to write till then — I wonder whether any
kind souls will ask me? I think I should work better if they would.
And as you 2 folks are going to dine out tomorrow & next day
— you know you might as well be kind to me if W^m dines at home.
It was sheer virtue & self denial that kept me away last night till
near your bed-time. I thought how poor H⟨arry⟩ would be bored
by the sight of my abominable mug; (a mug in high life means
a face) — and I spared him — You see if I do an act of virtue I
like to have the credit of it & am

                    Madams most obedient serviteur et frère

                               W M T.

[110] This note appears to have been written shortly before Thackeray's letter
to Mrs. Brookfield of June 30. Brookfield in the interval hinted that Thackeray should visit Mrs. Brookfield less frequently.

602.                    TO JAMES HANNAY [111]
                        29 JUNE 1849

Extract published in Hannay's *Brief Memoir of the Late Mr. Thackeray*, p. 13.

                                        Kensington June 29

My dear M^r Hannay

The publisher hasn't sent me the king,[112] and I ordered it of my bookseller here who forgot me: so that I'm as yet without a knowledge of any but No 1. part of w^h I thought was excellent —I hope the rest is as good     A naval captain told me of it the other day lauding it highly but saying the author was too savage.  I sup-

---

[111] Hannay (1827–1873) came to London in 1845 after five years' service in the Royal Navy as a midshipman. There he contributed to *The Morning Chronicle* and other publications and wrote several novels. In Thackeray he found a patron and friend by whom he was "loaded with benefits." "There was nothing more charming about Thackeray," he writes (*Brief Memoir*, p. 4), "than the kindly footing on which he stood with the younger generation. He was not a man to have a little senate; he held sycophants, and all who encouraged them, in contempt; his friends and acquaintances were of all varieties of class and character, and differed from him in their ways of thinking about everything.  But he made it a duty to befriend and cherish anybody in whose merit and sincerity he believed, however casual the accident which had brought them under his notice."  In October, 1852, Thackeray entrusted Hannay with the task of annotating *The English Humourists* (*Brief Memoir*, p. 25), and in later years he served him in various ways. Hannay repaid this kindness by the discriminating essays he devoted to his master, his *Brief Memoir* and *Studies on Thackeray* (London, 1869).  He spent the last fifteen years of his life as British Consul at Barcelona.

I have been able to trace only one of Thackeray's several letters to Hannay, but a fragment of another, quoted in Hannay's *Brief Memoir* (p. 19), should be recorded.  Thackeray is writing in August, 1854, to thank Hannay for a copy of his *Satire and Satirists*: "I hate Juvenal, I mean I think him a truculent brute, and I love Horace better than you do, and rate Churchill much lower; and as for Swift, you haven't made me alter my opinion.  I admire, or rather admit, his power as much as you do; but I don't admire that kind of power so much as I did fifteen years ago, or twenty shall we say.  Love is a higher intellectual exercise than Hatred; and when you get one or two more of those young ones you write so pleasantly about, you'll come over to the side of the kind wags, I think, rather than the cruel ones."

[112] *King Dobbs; Sketches in Ultra-Marine* (1849), which Hannay dedicated to Thackeray.

pose we all begin so — I know one who did: and who is sorry now for pelting at that poor old Bulwer & others, but it was in the days of hot youth when I was scarcely older than you are now.

I'm very glad you are in the country and like it  My grandfather had a little estate at Hadley[113] w^h ought to be mine (only to be sure he had the right to leave it to whom he liked) — and he lies buried there. I often meditate a trip into that country to look at my fathers birth place.

— I was very glad to hear from the Crowes that you were living and once more friendly with your family: they are the best friends for a man though not the pleasantest always. And I envy a man who has freshness enough in him left to be meditating heroic satires and reading Catallus in green lanes. I fancy some times I could do these things but Im afraid it's too late now — the London literary street walkers must come back to the flags. They are taken home and lead virtuous lives for a little — but they come back to the lamps and the gin-palace again — If you have a fair opening in a profession for Gods sake take it and dont depend on our's. I expect myself to be done in 3 or 4 years and then what is to happen?

This letter is not very lively: but I have just finished my number[114] & am fagged & unwell, having 20 letters to write, and not wishing to delay farther thanking you for yours. I am very much pleased indeed to have your good opinion and that you like and appreciate what I do. I wonder whether I shall ever set up a flag as I often thought of doing — if so, and you were inclined to serve I have always thought I would like to have you for a lieutenant. Believe me to be

Ever faithfully yours

W M Thackeray

I haven't thanked you for the dedication w^h was the purpose of

---

[113] Thackeray was named after his paternal grandfather, William Makepeace Thackeray, who had bought a residence at Hadley Green, near Barnet in Middlesex, in 1786, not long after returning to England from India. On his death in 1812 the house and grounds, which are described in *Memorials* (pp. 294–295), passed to his oldest son, William Thackeray.

[114] Number IX of *Pendennis*, chapters 27 to 29.

the note, but the P S always contains the cream of the correspondence. Thank you then very much.

603.          TO A. J. PAGET
            29 JUNE 1849

*Address:* A. J. Paget Esq^e | J Paget Esq^e The College | S^t Bartholomews
Hosp^t *Postmark:* 29 JU 1849. Hitherto unpublished.

Kensington

Dear Sir

   I cant help you in your search for the periodical[115] to w^h you
allude: and indeed had rather not: I dont think I wrote 1/2 a
dozen articles in it: and reprinted the best of them in the Paris
Sketch Book if I remember right.

Your very faithful Serv^t<br>W M Thackeray.

604.     TO MRS. ELLIOT AND KATE PERRY
            29 JUNE 1849

Hitherto unpublished.

29 June. Friday.

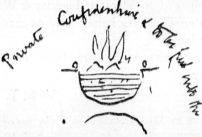

   Private. Confidential & to be put into the

My dear ladies

   I have only this minute done my work[116] and have leisure to ask
how you are — It is a week since one of you was taken unwell. Is

---

[115] See above, No. 148.
[116] Number IX of *Pendennis* for July, chapters 27 to 29.

she better now. Shall I come to Richmond to see her — to breakfast any day next week? I am free now for a little, as much as
that miserable villain can be said to be free who is flogged night
& day by a cruel tyrant who shall be nameless — and at
my age too — to be whopped so by a boy!

But enough of this. I am always yours

W M T.

605.               TO MRS. BROOKFIELD
                    30 JUNE 1849 [117]

*Address:* M^rs Brookfield | 15 Portman S^t | Portman Sq^re Published in *Col-
lection of Letters,* p. 69.

My dear lady I have 2 Opera boxes for tonight — pit box & for
the Huguenots at Covent Garden — where there is no ballet, and
where you might sit and see this grand opera in great ease and
quiet. Will you please to say if you will have it and I will send
or bring it —

Or if Miss Hallam [118] dines with you, may I come afterwards to
tea? Say yes or no. I shan't be offended only best pleased of course
with yes. I am engaged on Monday Tuesday & Wednesday nights
so if you go away on Thursday I shall have no chance of seeing you
again for ever so long.

I was to breakfast with M^r Rogers this morning but he played
me false. Good bye.

W M T.

[117] This date (given by Mrs. Brookfield in *Collection of Letters,* p. 69) is
confirmed by an announcement in *The Times* of June 30, 1849, that Mlle.
Grisi will appear in Meyerbeer's *Les Huguenots* at the Royal Italian Opera
that evening.

[118] Julia Maria Frances Hallam (d. 1888), one of the two surviving children
of Henry Hallam, and Mrs. Brookfield's niece. She married Captain Cator
(1816–1899), later (1880) Sir John Farnaby Lennard, first Baronet, in 1852.

606.             TO MRS. BROOKFIELD
                    1 JULY 1849

*Address:* M[rs] Brookfield. Hitherto unpublished.

My dear lady Are you better to day and able to see anybody. I wish instead of going to bed you had gone to the Huguenots: it was really the finest thing in the world. Where may one write to his Reverence?[119] I had the kindest letter from him and he told me what had offended him in the conduct of your most obedient Serv[t]. In one thing I was certainly wrong but not in the other as I can see. He had a fine night for sea, and cant be sick on such a beautiful Sunday morning. He told me that I ought to learn to eat a good breakfast: I think that was a hint that I shouldn't come so often to lunch somewhere — so I shant offer: but take a bun in my pocket after my morning's ride in the Park. I am engaged to dinner every day this week from tomorrow w[h] bores me for I should like to give up & go out of town now Madam goes. and I am always hers afftly

                    W M T.


607.     TO THE REV. WILLIAM BROOKFIELD
                    JULY 1849 [120]

Hitherto unpublished. My text is taken from a transcript made by Mrs. Fuller.

My dear Vieux,

I have begun 2 letters wh. have both been torn up because they *would* speak about a certain point: and here is No. 3. beginning in exactly the same way. What I want however to say is, about breaking a certain confidence — I am very sorry; I own it: I

---

[119] As was his custom at this time of the year, Brookfield had gone on a cruise in the revenue cutter *Vigilante* with Stephen Spring Rice. (*Mrs. Brookfield*, II, 289)

[120] This is the letter of apology to which Thackeray refers in his note of July 1.

couldn't help it. I was so greatly moved by the event that I blurted
it out to poor Harry the minute I saw him. I am tenderly interested
about an event which is to make the happiness of your dear wife's
life; how can I be otherwise? Pray God Almighty prosper the
child & mother & father. As for too much unreservedness: I can
only say I should have spoken to a Duchess so: not meaning any
harm, or to take any liberty. Pardon, cher vieux, que je t'ai blessé
d'aucune manière; & thank you for telling me. I am writing this
from my bed where I'm lying as one in agonies of shipboard. And
yet I did nothing to deserve my present attack, having been
moderate yesterday. I should like to hear that you've had a jolly
time — the wind was tremendous high here for 3 days & I thought
you would have frequent recourse to the [*sketch of a basin*] don't
you see how feeble this attempt at pleasantry and easy lightness is?
My dear old boy I want to shake hands with you very much, and
wish you were back from Cowes that I might do it, before I go out
of town myself to Paris somewhere or to Scotland.

My old and young folks are back: and will go to the Country
somewhere: so shall I to Richmond perhaps to do my number.
Try & make a run for Bonchurch when you are in the Island and
see White a visit from a Londoner does him all the good in life.


608.                 TO MRS. BROOKFIELD
                      7 JULY 1849 [121]

Hitherto unpublished.

My dear lady. I only write a word for I've got O such a splitting
headache, and I believe it came of going to Vauxhall last night
whither I went with Sartoris & Sartorissa — it was the stupidest
sight the lamps weren't bright at all the fire works perfectly dreary.
I felt myself like a demd exploded squib. There was no dinner at
Greenwich when I got down. Strutt had the cholera — I came back

[121] Mrs. Brookfield went to Southampton to stay with the Fanshawes on
Friday, July 6. She remained there until July 18, when her hosts took her
to Ryde on the Isle of Wight. (*Mrs. Brookfield*, II, 289–292) This letter
appears to have been written the day after she left London.

to London — I dined by myself & thought about you and read the life of Poet Campbell in the Quarterly Review.[122] I went to bed with aching head but I prayed for my dear sister and brother, I came down here to the Punch Office — Fancy the beasts proposing to me to go to the Isle of Wight with them on Monday! How dared they go for to aggravate me so?

Write me word soon dear lady that are you well and comfortable after your journeys. Mine wont take place so soon quite as I thought I had best finish No X of Pendennis[123] before going out on any pleasuring. The little & old folks are gone to a ship launch, and I end as I have begun by saying that I have got one of the handsomest headaches in all London.

But that don't prevent me from being always my dear lady's

W M T.

609.                    TO MRS. BROOKFIELD
                          JULY 1849 [124]

Published in part, *Mrs. Brookfield and her Circle*, p. 290, from which my text as far as *she was enthusiastic* is taken. Original of the remainder owned by Mrs. Fuller.

At Procter's was not furiously amusing — the eternal G[agiotti] bores one. Her parents were of course, there, the papa with a suspicious-looking little order in his button-hole, and a chevalier d'industrie air, which I can't get over. E[mma] didn't sing, but on the other hand Mrs. S[artoris] did. She was passionate, she was enthusiastic, she was sublime, she was tender — there was one note w.h she kept so long, that I protest I had time to think about my affairs, to have a little nap, and to wake much refreshed, whilst it was going on still — at another time overcome by almost unutterable tenderness she piped so low that it's a wonder one could hear at all — in a word she was mirobolante. the most artless affected good-

---

[122] "Dr. Beattie's Life of Campbell," *Quarterly Review*, June, 1849, pp. 32–81.

[123] For August, chapters 30 to 32.

[124] This letter was written shortly after that of July 7.

natured absurd clever creature possible — When she had crushed
Gagiotti who stood by the piano hating her and paying her the
most profound compliments — she tripped off on my arm to the
cab in waiting. I like that absurd kind creature. Drums are beating
in various quarters for parties yet to come off but I'm refusing any
more: being quite dun up — I am thinking of sending the old &
young folks to Clevedon. I'm sure M[rs] Robbins[125] & M[rs] Parr will
be kind to them, won't they?

M[rs] F[126] writes me word that you expect to hear from me so I
send this in a hurry: & hope & want so to know that you are pretty
well.[127]

---

[125] The former Maria Katherine Elton (d. 1899), an older sister of Mrs.
Brookfield, who had married Major George Robbins of Forest Lodge,
Southampton, in 1833.

[126] Mrs. Fanshawe.

[127] Mrs. Brookfield's reply to this letter has been printed in part: "I read
out your letter to Mrs. F. I should rather like, maliciously, to have witnessed
the Sartorissian crushment of the Gaggiotti.

"If you do send the children down to Clevedon, I am sure Maria and Julia
would like to see them often and your Mother too, but it sounds melancholy
their going there and you by yourself. I wonder where you will go?

"Mrs. F. is very kind to me. We often speak of you, she has a sincere
affection for you. They talk of her lingering on for two or three more years
only! and when she asked the doctor, 'Do you think it might be for ten years?'
he said, 'No, not the least possible,' so her life is ending very soon for us. But
she only looks forward with earnest desire to a happier state, about which she
never seems to have a fear, she speaks as trustingly as a child might do about
her Father. Dr. Locock told me a gentleman who sat opposite him lately introduced himself as knowing him through his friends at 15 Portman St. Viz
'The Thackeray! I was very proud to be asked to take wine by the man who had
created Becky.' I did not think the worthy man would have had the time to
read V. F.

"I have not heard from William since Penzance, when he was on his way
to Brest. I wish he was safely back again; he told me they had some very
rough weather, and that he could not say he had thoroughly enjoyed it.

"This was an exciting day to the doctors here, painfully bringing Cholera
very near to us, a lady patient of theirs, who was playing on the Pianoforte
till one this morning giving a party, — was taken ill to-day and died just
now." (Mrs. Brookfield, II, 290–291) Dr. Charles Locock (1799–1875),
later (1857) first Baronet, was a fashionable obstetrician who attended at the
birth of all of Queen Victoria's children.

610.     TO THE REV. WILLIAM BROOKFIELD
### 12 JULY 1849

*Hitherto unpublished.*

Punch Office, 85, Fleet Street.

My dear Vieux

I am starting from this port for Brighton[128] where I hope to hear of you and that you'll write me a word to the P. Office  The Old Club[129] is knocked up so I'm not certain yet where I shall go: but come and let us have some nights together after each has done his days work — God bless you. .

Yours

W M T.

611.       TO MRS. BROOKFIELD
### 13 JULY 1849

*Published in part, Collection of Letters, pp. 61–64, which is the source of my text as far as* in a day or two. *The next three sentences and the description of the drawing are taken from* Lambert Catalogue, *p. 44. The rest of the letter follows the last two pages of the original in the Morgan Library. First two pages owned by Dr. Rosenbach. The passage enclosed between daggers was overscored by Mrs. Brookfield.*

13 July 1849

From Brighton

Now for to go to begin that long letter which I have a right to send you, after keeping silence, or the next thing to silence, for a whole week. As I have nothing to tell about, it is the more likely to be longer and funnier — no, not funnier, for I believe I am

---

[128] Thackeray arrived in Brighton on July 12, as the next letter shows.

[129] Thackeray refers apparently to the Club House established in 1815 by Mr. Bedford as a successor to Raggett's famous Subscription-House. It was originally located in Steine Place and later moved to the South Parade. (John George Bishop, "*A Peep into the Past:*" *Brighton in the Olden Time,* Brighton, 1880, p. 123)

generally most funny when I am most melancholy — and who can be melancholy with such air, ocean, and sunshine? not if I were going to be hanged tomorrow could I afford to be anything but exceedingly lazy, hungry and comfortable. Why is a day's Brighton the best of doctors? I don't mean this for a riddle, but I got up hungry, and have been yawning in the sun like a fat *lazzarone*, with great happiness all day. I have got a window with a magnificent prospect, a fresh sea breeze blowing in, such a blue sea yonder as can scarcely be beat by the Naples or the Mediterranean blue; and have passed the main part of the morning reading O! such a stupid book, Fanny Hervey,[130] the new *intime* novel of the season, as good as Miss Austen's people say. In two hours I am engaged to dinner in London. Well, I have broken with that place thank Heaven, for a little, and shall only go back to do my plates and to come away. Whither to go? I have a fancy that Ryde in the Isle of Wight would be as nice a place as any for idling, for sketching, for daw-dling, and getting health; but the Rev. Mr. Brookfield must de-termine this for me, and I look to see him here in a day or two. . . . Your account[131] about yourself and Mrs. Fanshawe, cheers me immensely. I am counting the eggs you see, confidently, before they are etc. That particular image pursues me ceaselessly. [*Sketch of Mrs. Brookfield seated on a sofa with a baby, and Mr. Brookfield looking on*] . . . † I am tranquil and pleased that he should have his happiness; also those ⟨. . .⟩[132] if I were jealous of them why I ought to hate William and dont thank God but have a pleasure myself all day in thinking that you & he ⟨. . .⟩ have a happy marriage.†

There's only 1 man staying at this house: and he asked me at breakfast in a piteous tone to let him dine with me: if we were 2 he said the rules of the Club would allow us a joint as if this luxury

[130] *Fanny Hervey, or the Mother's Choice* by Mrs. Stirling, 2 vols., London, 1849.
[131] No doubt the unpublished part of the letter of which a fragment is given above, No. 609.
[132] In this and the following hiatus there are respectively about six and three words irrecoverably overscored.

would tempt the voluptuary who pens these lines — He is come down here suffering from indigestion and with a fatal dying look w^h I've seen in one or two people before. He rushed wildly upon the joint and devoured it with famished eagerness — He said he had been curate of S^t James's Westminster: whereupon I asked if he knew my friend Brookfield — my successor says he — very able man very good fellow married a very nice woman — upon my word he said all this: and of course it was not my business to contradict him. He said — no he didn't say but the waiter said without my asking — that his name was M^r Palmer. and then he asked if Brookfield had any children? So I said not and began to ask about his own children — How queer it seemed to be talking in this way! And what 2 1/2d incidents to tell! but there are no others. Nobody is here — the paper this m^g announces the death of dear old Horace Smith[133] that good serene old man who went out of the world in charity with all in it, and having shown through his life as far as I know it, quite a delightful love of Gods works and creatures — a true loyal Xtian man. So was Morier of a different order but possessing that precious natural quality of Love w^h is awarded to some lucky minds — such as these, Charles Lamb's[134] & one or 2 more in our trade — to many amongst the parsons I think — to a friend of yours by the name of Makepeace perhaps, but not unalloyed to this one — O God purify it, and make my heart clean — After

dinner and a drive on the sea shore I came home to an evenings reading w^h took place as follows    It is always so with my good intentions, and I woke about dawn and found it was quite time to go to bed. But the solitude and idleness I think is

---

[133] On July 12. Morier had died on March 19.

[134] FitzGerald wrote to Charles Eliot Norton that Thackeray had once called Lamb, " 'Saint Charles,' . . . while looking at one of his half-mad Letters, and remember[ing] his Devotion to that quite mad Sister" (*Letters and Literary Remains*, ed. Wright, III, 228). The letter in question was that from Lamb to the Bartons of December 1, 1824, published in *The Letters of Charles Lamb*, 3 vols., ed. E. V. Lucas (London, 1935), II, 446–448.

both cheerful & wholesome. I've a mind to stay on here and begin to hope I shall write a stronger number of Pendennis than some of the last ones have been.

The Clevedon plan was abandoned before I came away. Some place in S. Wales I forget what was fixed upon by the old folks. I would go with them but one has neither the advantage of society nor of being alone, and it is best to follow my own ways. What a flood of egotism is being poured out on you — Well, I do think of some other people in the world besides myself — Can you guess the name of one of them? Of a second you cant guess the name, because that personage has not a name as yet. May the Ruler of today and tomorrow watch over both: and bless my dear lady.


612.            TO MRS. BROOKFIELD
            15–16 JULY 1849 [135]

Published in part, *Collection of Letters*, pp. 81–83. My text of the first two paragraphs is taken from a transcript made by Mrs. Fuller. First two pages of the original owned by Dr. Rosenbach, last two in the Morgan Library.

Monday.

My dear Lady, I must tell you that I have managed with the very greatest difficulty to overcome a sore temptation this morning and it's a wonder that I am not at Ryde at this time where I might have gone. The morning was so lovely that I could hardly resist coming and I would, as I own, but for you. There was a Cockney excursion from here to Portsmouth 2000 people or more. I had more than a mind to go just to say How do you do and God bless you and come back again, by the night train. But I thought you would be just landing, and be occupied with your relations and I might be de trop. But when you are settled and as soon as you think I may come, do write to me if you please. Remember I'm only about two hours off, and that I only want ever so little a hint to be with you. Surely I might run over to the island, and put up at the Inn for a night or two. What a comfort it would be to me to see you

[135] Mrs. Brookfield received this letter on July 17 (*Mrs. Brookfield*, II, 292).

for an hour and shake hands, and after working hard as I'm
doing now have a holiday. Not that I'm doing much, though I get
up at 6 in the morning: but though I can make a sacrifice as you see,
my mind isn't easy after it — I've been many hours writing two
pages, and thinking where I might be instead of being here. Yet
I like this solitude, like the early waking and rising: am determined
that Mr. Pendennis shan't dawdle any more, and that I'll do something to fetch up my languishing reputation, something uncommonly spirited, sarcastic, pathetic, humorous, it must be. Can you
give me a hint or two? a guinea for a hint or two. Wednesday 18th
is my birthday. 38 if you please. What will you give me for a
birthday present? What wouldn't I give to see this day as I wish
it in 1850? I can't help talking about it because I can't help thinking
about it — I want and long for you so to be happy. My first feeling
was one of intense rage and jealousy which kept me awake the whole
night (you see some people are jealous as well as other people) but
I grew to be much more wholesome in 24 hours and to wish for this
event more fiercely than anybody does except you I believe. I mean
that when I was a Papa myself or about to become one, I used to
accept the position with a great deal of equanimity and supposed
that other fathers are similarly pretty easy. I'm disappointed not
to have heard from his Reverence as yet. I had hoped to hear from
him a friendly line. I want it very much.

Surely this is as stupid a letter as mortal man can write. The
truth is I can't get the Ryde excursion out of my head, and keep
thinking on how much pleasanter it would be to talk than write
to you.

What you say about Mʳˢ [Fanshawe] being doomed does not
affect me very much I'm afraid — I don't see that living is such a
benefit and could find it in my heart prettily readily to have an end
of it — after wasting a deal of opportunities and time and desires
in vanitarianism — What is it makes one so blasé & tired I wonder at 38 Is it pain or pleasure? present solitude or too much
company before — both very likely — You see I am here as yesterday gloomy again and thrumming on the old egotistical string.
But that I think you will be pleased to have a letter from me, dear

lady, I'd burn these 2 sheets or give my blue devils some other
outlet than into your kind breast. Here are some verses wͪ I have
been knocking about and are of the same gloomy tendency — You
must know that I was making a drawing wͪ was something like you
at first but ended in a ⟨fat jolly⟩ face that is not in the least like
yours: whereupon the Pote ever on the watch for incidents, began.

### A Failure.

Beneath this frank and smiling face
You who would look with curious eye
The draughtsmans inward mind to spy
Some other lineaments may trace
Ah many a time I try & try
Lady, to represent their grace.

Dear face! the smile with wͪ tis lit
The mantling blush, the gentle eyes
Each individual feature lies
Within my heart so faithful writ
Why fails my pencil when it tries
Continually to copy it?

. . . . . . . . . . .

I look upon the altered line
And think it ever is my lot
A something always comes to blot
And mar my impossible design
A mocking Fate that bids me pine
And struggle and atchieve it not

Poor balked endeavour incomplete!
Poor feeble sketch, the world to show
While the marr'd truth lurks lost below.
Whats life but this? — a cancelled sheet
A laugh disguising a defeat,
Let's tear and laugh and own it so —

(Here lines may be in-
serted ad lib: compli-
mentary to the person

Exit with a laugh of demoniacal scorn — But I send the wery
original drawing to these wery original verses — Do you know

writing them down has given me a great comfort: and liberty to see how absurd they are?

613.     TO MRS. CARMICHAEL-SMYTH
18 JULY 1849

*Address:* Mʳˢ Carmichael Smyth | Lough Arne | Carmarthen. *Postmarks:* BRIGHTON JY 18 1849, CARMARTHEN JY 20 1849. Published in part, *Biographical Introductions,* II, xxxvi.

Brighton. July 18. 1849.

My dearest Mammy

You must have a line on this lamentable anniversary to say that I bless and love my dearest old Mother always and in spite of every kind of waywardness selfishness good fortune evil ditto — I have been at work to very little purpose though jusqu'à present but stopping in my room from seven o'clock until 5 almost every day, and going to bed & to sleep with great comfort at 9 1/2 or so: I could easily accustom myself to that or to any other kind of life; and with the help of that blessed invention sleep accommodate myself to almost any existence but I find one is not very brilliant in these times of absolute ease. I suppose the mind requires torpor too at any rate my brains have almost refused to work these last 3 or 4 days; but are beginning now at last to get into play. This is written in Mʳ Inspector Brookfields company in the Brighton National School room,[136] with a score of little and 3/4 grown people writing examination-papers round about. Dont be alarmed Mʳˢ Inspectress isn't here — nor did I know that the husband was coming until yesterday — He has been a fortnight's cruise was very uncomfortable and the skin of his nose came off ever so many times. What do men go acruising for? But he looks healthier for it — & so am I for Brighton. I must go up to town on Saturday to do my plates; and then to finish my number somewhere or other —

---

[136] Brookfield rejoined Thackeray late in the evening, "at his club where he was entertaining two dragoons with the wicked weed and wickeder distillation," and the two men dined together the following day (*Mrs. Brookfield,* II, 292–293).

w$^h$ isn't near done. I woonder could I do 2 next month? If I could I'd be off for September somewhere — but thats too great a piece of luck to hope for: the invention seems to fail for one number almost how much more for 2.

I will write about Mary Rees to my friend Jas Harly[137] — but my mind misgives me that he was not the Director who got me my free passage but that it was done through Tennents interest however nothing will be easier than to write a pooty letter and try.

How do you like your Welsh retreat? I wish I knew how to hunt shoot course or play at cards — Depend on it those were very sensible people who invented and practised those recreations, and thereby kept themselves out of a great deal of ugly mischiefs — I have for a wonder not met with a single soul de connoissance here, have dined alone every day; And have spent most of the time reading novels — Alexandre Dumas is wonderful. He kept me on the stretch for nearly nine hours one day.[138] What wouldn't I give to have his knack of putting a story together: and yet in degree the I is infinitely below the other. But the business-habit is the thing I admire in him.

God bless my dearest little women and my dear old G P. I'm really very much easier in my absurd mind: healthy in my body: quite ready for a lark whenever it may turn up, and not minded in the least to break my heart. I was much worse this time last year, and can see by the watermarks how much lower the tide is.

God bless all and today especially my dearest old Mother.

W M T.

[137] James Hartley.
[138] Thackeray's cult of the novels of Dumas père is the subject of chapter 9 of my *Thackeray and France*.

614.                 TO MRS. BROOKFIELD
                     24 JULY 1849 [139]

Published in part, *Collection of Letters*, pp. 54–55. The passage between
daggers has been overscored by Mrs. Brookfield.

                                    Refawrm Club. Tuesday.

My dear Lady — I write only a word and in the greatest hurry
to say Im very well in health. I've been at work & have written
somewhat and done my two plates, which only took two hours, and
now that they're done I feel that I want so to come back to Ryde,
I must get a rope or a chain to bind myself down to my desk here.
I've nothing you see to say: but I found half a dozen lines from
you on coming home all the world is out of town — M$^{rs}$ Procter
not at home perhaps to my visit — dear kind K. Perry whom indeed
I like with all my heart just packing to go to Brighton — my
Chesterfield Street loves flown away to Tunbridge Wells: & so
I'm alone, and miss you. I sent your packidge off to Harry this
morning. The lucky rogue tomorrow I suppose he will see Madam,
and all those kind Ryde Folks. Tell them if you please how very
grateful I am for their good nature — I can't help fancying them
relations rather than friends — † I met on the pier as I was running
for the dear life, the great Dickens with his wife his children his
Miss Hogarth all looking abominably coarse vulgar and happy and
bound to Bonchurch where they have taken one of White's houses
for the summer † — I got some dinner at 10 1/2 o'clock I drank to
the health of Madame ma bonne soeur — I hadn't the courage to
go home till past midnight, when all the servants got out of bed
to let me in. There was O such a heap of letters — I send you a
couple w$^h$ may amuse you. Send me Colonel Ferguson's back if you
please as I must answer him — but I dont think I shall be able to
get away in August to Scotland. Who can the excoriated female

[139] We learn from one of Mrs. Brookfield's notes to *Collection of Letters*
(p. 54) that Thackeray went from Brighton to Ryde, where he spent several
days with her and with Mr. and Mrs. Arthur Elton. This letter was written
the day after his return to London, on Tuesday, July 24.

be who imparts her anguish to me? — What raw wound has the whip of the satirist been touching? Will you go & sit upon that plank and look out at the pleasant green & the sea and the sunshine? — I would give twopence to be upon it even without the shawl: and I was sitting with my Frenchmen at 3 o'clock, I thought to myself O Lor M͟r Makepeace how much better you were off yesterday.

The travellers to Wales had a severe rough passage in boats and steamers and the post takes 2 days so that it must be an awfle way off.

Goodbye dear lady Godbless every kind person of all those who love you — I feel here you must know, just as I used five and twenty years ago at school the day after coming back from the holydays. If you have nothing to say to me pray write, if you have something of course you will. Tell Missy[140] that I intend to write to her some day the most beautiful letter; and that she will make a fortune at the sale.

Good bye. Godbless you. Shake hands — So the Captain is coming to dinner to day? The lucky rogue! I am always my dear lady's sincere

W M T.

615.          TO LADY EDDISBURY
                 JULY 1849 [141]

Hitherto unpublished.

Dear Lady Eddisbury. You are quite wrong in thinking M͟r Brown[142] an ungrateful wretch. He has been out of town and awfully busy whilst in the metropulus: Another day passes and he can't come to pay his duty to you, being forced by an odious en-

[140] Maria Agnes Elton.
[141] This letter was written shortly after the birth of Lady Eddisbury's fifth daughter on July 25, 1849. The baby died a few days later.
[142] That is, Thackeray.

gagement to ride with a young lady as soon as his day's work is
over. But the venerable man blesses+ the babby and its Mamma
in his heart: and longs to behold the latter.

A printers divvle opportunely comes, and is the bearer of this
to your Ladyship.

+By reading the words 'in his heart' immediately after the word
'blesses', a sentence w^h would be otherwise absurd & nonsensical
(for I have not the least wish to behold my own heart) becomes
intelligible & not inelegant.

I purposely omit making any enquiries about the health of any
young ladies: because perhaps you would not like to think of any
but your youngest daughter just now. If it be true and who can
doubt the words? that a man is blessed who has his quiver full of
children[143] in what a state of earthly happiness the Under-Secretary-
for Foreign Affairs must be! —

[For fragments of a letter to Kate Perry, July, 1849, see letter 6, Appendix
XXVI.]

[143] *Psalms,* 127, 5.

616.                    TO ADELAIDE PROCTER
                          5? AUGUST 1849 [144]

Hitherto unpublished. My text is taken from the transcript given Lady Ritchie
by George Murray Smith.

Kensington.

Sunday evening.

My dear Adelaide,

Where is the letter I nearly wrote you the day before yesterday on receipt of the beautiful purse? It was finished all but ever such a little bit on Friday when I had to go and wish somebody Good bye who was going out of town. Since then writing for love has been impossible. I was ill all yesterday with a headache,* and have been writing till this minute to-day (at five o'clock) but I do not like the splendid purse the less for that, nor am I less thankful to the giver. I shall keep it and value it sincerely and hope that the donor for whom I had a regard ever since the time when my head was black and she wore a pinafore, and the owner of the purse will be good friends until we stop altogether. Your parents have been of the best friends I have ever had. Twelve years ago when I was a poor struggling fellow they were just as good to me as now when — when I'm a poor struggling man still: with a little additional stock of reputation and a vast deal more care and doubt. How much one has gone through since one knew them to be sure! I can't help tracing over the ground from that distant landmark — nearly the third part and all the busiest part of my life lies within it. I've made in that time about 100000 acquaintances and two sets of intimate friends beside those in your house.[145] I suppose one won't make any more now. I feel so good-naturedly indifferent to new people, that I can't expect them to have any more than in-

* A headache brought on by going to Vauxhall I believe and sitting up very late: not by any excess of either feasting or grief.

[144] Parliament was prorogued on Wednesday, August 1, in 1849 (*Times*, August 2). This letter appears to have been written the following Sunday.
[145] The Brookfields and their friends, and the Elliots and their friends.

difference for me, and don't care if they do or don't, that's the truth:
or 2d for reputation except for the substantial part of it, or for
any except a very very few people. If it[146] had been a new acquaintance who as I thought hesitated about [*Sketch*] I shouldn't have
been hurt in the least or made a bluster. Thank God I was wrong.

I wonder whether it is the conclusion of the season, or everybody
being out of town, or the Lord Mayor's dinner yesterday (where
I drank wine and water think of that!) or the remnants of yesterday's headache or the lassitude produced by writing all day against
the will that makes me so profoundly egotistic and melancholy?
But I can't delay writing any longer to thank you for the splendid
present: and if I am happy or otherwise (or out of humour which
if you please, Miss, is very rare indeed) I must show it. So you
get me at an unlucky minute with a black-edged border round me,
and a dismal news within. Excuse my lugubriousness — I can't
grin when I'm melancholy: and Tom Fool at home is known to
have occasional fits of depression. By the way, I had to send for
my neighbour, Mr Merryman[147] — I declare he comes in quite pat
to make the joke.

But tomorrow I'll perfectly astonish everybody with the liveliness of my rattle. Forster shan't be anything to me in his lightest
moods. And now farewell, and believe me, my dear Adelaide,

Yours till death,

[*Sketch*]

617.            TO MR. AND MRS. PROCTER
                      AUGUST? 1849

Hitherto unpublished. My text is taken from a transcript given Lady Ritchie
by George Murray Smith.

My dear Procter, and also my dear Mrs ditto,

Much thanks for your note. I was coming on Saturday to
speak about it and to settle some day for dining: but I received a

---

[146] The transcript reads *I*.
[147] See above, No. 448.

letter from my Mother alarming me rather about the health of the old step-father, and I don't like to settle anything until I hear again from them. It may be that I shall have to go down to Wales to my Mother: and this of course at a sudden warning. I wish they had not gone to such a distant and difficult place as South Wales — it takes two days to get at it and I could travel to Paris and back in the time.

I should have written earlier of course, only I thought every day that I should see you.

Always affectionately yours,
W. M. Thackeray.

618.          TO LADY EDDISBURY
              18 AUGUST 1849

Hitherto unpublished.

Kensington. Saturday. 18. August

Dear Lady Eddisbury    Thank you very much for writing to me; I was as grateful to get your kind letter, as I was shocked when I found what an occasion I had taken to send my own.[148]  Indeed you do me no more than justice in saying that I have a kind heart towards Mothers & children: I was so unhappy myself as a child that I don't think I have said a rough word to one twice in my life — and for you and your family how should I have anything but a sincere liking & cordiality? You have been too kind to me to allow of any other feeling: and I am glad that you think I wish you all sincerely well. I hope you will have a pleasant holyday in Cheshire, and am always dear Lady Eddisbury Yours most truly

W M Thackeray

[148] See above, No. 615.

619.     TO LORD HOLLAND
          29 AUGUST 1849

*Hitherto unpublished.*

Folkstone. Wednesday m<sup>g</sup>

Dear Lord Holland

I got a letter yesterday to say that a dear old relation of mine[149] was in extremis at Paris, and I am so far on my way thither to give her a parting shake of the hand. I am sorry to be obliged to refuse your hospitality for to day.

Always very faithfully yours
W M Thackeray


620.     TO CHARLOTTE RITCHIE
          29 AUGUST 1849

*Hitherto unpublished.*

Hotel Bristol. Wednesday night.

My dear Charlotte. I have two letters to you half written in my desk, but the subject was so melancholy that indeed I hadn't courage to finish them, hoping always to come & pay my dear Aunt a visit my dear Aunt who has always loved me so kindly. I was just finishing my month's work[150] yesterday when your letter came, and as soon as I had done I set off, and hope to see you all in the morning. But I should be glad to know how you are all first, and to have a line from you — ever affectionately yours

W M Thackeray

[149] Mrs. Halliday.
[150] Number XI of *Pendennis* for September, chapters 33 to 36.

621.        TO MRS. CARMICHAEL-SMYTH
30 AUGUST 1849

*Address:* M^rs Carmichael Smyth. | Lough Arne | S. W. *Postmarks:* AU 31
1849, ST. OLEARS SP. 1 1849. Hitherto unpublished.

Hotel Bristol. Place Vendome.
Thursday.

My dearest Mammy I got in here at 12 last night, and am very
glad I came to see my good old Aunt, & the 2 girls[151] who were
as kind and cordial as they always are. Then I went to see D^r
Halliday, who is not long for this world I should think, having
all sorts of inflammatory complaints & symptoms, not eating, not
going out, and greatly depressed about M^rs Halliday. She has been
wandering in her mind for weeks past: very seldom recognizes anybody: was better yesterday, but is worse again today. I saw her in
her bed, asleep and groaning an old old woman — it was rather
an awful sight: and I am glad I set out to be here and pay the
last duties to one of our race w^h is dropping away. Charlotte
Ritchie says that 2 days ago, she was wandering and fancying she
was in the boat with my father dying[152] — it affected me. I think
this is all I have to say: but I shall stay on until the end comes — I
may do my next months work[153] or the best part of it here: and
whilst I'm writing am thinking about an article for Punch w^h must
be done too in the course of the evening & tomorrow morning.
What a queer world it is. I write by this post to M^r Hartley begging him to help in the Miss Rees affair, but I don't know whether
he can; I will contribute 10£ though towards the passage if that

[151] Mrs. Ritchie, Charlotte, and Jane.
[152] "Richmond Thackeray," writes Mrs. Fuller, "died of a lingering fever.
Towards the end he was carried on board a ship in the Ganges in the hope
that the cooler air of the river might save his life. His wife and his sister, Mrs.
Halliday, nursed him."
[153] Number XII of *Pendennis*, chapters 37 to 38, which was not published
until the following January. The article for *Punch* is "What Mr. Jones saw
at Paris" (September 8, pp. 100–101). It has not previously been identified
as Thackeray's.

will do. God bless you all: let me hear quickly please that all is
well: and that my young women are not barking & biling with
each other. O where is that paragon governess whom we want to
keep them in order? Goodbye.

W M T.

622.       FROM MRS. BROOKFIELD
1 SEPTEMBER 1849

My text is taken from *Mrs. Brookfield and her Circle*, pp. 294–295.

1 Sept., 49.

My dear Sir,

It was kind of you to send the little note with G. B. Y. Just as
I received it Totty Fanshawe came in, having come to spend ten
days in London. I was pleased to have her, she comes out most
companionably, and is like her mother in many ways. She spent
the day with me on Wednesday, and we went together to the
Vernon Gallery, which I had never seen, and I took up a *connoisseur*
air to point out the best pictures to my young friend who is fond
of drawing.

Yesterday was William's birthday and also Harry Hallam's and
by a curious coincidence Stephen Spring Rice's, who wrote to propose dining here, but called and breakfasted instead, his father
having made up a family dinner in his honour at home — he enquired affectionately after you and declares he never sees you which
he laments, and he praises Pendennis more than anybody. We had
the new number yesterday. I should think people would like it,
as it is of the amusing order. But you are rather hard upon the
people who have not good Cooks or Butlers of their own, at least
I think that they would be justified in thinking you were scoffing
at them.

I have just had Mrs. Fry's memoirs to read. On her death-bed
she says, "I can say one thing that since I was 17, when first my
heart was touched, I have never wakened or gone to sleep, without

my first and last thought being how best I might serve my Lord," [154]
and this as a deliberate death-bed assertion is very striking, as she
had Mr. Fry and I don't know how many children who might have
been expected to distract her thoughts occasionally.

We had three of the Council Office men[155] to dine yesterday, one
of them brought a friend, Mr. Clough, who seemed to know you,
and I tried to talk with him, but he has the most peculiar manner
I almost ever saw. His eyes cut one through and through, twenty
times sharper than Sir Alexander Duff, who has that way of scruti-
nising one. Mr. Clough sat at the foot of my sofa with this keen
expression of investigation, but I determined not to mind and only
thought him ununderstandable.


623.                    TO MRS. BROOKFIELD
                    2–3 SEPTEMBER 1849

*Address:* M<sup>rs</sup> Brookfield | 15 Portman St | Portman Sq<sup>re</sup> London. *Postmarks:*
PARIS 3 SEPT. 49, 4 SP 1849. Published in part, *Collection of Letters*, pp.
81, 83–85; facsimile of the first four pages after p. 80.

                                        Sunday 2 Sep.<sup>t</sup>
Madam's letter made a very agreeable appearance upon the
breakfast table this morning when I entered that apartment at 11
o'clock. I dont know how I managed to sleep so much, but
such was the fact — after a fine broiling hot day's utter idleness
part of w.<sup>h</sup> was spent on the sofa, a little in the Twillery gardens
where I made a sketch thats not a masterpiece but praps Madam
will like to see it: and the evening very merrily with the Morning
Chronicle the Journal des Debats[156] and Jules Janin at a jolly little
Restaurateur's on the Champs Elysées at the sign of the Petit

---

[154] Mrs. Fry spoke these words in 1843, two years before she died (*Memoirs
of the Life of Elizabeth Fry*, ed. by two of her Daughters, 2 vols., Philadelphia,
1847, II, 495). Mrs. Brookfield condenses the original statement.
[155] Men from the Privy Council Office, and, more particularly, from the
Office of the Committee of Council on Education, Brookfield's headquarters as
a School Inspector.
[156] That is, Tom Fraser and John Lemoinne.

Moulin Rouge. We had a private room & drank small wine very gaily looking out into a garden full of green arbours in almost every one of w^h were gentlemen & ladies in couples come to dine au frais, and afterwards to go & dance at the neighbouring dancing garden of Mabille. Fiddlers and singers came and performed for us: and who knows I should have gone to Mabille too, but there came down a tremenduous thunder-storm with flashes of lightning to illuminate it, w^h sent the little couples out of the arbours, and put out all the lights of Mabille. The day before I passed with my aunt & cousins, who are not so pretty as some members of the family; but are dear good people with a fine sense of fun and we were very happy until the arrival of two newly-married Snobs, whose happiness disgusted me and drove me home early, to find 3 acquaintances smoking in the moonlight at the hotel door, who came up and passed the night in my rooms — No I forgot, I went to the play first: but only for an hour I couldn't stand more than an hour of the farce w^h made me laugh while it lasted, but left a profound black melancholy behind it. Janin said last night that life was the greatest of pleasures to him, that every morning when he woke he was thankful to be alive (this is very tolerably like him) that he  was always entirely happy, and had never known any such thing as blue devils or repentance or satiety. I had great fun giving him authentic accounts of London. I told him that to see the people boxing in the streets was a constant source of amusement to us; that in November — you saw every lamp post on London Bridge with a man hanging from it who had committed suicide — and he believed everything.[157] Did you ever read any of the works of

[157] Thackeray pursued this hoax when Janin came to England. "Some years ago," he writes in *The Roundabout Papers* (*Works*, XII, 305), "a

Janin? — No? Well he has been for 20 years famous in France: and he on his side has never heard of the works of Titmarsh, nor has anybody else here and that is a comfort. I have got very nice rooms but they cost 10 francs a day: and I began in a dignified manner with a domestique de place, but sent him away after two days: for the idea that he was in the anteroom ceaselessly with nothing to do, made my life in my own room intolerable, and now I actually take my own letters to the post. I went to the Exhibition, it was full of portraits of the most hideous women, with inconceivable spots on their faces of w$^h$ I think I've told you my horror: and scarcely 6 decent pictures in the whole enormous collection: but I had never been in the Tuilleries before, and it was curious to go through the vast dingy rooms by w$^h$ such a number of dynasties have come in & gone out — Louis XVI. Napoleon, Charles X. Louis Philippe have all marched in state up the stair case with the gilt balustrades, and come tumbling down again presently. — Well I wont give you an historical disquisition in the Titmarsh manner upon this but reserve it for Punch — for whom on Thursday an article that I think is quite unexampled for dullness even in that Journal, and that beats the dullest Jerrold. What a jaunty off hand satiric rogue I am to be sure — and a gay young dog! I took a very great liking and admiration for Clough. He is a real poet and a simple affectionate creature — Last year we went to Blenheim from Oxford[158] (it was after a stay at Cl—ved—n C—rt the seat of Sir C— E—n B—t) and I liked him for sitting down in the Inn yard and beginning to teach a child to read off a bit of Punch w$^h$ was lying on the ground — Subsequently he sent me his pomes w$^h$ were rough but contain the real genuine sacred flame I think. He is very learned: he has evidently been crossed in love:

---

famous and witty French critic was in London, with whom I walked the streets. I am ashamed to say that I informed him (being in hopes that he was about to write some papers regarding the manners and customs of this country) that all the statues he saw represented the Duke of Wellington. That on the arch opposite Apsley House? the Duke in a cloak, and cocked-hat, on horseback. That behind Apsley House in an airy fig-leaf costume? the Duke again. That in Cockspur Street? the Duke with a pig-tail — and so on. I showed him an army of Dukes."

[158] See above, No. 519.

he gave up his Fellowship and university prospects on religious scruples. He is one of those thinking men, who I daresay will begin to speak out before many years are over, and protest against Gothic Xtianity. — that is I think he is — Did you read in F. Newman's book?[159] There speaks a very pious loving humble soul I think, with an ascetical continence too — and a beautiful love and reverence — I'm a publican and sinner; but I believe those men are on the true track. — and — and I won't say any more to my dear lady who is still of the Gothic believers. The sight of the old aunt in bed was very awful — it was her custom to turn out two or three months ago in the utmost splendor & crinolines, with a chestnut front, a pearly set of teeth, and a carmine complexion — there in bed lay an old lean gray pale toothless woman tossing & moaning feebly — May God be merciful to us. When I last dined with my aunt Ritchie[160] her husband sate at the head of the table — now there's only his bust in the room and the old gentleman has disappeared out of this world altogether. They all got a great shock they told me by reading in Galignani that W M Thackeray was dead & thought it was I — indeed 2 W T's have died within the last month. Eh bien? There's a glum sort of humour in all this I think and I grin like a skull — As I sent you a letter to my Mamma, here is a sermon to Anny wh please put in the post for me. I think about my dear honest old Fatty with the greatest regard and confidence — I hope please God that she'll be kept to be a companion & friend to me — You see I work in the Herschel[161] — Give my love to Harry when you write to him & to Mrs F. & to Missy — I haven't time to transact letters to them to day or I should take

[159] Thackeray probably refers to *The Soul; her Sorrows and her Aspirations* (1849) by Francis William Newman (1805–1897), whose *Phases of Faith* (1850) is the basis of Thackeray's comparison between him and his famous brother, later Cardinal Newman, in chapter 61 of *Pendennis* (*Works*, II, 615–616).

[160] During his visit of February, 1849. John Ritchie died during the following month.

[161] It would appear from Mrs. Brookfield's reply (see below, No. 624) that Thackeray refers to Sir John Frederick Herschel (1792–1871). She writes of Ainsworth that he once offered to shake hands with Hallam, saying " 'I am Mr. Ainsworth,' as if he had been Herschel at the least."

advantage of the traveller who carries this here, and glory in saving 20ᵈ by that stratagem. And I'd have ye to know Madam, that I wish I was going to dine at Portman Street this day as I did this day week — but that as I cant why I'll be a man and do my jewty: and that I hope that you are well and hopeful: and that I begin & end my day with a G B Y. Bon Soir William. Bon Soir Madame.

W M T.

Monday. The man who was to carry my letter yesterday fled without giving me notice, so Madam loses the sermon to Anny the pretty picture &c. I haven't the courage to pay the postage for so much rubbish. Isn't it curious, that a gentleman of such expensive habits should have this meanness about paper & postage? The best is that I spent 3 francs in cab-hire hunting for the man who was to carry my 2 franc letter. The follies of men are ceaseless — even of comic authors who make it their business to laugh at the follies of all the rest of the world

What do you think I did yesterday night? If you please Mum I went to the play:[162] and I suppose because it was Sunday was especially diverted and laughed so as to make myself an object in the stalls — but it was at pure farcicality not at wit — The piece was about the pleasure excursion to London; and the blunders and buffoonery mingled made the laughter — 'Eh oui, nous irons à Greenwich, manger un excellent Sandwich' was a part of one of the songs.

My poor Aunt is still in life but that is all. She has lost quite her senses. I talked for some time with her old husband, who has been the most affᵗᵉ of husbands to her — and who is looking on he being 72 years old himself with a gloomy resolution, and awaiting the moment wʰ is to take away his life's companion     I wonder whether she will leave me any money? She is rather well to do. But I have never courted the kind old soul — on the contrary: and

---

[162] Thackeray went to the Vaudeville, where he saw *Une Semaine à Londres, ou les trains de plaisir* by Éléonore Tenaille de Vaulabelle [Jules Cordier] (1802–1859) and Louis François Nicolaie, called Clairville (*Moniteur universel*, September 1).

don't feel much excited about the event one way or other. But it would be a comfort rather to have Anny & Minny provided for. I don't think I care personally otherwise. Madam, you don't tell me whether you are pretty well, w^h I should like very much to know. I think it seems about a year since this day week, when W^m wouldn't come to dinner with me, and we had if I remember aright rather a pleasant evening of talk & smoking: but it's so long so very long ago that I forget. As for Pendennis I began upon no 7 to day, & found a picture w^h was perfectly new and a passage w^h I had as utterly forgotten as if I had never read or written. This shortness of memory frightens me and makes me have glum anticipations — Will poor Anny have to nurse an old Imbecile of a father some day — who will ramble incoherently about old days, and people whom he used to love? — What a shame it is to talk such gloomy stuff to my dear lady. Well, you are accustomed to hear my chatter gloomy or otherwise as my thoughts come up. I fancy myself by the dear old sofa almost, as I sit here prating: and shut my eyes and see you quite clear. I'm glad you have been doing works of art with your needle. I've got a pretty present in my i for you. When shall I give it you? W^m Harrison Hainsworth Esq^r is here; we dined next each other at the 3 Freres yesterday, and rather fraternized. He showed a friendly disposition I thought and a desire to forgive me my literary success. But beyond a good humoured acquiescence in his good will, I don't care. I suppose one doesn't care for people: — only for a very very few. A man came in just now who told me he had heard how I was dead — I began to laugh and my laugh meant 'Well old fellow you didn't care did you?' And y should he? How often I must have said & said these things over to you. Oui Madame Je me repète, Je me fais vieux, J'oublie, je radote, Je ne parle que de moi. Je vous fais subir mon égoisme, ma mélancolie — le jour viendra t il ou elle vous gênera? Eh, mon dieu; — ne soyons pas trop curieux — demain viendra, aujourdhui s'oubliera — pourquoi ne vous vois je pas aujourdhui? — I think you have enough of this for to day — so Goodbye. Goodbye M^r Williams. I fancy the old streetsweeper at the corner is holding the cab. I take my at and stick. I say

Goodbye again — the door bangs finally. Here's a shilling for you old street-sweeper — The cab trots solitary into the Park — Je fais de la littérature ma parole d'honneur — du style — du Sterne tout pur — O vanitas vanitatum! — God bless all.

W M T.

624.                    FROM MRS. BROOKFIELD
                       4? SEPTEMBER 1849 [163]

My text is taken from *Mrs. Brookfield and her Circle*, pp. 296–298.

When you suggested you may end in a fatuous old age without memory, &c., I merely thought how much better suited I should be for a friend to you when you are brought a little more to my level; and perhaps when you are in that state you will see what a nice provision you have made in securing an idiotic sister in your comparative early life instead of a Miss B——, who might be bored by the second childhood, while I should have such a comfortable sympathy with it that we should get on very well together.

But I wish you could be made independent of having to work so constantly. I sometimes imagine legacies from unknown individuals coming in to me, and I make the handsomest settlements in an anonymous manner upon Annie and Minny. I wish they would come true some day and that I could "hand you over your freedom," which is a phrase I have heard applied to some kind of privilege awarded to citizens.

I heard from Arthur[164] to-day, a long letter, containing a long critique on V. F., which he never regularly read through until just now — they have been such absurd Dickensites under Julian Young's[165] guidance, that with every personal *prestige* for you,

---

[163] This is Mrs. Brookfield's reply to Thackeray's letter of September 2–3 and was evidently received by him before he posted his letter of September 4–6.

[164] Arthur Elton.

[165] The Rev. Julian Charles Young (1806–1873), at this time Rector of Southwick in Sussex, author of *A Memoir of Charles Mayne Young, tragedian; with extracts from his son's journal* (1871).

they thought one periodical-luxury sufficient, and have always plodded on in the old track, and that one being Mr. Dickens'. However, Arthur allows that he never fully appreciated your powers as an author, till now, although he complains of an occasional "morbid cynicism" and too constant imputation of background and unworthy motives to all the actions of men — he is much impressed with the Author's admirable talents, "wit, graphic powers, touches of feeling," "fragmentary traces of reverence," "strong and honest indignation against cant, worldliness," &c., &c., &c. I have copied you out quite a wedge of praise which will fall mildly before you as coming from the mild country gentleman. I am amused at your having Mr. Ainsworth at Paris — he was at Venice when we were there, and was always called "Tiger or Tig" by Uncle Hallam, who did not know who he was till he came up one day and proffered the hand of fellowship to uncle H. on the ground of their mutual authorship. "I am Mr. Ainsworth," as if he had been Herschel at the least, and we sat together in the Place St. Mark, eating ices and discussing you, and I recollect saying you had "such an affectionate nature," which Mr. Ainsworth made me repeat about 3 times, pretending not to hear, and I felt I had thrown pearls before swine and been unnecessarily frank in my praise of you, and began to think he might very possibly have a feeling of jealousy about you as an author, tho' it would be ludicrously presumptuous in him — as of all detestable writing his is the worst, I think. Mr. P.[166] is in Paris . . . there is a great deal of worthiness in him *au fond* — am I not quite Mrs. Gore-like in my little French words to-day? tho' he does hem and hesitate before he can bring out a title, so awful is it in its attractiveness in his eyes. Forgive this nonsense, I wish I could make you laugh even if it were only at me. Why did you not send me the sermon to Annie, you need not have paid it, if you were determined to be stingy that is no reason why I should dislike paying postage; on the contrary, as my writing is too large to be over suited to underweight letters, I am quite hardened to all postal expenses.

[166] Tom Parr. See below, No. 627.

625.                 TO MRS. BROOKFIELD
                    4–6 SEPTEMBER 1849

*Address:* M<sup>rs</sup> Brookfield | 15 Portman S<sup>t</sup> | Portman Sq<sup>re</sup> London. *Postmarks:*
6 SEPT. 49, 7 SP 1849. Published in part, *Collection of Letters,* pp. 85–89.

Tuesday.

Perhaps by my intolerable meanness and blundering you will
not get any letter from me till tomorrow. On Sunday the man
who was to take the letter failed me: yesterday I went with it in
a cab to the Grande Poste w<sup>h</sup> is a mile off, and where you have to
go to pay: the cab horse was lame and we arrived 2 minutes too
late — I put the letter into the unpaid letter-box I dismissed the
poor old broken cab horse behind which it was agonizing to sit: in
fine it was a failure. When I got to dinner to my aunts, I found
all was over M<sup>rs</sup> Halliday died on Sunday night in her sleep quite
without pain or any knowledge of the transition — I went and sate
with her husband an old fellow of 72: and found him bearing his
calamity in a very honest manly way. What do you think the old
gentleman was doing? Well, he was drinking gin & water & I had
some too — telling his valet to make me some. The man thought
this was a master stroke of diplomacy, & evidently thinks I have
arrived to take possession as heir: but I know nothing about money
matters as yet, and think that the old gentleman at least will have
the enjoyment of my aunts property during life. He told me some
family secrets in w<sup>h</sup> persons of repute figure not honorably. Ah
they shock one to think of. Pray have you ever committed any
roguery in money-matters? Has William? Have I? I am more
likely to do it than he that honest man: not having his resolution
or self denial: but I've not as yet — beyond the roguery of not
saving perhaps w<sup>h</sup> is knavish too. Im very glad I came to see my
dearest old Aunt. She is such a kind tender creature — Laws bless
us, how fond she would be of you! I was going to begin about W<sup>m</sup>
& say Do you remember a friend of mine who came to dine at the
Thermes, and sang the song about the Mogul & the Blue Bottle
Fly? — but modesty forbade: and I was dumb.

Since this was written in the afternoon, I suppose if there has been one virtuous man in Paris it is Madam's most obajient servant. I went to sit with M.ʳ Halliday, and found him taking what he calls his tiffin in great comfort (Tiffin is the meal w.ʰ I have sometimes had the honour of sharing with you at one o'clock) and this transacted & I did not have any tiffin having consumed a good breakfast 2 hours previously, I went up a hundred stairs at least to Miss Bess Hamerton's airy apartment and found her & her sister & sate for an hour. She asked after you so warmly that I was quite pleased. She said she had the highest respect for you and I was glad to find somebody who knew you, and all I can say is if you fancy I like being here better than in London, you are in a pleasing error, and once at least in every day I want to see you — but you must calculate how long once is & at what o'clock in the morning it begins and when it ends. Then I went to see a friend of my mothers: then to have a very good dinner at the Café de Paris where we had potage à la Poupard (think of Poupard soup we had it merely for the sake of the name & it was uncommonly good) then back to old Halliday again, to bawl into his ears for an hour & a half, then to drink tea with my aunt — why life has been a series of sacrifices to day, & I must be written up in the book of good works: for I sh.ᵈ have liked to go to the play & follow my own devices best, but for that stern sentiment of duty w.ʰ fitfully comes over the most abandoned of men at times. All the time I was with M.ʳ Halliday in the morning, what do you think they were doing in the next room? It was like a novel. They were rapping at a coffin in the bed room: but he was too deaf to hear, & seems too old to care very much. Ah dear lady I hope you are sleeping happily at this hour. And I will go & sleep too, & you & M.ʳ Williams, & another party who is nameless, shall have all the benefits of an old Sinner's prayers. †.

I suppose I was too virtuous on Tuesday — for yesterday I got back to my old selfish ways again and did what I liked from morning till night. This self indulgence though entire was not criminal — at first at least but I shall come to the painful part of my memories presently — all the forenoon I read with intense delight a novel

called Le Vicomte de Bragelonne,[167] a continuation of the famous
Mousquetaires and just as interesting keeping one panting from
volume to volume and longing for more. This done and after a
walk and some visits read more novels David Copperfield[168] to wit,
in w^h there is a charming bit of insanity, and w^h I begin to believe
is the very best thing the author has yet done — Then to the
Variétés Theayter to see the play of the Caméléons[169] after w^h
all Paris is running — a general satire upon the last 60 years.
Everything is satirized Louis XVI, the Convention, the Empire,
the Restoration, & the Barricades at w^h these people were murdering
each other only yesterday — Its awful — immodest — surpassed
my cynicism altogether — at the end of the piece they pretend to
bring in the Author, and a little child who can just speak comes in
and sings a satiric song in a feeble tender infantine pipe — w^h
seemed to me as impious as the whole of the rest of the piece.
They dont care for anything — not religion not bravery not liberty
not great men not modesty — Ah Madam What a great moralist
somebody is, and what moighty foine principles entoirely he has!
— But now with a blush upon my damask cheek I come to the
adventure of the day — You must know I went to the play with an
old comrade of mine Roger de Beauvoir[170] an ex dandy and man of
letters who talked incessantly during the whole of dinner time as I

[167] Which Dumas had published in 1848.
[168] Number V, chapters 13 to 15. The "charming bit of insanity" is, of
course, Mr. Dick, who first appears in chapter 13.
[169] Les Caméléons, ou soixante ans en soixante minutes, a vaudeville in seven
scenes by Clairville, Bourdois, and Dumanoir.
[170] Edouard Roger de Bully (1809–1866), called Roger de Beauvoir, the
author of many romantic plays, novels, and poems. He and Thackeray were
old friends, according to the Comtesse Dash [Gabrielle Anne Cisterne de
Courtiras, Vicomtesse de Saint-Mars] (Mémoires des autres, 6 vols., Paris,
n. d., V, 87–88), who often saw them together in the middle eighteen-thirties.
She writes of the Thackeray of that time: "Il faisait des aquarelles, des marines,
et il avait beaucoup de peine à gagner sa vie avec son pinceau, lui qui sa plume
a rendu depuis si riche.

"C'était alors un jeune homme assez fantasque, rempli d'esprit et d'humour;
il avait un vrai talent pour la caricature et la saisissait en perfection. Il causait
par boutade, mais quand il était en verve, il avait des drôleries tout à fait
françaises qu'il débitait avec le flegme de sa nature."

remember, though I cant for the life of me recal what he said —
Well we went together to the play, and he took me where W$^m$
would long to go to the Greenroom I have never been in a French
Greenroom before & was not much excited: but when he proposed
to take me up to the loge of a beautiful actress with sparkling eyes
and the prettiest little retroussé nosy posy in the world, I said to
the regisseur of the theatre Lead on, and we went through passages & up stairs to the loge w$^h$ is not a box but O gracious goodness
a dressing room!

She had just taken off her rouge her complexion was only a
thousand times more brilliant — perhaps a peignoir of black satin
w$^h$ partially enveloped her perfect form only served to heighten
&cs w$^h$ could but partially &c. Her lips are really as red as &c, &
not covered with paint at all. Her voice is delicious — her eyes
O they flashed &c, upon me, & I felt my &c beat so that I could
hardly speak — I pitched in (if you will permit me the phrase) 2
or 3 compliments however, very large & heavy of the good old
English sort, — and Oh Mon Dieu! She has asked me to go and
see her! Shall I go or shan't I? Shall I go this very day at 4
o'clock or shall I not? Well I won't tell you. I'll put up my letter
before 4: and keep this piece of intelligence for the next packet.

The funeral takes place tomorrow, and as I dont seem to do
much work here, I shall be soon probably on the wing: but perhaps
I will take a week's touring somewhere — about France to Tours
& Nantes perhaps or elsewhere, or anywhere I don't know, but I
hope before I go to hear once more from you. Im happy indeed
to hear how well you are. What a shame it was to assault my dear
lady with my blue devils — The worst of it is its all perfectly
true and reasonable what I wrote — Who can help looking to the
day of failing powers? But if I last a few years no doubt I can
get a shelter somewhere against that certain adversity — And so
I oughtn't to show you my glum face or my dismal feelings —
That's the worst of habit and confidence, you are so kind to me
that I like to tell you all; and to think that in good or ill fortune,
I have your sympathy. Here's an opportunity for sentiment —
Heres just a little bit of the page left to say something neat and

pretty — Madame Je les méprise les jolis mots vous en ai-je jamais fait de ma vie? — Je les laisse à M. Bullar et ses pareils — J'en ferai pour Mademoiselle Page, pour la ravissante la sémillante la frétillante Adèle (c'est ainsi qu'elle se nomme) mais pour vous? — Allons — partons — il est quatre heures — fermons la lettre — disons adieu à l'ami et à Madame — Vous m'écrirez avant mon départ n'est-ce pas? Allez bien, dormez bien, marchez bien s'il vous plait — et gardy mwaw ung petty moreso de voter cure.

W M T.

626.                TO MRS. BROOKFIELD
                   9 SEPTEMBER 1849

*Address:* M<sup>rs</sup> Brookfield | 15 Portman S<sup>t</sup> | Portman Square. London. *Postmarks:* LIGNE-DE-CALAIS 9 SEPT. 49, 10 SP 1849. Hitherto unpublished.

My dear lady — As my mother wants a line from me, and it will cost me no more to write on 2 1/2 sheets than one whole one, common economy suggests that I should write you a line to say that I am pretty well and leading on before a dismal but dutiful life — I go & sit with the deaf old Scotch widower every night, & with my aunt afterwards. This is not very amusing, but the sense of virtue and self denial tickles one as it were, and I come home rather pleased to my bed of a night. I shall stay here for a few days more; — my tour will be to Boulogne probably where I shan't find the Crowes who are going away, but shall have M<sup>rs</sup> Procter; and next week will see me back in London probably working away in the old way. Yesterday I went a little way into the country to see Miss Ricketts's husband my old friend Stevens — They have just got a little son a beautiful child, and the happiness of this couple was pleasant albeit somewhat painful to witness. She is a very nice elegant accomplished young lady adoring her Augustus who is one of the best & kindest of old snobs. We walked across vines to the coach at 7 1/2 o'clock, after an evening of 2 1/2 hours w<sup>h</sup> was quite enough for me — She is a little thing & put me in mind of my own wife somehow. Give M<sup>rs</sup> F. with my respectful love a good account of her cousin. I am bound to day to another country place, but don't like the idea of it — tomorrow I dine with M<sup>r</sup> T. B. Macaulay[171] who is stopping in this hotel — And what else has happened? I have been to see the actress — who received us in a yellow satin drawing room, and who told me she had but one fault in the world that she had *trop bon coeur* — and I am ashamed to say that I pitched still stronger compliments than before, and I daresay she thinks the enormous old Englishman is rapturously in love with her — But she will never see him again that faithless giant — I am past the age when Fotheringays inflame: but I shall pop her & her boudoir into a book someday and that will be the end of our transactions. A good character for a book, accompanied us to the funeral — an expatriated parson, very pompous & feeble-minded, who gets his living by black jobs entirely & attends all the funerals of our countrymen. He has had a pretty good season, & is tolerably cheerful. I was struck by 'Behold I show you a mystery' & the noble words subsequent.[172] but my impression is that S<sup>t</sup> Paul fully believed that the end of things and the triumph of his adored Master, was to take place in his own time, or the time of those round about him — surely S<sup>t</sup> John had the same feeling, and I suppose that this secret passed fondly among the initiated, and that they died hoping for its fulfilment. Is this heresy? let his Reverence tell me. Madame, if you will be so diffident about your compositions, there is no help for it. Your

---

[171] Thackeray, who set a high value on Macaulay's writings, was on excellent terms with the historian from this time forth. His "Nil Nisi Bonum" (*Works*, XII, 173–179) was perhaps the most notable of the memorial tributes called forth by Macaulay's death in the last days of 1859, and but for his own death four years later he would no doubt have executed his plan of carrying Macaulay's history through Queen Anne's reign. Francis St. John Thackeray (*Temple Bar*, 1893, p. 377) relates that at a dinner given by Thackeray in the early days of 1860, "the conversation turning upon the historian, someone began to speak of him in depreciating language, when the host interposed and would not allow it to go on. 'He was a giant,' I recollect his crying out."

[172] The Episcopal Order for the Burial of the Dead includes the lesson: "Behold, I shew you a mystery; We shall not all sleep, but we shall all be changed, in a moment, in the twinkling of an eye, at the last trump: for the trumpet shall sound, and the dead shall be raised incorruptible, and we shall be changed" (*I Corinthians*, 15, 51–52).

letter made me laugh very much and therefore made me happy. Pray God you may be so dear lady, & happier still ere long. When I saw that nice little M^rs Stevens with her child yesterday, of course I thought about somebody else — the tones of a mother's voice speaking to an infant play the deuce with me somehow — that charming nonsense and tenderness work upon me, until I feel like a woman or a great big baby myself fiddledydee — So M^rs Fanshawe scolds you does she? this is by way of transition from the sentiment — What do you think her abominable old father has done? He has consoled himself for the loss of his late lady already, & with a young creature of 15 — I'm sorry I have written this, now it is on the paper — It looks wrong & oughtnt to be said: if you please erase it: and consider it unsaid — Madame Marvy is coming to me tomorrow morning with some pocket handkerchiefs the pick of all Paris for cheapness: but I think I shall choose white ones and not those with coloured borders in spite of your orders. And here the paper is full and we come to the final G B Y. G B Y 3, G B M 2. I am always my dear W J B's S F & A B.

W M T.

If you dare to peep into the enclosed you'll see a letter to Miss Minny.[173] please to let me O you for a stamp once more.

[For fragments of a letter to Mrs. Brookfield, 11 September, 1849, see letter 7, Appendix XXVI.]

627.          TO MRS. BROOKFIELD
                    13 SEPTEMBER 1849

Published in part, *Collection of Letters*, pp. 92–93.

Thursday Ev^g

My dear lady. This letter does not count though it is most probbly the last of the series — yesterday I couldn't write for I went to Chambourcy in the morning to see those 2 poor Miss

---

[173] This letter has not been preserved.

Powers, and the poor old faded and unhappy Dorsay:[174] & I did not return home till exactly 1 minute before post time, perhaps 2 late for the letter w^h I flung into the post last night. And so this is the last of the letters and I am coming back immediately — the last anything is unpleasant I had almost hoped to have heard from you though once more. I was to have gone tomorrow for certain to Boulogne at least: but a party to Fontainebleau was proposed by whom do you think? by the President[175] himself. I'm going to dine with him to day, think of that. I believe I write this for the purpose solely of telling you this — The truth is I have made acquaintance here with Lord Douglas,[176] who is very good natured, and I suppose has been instigating the President to these hospitalities — I am afraid I disgusted Macaulay yesterday at dinner at Sir George Napiers:[177] we were told that an American lady was coming in the evening, whose great desire in life was to meet the Author of Wanaty Fair and Author of the Lays of A. Rome, so I proposed to Macaulay to enact me, and let me take his character — but he said solemnly that he did not approve of practical jokes, & so this sport did not come to pass. Well, I shall see you at any rate for some days before the 23^d: and I hope you will be happy

---

[174] After the death of Lady Blessington on June 4, 1849, the Miss Powers and Count D'Orsay went to live in the country house of his sister and her husband, the Duc and Duchesse de Grammont (Sadleir, *Blessington-D'Orsay*, pp. 352–354).

[175] Louis Napoléon, who had been elected President of the French Republic on December 10, 1848.

[176] William Alexander Hamilton (1811–1863), styled Marquess of Douglas, later (1852) eleventh Duke of Hamilton and eighth Duke of Brandon. Lord Douglas, who had married Princess Marie of Baden in 1843, lived chiefly in Paris and Baden even after his father's death put him in possession of the magnificent establishment of Hamilton Palace. His attempt in an uncongenial age to lead the life traditional to a *grand seigneur* caused Lord Brougham to call him "Very Duke of Very Duke," for he seemed to his contemporaries inordinately proud of his distinguished lineage and of the immense Hamilton properties, which, despite the sale of his Lancashire estates in 1853 for £329,800, were worth £140,642 annually three decades later. The part played in *Esmond* by his ancestor, the fourth Duke of Hamilton, will be recalled. See Lord Lamington, *In the Days of the Dandies*, pp. 108–139; and G. E. C., *Complete Peerage*, ed. Gibbs and others, VI, 274–275.

[177] Lt. General Sir George Thomas Napier (1784–1855).

at Southampton enjoying the end of the autumn: and I shall be glad to smoke a pipe with old M^r Williams too, for I don't care for new acquaintances, whatever some people say, and have only your house now where I am completely at home — I've been idle here but I've done plenty of dutifulness, haven't I? I must go dress myself and tell old D^r Halliday that I am going to dine with the President, that will please him more than even my conversation this evening, and the event will be written over to all the family before long be sure of that. Dont you think M^r Parr will like to know it, and that it will put me well with him? perhaps I shall find the grand cross of the Legion of Honour under my plate. I will put it on and come to you in it in that case. I was going to have the impudence to give you a daguerreotype of myself w^h has been done here — very like & droll it looks — but it seemed to me too impertinent and I gave it to somebody else. I've bought W^m 4 glasses to drink beer out of; since I never can get one of the silver ones when I come — dont let him be alarmed these only cost a shilling apiece, and 2 such loves of EaudeCologne bottles for M^rs Procter, and for my dear M^rs Brookfield I've bought a diamond necklace & earrings, — no Ive bought you nothing but the hand-kerchiefs but I hope you will let me give you those — wont you?

I *am* very sorry for Turpin. I *do* feel an interest in her and I think she is very pretty — all this I solemnly vow & purtest. My paper is out — theres the last corner of the last letter — and the burthen of all is G B Y. God keep my dear lady happy and well. Ah I wonder who will ask me to dine on Monday next.

W M T.

628.　　　　　　　　TO MRS. PROCTER
　　　　　　　　18 SEPTEMBER 1849

Hitherto unpublished. My text is taken from a transcript given Lady Ritchie
by George Murray Smith.

　　　　　　　　　　　　　13, Upper Harley Street,
　　　　　　　　　　　　　Tuesday evening.

My dear Mrs Procter,

　I can't come to see you because I am so cruelly hurt, not in my
feelings but in my ancle which is strained and on a cushion.[178]　I
hope not for long though. Bad yesterday. Bed today. Better tomorrow. Well on Thursday when I will pay off a young woman
whom I am asked to meet at dinner. Now don't let her cry off on
purpose to give me the advantage of a — fiddlededee never mind.
Another gentleman is to be there — young, single, of a good family
and fortune. I think I need say no more. Well, you really are not
angry that I called you &c? I am though. I didn't mean the words
a bit and was scared directly I had dropped them out of my mouth.

　I fell asleep writing Pendennis to-day having ceaseless visitors
upstairs in bed until near three o'clock — the last (at last) L. Hunt's
son[179] with a piteous tale about his father's mishap — a crash is
coming but he only owes £220 — however I have no money and
recommended the Law as a protection.

　I dined with Lady Rodd yesterday who asked the elder folks

　　[178] Thackeray's ankle had given way beneath him while he was at a dinner
party at Lady Rodd's on Monday, September 17, and he was forced to go
home and send for Dr. Elliotson, who at once put him to bed (see Appendix
XXVI, letter 8). The progress of his illness — diagnosed as cholera —
from which his recovery was for a time in doubt, may be traced in the letters
of the Brookfields, who helped to take care of him until his mother returned
from Wales. On September 24 he appeared to have turned the corner; three
days later he was no worse; but on October 1 it was felt that he was not
recovering as rapidly as he should. On October 3 he had a very bad night,
and the doctors worried about "some former complaint." He thought himself
that the end was "possibly near at hand." (*Mrs. Brookfield*, II, 298–303)
By October 15, however, he was out of danger.
　　[179] Thornton Leigh Hunt (1810–1873), a London journalist who had been
Thackeray's colleague on *The Constitutional*.

but I was obliged to come away with my foot in one of the Admiral's slippers. Fancy having both there!

I wish you are well, and am yours ever,

W. M. Thackeray.

[For fragments of a letter to Mrs. Brookfield, 18 September, 1849, see letter 8, Appendix XXVI.]

629.          TO SIR FREDERICK POLLOCK
SEPTEMBER 1849 [180]

Hitherto unpublished.

My dear Lord Chief,

Im too ill for dinner next Sunday have had severe bilious fever & a hard time of it — So I write to say how you must dine without me & that it is most probable I shant dine at all. I salute you & all your home.

W M Thackeray

630.          TO SIR FREDERICK POLLOCK
29 SEPTEMBER 1849 [181]

Hitherto unpublished.

Saturday

Private & Confidential.

My dear Lord Chief  I have had 10 dreary days and I think about that Haunch of Venison tomorrow with feelings w$^h$ may be more readily &c than &c. — No — it is not about the Haunch its about some venison broth of old old times w$^h$ was so good that I think if I could get any I should be well with a skip hop & jump. It w$^d$ n't be good for me for 2 or 3 days — but then! — O!

[180] This note was written a day or two before Thackeray's note to Pollock of September 29.
[181] The second Saturday after Thackeray became ill was September 29.

631.                    TO MRS. BROOKFIELD
                        OCTOBER 1849 [182]

Hitherto unpublished.

Ma chere Dame  Le monstre de Docteur m'afflige horriblement
Comme à Sancho,[183] il m'enlève mon potage.  Mais au reste tout va
tres bien

                              Adieu bonne nuit [?]
                              A moy aussy


632.                    TO MRS. CARLYLE
                        OCTOBER 1849

Hitherto unpublished.

Dear Mrs Carlyle
    I am getting better & am susceptible of seeing ladies, but I cant
write as yet
              Yours ever
              W M T.


633.              TO THE REV. WILLIAM AND
                  MRS. BROOKFIELD
                  OCTOBER 1849

*Address:* Mr & Mrs Brookfield.  Hitherto unpublished.

    My dear Vieux.  You & Madam will rejoice to hear that I slept
very well, & am though not near well a great deal better
                        Always your affte.  W M T.

    [182] This and the next four letters were written between September 30,
when Thackeray presumably received the venison soup that he had asked
Pollock to send, and October 15, when he was well on his way to recovery.
    [183] See *Don Quixote*, Part IV, chapter 47.

634.                  TO MRS. PROCTER
                      OCTOBER 1849

Hitherto unpublished. My text is taken from a transcript given Lady Ritchie
by George Murray Smith.

Dear Mrs Procter,

I am still in bed mending but very slowly and hardly able to
hold a pen.

                      From,
                W. M. T.


635.                  TO MRS. PROCTER
                      OCTOBER 1849

Hitherto unpublished. My text is taken from a transcript given Lady Ritchie
by George Murray Smith.

Please I should like some jelly, not rich but good nourishing
cowsfoot jelly with Madeira. Law, here's your servant just been
and gone. Thanks for grapes and flowers.


636.         TO MRS. CARMICHAEL-SMYTH
             15 OCTOBER 1849 [184]

Hitherto unpublished.

Monday.

My dearest Mammy  Yesterday we had tripe & onions to day
broth. We get on famously but slowly & though Im quite comfortable Im very weak  G. b. all.

                      W M T

[184] It appears from the next letter that Thackeray's mother arrived in London shortly before Wednesday, October 17. The uncertain development of
his illness had prevented his friends from informing Mrs. Carmichael-Smyth
of the seriousness of her son's condition until he was out of danger. When

637.                  TO MRS. GIBSON
                   17 OCTOBER 1849

Hitherto unpublished.

                                    Kensington Wednesday
    Thank you very much for your kindness dear M^{rs} Gibson, I am
beginning to rally, but the strength is slow to return after near 4
weeks of bed & fever.  My mother is with me & children and I am
in very good charge, but I shall be very glad that you should come
to Kensington because then I shall be assured that you are well
                        Yours always sincerely
                           W M Thackeray


638.                  TO MRS. PROCTER
                   17 OCTOBER 1849


Hitherto unpublished.  My text is taken from a transcript given Lady Ritchie
by George Murray Smith.

                                      Wednesday.
                                    October 17.
My dear Mrs. Procter,
    I hope you are very well.  I am pretty well.  I have been ill in bed
for four weeks, and had to take a great deal of medicine, but as

---

news of his ordeal at last reached Major and Mrs. Carmichael-Smyth in Wales,
they "set off in a carriage," writes Lady Ritchie, "driving across country, and
taking us with them.  At Monmouth, I remember, when we were driving
through the town, the bells were tolling, and the people, dressed in black,
were streaming into the churches.  It was a day of prayer and solemn humiliation, which had been appointed for the cholera.  At Gloucester that night
my grandmother left us and started off ahead: I think just after she left us
better accounts came in.
    "We travelled to Kensington with our grandfather next day.
    "How thin and changed, with what great wan eyes my father looked at us
when we reached home and were allowed to go up to his room to see him
in his bed." (*Biographical Introductions*, II, xxxvii) The "better accounts" of
which Lady Ritchie writes may well be this note.

the Doctor said it was good for me, I took it like a good boy and am now better.

When I was ill a kind lady came and brought me some nice grapes, I ate and liked them very much. Then she went to her cook and said: Cook, make some jelly for a little boy who is ill." I ate all the jelly, and O, it was very good. Then she sent me some turtle soup which I would like to eat too, but the Doctor will not let me, and though I am very sorry I do not cry. Is not this being good? Well, you see though I am not well enough to sit up much yet, I am well enough to begin to be a tom-fool, and that is a great point gained. All the rest will follow in due season, and I hope to be quite strong and frisky before long. What a kind world it is, what kind folks in it, what a number of kind friends some people have. I like to write a line to one of the kindest of all and to say, dear Mrs Procter, how sincerely and affectionately I am yours,

W. M. T.

639.            TO MRS. BROOKFIELD<br>23 OCTOBER 1849 [185]

Published in *Collection of Letters*, p. 72.

63 East S<sup>t</sup> Brighton.

My dear lady Yestirrdy I had the courage to fly to Brighton, I've got a most byootiful lodging and had a delightful sleep. I write a line at 7 o'clock of the morning to tell you these good news.

Gby.

[185] Mrs. Brookfield received this letter on October 23. Thackeray was accompanied to Brighton by his servant John. (*Mrs. Brookfield*, II, 303)

640.  **TO ANNE AND HARRIET THACKERAY**
23 OCTOBER 1849

Hitherto unpublished.

My dearest Shildren

You'll be glad to hear so far that I made a good journey — and am extremely well this morning and

Your affectionate Papa always

641.  **TO MRS. BROOKFIELD**
23 OCTOBER 1849

*Postmarks:* BRIGHTON OC 23 1849, 24 OC 1849. Published in *Collection of Letters*, pp. 72–73.

63 East Street, Tuesday.

This mornings you know was not a letter, only to tell you that I was pretty well after my travels, and after the letter was gone thinks I the hand-writing is so bad & shaky she will think I am worse and only write fibs to try & soothe her — but the cause of the bad writing was a bad pen and impossible ink — See how different this is — though Ive not much to say now, only that I have been sitting on the Chain-pier in a Bath Chair for 2 hours, and feel greatly invigorated and pleasantly tired by the wholesome sea breeze. Shall I be asleep in 2 minutes I wonder? I think I'll try, I think snoring is better than writing. Come let us try a little doze.

A comfortable little doze of a quarter of an hour, since then a somewhat fatiguing visit from the Miss Smiths, who are all kindness and look very pretty in their mourning. I found acquaintances on the pier too and my chair anchored alongside of that of a very interesting nice little woman M^rs Whetmore so that there was more talkee talkee — Well, I wont go on writing any more about my ailments & dozes and fatigues, but sick folks are abominably selfish. Sick men that is. And so God bless my dear lady.[186]

W M T.

642.                    TO MRS. BROOKFIELD
                       25 OCTOBER 1849

Published in part, *Collection of Letters*, p. 73.

Thursday.

I cant write you long dear lady I have 2 notes to my mother daily and a long one to Elliotson &c — but I am getting on doucement; like the change of air exceedingly, the salt water baths, & the Bath Chair Journies to the Pier, where its almost as fresh as being at Sea. But do you go on writing, please, and as often as you can for it does me good to get kind letters. God bless you and good night is all I can say now, with my love to his Reverence from

Love to Arry.                              W M T.

[186] Mrs. Brookfield's reply to this note has been printed in part: "I must write so as to keep you in mind of telling me how you go on. I wish you would make John tell people not to talk while you are *airing yourself* as it will do away with the good of the sea-breezes if you are tired with talking, even to the fascinating Mrs. W[hetmore]. You will see Mrs. Elliot, I suppose, to-morrow, as she set off for Brighton to-day, and by her your Mother has sent a pamphlet on Mesmerism, Dr. Elliotson wished you to read, showing you the cloven hoof of his besetting sin, now that you are recovering tho' he kept it so well under control before, and a small wedge of soup which she said had been forgotten when you went down. I called in Young St. to-day and brought Anny and Minny back with me, packed three in a Hansom. They are sitting here buried each in a book while I write, and they send their love to you. I am going to make them chaperon me to Russell Square to call on Virginia Garden who is ordered to Malaga for the winter, being threatened with consumption. If you make your expedition to Cadiz with Mr. Baring you may fall in love with her; they have had Alfred Tennyson staying with them in Edinburgh, and are highly pleased by his writing to the lady by her Christian name. Your Faithful Admirer, Miss Dobson, has written to beg to know if you are really ill, and to make great outcry at their desolation for want of Pendennis, 'tell me of *Thackeray*; it is too horrible to put "*Mr.*" before his name,' and she wishes very kindly to come and stay with me. I daresay she would gladly come to *you* as Cook or shoeblack or Coachman all in one, she

643.                     TO MRS. PROCTER
                         26 OCTOBER 1849

Hitherto unpublished.

Friday Morning. 63 East St. Brighton.

My dear Mʳˢ Procter  I must write you ever so little a letter if
but to say my illness hasn't driven my friends out of my mind
entirely — I have often wanted to write, but of nights I'm often
in a blank doze, often with three or four letters wʰ I must write —
in fact the pen don't flow so freely now as it used: and Im easily
jaded and weary. You see this is a very glum way to begin — but
the truth is I am getting monstrous tired of my solitude: though
I have the most beautiful view out of window, and find the evenings
dismal, though I commonly fall asleep directly after dinner. But I
am grown very much stronger can walk a good bit, and advance
though slowly no doubt towards recovery. It will be a long time
before I am my own man again to use the phrase of the poet,[187]
and I look forward to a pretty long career of diet and sofa & so
forth.

There are plenty of acquaintances here who are kind to me, there
is the Miss Smiths & Mʳˢ Smith; there is Mʳˢ Cunningham who
sends me good jelly & soup. But que voulez-vous? Jelly & soup
are not all. I wish there were some Xtians here of my persuasion
— to make the days pass by rational conversation. I have Mʳˢ F.
Elliot, one of the kindest of creatures and when we are together we
talk & are merry — but its only for a short time, when I relapse
into my usual sombre state of mind.

Luckily, somebody, is it you?, has this day sent an immense jar
of turtle from Bond Street. This will render existence tolerable — fiddlesticks and what nonsense am I writing? thats why I
dont like to write to people in my present condition, I don't appear

really is very warm in her feelings. Pray be very martyrising upon yourself
about your health." (*Mrs. Brookfield*, II, 304–305)
    [187] Perhaps Thackeray has in mind *Macbeth*, III, iv, 107–108.

to advantage, but am conscious of being horridly unamiable & selfish.

There's a glorious sun blazing outside in a sky of cloudless hazure — Would you recommend me to go out & face it or is it a rascally East Wind? — the Pier is as good as being on board ship, with the blessing of no calling for the steward, & if its decently warm I go & sit there and fancy I inhale health every hour. But for all that, a little bird tells me that I shant be away from home very long, for I myself am a very erratic little bird and anxious to be on the wing.

My love to Procter and Adelaide and the young folks and mind and remember me most kindly to dear kind old Adelaide Sartoris. Tom Taylor never once came near me; & told Lady Duff in the midst of a talk By the bye Thackeray has been dangerously ill — I have often said that I myself had no heart, w^h is a lie, but T T beats me altogether. God bless you my dear friend, always gratefully yours

W M Thackeray

644.            TO ANNE THACKERAY
                  OCTOBER 1849

Hitherto unpublished.

My dearest Fat.

The sea air does me all the good in the world and I know that you & Minny will be glad to have so much news of your loving
Father.

Any letters may be sent to me tomorrow but not after — Im very busy & have been writing[188] the whole day.

[188] Not *Pendennis*, but *Rebecca and Rowena*. See below, No. 661.

645.    TO ANNE AND HARRIET THACKERAY
OCTOBER 1849

Hitherto unpublished.

My dearest little Misses

I send you many kisses. I've scarce done more than look at the sea out of window but I've done a good days work yesterday and after that I'm always better, and I hope to do another today: and I write to say that I dont know exactly when I shall be at home but that I'm your affte Papa.

What a delight on opening Miss Annys enclosure! — It contained 2 very good letters though. And the other letter is very interesting I'll keep it and show it [to] Miss Anny & Miss Minny praps some day. I've had a famous days work again to day: and been to church too.

If you write to Granny tell her Im tremendously busy   I can hardly hold my pen now tant j'ai écrit.


646.      TO MARY AGNES ELTON
OCTOBER 1849

Hitherto unpublished.

Brighton. 63 East Street.

My dear Missy

I began to write you a letter weeks ago, as M^{rs} Brookfield can tell you for I wrote it at her house, but I stopped, for I thought I had put too much fun and nonsense into the letter,.and that I had no right to write to a young lady nothing but nonsense & stuff. Since then I have been so ill that there was a very great chance that I never should write sense or nonsense any more; but I am now much better, and getting stronger I think in the sea air. I go and sit on the pier in a Bath Chair (think of that! you may make a picture of me if you like) and enjoy the fresh breeze immensely, and I must tell you that I am not such a load to pull as I was, for

indeed my legs are no thicker than this

Yesterday I had a Clevedon pheasant for dinner Captain Robbins shot it on purpose for me; and it was so good that I am happy
to say he shot two. Everybody has been so kind to me whilst I was
ill, that I declare I am quite surprized there are so many good
people — every body except 2 wicked servants, who were cheating
and robbing me, and whom I have whisked out of the house with
a tremendous scolding. I think this is all my news, you see it is
but a scanty budget, but we must pay our debts in such coin as
we have.

I have often and often thought about you & the children, and
it would do me good to see you again, kiss any body for me who
will let you; & give my best love to your Mamma & Mʳ Elton from

Your very sincere friend<br>W M Thackeray

647.        TO THE REV. WILLIAM AND
              MRS. BROOKFIELD
              31 OCTOBER 1849

Published in *Collection of Letters*, pp. 93–94.

October 31.

My dear Monsieur & Madam Harry[189] says you will not eat your
dinner well if I don't write and tell you that I am thriving: and
though I don't consider this a letter at all but simply a message, I
have to state that I am doing exceedingly well, that I ate a mutton
chop just now in Harrys presence with great gusto, that I slept 12
hours last night, and in fact advance by steps, wʰ grow every day
more firm, towards convalescence     If you will both come down
here I will give you beautiful rooms and the best of mutton — I

[189] For Harry Hallam's visit to Thackeray in Brighton, see below, No. 725.

shall stop till Monday settingly, after w^h I may probbly go to the Club.

Gby both on you.

W M T.

[For fragments of a letter to Mrs. Brookfield, 3 November, 1849, see letter 9, Appendix XXVI.]

648. TO MARIA HAMERTON
5 NOVEMBER 1849

Published in *Unpublished Letters by W. M. Thackeray*, ed. Shorter, pp. 10–11.

Kensington Nov^r 5/.

My dear Maria

When I was recovering from my illness the other day, I think a dozen of my friends who know that I spend all the money I make, made me offers of service w^h I accepted very gratefully. My mother has been just reading to me your letter speaking of poor Bess's weakness and illness, and that she requires dainties to coax her appetite — She ought to have a carriage to drive in if she has a mind — and I think I would be ungrateful to my friends and to God Almighty who has sent me so many kind ones, if I didn't beseech you to let me help a little towards your sister's comfort — I remember always what a kind friend she was to me and my children, and pray her to let me bring her a little ease — You'll fancy that I am going to offer you something magnificent after this — but it is only a 10£ note w^h I shan't miss in the least and w^h if it can help to make the little quatrième more comfortable will make me very happy indeed    With my best regards to Bess believe me always my dear Maria

Your most sincere old friend
W M Thackeray

Delisle lives Rue de la Chaussée d'Antin 24 or 26 I think.

649.                TO EYRE CROWE
                    7 NOVEMBER 1849

My text is taken from a facsimile in Eyre Crowe's *Thackeray's Haunts and Homes* (London, 1897), p. 59, where the date is also recorded.

                                        Kensington. Wednesday.
My dear Eyre

Come to me as soon as pawsable, and let us work off that set of texts for Bogue.[190] I think I could dictate some and you could supply more and we could be soon done with the dem bugbear.

                        Ever yours
                        W M T.

Come in the earliest morning you can to breakfast; bring the plates with you & let us go to work.


650.                TO MRS. RITCHIE
                    19 NOVEMBER 1849

*Address:* M^rs Ritchie | Rue Montagne. Fbg S^t Honoré | Paris. *Postmarks:* 19 NO 1849, 20 NOV. 49 CALAIS. Published in part by Mrs. Cornish, *Family Letters,* pp. 14–15.

My dear Aunt  Of course I cede my picture[191] to you with a very great deal of pleasure. I recollect it quite well as a child in India, and admiring above all how the stick was painted, w^h was made to look as if it was polished & shone — what strange things the memory chooses to keep hold of!  Your reminiscences are of a very different sort about the picture: it brings back spring and youth to you and all the affectionate histories connected with them; it can only

[190] David Bogue (1812?–1856) assumed the management of the book and print shop of Charles Tilt on the latter's retirement. The "texts" of which Thackeray writes were to accompany Marvy's engravings.

[191] A portrait of William Makepeace Thackeray, Mrs. Ritchie's father and Thackeray's grandfather, which is reproduced in *The Ritchies in India,* opposite p. 6.

be an ancestor to me. I have not liked to hang up my father here at Kensington: his successor being in the house or visiting it constantly: and though the good old Major would not mind, I think my mother would not be over well pleased to see the picture hanging up. The poor soul is in bed very ill indeed a cripple with the severest attack of rheumatism, and without rest night or day: the way in w.<sup>h</sup> her husband attends her is something admirable and affecting to witness, I dont know how he sleeps for a week past, but he lies on the edge of her bed on w.<sup>h</sup> she is restless and moaning, and wont go to another room. Thank God however my mother is better, and this dismal attack I hope is drawing to an end. The children are very well meanwhile: they & I breakfast every morning together (I in my bed it must be confessed) and I see more of them than I have almost ever done. Anny is grown to be almost a young woman, & will soon be a capital companion for me — We went yesterday & atchieved the ascent of Highgate Hill, with a broken-winded horse I have got who suffered wofully in the journey, and lighted upon all the little Irvines at their dinner of w.<sup>h</sup> we ate ravenously (I am eating all day now): but the ladies were away on a shopping excursion into London, and we lost them. Charlotte Low[192] showed us the new baby with great pride: a sweet little thing it was too, placid & waxen-faced; & there is one of the other children, Augusta,[193] the very image of what her mother was when we were all young folks in Southampton Row[194] — I think that Southampton Row was the only part of my youth w.<sup>h</sup> was decently cheerful, all the rest strikes me to have been as glum as an English Sunday.

Thank D.<sup>r</sup> Halliday very much for his offer of the rooms, I should like exceedingly to come to Paris, were I a little bit stronger, & could I get over those 12 hours of railroad: but 2 from Brighton shook me the other day a good deal: to be sure that is a fortnight

---

[192] Oldest daughter (d. 1853), *Genealogy* (95), of John and Augusta Low. She married Sir John Theophilus Metcalfe (1828–1883), fifth Baronet, *Genealogy* (96), in 1851. The new baby was the last child of Colonel and Mrs. Irvine.

[193] Augusta Georgiana Low, *Genealogy* (97), Charlotte's younger sister.

[194] See *Memoranda*, The Ritchies.

ago, since when I am quite a changed man, thrice as strong, &
mending as fast as may be since I have thrown the physic-bottles
out of [the] window. D^r Elliotson said I had intermittent fever
& gave me quantities of quinine: but it was the quinine that gave
me the fever for the day after I rebelled, and substituted pale ale
for it, all the feverish symptoms took their leave, and I have been
mending ever since under the latter regimen. As I lie here and
think about going to Paris I long to be off at once, and to call John
to pack my portmanteau: — but I must wait until I can enjoy
myself a little, for after this dismal season of illness I want to make
merry — Goodbye dear Aunt I am always affectionately yours and
my cousins  W M T.

651.                TO DAVID BOGUE
                  21 NOVEMBER 1849

Hitherto unpublished.

                               13 Young S^t Kensington
                                  21 November.
Sir

    The story of Stubb's Calendar[195] has been already reprinted by
me, in the 'Comic Tales & Sketches' published by Cunningham in
1840 — It is my copyright, as all my works have been by verbal
agreements with the publishers for whom I wrote, with the exception of certain contributions to the 'Heads of the People' about
w^h I forgot to make a stipulation: though I am advised that I can
with perfect safety republish these latter in case I sh^d think fit so
to do.

    I regret that I cannot consent to the republication of the Stubbs
story, under the present circumstances.

    I am working at the text for M. Marvy's engravings, & hope

    [195] Which Bogue's predecessor, Tilt, had first published in *The Comic
Almanack for 1839*.

very shortly to deliver it to you.  Nothing but illness w<sup>d</sup> have
prevented me from executing this task before now.

Your obdt Serv<sup>t</sup><br>W M Thackeray

<br>

652.                    TO ?
29 NOVEMBER 1849

Hitherto unpublished. My text is taken from a transcript supplied by Mr.
Beyer, who owns the original.

13 Young S<sup>t</sup> Kensington Sq<sup>re</sup> 29 Nov.

My dear Madam      Your very kind invitation can't I am sorry
to say be accepted just now, for I have a sick house w<sup>h</sup> I do not like
to leave, and as soon as I am free I am engaged to more than one
friend to whom I am under the strongest promises.[196]  But I hope
you will let me keep your hospitable offer in mind, as I do the

---

[196] Among Thackeray's engagements was a dinner with George Smith on
December 3 (Wise and Symington, *The Brontës*, III, 55–56).  Charlotte
Brontë was passing three weeks with Smith and his mother at 4 Westbourne
Place.  At her request the publisher called on Thackeray, whom he had not
previously met, and invited him to make her acquaintance.  "I told Thackeray
there would be no one with us excepting Sir John Forbes," Smith relates,
"and explained that Miss Brontë was incognita in London, and begged him
not to say a word to indicate his knowledge of her identity as the authoress of
'Jane Eyre.'  He replied in his large way: 'I see!  It will be all right: you are
speaking to a man of the world.'

"But unhappily it was not all right.  When the ladies had left the dining-
room I offered Thackeray a cigar.  The custom of smoking after dinner was
not common then, but I had been told he liked a cigar, and so provided for
his tastes.  To my dismay, when we rejoined the ladies in the drawing-room,
he approached Miss Brontë and quoted a familiar and much-criticised passage
from 'Jane Eyre.'  It was that in which she described 'the warning fragrance'
which told of the approach of Mr. Rochester:

> " 'Sweetbriar and southern wood, jasmine, pink and rose, had
> long been yielding their evening sacrifice of incense.  This new scent
> was neither of shrub nor flower.  It was — I knew it well — it was
> Mr. Rochester's cigar!'

"The quotation, in one sense, was happy enough, and it did credit to Thackeray's memory of 'Jane Eyre'; but not to his memory of his agreement with

many kind and friendly things you are pleased to say of me, and on some future day pay a visit to you in Lincolnshire

Always most faithfully yours

W M Thackeray.

653.      TO JOSEPH CUNDALL
DECEMBER 1849

Hitherto unpublished.

## Dear Mʳ Cundall

The gentleman[197] whom I had engaged to get some biographical notices for Mʳ Marvy's sketches is gone to France, hence my delay

---

me. Miss Brontë's face showed her discomposure, and in a chilly fashion she turned off the allusion. But I was almost as much discomposed as Miss Brontë by this sudden assault on what she was so anxious to guard — her identity as the authoress of 'Jane Eyre.' She cast an accusing look at me.

"Thackeray, however, had no sense of either awkwardness or guilt. From my house he went to the smoking-room of the Garrick Club and said: 'Boys! I have been dining with "Jane Eyre"!' To have her identity expounded in the smoking-room of the Garrick Club was the last experience which the morbidly shy and sensitive little lady would have chosen." ([Leonard Huxley], *House of Smith, Elder*, pp. 67–68)

Thackeray has left his own account of this meeting with Miss Brontë. "I saw her first," he writes in *The Roundabout Papers* (*Works*, XII, 188), "just as I rose out of an illness from which I had never thought to recover. I remember the trembling little frame, the little hand, the great honest eyes. An impetuous honesty seemed to me to characterise the woman. Twice I recollect she took me to task for what she held to be errors in doctrine. Once about Fielding we had a disputation. She spoke her mind out. . . . She formed conclusions that might be wrong and built up whole theories of character upon them. New to the London world, she entered it with an independent indomitable spirit of her own; and judged of contemporaries, and especially spied out arrogance or affectation, with extraordinary keenness of vision. She was angry with her favourites if their conduct or conversation fell below her ideal. Often she seemed to me to be judging the London folk prematurely: but perhaps the city is rather angry at being judged. I fancied an austere little Joan of Arc marching in upon us, and rebuking our easy lives, our easy morals. She gave me the impression of being a very pure, and lofty, and high-minded person. A great and holy reverence of right and truth seemed to be with her always. Such, in our brief interview, she appeared to me."

[197] Eyre Crowe. See above, No. 649.

during the last month — but this month at any rate I promise you that the work shall be done, and always keep my promises.

I hope Mʳ Bogue will settle with Mʳ Marvy — what is it that I am to be paid for my contributions? It is a very difficult task to perform.

Yours<br>W M Thackeray

654. TO EDWARD CHAPMAN
DECEMBER 1849

*Hitherto unpublished.*

My dear Chapman

I send all. The book ought to make 100 pages;[198] it can easily be done by cutting 2 lines off each present page.

Please to send 50 £ to Lubbocks — The book has cost me more time than all the rest.

Yours<br>W M T.

655. TO EDWARD CHAPMAN
DECEMBER 1849

*Address:* E. Chapman Esqʳᵉ *Hitherto unpublished.*

R & R<br>or Romance on Romance.

The preface beginning 'Thou readers &c to be expunged in future advertisements.

What the devil have you gone & done?
Why the devil didnt you send me proof

[198] Of the Christmas books published for Thackeray by Chapman and Hall only one, *Rebecca and Rowena* (which extends to 102 pages), contains more than 54 pages. This story appeared in December, 1849.

You have gone & printed the preface[199] with the
advertisement — spoiled my point: offended
D.ʳ Elliotson & annoyed me beyond measure

656.          TO EDWARD CHAPMAN
                  DECEMBER 1849

*Address:* E. Chapman Esq.ʳᵉ | 186 Strand. Hitherto unpublished.

My dear Chapman — Have you done the little job w.ʰ I requested? Doyle writes in great indignation sorrow rather about the
cuts — The title as I wrote, and rewrote and recorrected is R & R
*or* Romance on Romance not *A*[200] — Please to send me a copy or
2 as early as poss: that and an answer to the above query.

                                        Yours
                                        W M T.

657.          TO MRS. BROOKFIELD
                  DECEMBER 1849

*Address:* M.ʳˢ Brookfield. Hitherto unpublished.

My dear lady. The weather is so fine and cheerful that I have
made my mind up to go down to Brighton tomorrow or somewhere
where I can be alone and think about my friend M.ʳ Pendennis
whom I have been forced to neglect. I have been working now
until 7 o'clock and am dead beat — having done a poor drivelling
days work — writing too much — hipped hacked & blue devilled —
I passed Portman S.ᵗ after an hours ride in the Park but hadn't
time to come in — the infernal task master hanging over me — So

---

[199] Thackeray explains in his preface, dated December 20, 1849, how he
came to write *Rebecca and Rowena*: "But passing many hours on a sofa of
late, recovering from a fever, and ordered by DR. ELLIOTSON (whose skill
and friendship rescued me from it) ON NO ACCOUNT to put pen to paper,
I, of course, wished to write immediately, — for which I humbly ask the
Doctor's pardon."

[200] This mistake has never been corrected.

I gave my bridle reins a shake — and plunged into doggrel — Good
bye — God bless you — Come soon back both of you — Write to
me, wont you? — I wish a merry Christmas for you and am always
yours.

W M T.

[For a fragment of a letter to Mrs. Brookfield, 8 December, 1849? see letter
10, Appendix XXVI.]

658.                 TO MRS. BROOKFIELD
                     25 DECEMBER 1849

*Address:* Mᵣˢ Brookfield. Published in *Collection of Letters,* pp. 95–96.

I stop in the middle of Costigan²⁰¹ with a remark applied to
readers of Thos a Kempis²⁰² and others — wʰ is — I think that
cushion-thumpers and high & Low Church extatics have often carried
what they call their love for △ to what seems Impertinence to me.
How good my — has been to me in sending me a back-ache — how
good in taking it away: how blessed the spiritual gift wʰ enabled
me to receive the sermon this morning — how trying my dryness
at this afternoons discourse &c — I say it is awful and blasphemous to
be calling upon Heaven to interfere about the 1000 trivialities of a
man's life — that — has ordered me something indigestible for dinner (wʰ may account for my dryness in the afternoon's discourse.) to
say that it is Providence that sends a draught of air behind me wʰ
gives me a cold in the head, or superintends personally the action
of the James's powder wʰ makes me well — Bow down, Confess,
Adore, Admire and reverence infinitely Make your act of Faith and
trust  Acknowledge with constant awe the Idea of the Infinite
Presence over all, — but what impudence it is in us to talk about
loving God enough if I may so speak — Wretched little blindlings
What do we know about Him? — Who says that we are to sacrifice

²⁰¹ Chapter 42 of *Pendennis,* published in number XIII for February.
²⁰² Thomas à Kempis (1380–1471), the Augustinian monk who is supposed
to have written *De Imitatione Christi.*

the human affections as disrespectful to God? — the Liars? — the wretched canting Fakeers of Christianism the Convent & conventicle dervishes — they are only less unreasonable now than the Eremites and holy women who whipped & starved themselves, never washed and encouraged vermin for the Glory of God — Washing is allowed now, and bodily filth and pain not always enjoined: but still they say 'Shut your ears and dont hear music close your eyes and dont see nature and beauty Steel your hearts and be ashamed of your love for your neighbour' — and timid fond souls scared by their curses and bending before their unending arrogance & dullness, consent to be miserable, & bare their soft shoulders for the brutes' stripes according to the nature of women. You dear Suttees — you get ready and glorify in being martyrized. Nature truth love protest day after day in your tender hearts, against the stupid remorseless tyranny w^h bullies you. Why, you dear creature — what a history that is in the Thos a Kempis book. The scheme of that book carried out would make the world the most wretched useless dreary doting place of sojourn — there would be no manhood no love no tender ties of mother & child no use of intellect no trade or science — a set of selfish beings crawling about avoiding one another, and howling a perpetual miserere. We know that deductions like this have been drawn fom the teaching of J.C: but Please God the world is preparing to throw them over. And I won't believe them though they are written in ever so many books, anymore than that the sky is green or the grass red. Those brutes made the grass red many a time fancying they were acting rightly — amongst others wells the blood of the Person who was born to day —

Good bye dear Lady & my dear generous old W^m

659.            TO MRS. MONTGOMERY
                31 DECEMBER 1849

Hitherto unpublished.

                            Kensington. 31 Dec.ʳ 1849.

Dear Mʳˢ Montgomery

I am just come back from Oxford & find your polite favour; but
I am engaged for New Years day to Mʳ Hallam since a long time:
and can only wish you the compliments of that season under my hand
and seal. Are all your visits over? It will be a comfort to a man
so passionately fond of tea to think that you are.[203] How can you
think I have forgotten the brown bread & butter? may I never
swallow a tartine again when I do.

I wish you and Alfred and those little fairies a very merry New
Year and am always faithfully yours dear Mʳˢ Montgomery

                    W M Thackeray


660.            TO CHARLOTTE LOW
                31 DECEMBER 1849

My text is taken from John W. Irvine's "A Study for Colonel Newcome,"
*The Nineteenth Century*, XXXIV (1893), 586.

                    Kensington: Dec. 31, 1849.

My dear Charlotte, — There is no answer to such an afflicting
letter as yours — for who can offer any consolation to a tender and
devoted wife bereaved of her greatest earthly treasure? I think
we have scarce a right even to offer condolence. May God Almighty
help and comfort your dear aunt[204] under her calamity. The pang
which makes the parting with such a man, so upright, so honest,
so pure-minded, so tender-hearted, inexpressibly bitter to the woman
who has possessed his entire confidence and affection (and knows

---

[203] Possibly Thackeray intended to write *they are.*
[204] Charlotte Low was living at Little Holland House with Mrs. Irvine,
whose husband had just died.

his goodness infinitely better than we) must yet after the first keenness yield to thoughts more comforting. Where can a good and
pious man be better than in the presence of God? away from ill
and temptation and care, and secure of reward. What a comfort to
think that he, who was so good and so faithful here, must be called
away to dwell among the good and just for ever?

There never seems to me to be any cause for grief at the thought
of a good man dying, beyond the sorrow for those who survive
him, and trusting in God's mercy and wisdom, infinite here and
everywhere, await the day when they too shall be called away.

Goodbye, my dear Charlotte, write to me if I can be of any
service, and believe me always,

Affectionately yours,

W. M. Thackeray.

## 661.   TO WILLIAM EDMONDSTOUNE AYTOUN
### 1849?

*Address:* W. E. Aytoun Esq<sup>re</sup> | 113 Jermyn S<sup>t</sup> Published in part, *Daily
Telegraph*, July 18, 1894.

13 Young S<sup>t</sup> Kensington.

My dear Aytoun

'When the bee is in the bonnet and the heather on the brae
And the lilting Bubblyjocky[205] carols forth an ilka spray
When the Haggis in the muirland and the Estrich on the tree
Sing their matins at the sunset dost thou think my Jean of me?

I have been just reading the sweet poetry of the Incas daughter[206]
— and want to know about Saturday. Is it an engagement? I have
2 of the pleasantest dinners possible to choose out of if yours does
not come off, and beg to know instanter.

[205] A turkey, according to Walter William Skeat (*Notes and Queries*, Eighth
Series, VI, 1894, p. 85), who humorously thinks "the Haggis in the muirland"
a fine image.

[206] This is presumably a reference to *The Bon Gualtier Ballads*, an illustrated
edition of which was published in 1849, although "The Cadi's Daughter,"
the only "daughter" poem in the collection, is Spanish, not Spanish-American.

I had rather, mind, have your's: but am good for most days next week if Saturday should not suit you.

Yours ever

W M Thackeray.

I have just got a card from Maquet[207] who is Lieutenant of Alexander Dumas wouldn't Alexander be fun?

662.     TO MRS. BROOKFIELD
1849 [208]

Published in *Collection of Letters*, pp. 25–26.

I was making this doggrel instead of writing
my Punch this morning. Shall I send it or no?

Tis one o'clock, the boy from Punch is sitting in the passage here, it used to be the hour of lunch at Portman Street near Portman Squeer. O stupid little Printers boy I cannot write my head is queer; and all my foolish brain's employ is thinking of a lady dear. It was but yesterday & on my honest word it seems a year, as yet that person was not gone as yet I saw that lady dear — She's left us now, my boy, and all this town this life is blank and drear Thou Printer's devil in the hall, didst ever see my lady dear? — You'd understand you little knave I think if you could only see her why now I look so glum and grave for losing of this lady dear. A lonely man I am in life, my business is to joke & jeer, a lonely man without a wife God took from me a lady dear. A friend I had and at his side, the story dates for seven long year;) one day I found a blushing bride a tender lady kind and dear. They took me in they pitied me they gave me kindly words & cheer, a kinder welcome who shall see than yours O friend & lady dear?

The rest is wanting ——

[207] Auguste Maquet (1813–1888), Dumas's collaborator in many of his most famous novels.

[208] This letter was written seven years after Thackeray's first meeting with Mrs. Brookfield in 1842.

663.                TO MRS. BROOKFIELD
                         1849

*Address:* M<sup>rs</sup> Brookfield. Hitherto unpublished.

My dear lady. Having to send into your neighbourhood this morning, I should be very glad also to know that you were better and had a comfortable night. William & Makepeace couldn't eat their dinners without you: and the latter went to bed at 10 o'clock. He has also been compelled to refuse the dinner at M<sup>r</sup> Hallams, having been invited by M<sup>rs</sup> Elliot (Mark the spelling) two days before.

Pray send me word that you are better — I shan't be able to be funny if you are unwell.

664.                TO MRS. BROOKFIELD
                         1849

Hitherto unpublished.

                              Tuesday night.
My dear lady. I hope you had a pleasant drive to day and that you are well. And will you be at home at 2 tomorrow when I will call on my way to the Railroad, and say good bye till Saturday?
                         Yours always
                         W M T.

665.                TO MRS. BROOKFIELD
                         1849

*Address:* M<sup>rs</sup> Brookfield. Hitherto unpublished.

My dear lady I am going out of town to dine with old Miss Berrys and shall be hard at work until then. But before going away I should be glad to know that you are better than you were yesterday, when you *would* go down to dinner in spite everythink and everybody.

How surprized the printers will be this month with the early Pendennis! What can be going to happen to me? the best thing now w^d be to hear that you are pretty well.

Always yours

W M T.

666.     TO MRS. BROOKFIELD
1849? [209]

*Address:* M^rs Brookfield. Hitherto unpublished.

Thursday.

My dear Lady     A note comes asking me to dine tomorrow with M^r Benedict close by you at no 2 Manchester Square to meet M^me Jenny Lind.

I reply that a lady is coming to dine with my mother whom I must of course meet: but that I hope M^rs Benedict will allow me to come to her in the evening with my mamma and this lady under each arm, and I promise they will look and behave well.

Now suppose M^rs S & I were to come and dine with you, or my mother alone if you like to have her better? — yes, that would be best — and I could come at nine o'clock and accompany you to the Swedish Nightingale.

I am as usual

Your obedient Serv^t

Clarence Bulbul.[210]

---

[209] This and the five succeeding notes appear to have been written during the visit of Major and Mrs. Carmichael-Smyth to London between April and July, 1849.

[210] Cf. "The Lion of the Street" in "Our Street," *Works,* IX, pp. 57–58.

667.    TO THE REV. WILLIAM BROOKFIELD
1849?

Hitherto unpublished.

                                        Saturday.
My dear Vieux

I am going to Lady Pumicestone's[211] to night, and shant be out
time enough to smoke a pipe with you. If you've no evening service tomorrow will you come & dine? At 6 1/2 — Neate an Oxford
man, and Jorrocks[212] whom we had last year are coming — Come
after sarvice of you cant come to dinner to

                            Yours
                            W M T.


668.    TO THE REV. WILLIAM BROOKFIELD
1849?

Published in *Collection of Letters*, p. 30.

Va diner chez ton classique ami tant renommé pour le Grec —
Je ne pourrai mieux faire que de passer la Soirée avec une famille
que J'ai negligée quelque peu — la mienne — Oui, Monsieur, dans
les caresses innocentes de mes enfans chéris, dans la conversation
édifiante de Monsieur mon beaupère, Je tacherai de me consoler
de ta seconde infidelité. Samedi Je ne puis venir: J'ai d'autres
engagemens auxquels Je ne veux pas manquer. Va. Sois heureux.
Je te pardonne.

                            Ton mélancolique ami
                            Chevalier de Titmarsh.


[211] Lady Palmerston.
[212] Robert Smith Surtees (1803–1864), author of *Jorrocks' Jaunts and
Jollities* (1838) and other sporting novels.

669.                TO LADY EDDISBURY
                        1849? [213]

Hitherto unpublished.

Dear Lady Eddisbury

I have but this scrap of paper to thank you for the voucher
I have borrowed 13/ w$^h$ with 8/ I had of my own; will get the
ticket from Mitchels: and having credit with a tailor for whom I
occasionally do something in my way (need I mention the eminent
city firm of M—ses and S—n?) I have ordered a new coat waistcoat and sm—ll cl—thes w$^h$ are to be at home on Monday evening.
These with my hat ironed up, and my gloves w$^h$ the maid is
working up with India rubber, will I flatter myself make of me not
the *least* elegant object in the *giddy but benevolent throng* and
render me not unworthy of the patronage of Lady Eddisbury. I
shall not ave my air curled only hoiled and turned and just a little
pink or picotee in my button hole will I have no doubt set me hup
as a reglar *man of fashion.* A segar looks well — not to smoke so
much as to ave it in your mouth and give you a *distangy air.* I've
seen many gents about *the Parks and West End* with 'em. And so
ornamented I ope you'll permit me to ingage your ladyship for
the very fust Miniwet.

It is most kind of you to treat me as a *younger brother.* Give my
best regards to *my charming nieces* from their *venerable Uncle.*

                        W M T

Since the above was written I have sent for a 1/2 quire of paper,
and read how your ladyship is going to have an oakleaf quadrille.
May I recommend my friends in the city for the costumes? of w$^h$
a sketch is respectfully forwarded.[214]

[213] Thackeray became acquainted with Lady Eddisbury early in 1849, and
her husband became Lord Stanley of Alderley in October, 1850. This letter
may have been written either year.
[214] The accompanying sketch has not been preserved.

670.            TO LADY EDDISBURY
                    1849?

Hitherto unpublished.

Dear Lady Eddisbury Am I to dine with you to day? If you wouldn't like me, a banyan day would be of great service to me, and I would gladly come to tea — But for tea or dinner or any other occasion of life

I have the honor to subscribe myself
Your ladyships very faithful
and obliged
humble Serv.ᵗ

671.            TO MRS. FANSHAWE
                    1849?

*Address:* M.ʳˢ Fanshawe.  Hitherto unpublished.

My dear M.ʳˢ F.

If you please how does every body do? I cant write for love to day, being engaged in writing for money till 2 o'clock, when me and the gals and their Granny are going to the Zoological gardens
Thanks for the letters, and G b all

W M T.

672.            TO MRS. FANSHAWE
                    1849?

Hitherto unpublished.

My dear M.ʳˢ F.

Mamma will come for Totty and I will try and pay you my respects in the course of the day. Yours at work

W M T.

673.          TO RICHARD MONCKTON MILNES
1849

My text is taken from Reid's *Life of Lord Houghton*, I, 427.

You are a good and lovable adviser and M. P., but I cannot get the Magistrate's place, not being eligible. I was only called to the Bar last year,[215] and they require barristers of seven years' standing. Time will qualify me, however, and I hope to be able to last six years in the literary world; for though I shall write, I dare say, very badly, yet the public won't find it out for some time, and I shall live upon my past reputation. It is a pity, to be sure. If I could get a place and rest, I think I could do something better than I have done, and leave a good and lasting book behind me; but Fate is overruling. I have written to thank L. for his kind letter, and to beg him to remember me if any opportunity occurs of serving me. I wonder whether Lord Palmerston could? But I would rather be in London. Thank you for thinking of me, and believe that I am grateful.

Always yours, dear Milnes,

W. M. Thackeray.

[For fragments of a letter to Mrs. Brookfield, dated 1849, see letter 11, Appendix XXVI.]

[215] Thackeray was called to the bar by the Middle Temple on May 26, 1848. In order to meet the requirement that a London magistrate be a barrister of seven years' standing, he kept his name plate on the door of 10 Crown Office Row from 1849 to 1851 and on the door of 2 Brick Court from 1853 to 1859. (Hugh H. L. Bellot, *The Middle and Inner Temple*, London, 1902, p. 80) He never occupied either of these chambers, and it is unlikely that he looked into them more than once or twice a year. Consequently Tom Taylor's poem "Ten, Crown Office Row" cannot concern Thackeray, as Lewis Melville (*William Makepeace Thackeray*, I, 82–83) asserts.

674.                    TO MRS. MONTGOMERY
                                1849?

Hitherto unpublished.

                                        Kensington. Saturday.
Dear Mrs Montgomery.
    May I if you please come directly after dinner on Monday?
I must really dine at home on that day with parents & children,
who have been away for a month & have not seen me at dinner for
a week since their return.
    Then I shall be able to tell you what a lady says whom you have
been to visit: and who admired your writing before she saw you.
                                Most faithfully yours
                                        W M Thackeray


675.                    TO MRS. PROCTER
                            3 JANUARY 1850

Hitherto unpublished. My text is taken from a transcript given Lady Ritchie
by George Murray Smith.

                                        January 3, 1850.
My dear Mrs Procter,
    I will come with very much pleasure on Sunday and I should
like to have Carlyle and Reeve over again only I know it's wrong
and impossible.
                        Always yours,
                            W. M. T.

    I think this is the night of Patmore's tea, how sorry I am that
I am going to dine at home.

676.     TO LADY CASTLEREAGH
3 JANUARY 1850

Hitherto unpublished.

Kensington. Jan 3. 1850.

Dear Lady Castlereagh

I am very sorry to hear that you are still a prisoner and should have liked very much to have been allowed to visit your place of captivity on New Years Day, and wish you better health for 1850, and, (extending my arms over your couch with my fine eyes lifted towards the ceiling) to have given you an old man's blessing. Pray accept the same at this writing, it is a benediction, like the homœopathic remedies, that mayn't do any good, but at least it can't do any harm.

How artful of you to say you *were just going to read* Rebecca & Rowena! Ah Madam, do you suppose that I am not acquainted with that stratagem? When we get a book from the author and suspect, from his known character and from the common chances of life, that the book is stupid, we are always *going to read* it. But why should I complain at being served as I serve my neighbours?

I have very bad news about the trip to Paris. No money. All gone to pay bills. No Paris: no fun this month — Life is made up of disappointments and behold here is one. But there are compensations too, and there's Monday still to look forward too I shall come with my usual fine appetite and alacrity and am till Monday, and for all the rest of the year

Yours very faithfully dear Lady Castlereagh
W M Thackeray

677.                 TO JAMES SPEDDING
                        5 JANUARY 1850

Hitherto unpublished.

                                        Kensington Jan 5. 1850.

My dear Spedding

Although I didn't do that w^h I ought to have done, you know
we don't in the prayer-book,¹ and I was very glad to hear from you
and that you were pleased to remember me. Well, another reason
why I did not answer was that the other day Fitz came grumbling
& growling into my room, and said you were expected instantly in
London: and I thought that &c &c — there's no use in going on
with excuses: w^h are seldom good for anything unless they are lies,
and these I never employ for common use.

I have got back nearly to my former flesh and strength, and rattle
about London pretty much in the old way — out 4 times a week
like a gay young dog. I had a severe bout of it and was very
nearly transmitted to the next world: but behold there is a reprieve,
and I am left to blunder on yet a little longer. I'm not satisfied
with what I do either as a man or a literary man — I will not bother
you with forebodings though. I have been now 3 days trying to
write an article for Punch² and not canning. The fun goes out of
a man at 40: where are the jokes that came in such plenty? Ah me
as Tom Carlyle says he was here the other day and very kind. I
wish you could have heard him though, in a different mood, at
Procter's.³ He fell foul of Reeve, who had a stiff white neckcloth,
w^h probably offended the Seer. He tossed Reeve and gored yea
as a bull he chased him and horned him: for an hour or more he
pitched him about ripping open his bowels and plunging his muzzle

¹ See "General Confession," *Book of Common Prayer.*
² "Hobson's Choice," *Punch,* January 12, pp. 11–12.
³ The other guests at this dinner, which took place on December 19, were
Mrs. Carlyle, Harriet Martineau, and Kinglake. It is described in David A.
Wilson's *Carlyle at his Zenith* (London, 1927), pp. 235–236. Reeve wrote
in his diary under this date, "Carlyle was so offensive I never made it up
with him" (*Memoirs,* ed. J. K. Laughton, I, 217).

into Reeves smoking entrails. Reeve had to appear perfectly good-humoured all the time of the operation, and indeed bore it with wonderful face & patience. I dont think I know of anything else. I am going to breakfast with Macaulay. Rogers is all but extinct and flickers so feebly that you would fancy that old lamp must go out with a puff. The Sterling Club[4] is called the Tuesday Club: but as there are no lords I don't go. Alfred has taken rooms in Forster's house. The Queen Dowager is dead much lamented.[5] My shaving water is getting cold. The Elliots are well and kind. My dear Inspectress of schools beautiful as ever. is about very soon to become a Mamma. A comic poet[6] once singing of an Irishwoman said 'Children if she bear blest will be their daddy' And indeed I can conceive few positions more agreeable than his who is called upon to perform the part of husband to so sweet a creature. Good bye my dear Spedding I wish you a happy Year: and am ever truly yours

W M Thackeray

678.  TO JOHN DOUGLAS COOK
8 JANUARY 1850

*My text is taken from* The Morning Chronicle, *January 12, 1850.*

To the EDITOR of the MORNING CHRONICLE.

Sir, — In a leading article of your journal of Thursday, the 3rd instant, you commented upon literary pensions and the status of

---

[4] An informal society founded in 1838 by John Sterling with Spedding as its secretary. It was first called the Anonymous Club and later, after its founder had left England, the Sterling Club. Thackeray was not an original member. See Carlyle's *Life of John Sterling*, part II, chapter 6.

[5] Queen Adelaide, the widow of William IV, died on December 2, 1849.

[6] Thackeray himself, the next to the last stanza of whose "Peg of Limavaddy" runs:

> Married if she were
> Blest would be the daddy
> Of the children fair
> Of Peg of Limavaddy.

(*Works*, XIII, 33).

literary men in this country, and illustrated your argument by extracts from the story of "Pendennis," at present in course of publication.[7] You have received my writings with so much kindness, that, if you have occasion to disapprove of them or the author, I can't question your right to blame me, or doubt for a moment the friendliness and honesty of my critic; and, however I might dispute the justice of your verdict in my case, I had proposed to submit to it in silence, being indeed very quiet in my conscience with regard to the charge made against me.

But another newspaper of high character and repute takes occasion to question the principles advocated in your article of Thursday; arguing in favour of pensions for literary persons, as you argued against them; and the only point upon which the *Examiner* and the *Chronicle* appear to agree unluckily regards myself, who am offered up to general reprehension in two leading articles by the two writers: by the latter, for "fostering a baneful prejudice" against literary men; by the former, for "stooping to flatter" this prejudice in the public mind, and "condescending to caricature (as is too often my habit) my literary fellow-labourers, in order to pay court to 'the non-literary class." [8]

The charges of the *Examiner* against a man who has never, to his knowledge, been ashamed of his profession, or (except for its dulness) of any single line from his pen — grave as they are, are, I hope, not proven. "To stoop to flatter" any class is a novel accusation brought against my writings; and as for my scheme "to pay court to the non-literary class by disparaging my literary fellow-labourers," it is a design which would exhibit a degree not only of baseness but of folly upon my part of which, I trust, I am not capable. The editor of the *Examiner* may perhaps, occasionally

[7] The *Chronicle's* criticism was provoked by the literary dinner described in chapter 34 of *Pendennis*, and by Warrington's question to Pen about it: "And now . . . that you have seen the men of letters, tell me, was I far wrong in saying that there are thousands of people in this town who don't write books, who are, to the full, as clever and intellectual as people who do?" (*Works*, II, 340)

[8] Paraphrased from Forster's article, "Encouragement of Literature by the State," in *The Examiner* of January 5.

write, like other authors, in a hurry, and not be aware of the conclusions to which some of his sentences may lead. If I stoop to flatter anybody's prejudice for some interested motives of my own, I am no more nor less than a rogue and a cheat; which deductions from the *Examiner's* premises I will not stoop to contradict, because the premises themselves are simply absurd.

I deny that the considerable body of our countrymen described by the *Examiner* "as the non-literary class" has the least gratification in witnessing the degradation or disparagement of literary men. Why accuse "the non-literary class" of being so ungrateful? If the writings of an author give a reader pleasure or profit, surely the latter will have a favourable opinion of the person who so benefits him. What intelligent man, of what political views, would not receive with respect and welcome that writer[9] of the *Examiner* of whom your paper once said that "he made all England laugh and think?" Who would deny to that brilliant wit, that polished satirist, his just tribute of respect and admiration? Does any man who has written a book worth reading — any poet, historian, novelist, man of science — lose reputation by his character for genius or for learning? Does he not, on the contrary, get friends, sympathy, applause — money, perhaps? — all good and pleasant things in themselves, and not ungenerously awarded as they are honestly won. That generous faith in men of letters, that kindly regard in which the whole reading nation holds them, appear to me to be so clearly shown in our country every day, that to question them would be as absurd as, permit me to say for my part, it would be ungrateful. What is it that fills mechanics' institutes in the great provincial towns when literary men are invited to attend their festivals? Has not every literary man of mark his friends and his circle, his hundreds or his tens of thousands of readers? And has not every one had from these constant and affecting testimonials of the esteem in which they hold him? It is of course one writer's lot, from the nature of his subject or of his genius, to command the sympathies or awaken the curiosity of many more readers than

[9] Fonblanque.

shall choose to listen to another author; but surely all get their hearing. The literary profession is not held in disrepute; nobody wants to disparage it; no man loses his social rank, whatever it may be, by practising it. On the contrary, the pen gives a place in the world to men who had none before — a fair place fairly achieved by their genius; as any other degree of eminence is by any other kind of merit. Literary men need not, as it seems to me, be in the least querulous about their position any more, or want the pity of anybody. The money-prizes which the chief among them get are not so high as those which fall to men of other callings — to bishops, or to judges, or to opera singers and actors; nor have they received stars and garters as yet, or peerages and governorships of islands, such as fall to the lot of military officers. The rewards of the profession are not to be measured by the money-standard: for one man spends a life of learning and labour on a book which does not pay the printer's bill, and another gets a little fortune by a few light volumes. But, putting the money out of the question, I believe that the social estimation of the man of letters is as good as it deserves to be, and as good as that of any other professional man.

With respect to the question in debate between you and the *Examiner,* as to the propriety of public rewards and honours for literary men, I don't see why men of letters should not very cheerfully coincide with Mr. *Examiner* in accepting all the honours, places, and prizes which they can get. The amount of such as will be awarded to them will not, we may be pretty sure, impoverish the country much; and if it is the custom of the State, to reward by money, or titles of honour, or stars and garters of any sort, individuals who do the country service, and if individuals are gratified at having sir, or my Lord, appended to their names, or stars and ribbons hooked on to their coats and waistcoats, as men most undoubtedly are, and as their wives, families, and relations are; there can be no reason why men of letters should not have the chance, as well as men of the robe or the sword; or why, if honour and money are good for one profession, they should not be good for another. No man in other callings thinks himself degraded by receiving a reward from his Government; nor surely need the literary man be more squeamish about pensions, and ribbons, and titles, than the ambassador, or general, or judge. Every European State but ours rewards its men of letters; the American Government gives them their full share of its small patronage; and if Americans, why not Englishmen? If Pitt Crawley is disappointed at not getting a ribbon on retiring from his diplomatic post at Pumpernickel; if General O'Dowd is pleased to be called Sir Hector O'Dowd, K.C.B., and his wife at being denominated my Lady O'Dowd; are literary men to be the only persons exempt from vanity, and is it to be a sin in them to covet honour?

And now, with regard to the charge against myself of fostering baneful prejudices against our calling — to which I no more plead guilty than I should think Fielding would have done if he had been accused of a design to bring the Church into contempt by describing Parson Trulliber — permit me to say, that before you deliver sentence it would be as well if you had waited to hear the whole of the argument. Who knows what is coming in the future numbers of the work which has incurred your displeasure and the *Examiner's*, and whether you, in accusing me of prejudice, and the *Examiner* (alas!) of swindling and flattering the public, have not been premature? Time and the hour[10] may solve this mystery, for which the candid reader is referred "to our next." [11]

That I have a prejudice against running into debt, and drunkenness, and disorderly life, and against quackery and falsehood in my profession, I own; and that I like to have a laugh at those pretenders in it who write confidential news about fashion and politics for provincial *gobemouches*; but I am not aware of feeling any malice in describing this weakness, or of doing anything wrong in exposing the former vices. Have they never existed amongst literary men? Have their talents never been urged as a plea for improvidence, and their very faults adduced as a consequence of their genius? The only moral that I, as a writer, wished to hint in the descriptions against which you protest, was, that it was the duty of a literary man, as well as any other, to practise regularity and sobriety, to

[10] *Macbeth*, I, iii, 147.
[11] Number XIII of *Pendennis* for February, chapters 39 to 41.

love his family and to pay his tradesmen. Nor is the picture I have drawn "a caricature which I condescend to," any more than it is a wilful and insidious design on my part to flatter "the non-literary class." If it be a caricature, it is the result of a natural perversity of vision, not of an artful desire to mislead: but my attempt was to tell the truth, and I meant to tell it not unkindly. I have seen the bookseller whom Bludyer robbed of his books: I have carried money, and from a noble brother man-of-letters, to some one[12] not unlike Shandon in prison, and have watched the beautiful devotion of his wife in that dreary place. Why are these things not to be described, if they illustrate, as they appear to me to do, that strange and awful struggle of good and wrong which takes place in our hearts and in the world? It may be that I work out my moral ill, or it may be possibly that the critic of the *Examiner* fails in apprehension. My efforts as an artist come perfectly within his province as a censor; but when *Mr. Examiner* says of a gentleman that he is "stooping to flatter a public prejudice," which public prejudice does not exist, I submit that he makes a charge which is as absurd as it is unjust; and am thankful that it repels itself.

And, instead of accusing the public of persecuting and disparaging us as a class, it seems to me that men of letters had best silently assume that they are as good as any other gentlemen; nor raise piteous controversies upon a question which all people of sense must take to be settled. If I sit at your table, I suppose that I am my neighbour's equal, as that he is mine. If I begin straightway with a protest of "Sir, I am a literary man, but I would have you to know I am as good as you" which of us is it that questions the dignity of the literary profession — my neighbour who would like to eat his soup in quiet, or the man of letters who commences the argument? And I hope that a comic writer, because he describes one author as improvident, and another as a parasite, may not only be guiltless of a desire to vilify his profession, but may really have its honour at heart. If there are no spendthrifts or parasites amongst us, the satire becomes unjust; but if such exist, or have existed, they are as good subjects for comedy as men of other callings. I

---

[12] No doubt Maginn.

never heard that the Bar felt itself aggrieved because *Punch* chose to describe Mr. Dunup's notorious state of insolvency, or that the picture of Stiggins in "Pickwick" was intended as an insult to all Dissenters; or that all the attorneys in the empire were indignant at the famous history of the firm of "Quirk, Gammon, and Snap:" [13] are we to be passed over because we are faultless, or because we cannot afford to be laughed at? And if every character in a story is to represent a class, not an individual — if every bad figure is to have its obliged contrast of a good one, and balance of vice and virtue is to be struck — novels, I think, would become impossible, as they would be intolerably stupid and unnatural, and there would be a lamentable end of writers and readers of such compositions. — Believe me, Sir, to be your very faithful Servant,

W. M. THACKERAY.

Reform Club, Jan. 8.


679.          TO ABRAHAM HAYWARD
25 JANUARY 1850

Hitherto unpublished.

Jan 25. Kensington.

My dear Hayward.

I ought to have written before to thank you and Milman only I oughtnt to thank *Milman[14] & oughtnt to know anything about the proposal[15] I believe, as it emanates from the Committee and not from the Individual    And there is another good reason why I'm not very anxious — It is that I am very poor at this 'writing' and want my money to pay my bills. However if I'm elected I think I can find the 30 guineas or whatever it is in mine or somebody else's

* Is it M.ʳ or D.ʳ Milman?

[13] In Samuel Warren's *Ten Thousand a Year*.
[14] Henry Hart Milman (1791–1868), the historian, who had become Dean of Saint Paul's in 1849.
[15] To have Thackeray elected to the Athenæum Club.

pocket: and have no right to refuse such a kind offer from such a backer.

The words in Pendennis are untenable be hanged to them: but they were meant to apply to a particular class of literary men, *my* class who are the most ignorant men under the Sun, myself included I mean. But I wrote so carelessly that it appears as if I would speak of all, & even if it were true I ought never to have written what I did,

Yours ever<br>W M Thackeray.

680.            TO ABRAHAM HAYWARD
                  1 FEBRUARY 1850

Published in *A Selection from the Correspondence of Abraham Hayward*, I, 144–145.

Kensington. Feb 1. 1850.

My dear Hayward.

Thank you for your kind note.[16] I was quite prepared for the issue of the kind effort made at the Athenæum in my behalf: indeed as a satirical writer, I rather wonder that I have not made more enemies than I have — I don't mean enemies in a bad sense, but men conscientiously opposed to my style, art, opinions, impertinences & so forth. There must be thousands of men to whom the practice of ridicule must be very offensive: doesn't one see such in

[16] In his letter to Thackeray Hayward no doubt repeated what Milman had written to him on January 30: "I cannot say how much I am annoyed by the failure in my attempt to bring in Thackeray at the Athenæum. But there is no counting on the stubborn stupidities of man. One voice, you know, excludes, and among eighteen committee-men that there should not be one self-conceited — I must not fill up the sentence. We are bound not to reveal the secrets of our *Conciliabulum*, but I may say that it was curious to see Macaulay and Croker rowing together in my boat, with Mahon, &c. &c. If I had not thought myself sure of my success, I should not have subjected Mr. Thackeray to the chance of rejection. Pray assure him of my regret and disappointment. . . . Every man whose opinion Mr. Thackeray would value was with him." (H. E. Carlisle, ed., *A Selection from the Correspondence of Abraham Hayward*, I, 143)

society or in one's own family? — persons whom Nature has not gifted with a sense of humour? Such a man would be wrong not to give me a blackball or whatever it is called — a negatory nod of his honest respectable stupid old head. And I submit to his verdict without the slightest feeling of animosity against my judge. Why, Doctor Johnson would certainly have blackballed Fielding, whom he pronounced 'a dull fellow Sir a dull fellow' [17] — & why shouldn't my friend at the Athenæum? About getting in I do not care 2$^d$: but indeed I am very much pleased to have had 2 such sureties as Hallam and Milman; and to know that the gentlemen whom you mention were so generous in their efforts to serve me. What does the rest matter? If you should ever know the old gentleman (for old I am sure he is, steady and respectable) who objects to me, give him my best compliments, and say I think he was quite right to exercise his judgment honestly, and to act according to that reason with w$^h$ Heaven has mercifully endowed him. But that he would be slow, I wouldn't in the least object to meet him: and he in his turn would think me flippant &c — enough of these egotisms. Didn't I tell you once before that I feel frightened almost at the kindness of people regarding me? May we all be honest fellows and keep our heads from too much vanity. Your case was a very different one, your's was a stab with the sharp point; and the wound I know must have been a most severe one — So much the better in you to have borne it as you did. I never heard in the least that your honor suffered by the injury done you, or that you lost the esteem (how should you?) of any single friend, because an enemy dealt you a savage blow. The opponent in your case exercised a right to do a wrong: whereas in the other, my Athenæum friend has done no earthly harm to any mortal, but has established his own character, & got a great number of kind testimonials to mine.

Always dear Hayward yours very truly<br>W M Thackeray

[17] Thackeray apparently had in mind the following passage from Boswell's *Life of Johnson* (ed. George Birkbeck Hill and L. F. Powell, 6 vols., Oxford, 1934-40, II, 173-174): "Fielding being mentioned, Johnson exclaimed,

681.        TO MRS. BROOKFIELD
            4 FEBRUARY 1850 [18]

Hitherto unpublished. *Endorsed:* Feb 4.

My dear lady. I dont think I shall come to day to see you but
if you please will you tell your husband when you write this
evening that my dinner for Thursday is off     I send back the
book of devotions, w^h set me off last night in a most profound sleep:
I am always

                                        Yours
                                        W M T.

682.   FROM THE REV. WILLIAM BROOKFIELD
            26 FEBRUARY 1850

Hitherto unpublished.

                                        15 Portman S^t
                                        26 Feb 1850

My dear T.

It's a wench & came at 12.30 P. M. this day.[19] Both seem well.
Y^rs affly

            W H B

---

'he was a blockhead;' and upon my expressing my astonishment at so strange
an assertion, he said, 'What I mean by his being a blockhead is, that he was a
barren rascal.' "

[18] The tone of this letter places it between November, 1848, and September,
1851. Since Thackeray was in Paris on February 4 both in 1849 and 1851,
1850 is the only possible year.

[19] "BIRTHS . . . On Tuesday, the 26th inst., at 15, Portman-street,
Portman-square, Mrs. William Henry Brookfield, of a daughter" (*Times*,
February 28).

683.          TO MAGDALENE BROOKFIELD
26 FEBRUARY 1850

*Address:* Miss Brookfield | care of M^rs Denton | 15 Portman S^t | Portman Sq^re.
London. Hitherto unpublished.

13 Young S^t Kensington.
Feb 26. 1850.

My dear Miss Brookfield

I send you my very best love and compliments upon your appearance in this world, where I hope you will long remain, so as
to make your Mamma & Papa happy. Sometimes they will talk to
you perhaps, about a gentleman who was a great friend of theirs
once. He was a writer of books w^h were popular in their day, but
by the time you are able to read this they will be quite forgotten.
Therefore the author himself did not much care about them: and
he does not in the least wish you to read them. But what he would
like you to remember is that he was very fond of your dear mother,
and that he and your Papa were very good friends to one another,
helping each other as occasion served in life.

And this gentleman who has 2 daughters of his own and likes
them very much, was at your house a quarter of an hour before
you were born to day; and he drank your health in a glass of
Burgundy wine at night; and he prays heartily to God Almighty
for the welfare of yourself and your dear mother and your father.
And so Good bye my dear little girl, and believe me to be your
affectionate friend

W M Thackeray

684.    TO THE REV. WILLIAM BROOKFIELD
26 FEBRUARY 1850

*Address:* Rev^d W. H. Brookfield | 15 Portman S^t | Portman Sq^re. *Postmark:* FE 26 1850. Hitherto unpublished.

My dear Vieux

    I give thee joy. Will you kindly forward the enclosed.[20]
Ever yours<br>W M T

685.    TO MRS. FANSHAWE
27 FEBRUARY 1850

*Address:* M^rs Fanshawe. Hitherto unpublished.

27 Feb.

My dear little F

    I should be very much pleased, please, to hear that your friends have had a good nights rest, and that their nurse (I mean you) is pretty well. Distribute my blessings freely amongst the family. And when may Totty come here and spend a day or two & night or two in a bed with Anny who wants her very much? — They have slept in the same bed together before it appears, & Anny says she has not grown any fatter since.

    I wrote a letter to Miss Brookfield last night w^h I sent enclosed to her Papa. God bless them all says
Yours<br>W M T.

[20] Thackeray's letter of February 26 to Magdalene Brookfield.

686.                    TO MRS. BROOKFIELD
                        28 FEBRUARY 1850

Published in part, *Collection of Letters*, pp. 102–104.

Feb. 28.

After hearing that Miss ~~Brookfield~~ was doing well in the arms
of her mamma; if you please I rode in the Park on Tuesday, where
there was such a crowd of carriages along the Serpentine that I
blushed to be on horseback there, and running the gauntlet of so
many beauties. Out of 1000 carriages I didn't know one w$^h$ was
odd and strikes one as showing the enormity of London. Of course
if there had been anybody in the carriages I should have known
them but there was nobody positively nobody — (this sentence is
not as neatly turned as it might have been; and is by no means so
playfully satirical as could be wished.) Riding over the Serpentine
bridge six horsemen with a lady in the middle came galloping upon
me and sent me on to the footpavement in a fright, when they
all pulled up at a halt and the lady in the middle cried out How
do you do M$^r$ &c. The lady in the middle was pretty M$^{rs}$ Liddell,[21]

[21] The former Lorina Reeve, whom Henry George Liddell (1811–1898)
married in 1846. Thackeray and Liddell had been good friends at Charterhouse, which they both entered in 1823. The two boys sat next to each other
in the second form, and Liddell later wrote of their association: "*He* never
attempted to learn the lesson, never exerted himself to grapple with the
Horace. We spent our time mostly in drawing, with such skill as we could
command. His handiwork was very superior to mine, and his taste for comic
scenes at that time exhibited itself in burlesque representations of incidents
in Shakespeare. I remember one — Macbeth as a butcher brandishing two
blood-reeking knives and Lady Macbeth as the butcher's wife clapping him
on the shoulder to encourage him." (Henry L. Thompson, *Henry George
Liddell*, p. 8) Thackeray lost sight of Liddell in 1829, when his friend left
Charterhouse for Oxford, and did not encounter him again until he became
Headmaster of Westminster School in 1846, a post he held until 1855. "After
that," Liddell recalls (pp. 8–9), "[Thackeray] often used to join Mrs. Liddell
and myself when riding in Rotten Row. On one occasion he turned to her
and said: 'Your husband ruined all my prospects in life; he did all my Latin
verses for me, and I lost all opportunities of self-improvement.' It is needless
to add that this was a pure fiction — I had trouble enough to do my own

she made me turn back with the 6 horsemen — of course I took
off my hat with a profound bow and said that to follow in her
train was my greatest desire — and we rode back all through the
carriages, making an immense clatter and sensation w$^h$ the lady in
the middle her name was M$^{rs}$ Liddle enjoyed very much. She
looked uncommonly handsome, she had a gentleman with mustachios on each side of her; — I thought we looked like Brighton
bucks or provincial swells and felt by no means elated — Then we
passed out of Hyde Park into the Green do, where the lady in the
middle said she must have a canter and off we set the mustachios,
the lady & myself skurrying the policemen off the road and making
the walkers stare. I was glad when we got to S$^t$ James Park gate
where I could take leave of that terrific black eyed beauty, and
ride away by myself and think of my dear lady. Dear brave old
Liddell! he has passed 20 years at Oxford, he is full of learning
and honour and simplicity, and has taken a 3$^d$ rate provincial lady
(rather first rate in the beauty line though I think) for a wife. They
are like couples in the old comedies — I wonder whether they will
be of use to any present writer? — After saying this about them you
see Maam you have me in your power: you have but to hand over
this letter to M$^{rs}$ L: and that instant she'd tear my eyes out. As
I rode home by the Elliots door I longed to go in and tell them
what had happened and how it was your little girls birthday but
I didn't and came home and drank her health instead and wrote
her a letter, and slept sound — Thank God you did too, madame,
ma bonne soeur.

---

verses. At this time *Vanity Fair* was coming out in monthly parts in its well-
known yellow paper covers. He used to talk about it, and what he should do
with the persons. Mrs. Liddell one day said, 'Oh, Mr. Thackeray, you must
let Dobbin marry Amelia.' 'Well,' he replied, 'he shall; and when he has got
her, he will not find her worth having.' " From 1855 until 1891 Liddell was
Dean of Christ Church College, Oxford. Thackeray's testimony to the somewhat overpowering nature of the wife's personality is confirmed by the following couplet from the unpublished *Masque of Balliol*, cited in *The Oxford
Dictionary of Quotations*, p. 528:

I am the Dean, and this is Mrs. Liddell;
She is the first and I the second fiddle.

Yesterday (after writing for 3 hours or so) what did I go out for to see? — first the Miss Jingilbys looking very fresh and pretty (you see we have consolations) then a poor fellow[22] dying of consumption. He talked as they all do with a jaunty lively manner as if he should recover — his sister sate with us looking very wistfully at him as he talked on, about hunting, and how he had caught his cold by falling with his horse in a brook and how he sh$^d$ get better by going to S$^t$ Leonards and I said of course he would, and his sister looked at him very hard. As I rode away through Brompton I met 2 ladies not of my acquaintance in a Brougham, who nevertheless ogled and beckoned me in a very winning manner w$^h$ made me laugh most wonderful. O you poor little painted Jezebels thinks I, do you think you can catch such a grey headed old fogy as me? poor little things — Behind them came dear honest kind Castlereagh galloping along: and we pulled up & shook hands, that good fellow was going on an errand of charity & kindness — Consumption Hospital — woman he wants to get in — & so forth. Theres a deal of good in the wicked world. isn't there? This man was driving about with Madame Jezebel Grisi a few years ago: and fighting duels about her:[23] the same honest soul then as now,

[22] Charles Thomas Irvine (1827–1850). His younger brother, John Irvine, writes (*Nineteenth Century*, XXXIV [1893], 585) that Charles used to meet Thackeray "at Little Holland House and go to him in Young Street. He had always been delicate, and died of phthisis at Brompton July 13, 1850, active mischief having been set up from his having got drenched out hunting in Leicestershire in November 1849 and gone on in his wet clothes."

[23] The circumstances of this duel, which took place in June, 1838, were described to Sir William Fraser by George Bentinck: "Lord Castlereagh had been paying attentions for some time to Madame de Melci, known universally by her stage name as Madame Grisi. These became so conspicuous that Monsieur de Melci, who was living in Paris, separately from his wife, was compelled to take notice of the matter: M$^r$ Bentinck was at the Castle Hotel, Salt Hill, for Eton Montem, when a letter came from Lord Castlereagh, stating that he had been challenged by Madame Grisi's husband. M$^r$ Bentinck hoped that M. de Melci might be by his social position unable to demand satisfaction. He found, however, on the contrary, that he was a man of good social standing, and a gentleman; and, what he regretted very much more, had the reputation of being 'a dead shot.' Under these circumstances he negociated that they should fight with pistols which neither combatant had seen before: and he endeavoured to procure a pair that were not easy to fire. On taking

when he goes to Church every day; and people sneer at him and say he's mad: because he says his prayers and believes with all his simple heart; and devotedly loves a woman. What a mixture of motives we have though! I'm sure it's partly because he is a Lord that I like that man: but its his lovingness manliness and simplicity w.ʰ I like best. Then I went to Chesham place[24] where I told them about things — You ought to be fond of those two women they speak so tenderly of you. KP is very ill and can scarcely speak with a sore throat — They gave me a pretty bread-tray w.ʰ they have carved for me with wheat ears round the edge and

 in the centre. — O yes, but before that I had ridden in

the park and met dear old Elliotson thundering along with his great horses at 10 miles an hour, the little oss trotted by the great osses quite easily though, and we shook hands at a capital pace, and talked in a friendly manner. and as I passed close by your door why I just went in & saw W.ᵐ and M.ʳˢ F. I should have liked to hear the baby squall but she didn't. I thanked G to hear you were so well.

Then at 8 o'clock a grand dinner in Jewry.[25] M.ʳˢ Montefiore 2

their stand, he demurred to several of the conditions; yielding them one after another; but eventually settling the matter so that he should give the word to fire. He told me that he was afraid it was all over with 'poor Cas.' The combatants were bound to hold their pistols muzzle downwards until the word was given: he said 'I saw de Melci's right hand move a little; enough to give me the excuse for saying "Monsieur de Melci! il faut que le pistolet touche au pantalon." I then instantly gave the word to fire.' Lord Castlereagh fired in the air: M. de Melci at the same moment fired: and shot Lord Castlereagh through the wrist, which was raised at the side of his head, holding his discharged pistol muzzle upwards." (Sir William Fraser, *Hic et Ubique*, London, 1893, pp. 37–38)

[24] Where the Elliots and Kate Perry lived.

[25] Mrs. Disraeli was present at this dinner, of which her husband noted: "The Hebrew aristocracy assembled in great force and numbers, mitigated by the Dowager of Morley, Charles Villiers, Abel Smiths, and Thackeray. I think he will sketch them in the last number of *Pendennis*." (Wilfrid Meynell, *Benjamin Disraeli*, London, 1903, p. 22) Thackeray mentions the following members of the "Hebrew aristocracy": Henrietta Montefiore (1790–1866) and her sons, Joseph Mayer Montefiore (1816–1880) and Nathaniel

Drawn at Chesham Place.          The Miss Perrys at home.

MRS. ELLIOT AND KATE PERRY AT CHESHAM PLACE
*From a sketch by Thackeray*

young Israelites her sons, Sir A. Rothschild Sir I. L. Goldsmid Lady G & Miss G about to marry M.ʳ Nat. Montefiore. Is it not a pretty name? The prétendue pleasant looking clever and well bred — a very plain but pleasant Hierosolymite lady to go down to dinner with sister to Lady Rothschild    they are all each others uncles cousins wives nieces & so on and the women as I've said to you very nice. My! what a fine dinner what plate and candelabra what a deal of good things and sweet meats especially wonderful. The Christians were in a minority. Lady Charlemont[26] beautiful serene stupid old lady. (She asked isn't that the great M.ʳ Thackeray? O my stars think of that!) Lord Marcus Hill celebrated as a gourmand — kindly told me of a particular dish w.ʰ I was not to let pass something à la Pompadour very nice — Charles Villiers Lady Hislop & pretty little Hatty Elliot & Lady Somebody: and then I went to Miss Berry's.[27] Kinglake Phillips[28] Lady Stuart de

---

Montefiore (1819–1883); Sir Anthony Rothschild (1810–1876); Sir Isaac Lyon Goldsmid (1778–1859), Lady Isabel Goldsmid (d. 1860), and Emma Goldsmid (d. 1902). The marriage between Montefiore and Miss Goldsmid took place on May 7. The sister of Thackeray's friend Lady Rothschild was Mrs. Charlotte Montefiore (1818–1854).

[26] Lady Anne Charlemont (d. 1876), wife of the second Earl; Arthur Marcus Cecil Hill (1798–1863), third son of the second Marquess of Downshire, styled Lord Marcus Hill, later (1861) third Baron Sandys; Harriet Elliot (d. 1855), fifth daughter of the second Earl of Minto.

[27] Mary Berry (1763–1852) and her sister Agnes (1764–1852) had made their house at 8 Curzon Street a center of fashionable and literary society for nearly twenty years. Thackeray liked both the grave and learned Mary and the lively, pretty Agnes, and he enjoyed meeting in their *salon* many of the friends he was accustomed to see at Chesham Place. Yet his sense of what the sisters had been was perhaps an even stronger attraction to him than what they were. "A few years since," he wrote (*Works*, VII, 621) of Mary Berry in 1855, "I knew familiarly a lady who had been asked in marriage by Horace Walpole, who had been patted on the head by George I. This lady had knocked at Doctor Johnson's door; had been intimate with Fox, the beautiful Georgina of Devonshire, and that brilliant Whig society of the reign of George III.; had known the Duchess of Queensberry, the patroness of Gay and Prior, the admired young beauty of the Court of Queen Anne. I often thought, as I took my kind old friend's hand, how with it I held on to the old society of wits and men of the world."

[28] Tom Phillips, an artist popular in the London world.

Rothesays[29] Lady Waterfords mother Colonel Damer[30] — There's a day for you. Well, it was a very pleasant one and perhaps this gossip about it will amuse my dear lady.

687.                    TO MRS. BROOKFIELD
                       1–2 MARCH 1850

Published in part, *Collection of Letters*, pp. 131–132.

Friday.

My dear lady I have no news to give for these 2 days: but that I have been busy and done nothing. Virtue doesn't agree with me well, and a very little domestic rose-leaf rumpled puts me off my work for the day. Yesterday it was I forget what, to day it has been the same reason: and lo Saturday cometh and nothing is done. How curious it will be to see you, realizing your nine years' dream at last, with that dear little baby for your constant thought and occupation! How much would you sell it for? — you who had misgivings about your love for it (though you didn't say so) a fortnight ago. God keep you both well. It reads very odd and pleasant in print in the Times & Daily News 'M$^{rs}$ W. H. Brookfield of a daughter' [31] — the first of many announcements of that nature, for you are going to be healthier and happier than you have been all your life, and I daresay to educate an awful family. I feel like an old woman in thinking about you, and talk as such — you know it has been agreed that at one time of my existence I must have been a woman — darling duck, what a beauty I must have been! We have been to the Zoological gardens this fine day, and amused ourselves in finding likenesses to our friends in many of the animals — Thank Evns, both of the girls have plenty of fun and humour,

[29] The former Lady Elizabeth Margaret Yorke (d. 1867), third daughter of the third Earl of Hardwicke, who in 1816 had married Sir Charles Stuart, later (1828) first Baron Stuart de Rothesay. Their second daughter married the third Marquess of Waterford in 1842.

[30] Colonel George Lionel Dawson Damer (1788–1856), third son of the first Earl of Portarlington.

[31] See above, No. 683.

yours ought to have from both sides of the house; and a deal of
good besides if she do but possess a mixture of W^m's disposition and
your's — He will be immensely tender over the child when nobody's by, I'm sure of that: no father knows for a few months what
it is: but they learn afterwards — It strikes me I have made these
statements before.

We had a dull dinner at Lady Ashburton's, a party
of Barings chiefly — and O such a pretty one — blue
eyes gold hair alabaster shoulders and such a splendid display of them! Venables was there very shy
and grand looking and awkward — How kind that
man has always been to me — And a M^r Simeon[32] of the Isle of
Wight an Oxford man who won my heart by praising certain parts
of Vanity Fair w^h people won't like. Carlyle glowered in in the
evening: and a man who said a good thing speaking of a stupid
place at the sea side Sandwich I think    Somebody said Cant
you have any fun there? O yes Corry said 'but you must take it
with you' — a nice speech I think not only witty but indicating a
gay cheerful heart. I intend to try after that: we intend to try
after it: And by action and so forth get out of that morbid dissatisfied condition. Now I'm going to dress to dine with Lord
Holland — My servant[33] comes in to tell me it's time. He's a

---

[32] Cornwall Simeon (1820–1880), third son of Sir Richard Godin Simeon,
second Baronet, of the Isle of Wight, who had taken his B. A. and M. A.
degrees at Oxford in 1842 and 1844; Henry Thomas Lowry-Corry (1803–
1873), second son of the second Earl of Belmore, who was M. P. for Tyrone
from 1826 to 1873 and First Lord of the Admiralty in 1867 and 1868.

[33] S. James, the best of Thackeray's long succession of servants, remained
with him until the summer of 1852. "De la Pluche was devoted to my
father," Lady Ritchie (Chapters, pp. 84–86) writes of this paragon, "and
next to him he seemed the most important member of the household. He
was more than devoted. We used to think he was a sorcerer. He used to
guess at my father's thoughts, plan for him, work for him, always knew before-
hand what he would like far better than we ever did. I remember that we
almost cried on one occasion, thinking that our father would ultimately prefer
him to us. He used to write to the papers and sign his letters, 'Jeames de la
Pluche, 13 Young Street.' 'Like to see my last, miss?' he used to say, as he put
down a paper on the schoolroom table. He was a very good and clever man,
though a stern ruler. My father had a real friendship and regard for him, and

capital man an attentive alert silent plate-cleaning intelligent fellow. I hope we shall go on well together and that I shall be able to afford him — Mark the dellixy of my attention, I write large so that Madam need not fatigue her eyes or put her spectacles on. Ah Madam I shall be glad when I can see you through mine. I picture you walking in the Park sometimes with a behind — Haven't I done the Baby prettily? Well Goodbye Godbless you — I dont like to go away but linger on shaking hands with you.

Boz is capital this month [34] — some very neat pretty natural writing indeed — better than somebody else again. By Jove he is a clever fellow, and somebody else must and shall do better.

Quite pleasant dinner at Lord Hollands — leg of mutton that sort of thing home to bed at 10 1/2 — and tomorrow to work really & truly. Let me hear please that you are going on well and I shall go on all the better.

---

few of his friends ever deserved it more. He lived alone downstairs, where he was treated with great deference, and had his meals served separately, I believe. He always called my father 'the Governor.' He was a little man, and was very like Holbein's picture of Sir Thomas More in looks. I remember on one occasion coming away from some lecture or entertainment. As we got out into the street it was raining. 'It has turned cold,' said my father, who was already beginning to be ill. At that moment a voice behind him said, 'Coat, sir? Brought it down;' and there was De la Pluche, who had brought his coat all the way from Kensington, helping him on with it. My father thanked him, and then felt mechanically in the pocket for a possible cigar-case. 'Cigar? Here,' says De la Pluche, popping one into my father's mouth, and producing a match ready lighted." There are many traits of James in John Howell, the literary butler of Thackeray's *The Wolves and the Lamb*.

[34] Number XI of *David Copperfield*, chapters 32 to 34, which appeared late in February, concurrently with number XIV of *Pendennis*, chapters 42 to 44.

688.          TO MRS. BROOKFIELD AND
                  MRS. FANSHAWE
                  5 MARCH 1850

*Address:* M^rs Fanshawe | 15 Portman St. | Portman Square. *Postmark:* MR
18(49). Published in part, *Collection of Letters*, pp. 104–105.

Hotel Bristol. Place Vendome. Tuesday.

My dear ladies    I am arrived just this minute safe and
sound under the most beautiful blyew Sky, after a fair passage and
a good night's rest at Boulogne, where I found what do you think,
a letter from a dear friend of mine dated September 13,[35] w^h somehow gave me as much pleasure as if it had been a fresh letter
almost and for w^h I am very much obleeged to you. I travelled
to Paris with a character for a book, Lord Howden,[36] the ex-beau
Caradoc or Cradock a man for whom more women have gone distracted than you have any idea of — so delightful a middle-aged
dandy! — Well, he will make a page in some book someday. In
the meantime I want to know why there is no letter to tell me
that Madam is getting on well — I should like to hear so much.
It seems a shame to have come away yesterday without coming to

[35] Thackeray had last visited Paris in September, 1849. He is no doubt
referring to Mrs. Brookfield's reply to his letter of September 9.

[36] John Hobart Caradoc (1799–1873), second Baron Howden, the soldier
and diplomat. His youth, after he left Eton in 1815, was passed chiefly at
Paris, where he was known as "*le beau* Caradoc." What might have been the
great *coup* of his life, his marriage in 1830 to the Russian heiress, Princess
Bagration, failed when Nicholas I confiscated his wife's estates and exiled her
from Russia for marrying a foreigner. The marriage turned out unhappily but
did not interrupt Caradoc's career of gallantry. It is recorded by Lord Lamington (*In the Days of the Dandies*, p. 90) that when the Beau was wounded at
the Siege of Antwerp in 1832 "and for some months appeared with the sleeve
of his coat cut open and tied with ribbons, . . . the ladies had their sleeves
slashed in a similar manner," calling the new fashion the "*manche à la
Caradoc.*" Thackeray met Lord Howden in the interval between his appoint-
ments as Minister to Brazil and Ambassador to Madrid. He was recalled from
Spain in 1858 and retired with his mistress to the Casa Caradoc, his estate
in southern France. See Robert E. C. Waters, *Genealogical Memoirs of the
Extinct Family of Chester of Chicheley* (London, 1878), pp. 684–689.

ask. It was the suddenest freak — done packed and gone in 1/2 an hour, hadn't time even to breakfast — and as I couldn't see my lady and as I mightn't see her nuss, to get news of her, and as I really wanted a little change & fresh air for my lungs, I think I did well to escape: and to say my prayers for her on this side of the channel. Get well and come down stairs quickly please, nurse that pooty little baby and be happy please, and dont fancy that I am come here to forget you, quite the reverse — the chain pulls tighter the farther I am away from you. and I dont want to break it, or to be other than my dear sisters most faithful Makepeace to command. You wont go to Clevedon before I come back will you? Godbless you all. I send this by the M. Chronicle's packet — dont be paying letters to me but write and write away and never mind the expense M^rs Fanshawe.

W M T.

[For fragments of a letter to Mrs. Elliot and Kate Perry, 5 March, 1850, see letter 12, Appendix XXVI.]

689.            TO ANTONIO PANIZZI
10 MARCH 1850

*Address:* A. Panizzi Esq^re. | British Museum | London. *Postmarks:* PARIS 10 MARS 50, 11 MR 1850. Hitherto unpublished.

Hotel Bristol. P. Vendome. Paris 10 March

My dear Panizzi

I went yesterday to the Bibliothèque Nationale and asked for 2 or 3 books at a venture. I asked for Southeys Book of the Church & Cobbetts Church History but wrote down the 2 names on the same paper. At the same time on another paper I wrote for a French Life of Thomas a Beckett.

I said I did not know what authors to consult on the life of this Saint, and asked if I might see a catalogue. The librarian replied that I might have the book w^h I wanted, at the same time mentioning three or four lives of the Saint in Latin French & English.

Then I asked for a French book resembling Watt's Bibliotheca Britannica — w.ʰ latter was presently brought to me, to be consulted at the counter where the Librarian sits. There seemed to be no objection to give me several volumes. Many of the readers at the tables had 3 or 4 or more books about them, though the major part had but one volume. The printed rule of the library is that except in reserved cases only one volume shall be given. This is on account of the numbers of readers, and because any one may read who likes: the friend who went to the Library with me had a pamphlet taken from his hand at the porter's lodge as we entered, — the porteress saying that no books could be taken out of the library without an authorization.

For the accommodation of applicants for books, there were 2 pens and an inkstand. I had to wait several minutes before I could get the use of one of the pens.

Cobbett's *Reformation* I had asked for Cobbett's History of the Church, was brought after 38 minutes waiting. I got it at the desk or counter

I waited twenty minutes more and asked for the other volumes — Southey I could not have as I had put it on the same paper with Cobbett: and the Life of S.ᵗ Thomas a B: was not to be found — Here is the ticket.

The accommodation is so entirely inferior to that w.ʰ the British Museum gives us: that comparisons are quite out of the question. The catalogue you consult is the librarian of whom however learned one cannot ask too many questions and on whom there is a constant pressure of applicants. If I had to write on a French subject, the French Revolution for example, I would go to London for the books (as I told you I did before when I was writing a Review article on the French Restoration[37]) rather than apply here, where instead of a catalogue at my orders, I must trust to the good memory and complaisance (both of w.ʰ are very great) of the librarian.

I think there were not more readers than I have seen at the

[37] See below, Appendix VIII.

B. M — the tables were however full, the conveniences nothing like those w^h we have at home.

I asked to get back my ticket for Southey & Cobbett, but an aid-librarian said it was buried under a heap of other tickets, pointing to them. And I suppose that a repetition of the experiment with any other books would lead to pretty much the same result.

Always faithfully yours<br>W M Thackeray

[For fragments of a letter to Mrs. Elliot and Kate Perry, 12 March, 1850, see letter 13, Appendix XXVI.]

690.          TO MRS. BROOKFIELD<br>18–20 MARCH 1850

*Address:* M^rs Brookfield | 15 Portman S^t | Portman Sq^re *Postmark:* MR 21 1850. Published in part, *Collection of Letters*, pp. 109–110.

Madam and dear lady.     If I've no better news to send you than this pray dont mind but keep the inclosure safe for me agin I come back w^h wont be many days now p. G. I had thought of setting off tomorrow, but as I have got into working trim I think I had best stop here and do a great bit of my number[38] before I unsettle myself by another journey &c — I have been to no gaieties for I have been laid up with a violent cold and cough, w^h kept me in my rooms too stupid even to write: but these ills have cleared away pretty well now, and I'm bent upon going out to dinner au cabaret, and to some fun afterwards I dont know where: nor scarce what I write I'm so tired — I wonder what will happen with Pendennis and Fanny Bolton? Writing it and sending it to you somehow it seems as if it were true — I shall know more about them tomorrow but mind mind and keep the MS — you see its 5 pages 15£ by the immortal Gods!

I dined at some very stupid but splendid Americans lately, the

[38] Number XV for April, chapters 45 to 47. Pen's flirtation with Fanny Bolton begins in chapter 46.

gentleman took care to tell me his family were on the losing side in the War of Independence, and Lor! how he does love a Lord! I'm asked to a marriage tomorrow — a young Foker of 22 with a lady twice a widow & once a runaway M$^r$ Webster — M$^{rs}$ Fitzroy Somerset[39]     The pen drops out of my &, its so tired but as the Ambas: bag goes for nothing I like to say How do you do and remember me to Miss Brookfield and to shake hands with William God bless you all

W M T.

Tuesday

This note w$^h$ was to have gone away yesterday was too late for the bag: and I was at work too late to day to write a word for anything but Pendennis. I hope I shall bring a great part of it home with me at the end of the week and in the mean time dont put you to the trouble of the MS, w$^h$ you see I was only sending because I had no news and no other signs of life to give. I have been out to the play to night and laughed very pleasantly at nonsense until now: when I'm come home very tired and sleepy, and write just one word to say Good night to my dear lady. I'm going away & am rather sorry for it I think: for I shall only have the pleasure of seeing you for a day or two when you will go to Clevedon, I know, for ever so long. Well, I hope you'll enjoy the Spring-time there and that Miss Brookfield will flourish God bless her and her Mamma. They say theres to be another Revolution here very soon: but I shall be across the water before that event: and my old Folks will be here instead — You must please to tell M$^{rs}$ Fanshawe that I am over head and ears in work and that I beg you to kiss the tips of her gloves for me. There's another letter for you begun somewhere about the premises: but it was written in so gloomy and egotistical a strain that it's best burnt. I burned another yesterday written to Lady Ashburton because it was too pert and like Major Pendennis — talking only about Lords and great people in an easy off hand way. I think I only write naturally to one person

[39] "MARRIED . . . On the 19th inst., at the British Embassy, Paris, Henry, eldest son of the late Sir Henry Webster, to Emilie Louise, relict of the late Major-General FitzRoy Somerset." (*Times*, March 23, 1850)

now and make points and compose sentences to others: that's why you must be patient, please, & let me go on twaddling and boring you.

Harrys late bride Miss Guizot[40] was married yesterday in the midst of a huge crowd. And I couldn't go to the other wedding to day because I was too busy with my business. This is not interesting is it nor amusing nor yet too sentimental? — only stupid but I like to say good night and Gby before I go to roost.

Wednesday. I send this scrap by a newspaper Correspondent just to say I'm very well and so awfully hard at business that Ive no time for more than Gby. I shall go away on Saturday probably.

691.                    TO MRS. BROOKFIELD
                        27 MARCH 1850

Published in part, *Collection of Letters*, p. 67.

My dear lady. Have you had a good night and are you pretty better this morning? It is so fine that I could not help ordering the oss and taking a ride — My mother will come and see you to day — and I shall be very happy when the day comes that we may have a talk together. On Monday I had 2 letters from you — one came from Paris and the other was written on the day I went away — Thank you for it. I hadn't the heart to read it till Monday: and until I had got up my courage at 12 o'clock when I thought the Xning would be taking place, and said Amen here.

I am going to dine at the Berrys to day and to Lady Ashburton's at night. I dined at home 3 days running, think of that! — This is my news it isn't much is it? I have written a wicked number of Pendennis but like it rather. It has a good moral I believe, although to some it may appear naughty.

Big Higgins who dined with me yesterday offered me what do

[40] "Hier a eu lieu, au temple de l'Oratoire, la célébration du mariage de M. de Witt avec Mlle Henriette Guizot. . . . On remarquait auprès de M. Guizot, M. de Broglie père, M. de Broglie fils, Mme de Lieven, etc." (*Moniteur universel*, March 20, 1850)

you think? — If, says he, you are tired & want to lie fallow for a year come to me for the money. I have much more than I want! Wasnt it kind? I like to hear and to tell of kind things.

Dont trouble yourself to write if its dangerous but get well as soon as ever you can: and be happy always. I give my compliments to Miss Brookfield and am yours as usual

W M T.

692.       TO MRS. SARTORIS
28 MARCH 1850

Hitherto unpublished. My text is taken from a transcript supplied by Mrs. Fuller.

Kensington, March 28.

My dear Mrs. Sartoris,

I wish I could pay you a visit in the country but I have just had a little holyday in Paris, and am on duty again at home in London for some time at least, with an immense deal to write and to do, and a fine cough and cold to keep me company in this bitter weather. I came back on Saturday and have been writing for money ever since: please excuse me for not having sooner acknowledged your kind note.

What is this, I hear that you have let your house? I'm sorry to lose it. I never had anything but kindness and friendliness in it. I get scolded in some houses. The other day somebody in Harley Street[41] with whom I couldn't dine because I had promised them at home said "You won't come because, we haven't got a Lord." Who could it be I wonder?

I could not see Paris, for the old friends and dinners which would take no denial: scarcely any theatres and fun. I went to hear Sontag whom the polite world received with immense kind-

[41] Mrs. Procter. FitzGerald was troubled by similar misgivings. He wrote to Frederick Tennyson on April 17 of this year: "Thackeray is in such a great world that I am afraid of him; he gets tired of me: and we are content to regard each other at a distance" (*Letters and Literary Remains*, I, 295).

ness, but what I admired most was some of the girls of the Conservatoire singing just a few notes by way of a chorus to one of her songs. O how much fresher their voices were than hers! O how much better it is to be young than to be anything else, ever so good, or clever, or rich! Is this true or quite the reverse? When you are forty[42] please lock up the piano and never sing another note until you are sixty. It doesn't do to have a "beautiful voice, considering" a beautiful gown only it's tarnished, a beautiful mirror only it's cracked.

I went to see a charming comedy "Gabrielle" by Augier [43] of which the moral is quite nice and proper. Strange to say the husband is made the interesting character in the piece. These people have freaks of virtue sometimes and relish occasional morality as epicures sometimes eat roast leg of mutton, Then on the other hand I saw a play at the Vaudeville, where I think the morals and the petticoats were scantier than I ever knew them. How they did jest and leer and grin! if they were going to the guillotine tomorrow (and why not?) they would still pass the night in kissing and grinning and leering.

Mind I dont mean in the least to say that I'm more moral than they are — only more melancholy. This begins to look very much as if it were written for print and as if I should send it down before posting, to my clerk to copy it. But I didn't see anything else but the theatres and a few dinner parties when I was at Paris. I've no information or sound practical views. The only books I read are novels and trash.

What should a man talk about who lives upon tarts and puffs, but puffs and tarts? Is it pleasant at the country chez vous? For a settler very likely — you paint your life in grey, and sing it to a humdrum tune, sweet low and not unpleasant. But after all I suppose people go to sleep after dinner over their books. I do when I want to pass the evening virtuously.

[42] Mrs. Sartoris was born in 1814.
[43] The first of the notable comedies of Émile Augier (1820–1889). Though its *première* had taken place in 1849, it was still being shown at the Théâtre de la République.

Last night I went to dinner and afterwards to tea and afterwards to the Club to write the last page of Pendennis and afterwards to smoke a cigar. At 11 1/2 at night when I was going to work I left old Poodle Byng[44] who had been at the other 2 places trotting off to a 3ᵈ What a queer routine. What a different one from yours! — And here at the end of the paper I discover that I've had nothing to say: but thank you and Good bye. I am Always sincerely your[s] Dear Mrs. Sartoris

W. M. Thackeray.

693.                 TO MRS. BROOKFIELD
                    29 MARCH 1850 [45]

Published in part, *Collection of Letters*, pp. 141–142.

Good Friday —

Yesterday evening in the bitter blast of the breeze of March a cavalier whose fingers were so numbed that he scarce could hold the rein of his good steed might have been perceived at a door in Portman Street in converse with a footman in dark green livery and whose buttons bore the cognizance of the well-known house of Brookfield.[46] Clouded with care and anxiey at first, the horsemans countenance (a stalwart and grey-haired man he was by our lady and his face bore the marks of wounds received doubtless in early encounters) presently assumed a more cheerful aspect when he heard from the curly-pated servitor whom he interrogated, that his Ladys health was better. 'Gramercy he of the steed exclaimed 'so

---

[44] Frederick Gerald Byng (1784–1871), fifth son of the fifth Viscount Torrington, one of the last surviving Regency dandies. Lady Bath and Georgiana, Duchess of Devonshire, had named him "Poodle" because of his thick, curly hair. See Lewis Melville's *The Beaux of the Regency*, 2 vols. (London, 1908), II, 175–179.

[45] Good Friday fell on March 29 in 1850. In 1851, the only other year in which this letter could conceivably have been written, Good Friday came on April 18.

[46] The whole of this paragraph, it will be noted, is written in the style of "Barbazure" (*Works*, VI, 501–509), Thackeray's parody of the fiction of G. P. R. James.

that she mends I am happy, happier still when I may behold her.'
Carry my duty, Fellow to thy mistress's attendant and tell her
that Sir Titmarsh hath been at her gate' — It closed upon him. The
horseman turned his charger's head homewards and soon was lost
to view in the now lonely Park.

I should be glad to hear that you are still better if you please
Mum this morning, and a message even to that effect will please
me. I've been to Church already with the young ones: had a
fine ride in the country yesterday: am going to work directly this
note goes off and am exceedingly well and jolly in health. I think
this is all my news: I cant go to dine with the lady opposite[47]
having one or two here. La Granja[48] would be a very pleasant
house for his reverence — to bait[49] at when he is on visitation in
Hampshire and I'll hear more about the schoolmistress before
many days are out. *This* lady when she is ill receives her friends
in her bed-room. I was introduced to that chamber of delight on
Wednesday night. I had a little note from Totty last night and
grieve to hear that dear kind little F is still so unwell. Mrs
Elliot has been very bad but is mending. I dined there last night.
She was on the sofa and I thought about her kind face coming into
me alongside of another kind face) when I was ill. What numbers
of good folks there are in the world. F. Elliot would do anything
I believe to help me to a place: old Miss Berry is very kind too
nothing can be kinder. But I will go back to my poetry for Punch[50]
such as it is and say Gby to my dear lady and Miss Brookfield
and Mr

## W M T.

[47] Thackeray's letter is written on the third and fourth pages of the following note, to which the hand points:
   "Will you dine with us a small dinner in all ways at 1/4 8 tomorrow —
          Yrs truly
              Har. Ashburton
   Thursday —
   I want you to help me about a School mistress thro' Mr Brookfield
   whom I don't know personally."
[48] The Grange at Alresford in Hampshire, the Ashburtons' country seat.
[49] Thackeray wrote *bate*.
[50] These verses were apparently not finished.

694. TO MRS. FANSHAWE
MARCH? 1850 [51]

Published in part by Frances Brookfield, "William Makepeace Thackeray and his Friends," *Munsey's Magazine*, December, 1911, p. 368.

### Anecdote.

Poor Thackeray in his life time had a great regard (indeed he was rather a general admirer of the sex) for the wife of an esteemed clergyman the Rev$^d$ C. Fanshawe afterwards Bishop of Bundlecund: Before his elevation to the episcopate M$^r$ F lived in humble though genteel apartments near P—rtm—n Square — and the Author of Vanity Fair calling one day and finding M$^{rs}$ F. too unwell to receive his visit, asked for pen ink & paper & dashed off the following

### Impromptu.

Ive come for the twentieth time I think to ask to know how be you, and consider it very hard indeed that Im not allowed to see you — And as I cant I should like to sit on the stair case landing near you, and vith my vicked jokes and vit to enliven you and cheer you — But then as you have lost your woice you know I couldnt hear you — And as you and Totty have your night caps on, to see you would distress you: and to enter into a lady's bed-room! Good lor I mustn't press you! So I send you my love, my kind little F, and heartily pray God bless you.

There is nothing in the lines to give any indication of the talent w$^h$ this to us overrated writer was said to possess: but they at least show that in the midst of all his irregularities eccentricities, nay crimes his heart was not altogether devoid of kind feeling at this period of his career.

Its melancholy end is well known. Who would have thought in 1850 that this man whom the great world received and who had

---

[51] This letter appears to have been written while Mrs. Fanshawe was in London helping Mrs. Brookfield to convalesce after the birth of Magdalene.

many friends and well-wishers should perish a convict in Norfolk Islands?

Hogson's Anecdotes of the Press, & the Literary
Men of the 19th Century.

695.          TO JOHN FORSTER
          3 APRIL 1850

Hitherto unpublished.

Kensington April 3. 1850

My dear Monsieur I shall come with great pleasure but like an Ass I burned the note and forgot the hour.

Yours ever

W M Thackeray

P.S You can't write as small as this.[52]  I can write much smaller.

P.S. 2 I come though I think it will be a bore: but the old fellow was uncommonly kind to me when I was a boy and I like him very much. And I think it is exceedingly good and kind-hearted of you to ask him and that you ought to be supported and that you get more benevolent every day. and that it was very kind of your mother to wait for a day before she gave you birth. And I wish you many happy returns of your birthday,[53] Dickens of his marriage-day, & both of you of the day previous.

696.     TO THE REV. WILLIAM BROOKFIELD
          APRIL? 1850 [54]

Address: Rev[d] W. H. Brookfield. Published in *Collection of Letters*, pp. 58–59.

My dear Vew

I wish you would go & call on Lady Ashburton. Twice Ashburton has told me that she wants to make your acquaintance

[52] The whole of this note is written in Thackeray's minute hand.
[53] Forster was born and Dickens was married on April 2.
[54] Thackeray probably wrote this note not long after his letter of March 29,

and twice remarked that it w^d be but an act of politeness in you
to call on a lady in distress who wants your services. Both times
I have said you were uncommonly proud & shy and last night told
him he'd best call on you: w^h he said he should hasten to do. But
surely you might stretch a leg over the barrier when theres a lady
actually beckoning to you to come over & such an uncommonly good
dinner laid on the other side. There was just a vacant place yesterday as you might ave ad: and such a company of jolly dogs! Con:
S^t Davids⁵⁵ Harry Hallam, (S^r) & ever so many more of our set.
Do go if you can, and believe me to be     Yours

A. Pendennis. Major H. P.

697.          TO MRS. BROOKFIELD
              26–30 APRIL 1850

Published in part, *Collection of Letters*, pp. 97–98 and 115–117.

I was too tired to talk to Madam when I sent away the packet of
MS ⁵⁶ to day: I'm not much better now, only using her as a passe-
temps at a Club 1/2 an hour before dinner. That's the way we
use women. Well, I was rather pleased with the MS I sent you
to day. It seems to me to be good comedy. My mother would have
acted in just such a way if I had run away with a naughty woman
— that is I hope she would — though praps she is prouder than I
am myself. I read over the first part of Pen to day — all the
Emily Costigan part and liked it, I'm glad to say: but am shocked
to think that I had forgotten and read it almost as a new book —
I remembered allusions w^h called back recollections of particular

in which he suggests that it would be to Brookfield's advantage to know the
Ashburtons. Brookfield presumably made their acquaintance some time before
October 15, when he paid the first of his many visits to the Grange (*Mrs.
Brookfield*, II, 322–323).
  ⁵⁵ Connop Thirlwall (1797–1875), Bishop of St. Davids, author of *A History of Greece* (1835–1844).
  ⁵⁶ Number XVI of Pendennis, chapters 48 to 51.

states of mind. The first part of that book was written after Clevedon in '48 [57] — que de souffrances! I'm quiet now, Madam, and
you dear Sister I pray God nightly & daily for you & your husband
and your child — May all 3 of you be happy. And there's no reason
why you shouldn't, Please God — You & all the little ones to
come. — I should like to go & shake hands with poor old ⟨. . .⟩[58]
but he flies from me. What a wholesome thing, fierce mental occupation is — better than dissipation to take thoughts out of one —
only one cant always fix the mind down and other thoughts will
bother it. Yesterday I sate for 6 hours & could do no work. I
wasn't sentimentalizing but I couldnt get the pen to go: and at
4 rode out into the country and saw whom do you think? O lâche,
coward, sneak & traitor — that pretty M^rs Merivale[59] I wrote you
about — She is very pretty and very well: but it wont do — I am
an extinct crater and my volcano is poked out. The night before
in the same way restless and wandering à l'aventure (admire my
constant use of French terms) I went to M^rs Prinseps and saw
Virginia then to Miss Berrys and talked to L^d Lansdowne who was
very jolly & kind and hasn't recognized the story: [60] then to Lady
Ashburton, where were Jocelyns [61] just come back from Paris my
lady in the prettiest wreath — We talked about the Gorham Controversy[62] I think and when the Jos's were gone, about John Mill's

[57] See above, No. 517.
[58] This name has been irrecoverably overscored by Mrs. Brookfield.
[59] The wife (d. 1881) of Herman Merivale (1806–1874), a barrister and
writer who was permanent Under-Secretary of State for the Colonies from
1848 to 1860 and permanent Under-Secretary for India from 1860 till his
death. The Merivales and their children were long among Thackeray's closest
friends.
[60] I cannot explain this allusion.
[61] Robert, styled Viscount Jocelyn (1816–1854), oldest son of the third
Earl of Roden, and his wife, the former Lady Frances Cowper (d. 1880).
[62] George Cornelius Gorham (1787–1857) was in November, 1847, presented with the vicarage of Brampford Speke near Exeter. The Bishop of
Exeter, who examined him in the following December and March, found his
views on baptismal regeneration unorthodox and refused to institute him.
Gorham took the case to court, and after a series of actions a verdict in his
favor was at last rendered on June 11, 1850. The religious world was keenly
interested in the Gorham dispute throughout its development.

noble article in the Westminster Review[63] — an article w.ʰ you mustnt read because it will shock your dear convictions but wherein as it seems to me a great soul speaks great truths. It is time to begin speaking truth I think — Lady Ashburton says not — Our Lord spoke it and was killed for it: and Stephen and Paul who slew Stephen. We shuffle, and compromise, & have Gorham controversies, and say let things go on smoothly, and Jock Campbell writes to ye Moʳ Superior and Milman makes elegant after-dinner speeches at the Mansion House — Humbugs all — I am become very stupid and rabid — Dinner time is come — Such a good dinner truth be hanged let us go to Portland Place.[64]

The good dinner on Friday was very pleasant and quiet with old acquaintances: the ladies MP's wives, took me aside and asked confidentially about the fashionable world, in w.ʰ it is supposed, I believe, that I live entirely now; and the wonder is that people don't hate me more than they do, I tried to explain that I was still a man, and that among the ladies of fashion a lady could but be a lady and no better nor no wusser. God bless you Are there any better ladies than you and Pincushion?[65] Anny has found out that quality in the 2 of you with her generous instinct, I had a delightful morning with her on Sunday, when she read me the Deserted Village and we talked about it. I couldn't have talked with her so with anybody else (except perhaps U) in the room. Saturday what did I do? I went to Punch and afterwards to the play to see a piece of the Lady of Lyons performed by that butcher of a Mʳ Anderson.[66] Before that to the Water Colour Society w.ʰ

[63] "The Church of England" (*Westminster Review*, April, 1850, pp. 165–218), an appeal for church reform in which the thesis is maintained that "what alone the Church cares to teach has ceased to be the real religion of this nation" (p. 217). The article was written, not by Mill, but by James Martineau, and is reprinted in his *Essays, Reviews, and Addresses*, 4 vols. (London, 1890–1891), II, 47–118.

[64] No doubt to the home of Thackeray's friend Robert Hollond, 63 Portland Place (*Royal Blue Book*, 1851).

[65] Mrs. Fanshawe, so called because of her small stature.

[66] James Robertson Anderson (1811–1895), manager of Drury Lane from 1849 to 1851, appeared as Claude Melnotte in Bulwer-Lytton's *The Lady of Lyons* on Saturday, April 27, 1850 (*Times*).

was chock full of bishops and other big wigs, & among them Sir Robert Peel elaborately gracious — conversation with Lady Peel — about 2000 people looking on — bows grins grimaces on both sides followed by an invitation to dinner next Saturday. The next person I shook hands with after Sir R Peel — was, whom do you think? M^rs Rhodes[67] of the Back Kitchen. I thought of you that very instant, & to think of you dear lady is to bless you, & I'm thinking of you now in bed, after coming home from the Berrys where was a great assembly of polite persons. Lady Morley whom you love, we laughed and cracked away so that it would have made you angry — my dear Elliot & Perry, Lord Lansdowne, Carlisle[68] ever so many more — O! Stop! after Water Colour on Saturday M^r Hallam asked me to dinner. I felt for poor Harry. I accepted. He & Lord Mahon[69] & Miss Julia went & admired a picture, O such a spoony picture! It inwardly pleased me to see the great historians drivelling so.

Sunday went to Hampstead with the infants who dined at the Crowes I went to Higgins very pleasant little party sorry his Reverence wouldnt come.

And this w^h is I believe Monday I was alarmed at not getting my MS back, I drew woodblocks all day; rode in the Park for 3 hours without calling or visiting anywhere came home to dinner & went out to the Berrys and am back again at 12 to say G B Y.

Tuesday. Your Sundays letter only came in this morning. I am sorry to see my dear lady writes tristely, but I would rather you would write sorrowfully if you feel so than sham gaiety or light-heartedness. What's the good of a brother to you if you can't tell

[67] The widow of William Rhodes, who succeeded her husband as the proprietor of the Cider Cellar, a public house at 20 Maiden Lane, Covent Garden. This tavern figures in chapter 30 of *Pendennis* as the "Back Kitchen." See above, No. 515.

[68] George William Frederick Howard (1802–1864), seventh Earl of Carlisle, a Whig statesman and patron of letters.

[69] Philip-Henry Stanhope (1805–1875), styled Lord Mahon, later (1855) fifth Earl Stanhope, author of a *History of England from the Peace of Utrecht to the Peace of Versailles* (1836–1858), a *History of England, comprising the Reign of Queen Anne until the Peace of Utrecht* (1870), and many other historical works.

him things? If I am dismal dont I give you the benefit of the dumps? Ah I should like to be with you for an hour or two, and see if you're changed and oldened in this immense time that you have been away. But business and pleasure (likewise expediency & the not being asked) keep me here nailed. I have an awful week of festivities before me. To day Shakspeare's birthday at the Garrick Club, dinner and speech — lunch Madame Lionel Rothschild     ball Lady Waldegrave [70]     She gives the finest balls in London & I've never seen one yet — tomorrow of 5 invitations to dinner the first is M<sup>r</sup> Marshall — The D of Devonshire's Hevening party Lady Emily Dundas's[71] ditto — Thursday Sir Anthony Rothschild — Friday the domestic affections, Saturday Sir Robert Peel, Sunday Lord Lansdowne — Isn't it curious to think (it was striking my great mind yesterday as Anny was sorting the cards in the chimney glass) that there are people who would give their ears or half their income to go to these fine places. I was riding with an old Bailey Barrister yesterday in the park and his pretty wife (On les aime jolies Madame) — he apologized for knowing people who lived in Brunswick Square, and thought to prove his gentility by calling it 'that demmed place'. I've only known 1/2 a dozen ⟨. . .⟩ [72]

[70] The former Sarah Whitear (d. 1873), second wife of the eighth Earl Waldegrave.

[71] The wife of Rear-Admiral Sir James Whitley Deans Dundas (1785–1862), later (1855) G. C. B.

[72] The rest of this letter has not been preserved.

698.                        TO BENJAMIN LUMLEY
                               13 MAY 1850

Facsimile of several sentences in Lawrence B. Phillips's *Autographic Album*
(London, 1866), p. 91.

                                Kensington. Monday 13 May.
My dear Lumley,

   I was prevented from coming to pay you my visit yesterday, for
my groom had taken French leave, and I had nobody to drive me
to & from the Chancellors.[74] And I wanted to see you very much
indeed, to beg & pray you to ask me to meet Madame Sontag, I
met her & M de Rossi at Lady Molesworth's at dinner and thought
her delightful: and I want to know where the Countess Rossi
lives and to cultivate her acquaintance and to meet her wherever
I can. The worst of it is that I get entangled in the folds of the
dinner-cloth every night, and can't get to the Opera to hear her.
         Believe me my respected and complimentary friend
                            Always yours
                            W M Thackeray


699.                         TO MRS. BAYNE
                               15 MAY 1850 [75]


*Address:* M\ʳˢ Bayne | 40 York Terrace | Regent's Park. *Postmark:* MY 16
1850. Hitherto unpublished.

                          Kensington.   Wednesday.
My dear Mʳˢ Bayne

   I had engaged myself to Eton for the 4 of June, but all engagements must give way before such a letter as yours, and I shall

   [74] No doubt the Earl of Carlisle, who the previous March had succeeded
Lord Campbell as Chancellor of the Duchy of Lancaster in Lord John Russell's
ministry. Thackeray does not appear to have known Lord Cottenham, the
Lord Chancellor.
   [75] This note was written on Wednesday, May 15.

gladly be one of your first party. You know that your house has a high character to keep up and that your predecessor was and is a famous banqueteer.[76] A noble emulation I know will distinguish you and I look forward with great anxiety to the day of trial. It is very kind of you to ask me, and forgive my remissness in not calling but you know that my avocations are many, and that even if I don't call I am

Most truly yours

W M Thackeray

700.      TO MRS. FANSHAWE

MAY 1850

Hitherto unpublished.

My dear M^rs

My darlings shall set off from Waterloo Station by the 1 o'clock train tomorrow DV. And they will bring nobody with them, nor no maid nor nothink.

And there's no use in meeting them even, for Anny will be instructed to call a coach and say to the Driver Driver drive to 3 West Marlands.

And I am yours thankfully & Fanshawe's very much obliged

W M T.

701.      TO ANNE THACKERAY

22? MAY 1850 [77]

Hitherto unpublished.

My dearest Nan I am so busy with my work and so tired of writing that I can only write you a line or two. I'm delighted that

[76] Thackeray's friend John Kenyon had formerly lived at 40 York Terrace (*Post Office London Directory*, 1847).

[77] This is the first of three letters from Thackeray to his daughters, who were visiting the Fanshawes in Southampton. It was written shortly before

you are so happy and that you enjoy yourself & that your friends are so kind to you. The way to have friends is to like people yourself you see; and I hope you will have and keep a plenty.

I have been at home 3 whole days think of that not going out at least until near 8 o'clock to dinner: so that my work[78] is pretty well advanced and will be done by Sunday evᵍ I trust. Then comes printing & proof correcting & so forth, and by Thursday I hope to see you young folks again and bring you back. I must dine with the Chief Baron on the 31 May. Or can Mʳˢ F afford to keep you till Saturday when I wᵈ come down and we would take a small trip to the I of Wight or somewhere? Please Mʳˢ F:write me a word on this subject.

Miss Trulock has had a good offer of 100 a year and Im afraid must leave us — there will be the business to do over again, the same perplexities botherations uncertainties Why dont you get a little older and do without a governess? You will some day when you'll spell excursion with an S not a T.

Don't make doggrel verses and spell badly for fun. There should be a lurking prettiness in all buffoonery even, and it requires an art wʰ you dont know yet to make *good* bad verses — to make bad ones is dull work.

And don't scribble faces at the bottom of your letters to ladies — They shouldn't be done unless they are clever — they are not respectful or ladylike else do you understand? I like you to make jokes to me because I can afford to tell you whether they are bad or good or to scold you as now: but Mʳˢ Brookfield is too kind to do so: and when you write to her or to any other lady you should write your very best — I dont mean be affected and use fine words, but be careful grateful and ladylike.[79]

---

Sunday, May 26, most probably Wednesday, May 22, for operas with ballets were given at both Her Majesty's and the Royal Italian Opera House on Tuesday, and there was no performance at either theatre on Monday or Wednesday (*Times*).

[78] Number XVII of *Pendennis* for June, chapters 52 to 54.

[79] Lady Ritchie has written at the bottom of the last page of the original: "I never write an untidy letter but I think of this one — alas it has not yet made me into a tidy woman."

I did not dine till 9 o'clock last night and went to the Opera afterwards but the ballet bored me and I came away pretty soon. I think that's all I know. And so God bless you and my dearest Minikin: and our friends who receive you so affectionately, & farewell

W M T.

702.   TO ANNE AND HARRIET THACKERAY
26 MAY 1850 [80]

Published in *Thackeray and his Daughter*, pp. 33 and 36.

My dearest Fattyminny  As I have not written a single word this day I think I may have a five minutes' talk to your ladyships. You went to S$^t$ Mary's church I suppose. I recollect it in the year 1817 when I was a miserable little beggar, at school at the Polygon under an odious little blackguard who used to starve and cane us.[81] Times are changed since then and you young women have not had much starving or scolding in the course of your easy lives. Whilst you have been at Church I have at least been doing no manner of work: for I have been at Richmond all day dawdling in the sun under a tree, or making sketches for the Miss Berrys with my goold pen. The ease and tranquillity were very refreshing after the hard work of the past 4 or 5 days. I looked about to see if there were tempting looking lodgings anywhere about: But the prices are very heavy for good rooms, and if Miss Trulock is going away what the deuce are we to do? — A plague upon such misadventures. As I think over matters just now, I shant be able to go to the I of Wight with you, and I dont see why you shouldn't travel back as safely as you went. So you must please to write and say by what train you'll come away on Thursday, and the carriage and your Papa, or else James his Vice-regent upon earth, shall be at Waterloo Station to meet you.

I am going out of town tomorrow evening to stay over Wed-

[80] This letter was written on the first Sunday after May 22.
[81] See above, No. 2.

nesday, & to return on Thursday — Shall I get a new Governess or shall I send you to school after the midsummer holy days. I do believe the latter would be the best plan — and then you'd learn something. As it is — ballottées from one Governess to another now at London & next at Aix la Chapelle, your young days pass away without any larning — and in fine I'm in a great puzzle concerning you. That is all I have to say I think. It isn't very amusing or very wise is it?

Give my love to your Aunt Fanshawe and a kiss to Totty: and remember young ladies that I'm always your affectionate father.

W M T.

703.          TO JOHN FORSTER
              30 MAY 1850

Hitherto unpublished. *Endorsed:* May 30/50.

                                        Thursday

My dear F. I'm your[s] at 1/2 past 6 and ever after

                              W M T.

I didnt answer yesterday being outatown

704.     TO ANNE AND HARRIET THACKERAY
              3–5 JUNE 1850 [82]

Hitherto unpublished.

My dearest young ones   You seem to be very happy at Southampton and enjoying your holyday famously. Dont you feel very grateful to the kind friends and the new acquaintances who are giving you so much pleasure? I do, and Anny will please to thank Dʳ W. Bullar very sincerely for me, for his kindness and attentions and the time he has bestowed on you. When you come back to London, we'll go to the British museum some day, and read an account of Romsey Abbey in Dugdale's Monasticon [83] or elsewhere,

[82] The date of this letter is set by Thackeray's reference to Mrs. Bayne's dinner on June 4, the first that she gave at 40 Oxford Terrace. See above, No. 699.

[83] The *Monasticon Anglicanum* (1655–1673) of Sir William Dugdale (1605–1686) and Roger Dodsworth (1585–1654).

and see who founded it and of what order the nun was whose red braids you saw so many hundred years after her soul had gone to its account and her brains and her body were eaten up by the worms, or turned into grass and daisies w^h the convent cows munched up perhaps or the convent-gardener mowed down. The cows became beef and passed away as meat for the poor at the convent gate: and the convent gardener was mowed down too at his turn; and who would have thought that the poor carroty hair grew on the nun's scalp for you and me to moralize about five hundred years after Sister Redhead was laid in her omnibus-box? Over the round Saxon arches with cumbrous ornaments and hideous barbaric carving, the Norman builders sprung their graceful shafts and slim pointed arches: Harry VIII came and gutted the nun's treasure boxes and seized their plate and their pyxes and their sacred trinkets and relics and pretty fond superstitious gimcracks, and turned them and their worship out of doors: and the Honorable and Reverend Gerard Noel [84] is parson at Romsey I believe and son of the late Earl of Gainsborough. You see there's a time for the round arch and the pointed arch and the Reverend Gerards pulpit and at each period according to the best of their power & belief the various occupants of the place worship Our Father in Heaven: and die off and are replaced by men of other ages and modifications of opinion. The truth is in all let us hope but the *whole* truth? The Whole Truth is what we worship and bow down to, and dont know

I wrote so far two days ago. It wasn't very amusing was it Miss Minny? and since then I have hardly been at home except to sleep and as busy at breakfast-parties visits dinner-parties and so forth as if they were the business of life, and so they are with some people.

Miss Trulock is not going away. She has agreed to remain with us, and so your plan for going to school at Southampton young ladies is knocked on the head. It never could have taken place though I should have liked it very much, and that you should have

---

[84] The Rev. Gerard Thomas Noel (1782–1851), second son of Sir Gerard Noel-Noel, had been Vicar of Romsey since 1840. His older brother, Charles Noel, was created Earl of Gainsborough in 1841, and Gerard was henceforth permitted to use the courtesy prefix "Honourable." In the same year he married Susan Kennaway (d. 1890), daughter of the Devon baronet whom Thackeray had known as a boy.

the watchfulness and affection of such a dear schoolmistress. But there were reasons against the plan, w<sup>h</sup> I wont trouble your lady-ships with. If there's a nice country lodging near Southampton, perhaps we might spend a part of the autumn there. But you have got to see Granny at Aix la Chapelle most likely: at least if she goes there. I may take you there possibly and leave you and make a little tour by myself. When does M<sup>rs</sup> F. go on her visiting? and when are you coming back? I dont want to hurry you: but you mustn't inconvenience those kind friends

The garden has been raked the weeds pulled out and the lawn mown. Who do you think did it? James the Viceregent: and with what? He mowed it with a dessert knife! I have been into the country 3 times, to Richmond, to Croydon, to Weybridge where I passed all last Sunday very happily seeing some of the most pleasant if not quite the most beautiful landscapes in the world.

Yesterday I went to breakfast with the Bishop of Oxford [85] to see the hippopotamus,[86] to Hampstead, and to dinner afterwards with M<sup>rs</sup> Bayne who has taken a nice new house: and wishes much for the company of you young ladies. Miss Brookfield has been waksynated and her Mamma from her. I have been out to breakfast this morn-ing and am going to 3 evening parties to night after dinner: at the houses of people who would be very much offended if I didn't go to them. My idle days are almost as hard as my busy days you see.

God bless you my dear women, and all who are kind to you.

W M T.

[85] Samuel Wilberforce (1805–1873), Bishop of Oxford from 1845 to 1869 and Bishop of Winchester from 1869 till his death. Thackeray had met this able and agreeable prelate at a dinner given by William Bingham Baring, later Lord Ashburton, March 23, 1848, Emerson being the guest of honor (A. R. Ashwell and R. G. Wilberforce, *The Life of the Right Reverend Samuel Wilberforce, D. D.*, 3 vols., London, 1880–1882, II, 9), and the two men saw each other often thenceforth in the London world. Cf. Ralph Leslie Rusk, ed., *The Letters of Ralph Waldo Emerson*, 6 vols., New York, 1939, IV, 43.

[86] The hippopotamus newly imported for the Zoological Gardens was a sensation of the London season in 1850. *Punch* devoted even more attention to it than to Lord Palmerston, the magazine's other *bête noir*.

705.        TO RICHARD MONCKTON MILNES
              11 JUNE 1850 [87]

My text is taken from Reid's *Life of Milnes*, I, 429.

13, Young St. Tuesday.

My dear Milnes, — Miss Brontë dines here tomorrow at 7.[88]
If you are by any wonder disengaged, do come to

Yours truly,

W. M. Thackeray.

[87] "Mr Thackeray. . . . made a morning-call and sat above two hours —,"
Charlotte Brontë writes from the Smiths' home at 76 Gloucester Terrace on
Wednesday, June 12, 1850, "Mr Smith only was in the room the whole
time. He described it afterwards as a queer scene; and I suppose it was. The
giant sat before me — I was moved to speak to him of some of his shortcomings
(literary of course) one by one the faults came into my mind and one by one
I brought them out and sought some explanation or defence — He did defend
himself like a great Turk and heathen — that is to say, the excuses were often
worse than the crime itself. The matter ended in decent amity — if all be
well I am to dine at his house this evening." (Wise and Symington, *The
Brontës*, III, 117–118)

[88] Lady Ritchie has left an inimitable account of this unhappy occasion:
"One of the most notable persons who ever came into our old bow-windowed
drawing-room in Young Street is a guest never to be forgotten by me, a tiny,
delicate, little person, whose small hand nevertheless grasped a mighty lever
which set all the literary world of that day vibrating. I can still see the scene
quite plainly! — the hot summer evening, the open windows, the carriage
driving to the door as we all sat silent and expectant; my father, who rarely
waited, waiting with us; our governess and my sister and I all in a row, and
prepared for the great event. We saw the carriage stop, and out of it sprang
the active, well-knit figure of young Mr. George Smith, who was bringing
Miss Brontë to see our father. My father, who had been walking up and
down the room, goes out into the hall to meet his guests, and then, after a
moment's delay the door opens wide, and the two gentlemen come in, leading
a tiny, delicate, serious, little lady, pale, with fair straight hair, and steady
eyes. She may be a little over thirty; she is dressed in a little *barège* dress
with a pattern of faint green moss. She enters in mittens, in silence. in seriousness; our hearts are beating with wild excitement. . . . The moment is
so breathless that dinner comes as a relief to the solemnity of the occasion,
and we all smile as my father stoops to offer his arm; for, genius though she
may be, Miss Brontë can barely reach his elbow. My own personal impressions
are that she is somewhat grave and stern, specially to forward little girls who
wish to chatter; Mr. George Smith has since told me how she afterwards re-

[For a fragment of a letter to Mrs. Brookfield, June, 1850? see letter 14, Appendix XXVI.]

---

marked upon my father's wonderful forbearance and gentleness with our un-called-for incursions into the conversation. She sat gazing at him with kindling eyes of interest, lighting up with a sort of illumination every now and then as she answered him. I can see her bending forward over the table, not eating, but listening to what he said as he carved the dish before him."

Among the guests at the reception that followed were Mrs. Brookfield, the Carlyles, Mrs. Procter and her daughter, Mrs. Elliot, and Miss Perry; Milnes was invited, Lady Ritchie notes, but did not come. "It was a gloomy and a silent evening. Every one waited for the brilliant conversation which never began at all. Miss Brontë retired to the sofa in the study, and murmured a low word now and then to our kind governess, Miss Truelock. The room looked very dark, the lamp began to smoke a little, the conversation grew dimmer and more dim, the ladies sat round still expectant, my father was too much perturbed by the gloom and the silence to be able to cope with it at all. Mrs. Brookfield, who was in the doorway by the study, near the corner in which Miss Brontë was sitting, leant forward with a little commonplace, since brilliance was not to be the order of the evening. 'Do you like London, Miss Brontë?' she said; another silence, a pause, then Miss Brontë answers, 'Yes and No' very gravely. . . . My sister and I were much too young to be bored in those days; alarmed, impressed we might be, but not yet bored. A party was a party, a lioness was a lioness; and — shall I confess it? — at that time an extra dish of biscuits was enough to mark the evening. We felt all the importance of the occasion; tea spread in the dining-room, ladies in the drawing-room; we roamed about inconveniently, no doubt, and excitedly, and in one of my excursions crossing the hall, after Miss Brontë had left I was surprised to see my father opening the front door with his hat on. He put his fingers to his lips, walked out into the darkness, and shut the door quietly behind him. When I went back to the drawing-room again, the ladies asked me where he was. I vaguely answered that I thought he was coming back. I was puzzled at the time, nor was it all made clear to me till long years afterwards, when one day Mrs. Procter asked me if I knew what had happened. . . . how finally, after the departure of the more important guests, overwhelmed by the situation, my father had quietly left the room, left the house, and gone off to his club." (*Chapters*, pp. 60–65)

If Miss Brontë was silent on this occasion, she was not unobservant. "One of Mr. Thackeray's guests was Miss Adelaide Procter," writes George Smith, "and those who remember that lady's charming personality will not be sur-prised to learn that I was greatly attracted by her. During our drive home I was seated opposite to Miss Brontë, and I was startled by her leaning for-ward, putting her hands on my knees, and saying 'She would make you a very nice wife.' 'Whom do you mean?' I replied. 'Oh! you know whom I mean,' she said; and we relapsed into silence. Though I admired Miss Procter very much, it was not a case of love at first sight, as Miss Brontë supposed." (*George Smith, A Memoir*, pp. 98–99)

706.                        TO ?
                         JUNE 1850 [89]

Hitherto unpublished.

Madam    Miss Bronte's address is 76 Gloucester Terrace at
the back of Westbourne Terrace    Zoe's I dont know and I am
your obedient Serv.t W M Thackeray


707.   TO THE REV. ROBERT MONTGOMERY [90]
                    15 JUNE 1850

Address: Rev.d R. Montgomery | 51 Torrington Square. Postmark: JU 17
1850. Hitherto unpublished.

                              Kensington.   June 15.
My dear M.r Montgomery
    Thank you for the paper. I don't remember the word 'faint'
as applied to M.r Newman's sinner,[91] but the account you give of
the bearing and tendency of the discourse is very correct, and I for
one am very happy to have heard the preacher. A man who admits

[89] Charlotte Brontë stayed with George Smith and his mother at 76
Gloucester Terrace only in June, 1850. When she returned the following
year, her friends' house had been renumbered 112. (Huxley, The House of
Smith, Elder, p. 61; Royal Blue Book, 1851)
[90] Montgomery (1807–1855) long remained one of the most popular of
Early Victorian poets, despite Macaulay's celebrated attack on his verse in
The Edinburgh Review of April, 1830. From 1843 until his death he was
minister of Percy Chapel in the parish of St. Pancras. It should not be thought
that Thackeray had any sympathy with his theological views. When Richard
Bedingfield (Cassell's Magazine, II, 14) reported that he "had heard Robert
Montgomery in the pulpit, expressing himself on the subject of Adam's trans-
gression, saying, 'The squalling of an infant is an illustration of original sin,'
[Thackeray] observed, 'Did he say so? by Jove! He must be a beast! But
he is a clever fellow to have said it!'"
[91] Thackeray had evidently been to the eighth of a series of lectures given
by Newman at the Oratory Church, King William Street, Strand, beginning
on May 9. The passage under discussion, perhaps the most debated in all of
Newman's writings, follows: "Take a mere beggar-woman, lazy, ragged, and
filthy, and not over-scrupulous of truth — (I do not say she had arrived at

that a lousy lying beggarwoman who goes to confess and says her prayers is more likely of salvation than a good wise honest humble conscientious man earnestly trying to fulfil his duty: a man who glories in asserting that every scoundrel who has been executed at Rome goes straightway and secure with the sacerdotal passport to Heaven, while his denouncer very likely goes to the Devil ought *to be let go on.* The more he preaches in this way, the better for the Truth: the more he shows what the figure is under those fine copes and embroideries and behind all that chandlery and artificial flower-show, the better for the people who are now attracted by the splendour and the ceremonial and the sweet-chanted litanies and the charm of the orators rhetoric Put out the lights and lock up the incense pots     Stop the organ and take off the priests fine clothes — and when we come to M^r Newman's naked beau ideal, it seems to me we get at a creature so hideous degraded and despicable, that the public scorn will scout him out of the world again. And, as the priest himself in the pulpit or preaching box likes evidently a little mischief and to keep his congregation in a grin, I suppose we may enjoy a little fun on our part too, in thinking, while Newman makes such dismal admissions & lets such *ugly cats out of* the bag w^h he ought to keep close — how D^r Wiseman must be pleased — as he sits listening by Newman is a child of the Church but he is an *Enfant Terrible* — and tells things w^h his Mamma would best like kept quiet

Always faithfully yours

W M Thackeray

---

perfection) — but if she is chaste, and sober, and cheerful, and goes to her religious duties (and I am supposing not at all an impossible case), she will, in the eyes of the Church, have a prospect of heaven, which is quite closed and refused to the State's pattern-man, the just, the upright, the generous, the honourable, the conscientious, if he be all this, not from a supernatural power — (I do not determine whether this is likely to be the fact, but I am contrasting views and principles) — not from a supernatural power, but from mere natural virtue" (*Certain Difficulties Felt by Anglicans in Catholic Teaching Considered*, 2 vols., London, 1918–1920, I, 249–250).

We learn from Father Ignatius Ryder of the Oratory that Newman "was fond of Thackeray, reading faithfully everything that he wrote down to the last unfinished work," and a letter of December 28, 1850, testifies that Thack-

708.                    TO MRS. STRUTT
                        21 JUNE 1850 ?

Hitherto unpublished.

Kensington.  June 21.

Dear Mʳˢ Strutt

On Friday I leave town and its fleshpots, and fly away to the country somewhere; so that I can't have the pleasure of dining with you on the 2ᵈ I'm going, is it to Switzerland or to the sea side in Devonshire?  That is not clear: but first to Paris to resume possession of my family.

Yours always dear Mʳˢ Strutt

W M Thackeray.

709.              TO MRS. BROOKFIELD
                  6 JULY 1850 ⁹²

Facsimile published in *Collection of Letters*, between pp. 110 and 111.

Dieppe
Hotel Morgan

For once there is some good in being in France, dear lady, for I can write you a line on a Saturday night & know that it will travel through Sunday and reach you some time the next day.  As yet the journey hasn't done me any good, on the contry stirred up my inward man and made me ill — I was in bed the greater part of yesterday & to day and when I went to look at the town and sea wʰ are very pretty only saw them with such bilious eyes as a man deserves who dines out every day of his life.  Why didn't I accept your invitation on Wednesday wasn't it Wednesday? — it seems to me

eray's comparison of his career with that of his brother Francis in chapter 61 of *Pendennis* did not escape his attention (Wilfrid Ward, *The Life of John Henry Cardinal Newman*, 2 vols., London, 1912, II, 355, and I, 625). For the letter that he wrote on Thackeray's death, see *Memoranda*, Mary Holmes.

⁹² Thackeray left Dieppe on Thursday, July 11 (see App. XXVI, July 11, 1850).  This letter was written the previous Saturday.

about 2 years since Wednesday — I thought I'd been to see you in
the day, that Im always made kindly welcome that Id no business to
come, and so instead went to the Ragg & Famish, where without
exceeding I had exactly 4 times as much wine as was good for me and
woke sick and ill and have been ill & sick ever since — here better —
please the pigs — for I took a delightful drive into the Country, &
saw a beautiful old Church and a charming landscape and an ancient
castle w^h interested me only a very little (You may pass over the
rest of this sentence and page if you please for I warn you that my
intention is to ménager you a surprise on the other side of the page
and all this is mere filling in as I have to do with my blocks in
Pendennis sometimes) Well I hire a gig and horse to drive me &
who do you think was my driver?

(I've drawn it shockingly ill though I took the gold pen — but
there was my Coachwoman a very lively pretty girl whose name
was Angelina Henrion and who told me she was heiress of fifteen

horses and six carriages w^h her Papa kept. As we were driving to
Arques we met one of the carriages and Angelina cried out Violà
Papa — and I thought Papa looked a little queer at seeing his
daughter drive a gentleman of forty. But she amused me with her
artless prattle, and Papa did not know that I was suffering from
something not at all unlike Cholera w^h made some of my grimaces
to Angelina ghastly to look at. However the drive did me good &
the beautiful air and scene and Angelina if you like. There came
to see me a lady before Angelina's arrival
you must [k]now, I found an elderly female
waiting in the Hotel passage who I instantly
knew to be the wife of the British clergyman of the place — an honest brandy and
water divine whom I recognized at once
(without having ever seen before) and whose
acquaintance I made on the packet. I shall
go to his Church tomorrow, and if he is free
to dine out of a Sunday, will fill his old skin
with strong drink. The continental parson
is a sort you don't know. Ah Mum! hes very different to the white
chokers of S^t James or Saint Margarets or Saint Montgomery's![93]
What a deal that woman has had to suffer what insults from
butchers and lodging house keepers whom his Reverence couldnt
pay. What hats have gone round for him — what struggles to be
respectable she has kept up since the day five & twenty years ago
when that croaking old woman was a pretty fresh young lass! —
Dont you see this is getting like a book? And am I not going to
be able to write naturally even to you — my dear lady? Since I
have been here I have read through 3 plays those of Beaumarchais
the Figaro cycle,[94] and 2 novels one in 6 volumes very impudent

[93] That is, Percy Chapel, St. Pancras, where the Rev. Robert Montgomery
was minister.

[94] *Le Barbier de Séville* (1775), *Le Mariage de Figaro* (1784), and *La
Mère coupable* (1792) by Pierre Augustin Caron de Beaumarchais (1732–
1799). The only novel in six volumes that Alexandre Dumas fils (1824–
1895) published is *Aventures de quatre femmes et d'un perroquet* (1846–
1847).

and amusing by Alexandre Dumas Fils — and I have had a letter
from M^r James, a composition as elegant as you could write or his
Reverence, and who forgot in my portmanteau just the things w^h
I told him to put there.

And now Maam I dont like to ask you to write to me because I
dont think I shall stop here very long, may come back by next
Mondays packet but that would perhaps hurt the feelings of my
old folks at Paris who might like to see me — and will you make
me a birthday present please — and it shall be a dinner on the 18
Ill see you off wish you well, and then — fire away at Pendennis.[95]

Coming here won't do — very moderate houses let at 50£ for
the season — then to go & come with my family is 20£ more —
where we may go to Boulogne & back for 6£ and get rooms for
25£. And so God bless you dear friend — and God bless all yours
prays your affectionate brother Makepeace.

There was a little girl of 10 in the Railroad going to Eastbourne
who was so beautiful that I had nearly gone after her, for I wanted
very little to decide me one way or other, and only came hither
because I saw by Bradshaw [96] in the morning that the boat started on
that day. But I think and hope I shall be better for the little
change. There's a play here tomorrow night Sunday, will you
come?

710.            TO MRS. BROOKFIELD
              13 JULY 1850 [97]

Published in part, *Collection of Letters*, p. 174.

My dear lady   I hope you will not object to hear that I am
quite well this morning. I should have liked to shake hands with
Harry before his departure: but I was busy writing at the hour

[95] Number XIX for August, chapters 58 to 60.
[96] *Bradshaw's Railway Gazette*.
[97] Harry Hallam went on the Midland Circuit a few days before July 18,
1850 (*Mrs. Brookfield*, II, 315). Performances of Meyerbeer's *Le Prophète*
were given on July 4 and 13 at the Royal Italian Opera House (*Times*).
Thackeray's statement that he is going to see the opera "again" must refer
to the second of these performances.

when he said he was going, and fell sound asleep here last night after a very modest dinner not waking until near midnight: when it was to late to set off to P. S.

What do you think I've done to day? I have sent in my resignation to Punch — there appears in next Punch an article so wicked I think by poor Jerrold,[98] that upon my word I don't think I ought to pull any longer in the same boat with such a savage little Robespierre. The appearance of this incendiary article put me in such a rage that I could only cool myself by a ride in the Park and I should very likely have reported myself in Portman S.t but I remembered how you had Miss Prince to luncheon and how I should be de trop.

Now I am going to work the rest of the mortal day until dinner time, when I go to see the Prophete again. But it would please me very much if you please, to hear that you were pretty well — Always faithfully de Madame le serviteur dévoué

W M T.[99]

[For a fragment of a letter to Mrs. Brookfield, 11 July, 1850, see letter 15, Appendix XXVI.]

711.     TO MRS. BROOKFIELD
22 JULY 1850

Published in part, *Collection of Letters*, pp. 52–53.

Monday.

My letter to day dear lady must needs be a very short one for the post goes in 1/2 an hour and I've been occupied all day with my own business and other peoples. At 3 o'clock just as I was in full work comes a letter from a protégée of my mother's, a certain Madame de Baurel informing me that she Madame de Baurel had

[98] The offending article was presumably withdrawn, for Thackeray continued to contribute to *Punch*.

[99] Mrs. Brookfield's reply to this letter is given in part in *Mrs. Brookfield*, II, 314–315: "I am very glad you are well again, and I cannot feel sorry for the resignation from *Punch*, which is really a grand thing to have done as a

it in view to commit suicide immediately unless she could be in some
measure relieved or releived w<sup>h</sup> is it? from her present difficulties
— so I have had to post off to this Madame de Baurel, whom I
expected to find starving, and instead met a woman a great deal
fatter than the most full fed person need be, and having just had
a good dinner. But that did not prevent her, the confounded old
fiend, from abusing the woman who fed her and was good to her:
from spoiling the 1/2 of a days work for me and taking me of a
fool's errand. I was quite angry instead of a corpse perhaps to find
a fat & voluble person who had no more idea of hanging herself to
the bedpost than you or I have. However I got a character in
making Madame de Baurels acquaintance and some day she will
turn up in that inevitable repertory of all ones thoughts and experiences que vous savez. Thence as it was near, I went to see a
sick poetess who is pining away for love of Savile Morton that you
have heard tell of, and who, literally has been brought near to the
grave by that amorous malady. She is very interesting somehow,
ghastly pale and thin, recumbent on a sofa, and speaking scarcely
above her breath. I wonder though after all, was it the love or
was it the bronchitis or was it the chest or the spine that was affected?
all I know is that Don Savilio may have made love to her once
but has tried his hand in other quarters since      And you know one
does not think the worse of a man of honour for cheating in Affairs
of the heart — The numbers that I myself have — fiddledydee —
this is nonsense. The Refawrum banquet was very splendid and
dull enough: a bad dinner and bad wine and pretty fair speaking:
my friend fat James[100] being among not the least best of the
speakers. They all speak in a kind of singsong or cant without w<sup>h</sup>

---

testimony, — but they ought to cut out the Jerrold article and make you
come back.

"I took a turn in the park, but was soon knocked up, it was so hot.

"Poor Harry went off with a dismal face, and I am very dismal too. I
am glad you will have the *Prophete* to-night. Pray don't make yourself ill
again, I mean I hope you take proper care of yourself."

[100] William Milbourne James. The banquet was given on July 20 in
honor of Lord Palmerston, "to express their confidence in his policy, and in
commemoration of his late triumph in the House of Commons" (Joseph
Irving, *The Annals of our Time*, London, 1871, p. 306)

I suppose it is impossible for the orator nowadays to pitch his sentence, and Madam you are aware that the Romans had a pipe when they spoke — not a pipe such as your husband uses: but a pitch pipe. I wanted to have gone to smoke a last calumet at poor dear old Portman S.ᵗ but our speechifyers did not stop till 12 1/2, and not then but the best of them had fired off by that time, and I came off.

Yesterday after devoting the morning to composition I went & called on — the Rev.ᵈ W H Brookfield whom I found very busy packing up and wishing me at Jericho, so I went to the Miss Leslies and Captain Morgan the American Captain and then to dine at Hampstead,[101] where the good natured folks took in me & the 2 young ones: finally in the evening to Lady Tennents where I have been most remiss in visit paying for I like her & she was a kind old friend to me. To day I'm going to dine with the Dowager Duchess of Bedford,[102] afterwards to M.ʳˢ Procters, afterwards to Lady Granvilles — here you have your humble Servants journal and you see his time is pretty well occupied. I have had a good deal of the children too and am getting on apace with my number though I don't like it. Shall I send you some of it? No I won't. Or if I do a very good piece indeed perhaps I may.

I think we shall go to Brighton. I think you'll be away six weeks at least. And I hope to hear that my dear lady is well that she's cheerful that shes doing her duty with all her might, and that she remembers her affectionate old friend Makepeace who begins and ends his days with a G. B. Y.

[101] With the Crowes.
[102] The former Lady Georgiana Gordon (1781–1853), youngest daughter of the fourth Duke of Gordon and widow of the sixth Duke of Bedford.

712.                TO MRS. BROOKFIELD
                     26 JULY 1850 [103]

Published in part, *Collection of Letters*, pp. 98–99. The word enclosed
between daggers was overscored by Mrs. Brookfield.

My dear lady  I hope you are better, are you?  I have had a
bad week, and a most cruel time of it this month, my groans were
heart-rending, my sufferings immense, I thought no XIX would
never be born alive — It is, but stupid ricketty and of feeble intellect I fear.  Isn't that a pretty obstetrical metaphor?  Well, I
suppose I couldnt get on, because I hadn't you to come and grumble
to.  You see habit does so much, and though there is Blanche
† Stanley † to be sure,[104] yet shall I tell you I will though perhaps
you won't believe it that I haven't been there for a month.  And
what a singular thing it is about my dear friend Miss ⟨. . .⟩[105] that
I never spoke to her but once in my life when I think the weather
was our subject, and as for telling her that I had drawn Amelia
from anybody of our acquaintance I should have as soon thought
of — of what?  I have been laboriously crossing all my ts see, and
thinking of a simile.  But it's good fun about poor little Blanche —
Does anybody suppose I would be such an idiot as to write verses
to her?  I never wrote her a line.  I once drew one picture in her
music-book, a caricature of a spoony song in wʰ I laughed at her,
as has been my practice alas.  But I'll serve out Miss ⟨. . .⟩ and tell
Lady Ashburton of her I think.  The only person to whom I remember having said anything about Amelia was the late Mʳˢ Ban-
croft as I told you, and that was by a surprize.  I tell you everything.  I dont think I ever went to Lady Eddisbury without a
telling of you or anywhere else if you'd like to know.  The Duchess
of Bedford was very pleasant a kind frank friendly old lady and

[103] Thackeray wrote this letter on the Friday after he completed number
XIX of *Pendennis*, almost certainly July 26, the last Friday in the month.
[104] See *Memoranda*, The Stanleys of Alderley.
[105] Here and elsewhere in the letter Mrs. Brookfield has overscored this
name beyond recovery.

a nice simple society. She asked me to Scotland and I may go perhaps. I would if you would take M^rs Fanshawe's house, and take
the children & Miss Trulock to live with you for a month.[106] I want
them to love you, and wisey wussy. For what else do I care — let
it be known from China to Peru,[107] but them and my dear lady?
Lady John Russell was at Campden Hill — and I won her heart
by admiring her verses to the Duchess who told her. Afterwards
was a great drum at Lady Granville's where there was all the polite
world; and after that on Wednesday Grand Concert Lady Shelburne[108] Lansdowne House — intimate conversation with Lord
Palmerston — Duchess of Beaufort[109] uncommonly civil and confidential — Lady Duff the only woman in the room out of mourning
& she in a tawdry rainbow-gown particularly odious; didn't hear
a word of the music. Yesterday after a hard days labour went out
to Richmond dined with old Miss Berrys Lord Brougham there,
enormously good fun boiling over with humour & mischief the
best and wickedest old fellow I've met I think. And I was better
in health than Ive been for a fortnight past. O how I should like
to come on Sunday by the Excursion train price 5/ and shake hands
and come back again! I've been writing Pen[110] all the morning
and reading back numbers in order to get up names &c w^h I'd forgotten. I lit upon a very stupid part I'm sorry to say: and yet how
well written it is. What a shame the Author dont write a complete

[106] On July 31 Mrs. Brookfield wrote to her husband from Southampton:
"I heard from Mr. Thackeray proposing that the children and their governess
should join us in taking lodgings and keeping house here, as they would be
all the better for change of air, but I have said in answer that nothing is yet
decided, and I fancy you would feel rather bored by the governess, however
much she might stick to her schoolroom" (*Mrs. Brookfield*, II, 317). The
visit was nevertheless arranged, and early in August Annie and Minnie accompanied by Miss Trulock went to Southampton. Thackeray passed two
weeks there at the Dolphin Inn, returning to London on August 20, and
Brookfield was also on hand for a few days before departing on his annual
cruise with Spring Rice in the *Vigilante* (*Mrs. Brookfield*, II, 317–320).

[107] See the opening couplet of Dr. Johnson's *The Vanity of Human Wishes*.

[108] The second wife (1819–1895) of Henry Petty-FitzMaurice, styled
Earl of Shelburne, later (1863) fourth Marquess of Lansdowne.

[109] The second wife (d. 1889) of the seventh Duke of Beaufort.

[110] Number XX for September, chapters 61 to 63.

good story. Will he die before doing so, or come back from America & do it? And now on account of the confounded post regulations I shant be able to hear word of you till Tuesday. It's a sin and a shame to cut 2 days out of our week as the Pharisees do and I'll never forgive Lord John Russell,[111] never — The young ladies are now getting ready to walk abroad with their dear Par — God bless Magdalenes little tooth. Its but a hasty letter I send you, dear lady, but my hand is weary with writing Pendennis, and my head boiling up with some nonsense that I must do after dinner for Punch.[112] Isn't it strange that, in the midst of all the selfishnesses, that one, of doing one's business, is the strongest of all? What funny songs Ive written when fit to hang myself! To day I read a bit w[h] was done when I thought you were lying in — early one grey morning, but that's solemn & pretty. You said it was, — about 'the child to be born into the world & take it's part of' in — [113] God bless the child and its parents. And Heaven mend that Miss ⟨. . .⟩ Ill sarve her out when ever I catch her as sure as my name is Makepeace.

713.     TO THE REV. ROBERT MONTGOMERY
3 AUGUST 1850

*Address:* Rev[d] R. Montgomery | Torrington Square. Hitherto unpublished.

Saturday. August 3.

My dear M[r] Montgomery

I am rather tardy in acknowledging your kind present[114] but it reached me when I was in the agonies of my monthly labour, and when the songs of all the poets of Parnassus wouldn't have been heard by me. Nor have I had time since yesterday, when I began to

---

[111] Lord John Russell, as Prime Minister, was indirectly responsible for the objectionable regulations.

[112] "Mr. Malony's Account of the Ball," *Punch,* August 3.

[113] The last paragraph of chapter 44 of *Pendennis* (*Works,* II, 441), which concluded the number for March, 1850.

[114] There is nothing to indicate which of Montgomery's many volumes of verse was sent to Thackeray.

be free for a little again, to sit down to the perusal of the volume w.<sup>h</sup> I promise myself to read by the shore of the farsounding sea at Brighton next week whither I'm going for a holyday:<sup>115</sup> and with a box of good books for recreation and instruction. It was not fair to judge of you or any man by his works at nineteen, though many men would be proud to have been able to write as you did then, at any period of their lives. And it will give me great pleasure to know your works better & you in your works, as I promise myself to do ere many days are over.

    With my very best regards to your circle, believe me my dear Sir

Most truly yours

W M Thackeray

[For fragments of a letter to Mrs. Brookfield, 21 August, 1850, see letter 16, Appendix XXVI.]

714.          TO EDWARD CHAPMAN

22 AUGUST 1850

Hitherto unpublished.

Kensington.   August 22.

Dear Chapman

    If I do a Xmas book with you this year, the price will be 150£ for an edition of 3000. Of course I have spoken to no other publisher as yet on the subject but I think I have a right to a shilling per copy of a 5/ & often 7/ book: and intend to stipulate for that sum with my publisher.

    The book will be the foreign tour before projected; and I should be glad to hear in a day or 2, whether you are disposed to treat.<sup>116</sup>

Always yours

W M Thackeray

<sup>115</sup> Actually he went to Southampton.

<sup>116</sup> Chapman and Hall declined Thackeray's offer, and *The Kickleburys on the Rhine* was published by Smith, Elder, and Co.

715.                    FROM MRS. BROOKFIELD
                       22 AUGUST 1850 [117]

Hitherto unpublished. The passage enclosed between daggers has been in part
overscored and in part cut away by Mrs. Brookfield.

Aug⁺ 22.

My dear brother Wᵐ It was very kind of you to write in the
midst of your H. C. & it made me very happy to have yʳ letter. We
have had too much rain for driving out — since you went away,
about 3 weeks ago — Yesterday Anny & Minny seemed to be at
work all day during the rain till 4 1/2, when J. Bullar came in, &
staid to dine — & we all walked through the mud of Fitzhugh
Field & down by the water calling in at Prospect place I went with
her to hear Maurice [118] at Lincoln's Inn on Sunday — he interpreted the verse "By his knowledge shall my righteous servant
justify many" [119] — to mean by his knowledge of our temptations
& of our weakness — & indeed of our whole human nature, which
he had taken on himself that he might have this complete knowledge of what is in man. I liked the sermon but his voice is bad
& one loses half the sentences by the echoes in the Chapel — & "I
don't take the least interest in Maurice" — I can fancy your saying
— but I should tell you about him if I saw you, so I only write
as I speak. † ⟨. . .⟩ [120] my telling you that I ⟨. . .⟩ † to borrow some
books & bringing Dʳ Wᵐ back to tea — Magdalene was so cold
we had a fire which she seemed greatly to approve of, & when she
was gone to bed & Dʳ Bullar departed I read an article on Pendennis in the North British Review [121] — have you read it? I

---

[117] Excerpts from Thackeray's letter of August 21, to which this is a reply,
are given in Appendix XXVI.

[118] John Frederick Denison Maurice (1805–1872), the Unitarian and
Christian Socialist, had been Chaplain of Lincoln's Inn since 1846.

[119] *Isaiah*, 53, 11.

[120] About three and ten words respectively are missing in this and the following hiatus.

[121] "Pendennis — The Literary Profession," *North British Review*, August,
1850, pp. 335–372.

wonder who wrote it — he is very vehement in clearing you from the charge of writing down literary men — & puts in y.r letter to the M. Chronicle [122] in a note — it is a very sensibly written article & evidently by a staunch admirer of yours; — I read out a good deal of it to Anny & Miss Trulock — was not that couragious? Today we have been at the School in the morning & since then I had two or three visits to pay, & have come in so tired I have no power left for talking — Miss Anna Dick begged I w.d tell you that her whole happiness for life depended upon your not making Laura marry "Such a wretch" as Pendennis but that she should marry "that dear Warrington" — & yet she thought Pen: not quite bad enough to be married to Blanche — Miss Dick was evidently quite in a little excitement about it, so I am bound to repeat the message. — I expect his Reverence at about seven this Eveg. & he thinks of remaining here till Tuesday — Miss Ogle has just called & taken me a drive & left me no time for more writing as I must put this in the Post before dinner. I shall be very *very* glad when you come back [123] — God bless you my dear kind brother — The children are quite well & we get on very comfortably. Goodbye.

716.           TO MRS. BROOKFIELD
               24? AUGUST 1850 [124]

Published in part, *Collection of Letters*, pp. 127–128.

My dear lady

As the Sunday post is open again, I write you a word of good bye & send a little commission. Please to give D.r Bullars Infirmary 30/ for me and the children: or put that sum into his money-box at P. Place as a little remembrance of our jolly jolly day at Lyndhurst: & Miss Trulock will give you 4£ out of her cheque instead of two pound ten of it: and pay you faithfully besides our 1/2 of

---

[122] See above, No. 678.

[123] Thackeray planned a trip to the continent.

[124] This note appears to have been written on the Saturday after Thackeray's return from Southampton on Tuesday, August 20.

the expenses of the house bills and house. I tried my very hardest to compose my mind and a ballad in the railway, but it was no use; and I haven't the courage actually to go home until night. I start for Antwerp at 9 tomorrow morning — shall be there at 6 or so Monday and sleep probbly at Cologne or Bonn on Monday night — and if anybody chooses to write to me at Frankfort o/m poste restante, I shall get the letter I daresay. Shall I send you Lady Kickleburys tour? I will if its at all funny or pleasant but, I doubt if it'll do for letters well — O how glum and dingy the city looks and smoky and dreary! — Yesterday as I was walking in the wood with Mʳˢ Procter looking at the columns of the fir-trees, I thought of the pillars here and said This place is almost as lonely as the Reform Club in September — but the difference to the feeling mind is very great betwigst the 2 solitudes and for one I envy the birds in the Hampshire boughs. — What rubbish! I'm trying to get the day through. I've had my hair cut: I've tried to read a book and am determined, Madam, to be as happy as possible in a word — The Duchess of Sutherland ¹²⁵ asked me to Scotland to the deuce knows whither in the Highlands: but its too far all that — too much white neckcloths and society — it wᵈ be better to walk by your chair — or to go to Brighton wʰ I choose in preference to other places because it will give me a chance of shaking your hand sometimes. And is it very severe discipline they're going to put you under? And is W: Bullar going to work upon you with his simple mysticism? I don't know about the Unseen World, the use of the Seen World is the right thing I'm sure — it is just as much God's work and creation as the kingdom of Heaven with all the angels — How'll you make yourself most happy in it? how know at least the greatest amᵗ of happiness compatible with your condition? by despising to day and looking up cloudwards? Pish. Let us turn God's to day to its best use as well as any other part of the time He gives us. When I am on a cloud singing, or a pot boiling — I will do my best — and here

¹²⁵ The former Lady Harriet Howard (d. 1868), daughter of the sixth Earl of Carlisle, who had married George Granville (1786–1861), second Duke of Sutherland, in 1823.

[if] you are ill you can have consolations, if you have disappointments you can invent fresh sources of hope and pleasure — I'm
glad you saw the Colours and that they gave you pleasure — and
that noble poetry of Alfreds gives you pleasure (Im happy to say
Mum I've said the very same thing in prose that you like in the
very same words almost) [126] — the bounties of the Father I believe
to be countless and inexhaustible for most of us here in life — Love
the greatest Art (w^h is an exquisite and admiring Sense of Nature)
the next. By Jove, I'll admire, if I can, the wing of a cocksparrow
as much as the pinion of an archangel and adore God the Father
of the Earth earthy first, waiting for the completion of my senses
and the fulfilment of His intentions towards afterwards when this
scene closes over us.

So when Bullar turns up his i to the cieling — I'll look straight
at your dear kind face, and thank God for knowing that, my dear:
and though my nose is a broken pitcher yet lowandbyold there's

a well gushing over with kindness in my 🫀 where my dear

lady may come and drink. God bless you and W. and little Maude.


717.     TO ANNE AND HARRIET THACKERAY
              15 SEPTEMBER 1850

*Address:* Miss Thackeray | 13 Young street. Kensington | London. | Angle-
terre. *Postmark:* BRUXELLES 15 SEPT 1850. Published in part, *Thackeray and his Daughter*, pp. 36–38.

                    Hotel de Suède. Brussels. Sunday 15 Sep^t

My dearest young women I am so far on my way home and
my journey has been but a little one: only to Hombourg [127] and

---

[126] It would appear from a later letter (see below, No. 825) that Mrs.
Brookfield had been pleased by the last stanza of section XXVII of *In
Memoriam*, published the previous June:

          I hold it true, whate'er befall;
          I feel it, when I sorrow most;
          'Tis better to have loved and lost
          Than never to have loved at all.

I have been unable to find the passage in his own works of which Thackeray
speaks.     [127] The Rougetnoirbourg of *The Kickleburys on the Rhine*.

back again where we stopped for 5 days pretty pleasantly doing nothing, reading novels, making sketches, seeing the people drink the waters and gamble at the tables. I tried my luck once or twice and think I won about 5 shillings altogether: but I'm glad I came as it has given me what I wanted for my Xmas book. What I should have liked best w^d have been the society of Miss Anny & Miss Minny — no of Minny some 2 years later. In 1852, when I'm back from America [128] and you are grown even bigger stronger & fatter than at present please God, we'll make a tour together, and admire the beautiful works of nature together. You may be very thankful both of you for possessing that faculty, the world is not 1/2 a world without it, and the more you indulge this pleasure (that's the beauty of it) the better you are. O, I saw such grand phenomena of sunrise at Cologne the other morning as I looked out of my window upon the river! It's useless to try and describe the scene in writing, but those magnificent spectacles of nature are like personal kindnesses from the Maker to us — and make one feel grateful — If your papa (to whom I present my best compliments) takes you to the play, don't you feel pleased & thankful? Let's acknowledge in the same way the kind provisions of Heaven that provides these delightful treats for all us children. As this is Sunday morning, theres no harm in making a little sermon.

I wandered about Frankfort fair, and this town yesterday w^h is smaller but handsomer and richer than Paris, looking for something to buy for you young ladies: but I could hit on nothing that I thought w^d be useful or that you would like very much, and I daresay shall come back empty handed — On Thursday or Friday you may look out for me, I think — I shall try for the next 2 or 3 days to be quiet here (my companion [129] leaving me to day) and

[128] This is Thackeray's earliest reference to his plan of lecturing in America on *The English Humourists of the Eighteenth Century.*

[129] Frederick Gale (1823–1904), Serjeant Lankin in *The Kickleburys on the Rhine* (*Mrs. Brookfield*, II, 343), was educated at Winchester and became a solicitor and parliamentary agent (Thomas Frederick Kirby, *Winchester Scholars*, London, 1888, p. 314). He was the author of *Echoes from the*

to come back with some of my month's work [130] done — Thats why I'm writing very early in the morning, that I may go breakfast quietly and have a quiet days work afterwards. Meanwhile you two young ladies will go down on your knees at church, & say your prayers for me — Won't you?

If the Reverend M[rs] Portman Street is come back you will please send or take this letter directly across the park to her with my love & say, that I only got her letter on Wednesday evening at Frankfurt, after having tried after it 5 days running: and, having some of Granny's ingenuity, I had managed in that time to conjure up to myself all sorts of evils as happening to you all. But the only evil was that M[rs] B's letter had got among the H's: where a kind clerk turned it out for me: and I vowed that I never would be alarmed again by no news nor will I until the next time. If M[rs] B's not come home, put this under envelope and send it to her: and state that the writer is well in health, fierce in appetite, and rather alarmingly getting fat. I saw a beautiful little brooch yesterday with a painting of a Magdalene upon it exquisitely done — and had a mind to buy it, and present it to Miss Alice, only it's a glum subject rather, and what has she as yet, poor little soul, to repent of?

I met lots of acquaintances at Hombourg from whom I was glad to get away — They are backbiting, slandering envying and bullying in that little place, as well as in greater cities, and as I don't profess to be better than my neighbours, I cant help thinking that I am a very paltry contemptible rogue. Or if we haven't the vices of meanness avarice and a narrow spirit, I suppose we have some others, that we deserve to be whipped for. And so good bye & God bless all.                              W M T.

If you get this on Monday I should like an answer — It will be here by Tuesday afternoon: and I shant go till Wednesday ev[g] or Thursday.

---

*Old Cricket Fields* (1871), *Modern English Sports* (1885), and a *Memoir of the Hon. Robert Grimston* (1885).

[130] Number XXI of *Pendennis*, chapters 64 to 66.

718.                    TO MRS. GORE
                        1 OCTOBER 1850

Hitherto unpublished.

Dear M^rs Gore. I only saw this morning the R S V P up at
the top of the note and the letters smote me to the ♡ . You
know when the note came that I was in my agonies, with the
Doctors in the house. I beg pardon for not writing before I waited
until I could say whether I could or couldnt come.

I am engaged to the Grange on Friday: and my purpose was
to come to you on Wednesday and pass in your society the cheerful interval.

Yesterday only comes a note from my old friend M^rs Prinsep
ordering me to be present at VIRGINIA'S marriage, to Lord
Eastnor tomorrow.[131] So that I have but Thursday left.

Shall I take the train at 1 from Waterloo, and may I come &
dine and sleep {with} — no no, what was I going to say? — at
Hamble Cliff on that day? Always yours
                                        W M Thackeray.


719.                   TO HENRY TAYLOR
                        3 OCTOBER 1850

My text is taken from Miss I. A. Taylor's "On Autographs. III," *Longman's
Magazine*, XVIII (1891), 257–258.

In Mr. Dickens's story that is coming out, there is a certain Mr.
Micawber addicted to getting into debt, and signing his name to
bills of exchange, and who, whenever he signs his name to a bill,
says, "Thank God that bill is settled." [132] When I find I have
done wrong, like Mr. Micawber I'm at least very eager to sign an
apology.

---

[131] Virginia Pattle married Charles Somers Cocks (1819–1883), styled Viscount Eastnor, later (1852) third Earl Somers, on October 2, 1850
[132] See chapter 36 of *David Copperfield*.

It is only about four hours since I found that I owed one to you.[133] I have long been aware, by the reports of some friends, the estrangement of others, and the demeanour of some acquaintances, that a certain article of my writing had given great offence; but as I meant it in the most good-humoured spirit, and was actually proud of the absurd composition, I would not acknowledge

[133] "Mr. Thackeray is gone to Mrs. Gore's in Hampshire," Mrs. Brookfield wrote to her husband on October 3, "but before he went he had a letter from Lady Ashburton to put off his visit to the Grange telling him he had offended the Taylors, she could not say how, but she saw it wouldn't do for them to be at the Grange together. He had met Mr. Taylor at Miss Virginia Pattle's wedding, a few days ago [sic], and told him he should meet him again at the Ashburtons', and thought he seemed friendly enough, so he wrote a letter to Lady A. with a picture of a Donkey let loose in a Chicken yard, and comparing it with his own flight of fancy in the objectionable *Punch* article, adding that he now thought 'the article had been unintentionally vulgar and impertinent.' After this he said he should not know whether they would write and ask him still to come to the Grange now; but he has at present proposed going there when you go on the fifteenth, and meantime was much bored at having to go down into Hants." (*Mrs. Brookfield*, II, 321)

The Taylors took offence at "The Proser. IV — On a Good-Looking Young Lady" (*Punch*, June 8, 1850, pp. 233–234), in which Virginia Pattle is described under the name of Erminia and Taylor (1800–1886), later (1869) knighted, the author of *Philip van Artevelde* (1834), appears as Timotheus. "By one of those kind freaks of favouritism which Nature takes," Thackeray had written of Miss Pattle, "she has endowed this young lady with almost every kind of perfection: has given her a charming face, a perfect form, a pure heart, a fine perception and wit, a pretty sense of humour, a laugh and a voice that are as sweet as music to hear, for innocence and tenderness ring in every accent, and a grace of movement which is a curiosity to watch, for in every attitude of motion or repose her form moves or settles into beauty, so that a perpetual grace accompanies her. . . .

"Well then, it happened the other day that this almost peerless creature, on a visit to the country, met that great poet, Timotheus, whose habitation is not far from the country house of Erminia's friend, and who, upon seeing the young lady, felt for her that admiration which every man of taste experiences upon beholding her, and which, if Mrs. Timotheus had not been an exceedingly sensible person, would have caused a jealousy between her and the great bard her husband. But, charming and beautiful herself, Mrs. Timotheus can even pardon another woman for being so; nay, with perfect good sense, though possibly with a *little* factitious enthusiasm, she professes to share to its fullest extent the admiration of the illustrious Timotheus for the young beauty." (*Works*, VI, 688)

that anybody had a right to be offended, and was quite indignant and angry that any one else should be so, and a few hours since I should have thought an apology a thing impossible, and that *I* was the injured party, and the innocent victim of a little social persecution.

But just before I came to the railroad I was referred to the unlucky paper in question by a friend of mine [134] who is not likely to be a very willing judge against me, and then, and not till then, I saw that I had been wrong. I meant no wrong as I say again. I write in a headlong way often as I speak, and I own and acknowledge now that [Mrs. Taylor] had cause of offence in that article, and I ask your forgiveness. It has done no wrong certainly; nobody, not fifty people at least, know what or who was meant, but I had no right to speak of [Mrs. Taylor] in that manner, and perfectly feel that the anger of [your wife's] friends is justifiable.

And having debated the subject in my mind during my railroad journey, and come to the conclusion of the rest of the world against myself that I have been guilty of a rudeness, I write an early and hasty line to you to express my contrition that I should have given you pain.

Believe me, dear sir,

Your very faithful servant,

W. M. Thackeray.

I shall stay here till over Saturday, and shall be very glad to learn that you forgive me.[135]

[134] Presumably Mrs. Brookfield.

[135] Taylor replied (*Longman's Magazine*, XVIII [1891], 258): "I believe that past proceeding of yours to have been as free from any ill intention as this present is full of frankness and generosity." Mrs. Carlyle, another guest at the Grange, tells the rest of the story. She wrote to her husband on October 5: "Thackeray is here — arrived yesterday, greatly to the discomfort of [Taylor] evidently, who had 'had the gang all to himself' so long. . . . Lady A. wrote he was to come after all, and went to Winchester to meet him, and [Taylor] sulked all yesterday evening, and to-day is solemn to death." (*Letters and Memorials of Jane Welsh Carlyle*, edd. Carlyle and Froude, I, 395) On October 8 she continued: "The Taylors are to be dispatched to-morrow. . . . Henry Taylor and Thackeray have fraternized finally, *not* 'like the carriage horses and the railway steam-engine,' as might have been supposed, but like

720. TO MRS. BROOKFIELD
3 OCTOBER 1850

*Postmarks:* SOUTHAMPTON 3 OCT. 1850, 4 OC 1850. Published in part, *Collection of Letters,* p. 136.

My dear lady Ive been at work till now its 8 o'clock. The house is very pleasant M^rs & Miss G bent on being so the dinners splendacious: and what do you think I did yesterday? Please to tell Spring Rice this with my best regards tomorrow — I thought over the confounded Erminia matter in the railroad and wrote instantly on arriving here a letter of contrition and apology to H. Taylor for having made what I see now was a flippant and offensive allusion to M^rs Taylor — I'm glad Ive done it: I'm glad that so many people whom I've been thinking bigotted and unfair and unjust towards me have been right and that I've been wrong — and my mind is an emence deal easier — Will you be happy at Hither Green? I pray you will my dear kind lady. My hearts very full and happy as I think of you and my young ones. God bless all.

721. TO MRS. BROOKFIELD
8 OCTOBER 1850 [136]

Published in part, *Collection of Letters,* pp. 155-156.

Amie — Please to prepare for a sad news w^h is that I have agreed to stay 2 days longer here and shant go till Thursday — And one of the reasons is an odd reason. Do you remember my telling you how my friend Gale at a dinner of Winchester big wigs had heard that I was a wretch with whom nobody should associate, that I had seduced a Governess by the name of Jane Eyre by whom I had

men and brothers! I lie by, and observe them with a certain interest; it is as good as a Play." (*New Letters and Memorials of Jane Welsh Carlyle,* 2 vols., London and New York, ed. Alexander Carlyle, with an introduction by Sir James Crichton-Browne, II, 24) See below, App. XXVI, October 1850.

[136] This letter was written two days before Thursday, October 10.

had ever so many &c? [137] The bishop [138] and a number of the clergy are coming here tomorrow and I thought I would like to make my appearance among them and give the lie to that story. And so I stay on for a couple of days, and will you write to me please by tomorrow's post and tell me that you are come back well. We've not had much fun. Yesterday I think was passed in eating chiefly: for it rained without, and I was quite glad to remain in my room the greater part of the day, & to make a good fire, and prepare myself for work. But I did none. It wouldn't come. Sleep came instead: and between it and the meals and reading Alton Locke [139] the day passed away. To day we have had a fine walk to Trench's parsonage,[140] a pretty place 3 miles off through woods of a hundred thousand colours and (I'm trying to get this pen into a writing condition but it wont) and the poet was absent but his good-natured wife came to see us, by us I mean me, Lady Ash. & Miss Farrer, who walked as aides de camp by my ladys poney — How is it that I find myself humbling before her, and taking a certain parasitical air as all the rest do? There's something commanding in the woman (she was born in 1806 you'll understand) and I see we all of us bow down before her. Why don't we bow down before you Ma'am? — Little Mrs Taylor is the only one who doesn't seem to Kotoo. I like Taylor whose grandeur wears off in ten minutes, and in whom one perceives an extremely gentle and loving human creature I think — not a man to be intimate with ever but to admire and like from a distance: and to have a sort of artistical good-will to — That's better than hating him in private: but I find Ive not yet forgiven Mrs Cameron for driving away from me — although I *was* disrespectful to Mrs Taylor. — What stupid stough I am writing to you! Am I thinking about something else? I daresay. I daresay I'm thinking that I stay on, not to meet the Bishop: but because, Wm being absent from home, its best that I should not be too much bothering my dear lady. But you know where I would be if I might.

[137] See above, No. 440.
[138] Charles Richard Sumner (1790–1874), Bishop of Winchester from 1827 till 1869.
[139] Which Charles Kingsley had published on August 17 (*Spectator*, p. 792).                         [140] See above, No. 62, July 2.

We have Carlyle coming down directly the Taylors go away and Major Rawlinson [141] arrives tonight: and, and — well what stuff and nonsense!  I don't know why for some time past Ive not been able to write to you: but what is there to say about the life here and at the Gores, and the history of walks and lunches and dinners? I'm ashamed of them somehow.  I've been reading in Alton Locke, Baillie Cochrane,[142] Kenealy's Goethe and a book on the Decadence of La France proved by figures, and showing that the French are not increasing in wealth or numbers near so fast as the English, Prussians, Russians — And Baillie Cochrane is an amusing fellow amusing from his pomposity and historic airs, and Alton Locke begins to be a bore I think and Kenealys Goethe is the work of a madcap with a marvellous facility of versifying and I should like Anny & Minny to go to my dear lady on Wednesday if you will have them and I send a kiss to your baby: and pray God to bless her mother — But this scrawl doesnt count I may write you one tomorrow mayn't I.

W M T.

722.      TO LADY EDDISBURY
OCTOBER 1850

Published in *Biographical Introductions*, II, xxxviii–xxxix.

Right Honorable!

Last Tuesday was a week when your Ladyships honour bade me to the pleasant new drinke of Tea w^h belikes me well (albeit a tost and ayle in the Cheshire fashion doe better suit me) I was awaye from my House at Kensington on a visit to my lady Ashburton at y^e Grange, my very good lady, and your ladyships billet did only reach me yesternight when I journeyed back from the Grange hitherward.  It were much pleasant to hear of what you saw

[141] Henry Creswicke Rawlinson (1810–1895), later a Major-General and (1891) first Baronet, the noted Assyriologist.
[142] Either *Ernest Vane* or *Lucille Belmont*, novels published in 1849 by Alexander Cochrane-Baillie (1816–1890), later (1880) first Baron Lamington; *Goethe, a New Pantomime* (1850) by Edward Vaughan Hyde Kenealy (1819–1880).

upon the River of Rhine and in Swisserland where I hear say the mountayns be cruel steepe: and a littel bird doe tell me that a fair lady your daughter did make sweet verses upon the Rhenus river and the snowy Alpine mountayns (whereof Master Milton do write).[143]  I doe dearly love all sweet things and would like to hear what that young lady did sing!  Alps do rhyme with 'scalps' and that be all I think: but Blaunche do rhyme with avalaunch and staunch, be it not so?

Your Ladyships noble sons [144] I did meet on the raylroad, and their pretty faces, and feathers in their hats, and pikes the w$^h$ they gallantly carried, and talk and jests did like me so well, that good lack, I could not but give them 10/ with my blessing remembring well when I was myself juvenis and all too glad of my elders' charitie.

I salute your ladyship reverently and the young ladies of your house: and pray you to bear in mind kindly

Your ladyships true Servant

S. Pips [145]

To the Right Honorable
    The Lady Eddisbury  my very good lady
at her house of Winnington Hall
                    in Cheshire

These with haste
    poste haste.

[143] If Thackeray intends a precise reference, it is probably to *Paradise Lost*, I, 351–355.

[144] Presumably Lady Eddisbury's three youngest sons: John Constantine Stanley (1837–1878), later a Colonel in the Grenadier Guards; Edward Lyulph Stanley (1839–1925), afterwards fourth Baron Stanley of Alderley and fourth Baron Sheffield; and Algernon Charles Stanley (1843–1928), from 1903 until his death Bishop of Emmäus, assistant at the Pontifical Throne, and Canon of St. Peter's, Rome.  For their personal traits, see Miss Nancy Mitford's preface to *The Ladies of Alderley*, an essay which tends to confirm Thackeray's maxim (*Works*, I, 175) that "if a man's character is to be abused, say what you will, there's nobody like a relation to do the business."

[145] This letter is not so much an imitation of Pepys as of the Pepysian text written by Percival Leigh to accompany Doyle's "Manners and Customs of the English," which was currently appearing in *Punch*.

[For fragments of a letter to Mrs. Brookfield, October, 1850, see letter 17, Appendix XXVI.]

723.       TO MRS. SARTORIS
OCTOBER–3 NOVEMBER 1850 [146]

Extract published in Lady Ritchie's *From Friend to Friend* (New York, 1919), pp. 49–50. My text is taken from a transcript supplied by Mrs. Fuller.

My dear Mrs. Sartoris. I won't sit down to eat your venison without thanking the givers thereof. It is at the fire now. Pray the Lord it will be good: I have a Cook not of the first order: the Brookfields, the Elliots, the F. Pollocks are coming to eat it and I have just walked across to a neighbour at Notting Hill: [147] not to ask him to dine but to borrow a bottle of port wine from him, which I ain't got any. Why did you put me to the expense of a dinner? You know I never would have had one but for the venison. Then there's currant jelly, French beans and all sorts of things to get. This pen and paper are abominable. You see my state of mind in a word — that's why I have not written sooner as common decency and gratitude and friendship ordered. I have no economy of time or anything else. My young one said to me just now Papa how will you get through your plates and your Punch and your Xmas book and your Pendennis? [148] "Why do you ask me that question? says I, flinging out of their school-room. I've been writing all day. Can't you leave me alone? I'll go downstairs and write a letter till the company comes if you've only those disagreeable questions to ask me. Thus it is our life wags away: and as I write I don't know whether I am grumbling or not, or really thankful to you for the venison (which may be spoiled in the dressing), I still think I would have preferred — no I dont care about game after all.

[146] This letter was begun in the latter part of October and finished on Sunday, November 3, shortly after Thackeray saw Macready in *Hamlet*.

[147] John Leech, who lived at 31 Notting Hill Terrace (*Royal Blue Book*, 1851).

[148] Number XXII for November, chapters 67 to 70.

Your description of your beautiful sister in law [149] was very picturesque. I should like to look better at that handsome lady. I passed yesterday morning upon the site of the Exhibition of '51. 1500 people were at work in the place and it seemed quite empty. What an enormous solitude it will be, after the first rush of visitors and when only 2 or 300 people are in the building!

Just as this was written, the company came, the venison was eaten up, and both roasted and hashed was pronounced excellent. Why didn't I write and thank the givers at once? I have been so hard at work almost ever since as to have no time for gratitude and letter writing, till now of a calm Sunday morning, the children being at Church, the window open, the sun shining, the house tranquil, the cigar lighted. We seldom get two hours tranquillity in London, and it's only in one room of the house that I can secure it, and that is [*hand and finger pointing to a little picture he has drawn of himself lying in bed smoking a cigar*]. It is curious to think that in this room and bed, one was all but dead this time last year, all but gone out of the world altogether, never more to write numbers of yellow coloured novels, never more to scuffle about in evening parties, or to hanker after vain desires, or to write grinning Punch articles with a heavy heart, or to chafe at social tracasseries and squabble with friends.

When you were a young girl learning to sing in that dismal little room in the Rue de Clichy,[150] were there any cares I wonder? I suppose there were; but the enjoyments were so great then to counter-balance them: a five franc dinner and a play on the Boulevards and a grenier à vingt ans [151] — what pleasures they were! Two or three nights ago I made a rush to the pit at the Haymarket to see Macready in Hamlet: [152] and the struggling outside

---

[149] Presumably Mrs. John Mitchell Kemble.

[150] Where Mrs. Sartoris, like her sister Fanny Kemble before her, had been sent to study music with a Miss Foster (Lady Ritchie, *From Friend to Friend*, p. 50).

[151] An echo of Béranger's "Le Grenier." See "The Garret," Thackeray's translation of this poem (*Works*, XIII, 142–143).

[152] The first of Macready's three farewell performances in *Hamlet* on October 30, 1850. (The other two were given on November 27, 1850, and

and the pushing and squeezing and battle at the money-hole were
well enough and like the old things: even till the curtain drew
up it was pretty pleasant in the pit: but when the play began and
old Hamlet came on with a gnarled neck and a rich brown wig over
his wrinkled old face, the youthful business disappeared altogether.
What a bore the play was! How I wished myself away smoking
a cigar! What a wretched humbug that old Hamlet seemed with
an undertakers tray on his head flapping about his eternal white
pocket handkerchief, and being frightened at that stupid old Ghost!
If the Ghost had to tell his story before Cockcrow why didnt he
tell it at once, instead of prosing about Murder most foul as in the
best it is, but in this case etc.? There was a young fellow who acted
Horatio, in a sort of manly stupid heavy dragoon way whom I
liked, and took to kindly; but Ophelia, Laertes! — suppose our
beloved monarch were to lose Prince Albert and marry his brother
the Duke of Saxe Cobourg two months after Albert's death, suppose I say a company of actors going to Windsor and acting a play
by the desire of the Prince of Wales full of the grossest allusions
to widows marrying, to marriage with a deceased husband's brother
and so forth — what a noise there'd be! What a pretty stratagem
for a clever Prince to employ! In plays and fairy tales they always
make those truculent ogres immensely stupid and I pity them
somehow. As for Claudius, bating the little affair with Hamlet
Senior, his conduct through the play is exceedingly decorous and
forbearing to the young Dane [*picture of Hamlet*] the enfant *terrible*. I was immensely relieved when they were all run through
the body. There came a farce afterwards, but the gaiety of that
was quite unbearable: and as the audience were encoring a drinking song, two gentlemen of 40 years of age left the theatre altogether. My dear old Fitz and I, how we used to go and see
Braham, and watch him with unwearied happiness twenty years
ago,[153] when your father had the theatre.

I can't call to mind anything more remarkable than the above

---

January 29, 1851.) The afterpieces on this occasion were *The Irish Diamond*
and *My Friend in the Straps*.
[153] See above, No. 57.

event to record — unless you'd have the history of a dinner at
Bradbury and Evan's yesterday: where the literary wags were assembled and where Dickens, Jerrold, Forster and your humble
servant sate sparring at each other. Would any of us, I wonder,
have liked Laertes's foil? Have you read David Copperfield? [154]
the artless rogue! that artless dodge makes me laugh (is it only
wicked things that make one laugh any more?) Did you see
Bouffé act the Gamin de Paris? [155] Everybody said it was just for
all the world like a real boy, and people wouldn't see the artless
grins, the artless rouge, the artless blond wig.

Last week I was at the marriage of a dear pretty honest girl
whom I've known ever since she was a child and been fond of;
and of course I was at Virginia's marriage. She looked beautiful
and has taken possession of Eastnor Castle, and her rank as Princess
and reigns to the delight of everybody. The paper's full. Good
bye my dear Mrs. Sartoris and believe that I am always

Yours W. M. T. and that I like very much the kind feeling you
show me.

724.                    TO DR. ELLIOTSON
                        4 NOVEMBER 1850

Hitherto unpublished.
                                    13 Young Sͭ Nov͞ 4.
My dear Doctor

Next month (D.V.) sees the completion of my story of Pendennis, w͒ would never most likely have been brought to a conclusion but for your skill and kindness to me this time last year.

May I dedicate the book to you? [156] It is but a compliment in
return for a life saved but I have no more than words and affectionate gratitude to offer and I hope you won't refuse them from

                        Yours ever faithfully
                        W M Thackeray

[154] Numbers XIX and XX for November, chapters 58 to 64.
[155] A comedy-vaudeville in two acts by Jean François Bayard (1796–1853)
and Louis Émile Vanderburch (1794–1862), first performed in 1836.
[156] See *Works*, II, xlv.

725.                    TO MRS. JAMES
                        NOVEMBER 1850

*Hitherto unpublished.*

My dear M^rs James

Let it be the 15^th if you please. I see by the Pocket Book it is Saint Machutus's day.[157] 13^th is S^t Britins's Do you know or care who they were? Have you read D^r Pusey about the vision of S^t Cyprian, or D^r Newman reported in the Times about 'the grave being opened, and                    coming forth?

As I was talking with Brookfield last night about our dear kind gentle boy Harry Hallam [158] who had the sweetest qualities and the most loving heart, and who when I was ill last year showed me the most kind and delicate proofs of affection & sympathy — I couldnt help thinking of that awful blasphemy and that this Newman is obliged to condemn the best and purest of all of us, his own mother, friends, brethren, — everybody. — Will we subscribe to that? Will we let that Lie go unquestioned among us? It seemed to me as if our very affection for that dear fellow gave the Doctor the lie: & proved what we hope & believe for him. He came a hundred miles last year to offer me money in case I sh^d be in want: he came down to see me at Brighton and gave me his arm for my first walk [159] — And lo — he's gone. — This seems very incoherent — I dont know why the words come to me, and seem like an insult on poor Harry's grave — and I dont know why I sh^d begin talking to you in this way answering a note to dinner but we dine and we die dont we? and we get suddenly stopped on the highroad by a funeral crossing it —

Meanwhile Ill come on the 15^th and am always sincerely yours

W M Thackeray

[157] St. Machutus Day is November 15, St. Britins Day November 13.

[158] Harry Hallam died at Siena on October 24 after a week's illness. The Brookfields received word of his death on November 4 (*Mrs. Brookfield*, II, 334).

[159] See above, No. 647.

726.                    TO MRS. FANSHAWE
                          NOVEMBER 1850

Hitherto unpublished.

My dear M$^{rs}$ Fans — A message from me instead of a letter
from Madam who is writing many letters and whom I want to
go & dine with the children (not with me) I shant be there for
one more time ere all things change. She has agreed to receive
Tom Parr into the house on Thursday; and other room there is
none except only poor Harry's w$^h$ I think W H B and she would
not like to make ready — The Hallams come back the next day
or the day following, & these people go to them I dont know,
they dont, for how long a time.[160] Madam is writing now to the
poor old man. What a change that death may make, what altered
plans in many selfish fortunes! I wish I could see your fce or
your handwriting sometimes my kind f Isn't it awful the death
of that poor boy — think of that last pang, feeling that he never
should see Her again. God bless him; the world is but a compromise is it? — and every one of us has more or less bleeding
wounds and mutilations.

God bless all of you. Couldnt you come & stay with us a little?
Theres plenty of room we sh$^d$ like it so much — on Thursday why
not

                          Ever Yours
                          W M T.

She w$^d$ have had you. Its I that prevented it.

[160] The Brookfields shut up their house and lived with Henry Hallam at
Wilton Crescent until some time after his son's funeral (*Mrs. Brookfield*, II,
337).

727.                TO MRS. CARMICHAEL-SMYTH
                        26–28 NOVEMBER 1850 [161]

Published in part, *Biographical Introductions*, II, xxxviii.

My dearest Mammy

Before I go to bed I must say one word of God bless you —
having completed my story this day and wrote finis: and very tired
weary & solemn minded. So I say God bless my dearest Mother
& G P, ere I try to go get some sleep.

— I've been in bed for the best part of 2 days since I wrote this
and asleep the greater part of the time — I was much done up
had a smart fever, boiled myself in a warm bath went without dinner slep 15 hours, ate no meat, treated myself to blue pill & an
elegant black composition this morning and am now as brisk as a
bee and as fresh as a daisy. I wanted very much to come with the
young ones to Paris for Xmas but dont know whether we shall
be able to make it out just at that season in consequence of the death
of my poor Aunt Mʳˢ F. Thackeray [162] — Her children being left
without a home now I couldnt but offer them one for the holydays
and I dont know yet whether they wᴸ come or no — I thought not
yesterday — but have a letter from young Edward [163] this morning
telling me when his holidays are and asking when he shall come
up about his cadetship. The oldest boy [164] is a very good clever

[161] This letter was written on November 26, when Thackeray finished the
final double number (chapters 71 to 75) and the preface of *Pendennis* (see
*Works*, II, xlviii), and on the second day following.

[162] Mrs. Francis Thackeray had died on November 18 (*Memorials*, p. 496).

[163] Edward Talbot Thackeray (b. 1836), *Genealogy* (69), for whom Thack-
eray secured a cadetship at Addiscombe through Sir John Cam Hobhouse.
He had a distinguished career in the Indian army, receiving the Victoria
Cross in 1857, and in 1862 married Amy Crowe, who had long lived with
Thackeray as an adopted daughter. See Vibart's *Addiscombe*, pp. 629–632,
and *Memorials*, p. 500.

[164] Francis St. John Thackeray (1832?–1919), *Genealogy* (67), who
writes ("Reminiscences of William Makepeace Thackeray," *Temple Bar*,
July, 1893, pp. 373–378) that his earliest recollections of his famous relative
date from the Easter holidays of 1849, 1850, and 1851, during each of which

hard-reading lad and is likely to get Kings [165] a hard matter now-adays when he'll do well — But if we dont come at Xmas will come a little later — I wont begin any new work without having a little time with you. How much did Lubbock lend you on the house? Think of my being able to buy it back again! I can — and carry on till my lectures [166] in spring. I've got a better subject for a novel [167] than any I've yet had — and am sorry to find have made a great number of enemies: but no man ever succeeded yet without such: & I must take my share (I cant write on this paper)

---

he spent a few days at 13 Young Street before going back to Eton: "I never visited, rarely saw him, at this time without having a sovereign slipped into my hand on leaving him. On one occasion, after I had my pocket picked in an omnibus, he emptied the whole of his purse into my hands. The exact amount, at this distant date, I do not remember, but it was much more than I had lost. This was when he was lying in bed, in one of his attacks of illness. On these delightful visits he would spare no pains in taking me to places of amusement — the play, or the pantomime — sometimes after an excellent dinner at the Garrick Club, where I remember his checking some one in the act of blurting out an oath, the utterance of which he would not tolerate in my presence. . . .

"In sight-seeing, whether visiting conjurors, or picture galleries, or other public places of entertainment, he was always, I think, studying faces and characters. But he must have put himself to a good deal of inconvenience; and the sacrifice of valuable time that he thus made I could understand afterwards, though I fear I did not appreciate it sufficiently at the time. Once, when he had taken me to the theatre and secured me a good place, after staying a little while, he said: 'Now I must leave you, and go and make a five-pound note.'"

[165] Francis Thackeray received his B. A. degree at Merton College, Oxford, in 1856.
[166] On *The English Humourists of the Eighteenth Century.*
[167] *Esmond.*

728.　　　　TO MRS. BROOKFIELD
　　　　　27 NOVEMBER 1850

Published in part, *Collection of Letters*, pp. 124–125. The passage enclosed between daggers was overscored by Mrs. Brookfield.

I could not come yesterday even to ring at the door: for I did not return until 8 o'clock from the visit to the Emigrant Ship [168] at Gravesend, and then had to work until 12 and polish off Pendennis. There are always 4 or 5 hours work when it is over: and 4 or 5 more would do it all the good in the world, and a second or third reading.

That emigrant business was very solemn and affecting; it was with difficulty I could keep my spectacles dry — amongst the people taking leave, the families of grave looking parents and unconscious children, & the bustle and incidents of departure — The cabins in one of the ships had only just been fitted up, and no sooner done than a child was that instant born in one of them — on the very edge of the old world as it were w$^h$ it leaves for quite a new country home empire. You shake hands with one or two of these people, and pat the yellow heads of the children (there was a Newcastle woman with 8 of them who interested me a good deal) and say God bless you — Shake hands — You & I shall never meet again in this world — Go and do your work across four months of ocean, and God prosper it — the ship drops down the river it gives us 3 great cheers as we come away in the steamer with heavy hearts rather, In 3 hours more M$^r$ W M T. is hard at work at Punch Office: M$^r$ Parson Quekett [169] has got to his night-school at S$^t$ Georges in the East: that beautiful gracious princess of a M$^{rs}$ Herbert is dressing herself up in diamonds & rubies very likely

[168] Thackeray's description of the scene aboard the *Derwent*, which sailed from Gravesend for Hobart Town, Tasmania, on November 26 (*Times*), calls to mind Ford Madox Brown's well-known painting "The Last of England."
[169] The Rev. W. Queckett was incumbent of Christ Church, St. George-in-the-East, Watney Street, Commercial Road (*Post Office London Directory*, 1847).

to go out into the world: or is she upstairs in the nursery reading
a good book over the child's cradle? O enormous various changing
wonderful solemn world! Admirable providence of God that creates such an infinitude of men — it makes one very grave and, † I
whisper to you ma soeur,† full of love and awe. I was thinking
about this yesterday morning before six when I was writing the
last paragraphs of Pendennis in bed and the sun walked into the
room, and supplied the last paragraph w^h ends with an allusion
about you, and w^h I think means a benediction upon W^m and your
child and my dear lady.[170] God keep you.


729.              TO WILLIAM ALLINGHAM
                     29–30 NOVEMBER 1850

My text is taken from *Letters to William Allingham*, ed. H. Allingham and
E. Baumer Williams (London, 1911), pp. 279–281.

My dear Mr. Allingham, — Months after date let me discharge
the debt I owe you and thank you for poems.[171] I began a letter
to you in September after reading the book, and waited and waited
intending to criticize at large and speak of what I liked and
doubted — but I doubted of one or two sentences of the criticism
too, and the letter never went and the months rushed after each
other. I've only finished *Pendennis* two days, and have been asleep
almost ever since.

I recognized you in *Household Words* the other day [172] — with
the Tennysonian cadence (who doesn't catch it who reads him?)
and the thoughts, observations and calmness your own. He has

---

[170] It seems likely that Thackeray refers not to the last, but to the next
to the last paragraph of *Pendennis*, in which he says of Laura: ". . . this
sweet lady is the friend of the young and the old; and her life is always passed
in making other lives happy" (*Works*, II, 752).

[171] *Poems* by *William Allingham*. See below, No. 737.

[172] Allingham's "Wayconnel Tower" appeared in *Household Words* on
November 16, 1850, p. 181. It was later reprinted, with some alterations,
in *Day and Night Songs — First Series* (1854).

just been here much excited about his court dress and sword (he says his legs are very good but we know what the Psalms say on that subject) [173] and as much pleased and innocent about it as a girl or a page. Everybody speaks well of his new wife [174] and of his affectionateness to her. . . . You have still time enough to heal old wounds and get new ones. I have passed my critical period I think and don't expect again to have my sleep disturbed by thoughts of any female.

This is not talking about your book. Well, I like it very much, that is all I can say, because the book seems to me true. I like its grey calm tones and solitary sweetness. I like a young fellow saddened by a great shock and bearing it with a manly gentle heart. I read it (in my own copy as well) at one of your chiefs', S. Spring Rice, who spoke in high terms not only of the Pote but of the Officer, which is always good for a young man to hear.

You're lucky to have a trade and to live out of this turmoil. It's pleasant enough for a man until he's successful: and then things go hard —

I tore off half a page here relating to my own literary woes, and egotistical plaints which are best put in the fire. I hope dear old Leigh Hunt won't take the loss of the laurels to heart after bidding for them so naïvely as he did in those pleasant memoirs.[175]

Do you see *The Leader* which his son Thornton writes? Thornton seems a fine fellow to me: wrong, very often, but looking after truth sacredly. But you mustn't have the paper at Ballyshannon, it would frighten people there: it does often shock even here: where we are not easily shocked and easily tired.

After making a great noise myself I begin to wonder why we have made so much to-do about the Cardinal.[176] Why shouldn't he come and set up a winking Virgin in the Strand? The claims

[173] "He delighteth not in the strength of the horse: he taketh not pleasure in the legs of a man" (*Psalms*, 147, 10).
[174] The former Emily Sellwood (d. 1896), whom Tennyson had married on June 13, 1850.
[175] Despite *The Autobiography of Leigh Hunt* (1850), Tennyson had been appointed Poet Laureate on November 19.
[176] Cardinal Wiseman.

of the Bishop of Oxford [177] (who is delightful company) are not much less preposterous: and Dr. Pusey says "quite right, it's not Popery the parsons have to fear but universal Protestantism." — Is it coming? — it must, to get rid of these Papists — the old sixteenth century Protestantism can fight them: they've the best of that battle.

I wish I weren't born in the time when the other is to take place, being of a lazy epicurean nature and woundily averse to fighting; but if it comes it must: and we must take up the cudgels on our side like the Paddies at Birkenhead the other day.[178] Ah me! Can't we be left aisy?

If I write you a stupid letter it is because I am tired and unwell: because I hate paying my debts: because I must pay you now if I've any honesty left. Shall I confess? — There's a letter of yours, I found it on returning from abroad, lying on my table below: and I've not dared to open the seal: it's like a dun: it's like Conscience upbraiding me. Well, to-morrow I'll have the courage to open it — I may now: and now Good night, and believe me. — Sincerely yours,

W. M. Thackeray.

Saturday. (the next morning that is) I have just read your note. I don't think it would answer — from your distance from London; [179] but if you'll send me any first chop bits I will send them to Mr. Lemon and try.

[177] Bishop Wilberforce. See above, No. 704.

[178] A dispatch in *The Times* of November 29 describes a riot that broke up a meeting of protest in Birkenhead two days earlier against the Papal Aggression.

[179] Allingham, who was at this time Principal Coast Officer of Customs in Belfast, evidently wished to contribute to *Punch*.

730.                 TO LADY POLLOCK
                    18 DECEMBER 1850

My text is taken from an Anderson Galleries Catalogue, February 24–25, 1930.

My dear Lady Pollock.

I did not know till last night why there is to be the breakfast at Hatton on Saturday; [180] and as my trip to Paris is delayed, I insist upon withdrawing my refusal; and whether you accept me or not, I shall be at the Church at Belfont at 11, and then you *must* ask me home to breakfast.

Wishing the bride every happiness and my best regards to her Papa. I am yours always most truly

W. M. Thackeray.

731.                      TO ?
                    22 DECEMBER 1850

Hitherto unpublished.

                                    Kensington December 22.
Dear Sir

I was on my way to Thurloe Square one day, when I met you riding in Brompton; & so thought I would take some other occasion of calling upon you. I have had very much to do since then, having had a more than double month's work [181] for my portion: or I should have ere this acknowledged your visit & thanked you for your pamphlet & your obliging note.

I read it with very much interest, as well for the subject of w^h you áre the historian, as for the perfect skill with w^h you have made our language your own.

Believe me, dear Sir, very faithfully yours

W M Thackeray

[180] Grace Anne, fifth daughter of Sir Frederick and Lady Pollock, married Henry Arthur Herbert on Saturday, December 21, 1850.

[181] The final (double) number of *Pendennis*, parts XXIII and XXIV, chapters 71 to 75, published for December, 1850.

732.                    TO MRS. BROOKFIELD
                       23 DECEMBER 1850

Published in part, *Collection of Letters*, pp. 129–130. The words between
daggers were overscored by Mrs. Brookfield.

White Lion. Bristol.
Monday.

My dear Lady. With the gold pen there's no knowing how and
what I write — the handwriting is quite different and it seems as
if one was speaking with a different voice. Fancy a man stepping
up to speak to you in stilts & trying to make a bow, or paying you
compliments through a Punch's whistle — Not that I ever did pay
you a compliment you know: but I cant, or I shan't be able for a
time or two to approach you naturally, and must skate along over
this shiny paper. I went to Clevedon & saw the last rites performed
for poor dear Harry.[182] I went from here and waited at Candy's
till the time of the funeral in such cold weather! Candy's shop was
full of ceaseless customers all the time — there never was a little
boy buying candles or an old woman with the toothache (only look
(the last word is look) at the paper) all the time I was there — at
last the moment drew nigh, and Tinling in a scarf & hatband driving
himself down from the Court passed the shop & I went down to
the Church. It looked very tranquil and well ordained, and I had
half an hour there before the procession came in view — Those
ceremonies over a corpse the immortal soul of a man being in the
keeping of G   ., and beyond the reach of all undertakers always
appear to me shocking rather than solemn, and the horses and the
plumes gave me pain — The awful moment was when the dear
old father the coffin being lowered into the vault where so much
of his affection and tenderest love lies buried went down into the
cave, and gave the coffin a last kiss. There was no standing that
last most affecting touch of Nature.

Then we went back to Clevedon Court where everybody was

[182] Harry Hallam was buried on December 23 (*Mrs. Brookfield*, II, 339–
340).

very kind, and where Aggy & Beatrice [183] and I had a great talk and play. It's odd how one can make fun & dance with other folks children and not with one's own — I cant be jocular with them somehow. M^r Hallam who had been † out of town † up stairs came down after an hour or two, and I was so sorry that I had decided on coming back to Bristol when he asked whether I wasn't going to stay? Why didn't I? I had written & proposed myself to Dean Elliot [184] in the morning personally, & I find he is out of town on returning here, in the coldest night to the most discomfortable inn, writing paper, gold pen.

There was a great fog and in the walks and terrace one could scarcely see anything. Arthur [185] your uncle the Captain & your father and Parr and T—nd—l how do you spell his name? and W^m who was very much affected and F. Lushington [186] made the funeral party — M^rs Elton was very kind and hospitable and I like her always though she *didnt* ask me to Clevedon with the children, but I suppose there is no room for me, and it will be better that I should go to Paris with A & M whilst you are in your old home quarters — My dear Sister what matters a week or 2 more or less? Duty Duty is the word: and I hope & pray you will do it *cheerfully* Now it is to comfort & help the weak hearted: & so may your comforter & helper raise you up when you fall. I wonder whether what I said to you yesterday was true? [187] I know

[183] Mary Agnes and Laura Beatrice Elton, daughters of Mrs. Brookfield's brother Arthur.

[184] The Very Rev. Gilbert Elliot (1800–1891), D.D., Dean of Bristol, was an older brother of Thackeray's friend Thomas Frederick Elliot.

[185] Arthur Elton, Henry Hallam, Captain Robbins, Sir Charles Elton, Tom Parr, and Thomas Onesiphorus Tyndall (d. 1869), who had married Mrs. Brookfield's sister Caroline Lucy Elton in 1844.

[186] Franklin Lushington, a classmate of Harry Hallam at Trinity College, Cambridge.

[187] This allusion is explained in the few lines of Mrs. Brookfield's letter to Thackeray of December 21 which have been printed: "There is not much to say except that I woke up with the recollection of your little scolding, and determined not to give way too much to dismal thoughts. They are all gone to Clevedon and Julia and I remain alone. I hope to-morrow Anny and Minny may come here to see me. I think Julia felt touched by your going down for the funeral.

what I think about the famous chapter of S.<sup>t</sup> Paul that we heard to day — one glory of the Sun & another of the moon, and one flesh of birds & one of fishes and so forth [188] — premature definitions — yearnings and strivings of a great heart after the truth. — Ah me — When shall we reach the truth? How can we with imperfect organs? But we can get nearer & nearer or at least eliminate false-hood.

Tomorrow then for Sir Joncamobbus.[189] Write to me there dear Sister I know you will. And tell me you are cheerful: and that your baby is well and that you love your affectionate old brother. When will you see the children? Tomorrow I hope: and now I will go (I'm obliged to write with fierce desperation on this dreadful paper) I will go to bed & pray as best I can for you and yours and for your nieces and your faithful old Makepeace

It writes here but on the
other side it wont mark
without agonies
GBY.

733.                    TO ANNE THACKERAY
                        24 DECEMBER 1850

Hitherto unpublished.

My dearest Fat. This will be one more of those disappointments w.<sup>h</sup> are blighting always your miserable existence: I dont know M.<sup>rs</sup> Lewes's [190] address — and have wrote the enclosed for her apropos of that handsome article in the Leader. If you have not sent

"I went to-day to kneel down by the coffin and to remember what a kind creature had been taken from us." (*Mrs. Brookfield*, II, 337)

[188] *I Corinthians*, 15, 39 and 41, which forms part of "The Order for the Burial of the Dead" (*Book of Common Prayer*).

[189] Sir John Cam Hobhouse (1786–1869), later (1851) first Baron Broughton, the liberal statesman, writer, and intimate friend of Byron. Thackeray was his guest from December 24–28 at his estate of Erle Stoke, Westbury, Wiltshire.

[190] The wife of George Henry Lewes; her husband's article in *The Leader* was presumably a review of *Pendennis*.

it to Granny yet: I should like you to show it to the Brookfields:
and that you and Minny should go there tomorrow taking this
with you if you like to M$^{rs}$ B; and wishing our love and a happy
Xmas to all of them. I wrote her a note yesterday, & will again
from Erlstoke [191] — You might go to Wilton Crescent just before
you went to Aunt Mary. Look out Sir J. Hobhouse's address in
the Court Guide: and forward letters to me.

Yesterday passed away pretty well: it was very affecting to see
M$^r$ Hallam go down into the vault, to have one last look at the
grave of his dear Son. But the ceremonial and the scarfs, and
feathers and hatbands of the Funeral annoyed me — One wished it
could have been done without all that old-world mummery. When
I am buried, you will have the goodness to remember that there
are no hatbands scarfs or feathers — and that unless black coaches
have come down in price by that time, the people go in cabs.

I intended to have passed the evening with D$^r$ Elliot but he
was away, so I went to bed early to one of my big sleeps —

God bless my dear women: and all who love us and give us all
a happy Xmas —

## W M T.

[191] "Thackeray, the author of 'Pendennis,' is also staying with me," Lord
Broughton (John Cam Hobhouse) noted in his diary on December 24. "He is
a most agreeable man, very tall and big, with a broken nose, and always wears
spectacles. He gave my daughter a specimen of his power of sketching by
making a frontispiece to 'Pendennis' in pen and ink.

"He spoke of his literary labours without reserve, and said he lived on
them. He is going to America to give lectures on English literature or to write
a book." (*Recollections of a Long Life*, 6 vols., London, 1909–1911, VI, 266.)

734.                    TO MRS. BROOKFIELD
                    26 DECEMBER 1850 [192]

Published in part, *Collection of Letters*, pp. 100–101.

Thursday.

As I am not to come back till Saturday, and lest you should think that any illness had befallen me dear lady I send you a little note. This place is as handsome as man could desire, the park beautiful, the quizeen and drinks excellent, the landlord most polite and good natured, with a very winning simplicity of manner and bonhommie and the small select party tolerably pleasant. Charles Villiers, a bitter Voltairian joker, who always surprizes one into laughter — Peacock [193] — did you ever read Headlong Hall & Maid Marian? — a charming lyrical poet and Horatian satirist he was when a writer; now he is a whiteheaded jolly old worldling and Secretary to the E. India House full of information about India and everything else in the world. There are 4 or 5 more, 2 young lords, one extremely pleasant gentlemanlike and modest who has seen battles in India and gives himself not the least airs — and there are the young ladies, 2 pretty little girls [194] with whom I dont get on very well though — Nor indeed with anybody over-well. There's something wanting, I can't tell you what: and I shall be glad to be on the homeward way again but they wouldn't hear of my going on Friday, and it was only by a strong effort that I could get leave for Saturday. *This* paper you see is better I bought it regardless of expense — half a ream of it — at Bristol. That Bristol terminus is a confounding place — I missed the train I was to go by: had very nearly gone to Exeter and was obliged to post 25 mile: in the dark from Chippenham in order to get here too

[192] This letter appears to have been written while Thackeray was staying with Sir John Cam Hobhouse. Thursday was December 26.

[193] Thomas Love Peacock (1785–1866), the novelist, Chief Examiner of the East India Company from 1836 to 1856.

[194] Hobhouse's daughters, Charlotte, who married Dudley Wilmot Carleton, fourth Baron Dorchester, in 1854, and Sophia, who married John Strange Jocelyn, later fifth Earl of Roden, in 1851.

late for dinner. Whilst I am writing to you what am I thinking of? — something else to be sure and have a doggrel ballad about 'a yellow Post Chay' running in my head w^h I ought to do for M^r Punch.[195]

We went to the little Church yesterday, where in a great pew with a fire in it, I said the best prayers I could for them as I am fond of. I wish one of them would get well: and that her period of trial was over, and that of rest could arrive for you. You might be comfortable for a little at Bournemouth, mightn't you? I must give my young ones 3 or 4 weeks at Paris: and may go a travelling myself during that time, for I think my dear old Mother will be happier with the children and without their father: and will like best to have them all to herself. Bon Dieu is that the luncheon-bell already? I was late at dinner yesterday and late at breakfast this morning — It is eating and idling all day long: but not altogether profitless idling — I have seen winter woods winter landscapes, a kennel of hounds, jolly sportsmen riding out a hunting, a queer little country church with a choir not in surplices but smock frocks and many a sight pleasant to think on — I must go to lunch and finish after, both with my dear lady, and the yellow pochay.

Will M^r & M^rs Brookfield come and dine with M^r Thackeray on Saturday? He will arrive by the train w^h reaches London at 5.25: and it would be very very pleasant if you could come — or one of you man or woman. Meanwhile I close up my packet with a G. b. y. to my dear lady and a kiss to Miss Brookfield and go out for a walk in the woods with a noble party that is waiting down stairs. The days pass away in spite of us, and we're carried along the rapid stream of time you see. And if days pass quick, why a month will, and then we shall be cozily back again in London once more and I shall see you at your own fire or lying on your own sofa, very quiet and calm after all this trouble & turmoil. God bless you dear lady & W^m and your little maiden.

W M T.

[195] This ballad does not appear to have been written.

735.          TO ROBERT SMITH SURTEES
                 29 DECEMBER 1850

Hitherto unpublished.

Kensington.  Sunday 29 Dec<sup>r</sup>

My dear Surtees

I send on your note to Leech reproaching myself as I see your
hand-writing with benefits not forgot but unacknowledged.  I ought,
of course I ought, to have thanked you for your presents of books:
and to have written to you — but there came a journey in the
autumn, and then such hard work afterwards that writing for any-

thing but money was out of the question I
mean that the sight of a pen becomes odious
to a man after some periods of labour and
he can't take it up except in compulsion.  Can
you?  felix ter et amplius [196] you who can
afford to jaunt & jollify when you like only,
and never miss a days sport, but when you
choose it.  Sir, when I came back from the
country to the bosom of my family last night
there was the printers devil waiting in the
Hall.  He's always there.  always waiting.
I'm surprized we get any letters written at
all.

As you only read books in a lump, I'll send you Pendennis with
my very best regards and hope it may serve to set you to sleep
these winter evenings.  I dont know whether it is stupid as a whole.
I am sure the binders are stupid who have put the dedication and
preface into the second volume, but please when it comes accept it
faults and all, and may you live a many score merry Xmases prays

Yours very truly

W M Thackeray

[196] Horace, *Odes*, I, 13, l. 17.  Surtees's first book was *Jorrocks' Jaunts and
Jollities* (1838).

736.    TO GEORGE MORLAND CRAWFORD [197]
DECEMBER 1850?

My text is taken from *The New York Tribune*, December 13, 1885.

You will find much to remind you of old talks and faces — of William John O'Connell,[198] Jack Sheehan and Andrew Archedecne [199] — in this book. There is something of you in Warrington,

[197] This letter was sent to Crawford (d. 1885), with a presentation copy of *Pendennis*. Crawford, we learn from an account of his career in *The New York Tribune* (December 13, 1885), "was born in the charming Kent manor of Chelsfield Court, of which he was to be the lord. He was an eldest son and heir to an entailed estate of which an extravagant father had a life interest. But to prevent the paternal interest being sold by creditors and his sisters going out as governesses, he became responsible for the load of debt. He at first asked that £200 a year might be left him to be able to wait at the bar, to which he had been called, for clients. But his mother wept and asked what was to become of the helpless part of the family. He consulted a religious old barrister of whom he had been the pupil, and was told not to grieve his parents and 'trust to God to make good the sacrifice.' This counsel he adopted. Part of his subsequent life was brought by his friend Thackeray into 'The Adventures of Philip' and 'Pendennis.' At Lincoln's Inn Mr. Crawford belonged to the brilliant set which used to dine on Saturdays at Judge Talfourd's, and he knew most of the barristers who rose to eminence in his time, and the foremost authors and orators. He was beginning to win a high reputation as a Chancery barrister when London fog gave him a sore throat." It was at about this time that Saville Morton was murdered (see *Memoranda*), and Crawford, at Thackeray's suggestion, applied for Morton's post as Paris correspondent of *The Daily News*. He filled this position with great distinction until his death thirty-three years later.

[198] No doubt a transcriber's error for Morgan John O'Connell.

[199] It would appear from the account of Arcedeckne in Jeaffreson's *A Book of Recollections* (I, 329–331) that Thackeray's portrait of him as Foker was decidedly flattering. He was an idle man-about-town, living on a small inherited fortune, whom Thackeray saw chiefly at the Garrick Club. His relations with Thackeray are amusingly described by Sir Francis Cowley Burnand (*Pall Mall Magazine*, XVIII, 327–328): ". . . Arcedeckne was a most eccentric character, a genuine low comedian off the stage. . . . During the last years of his comparatively short life, Arcedeckne and myself were great 'chums.' He used to amuse me immensely, especially with his Garrick Club stories and his reminiscences of Thackeray. . . . Arcedeckne 'owed' Thackeray 'one' on account of his having used him as his model for Foker in 'Pendennis,' and he never lost an opportunity of scoring off the great novelist, of whom, however, he invariably spoke with affectionate familiarity

but he is not fit to hold a candle to you, for, taking you all round, you are the most genuine fellow that ever strayed from a better world into this. You don't smoke, and he is a consumed smoker of tobacco. Bordeaux and port were your favourites at 'the Deanery' and 'the Garrick,' and War. is always guzzling beer. But he has your honesty, and like you could not posture if he tried. You have a strong affinity for the Irish. May you some day find an Irish girl to lead you to matrimony. There's no such good wife as a daughter of Erin.

W. M. T.

---

as 'Old Thac.' Occasionally, and only when in a very mischievous yet genial mood, would Arcedeckne address him as 'Thac my boy!' He would select a moment when Thackeray, towering above little podgy Arcedeckne, was standing in the smoking-room with his back to the fire and his coat tails spread out, his mind occupied with some work the proofs of which were probably in the pockets he was warming, when Arcedeckne would furtively enter, look round, pretend not to see him, and then, as he reopened the door preparatory to taking his departure, he would look back and say, in his grating, nasal voice, 'Hallo! Thac my boy! gettin' inspiration, eh?' and then *exit quickly*.' It was a delightful illustration of 'dignity and impudence.' At other times Arcedeckne would wait until Thackeray had comfortably settled himself with a cigar in a large armchair, and just when he had assumed his favourite attitude of lounging back, head in air, and right leg crossed over his left, the sole of his boot being well *en évidence*, the original of Foker would sneak in, humming to himself some popular air, — his favourite was the song of 'Villikens and his Dinah,' — while carrying an unlighted cigar in his left hand and a match in his right. Then, as he passed the peacefully meditative giant, pigmy Arcedeckne, pausing awhile in his humming, would exclaim, with a sort of cheery grunt, 'Hallo! Thac my boy!' and, as if obeying an irresistible inspiration, would sharply strike the match on the sole of Thackeray's boot, light his cigar, and then hurriedly limp out of the room (he was a bit gouty) without saying another word, leaving Thackeray speechless at this 'confounded liberty.' 'Awfully good chap was old Thac,' Arcedeckne used to say, when subsequently narrating this and similar anecdotes: 'Lor' bless you, he didn't mind me a bit. But I *did* take it out of him now and again. Never gave him time for a repartee.' "

737.                TO EDWARD CHAPMAN
                        1850 [200]

Hitherto unpublished.

Dear Chapman

A young Irish man a M^r Allingham has come up to town with a volume of poems of such good mark that any publisher may be proud to act as Master of Ceremonies to them and introduce them to the world. I've only seen him once through the introduction of Leigh Hunt, and like him, and should be glad if you would be his man of business. He is ready to pay the expenses of the publication he says and of course I have warned him not to expect a fortune.

Will you see him on Monday if he calls introduced by

                        Yours very truly
                        W M Thackeray

738.                TO MRS. BROOKFIELD
                        1850? [201]

My text is taken from *The Critic*, New Series, VIII (1887), 179.

My dear Mrs. Brookfield: — I have just been to Mrs. Pratt the worsted lady, and have told her how the jacket is too small. She will send somebody this ev'g or tomorrow and I hope that person will be able to remedy the defect: and that the little jacket will keep its owner warm through the winter. Believe me dear Mrs. Brookfield always truly yours.

                    W. M. Thackeray.

[For record of another letter to Mrs. Brookfield in 1850? see letter 18, Appendix XXVI.]

[200] This note was evidently written during the early months of 1850. A first volume of poems by William Allingham (1824–1889) was published later in the year by Chapman and Hall. See above, No. 729.

[201] It seems likely that the jacket which this letter concerns was for Magdalene Brookfield's use during the winter of 1850–1851.

739.                        TO MRS. GORE
                                1850

Hitherto unpublished.

                                          Kensington.  Sunday.

My dear M<sup>rs</sup> Gore

If it weren't the working time I would come & tell you that I
have read the Hamiltons [202] and have been not only pleased by it,
I mean for cleverness & so forth, but amused by it; and that is a
great thing for a professional man to own  I wish to goodness you
could say as much for me.  But its not to be done I'm afraid.

I liked the part of the death of George IV & the babby very
much — the touch of kindness gives a sort of chance & hope for
the poor old departing reprobate, and gives him a drop of water
in that warm place between w<sup>h</sup> and Abraham's bosom there is a
great gulph fixed.[203]  What an awful radical you are Ma'am or
you was!  There's tremendous revolutionary sentiments in the
Hamiltons.  Susan is a party after my own sort — mild and sweet
charming but not inebriating  I should like to have such a woman
to bully.  She would like it so too.

And I think some critics who carped at some writers for talking
too much about fine company ought to hold their tongues.  If you
live with great folks, why should you not describe their manners?
There is nothing in the least strained in these descriptions as I now
think — and believe it was only a secret envy & black malignity of
disposition w<sup>h</sup> made me say in former times this author is talking
too much about grand people, this author is of the silver fork school,
this author uses too much French &c [204]  There's none in this book
to speak, perhaps that's why you sent it to me you malicious woman,

[202] Mrs. Gore's *The Hamiltons, or the New Era* was first published in
1834 and reprinted in 1850.
    [203] *Luke,* 16: 22–26.
    [204] See "Lords and Liveries," Thackeray's parody of Mrs. Gore's fiction in
*Novels by Eminent Hands,* and his review (hitherto unidentified) of Mrs.
Gore's *Sketches of English Character* in *The Morning Chronicle* of May 4,
1846.

and the only point I object to is perhaps a too frequent use of the note of hadmiration! After all one must object to something. I didn't think Hopes drawing room chairs were handsome enough — thank G — one can find a hole in every body's coat.

Madam, about Kingsley the Rev^d C. Kingsley J^r is a writer of great power and poethry in Frasers Magazine,²⁰⁵ not a contributor to the Times. Shall he have your book? If so I'll forward it to Parker. Kingsley is a Xtian chartist or very near it I believe, & I am

> Your grateful but neglectful servt to command
> W M Thackeray

740. TO MRS. CARMICHAEL-SMYTH
3 JANUARY 1851

*Address:* M^rs Carmichael Smyth. | 95 Fbg. S^t Honoré | Paris. *Postmark:* 3 JA 1851, PARIS 4 JANV. 51. Hitherto unpublished.

My dearest Mammy     Such a tempest is blowing in London today that until it's end I dont fancy tempting the waves or crossing the water, and instead of coming away tomorrow night as we had thought, it will probably be Monday before we start. Besides I have a fine sore throat w^h I want to cure before commencing the journey. So we shall come on you like thieves in the night: and you'll have the pleasure of roosting your young ones under your wings once more: and for 2 or 3 weeks. Then you'll come to us in May, won't you, for the lectures? and when I'm gone to America, you'll have a long spell of them. Jeames & I will go into lodgings somewhere in the neighbourhood: Will you take them? — The Madeleine would be a good quarter, or any place near where there is plenty of light and a decent shelter. I shall bring some books and try and read very hard. I'm afraid one is past that now, and the power of application no stronger than it ever was in me.

---

²⁰⁵ *Yeast, a Problem* was first published in *Fraser's Magazine* between July and December, 1848.

Poor little Chéri is here for a day or 2, a kindly little creature old fashioned [1] and weakly poor child: and affecting somehow. I'll go see Mary today: and she is to have the benefit of the fly during my absence in foreign parts. The children all go to Lady Carmichael to night: and speak in terms of not much enthusiasm of their Xtmas dinner at Mary's     Mine was pleasant enough though I had rather have been at home: but I didn't like to refuse the kind giver of the cadetship.[2] He is the kindest of hosts: with the best of cellars and a comfortable house where people may do very much as they like. I was at work for the chief part of the days I was there: and when I'm not busy, write letters all the morning: by half dozens at a time about everybody's business — plague take it. Anny will be letter-writer in a year or two, and taught to forge her father's hand writing — Stop — I was going to say Wouldnt D$^r$ Halliday take me in for a day or two: but it's best not. The best way is to find a lodging: have out papers & books and go to work. We must make the great coup this time: and save that sum of money.

I am very glad to find that Morton's enemy M$^r$ Wheble the second of the other chap has left Paris. I dont see how old M. could have helped an explanation with that fellow. Charles's was by far the sensiblest letter of the bunch I think & mine the worst & most quarrelsome, not as against Campbell but Wheble — Poor Morton has a genius for scrapes such as no man out of Ireland ever can hope for: & the wonder is that he has lasted up to 40 years of age with a whole skin — Why he is always in some feminine mischief, and has kicked lots of whatdyoucallums besides Forbes Campbells — Goodbye my dear old G P and Granny say we all till next week.

[1] ". . . it is to be lamented of this young gentleman," observes Miss Cornelia Blimber of little Paul in chapter 14 of *Dombey and Son,* "that he is singular (what is usually termed old-fashioned) in his character and conduct, and that, without presenting anything which distinctly calls for reprobation, he is often very unlike other young gentlemen of his age and social position."

[2] See above, No. 727.

741.       TO MRS. PROCTER
JANUARY 1851? [3]

*Hitherto unpublished. My text is taken from a transcript given Lady Ritchie by George Murray Smith.*

My dear Mrs Procter,

I shall try and see you tomorrow. I can't come to dinner. I'm going to Paris on Tuesday. Don't have a farewell dinner to Revel.[4] Don't bid anybody good bye. Don't be sorry at parting with anybody. Don't care for anybody except your own family circle in which all true affection ought to centre. Ad—you.

W. M. T.

742.       TO MRS. PROCTER
6 JANUARY 1851?

*Hitherto unpublished. My text is taken from a transcript given Lady Ritchie by George Murray Smith.*

My dear Mrs Procter,

The printers kept me till Saturday morning and then I could not leave my bed with illness which has occupied me till now, Monday.

I am so beat that I feel as if I had no pluck to go to Paris. Perhaps I may be stronger tomorrow and go: perhaps give it up: but what will happen to your parcel for Stevens?

Believe me,

Your unfortunate friend,

W. M. T.

[3] The place of this and the following note in the Procter sequence suggests that they were written just before Thackeray departed for Paris early in January, 1851.

[4] Emily de Viry, widow of Charles de Viry and half-sister of Mrs. Procter, afterwards married the Count Adrien de Revel, Sardinian ambassador to England. A week after their marriage, both died of the cholera in Italy. (Frances Ann Kemble, *Records of Later Life*, p. 521.)

743.              TO ABRAHAM HAYWARD
                     6 JANUARY 1851

Hitherto unpublished.

                                13 Young S͟t Kensington. Jan 6.
My dear Hayward

Here are the volumes of w͟h you have always befriended the
author. I only found them on my return from the country and
when you get them, shall be at Paris for a week or two — With
them comes what I know you'll disapprove — a little controversy
with the Times [5] but I *couldn't* forego the chance: and the whole
story is strictly true strange to say & the publishers of the Xmas
book did actually sell the last copy (& send me a 50£ note too)
on the day when the Times article appeared. Be hanged to them!
I send out a strong man and they leave him alone: but I send out
a poor little boy and they rush out on him and thump him — Vale

                         Yours ever

                         W M Thackeray —


744.                 TO MRS. PROCTER
                      8 JANUARY 1851 [6]

Hitherto unpublished. My text is taken from a transcript given Lady Ritchie
by George Murray Smith.

My dear Mrs Procter,

I'm only come to say good bye. My cab is at the door and my
bag is on the box [7] — and I wanted to say that I was busy till 9

[5] See "An Essay on Thunder and Small Beer," Thackeray's preface to the
second edition of *The Kickleburys on the Rhine* (*Works*, IX, 161–168).
According to Henry Sutherland Edwards (*Personal Recollections*, pp. 38–39),
the writer of *The Times'* article which Thackeray attacked was Charles Lamb
Kenney, who shortly afterward "confessed his fault, and was at once forgiven."
Lady Ritchie writes that it was this "rather short, good-looking man, with a
fair, placid face" who served as a model for Thackeray's drawings of Pendennis (*Biographical Introductions*, II, xxxiii).

[6] This note was written the Wednesday after Friday, January 3.

[7] See above, No. 293.

o'clock on Monday and so couldn't come, and went to bed at 9 last night quite tired out — and now I'm actually gone for a fortnight or perhaps more: and am going to see L. Napoleon Lamartine and all the Parisian lions. I hope it will be very good fun. But I don't much fancy it will.

Meanwhile I am yours always,<br>W. M. T.

I am rather glad you weren't here as I hate taking leave.

745.    TO MRS. BROOKFIELD
9–12 JANUARY 1851

Published in part, *Collection of Letters*, pp. 105–109.

Hotel Bristle. P. Vendome.

Madam, One is arrived; one is at his ancient lodging of the Hotel Bristol; one has heard the familiar clarions sounding at nine hours and a half under the Column; the place is whipped by the rain actually and only rare umbrellas make themselves to see here and there. London is grey & brumous but scarcely more sorrowful than this. For so much, so love I these places, it is with the eyes that the sun makes itself on the first day at Paris: one has suffered one has been disabused but one is not blased to this point that nothing more excites nothing amuses. The first day of Paris amuses always. Isn't this a perfectly odious and affected style of writing? [8] Wouldnt you be disgusted to have a letter written all like that? Many people are scarcely less affected though in compoging letters and translate their thoughts into a pompous unfamiliar language as necessary & proper for the circumstances of letter writing. In the midst of this sentiment — Jeames comes in having been employed to buy pens in the neighborhood, and having paid, he said 3 francs

[8] It amused Thackeray to translate French literally into English, and he occasionally wrote whole articles in this vein for *Punch*. See "M. Gobe-mouche's Authentic Account of the Grand Exhibition," *Works*, VI, 197–200, and "From the Own Correspondent of the Moniteur des Boulevards," *Punch*, March 8, 1851, p. 93.

for 20 — I go out in a rage to the shop, thinking to confound the woman who had cheated him: I place him outside the shop and entering myself ask the price of a score of pens — One franc says the woman — I call in James to confront him with the trades-woman — She says, I sold Monsieur a box of pens he gave me a 5 franc piece — I returned him two 2 franc pieces — and so it was only Jeames never having before seen a 2 franc piece thought that she had given him back 2 franc-pieces — and so nobody is cheated and I had my walk in the rain for nothing.

But as this had brought me close to the Palais Royal where there's the Exhibition of pictures I went to see it: wondering whether I could turn an honest penny by criticising the same. But I find Ive nothing to say about pictures: a pretty landscape or two pleased me: no statues did: some great big historical pictures bored me — This is a poor account of a Paris Exhibition isn't it? Looking for 1/2 a minute at a work w$^h$ had taken a man all his might and main for a year, on w$^h$ he had employed all his talents and set all his hopes and ambition: about w$^h$ he had lain awake at night very probably and pinched himself of a dinner that he might buy colours or pay models — I say it seems very unkind to look at such a thing with a yawn and turn away indifferent: and it seemed to me as if the cold marble statues looked after me reproachfully and said 'Come back, you Sir, don't neglect me in this rude way: I am very beautiful, I am indeed. I have many hidden charms and qualities w$^h$ you dont know yet, & w$^h$ you would know and love, if you would but examine a little.' But I didn't come back — the world didn't care for the hidden charms of the statue, but passed on and yawned over the next article in the Catalogue. There is a moral to this fable I think, and that is all I got out of the exhibition of the Palais Royal.

Then I went to beat up the old haunts, and look about for lodg-ings w$^h$ are awfully scarce and dear in this quarter. Here they can only take me in for a day or two: and Im occupying at present 2 rooms in a gorgeous suite of apartments big enough and splendid enough for the Lord Chief Baron and all his family [9] — Oh but

[9] Sir Frederick Pollock had twenty-four children.

first, I forgot, I went to breakfast with Bear Ellice [10] who told me
Lady Sandwich had a grand ball, and promised to take me to a
swoary at M. Duchatel's — I went there after dining at home —
splendid hotel in the Fbg S<sup>t</sup> Germain: magnificent droaring room:
vulgar people I thought — The walls were splendidly painted —
C'est du Louis XV ou du commencement de Louis XVI the host
said. Blagueur! the painting is about 10 years old and is of the
highly-ornamental Café School — It is a Louis Philippest house
and everybody was in mourning for the dear Queen of the Bulgiums
I suppose — The men as they arrived went up & made their bows
to the lady of the house, who sate by the fire talking to other 2
ladies, and this bow over the gentlemen talked standing to each
other. It was uncommonly stewpid. Then we went off to Lady
Sandwich's ball. I had wrote a note to her Ladyship in the morning
and received a kyind invitation — Everybody was there — Thiers
Molé and the French Sosiatee: and lots of English. The Castlereaghs very kind and hearty my lady looking very pooty indeed
and Cass — mark the easy grace of Cass — well and clear sighted
— L<sup>d</sup> Normanby & wife exceeding gracious — Lady Waldegrave
— all sorts of world — and if I want the reign of pleasure it is here
it is here. Gudin [11] the painter asked me to dine today & meet
Dumas w<sup>h</sup> will be amusing I hope.

And I forgot to say that M<sup>r</sup> Thomas Fraser says that M<sup>r</sup> Inspector Brookfield is the most delightful fellow he ever met. I
went to see my Aunt besides all this and the evening & the morning was the first day.

Sunday m<sup>g</sup> I passed the morning yesterday writing a scene of a

---

[10] Edward Ellice (1781–1863), merchant and Whig politician, known as
"the Bear" because of his connection with the Canadian fur trade; the former
Lady Mary Paget (d. 1859), who had married the seventh Earl of Sandwich
in 1838; Charles Duchâtel (1803–1867), an Orleanist politician who had
retired from public life after the fall of Louis Philippe in 1848; Queen
Marie Louise (d. 1850), daughter of Louis Philippe, who had married Leo-
pold I of Belgium in 1832.

[11] Théodore Gudin (1802–1880), a marine painter who had enjoyed
Louis Philippe's special favor. His vogue declined rapidly during the Second
Empire.

play [12] so wicked witty and diabolical that I shall be curious to know if it's good: and went to the pictures again and afterwards to Lady Castlereagh and other polite persons finishing the afternoon dutifully at home and with my aunt & cousins whom you'd like. At dinner at Gudins there was a great stupid company and I sat between one of the stupidest and handsomest women I ever saw in my life and a lady to whom I made 3 observations w[h] she answered with Oui Monsieur and Non Monsieur, and then commenced a conversation over my back with my handsome neighbour. If this is French manners, says I, civility be hanged and so I ate my dinner and did not say one word more to that woman. But there were some pleasant people in spite of her: a painter with a leonine mane — M. Gigoux [13] that I took a liking to: an old General jolly and gentlemanlike: a humourous Prince agreeable and easy, and a wonderful old buck who was my pleasure. The party disported themselves until pretty late and we went up into a tower fitted up in the Arabian fashion and there smoked, w[h] did not diminish the pleasure of the evening. M[rs] Lock [14] the Engineer's wife brought me home in her Brougham, the great Engineer sitting bodkin and his wife scolding me amiably about Laura & Pendennis. A handsome woman this M[rs] Lock must have been when her engineer married her: but not quite up to her present aggrandized fortune — in manners and turnout I mean. Some people have not such good manners as some other people and M[rs] Lock had a blew satting gownd w[h] it was a most estraordinary raiment indeed —

My old folks seem happy in their quarters and good old GP bears the bore of the children constantly in his room with great good humour. But ah somehow its a dismal end to a career. A famous beauty and a soldier who has been in 20 battles and led

[12] A drama in blank verse about Bluebeard which was never finished. It is summarized in Professor Dodds's *Thackeray*, pp. 75–77. The manuscript is owned by Dr. Rosenbach.

[13] Jean François Gigoux (1806–1894), a painter of the romantic school who began to exhibit in 1831.

[14] The wife (d. 1866) of Joseph Locke (1805–1860), a noted railway engineer who built many important lines in England and France.

a half dozen of storming parties to end in a garret — and its not the
poverty I mean but the undignified dignity, the twopenny toadies,
the twaddling mean society and — here comes James to say that the
letters must this instant go. And so God bless you and your husband and little maiden, and write soon my dear kind lady to

W M T.

746.　　　　　　　TO MRS. BROOKFIELD
　　　　　　　　　13–16 JANUARY 1851

Published in part, *Collection of Letters*, pp. 111–115. The words enclosed
between daggers were overscored by Mrs. Brookfield.

My dear lady　　Do you see how mad everybody is in the
world, or is it my own insanity? Yesterday when it became time
to shut up my letter I was going to tell you about my elders, who
have got hold of a mad old Indian woman, who calls herself Aline
Sultane d'origine Mogole who is stark staring mad and sees visions
works miracles, que sais je? the old fool is mad of sheer vanity, and
yet fool as she is my people actually believe in her, and I believe
the old gentleman goes to her everyday. Today I went to see
Dorsay who has made a bust of Lamartine who too is mad with
vanity. He has written some verses [15] on his bust — he asks who is
this? is it a warrior, is it a hero, is it a priest, is it a sage, is it a

---

[15] "Au Comte d'Orsay," the first two stanzas of which read:

Quand le bronze, écumant dans ton moule d'argile,
Léguera par ta main mon image fragile
A l'œil indifférent des hommes qui naîtront,
S'ils promènent leurs doigts dans ces tempes ridées
Comme un lit dévasté du torrent des idées,
Pleins de doute, ils diront entre eux: De qui ce front?

Est-ce un soldat debout frappé pour la patrie?
Un poëte qui chante, un pontife qui prie?
Un orateur qui parle aux flots séditieux?
Est-ce un tribun de paix, soulevé par la houle,
Offrant, le cœur gonflé, sa poitrine à la foule,
Pour que la liberté remonte pure aux cieux?

(*Œuvres complètes de Lamartine*, 41 vols., Paris, 1860–1866, V, 87–88)

tribune of the people, is it an Adonis? — meaning that he is all these things — verses so fatuous & crazy I never saw. Well, Dorsay says they are the finest verses that ever were written & imparts to me a translation w$^h$ Miss Power has made of them: and Dorsay believes in his mad rubbish of a statue w$^h$ he *didn't* make — believes in it in the mad way that madmen do, that it is divine and that he made it: — only as you look in his eyes you see that he doesn't quite believe, and when pressed hesitates & turns away with a howl of rage. Dorsay has fitted himself up a charming atelier with arms and trophies pictures and looking glasses — the tomb of Blessington the sword & star of Napoleon and a crucifix over his bed: and here he dwells without any doubts or remorses, admiring himself in the most horrible pictures w$^h$ he has painted and the statues w$^h$ he gets done for him. I'd been at work till 2 all day before going to see him, and thence went to Lady Normanby who was very pleasant and talkative, and then tramping upon a half dozen of visits of duty. I had refused proffered banquets in order to dine at home but when I got home at the dinner hour everybody was away: the bonne was ill and obliged to go to the country, and parents and children were away to dine with a M$^{rs}$ Colmache, a good woman who writes books, keeps a select boarding house for young ladies who wish to see Parisian society and whom I like but can't bear because she has the organ of admiration too strongly — Papa was King, Mamma was Queen in this company, I a sort of Foreign Emperor, with the princesses my daughters: by Jove it was intolerably painful. And I must go to her Soirée tomorrow night too: and drag about in this confounded little Pedlington.[16] Yesterday night (I am afraid it was the first day in the week) I dined with Morton and met no less than 4 tables of English I knew, and went to the play. There was a little girl acting who made one's heart ache: the joke of the piece is that the child who looks about 3 is taken by the servants to a casino, is carried off for an hour by some dragoons & comes back having learned to smoke, to dance slang dances, and sing slang songs, — poor little rogue! She sang

[16] See John Poole's *Little Pedlington and the Pedlingtonians*, 2 vols. in one, London, 1839.

one of her songs from an actors arms — a wicked song in a sweet little innocent voice. She will be bought & sold within 3 years from this time, and won't be playing at wickedness any more. I'll shut up my desk, and say Gb all little girls that you & I love, and their parents. God bless you dear lady. Are you asleep now at 1 o'clock? and without drowsy syrups? [17] — I have got a very amusing book, The Tatler newspaper of 1709 and that shall be my soporific I hope. I have been advancing in Bluebeard but must give it up: its too dreadfully cynical and wicked. Its in blank verse & all a diabolical sneer. Depend upon it Helps is right [18] — Come, lets be off. Gby.

Wednesday. If I did not write yesterday it is because I was wickedly employed. I was gambling until 2 o'clock this morning, playing a game called lansquenet w.h is very good gambling and I left off as I had begun very thankful not to carry away anybody's money or leave behind any of my own. But it was curious to watch the tempers of the various players, the meanness of one, the flurry and excitement of another, the difference of the same man winning & losing — all w.h I got besides a good dinner and a headache this morning. Anny & Minny and my mother came to see me yesterday. I dont think they will be so very eager for Paris after 3 weeks

---

[17] *Othello*, III, iii, 331.

[18] This allusion to Arthur Helps (1813–1875), later (1872) K. C. B., author of *Friends in Council* (1847) and Clerk of the Privy Council from 1860 until his death, is explained in a letter of January 8 from Mrs. Brookfield to her husband: "I dined with the Elliots yesterday, only Mr. Helps and Mr. Gale (Sergt. Lankin of the Kicklebury book). . . . After dinner Mr. Helps began talking of Mr. Thackeray, 'Is he an amiable man? I want to know, for his books don't give me the impression that he is.' The Elliots all answered very warmly as to amiability, when the door opened and 'Mr. Sloane' was announced. 'It's not my joke, but Brookfield's,' Mr. Thackeray said, as he came into the room, but it made a laugh, while poor Helps looked amusingly guilty at his appearing so." (*Mrs. Brookfield*, II, 343–344) Kate Perry tells the same story, with more elaborate dialogue and a slightly different setting, in *Collection of Letters*, pp. 181–182. It should be explained that the name Thackeray had adopted belonged to the most detested man in London. The trial of George Sloane and his wife for the calculated brutality to which they had subjected their sixteen-year-old servant girl began on December 5, 1850, and concluded, with a sentence of two years' imprisonment for both defendants, on February 5, 1851. (*Annual Register*, 1850, II, 144–149)

here — the simple habits of our old people will hardly suit the little women — Even in my absence in America I dont quite like having them altogether here. I wonder if an amiable family as is very kind to me will give them hospitality for a month? — I was writing Bluebeard all day very sardonic and amusing to do, but I doubt whether it will be pleasant to read or hear, or even whether it is right to go on with this wicked vein. And also I must tell you that a story [19] is biling up in my interior, in w^h there shall appear some very good lofty and generous people. Perhaps a story without any villain in it would be good, wouldn't it?

Thursday. Thanks for your letter Madame — If I tell you my plans & my small gossip I dont bore you do I? You listen to them so kindly at home that I've got the habit you see. Why dont you write a little handwriting & send me yours? — This place begins to be as bad as London in the season there are dinners and routs for every day & night. Last night I went to dine at home with bouilli beef and ordinaire and bad ordinaire too — but the dinner was just as good as a better one and afterwards I went with my mother to a sworry, where I had to face 50 people of whom I didn't know one and being there was introduced to other soirée-givers — be hanged to them and there I left my Ma, and went off to Madame Gudin's the painters wife, where really there was a beautiful ball and all the world — all the English world that is: and tonight it is the President's ball if you please & tomorrow & the next day & the next more gaieties. It was queer to see poor old Castlereagh in a dark room keeping aloof from the dancing and the gaiety and having his thoughts fixed on Kingdom Come and Bennett [20] Confessor & Martyr; while Lady Cas who led him into his devotional state, was enjoying the music and the gay company as cheerfully as the most mundane person present. The French people all talk to me about Ponche when I am introjuiced to them,

---

[19] *Esmond.*

[20] The Rev. William James Early Bennett (1804–1886), about whom the ritualist controversy centered at this time. He had resigned as minister of St. Barnabas, Pimlico, on December 4, 1850, because of the scandal occasioned by the elaborate ceremonies he introduced into his services.

w$^h$ wounds my vanity, w$^h$ is wholesome very likely. Among the notabilities was Vicomte d'Arlincourt [21] a mad old romance-writer, on whom I amused myself by pouring the most tremendous compliments I could invent. He said J'ai vu l'Écosse Monsieur mais Valter Scott n'y étoit plus, hélas! I said Vous y étiez Vicomte, c'étoit bien assez d'un — On w$^h$ the old boy said I possessed French admirably and knew to speak the prettiest things in the prettiest manner. I wish you could see him. I wish you could see the world here. I wish you & W$^m$ were going to the play with me to night — to a regular melodrama far away on the Boulevard, and a quiet little snug dinner *au banquet d'Anacréon*. The banquet d'Anacréon is a dingy little restaurant on the boulevard where all the plays are acted; and they tell great things of a piece called Paillasse [22] in w$^h$ Lemaitre performs. Nous verrons, Madame, nous verrons — But with all this racket and gaiety, do you understand that a gentleman feels very lonely? I swear I'd sooner have a pipe and a gin and water soirée with somebody than the best of the President's orgeat — I go to my cousins for 1/2 an hour almost every day — You'd like them better than poor † Mary Carmichael † whom you wont be able to stand at least if she talks to you about her bodily state as she talks to me. What else shall I say in this stupid letter? — I've not seen any children so pooty as Magdalen that's all. I've told Anny to write you: and I'm glad M$^{rs}$ Fan is going to stay: and I hear that several papers have reproduced the Thunder & Small Beer article: and I thank you for your letter, and pray the best prayers I am worth, for you and your husband & child my dear lady.

W M T.

[21] Charles Victor Prévot (1789–1856), Vicomte d'Arlincourt, a poet and novelist who had some success during the Restoration. Thackeray reviewed his *The Three Kingdoms* in a hitherto unidentified article for *The Morning Chronicle* on April 4, 1844.

[22] A five-act drama by Adolphe Philippe (1811–1899), called Dennery, and Marc Fournier (1803–1880), first performed on November 9, 1850. Frédéric Lemaître (1800–1876), who created the title role of *Robert Macaire* (1834), was one of the best-known actors of his day. See *Works*, V, 151–152.

747.            FROM MRS. BROOKFIELD
                 14 JANUARY 1851

Hitherto unpublished.

                                              Tuesday.

My dear brother W.<sup>m</sup> I want to write to you because I think you
will expect to hear, but there seems to have been nothing to say
during the six weeks that you have been gone. I was very glad to
have your letter yesterday, & began an answer to it, but there was
an *untowardness* of circumstances — springing out of W<sup>m</sup>'s arrival
at 11 o'clock Sunday night — the day before he was expected, &
finding my brother in law George Robbins comfortably tucked up
in his bed down stairs, & only the dismal attic available for himself.
All *would* have been spic & span for him next day, as George had
taken me by surprise & asked for a bed only 1/2 an hour before
W<sup>m</sup> arrived — but I was weak in giving up the sacred room of the
house to anybody — However it has all smoothed away now, & I
can write to you with a quiet mind today — only I have no M<sup>me</sup>
Duchatel soirées to describe. I have been reading M<sup>me</sup> de Maintenon, [23] & hating her more & more, with her cold calculating morality & time serving friendships. — M<sup>r</sup> Doyle & M<sup>r</sup> Lemesurier
were much excited about Laura & Pendennis last night — they
thought she ought not to have gone back to him after once loving a
man of so much higher a nature — & that you might have killed off
M<sup>rs</sup> Warrington & let Pen: be punished at last — They seem to think
"Thunder & small beer" [24] very clever. I have not yet read it, as
W<sup>m</sup> left it at Clevedon by accident — Adelaide Procter has been
here & described the reconciliation with her mother, which seems
to have been a successful *coup*. — The Fanshawes have taken a
house in James St. close to the Paddington Terminus & intend to
be here till April which is pleasant news, though they will be a
good way off from us — I saw the dear old carriage filled with
ladies & Cheri, wheeling past Sussex Terrace yesterday — it was

[23] Probably *Lettres de Mme. de Maintenon* (1752–1756).
[24] See above, No. 742.

*something* even to see that — but I get on pretty well & I am rather stronger & able to walk better. Baby is much better & really getting as fat as ever — give my best love to Anny & Minny; I hope they are very happy with their Granny — Anny promised to write to me, & I should be very glad to hear from her, when she is in the humour for a letter. Col: Carmichael has just been here. I like his face & he was most courteous & friendly — he talked of his "good cousin "Bill Thackeray" — & your kindness in lending y^r carriage for Madame, who sent messages that she w^d call on me, when she is a little stronger — W^m came in to converse with Col. C. & they were getting on very well when all the M^rs Hoares & Miss Peirce came in & they are only just gone now; & I am expecting Locock today, who will be here very likely before this is finished. I am glad you have some people you like at Paris — you don't say how your throat is? — I hope *well* by this time. I don't think you suffer much from having to talk with mere strangers who don't suit you — I mean that you w^d do it always cheerfully & readily & not find it the up hill work it is to me — M^rs F. says I am not enough of a Christian Socialist yet & that one *ought* to have some points of sympathy with all human beings so as to find no one really a bore.

I say my prayers for you every night & morning & feel very thankful for all your affection Bless you dear friend may God bless you & take care of you always. —

748.     FROM MRS. BROOKFIELD
           JANUARY 1851 [25]

My text is taken from *Mrs. Brookfield*, pp. 344–346.

This is about the smallest hand I can achieve, with my arm in a cramp. All persons have not your facility in penmanship you know.

I wish to read Bluebeard very much, and I should like you to write a novel to startle Helps and such like objectors who think

[25] This is Mrs. Brookfield's reply to Thackeray's letter of January 13–16.

your heart does not keep pace with your head (a graceful phrase).
You know how glad I should be to have the children for any or
all the time that you are in America, and William would like it
too. He has been immersed in the Inspectors' conference all the
week. We had three at dinner yesterday, and Mr. Lingen, and
Mrs. F[anshawe] and your faithful D[obbins], who came in her
youngest and most fashionable attire, evidently hoping to see her
anonymous receiver of letters, but when everybody was arrived
but you, she turned to me with an assumed air of indifference and
"Tell me, dear lady, how is Mr. Thackeray?" I felt malicious as
I said, "Oh he is at Paris." Why could I not have been sympa-
thising instead? She looked discomfited, but rallied in a few
minutes and afterwards talked of her isolated position in Lincolnshire, only knowing celebrated men of the day by name, and "one
can only get to know them by writing to them, but if *they* don't
answer of course it falls to the ground," she said, and I looked
perfectly stolid, as if I did not in the least understand. I was
thinking over your chafing against the petty homage and the small
sets at Paris, and debating whether you ought not to chafe *as much*
against the adulation on a grand scale, but I merely throw this out.
I don't think you care about the sublimer flatteries in the least, but
it does not irritate you in the same way. I am just going out to pay
stupid visits. We asked the R.'s to dine yesterday and Mr. R.
(husband of William's Lady Cecilia) wrote me such a pert note to
decline, beginning "Dear Mrs. JOB," I had literally only met him
about three times, I sent it to Mr. Spring Rice, who hates him for
marrying his cousin and said in my note "he has given me a distaste
for my initials." "Will you throw away a jewel because a snail
has left its slime on it?" replied Mr. Spring Rice. "Your initials
are so dear to so many of us you ought to think twice or three
times before you give them up." Was not this gallant? He has
been much fascinated by Lady G——'s "fine generous manner"
and is in high intimacy with Mrs. Cameron. When you talked of
all the world being mad I was amused by Sir Alex. Gordon's so-
lution of the S[artoris] *ménage*, "Mrs. S[artoris] mad, bless my
soul she is as sane as I am. *He's* mad and fancies she is."

Magdalene is quite fat and rosy, but has cut her sixth tooth and very nearly stands by herself; I shall like to see Anny and Minny back again, and to hear their account of their visit. How much I should like to have them when the awful American expedition takes place!

[For fragments of two other letters to Mrs. Brookfield in January, 1851, see letters 19 and 20, Appendix XXVI.]

749.          TO THÉODORE GUDIN
              JANUARY 1851

*Address:* Monsieur Gudin.  Hitherto unpublished.

Mon cher peintre. Que s'est il passé avant-hier apres le festin? Brougham en fuite, Vigier parti, nous avons fumé, causé, bu du grog, n'est-ce-pas? M'avez vous invité pour diner encore aujourd-hui? Ai-je accepté? est ce un rève? Non — Je ne veux pas me prévaloir une seconde fois de votre hospitalité toute royale — Gardons toujours le souvenir du premier diner

                    Tout à vous mon cher Gudin
                    W M Thackeray

750.          TO THÉODORE GUDIN?
              JANUARY 1851?

Hitherto unpublished.

I find in a bad book of costumes this dress worn by M^{rs} Louis the Fourteenth. Ropes of jewels round the hair. Jewellery ad liber-tam down the Stomacher & front of the petticoat w^h is probably of a stiff & splendid damask. The outer garment a dark velvet or brocade figured, looped up with emeralds smaragds and other cornelians, and with *bouffans* (I flatter myself that's the word of pink satting. A long queue probably completed this costume; but it's not given in my print.

I sent your note to M Jules Janin on Saturday and my messenger
goes to him for an answer.  Shall I come without him on Sunday?
I am always your obdt Servt

        W M Thackeray.

751. TO MRS. BROOKFIELD
21 JANUARY 1851 [26]

Published in part, *Collection of Letters*, pp. 79–80.

On Sunday I took a carriage and went to Stevens in the country — M^rs S again in a highly interesting situation — the jolly old nurse who has been in the Ricketts family 120 years or more or less talked about Miss Rosa, and remembered her as the flower of that branch of the family and exceedingly pretty and with a most lovely complexion — and then I told them what a lubly jewel the present Miss Rosa was; and how very fond I was of her mamma: and so we had a tolerably pleasant afternoon, and I came back and sate again with M^r Thomas Fraser. Yesterday there was a pretty little English dance next door at M^rs Errington's; [27] and an English country dance being proposed one of the young bucks good-naturedly took a fiddle and played very well too and I had for a partner Madame Gudin [28] — the painters wife — I think I mentioned her to you didn't I? — She is a daughter of Lord James Hay, — a very fair complexion and jolly face — and so with the greatest fear and trepidation (for I never could understand a figure) I asked her, & — and she refused, because she tells me that she too is in an int—r—st—ng &c — and I am sure I was very glad to be out of the business. She is a jolly fat dumpy good-humoured oldish woman — and neither by age or figure good for dancing.

I went to see a play too last night, and the new comedian Mademoiselle Brohan [29] of whom all the world is talking — a

[26] This letter was written the Tuesday before Saturday, January 25, when Mrs. Brookfield received it.
[27] The wife of John Edward Errington (1806–1862), a railway engineer who was the friend and associate of Joseph Locke.
[28] The former Louise Margaret Gordon Hay (d. 1890), who had married Gudin in 1844. She was the second daughter of General Lord James Hay (1788–1862), second son of the seventh Marquess of Tweeddale.
[29] Émilie Brohan (1833–1900), later (1854) Madame Uchard, who had made her début at the Théâtre Français on October 13, 1850, with notable success.

beautiful young woman of 17 looking 25, and I thought vulgar intensely affected and with a kind of stupid intelligence that passes for real wit with the pittites who applauded with immense enthusiasm all her smiles and shrugs and gestures and ogles — But they wouldn't have admired her if she hadn't been so beautiful: if her eyes weren't bright and her charms undeniable. I was asked too by some of the young English seigneurs here to go to an actress's ball: where there was to be a great deal of Parisian beauty, w$^h$ a cosmophilite ought to see perhaps as well as any other phase of society. But I refused Mad$^{me}$ Osy's ball — my grey head has no call to show amongst those young ones and, as in the next novel we are to have none but good characters, what is the use of examining folks who are quite otherwise.

Meanwhile, & for 10 days more, I must do my duty and go on feeling deucedly lonely in the midst of the racketting and jigging — I am engaged to dinner for the next 3 days and on Friday when I had hoped to be at home, my mother has a tea party — and asked trembling (for she is awfully afraid of me) whether I would come? Of course I'll go — and the sense of inspiring terror makes me more awfully glum and discomfortable — in fact my best plan w$^d$ have been to have made the tour I spoke about, and to have kept out of this place, and left my poor women at their ease.

Magdalene's shoes will be home tomorrow — & I think I'll go out now: and say Goodbye and pray God bless you & all yours my dear lady. If you see the Elliots give them all sorts of kind words from me, and so to little f: [30] and *don't* write me gay letters nor long ones unless you are strong & well.

W M T.

[30] Mrs. Fanshawe.

My dear Gudin    I have dined so much so well & so often with you
since my arrival here, that this time I must refuse: and go to my
mother whom I have scarcely been able to see anything in consequence
of the tyrannical hospitality of you Parisians

You who are such a good father, I know have been a good son in
your time, and so I know you will let me off.

                                                        ever yours
I wish I hadn't begun to                                W M T.
colour Mrs Punch, for the
ink has run & played the deuce with her beauty.

752.                  TO THÉODORE GUDIN
                         JANUARY 1851

Hitherto unpublished.

My dear Gudin  I have dined so much so well & so often with you
since my arrival here, that this time I must refuse: and go to my
mother of whom I have scarcely been able to see anything in consequence of the tyrannical hospitality of you Parisians

You who are such a good father, I know have been a good son in
your time, and so I know you will let me off.

                         ever yours
                         W M T.

I wish I hadn't begun to colour M^rs Punch, for the ink has run
& played the deuce with her beauty.


753.                  FROM MRS. BROOKFIELD
                         29 JANUARY 1851

My text is taken from *Mrs. Brookfield*, pp. 346–348.

                                        29 Jan., 51.

I was very glad to have your kind letter on Saturday and thank
you for it very much. I am getting better now, but poor Magdalene has been imprisoned in the nursery with a cold and cough, so
that all her good looks will be gone just when I want her to *become*
her new shoes and to elicit approbation for fatness and prettiness
from her uncle Makepeace and her cousins the young ladies, to
whom give my best love. Yesterday I went to Wilton Crescent,
walked all the way there, and arrived in time to take their carriage
to Chesham Place, where I staid an hour with "Kate and Jane," [31]
they are very anxious to see you again, and very glad you are

---

[31] Wilton Crescent was the home of the Hallams (see above, No. 726).
"Kate and Jane" refers to Kate Perry and Mrs. Frederick Elliot, both of whom
lived at 37 Chesham Place.

coming back so soon. William liked his dinner there, and struck up a flirtation with the eldest little Perry,[32] who told her aunt afterwards, that no grown up gentleman had ever talked to her for so long together before, and she was sure Mr. Brookfield sympathised in Mr. Bennett's misfortunes, for he said "Poor Mr. Bennett" so feelingly.

We were amused with Beatrice [33] last night. William was singing the Nigger song, "Old Uncle Ned has long been dead and is gone where the good niggers go." [34] "Where is that?" Beaty asked. "Why, where do good Bishops go, my dear?" "Where do they go? Oh! to *Rome*!" which would seem to supersede Heaven in the mind of the younger generation.

I can't say I much like the Memoir,[35] it seems very short and bald, and as if it were intended for the public instead of intimate friends.

I went to the Miss Berrys on Saturday, they were very cordial, and the Elliots were so kind that I really quite love them. I don't mean *only* from that evening, but there is something so genial and good-natured about them, always the same, — and they really appear so fond of you. Mrs. Elliot is coming to take me to buy drawing room carpets to-day, you will find us just beginning our moving [36] when you come back. Miss Berry chiefly talked to me the other evening so that I hardly spoke to Agnes. She asked how much longer you would be at Paris *amusing* yourself. I said you declared you were going through the most exemplary round of duties visiting sick relations every day. She laughed and asked if your trumpeter was dead, that you praised yourself. Uncle Hallam seemed very sad as we came away together, but he was cheerful all the evening.

[32] Flora Perry, daughter of Sir Thomas Erskine Perry.
[33] Laura Beatrice Elton.
[34] From Stephen Foster's "Old Uncle Ned."
[35] A brief notice of Harry Hallam by his friends Henry Sumner Maine and Franklin Lushington, reprinted in Arthur Henry Hallam's *Remains in Verse and Prose*, ed. Henry Hallam (London, 1853), pp. xlvii–lx.
[36] To 64 Cadogan Place.

754. TO MRS. BROOKFIELD
31 JANUARY–2 FEBRUARY 1851

Published in part, *Collection of Letters*, pp. 151–153. The passage enclosed between daggers was overscored by Mrs. Brookfield.

A story with a moral. Last night I went to a party at the house of my mothers friend Madame Colmache (who introduced me to M^me Ancelot [37] the Authoress who was dying to see me said M^me C. — only I found on talking to M^me Ancelot that she didnt know who I was, and so was no more dying than the most lively of us) and coming downstairs with my Ma I thought to myself I'll go home and have an hour's chat with her, and try and cheer and console her, for her sad tragic looks melted my heart and always make me think I am a cruel monster: and so I was very tender & sentimental and, you see, caressed her filially as we went down. It was a wet night, and the fly was waiting, and she was just agoing to step in.

But there entered at the house-door a fiddler with his fiddle under his arm: whom when the dear old Mater Dolorosa beheld she said 'O that is M un tel who has come to play a duo with Laure.[38] I must go back & hear him,' and back she went, and all my sentimentality was gulped down: and I came home & sent the fly back 2 miles for her, with Jeames to escort her in the rain.

The moral is that women with those melancholy eyes & sad sad looks are not always so melancholy as they seem: that they have consolations, amusements, fiddlers &c ⟨in the w⟩orld and are not perpetually thinking of their children. Well, I am glad that she has her week's pleasure though it's at my expense and though I shall have but a glum dinner on the 1^st when I hoped to be so happy. Miss Magdalene's boots ⟨have just now⟩ come home and the woman who brought them was quite pleased with the funny little pretty things — there is a pair of pink and a pair of blyou.

[37] Mme. Virginie Ancelot (d. 1875), wife of the dramatist Jacques Ancelot, was the mistress of an important literary salon and the writer of many plays and novels.        [38] Laura Colmache.

Saturday. I must not cry out if your ladyship sends me no letters, provided you are well I am appy — as happy as I can be here w.ʰ is pretty well though I am bored daily and nightly and drag about sulkily from tea party to tea party. Last night my mother had her little T and they danced and it was not at all unpleasant quand on y etait. I found an old schoolfellow, looking 10 years younger than myself whom I remember older & bigger than me 28 years ago and he had got a charming young wife quite civilized and pleasant to talk to and the young ladies had their new frocks and looked tolerably respectable and exceedingly happy. They are to go to a party on Monday & another on Wednesday and on Thursday D V we shall be on the homeward road again. I had cuddled myself with the notion of having one evening to myself one quiet dinner one quiet place at the play: but my mother took my only evening and gave it to an old lady whom I dont want to see & who would have done very well without me — Was there ever such a victim? I go about from house to house and grumble everywhere. I say Thursday, D V. for what mayn't happen? My poor cousin Charlotte ⟨Ritchie⟩ has a relapse of rheumatic fever. My aunt is in a dreadful prostration and terror. "If anything happens to Charlotte, she says, I shall die. And then what will Jane do — I am glad Wᵐ ⟨Thackeray⟩ is here." There is a kind of glum pleasure, isn't there, in sitting by sick beds and trying to do one's best? I took the old G P to dinner at a Café before the soiree: he is very nice and kind and gentle. — Do you see how I have been putting tails to the G's & Y's? That is because I'm thinking of something else. I'm thinking that I should like to get a letter from you, and not an excuse for not writing. This paper lies in my desk since Tuesday. I've looked at it wistfully many & many a time, and wanted to begin talking: but I mustn't until Madam answers me — until she says 'My dear Sir I have only 3 minutes to save the post & say &c — If some folks letters were published as some folks dread after my & some folks' death — I think Posterity would smile rather. I would if I were Posterity — Well, on Wednesday I am going to dine with the Préfet de Police and afterwards to M.ˡˡᵉ Scriwaneck's ³⁹ ball — where I shall meet,

³⁹ Augustine Céleste Scriwaneck (1823–1909), the actress.

I an old fellow of 40, all the pretty actresses of Paris — Let us give a loose to pleasure. If it's wrong to attach oneself to honest women: let us go & live with the outlaws. If Virtue can only say My dear Sir I have but 2 minutes &c — let us hear what the other folks have to say for themselves.

Sunday. The stick of a fiddle! I dont intend to go to live with the outlaws    I intend to try and do the best I can, and take gratefully such a lot as Heaven sends me † ⟨. . .⟩; ⁴⁰ & I like & admire the intense affection of the child for her Gʳmother ⟨. . .⟩ it makes me think seriously about ⟨. . .⟩†? Anny rather wants to go to school. And when Im away, you'll have them on Sundays, won't you Aunt Jane? The school to wʰ I'm recommended is close by you in Chester Square. And so your little note ⁴¹ was interrupted again — and by Dʳ Locock I'm sorry for that. Mamma & I went to see the old lady last night. Lady Elgin,⁴² an honest grim big clever old Scotch lady, well read and good to talk to — dealing in religions of many denominations, and having established in her house as a sort of Director, Mʳ Caird, one of the heads of the Irvingites; a clever shifty sneaking man. I wish I had had your story of Manning, that wᵈ have been conversation: but your note didn't arrive till this morning, thank you & I hope you are very well. Yesterday was the 1ˢᵗ and I thought where I ought to have dined and where I should have liked to adined. But let us be thankful for what we get: and God bless all in your house. I hope you will like good old Miss Agnes.⁴³ I'm sure you will: and shall be glad that you belong to that kind and polight set of old ladies, and worthy gentlemen. Mʳ Wilkins too will approve of them I should

---

⁴⁰ The hiatuses in this passage are respectively of about nine, one, and fourteen words.

⁴¹ Mrs. Brookfield's letter of January 29, the text of which above is evidently not complete, since it does not include the story of Henry Edward, later (1875) Cardinal Manning, which Thackeray mentions.

⁴² Lady Elizabeth Elgin (d. 1860), widow of the seventh Earl of Elgin, a patron of the "Holy Catholic Apostolic Church" founded by Edward Irving in 1832.

⁴³ Miss Berry. Charles Foley Wilmot (1796–1852), second son of Sir Robert Wilmot of Osmaston, second Baronet, was a minor diplomatist who at one time served as Secretary of Legation to the Swiss cantons.

think. I dont know any better company than Foley Wilmot and Poodle Byng — I met my dear friend Miss Farrer the other night at the Duchess of Grammonts [44] — she is uncommonly good looking my dear friend — but she is odious and has a shy sarpentine look w$^h$ makes me frissoner — Pass quickly Sunday Monday Tuesday Wednesday. Shall I let Kensington with 10 beds to an Exhibition-seeing-party and live alone? Will you take a lodger who will lend you a fly to go to the parties w$^h$ you'll be continually frequenting? Ah, that would be pleasant    My cousin Charlotte was much better yesterday thank God, & her mother quiet — I've been visiting the sick here, 1,2,3, every day. I want to begin to write again very much. My mighty mind is tired of idleness, and ill employs the intervals of rest. My mighty body sleeps ten hours of nights: lolls upon easy chairs for other four: and smokes and yawns & dawdles over the paper: And then my mighty body takes a stroll — a very little lazy lazy stroll; and then it hulks in lady's drawing rooms, and then it has to dress itself for dinner; and then come tea parties and then comes sleep — and ever as I put the candle out, and ever as the morning wakens me, a gentle benediction guards my bed and whispers me good even and good day.

But I am interrupted by D$^r$ Locock — Goodbye my dear lady. Thank you for your note: & God bless all of you — What an emence emence time it seems since I saw you, and how glad I'll be to see my dear Elliots & my dear f & M$^r$ Wilkins, and Miss Brookfield in the new shoes.[45]

W M T.

[44] The former Anne Quintina Albertine Ida de Grimaud, sister of Count d'Orsay, who had married Antoine Agénor (d. 1855), Duc de Gramont, in 1818. At the Duchesse de Gramont's evening party Thackeray first met the ubiquitous Victorian gossip Sir William Augustus Fraser (1826–1898), fourth Baronet, who reports some interesting fragments of his conversation in his *Hic et Ubique*, pp. 146–178.

[45] The answer to this letter is partially printed in *Mrs. Brookfield* (II, 348–349): "Are you going among the actresses as a kind of retort for my dull letters? That is rather unworthy in you, if it is the case.

"I write to you very much as I talk, only I cannot express feelings as you do, who are always in the habit of expressing all kinds of emotions in writing.

755.                TO SAMUEL PHILLIPS [46]
                    9 FEBRUARY 1851

Hitherto unpublished.

                              Kensington. Sunday

My dear Mʳ Phillips

Thank you very much for your letter. I should have answered
it earlier but I was away at Paris whence I only returned on Friday
to find a heap of letters & a great deal of business to do. I am very
glad indeed to know that you are not the Author of that unlucky
criticism in the Times [47] — about wʰ I wasn't in the least angry,
for surely the Lord had delivered my enemy into my hands,[48] but
I think for the honor of our calling there are certain accusations wʰ
one is bound to meet and repel as rapidly and fiercely as possible,
and my unfortunate critic indulged in some of these. I wonder
when our people will learn to be civil to one another and conduct

---

Very commonplace things occur, and I can only describe them in a very
commonplace way. 'Posterity would smile' and would see a great deal to
marvel at in your giving your confidence and brilliant letters, and the time
spent in writing them, to a very dull everyday person, who can't spell 'vacil-
ating.'

"I have just come back from choosing a carpet and then a walk with
William to call on Miss C. Wynn's sister, Lady Doyle, and the widow, Mrs.
Lindesay, who has just escaped being pretty and is interesting looking. Mrs.
Procter was there calling and talked to William all the time till she took
leave, and we were speaking of other things when in came Mrs. Procter's
head at the door again, 'Before you *begin upon me* I want to tell Mrs. Brookfield Mr. Rogers wants to see her.' She was dressed in a suit of friar's grey
from mantle to gown and everything, with only a little bit of colour in her
bonnet, so that she looked better than I ever saw her.

"Now I have read over the first part of this letter I should very much
like to burn it. It seems to make such a fuss about the Actresses, why shouldn't
you go to their ball?"

Charlotte Williams-Wynn (d. 1869), Lady Sidney Doyle (d. 1867), and
Mrs. John Lindsay (d. 1878) were daughters of Charles Watkin Williams-
Wynn, second son of Sir Watkin Williams-Wynn, fourth Baronet.

[46] Phillips (1814–1854) was a miscellaneous writer who contributed literary reviews to *The Times* from about 1845 till his death.

[47] See above, No. 742.

[48] *Joshua*, 21, 44; *Judges*, 3, 28.

their controversies fairly and with honest courtesy? I am afraid
for a day or two, and I own it with a sincere regret that I thought
you were my enemy; and for this I beg your pardon. But I did not
think so on a second perusal of the Times Article: for I saw that
you *couldn't* have written so if you would: and that had you been
ill disposed towards me, I should have had a very different adver-
sary to encounter. Who are one's enemies? I am shocked and
pained daily in finding them: and remember but a very few years
back when I had none. Thank you very much for having friendly
dispositions towards me: and as for poor Pendennis, w^h is full of
blunders & slips and errors that I should like to recal (as I should
a number of such irrevocable faults in my life, as well as in my
books) — let him have justice dealt to him, and get the meed of
his deserts & shortcomings.

I am very glad to hear that you are better in health & spirits
and cheerful & industrious in your retirement

and am my dear Sir most faithfully yours

W M Thackeray

756.      TO MRS. CARMICHAEL-SMYTH
FEBRUARY–MARCH 1851 [49]

Hitherto unpublished.

And so my dearest old Mammy was in a panic about the night
passage from Calais, w^h is made every day of the year and is
almost as safe as the ride from the Fbg S^t Honoré to the Station?
— I wonder whether you have had other groundless panics about
our dear little women & the course in life of their Pa? What a
comfort they are those little women their goodness and kindness
to me is quite touching; we have had many walks and a good deal
of time together and it's always a pleasure to me to be with them
and talk with them. I dont think I have any news but that — the

[49] This letter was begun shortly after Thackeray returned from Paris on
February 7 and finished a few days after he spoke at Macready's farewell
dinner on March 1.

whirr of London life has begun as loud as ever, and I think I cant stand it and must go out to a little distance to Richmond Hampstead or some such place to be away from the constant turmoil, and get myself into a fit frame of mind for the lectures. I have been to Mary's of course & to Lady Carmichael, between w^h two little love I should think can be lost — and how the deuce you could have bred up such a woman as poor Polly passes my comprehension — She lays all the blame of the Wood ménage upon the poor wife and says that her conduct and cruelty to him has driven George to drink &c [50]    Lady Wood and old M^rs Timbs were asking for you & about poor George tother day, on the banks of the Serpentine river where I met them awalking. It's very hard that in order to defend their own share of the business C & M are obliged to hint M^rs Wood's character away, and make her out I don't know what — I wish I could feel more friendly & less hard-hearted towards them. But how to respect the husband or bear with the lunacies (for they are no less) of poor Polly? Charles goes about with a wonderful faith and madness too and narrates the perfections of his wife. He & She think there is no woman so clever charming stylish and ravishingly beautiful. Are we all battling with delusions equally monstrous? I had a kind letter from Eugenie [51] tother day who says she is happy in rather a plaintive way, and she speaks of the admirable *patience* of her husband — a queer quality for a bride to enlarge about. And I haven't answered her letter for I dont want a correspondence and I don't know whether to call her Christian or Sir. Honest M^rs Crowe wrote me a rich characteristic letter about the gown. She must owe it me for a little — Crowe *will* pay really &c. The Irish morals are not as the English morals, for all that I don't say the English morals are better. They are delighted because I passed some hours on a ballotting day at the Reform Club getting votes for Joe who was sure to be elected — and M^rs Crowe thinks that the 3 black balls he got 'may have been put in by Cobden Bright & Co' — the Co is admirable.

[50] Apart from the scanty information in Thackeray's letters, nothing appears to have transpired concerning this domestic drama.

[51] Eugenie Crowe.

Morris of the Times has asked me to dinner, and I'm going: and hearing that Forster had been ill I wrote him a kind & friendly letter [52] too and got quite a friendly reply. What is the meaning of enemies in this world, o mon dieu? My friend in the Times [53] I'm told was an Irishman w.<sup>h</sup> accounts for the animus against me, and relieves my mind for I like rather the Hirish to be bitter against me, at least am not angry that they should rail. Tizzy Revis having thrown over all her other adorers and promises is going to marry Captain Neald, Tennent's secretary at S.<sup>t</sup> Helena and goes out to that place incontinently     I had almost made a voyage to Madeira with poor Tennent who has a frigate to carry him to his destination, and [thought] of working my lectures there; but &c &c &c — When any man lectures on Titmarsh 100 years hence those &cs &c would make a queer text to write about — Thank God again & again for my dear little women, and the poor wife yonder.

What has happened since I wrote this ever so many days ago? Well, the old routine of the world and its wanities and three courses and claret almost every day — But the off days with the young ones are very pleasant and the walks and talks with them. I have been reading a good bit for my lectures: I have been elected at last into the Athenæum [54] where there's a beautiful library and too comfortable easy chairs — and there I go & read pretty well.

---

[52] I have not traced this letter.

[53] See above, No. 742.

[54] Thackeray, who had failed of election the previous year (see above, No. 680), was brought into the Athenæum Club on February 25, 1851. During the rest of his life he often worked in the Club's splendid library and ate at Hayward's table near the fire in the dining-room. "Frequently," it is reported, "he left looking tired out and worried, and would complain of the difficulty he found in disposing of this or that character, and declare despondingly that he knew what he was engaged in would fail. . . . [He was] beloved of the servants and even of the old cabman who drove him to the door." (Francis Gledstanes Waugh, *The Athenæum Club and its Associations*, London, n. d., pp. 33, 58–59, and 71–72) This last worthy appears to have been a favorite with Thackeray, for Fields relates that he one day saw the novelist "chaffing on the sidewalk in London, in front of the Athenæum Club, with a monstrous-sized, 'copiously ebriose' cabman, and I judged from the driver's ludicrously careful way of landing the coin deep down in his breeches-pocket, that Thackeray had given him a very unusual fare. 'Who

The young ones tell you the news of the day, how we went to Macreadys benefit: [55] I to the Macready dinner afterwards where I made a speech and didn't break down. It was pretty good I believe: but the reporters don't do the jokes justice. Anny & Minny made their appearance in the polight world yesterday at Lady Stanleys who dined here and spoke very kindly of Nanny. God bless her. Old Fitz is here staying for a day or two. I wish it might be for a month or two, We are young fellows when we meet: and I'm not spoiled for him — no nor for you my dearest old Mother. I have been to Mary again — more egotisms self-praises, and the old talk. She is crazy with vanity. Bob [56] is not admitted into her august presence: and spoke very glumly about the M$^r$ & M$^{rs}$ George Wood affair when we met in the park on Sunday. In that business, I think it is prudent that I should not put in my oar. I don't see what can be done until Wood is quite mad and recommend — (Here enters Charles at w$^h$ I put away the letter looking rather guilty — and we talk about the business — He produces a letter of M$^{rs}$ Wood's full of bad spelling & so forth, and queer confessions — Couldn't you give her a perfectly sensible advice — the mischief being done the marriage perfectly consummated — to leave off abusing Charles & Mary, as abuse of them can do no good, and can't undo the marriage — And — and

---

is your fat friend?' I asked, crossing over to shake hands with him. 'O, that indomitable youth is an old crony of mine,' he replied; and then, quoting Falstaff, 'a goodly, portly man, i' faith, and a corpulent, of a cheerful look, a pleasing eye, and a most noble *carriage*.' It was the *manner* of saying this, then, and there in the London street, the cabman moving slowly off on his sorry vehicle, with one eye (an eye dewy with gin and water, and a tear of gratitude, perhaps) on Thackeray, and the great man himself so jovial and so full of kindness! " (*Yesterdays with Authors*, p. 29)

[55] Macready's farewell appearance in *Macbeth* on February 26, which is described in *The Times* of the following day. At the dinner given to Macready on March 1, Thackeray proposed the toast, "To the health of Mrs. Macready and her family" (*Times*, March 3). "Was not Mr Thackeray's speech at Macready's Farewell Dinner peculiarly characteristic?" Charlotte Brontë wrote to George Smith on March 11. "I fancied so from the outline I saw of it in the papers. It seemed to me scarcely to disguise a secret sneer at the whole concern — the hero and his worshippers — and indeed Mr Macready's admirers exaggerate their enthusiasm." (Wise and Symington, *The Brontës*, III, 211)

[56] Robert Stewart Carmichael-Smyth.

there is Miss Anny singing at the piano in the next room, sometimes false, but with a pathetic sweetness in her honest voice — I
believe its a song of her own composing. We must get her some
lessons: and when we are all old it will be a comfort to hear her
sing of calm nights.

I had a big dinner yesterday: Miss Stanley and Swinton [57] the
painter asked me for it some days since when I was just in the
dinner giving mood; and it went off tolerably well — Lady Stanley
prodigiously gracious, and full of praises of everything — O, I've
said that before — They are making a dreadful thrumming on
the piano this hour & 1/2 in the drawing room, that's the fact: and
I don't like to interrupt them — and great comfort they are to me.

And I pack up this letter such as it is and ride with it a hoss
back to the F. O.[58] God bless you & G P.

W M T.

<br>

757.            TO MRS. JAMES
            FEBRUARY 1851 [59]

Hitherto unpublished.

Be so kind and let me off on Saturday if you please dear M[rs]
James. The Times has asked me to dinner for that day, and I have
refused the Times ever so often before until he fancies I won't
dine with him because he is not a Lord, and I have had a controversy a quarrel (in w[h] I got the best I think, did you see it?)
and should like a reconciliation; so that I hope you will see the
propriety of my breaking my plighted vow to you

Always yours
W M T.

who sends back the handkerchief of W M J.

[57] James Rannie Swinton (1816–1888), one of the most fashionable of
Victorian portrait painters.
[58] The Foreign Office.
[59] This note was written shortly after the preceding letter to Mrs. Carmichael-Smyth, in which Thackeray refers to his invitation from Mowbray
Morris of *The Times*.

758.                  TO MARK LEMON
                   15? FEBRUARY 1851 [60]

Hitherto unpublished.

                                   Kensington.  Saturday
My dear Lemon
   Last week I tried for 3 days the Sublime and 2 days this week
the ridiculous without result after either effort.  I am quite agashed
by the failure, & see that my Punch days are over.  I can't do it
no more.  But I hope nevertheless I may go on having a Wednesday dinner with you all now and again: and to pay B & E for
their hospitality some time or other by a stray contribution to the
old P P.
                          Yours always
                          W M T.


   Lord North used to be called the noble Lord in the Blue Riband.
Why should not Lord Pam;  the plucky minister, Lord Civis
            Romanus [61] be designated as the noble Lord in
            the White Feather?
                             or
            On Valentine's day our Venerable Prime Min-
            ister received a large envelope from Paris, w^h he
            opened eagerly — and found that it contained a
            beautiful WHITE FEATHER.  He has worn it at the
            house — thinks it most becoming


   Design for the British Lion opposite Buckingham Palace.

   [60] It seems likely that this letter was written the day after St. Valentine's
Day, Friday, February 14.
   [61] An allusion to Palmerston's great speech during the Don Pacifico debate
in 1850, which concludes with the words: ". . . whether, as the Roman, in
days of old, held himself free from indignity, when he could say *Civis
Romanus sum;* so also a British subject, in whatever land he may be, shall

A Story of a Cock & a Bull.

O Papa Papa I'm frightened of that dreadful bird!

John Bull. Nonsense child! I thought they used to call you plucky Pam.

Scene from the Rivals.[62]

Bob Acres. Look you Sir Lucius. Tisnt that I mind the word but if you had called me a poltroon ods daggers & balls but I should have thought you very ill bred.

———————

Bob Acres  Lord Palmerston K.G.
Sir Lucius O'Trigger  M$^r$ O'Punch.
Captain Absolute  His IMPERIAL MAJESTY, The Emperor L. N. K G.

———————

feel confident that the watchful eye and the strong arm of England will protect him against injustice and wrong."

[62] Act V, scene iii. No use was made of any of Thackeray's suggestions in *Punch*.

759.      TO HENRY THOMAS LOWRY-CORRY
10 MARCH 1851 [63]

Hitherto unpublished.

Kensington. March 10.

M^r Thackeray requests the honor of M^r Corry's company at
dinner on Tuesday April 1. at 7 1/2 o'ck.


760.      TO THE REV. WILLIAM BROOKFIELD
18 MARCH 1851

Published in *Collection of Letters*, p. 157.

March 18. Kensington.

My dear W^m I have just received your kind message and
melancholy news.[64] Thank you for thinking that I'm interested
in what concerns you, and sympathize in what gives you pleasure
or grief. Well, I don't think there is much more than this to say:
but I recal what you have said in our many talks of your father,
and remember the affection and respect with w^h you always regarded and spoke of him. Who would wish for more than honor
love obedience [65] and a tranquil end to old age? And so that generation w^h engendered us passes away & their place knows them
not: [66] and our turn comes when we're to say good bye to our
joys, struggles, pains, affections — and our young ones will grieve
and be consoled for us — and so on. We've lived as much in 40
as your good old father in his fourscore years, don't you think
so — and how awfully tired and lonely we are? I picture to myself
the placid face of the kind old father with all that trouble & doubt
over — his life expiring with supreme blessings for you all — for

[63] During the years Thackeray lived in Kensington, April 1 fell on a
Tuesday only in 1851.
[64] Brookfield's father died on March 17, 1851.
[65] *Macbeth*, V, iii, 25.
[66] *Job*, 7, 10.

you & Jane and unconcious little Magdalene prattling, and laughing, at Life's threshhold: and know that you will be tenderly
cheered & consoled by the good man's blessing for the three of
you; while yet, but a minute, but yesterday, but all eternity ago,
he was here living and suffering. — I go on with the paper before
me — I know there's nothing to say — but I assure you of my
sympathy and that I am yours my dear old friend afftly.

W M Thackeray

761.                 TO MRS. BROOKFIELD
                   18–19 MARCH 1851? [67]

Hitherto unpublished.

Are you ill ma soeur is anything the matter that you don't come
on Friday? I wrote you a long letter yesterday but I thought
shell come on Thursday I mustn't pester her with too many letters:
& so with a great gulp I swallowed the letter — I have just a note
from W^m, such a kind & affectionate one; though it brings me this
bad news. Be well, be well and happy, dear; for the sake of your
husband to whom I talk of you for hours, and of your brother who

 loves you O so well. Before I go to sleep — Let me
say God bless you two — My kind sweet gentle lady
I can't bear that you should be ill: Write me a word
as soon as ever you can & tell me that there is nothing
very bad.

Wensdy.

What have I been doing since these many days? I hardly know
— thinking about you chiefly I think; and wanting you back, as a
peevish babby wants back his nurse — there's a pretty simile, well
I wont say anything about the babby — but its a very nice nurse
— and I wish she were back.

[67] This note appears to have been begun on Tuesday, March 18, when
Brookfield wrote Thackeray of his father's death, and finished the following
day.

762.          TO MRS. CARMICHAEL-SMYTH
               26 MARCH 1851

Hitherto unpublished.

## March 26.

My dearest Mammy  Pleasant as the bag is you must please not
to wait for it, unless indeed you write tomorrow when it will be
just as quick as the post, and let us know that the threatening
pains diminish and the 'grumpiness' don't vex you      If you have
a desire for M$^r$ Capern why not come where he is to be found and
put yourself under his hands?  If you stay at Paris, and find walking doesn't suit you, why not ride?  Wouldn't I like to pay the fly,
thats all!  I am in hopes of making a very pretty little sum by the
lectures, and meanwhile haven't spent through the overplus of
last year.  I have been living in the last century for weeks past —
all day that is — going at night as usual into the present age; until
I get to fancy myself almost as familiar with one as the other; and
Oxford and Bolingbroke interest me as much as Russell & Palmerston — more very likely.  The present politics are behind the
world: and not fit for the intelligence of the nation.  The great
revolution's a coming a coming: and the man not here who's to
head it. — I wonder whether he's born and where he lives? — The
present writers are all employed as by instinct in unscrewing the
old framework of society, and get it ready for the Smash.  I take
a sort of pleasure in my little part in the business and in saying
destructive things in a good humoured jolly way.  They say there's
to be a wholesale secession at Easter, and a great corps of proselytes
will march over and be reconciled to our Mother of the Seven
Hills — The ground is being cleared every day and the parties *se
dessinent* — Wonderful is the ferment w$^h$ this old Pope of Rome
has set us into — and not to be over yet for years upon years perhaps.  They say that while he makes such progress (undeniable it
is) in our country w$^h$ is surely the most faithful and religious in all
the world — all enlightened Italy is in a state of utter incredulity,
and scorns Pope and Popery entirely.  Our young ones may live

to see awful changes — but what? — Ah me: its not universal suffrage nor laws of parliamentary assemblies that can set us right. If they publish a little book called Yeast over the water get it and read it. It's written by Kingsley, the socialist parson, who wrote Alton Locke, and who has for his part pulled some awful screws out of the present social fabric — Sometimes I think it will crash down in our time, and knock your dearly beloved Son over. — I would write to you very [much] oftener if I could write cheerful letters to you. Why can't I? The most funny satirical letters about the world & the people I see would only make you glum. The children must amuse my dearest old mother; and thank God they do. We've been very happy in the absence of Trulock, chattering this morning. I can't speak to them before her: and when we dine together the poor lady gets up directly after the table cloth, and goes away and leaves us. I can't help my nature being so.

Mary was here yesterday in my absence and went all over the house, being supported Anny says by Miss Mark [68] — She has not been at home to me the last 2 times I have called: and kept hiding very likely, as not wishing to enter into the Wood affair. Bob wanted me to go to Hicks's, and see papers on the subject. But what can I do? Decide that they have been in the wrong? — What good will that do? Would they have me for an umpire? — not they. She will quarrel with everybody who doesn't agree with her make an injury out of a difference and fancy all sorts of wrong. She has a uterine disease, thats the fact, and her poor mind isn't sane. I see what her conversation is from the behaviour of Chéri; who looks hard & suspiciously and so forth. Well, on our side, our children laugh at her and at poor Charles. They can't help it: it's their sense of humour & justice: and I cant help laughing & cracking at what they tell me. She has bread & butter instead of bread at dinner & Mark's ⟨da⟩ughter, whats her name? butters it and her. Poor Poll⟨y . . .⟩ [69]     She seems very fond of me: & kisses and smacks me ⟨. . .⟩     I am glad of my dear old G P's

[68] One of the three daughters of Mark Wood Carmichael-Smyth.
[69] Two words have been torn away, both here and in the following hiatus.

six medals — do you know how I came to them? never mind the reasoning — but I do think I like other people to succeed in the world and am pleased with the fortune of those nearly akin to me by blood or friendship or circumstance. Addison wasn't though and Pope was an envious little devil: Swift liked his friends to succeed though he was a bad man, and scorned all the world except his own set: and Dicky Steele wasn't envious, though he was a sad loose fish — for w.h see lectures to be delivered — where? when? — about 20 May let us hope. And so God bless you. Write & say you are well — goodbye dear old GP

                                        W M T.


763.                    TO MRS. PROCTER
                        16 APRIL 1851? [70]


Hitherto unpublished. My text is taken from a transcript given Lady Ritchie by George Murray Smith.

                              13, Young Street,
                                 Kensington.
                                  April 16.
My dear Mrs Procter,

    Mrs Powell being about to retire from the place of Superintendent of the Lady's College, I should be very glad indeed if I could get your vote and interest in favour of an old friend of my family.

    Miss Goodchild is the eldest daughter of the late John Goodchild Esq, the heir of a considerable estate long possessed by his ancestors in the county of Durham. Mercantile speculations and the failure of a Sunderland bank of which he was partner ruined Mr Goodchild and his widow and large family were finally left destitute.

    At this period of distress Miss Goodchild was the only member

[70] The place of this letter in the Procter sequence points to 1851, though 1850 is possible, since the Carmichael-Smyths' friendship with the Kennaways began when they moved to Larkbeare in 1825.

of the family who could exert herself for their benefit and to this end she employed herself for thirty years in literary pursuits or as governess or companion to ladies. My mother made her acquaintance twenty-five years ago when she was living with the family of the late Sir John Kennaway: and their friendship has ever since continued. I can say of Miss G. that she is not only a person of great merit and entitled to all the help which her friends can find for her, but that she is a lady, as I should think, perfectly well suited for the vacant post — good natured, sensible, energetic, well-read and well-bred.

If your interest is engaged for no other candidate I shall, be very glad indeed if you will take my word for the excellence and merits of Miss Goodchild

Believe me to be always, my dear Mrs Procter,

Most faithfully yours,

W. M. Thackeray.

764.          TO THOMAS JOHN MAZZINGHI
APRIL? 1851

My text is taken from *Thackeray in the United States*, II, 119.

My dear Mazzinghi, — I only find your letter here to-day and am very much grieved at its contents. If I can help you, I will. That is all I can say at present, for it requires time and chance and occasion to find work for a man. Perhaps there comes no chance, no occasion; that is the worst of it. In the meanwhile, is a little (a very little you understand, for I am always as poor as a church-mouse) present help wanted? My dear fellow in that case pray command me in this case and think that it is I who am thankful if I can aid you. Always truly yours, dear Mazzinghi,

W. M. Thackeray.

765. TO THOMAS JOHN MAZZINGHI
APRIL? 1851

Hitherto unpublished.

Kensington. Saturday.

My dear Mazzinghi

I am glad you applied to your old friend and I'm very glad that the old friend has the means to help you. If it hadn't been for friends' purses where should I have been now? The world is a good natured world to the good natured — I dont mean to say that men will perform sacrifices but they like to do kindnesses, and to be asked to do them, as witness the present writing.

Your fortress looks awful on paper: but I'm glad you prosper behind those grim walls & trenches. Fitz has been here once ill with a cold. I am busy going to give lectures — then to try America — and then if I can O if I can! but save a little money, to keep it. I couldnt attend to your note till last night & will send the next 1/2 note by Mondays post

Yours always
W M Thackeray

766. TO MRS. BROOKFIELD
29 APRIL 1851

Published in part, *Collection of Letters*, pp. 132–134.

April 29.

Madam and dear lady, Will you have a little letter to day or a long letter tomorrow for theres only half an hour to post time — a little letter today? — I dont wonder at poets being selfish, such as Wordsworth and Alfred — I've been for 5 days a poet, and have thought or remembered nothing else but my self and my rhymes and my measure [71] — If somebody had come to me and said M^rs Brookfield has just had her arm cut off I should have gone on with Queen of innumerable isles tidumtidytidumtidy and not stirred from the chair — the children and nobody haven't seen me except at night — and now though the work is just done (I'm just returned from taking it to the Times Office) I hardly see the paper before me, so utterly beat, nervous, bilious & overcome I feel. So you see you chose a very bad day Mum for a letter from yours very sincerely — if you were at Cadogan Place I would walk in I darsay, say God bless you, and then ask leave to go to sleep — Now you must be thinking of coming back to Pumlico soon for the lectures are to begin on the 15^th — I tried the great room at Willis's [72] yesterday, and recited a part of the multiplication table to a waiter at the opposite end so as to try the woice. He said he could hear perfectly: and I daresay he could but the thoughts somehow swell and amplify with that high-pitched voice and elaborate distinctness — as I perceive how poets become selfish I see how orators become humbugs and selfish in their way too: absorbed in that selfish pursuit and turning of periods — It is curious to take those dips into a life new to me as yet, and try it and come out and say how I like it isn't it? — Ah me — Idleness [is] best that is quiet and repose of mind, and somebody to love and be fond of, and nil admirari [73] in fine. The gentlemen of the G [74] tell me, and another auditor from the Macready dinner, that my style of horatory was conspicuous for consummate ease and impudence, I all the while feeling in so terrible a panic that I scarcely knew at the time what I was uttering, & didn't know at all when I sat down — This is

[71] Thackeray had been writing his "May-Day Ode," which appeared in *The Times* on April 30, 1851. The line he cites below is from the ninth stanza:

Oh! awful is that crown of yours,
Queen of innumerable realms
Sitting beneath the budding elms
Of English May!

[72] See below, No. 773.

[73] Horace, *Epistles*, I, vi, 1.

[74] Thackeray had spoken at the Garrick Club's annual Shakespeare dinner a few days before.

all I have to tell you about self and ten days w^h have passed away like a fever — Why if we were to let the poetic cock turn & run there's no end of it I think. Would you like me now to become a great — fiddlededydee — no more egotisms M^r Makepeace if you please.

I should have liked to see your master on Sunday but how could I & Lord I had such a headache and Dicky Doyle came and we went to Soyers Symposium and the Christial Palace [75] together where the great calm leviathan steam-engines and machines lying alongside like [a] great line of battle ships did wonderfully move me, and I think the English Compartment do beat the rest entirely and that (let alone our Ingynes w^h be incomparable) our painters artificers makers of busts and statuas do deserve to compare with the best foreign,— [76]

— This I am sure will interest and please Miss Brookfield very much. God bless that dear little lady. I would give 2^d to hear her say more tea — O — by the way — Can I have that young woman of whom Rossiter spoke? Mary goes away at the end of the week, and a cook is coming and I want a maid but have had no leisure to think of one, till now when my natural affairs and affections are beginning to return to my mind and when I am my dear ladys friend and servant, (and G B her)

W M T.

767.          TO MRS. BROOKFIELD
1 MAY 1851

Published in part, *Collection of Letters*, pp. 134–135.

Amie — I write you a little word after that Exhibition [77] from home, & why do you think I came home? for a letter from some-

---

[75] Where the Great Exhibition of 1851 was held.

[76] This sentence is written in the style of Percival Leigh's "Mr. Pips' Diary," which accompanied Doyle's "Manners and Customs of the English" in *Punch*. *Statuas* is Shakespearian; see *Richard III*, III, vii, 25.

[77] The inaugural ceremonies of the Great Exhibition are described in *The Times* of May 2.

body that I longed for: and was going away quite disconsolate at not finding it when Anny to whom I'd been talking mentioned that she had got & forgot one. But why havent you written all this time? What is the matter? Is W^m really unwell [78] at Southton? — It was I ordered Jane Elliot to write to you like a good dear soul as she is; the Ode has had a great success　What do you mean by an Ode as she calls, vive dieu Madame 'tis either an ode or nix. (the German for nothing) — and as for the Exhibition w^h dont interest me at all so much, it was a noble awful great love inspiring goose flesh bringing sight. I got a good place by good luck, and saw the whole affair of w^h no particular item is wonderful but the general effect the multitude the riches the peace the splendour the security the sunshine great to see — much grander than a coronation — the vastest & sublimest popular festival that the world has ever witnessed — What can one say about it but commonplaces? — There was a Chinese with a face like a panto-

mime mask  and  shoes who went up and

kissed the Duke of Wellington much to the old boys surprise, and the Queen looked not uninteresting and Prince Albert grave handsome & princely, and the Prince of W & the Princess Royal are nice children — very eager to talk and observe they seemed — and while the Archbishop was saying his prayer beginning with Paternoster (w^h sounded in that wonderful throng inexpressibly sweet and awful) 3  Romish priests were staring about with opera glasses: w^h made me feel as angry as the Jews who stoned Stephen —[79]

I think this is all I have to say: I'm very tired & the day not over for I have promised the children to take them to the play in recompense for their disappointment in not getting to the Exhibition w^h they had hopes of seeing through my friend Cole. God

[78] We learn from *Mrs. Brookfield* (II, 352) that after his father died, "Mr. Brookfield's health, always delicate, began to fail more rapidly, and a lung trouble was suspected. He went to Southampton in May to consult his old and trusted friends the Bullars."

[79] *Acts*, 7, 54–60.

MRS. BROOKFIELD AT CHESHAM PLACE

*From a sketch by Thackeray*

bless you — and you'll come back on the seventh will you? God
keep you that & all days my sister my lady.

W M T.

[For a fragment of a letter to Mrs. Brookfield presumably written in the
spring of 1851 see letter 21, Appendix XXVI.]

768.        TO MRS. PROCTER
1 MAY 1851

Hitherto unpublished. My text is taken from a transcript given Lady Ritchie
by George Murray Smith.

My dear Mrs Procter,

Will you send me a pooty little account of Mrs Jameson's writings and history? I can put it in a good way I think [80] and so it
shall be well seen by Lord John Russell. I saw her at the Exhibition to-day: let us hope that the great folks are sometimes
worth knowing and that we may get some good out of them now
and again.

Yours always,<br>W. M. T.

769.        TO ROBERT SMITH SURTEES
3 MAY 1851

Hitherto unpublished.

Kensington. May 3.

My dear Surtees

Information has reached me that you are in London, and I feel
glad & ashamed of myself: for having left undone those things
w^h I ought to have done [81] & omitted to write & thank you for your
books and send you my own. Sir, you who know the literary man

---

[80] Mrs. Procter and Thackeray wished to secure a pension for Mrs. Jameson
(1794–1860), the poetess.

[81] *Book of Common Prayer*, "General Confession."

(& I hope intend to subscribe many hundreds to the Guild of Literature & Art) [82] know how improvident literary persons are, careless in their habits, irregular in their business-transactions, wofully lazy when not urged by necessity. I dont know how long I should have gone on dawdling with my kind creditor not sending my promised book nor my letter, had not the news come that Surtees was in town when I knew I *must* write: if ever I wanted again to look you in the face. There — I've written — it's no such great difficulty when one sets about it, is it? and as for the matter of the book, the deuce is in it if I can't send mine to a man whose own books have given me so much pleasure — who sent me grouse when I was ill, who complimented me in print, who perhaps may take a ticket for my lectures, and who has always shown himself kind & friendly. I am over head & ears in business and pleasure just now, but I hope we may have a day together. Will the 8 May suit you? I have an old college friend another parson, and will look for a man or 2 more.

Yours ever dear Surtees<br>W M Thackeray

770.          TO MRS. PROCTER
          MAY 1851 [83]

Hitherto unpublished. My text is taken from a transcript given Lady Ritchie by George Murray Smith.

My dear Mrs Procter,

If I shouldn't be able to pay you a visit to-day, and I'm awfully busy, this is to say that I've been a waiting these two days for a letter from Lord John Russell which Lord Stanley has received in answer to our application: Lord S. promised: but hasn't sent it.

He says Lord John's letter is rather favourable: there are no pensions till June and no promise, but Lord Stanley thinks well of

[82] An organization to provide for superannuated writers and artists, of which Dickens was the moving spirit.

[83] This note was written shortly after Thackeray's letter of May 1 to Mrs. Procter.

our applicant; and you may be sure I backed her well when we talked about it.

Always yours,<br>W. M. Thackeray.

771.              TO MARK LEMON
                    MAY 1851

Hitherto unpublished.

Dear Sir

A little bit should be kept for the Grand Exhibition [84] — Is there to be a meet on Monday? I shall go to the W. Hall & try and get a par [85] or two. Please reply per po.

Yrs<br>W M T.

772.              TO DAVID MASSON [86]
                    6? MAY 1851

My text is taken from Flora Masson's "The Two Novelists: a Letter from Thackeray," *The Cornhill Magazine*, New Series, XXX (1911), p. 797.

Kensington. Tuesday M<sup>g</sup>

My dear Sir,

I received the N B Review [87] and am very glad to know the name of the critic who has spoken so kindly in my favor. Did I

[84] Thackeray dealt with the Exhibition of 1851 in two articles for *Punch* of May 10: "What I Remarked at the Exhibition" and "Monsieur Gobemouche's Authentic Account of the Grand Exhibition."

[85] I.e., paragraph.

[86] Masson (1822–1907), who had come to London in 1847, was at this time occupied with magazine writing and the compilation of textbooks for Robert Chambers. He was Professor of English Literature at London University from 1853 to 1865, editor of *Macmillan's Magazine* from 1859 to 1867, and Professor of Rhetoric and English Literature at the University of Edinburgh from 1865 to 1895. His name is kept alive today by his monumental *Life of Milton* (1859–1880).

[87] Masson's "*Pendennis* and *Copperfield*: Thackeray and Dickens" appeared in *The North British Review* of May, 1851, pp. 57–89. The maga-

not once before see your handwriting, in a note w.ʰ pointed out to
me a friendly notice of Vanity Fair [88] — then not very well known
or much cared for, and struggling to get a place in the world? If
you were the author of the article to w.ʰ I allude, let me thank you
for that too; I remember it as gratefully, as a boy remembers his
'tips' at school, when sovereigns were rare & precious to him. I
don't know what to say respecting your present paper comparisons
being difficult, & no two minds in the least alike. I think Mr.
Dickens has in many things quite a divine genius so to speak, and
certain notes in his song are so delightful and admirable, that I
should never think of trying to imitate him, only hold my tongue
and admire him. I quarrel with his Art in many respects: w.ʰ I don't
think represents Nature duly; for instance Micawber appears to
me an exaggeration of a man, as his name is of a name. It is delightful and makes me laugh: but it is no more a real man than my
friend Punch is: and in so far I protest against him — and against
the doctrine quoted by my Reviewer from Goethe too — holding
that the Art of Novels *is* to represent Nature: to convey as strongly
as possible the sentiment of reality [89] — in a tragedy or a poem or
a lofty drama you aim at producing different emotions; the figures

---

zine's editor, Alexander Campbell Fraser, sent copies both to Dickens and to
Thackeray, and Masson received a letter from the former dated May 9.
Thackeray's note was probably written on Tuesday of the same week.

[88] The first three numbers of *Vanity Fair* were briefly noticed in an essay
on "Popular Serial Literature" in *The North British Review* of May, 1847,
pp. 119–122.

[89] Masson distinguishes in his article (pp. 69–70) between real and ideal
styles in art. The aim of the former, he maintains, "is to reproduce pictures
that shall impress by their close and truthful resemblance to something or
other in real nature or life." The latter, on the other hand, "strikes, not by
recalling real scenes and occurrences, but by taking the mind out of itself
into a region of higher possibilities, wherein objects shall be more glorious,
and modes of action more transcendent, than any we see, and yet all shall
seem in nature." Thackeray is an artist of the real school, Masson continues,
but Dickens works in the ideal. If Thackeray should be praised for the veri-
similitude of his fiction, it is none the less a mistake to reproach Dickens
because his characters are not life-like. "Art is called Art, says Goethe, precisely because it is *not* Nature; and even such a department of art as the
modern novel is entitled to the benefit of this maxim" (p. 75).

moving, and their words sounding, heroically: but in a drawing-room drama a coat is a coat and a poker a poker; and must be nothing else according to my ethics, not an embroidered tunic, nor a great red-hot instrument like the Pantomime weapon. But let what defects you (or rather I), will, be in Dickens's theory — there is no doubt according to my notion that his writing has one admirable quality — it is charming — that answers everything. Another may write the most perfect English have the greatest fund of wit learning & so forth — but I doubt if any novel-writer has that quality, that wonderful sweetness & freshness w^h belongs to Dickens — And now I have carried my note out of all bounds and remain dear Sir

Yours very faithfully,

W. M. Thackeray.

[For a fragment of a letter to Mrs. Brookfield, 14 May, 1851, see letter 22, Appendix XXVI.]

773.                 TO  RICHARD  DOYLE
                       21 MAY 1851

My text is taken from *Thackeray in the United States*, I, 4.

My dear D, — I hope you will come to the tight rope exhibition to-morrow,[90] and send you a card. You and your friend will please to sit in distant parts of the room.

[90] "LECTURES on the ENGLISH HUMORISTS of the EIGHTEENTH CENTURY. — Willis's Rooms, King-street, St. James's — Mr. THACKERAY will deliver a series of SIX LECTURES on the English Humorists of the Eighteenth Century, their Lives and Writings, their Friends and Associates. The course will contain notices of Swift, Pope, and Gay, Addison, Steele, and Congreve, Fielding and Hogarth, Smollett, Sterne, and Goldsmith. The first lecture will be given THIS MORNING (Thursday) May 22 (to be continued on each succeeding Thursday), commencing at 3 o'clock. Tickets for the course of six lectures, £2 2s; single tickets, 7s 6d.; family tickets, to admit four, 21s: to be had at Mitchell's Library, 33, Old Bond-street; Sams' Library, 1, St. James's-street; Messrs. Chapman and Hall, Piccadilly; and Messrs. Smith and Elder's, Cornhill." (*Times*, May 22) The third lecture was postponed from June 5 to 12 at the petition of the

When you see me put my hand to my watch-chain, you will say, "God bless my soul, how beautiful!"

When I touch my neck-cloth, clap with all your might.

When I use my pocket-handkerchief, burst into tears.

When I pause say Brav-ah-ah-ah-vo, through the pause.

You had best bring with you a very noisy umbrella: to be used at proper intervals: and if you can't cry at the pathetic parts, please blow your nose very hard.

And now, everything having been done to insure success that mortal can do, the issue is left to the immortal Gods.

God save the Queen. No money returned. Babies in arms NOT admitted.

By yours ever,

W. M. T.

---

fashionable ladies in Thackeray's audience who wished to attend Ascot Races on the former date, and all following lectures were deferred one week.

THACKERAY PREPARING TO LECTURE

*From a caricature by an unknown artist*

774.        TO MR. AND MRS. CARLYLE
                23? MAY 1851 91

Hitherto unpublished.

My dear M^rs Carlyle my dear Carlyle you are both very kind
to me: and always have been my kind old friends and I am yours
in return very gratefully & sincerely indeed

                                W M Thackeray
                                Equilibrist and Tightrope
                                dance[r] in ordinary to the
                                nobility & the Literati

I think it was very kind of Mazzini 92 to ask.

                                T. O.

91 This note was probably written the day after Thackeray's first lecture.
92 Joseph Mazzini (1805–1872), the Italian revolutionist, a friend of the
Carlyles.

775.                    TO LADY CASTLEREAGH
                          23? MAY 1851

Hitherto unpublished.

                                        Kensington. Friday.

Dear Lady Castlereagh. You are very kind to send me your
good wishes when you are too unwell to bring them: and indeed
it's a very pleasant part of my success to know my friends' pleasure
in it. But if my kind subscriber cant come to me I can come to my
subscriber, and it would give me very great gratification indeed if
you would let me read my lecture to you as you lie on your sofa,
and if I could amuse an hour of your day. Any hour you please to
give me (at 3 today for instance?) I will come, & be only too glad.

                     Always most sincerely yours
                          W M Thackeray


776.                    TO ABRAHAM HAYWARD
                          23 MAY 1851

My text is taken from *A Selection from the Correspondence of Abraham
Hayward*, I, 119.

                                        Kensington,
                                        May 23rd. 1851.

O, most kind Hayward! Why do you go for to say that I
thought the words "Only a woman's hair" [93] indicated heartless-
ness? I said I thought them the most affecting words I ever heard,
indicating the truest passion, love, and remorse. I said, though
Swift announced himself in that letter to Bolingbroke as an *Am-
bitionist*, and took to the road and robbed — I say that your article
just read is a most kind, handsome, and gentlemanlike one, and
I'm glad to think I have such good friends and generous backers
in this fight, where all isn't generosity and good friendship and
fair play. Amongst the company I see that Lord D— was present;

[93] See *Works*, VII, 453.

how Lady D— must have been surprised!  But the truth is that
lectures won't do.[94]  They were all friends, and a packed house;
though, to be sure, it goes to a man's heart to find amongst his
friends such men as you and Kinglake and Venables, Higgins,
Rawlinson, Carlyle, Ashburton and Hallam, Milman, Macaulay,
Wilberforce looking on kindly.  Excuse egotism which means
thanks in this instance.

Always gratefully yours dear Hayward,

W. M. Thackeray.

777.    TO THE SECRETARY OF THE
ROYAL LITERARY FUND
26 MAY? 1851 [95]

Hitherto unpublished.

13 Young S̪ᵗ Kensington.  Monday.

My dear Sir

I thought my corrected copy of the Shorthand writers notes had
been returned some days since — Excuse the delay: there is only
one phrase wʰ contains an absurd error, the Queen is made to do
Mʳ Dickens *harm* instead of doing him honour.  Shᵈ the book be
printed, please to add this as an erratum deflendum.

Can you do anything for the gentleman whose letter & testi-
monial I enclose?

Believe me very faithfully yours

W M Thackeray

[94] Sir Francis Burnand (*Pall Mall Magazine*, XVIII, 329) describes an
incident that must have heightened these misgivings: "on Thackeray's expressing his fear lest his lecture should not prove a success, as his first start had
seemed to him a comparative failure, Arcedeckne, who among others had
been listening to him, sidled up to the door (his usual 'safe move,' reminding
me of the pugilist's dodge of 'going down to avoid a blow') and, looking
back sorrowfully as he went out, croaked, '*Ah! Thac my boy! you ought to
ha' 'ad a pianner*,' with which 'exit speech' he disappeared, chuckling."

[95] Thackeray had spoken at the dinner of the Royal Literary Fund on
Wednesday, May 14, 1851.  This note may reasonably be dated a week from

778.                   TO MRS. BUTLER
                      27 MAY? 1851

Hitherto unpublished.

                                    Garrick Club.
                                    Tuesday night.

My dear M^rs Kemble      I have made enquiries today regarding your benevolent project and I think you had best *not* make
that application about w^h you write to me.[96] This reply seems very
diplomatic and guarded, doesn't it? but I feel pretty sure that a
refusal would come if your request were made. And so I am
always sincerely yours

                              W M Thackeray

Thank you for your kind wishes about the lectures and your
kind shake of the hand [97] on the first awful occasion — I know you
wish me well and am grateful for the many many friends who have
helped to launch me.

---

the following Monday. The error that Thackeray remarks is corrected in the
*Report of the Royal Literary Fund* for 1851.

[96] I have been able to discover nothing about this application.

[97] Thackeray's allusion is most tactfully phrased. "He was to lecture at
Willis['s] Rooms, in the same room where I read," Fanny Kemble relates
(*Records of Later Life*, pp. 625–626), "and going thither before the time
for his beginning, found him standing like a forlorn disconsolate giant in the
middle of the room, gazing about him. 'Oh, Lord,' he exclaimed, as he shook
hands with me, 'I'm sick at my stomach with fright.' I spoke some words
of encouragement to him, and was going away, but he held my hand, like
a scared child, crying, 'Oh, don't leave me!' 'But,' said I, 'Thackeray, you
mustn't stand here. Your audience are beginning to come in,' and I drew
him from the middle of his chairs and benches, which were beginning to be
occupied, into the retiring-room adjoining the lecture-room, my own readings having made me perfectly familiar with both. Here he began pacing up
and down, literally wringing his hands in nervous distress. 'Now,' said I,
'what shall I do? Shall I stay with you till you begin, or shall I go, and
leave you alone to collect yourself?' 'Oh,' he said, 'if I could only get at that
confounded thing' (his lecture), 'to have a last look at it!' 'Where is it?'
said I. 'Oh, in the next room on the reading-desk.' 'Well,' said I, 'if you
don't like to go in and get it, I'll fetch it for you.' And remembering

779.      TO MRS. PROCTER
27? MAY 1851 [98]

Hitherto unpublished. My text is taken from a transcript given Lady Ritchie by George Murray Smith.

My dear Mrs Procter,

You thought something I said just as we parted on Sunday very odd, didn't you, and that I was very difficult to please? I was thinking about Forster at that time, whose conduct — not his article [99] — gave me a great deal of pain. He didn't say a sentence of praise without qualifying it: he who can praise so if he is let.

---

well the position of my reading-table, which had been close to the door of the retiring-room, I darted in, hoping to snatch the manuscript without attracting the attention of the audience, with which the room was already nearly full. I had been used to deliver my reading seated, at a very low table, but my friend Thackeray gave his lectures standing, and had had a reading-desk placed on the platform, adapted to his own very tall stature, so that when I came to get his manuscript it was almost above my head. Though rather disconcerted, I was determined not to go back without it, and so made a half jump, and a clutch at the book, when every leaf of it (they were not fastened together), came fluttering separately down about me. I hardly know what I did, but I think I must have gone nearly on all-fours, in my agony to gather up the scattered leaves, and retreating with them, held them out in dismay to poor Thackeray, crying, 'Oh, look, look, what a dreadful thing I have done!' 'My dear soul,' said he, 'you couldn't have done better for me. I have just a quarter of an hour to wait here, and it will take me about that to page this again, and it's the best thing in the world that could have happened.' With which infinite kindness he comforted me, for I was all but crying, at having, as I thought, increased his distress and troubles."

[98] This note appears to have been written two or three days after Sunday, May 25.

[99] Forster's review of the lecture on Swift (*Examiner*, May 24, pp. 325–326) set off one of the periodic quarrels that punctuated his association with Thackeray. Concerning himself chiefly with objections to details, he offered for the lecturer the damaging and gratuitous apology that "it is incident to this kind of literary entertainment that much should be sacrificed to effect." His notices of later lectures were slighter but no more conciliatory than his first article. They were marked, moreover, by a trivial controversy, in which the honors rested decidedly with Thackeray. On May 31 Forster regretted that in the lecture on Congreve no mention had been made of his tribute to Lady Elizabeth Hastings, that "to love her is a liberal education." When

And it grieves me to think that there should be that sort of rivalry and injustice among men, that a man whom I want to like and who has done me kindness, is bound by party-faction so — that I can't hold my hand out frankly to him and say: "you are an honest fellow — what do I care whether you like what I say or not? And I've promised to go and dine with him: and I *can't* tell him I'm satisfied with his conduct to me. Suppose Dickens or Bulwer had written and read that Swift-paper, fancy F's article about them! And it's I, that these fellows accuse of being artful and false — ah me! If I had an enemy I believe I should try most carefully to do him justice — but these? Well, if *we* ever come to be written about, will the critics say that I'm a rogue, I wonder? never satisfied with praise — scheming to prevent my rivals having it? No,

---

Thackeray next spoke, on June 12, he quietly set Forster right by assigning this epigram to Steele, its proper author (see number 49 of *The Tatler*).

This incident is reflected in a passage in the first edition of *Esmond* (II, 307–309). At the dinner which the ladies of Castlewood give for Harry in chapter 15 of the second book of that novel, Steele has occasion to claim the authorship of *Tatler* paper number 49.

" 'I always thought that paper was Mr. Congreve's,' cries Mr. St. John, showing that he knew more about the subject than he pretended to Mr. Steele, and who was the original Mr. Bickerstaffe drew.

" 'Tom Boxer said so in his Observator. But Tom's oracle is often making blunders,' cries Steele.

" 'Mr. Boxer and my husband were friends once, and when the captain was ill with the fever no man could be kinder than Mr. Boxer, who used to come to his bedside every day, and actually brought Dr. Arbuthnot who cured him,' whispered Mrs. Steele.

" 'Indeed, madam! How very interesting,' says Mr. St. John.

" 'But when the Captain's last comedy came out, Mr. Boxer took no notice of it, — you know he is Mr. Congreve's man, and won't ever give a word to the other house, — and this made my husband angry.'

" 'O! Mr. Boxer is Mr. Congreve's man!' says Mr. St. John.

" 'Mr. Congreve has wit enough of his own,' cries out Mr. Steele. 'No one ever heard me grudge him or any other man his share.' " Steele and Boxer here stand, of course, for Thackeray and Forster, *The Observator* for *The Examiner*, and Congreve and Dr. Arbuthnot for Dickens and Dr. Eliotson. Forster complained of this masquerade (see *Memoranda*), and Thackeray, perhaps judging that his rebuke had served its purpose, omitted the passage from the revised edition of *Esmond* published in 1858, thus rendering unintelligible an allusion to "the treachery of Tom Boxer" a few paragraphs further on.

by Jupiter. NO — and that question, Madam, is what's a biling up in my mind, and making me so sad and sorry about poor Forster.

I couldn't come to A. Sartour's [Sartoris's?] on Sunday, I was ill and went to bed at six o'clock: and I'm

Always yours,

W. M. Thackeray.

I'll speak about the pair of soles.

780.        TO MRS. PROCTER

29 MAY? 1851

Hitherto unpublished. My text is taken from a transcript given Lady Ritchie by George Murray Smith.

Thursday, M<sup>t</sup>

My dear Mrs Procter,

I went to the dinner at Forster's and am very thankful: I see the business in a better light now.[100] He was very angry and hurt, told me I was trying to please the women and coax the bishops, that we should see how long these reputations would last which some folks made, that in my lecture there wasn't a word of wit or humour — on which I lost my temper, for the attack was a very rude one, and said suppose when we come to Goldsmith I take your life [101] and show that there isn't a word of wit or humour there or any of Goldsmith's nature or his grace — for which explosion I should be very sorry only that the anger ended with it, and we parted the best friends. Well, this outbreak has left me pleased and happy rather than [otherwise] and given me the right opinion of my good kind old Forster. He's angry with me for succeeding; it personally chafes him: he's hurt at my getting

[100] Forster's reconciliation dinner, which appears to have been given on Wednesday, May 28, served its purpose only temporarily, for on July 5 Thackeray was again furious with his critic. See below, No. 791.

[101] Forster's *The Life and Adventures of Oliver Goldsmith* (1848). Thackeray lectured on Goldsmith on July 3.

on in society and knowing fine people; (poor old boy, I saw *his* one card to a great house stuck in his chimney glass) can't fancy but that I practise unworthy arts and boo [bow?] to the great: and heartily doesn't like or relish my writings and protests against their acceptance by the public. This you see is quite fair. Why the dickens should he like my writings, or I be angry with him for not liking them? I've no more right to quarrel with a man for that than for his liking a fig better than a peach. And as for his anger at the polite successes, one can bear that without much difficulty. But directly I see and think a man has a real honest opinion against me I respect it as any other opinion: and I think he has that: and no longer that he is fighting the babble [battle] of another man, but that he turns out against me sword and pistol on his own account and no other — which makes all the difference in the animus with which the quarrel is fought, and leaves men at full liberty to shake hands, and heartily too, as boxers do before they pitch in.

And you come to be the depositary of this because it's early morning and I can't sleep and because it is written in a better frame of mind I think than I had when I saw you last: at least I can think much better of a man whom I was forced then to think ill of, and now can regard him quite friendlily as a man in the opposition.

I've been reading the Spectator No 256 [102] this morning, and am yours always,

**W. M. T.**

---

[102] In which Addison observes, after rehearsing the trials attendant on success, "So inconsiderable is the satisfaction that fame brings along with it, and so great the disquietudes to which it makes us liable!"

781.    TO THOMAS WASHBOURNE GIBBS [103]
31 MAY 1851

*Postmarks:* May 31, 1851; June 1, 1851. My text is taken from Governor Wilbur L. Cross's edition of Sterne's *Works* (New York, 1904), X, xxxiv, where the postmarks are recorded.

13 Young St.
Kensington
May 31

Dear Sir

I thank you very much for your obliging offer, and the kind terms in w^h you make it. If you will send me the MSS I will take great care of them, and gratefully restore them to their owner.

Your very faithful Serv^t
W M Thackeray

782.                    TO MRS. BAYNE
5 JUNE 1851

Hitherto unpublished.

Kensington. June 5.

My dear M^rs Bayne

The reserved seats are for the subscribers to the series — how can I break in on their sacred precincts and let my outside friends come in? I'm sure you will agree with me that the arrangements of the *Salle* must rest with M^r Mitchell,[104] and see that I should have scores complaining if I were to grant privileges to one. There will be a better arrangement of chairs however, and many more people will I hope be able to obtain sitting and hearing room.

[103] A gentleman living at 5 Northumberland Buildings, Bath, who had discovered several important Sterne manuscripts, including the (then) unpublished *Journal to Eliza*, and offered to send them to Thackeray. See below, No. 795.

[104] John Mitchell, the impresario for Thackeray's lectures, had many years earlier published the novelist's first book, *Flore et Zéphyr*. See above, No. 91.

People heard quite well last lecture at the farthest corner of the room. How sorry I am that I can't help you. But mightn't Kenyon (he has 4, praise be to him) lend you a reserved place or 2?

Always sincerely yours

W M Thackeray

783.                    TO MRS. BAYNE
                        11 JUNE 1851

*Address:* M<sup>rs</sup> Bayne | York Terrace | Regents Park. *Postmark:* JU 11 1851. Hitherto unpublished.

Alas! dear M<sup>rs</sup> Bayne I am engaged not to a Duke but a publisher,[105] & always yours in an immense business

W M Thackeray

[105] "Mr Thackeray. . . . was here yesterday to dinner," writes Charlotte Brontë on June 14 from the home of George Smith and his mother at 112 Gloucester Terrace, "and left very early in the evening in order that he might visit respectively the Duchess of Norfolk, the Marchioness of Londonderry, Ladies Chesterfield and Clanricarde, and see them all in their fancy costumes of the reign of Charles II, before they set out for the Palace!" (Wise and Smyington, *The Brontës*, III, 247)

Miss Brontë had come to London on May 28 to hear Thackeray speak on Congreve and Addison the following day. "After the lecture," Smith relates, "Thackeray came down from the platform and shook hands with many of the audience, receiving their congratulations and compliments. He was in high spirits, and rather thoughtlessly said to his mother — Mrs. Carmichael Smyth — 'Mother, you must allow me to introduce you to Jane Eyre.' This was uttered in a loud voice, audible over half the room. Everybody near turned round and stared at the disconcerted little lady, who grew confused and angry when she realized that every eye was fixed upon her. My mother got her away as quickly as possible.

"On the next afternoon Thackeray called. I arrived at home shortly afterwards, and when I entered the drawing-room found a scene in full progress. Only these two were in the room. Thackeray was standing on the hearthrug, looking anything but happy. Charlotte Brontë stood close to him, with head thrown back and face white with anger. The first words I heard were, 'No, Sir! If *you* had come to our part of the country in Yorkshire, what would you have thought of me if I had introduced you to my father, before a mixed company of strangers, as "Mr. Warrington"?' Thackeray replied, 'No, you mean "Arthur Pendennis." ' 'No, I *don't* mean Arthur Pendennis!' retorted

784.            TO CHARLES LAMB KENNEY
                        19 JUNE 1851

Hitherto unpublished.

                                        Kensington. June 19.

Dear Kenney

I have already spoken with a French gentleman regarding a
translation of my lectures.

                        faithfully yours
                        W M Thackeray


785.                    TO MR. MOFFATT
                        2 JULY 1851

Hitherto unpublished.

                                        Wednesday.

Dear Moffatt.

I am much vexed to be obliged to throw myself over to day —
but I am not content with my last lecture, w$^h$ is to be given tomorrow; and I *must* do my best and devote the night to study instead of feasting.

                        Yours very faithfully
                        W M Thackeray

---

Miss Brontë; 'I mean Mr. Warrington, and Mr. Warrington would not have
behaved as you behaved to me yesterday.' The spectacle of this little woman,
hardly reaching to Thackeray's elbow, but, somehow, looking stronger and
fiercer than himself, and casting her incisive words at his head, resembled the
dropping of shells into a fortress.

"By this time I had recovered my presence of mind, and hastened to inter-
pose. Thackeray made the necessary and half-humorous apologies, and the
parting was a friendly one." (*George Smith, A Memoir*, pp. 99–100)

Miss Brontë attended four of Thackeray's lectures before returning to
Haworth late in June.

786.    FROM LORD STANLEY OF ALDERLEY
3? JULY 1851

Published in *Thackeray in the United States*, I, 365–366.

Dear Thackeray — I have just received a letter from Lord John Russell, informing me that the Queen has been pleased to grant a pension.of 100 l. a year to Mrs. Jameson and requesting me to inform her of it. As it was through your representations to me of the circumstances and condition of that lady that I brought her case before Lord Russell, I will trust to your kindness to make this communication to her, and to say how happy I am to have been in any degree the means of bringing forward the claims of one who is so well entitled to the consideration of her sovereign.

787.    TO LORD STANLEY OF ALDERLEY
4 JULY 1851

My text is taken from a transcript supplied by Mrs. Fuller.

Kensington.
July 4th., 1851.

My dear Lord Stanley.

Thank you for your letter and for making me the Bearer of the good news to Mrs. Jameson.

That was a lucky day when I met you at the Exhibition and interested you in her case: and I am glad to think that I have been the means ever so humble of helping this good woman to a quiet old age. I shall see Lord John on Saturday, and thank him *de vive voix* and I need not say that I am always.

Yours sincerely,
W. M. Thackeray.

788.                TO MRS. JAMESON
                       6 JULY 1851

Published in *Thackeray in the United States*, I, 366.

                              Kensington, July 6

My dear Mrs. Jameson, — I am very nearly as pleased as you
are, and shall gladly be your godfather to promise and vow the
necessary things in your name.  I saw Lord Russell yesterday and
thanked him, and told him how happy some people were made, and
what you said about your mother which touched the premier's
heart.  And I wish I had a couple of trustees and a pension

                       For yours very truly,
                          W. M. Thackeray


789.                TO MR. HAWKINS
                       7 JULY 1851

Hitherto unpublished. *Endorsed:* July 7ᵗʰ/ 51.

My dear Mr Hawkins

The last effort at Potry I made was for the 1 of May Exhibition [106] — The verses flow easily enough, but they took 5 days
of the hardest labour I ever endured in my life — clearing a
primaeval forest is nothing to it.

But if I can see my way into anything good — I'll do it for
honour & glory: but the verses, you see ought to be so *very* good,
and that sort is so very hard to do for

                       Yours most truly
                        W M Thackeray

[106] See above, No. 766.

790.          TO MRS. BROOKFIELD
              13–15 JULY 1851

Published in part, *Collection of Letters*, pp. 143–145.

The appy family has scarce had a moments rest since we left the
S$^t$ Katherines Wharf: [107] and this is wrote on board the steamer in
the Rhine with ever so many fine views at my back — Minny on
t'other side writing to her Granny and Anny reading her fathers
works in the Tauchnitz edition. It has not been a very brilliant
journey hitherto but the little ones are satisfied thats the main point.
The packet to Antwerp was awful a storm and a gib carried away
and a hundred women being sick on the cabin floor all night — the
children very unwell but behaving excellently, their pa tranquil
under a table and not in the least sick for a wonder — We passed
the day Friday at Antwerp, when I hope his Reverence came home
to you better, and it was very pleasant going about with the
children, walking & lionizing, and I wished &c &c — Yesterday we
got up at five and rushed to Cologne; to day we rose at 4 and
rush to Maynz. We shall sleep or at Wiesbaden or at Frankft to
night, as the fancy seizes me: and shall get on to Heidelberg then
to Basle, then to Berne & so on to Como. Milan. Venice. if it
dont cost too much money. I suppose you are going to church at
this time, and know the bells of Knightsbridge are tolling. Amie,
if I dont go to Church myself (but I do, here this instant opposite
the young ones) I know who will say a God bless me. I suppose
I've thought of you a good number of times. It seems a year since
I left. But it's passed pleasantly enough. Anny is famous. I hear
her bearing up against Minikin's ill humour & sarcasm in the next
room — Minny keeps all her claws for poor Nan. It's all smiles
& good humour for me. The little hypocrite! the little vixen!
the little woman! She has little Beckyfied ways and arts. It's
almost disloyal the way in w$^h$ I find myself observing her; and
rather pleased if my speculation regarding her subsequent conduct

[107] On the morning of Thursday, July 10 (*Mrs. Brookfield*, p. 362).

comes right. Thats what amused me in the Forster controversy,[108] that I knew from what he did, what he would do — poor dear old boy — and so I was in a rage last Saturday week — well, it seems impossible.

I bought Kickleburys, Rebecca & Rowena, & the Rhine Story, & read them through with immense pleasure. Do you know I think all 3 capital & R & R not only made me laugh but the other thing — here's pretty matter to send a lady from a tour! Well, I know you like to hear my praises and I am glad to send them to you — They are putting off a flat bottomed boat from the shore — they are putting out the tables for dinner. I will lock up my paper & finish my letter at some future halting-place: & say gby. dear lady

Wiesbaden. The first minute to myself since we came away: and that in a ground-floor closet, where it has been like sleeping in the street — the whole house passing by it — it is at the Hotel de la Rose. A & M are put away somewhere in the top of the house. And this minute at 6 in the morning on the parade they have begun music. The drive hither last night from the steamer was the most beautiful thing w^h has happened to us yet, and a view of the Rhine at sunset seen from a height as lovely as Paradise. This was the first fine day we have had: and the splendor of the landscape colours something marvellous to gaze upon. If Switzerland is better than this we shall be in a delirium. It is affecting to see Annys happiness: my dear noble creature. I sate with the children and talked with them about their mother last night. Minny's jealousy pains me — She is envious of Anny having an eye-glass now and is always looking through it: snappish with her before strangers — and t'other always magnanimous and gentle. On board the Antwerp steamer A was a little affected & ostentatiously useful — her reasoning being 'I am very plain & clumsy, I must try & make myself useful & liked by helping people' & so she did with all her might: and it's my pleasure to tell them how humble-minded their mother was, how humble-minded you are my dear lady. They bid me to the bath. I rise. I put on my scarlet gownd. I go.

Tuesday m^g again 6 o'clock. Heidelberg. After the bath and

[108] See above, No. 770.

the breakfast we discovered that we were so uncomfortable at that
most comfortable inn the Rose, without having the least prospect
of bettering ourselves that we determined on quitting Wiesbaden
though M^rs Stewart Mackenzie had arranged a party for us to see
the Dukes garden an earthly paradise according to her acc^t and
though in the walk ataking his waters whom should I see but ·T.
Parr Esq^re — and I promised to go & see him & your sister but
Dieu dispose — and we came off to Frankfort, and took a carriage
there for 2 1/2 hours and inspected the city, and then made for
Heidelberg w^h we reached at 6 1/2, too late for anything but dinner, and a sleep afterwards in the noisiest street I ever slep in —
And there were other causes for want of rest; and so I gat me
up at 5 and soothed myself with the pleasant cigar of morn. My
dear lady, the country is very pretty zwischen Frankfurt and
Heidelberg specially some fantastical little mountains the Mell-
bocus range, of queer shapes starting out of the plain capped with
darkling pine forests & ruined castles, covered with many coloured
crops — and based by peaceful little towns with old towers and
walls — and all these things as I behold I wish that Somebodys
eyes could see them likewise: and R! I should like a few days
rest and to see nothing but a shady wood and a tolerably stupid
book to doze over. We had Kingsley & his parents from Antwerp [109] a fine honest goahead fellow, who charges a subject
heartily impetuously with the greatest courage and simplicity, but
with narrow eyes, (his are extraordinary brave blue & honest) and
with little knowledge of the world I think. But he's superior to us
worldlings in many ways, and I wish I had some of his honest
pluck. And so my stupid paper is full; and I send my love to you
and yours — and I pray God bless my dear lady.

[109] Lady Ritchie describes the crossing with the Kingsleys in *Chapters*,
pp. 103–107.

791.          TO MRS. CARMICHAEL-SMYTH
                    15 JULY 1851

Hitherto unpublished.

Tuesday 15 July.

Heidelberg. My dearest Mammy This is written at 6 in the morning next door to those young ladies, who are dressing, and when they are packed and ready we are going to the castle to see it and to breakfast: and that done we shall go on to Baden, and stay a day or 2 if comfortable: but thats difficult in these watering places: and we came off from Wiesbaden in a sort of huff yesterday not being able to get rooms at the Inn bigger or more decent than cabin steamers. The Journey has been very pleasant indeed though, in spite of the storm & the sickness on board the Antwerp steamer, & my dearest Nanny enjoys it delightfully — not quite so much Minny who is scarce old enough — but she is very pleased in her way, and to see them makes me pleased, and we rush on very gaily together. It is not quite so dear as I thought. About 1£ a day for each will do it travelling & all: but there's no time as yet for reading or thinking or writing or anything but seeing sights. We are a head of the English invasion that is rather a comfort; that's to say more than every other person we meet in the railroads and inns is English, but not of our acquaintance: and so it's just the same as if we were among foreign barbarians — I saw the Chancellor [110] before I left London — no go. All those fine dreams about a place are mere dreams he wanted to speak to me about a

[110] Thomas Wilde (1782–1855), first Baron Truro, Lord Chancellor from 1850 to 1852. Mrs. Brookfield wrote to her husband that Thackeray had not gone with her to the Miss Berrys on July 9, "as the Chancellor had sent to beg a few words of conversation with him at half past four: which turned out to be a kind of early dinner, which he was begged to make his luncheon, all the while expecting the visit to end in a place. But at length when Lady Truro was gone off to some concert or engagement for which they had been dining early, the Chancellor slowly propounded his motives for requesting an interview, and they only turned out to be some literary scheme in which he wanted Mr. Thackeray to join, and he was disappointed." (*Mrs. Brookfield,* II, 362)

literary project w^h may or may not come to something. And I
slapped Forster's face (epistolarily) in a rage after 2 years treason,
& wrote to F. and threatened to bring out a rival paper, w^h brought
him & Fonblanque to their good behaviour: but this is 10 days
ago ever so far off, and I wonder now at the exasperation I felt.[111]
Good bye poor old F. I cant ever be friends with him again. He
is what he tries to fancy I am but he knows better, a traitor and
a sneak.

And here come the young ones with their bonnets on, and each
with her piece of letter for Granny: to w^h I add my scrap, and
she will get them on Friday about: when I shall be 40 years old:
and full of a deal of cares and pains very bearable, and schemes
that may come to nothing: and with a heart full of love still for my
dearest old Mother and G P. What shall we have for breakfast at
the Castle — What a noisy night it has been — what a bright sky
& fresh air — never mind the cares & the bugs. Come along young
ladies. God bless Granny & G P.

## 792.  TO MRS. BROOKFIELD
### 17–21 JULY 1851

Extract published in *The Orphan of Pimlico*, "Berne"; additions in *Collection of Letters*, pp. 146–150.

Thursday. 17. Yesterday was a golden day, the pleasantest of
the Journey as yet. The day before we got to Baden Baden; and
I had a notion of staying there 2 or 3 days having found an agreeable female acquaintance or 2 (Madame de Bonneval [112] Sister of
Miss Galway with whom we went to the Hippodrome, M^me Mart-
chenko, that nice Russian who gave me cigars & flattered me last
year) but the weather beginning to be bad, and the impure atmosphere of the pretty wicked gambling place not good for my young
ones, we came off by the Basle railroad — in the first class like

[111] I have not traced this letter.
[112] Caroline Gallwey (d. 1858), third daughter of Sir William Payne-
Gallwey, who had married Count Lionel de Bonneval.

princes — the most delightful Journey through the deliciousest landscape of plain & mountains w<sup>h</sup> seemed to Switzify themselves as we came towards here. And the day's rest here hasn't been less pleasant: though or perhaps because it rained all morning, and I was glad to lie on the sofa and smoke my cigar in peace. On Tuesday at Baden it was pretty — having been on duty for 5 days I went out for a solitary walk and was finding myself tant soit peu tired of my dear little companions: and met M<sup>me</sup> de Bonneval who proposed a little tea & a little society &c — and when I came back to the Inn — there was Anny with Minny on her knees & telling her a story, with a sweet maternal kindness & patience, God bless her — This touched me very much, and I didnt leave them again till bed time: and didnt go to the Rouge et Noir, & only for half an hour to M. & Madame de Bonneval, from whose society I determined to escape next day — And we agreed it was the pleasantest day we had had. And Minny laid out the table of the first class carriage (they are like little saloons & delightful to travel in) with all the contents of the travelling-bag, books, O de cologne, ink &c., and we had good trouts for supper at 9 o'clock, and today at 2 we walked out and wandered very pleasantly for 2 1/2 hours about the town and round it, and we are very hungry and we hope the dinner bell will ring soon; and tomorrow I am 40 years old; and hope to find at Berne a letter from my dear lady. You see one's letters must be stupid for they are written only when I'm tired, and just come off duty, but the sight of the young ones' happiness is an immense pleasure to me; and these calm sweet landscapes bring me calm and delight too — the bright green pastures, and the swift flowing river (under my window now) and the purple pine covered mountains with the clouds flickering round them. O Lord how much better it is than riding in the Park and going to dinner at 8 o'clock! I wonder whether a residence in this quiet would ennoble one's thoughts permanently? — and get them away from mean quarrels intrigues, pleasures? make me write good books — turn poet perhaps or painter — and get out of that baseness of London — in w<sup>h</sup> there's one good thing — ah one good thing — and God bless her always and always. I see my dear lady and her little girl — Pax be with them. Is it only a week ago that we are gone? it seems a year.

Berne. Saturday 19. Faucon. I must tell you that I asked at Heidelberg at the Post only by way of a joke, and never so much as expecting a halfpenny worth of letter from you: but here I went off to the Post as sure as Fate — Thinks I, it being my birthday (yesterday) there must be a little something waiting for me at the Poste Restante but the deuce a bit of a little something — Well — I hope you're quite well, and I'm sure you'd write if something didnt prevent you, and at Milan or at Venice I hope for better fortune. We had the most byooootiful ride yesterday from Basel going through a country w̲ʰ I suppose prepares one for the splendider scenery of the Alps — kind goodnatured little mountains not too awful to look at, but encouraging in appearance and leading us gradually up to the enormities w̲ʰ we're to contemplate in a day or two — a steady rain fell all day, but this as it only served to make other people uncomfortable (especially the 6 Belgian fellow-travellers in the bei-wagen, w̲ʰ leaked, and in w̲ʰ they must have had a desperate time) rather added to our own pleasure snug in the coupé. We have secured it for tomorrow to Lucerne and to day for the first time since our journey there's a fine bright sun out, & the sight we have already had of this most picturesque of all towns, gives me a zest for that fine walk w̲ʰ we are going to fetch presently. I've made only one sketch; but it is naught: best not make foolish sketches of buildings, but look about and see the beautiful pictures done for you by Nature beneficent. This is almost the first place I have seen, in Europe, where the women actually wear costumes — in Rome only the women who get up for the painters dress differently from other folks. Travelling as paterfamilias, with a daughter in each hand, I find I dont like to speak to our countryfolks, but give myself airs rather, and keep off from them — if I were alone I should make up to everybody — You don't see things so well à trois as you do alone. You are an English gentleman: you are shy of queer looking or queer-speaking people, you are in the coupé, you are an Earl, confound your impudence: if you had 5000 a year and were Tomparr Esqʳᵉ you could not behave yourself more highandmightily. Ah, I recollect, 10 years back a poor devil, looking wistfully at the few Napoleons in his *gousset,* and giving himself no airs at all. He was a better fellow than the one you know perhaps — not that our characters alter, only they develop, and our minds grow grey or bald &c. I was a boy, 10 years ago, bleating out my simple griefs in the Great Hoggarty Diamond. We have seen many pretty children, 2 especially sitting in a little tub by the roadside: but we agree that there's none so pretty as Baby Brookfield: we wish for her, and for her mother I believe. This is a brilliant account of a tour isn't it? — egotistical twaddle. I forget the lectures as much as if they had never been done, and my impression is that they were a failure. Come along young ladies we'll go walk till dinner time, and keep the remainder of this sheet (sacrificing the picture as after all why shouldn't we such a twopenny absurd thing?) & folding the sheet up in a different way — so goodbye, lady, & I send you a G & a B and a Y.

Lucerne. Monday m$^g$ We are in love with Berne. We agree that we should like to finish our lives there: it is so homely charming and beautiful without knowing it: whereas this place gives itself the airs of a beauty, and offends me somehow. We are in an inn like a town, the bells began at 4 in the morning 2 hours ago, & at present all the streets of the hotel are alive. We are not going up the Righi. Y should we go up a dimd mountain to see a dimd map under our feet? We are going on to Milan pretty quick. The day after tomorrow we shall sail down the Major Lake we hope to Sesto Calende and so to Milan — I wonder whether you've written to me to Como? — Well, I would have bet 5 to 1 on a letter at Berne: but such is life and such is woman that the philosopher must not reckon on either     And what news w$^d$ you have sent? That the baby is well that you have enjoyed yourself pretty well at Sevenoaks? &c. — I would give 6$^d$ to hear as much as that

Such is a feeble but accurate outline of the view out of my window at this moment and all the time I am drawing it (you will remark how pleasantly the firs & pastures in the foreground are indicated whereas I cant do anything with ink being black to represent the

snow on the mountains behind) I am making pretty dramatic
sketches in my mind of misfortunes happening to you — that you
are unwell, that you are thrown out of a carriage, that D$^r$ Locock is
in attendance, que sais je?

As for my dear young ones, I am as happy with them as possible.
Anny is a fat lump of pure gold — the kindest dearest creature as
well as a wag of the first order. It is an immense blessing that
Heaven has given me such an artless affectionate companion — we
were looking at a beautiful smiling innocent view at Berne on Saturday, and she said 'It's like Baby Brookfield' — there's for you:
and so it was like innocence and brightness &, & &cc &c. O may
she never fall in love absurdly and marry an ass! Luckily as she
has no money nor no beauty people won't be tempted: and if she
will but make her Father her confidant, I think the donkey wont
long keep his ground in her heart. And so the paper is full, and
must go to England without even so much as saying Thank you for
your letter. Good bye dear lady good bye Miss Brookfield good
bye M$^r$ Brookfield, says your aff$^{te}$ W M T. Aux Suisses July 21.

793.          TO MRS. CARMICHAEL-SMYTH
                        JULY 1851

Hitherto unpublished.

My dearest Mammy

I send you a scrap in the family bag, just to say that the young ones are happy and well and make me ditto that we are come to about the middle of our pilgrimage now, and shall stop at Venice, Vienna (*Autriche* mind if you write) where we hope we shall get a word from you — Prague, Dresden Leipzig and so with a rush home: when I must get to work again instantly preparatory to the great North American invasion — The cost of the trip is as near as possible 1£ a day for each. I have enjoyed it 10 times as much as I should alone, when I shouldn't have had the courage to make it probably, and should have yawned away a few weeks at a Rhine watering place — As it is I have not leisure to think about my plans, wʰ want pourtant thinking about, for I am never alone; and when we come home I'm too tired to think to advantage, or do anything but smoke and sleep: but the sights we now see are capital for future expenditure; and all the sights one sees are so much to the good. I think Berne was the most charming; but the whole of the Swiss week was a series of wonderful sights and golden days: and the best sight of all was the happiness of my dearest little women. If the musquitoes at Venice treat us with decency we shall bring to there for some days: and economize against the trip to Vienna, of wʰ the travelling expenses will be heavy. I haven't brought a single letter with me, and dont intend to see a single bigwig — One day, at Baden, I went out for an hour by myself: and on my return found Minny, who had been rather melancholy, sitting on Anny's knee, who was telling her a story. Thank God for this sweetness of temper, and almost maternal love wʰ fills my dearest old Anny's honest heart — We are royally lodged here at Milan, and instead of dining at the genteel table d'hôte today are going to have an Italian dinner in a suburb-garden, and perhaps to see a day theatre. We shall stop a night at Verona, and then Venice

and then homewards.[113] God bless my dearest old Mother & G P;
& I hope that your pear prospers and that your country quarters
are comfortable.

W M T.

794.                TO FREDERICK GALE
                     23 AUGUST 1851

Hitherto unpublished.

Kensington. August 23.

My dear Gale.

I send your boots and my blessing. I am very glad to hear of
what is going to happen to you and heartily wish health and happiness to a good fellow and his wife.

Always treat her as if she was the finest lady in England. Never
be rude to your wife: [114] that's the advice I give you. Not that I
fancy you will: but many men are, and ruin their homes by it. Did
you ever see my step-father & mother? I think not. Well, he is
70 odd & she 60. He pays her to this day as much deference, as
he did when he first stepped up to her at a Bath Ball in 1807,[115]
and asked her to dance. She was one of the most beautiful women
in the world — I am considered very like her. Those 2 folks are
to this day, though old, disappointed, and with many cares & crosses
in life, immensely happy in each others affection; and it's because
they have always respected each other.

I could shew you quite a different story and a ménage that promised every happiness, (where the man was a good fellow, & the

---

[113] Thackeray and his children returned to London by way of Weimar.
Their meeting with Thackeray's old friends Dr. Weissenborn and Frau von
Goethe is described in *Chapters*, pp. 107–117.

[114] Gale must have been somewhat bewildered to come upon this ex-
hortation to domestic courtesy in a letter of congratulation on his marriage.
Thackeray is thinking of the state in which he found the Brookfield household on his return from abroad. The inevitable quarrel between Brookfield
and Thackeray, preceded (as this letter testifies) by weeks of tension, appears
to have taken place shortly before September 24. See below, No. 797.

[115] See *Memoranda*.

woman a mere angel,) rendered miserable by the man forgetting he was a gentleman, and a lady's husband. So I say unto you, my dear old Gale, Be polite to your wife, as you are now at this present time of courtship.

Where's the marriage to be? I am nailed pretty much here now having business and 100 reasons but I should like to see you set out on your journey & with all my heart wish it may be a happy one.

Yours dear Gale most truly

W M Thackeray

I am only just back from 6 weeks abroad, with my children.

795.        TO THOMAS WASHBOURNE GIBBS
12 SEPTEMBER 1851

My text of the first page is taken from Sterne's *Works*, ed. Wilbur L. Cross, X, xxxv; of the last two pages from a facsimile in R. F. Sharp's *Architects of English Literature* (London, 1900), p. 284.

Kensington
12 September

Dear Sir

Immediately after my lectures I went abroad and beg your pardon for having forgotten in the hurry of my departure to return the MSS wh. you were good enough to lend me.[116] I am sorry that reading the Brahmin's letters to his Brahmine did not increase my respect for the Reverend Laurence Sterne.

In the printed letters there is one XCII addressed to Lady P. full of love and despair for my Lady & pronouncing that he had got a ticket for Miss XXX benefit that night, which he might use if deprived of the superior delight of seeing Lady P. I looked in the Dramatic Register (I think is the name of the book) to find what lady took a benefit on a Tuesday and found the names of 2, 1 at Covent Garden & one at Drury Lane on the same Tuesday evening and no other Miss's benefit on a Tuesday evening during

[116] See above, No. 781.

the season. Miss Poyntz I think is one of the names, but I'm 5 miles from the book as I write to you, and forget the lady's name & the day.

However on the day Sterne was writing to Lady P. and going to Miss ———'s benefit he is *dying* in his Journal to the Brahmine, can't eat, has the Doctor, and is in a dreadful way. He wasn't dying but lying I'm afraid [117] — God help him — a falser and wickeder man, its difficult to read of — Do you know the accompanying pamphlet? [118] (My friend Mr. Cooper gave me this copy, w$^h$ he had previously sent to the Reform Club, and has since given the Club another copy) — there is more of Yorick's lovemaking in these letters, with blasphemy to flavor the compositions, and indications of a scornful unbelief. Of course any man is welcome to believe as likes for me *except* a parson: and I cant help looking upon Swift and Sterne as a couple of traitors and renegades (as one does upon Bonneval [119] or poor Bem the other day) with a scornful pity for them in spite of all their genius and greatness.

With many thanks for your loan believe me dear Sir,

Very faithfully yours

W M Thackeray.

[117] Governor Cross (*Works of Laurence Sterne*, X, xxxvii–xxxix) has demonstrated that the letter to Lady Warkworth (later Lady Percy) which Thackeray cites was written on April 23, 1765, whereas the *Journal to Eliza* belongs to 1767. Thus in this instance, at least, Thackeray's charge of bad faith against Sterne is without foundation.

[118] *Seven Letters written by Sterne and his Friends, hitherto unpublished*, ed. William Durrant Cooper (1844).

[119] Claude Alexandre, Comte de Bonneval (1675–1747), a celebrated adventurer who climaxed his varied career by turning Moslem and becoming a Pasha of Turkey. I have been unable to identify "poor Bem."

796.　　　　　　　TO DR. JOHN BROWN
　　　　　　　　　21 SEPTEMBER 1851

Hitherto unpublished.

13, Young S!
Kensington.
Sep! 21.

My dear Sir  You have heard of my projected invasion of your
town, where I propose to mount my tub and send round my hat
in November or December next, if the good folk of Edinburgh will
hear me.  I told J. Blackwood how kind you had been on former
occasions, and he said that as an adviser and backer, guide philosopher & friend [120] in the coming venture I could have no better
person than yourself if you w? kindly act for me.  Will you be so
good as to think and say what I had best do: what public room I
can take, what prices I should charge; whether Glasgow could be
also favored with a visit &c.  The lectures were very much liked in
London: indeed I believe I had the best audience that ever was assembled to hear a man; Duchesses and great ladies came in spite
of the dog days and a very inconvenient room: and the heads of
my own profession with bishops bigwigs and parliament men.
Macaulay came to 5 lectures of the 6: and I hope that the reports
in the papers didn't give a good idea of them and couldn't.

I send my respectful compliments to M?s Brown and beg to hint
that my best backers in London were *the ladies*.  There were some
very pretty faces in the reserved seats.  Couldn't we have reserved
seats in Edinburgh at a pound, say, for the course of 6 lectures —
and 3/— for the unreserved places?  The great point is *not to fail*
better not to try at all than that.  Across the ingens aequor [121] a
failure anywhere here might injure me, and I hope out of this
harmless little scheme to turn a pretty penny for my children here
& in America.  I recommend myself to the Edinenses.[122]  O Grati

---

[120] Pope, *Essay on Man*, IV, 390.
[121] Horace, *Odes*, I, vii, 32.
[122] See above, No. 591.

Grataeque! I also will be gratus if you give me a friendly support once more.

Believe me always faithfully yours<br>
W M Thackeray

[For fragments of two letters to Mrs. Elliot and Kate Perry, dated 23? and 26 September, 1851, see letters 23 and 24, Appendix XXVI.]

797.          TO ANNE THACKERAY
24 SEPTEMBER 1851

*Address:* Miss Thackeray | 13 Young S^t | Kensington | W London. *Postmarks:* MATLOCK BATH SP 24 1851, 25 SP 1851. Hitherto unpublished.

My dearest Fat. I write to tell the place is pretty [123] and I'm quite well. Send letters tomorrow to

The Rutland Arms
Bakewell.
& God bless you

[For fragments of two letters to Kate Perry dated September, 1851, see letters 25 and 27, Appendix XXVI; and for fragments of a letter intended for Mrs. Brookfield and sent to Kate Perry the same month see letter 26, same.]

798.          TO ?
9 OCTOBER 1851

Hitherto unpublished.

Private.<br>
13 Young S^t Kensington.<br>
October 9. 1851.

Dear Sir

Pollock has enclosed to me your very kind letter, and I'll take leave frankly to answer it and tell you my wishes. The Liverpool

---

[123] After his quarrel with Brookfield (for an account of which see *Memoranda*) Thackeray left at once for the country, visiting Matlock Bath (seventeen miles north of Derby), Chatsworth House, Haddon Hall, and Bakewell.

Institutions both invited me, but their terms are impossible — I can't afford to take 5£ a lecture, or 10, for other places would then give me no more, and I have America, Edinburgh and London perhaps again in view.\ Mitchell gives better terms to M^rs Kemble than those even of the Philharmonic paying expenses of travelling, placarding, advertising, drums & trumpets, and giving half of the full proceeds.

James Haywood has sent me a notable requisition from Manchester where he backs me very kindly: the terms are to be 1£ for the 6 lectures for the reserved seats; 3/ for the unreserved places perhaps, I don't like to offer myself for less, lest the folks of other cities should grumble. I would cheerfully perform for nothing for the non-paying classes — but must keep my prices up for those who can afford to pay. And I should be very glad indeed if I could make some good terms at Manchester. I am told the Philharmonic is an enormous room, and could not hope to fill it at those prices: but it's important to me that they should be kept up I think and I would rather have a smaller room if that be feasible, and less money than sell my little wares (w^h are not good for public use and luxuries rather than necessaries) at a depreciated currency. As I don't intend to spend any of this money myself, but to keep it for some persons for whom I have a regard: I can afford to be a little more bold about money-matters than I hope I should otherwise be.

Thank you very much for your kind intentions in my favor, and be assured that I know the value of 'Incense' and shall receive it with a great deal of gravity and thanks too. And believe me

Yours very much obliged

W M Thackeray.

It w^d be in December or January that the affair would take place.

---

The only available records of his life during the next two weeks, a period of emotional crisis comparable to the autumn of 1840, are the extracts from his letters printed in Appendix XXVI.

799.　　　　　TO DR. JOHN BROWN
9 OCTOBER 1851

My text is taken from Alexander Peddie's *Recollections of Dr. John Brown*
(London, 1893), pp. 182–184.

Kensington,
October 9, 1851.

My dear Dr. Brown, — I find your letters on my return home
from the country, and thank you for them and your kindnesses all.

I don't know yet whether it will be December or January when
I shall behold Rutland Street and my friends there. I want to go
to Cambridge in November if the scheme is feasible, but can't move
in it until the vacation is over and my friends in Cambridge are
returned thither.

The gates of L'pool and Manchester are also open to me, and
I shall take these places either before or after Edinburgh, as seems
best to my advisers. Until the men are back at Cambridge, in about
a week, I can't, therefore, say when the Titmarsh Van will begin
its career. But as I don't intend to touch the proceeds of the lectures myself (beyond actual travelling charges) and resolutely
invest all the winnings for my two girls and their poor mother,
I'm bolder than I should be otherwise in the business, and determined to carry it through with brazen resolution.

In order to [achieve] this end you see I must work as if nothing
had happened, and am under stringent engagements to write a
novel [124] which will come out as I sail for America. Now to do
this I must have my own way, my own lodgings, factotum, liberty,
cigar after breakfast, etc., without all of which I can't work; and
the forenoon being spent in study, the afternoon in healthful exercise, *then* comes the evening when we will trouble Dr. Brown to

[124] "One day my father came in, in great excitement," writes Lady Ritchie
of *Esmond*. "'There is a young fellow just come,' said he; 'he has brought a
thousand pounds in his pocket. He has made me an offer for my book, it's
the most spirited, handsome offer, I scarcely like to take him at his word; he's
hardly more than a boy, his name is George Smith.'" (Huxley, *House of
Smith, Elder*, p. 69)

go down to the cellar for that etc., etc. You have brought me into very good company in print, I dare say there are good fish still in the sea.

With my best thanks and regards to Mrs. Brown, Believe me, yours most faithfully,

W. M. Thackeray.

Wood [125] shall be the man, and thank you.

800.     TO LADY STANLEY OF ALDERLEY
OCTOBER 1851 [126]

Hitherto unpublished.

Kensington. Wednesday

Dear Lady Stanley. I was vexed to be so unwell yesterday that I couldn't keep my promise to come to Grosvenor Crescent. [127] And I have made a cipher for your Countess; and I hope she will be as happy as a Queen: and I should much prefer her having a house within dinner-distance in London to a castle in Scotland however splendid or ancient. Has Hancock [128] sent those diamond ear-rings with my compliments? No? Then I shall withdraw my

[125] "George Wood, Music-seller, who took charge of the tickets, advertisements, and hall for the lectures" (Peddie, *Recollections of Dr. John Brown*, p. 184).

[126] This note was written not long after Thackeray's return to London on (or shortly before) October 9. Henrietta Blanche Stanley had married David Graham Drummond Ogilvy (1826–1881), seventh Earl of Airlie, at Alderley Park on September 23.

[127] The Stanleys' town house at 2 Grosvenor Crescent, Belgrave Square (*Royal Blue Book*, 1851).

[128] Thomas Hancock, jeweller, 17 New Bond Street (*Post Office London Directory*, 1847).

custom from the fellow; and import all my jewels from Golconda direct. And I hope that you will continue to be my friends until that ship comes. My daughters found the travelling case very useful indeed; and are grateful to the givers to whom they send their best thanks and regards. W$^h$ of them next I wonder will have a gold dressing-box from Papa, and make their Mother happy? Let us have more of those little parties, if you please, next season and let me make my remarks as before. Dear Lady Stanley, I congratulate you most sincerely and beg you to remember that I am always

Yours most truly<br>W M Thackeray

801.        TO WILLIAMS AND NORGATE [129]
25 OCTOBER 1851

Hitherto unpublished.

Kensington   October 25.

Gentlemen

I was about to call on you and beg you to communicate with M$^r$ Tauchnitz regarding my forthcoming novel. It will be published in February complete in 3 vols: and sheets as printed can be forwarded to Leipzig. But though not so large as Pendennis, I shall expect the same price w$^h$ I received from M$^r$ Tauchnitz for the foreign copyright of that work; as it will be published all at once, and as soon (within a few days) on the continent as in London. Believe me

Your very faithful Serv$^t$<br>W M Thackeray

Mess$^{rs}$ Williams & Norgate.

[129] Booksellers of foreign books at 14 Henrietta Street (*Post Office London Directory*, 1847).

802.　　　　　　TO LADY STANLEY
　　　　　　　28? OCTOBER 1851 [130]

Hitherto unpublished.

Kensington. Tuesday night.

My dear Lady Stanley.

I have often had that young lady in my mind who has been married a month or more, and for whom I have got a little two-penny memento from a very sincere friend of hers. I had a nice copy of Vanity Fair, the Tauchnitz Edition much prettier than the English, and sent it to a man to bind who gave me the most solemn promises that it should be ready by the 25 ult — but it was never ready for a week after and then came back such a homely ugly book that I couldn't think of sending it to a Countess as a present on such a festive occasion: and so got another book w.h has had to be bound and is now just come home. Tell me please how I shall send to Airlie Castle N. B. and if the lady there is well; and if you of Cheshire are happy too and not angry with me. I was within 25 miles of you for a day or two, & intended to come on but was too ill (parole d'honneur) to be in any body's house but my own. I am writing a book of cutthroat melancholy suitable to my state, and have no news of myself or any body to give you that shouldn't be written on black-edged paper and sealed with a hatchment. I would have written had it been otherwise; and asked to come to you but for the above dismal reasons. I am going to the Grange for 2 or 3 days at the end of the week, & then to Oxford & Cambridge barking about with my lecture thence to the modern Awthens. How far is Airlie Castle from Awthens? I'll take Vanity Fair to Edinburgh at any rate and send it if I can — the only cheerful face I have seen is Milnes's just come back and looking as if he quite liked being married: [131] he told us to night (this Madam is written in the loneliness of midnight) that M.rs Milnes insists on

---

[130] Since Blanche Stanley was married on September 23, this letter was presumably written the first Tuesday after Thursday, October 23.

[131] Milnes had married Annabella Hungerford (1814–1874), third daughter of the second Baron Crewe, on July 31.

his going to the Bloomer Ball [132] tomorrow. Do you know what Bloomers are in Cheshire? — It is a new kind of bonnet w.<sup>h</sup> the ladies wear. If I go to the ball and dance there I will write you about it, when the letter may be more cheerful than this one from yours very faithfully indeed

W M Thackeray

Carlyle's Life of Sterling [133] is delightful have you read it?

803.                    TO ANNE THACKERAY
                        29 OCTOBER 1851

*Address:* Miss Thackeray. Hitherto unpublished.

My dearest Fat.

Things went off very comfutably,[134] and I'm very glad I came down to shake hands with poor Brookfield and poorer M.<sup>rs</sup> B. She looks & is worse than he I think —

I send James to Cambridge today, if he wants money please Miss Trulock give him 2£ —

I bless my dear little gurgles and am their

Affectionate Father

W M Thackeray

Did I ever write to you in my own handwriting [135] before?

[132] A dispute as to whether bloomers were suitable garments for ladies was at this time agitating London society. See, for example, the reports of two lectures on "Bloomerism" in *The Times* for October 10 and 21.

[133] Although the opinion here expressed is at variance with that of the review of *The Life of John Sterling* in *The Times* of November 1, it was undoubtedly written by Thackeray, for his daughter Anne wrote in a letter of 1871 (*Thackeray and his Daughter*, p. 160): "The other day I met dear old Mr. Carlyle walking along, and I rushed after him to talk to him about his *Life of Sterling*. . . . I wonder have you ever come across my father's review of it in the *Times*?" The review is included in *Centenary Works*, XXV, 373–386.

[134] Thackeray is writing from the Grange, where the Ashburtons arranged a meeting between him and the Brookfields on October 29 (*Mrs. Brookfield*, II, 366). See Appendix XXVI for further information about this attempted reconciliation.

[135] This letter is in Thackeray's slanting hand.

[For fragments of two letters to Kate Perry, one dated October, 1851, the other 30 October, 1851, see letters 28 and 29, Appendix XXVI.]

804.        TO MRS. CARMICHAEL-SMYTH
            10 NOVEMBER 1851 [136]

Extract published, *Biographical Introductions*, VII, xvi.

Monday.

My dearest Mammy Before I go off on my circuiteering I must send you that letter that has been so often begun & burned in this month past: during w$^h$ I have not been the happiest mad wag in all England but in a very bearable condition of mind nevertheless and an easy frame of body. The Brookfield party is finally off for Madeira [137] and we met at the Grange and parted not friends, but not enemies — and so there's an end of it. And now the Oxford & Cambridge business begins, at Oxford Monday & Tuesday: at Cambridge Friday & Saturday, at home between days except next week when I go to old Sir Thomas Cullum who has asked me so often that I cant refuse any more. — Then in December for

[136] This letter was written on the Monday before Thackeray began his lectures at Cambridge, an announcement for which in Thackeray's hand is printed in the *Howe Proofs* (p. 250):
"Mr. Thackeray proposes to repeat at Mr. Swans assembly room, Cambridge, the lectures delivered in London in June–July last on The English Humourous Writers of the Last Century.
"The course will embrace notices of
    "Swift
    "Steele & the Society of the time of Q. Anne.
    "Congreve, Addison.
    "Prior, Gay, Pope.
    "Hogarth, Smollett, Fielding.
    "Sterne, Goldsmith.
"Tickets for the course of six lectures a guinea — single tickets five shillings. To be had at Mr Macmillans. The lectures will commence on Friday & Saturday evg. the 14 and 15 Novr. and will be resumed on the 2 ensuing Friday & Saturday evenings."
[137] The Brookfields left for Madeira on November 5, the ostensible reason for their trip being that it was "evident from Mr. Brookfield's state of health that he would not be able to winter in England" (*Mrs. Brookfield*, II, 363).

3 weeks to Scotland. Then in January at the Portman Square Rooms London, where they make me an offer of 150£ w.ʰ is pretty well, for 6 hours I think, and by the end of January my novel please God will be finished and I can go to America. I was thinking of sending the young ones to their Granny in December when I went Northwards: but it will be very dismal & lonely to be a month in London without them when I come back, so that they will hardly be with you before February, when they will spend I suppose a good half year in your nest. If all things go well I shall have made a pretty little start in the world by that time, and have saved enough money to keep them at least from starving. I dont see why not. God speed the campaign, w.ʰ opens tonight. Old Stoddart is my host at Oxford and I dont know how matters will go there: [138] of Cambridge I am surer expecting a great auditory there. It is curious isn't it to be arrived actually at the day when

[138] Before Thackeray lectured in Oxford, it was necessary that he secure the permission of the authorities. He accordingly applied to Dr. Frederick Charles Plumptre (1796–1870), Vice Chancellor of the University and Master of University College. Under the heading "Modern Literature at Oxford" *The Times* of November 18 reprints an account of his interview with this gentleman from an unidentified evening newspaper: " 'Pray what can I do to serve you, Sir,' inquired the bland functionary. 'My name is Thackeray.' 'So I see by this card.' 'I seek permission to lecture within the precincts.' 'Ah! you are a lecturer; what subjects do you undertake — religious or political?' 'Neither; I am a literary man.' 'Have you written anything?' 'Yes, I am the author of *Vanity Fair*.' 'I presume a Dissenter — has that any connexion with John Bunyan's book?' 'Not exactly; I have also written *Pendennis*.' 'Never heard of these works, but no doubt they are proper books.' 'I have also contributed to *Punch*.' '*Punch!* I have heard of that; is it not a ribald publication?' The upshot of this strange dialogue between the great popular master of the pen and the Master of University Coll., Oxon., was the requirement of a 'reference as to character' from this general favourite of the reading public, who, in deep consciousness of his comparative insignificance in the presence of so awful a Don, humbly gave the name of his particular friend the Bishop of the diocese, Samuel Wilberforce, which was held to be satisfactory." In fairness to Dr. Plumptre it should be mentioned that in *The Times* of November 21 he describes the greater part of this dialogue as "altogether the invention of the writer or his informant." As Charlotte Brontë suggests in a letter of November 30 to George Smith (Wise and Symington, *The Brontës*, III, 293), the informant can hardly have been anyone but Thackeray.

some money will be put by for the young ones? — they will probably be worth 30£ apiece to night.

Crowe dined with me yesterday and Lord Stanley whom I asked to meet him — I tremble about him. Joe has lost his place at the Daily News and Crowe has thrown up his [139] — Good God what are they to do? I see 50£ out of somebodys pocket before long. He is not to go yet: but his departure is decided; and then? its awful to think of the sword coming down — of the precipices we all walk on. I am on my knees to Stanley and Palmerston to get something for Crowe, who has been the best servant Lord P has ever had — but one stands aghast before the fate of these poor people, and cowardly self-love cries out Save Save Save — or you may starve too. So please God we will and do that work resolutely for the next year — I am very well in health I think, having staved off my old complaint, and the only thing that alarms me sometimes is the absurd fancy that now the money making is actually at hand some disaster may drop down and topple me over. But thats a fancy only.

Fonblanque dined here yesterday too and has *re*taken me into a great affection: but with poor Jack Forster it is well not to try to be friends again — it's best not to pick up some acquaintances when they are dropped.

The novel is getting on pretty well & gaily I mean — What I wrote a month ago is frightfully glum. And I shall write it better now that the fierceness of a certain pain is over. The truth is I've had an awful time of it: and don't know how miserable I was

---

[139] During 1851 *The Daily News* had steadily lost caste through the confusion of Eyre Evans Crowe's editorial policy. Though the general tone of the paper was liberal, not to say radical, Crowe continued to give expression to Lord Palmerston's support of the Napoleonic despotism in France. When it became apparent that the Whig ministry was tottering and that the position of Palmerston was particularly shaky, the proprietors of *The Daily News* determined to dispense with their editor's services. Just at this time Joseph Crowe fell ill and was confined for several weeks to his chambers in the Temple. Adducing his prolonged absence as the reason for their action, the proprietors ordered Crowe to give his son notice to quit the paper. Crowe thereupon resigned, and his resignation was at once accepted. (Sir Joseph Crowe, *Reminiscences*, pp. 96–98)

until I look back at such & such days. But I'm easy now. I wish the other folks were as happy: but they are both wretched I fear. Perhaps I'm rather ashamed of myself for taking things so easily. God bless you my dearest old Mother and G P: and now let's call a cab & go to Oxford. W M T.

In Kensington. The lady of S James [140] Esq. of a son.

805.                    TO MRS. PROCTER
                       10 NOVEMBER 1851

Hitherto unpublished. My text is taken from a transcript given Lady Ritchie by George Murray Smith.

                                        Monday,
                                            10, November.
My dear Mrs Procter,

I wish I could have come to see you before leaving town but the cab is at the door almost: and I didn't leave the desk till dinner time yesterday or Saturday. I'm off to Oxford and to Cambridge at the end of the week. It's curious to be arrived at the very day when a little money will be saved for the children isn't it? Please God they'll be worth £30 apiece to-night.

I'm very glad to hear Adelaide is better. A part of my cares went to Madeira last Wednesday — and I am always yours,

                                        W. M. Thackeray.

806.               TO MRS. CARMICHAEL-SMYTH
                    17–18? NOVEMBER 1851 [141]

Hitherto unpublished.                              .

                                    Monday & Tuesday.
My dearest Mammy. Where are other two letters that I have begun to you? They were very stupid and lie crumpling in pockets

[140] Thackeray's manservant.

[141] This letter was begun a week after Thackeray's letter of November 10, which he did not send.

or under heaps of papers. I have nothing to say that is of use to any one to say or to hear, and though I could fill pages with blue devils, of what good could that be to any one? and these are blue devils that I can't show to my mamma; as you could not tell me your secrets about G P — so the griefs of my elderly heart cant be talked about to you: and I must get them over as comfortably as I best may. As a man's leg hurts just as much after it's off they say: so you suffer after certain amputations; & though I go about and grin from party to party & dinner to dinner, and work a good deal and put a tolerably good face upon things I have a natural hang dog melancholy within — Very likely it's *a* woman I want more than any particular one: and some day may be investing a trull in the street with that priceless jewel my heart — It is written that a man should have a mate above all things  The want of this natural outlet plays the deuce with me. Why cant I fancy some honest woman to be a titular M^rs Tomkins?  I think that's my grievance: and could I be suited I should get happy and easy presently — It isn't worth while writing letters of this grumbling sort is it?  What can any body do for me?  Nobody can do nothing: for say I got my desire, I should despise a woman; and the very day of the sacrifice would be the end of the attachment.  And my dear girls are sitting in the next room busy with their innocent work and cheerful, and artless and tender as heart can desire — what a brute a man is that he is always hankering after something unattainable!  We had a good walk yesterday and went to see many polite folks. I was at Palmerston's the night before where all the world was — and tomorrow and tomorrow and tomorrow [142] — Sure I had much best put this rubbish in the fire. It was a general scorn and sadness w^h made me give up Punch I think more than any thing else — though I don't go with folks about the Times abuse of the President [143] — The latter articles have been measured and full of dignity I think, but the early writing was awfully dangerous.  What we have to do I think is not to chafe him but silently to get ready to fight him.

[142] *Macbeth*, V, i, 18.
[143] Louis Napoléon was at this time the object of nearly universal execration in the English press.

Fancy his going down to his Chambers with that article in the
Times in w<sup>h</sup> he was called cutpurse & his Uncle assassin and that
one of the Examiner on killing no murder and saying See Gentlemen the language of that perfidious Albion　　Shall we suffer
these insults or reply to them by war? Dont let us give any occasion
to it by calling names. But when war comes, then — then, O ye
Gods, there will be time for doing —

I asked young Leveson Lord Granville's Secretary if I might
send letters by the F O. and he said Yes but with an air as if he
didn't like it much — so I shall only send occasionally that way.
We must pay our own postidges for a little longer therefore. It
was Monday last I wrote that letter I didn't send after having been
the previous day and seen to my great satisfaction that your house
was let. It would not have been more convenient to me than this
one — a mile nearer London would: but I suppose I shall make
no changes until after the American trip — when I may bring back
a Negress you know and require another establishment — stuff and
nonsense. The fact is I think about that poor woman constantly
still — I don't write to her: and don't want. I've nothing to say.
All her family are on my side, did I tell you? M<sup>r</sup> Hallam dines
here next week [144] — and poor Brookfield has just had another and
I believe large legacy left him on acc<sup>t</sup> of his virtues by Miss Ogle
who believed that they were a model couple and he the most loving
of mankind — O, no Satire is as satirical as the world is — no humbug in books like those out of 'em,

It was time to dress for dinner yesterday when I got to the last
line, else the Lord knows whither my satirical vein might lead me.
Pleasant dinner Lord Castlereagh — my lady very kind, and has
invited the children to Ireland in the summer — it may be a pleasant fortnight for them at a grand house in the most byootiful
country possible. Poor Joe Crowe is just come in. The ruin of that

[144] Hallam wrote to Mrs. Brookfield on March 23, 1852: "You are behaving like a human angel. God knows how much I have thought of you,
sympathized with you, admired you; and Jane, strong words notwithstanding,
given you a certain degree of blame, but which is so interwoven with what
I do admire, that I might love you less were you more perfect." (*Mrs. Brookfield*, II, 376)

house is pretty near consummated. M^r Crowe has received final notice to quit the D News, and then what's to happen? — They have 220£ a year thats a comfort. 200 a year more than I have should misfortune come to me: and I have been recommending Joe and Joe's mother through him to sink at once — take a small house, and one maid, and never think about the dignities. Some folks think I care for them myself — but I would not in the least mind living in a lodging with my gals; and sh^d not lose a friend or a halporth of consideration I'm sure by it.

As for great society I like it. The air is freer than it is in small drawing rooms — Poor Forster & I met the other day, & shook sham-hands — Elliotson was at dinner who would scarcely speak to him & the poor old boy went away crestfallen rather    He has been elected at the Athenæum w^h has pleased him very much: and I am glad too, for I like him though I despise him. None of the men of my time Tennyson Fitz & the rest would stoop to a meanness or a cabal I am sure — These little folks are always scheming and suspecting. — I wish the new novel wasn't so grand and melancholy — the hero is as stately as Sir Charles Grandison — something like Warrington — a handsome likeness of an ugly son of yours — Theres a deal of pains in it that goes for nothing and my paper's full and I am my dearest Mothers & G P's affectionate son.

W M T.

807.          TO LADY STANLEY
          6 DECEMBER 1851

Hitherto unpublished.

Saturday. 6 Dec^r

My dear Lady Stanley: Thank you for your kindest of letters. I have sent the book off to Grosvenor Crescent for Madame la Comtesse [145] and *did* intend to have put the prettiest verses in the world the neatest thing! inside    But the neatest thing costs

[145] Henrietta Blanche Stanley, Countess of Airlie.

such a time to manufacture!  Nobody knows but the regular makers
of the article the cost & diffculty of it — and all my time is sold
for ever so long and I cant be writing for love but only for money.
I go northwards on Monday reaching Edinburgh that night and
mounting the tub next day: and my last lecture is on the 23ᵈ and
I am promised home for Xmas day to the children!  How to get
out of those obligations?  Indeed it would have given me otherwise a great pleasure indeed to have had a few days at Alderley and
seen the kind faces there *minus* that one to wʰ I used to be partial.

Though I went to dine with Lord John yesterday, I have no
news to give you.  Everybody is happy and d'accord at least about
one point in the new French Revolution [146] that Thiers is locked
up.  Not a soul of any party that I have seen but begins to grin at
the mention of that catastrophe: and even bear Ellis the ungrateful
Bruin has given his patron up.  I am in a fury with Punch for
writing the 'Old Pam' article agˢᵗ the Chief of Foreign Affairs.[147]
His conduct in the Kossuth affair [148] just suited my radical pro-
pensities: if he could have committed his government to a more
advanced policy, so much the better, and that ribald Punch must
go and attack him for just the best thing he has done: and just
when I wanted a favor of him too and now cant go & ask it.  Per-

haps you have not even heard of this Punch
Article at Alderley?  perhaps it has hurt nobody.

What a wonderful head-dress the French Am-
bassa — ditto had on yesterday!  Have you got
these up in Cheshire?

I think the lectures though odious will be
really a little fortune to me, that is that I may
carry off 100 or 150£ from every place where I deliver them, and
suppose they were delivered at 70 places how much would this
make?  May the Lord send me a good harvest.

[146] Louis Napoléon's *coup d'état* of December 2, 1851.
[147] The famous cartoon of Lord Palmerston as "The 'Judicious Bottleholder,' " which appeared in *Punch* on December 6, 1851, was accompanied
by an article called " 'Old Pam,' *Alias* 'The Downing Street Pet.' "
[148] When Louis Kossuth, a leader of the Hungarian rebellion against Austria
in 1849, came to England in October, 1851, he wished to thank Palmerston

I wanted your gentleman to dine with me and go and see a strange sight — a penny ball and diorama as well conducted as possible frequented by dancers of 14 & 15 married couples many of 'em — and giving a strange idea of the people. Have you got London Labour & the London Poor? [149] — for yourself only — Its better and more romantic than any romance including the forth-coming one of

Yours dear lady Stanley most truly<br>W M Thackeray

[For fragments of a letter to Mrs. Elliot and Kate Perry, November, 1851, see letter 30, Appendix XXVI.]

## 808.  TO ANNE AND HARRIET THACKERAY
### 9 DECEMBER 1851

My text is taken from *Thackeray and his Daughter*, pp. 100–101.

Barry's British Hotel<br>Queen Street, Edinburgh

My dear Little Gurgles, — Your dear Papa arrived last night at 9.30 and commissions me to tell you that he slept satisfactorily both in bed and about half the way down: losing the romantic scenery along the line and only waking up at the border to demm the railway man who asked for his ticket. Your father is already a good deal engaged to dinner: and his faithful servant James says that there is a very good subscription list for the lectures — but your Papa suspects that there will be more praise than money at this town.

The inn is very comfortable and the city splendid — the houses

---

for the protection the Foreign Secretary had extended to him two years earlier. Palmerston was with difficulty restrained from granting the desired interview, but he saw instead, to the great scandal of English conservatives, two radical delegations that called to express their gratitude for his services to Kossuth.

[149] A series of articles from *The Morning Chronicle* by Henry Mayhew, John Binny, and others, which were published as a book earlier in 1851.

grand — the streets broad and spacious, beyond anything in London, only there's nobody in 'em. This is the grand St. with 2 inhabitants.

I think this is all your Papa's news. His cough he hopes is a little better, and he writes this while waiting for Dr. Brown who is going to lionise him about the town [150] — He did a little of his novel this morning and he kisses his 2 darling gals with all his heart, and he sends his best regards to Miss Trulock and hopes you had a pleasant evening at Mrs. Bayne's. And so God bless you young women, prays

W. M. T.

[150] On December 10 Dr. Brown wrote to James Crum of Busby near Glasgow: "The great man has come, and *is* a great *man*, as well as *writer*. He is, in fact, greater as a man than as a writer, and he is big as well as great, six feet two and built largely, with a big, happy, shrewd head, and as natural in all his ways as you yourself, or the Black Prince up the way.

"But to business. He has been so surprised and pleased at his success last night that he longs to harry Glasgow of £100, and if sure of succeeding would give two or four forenoon Lectures. Wood is indifferent somehow, and throws cold water on it. Can you find out what is likely to be true about it? I know you would both like him, and you might take him out to Busby, and make him as happy as he would you. We had him at dinner yesterday all by himself." (*Dr. Brown*, p. 95) Thackeray lectured in Glasgow, but without notable success.

809.        TO MRS. ELLIOT AND KATE PERRY
                    10? DECEMBER 1851

Published in part, *Collection of Letters*, p. 142.

Mesdames.

You mustn't trust the honest 'Scotsman.' [151] He's such a frantic admirer that nothing less than 1000 people will content him. I had 100 subscribers, and 200 other people for the 1st lecture Isn't that handsome? Its such a good audience that I begin to reflect about going to America so soon. Why if so much money is to be made in this empire — not go through with the business & get what is to be had?

The Melgunds I saw at the Sermon: & the Edinburgh bigwigs in plenty. The M's live over the way. I'll go see them directly & thank them. And I like to tell you of my good luck, and am always yours and somebody's

W M T.


810.            TO ANNE THACKERAY
                    10? DECEMBER 1851

Hitherto unpublished.

My dear Nan.

Your dear Pa had 100 subscribers and about 200 more people at the 1st lecture — wh was very successful on the whole. And he begins to think America is farther off than it was: and that it will be a pity to leave England until some more money is taken out of it.

And he sends his gals his blessing wh they are a hundred pound richer today than they were yesterday at this time.

W M T.


[151] The leading Edinburgh daily, edited by Alexander Russel. See below, Appendix XVII.

811.            TO HARRIET THACKERAY
                      DECEMBER 1851

Hitherto unpublished.

My dearest Minikin

You needn't send me any more letters for I shall read them at home on Xmas day, I hope; and be home on Xmas eve. Though about this there is a leetle doubt: as there was some talk of giving a lecture for the ragged schools on Wednesday m<sup>g</sup> But this is only talk and I think nothing will come of it. I'm sorry James sent the paper w<sup>h</sup> said there were so few people: there were a great number every night and last night more than ever — near seven hundred. And I get so much compliments and praise and dinners luncheons & suppers that I wish I was home again: and wish the visit to the Grange was over. But it will be very pleasant when we are there: and you will see a great house with kind people in it and a beautiful park and fine gardens. And I have had a Daguerreotype done & think it almost as ugly as the picture in my room: and am come to the conclusion that M<sup>rs</sup> M<sup>c</sup>Cullagh [152] was quite right in her opinion about my beauty. But you see it doesn't matter — a face appears good-looking enough to those who love the owner of it: and who cares for the rest? I saw just now at breakfast a lady who was once such a beauty I was told that living in Russia she was obliged to be put privately on board a ship to be carried away from the Emperor Paul who wanted to run off with her — and this beauty is now a fubsy short old body with a front of hair and no more beauty than I have —

And now I have no more to say but that I am my dear women's affectionate old Father.

                        W M T.

[152] The wife of William Torrens McCullagh of 23 Cadogan Place, M. P. for Dundalk (*Royal Blue Book*, 1851).

812.        FROM DR. JOHN BROWN TO
            ANDREW COVENTRY DICK [153]
            22? DECEMBER 1851 [154]

My text is taken from Alexander Peddie, *Recollections of Dr. John Brown* (London, 1894), pp. 50–51.

23 Rutland Street

My dear Coventry, —

I wish you had been here for the last fortnight to have seen, heard, and known Thackeray, — a fellow after your own heart, — a strong-headed, sound-hearted, judicious fellow, who knew the things that differ, and prefers Pope to Longfellow or Mrs. Barrett Browning, and Milton to Mr. Festus,[155] and Sir Roger De Coverley to *Pickwick,* and David Hume's *History* to Sheriff Alison's; [156] and the 'verses by E. V. K. to his friend in town' [157] to anything he has seen for a long time; and 'the impassioned grape' to the whole works prosaic and poetical of Sir Bulwer Lytton. I have seen a great deal of him and talked with him on all sorts of things, and next to yourself I know no man so much to my mind. He is much better and greater than his works. His lectures have been

[153] Dick (d. 1870), for many years resident Sheriff of Bute, was one of Dr. Brown's oldest friends.

[154] Thackeray arrived in Edinburgh on December 8. If Dr. Brown's "fortnight" is to be taken literally, this letter was written on December 22.

[155] Philip James Bailey (1816–1902), whose *Festus* had appeared in 1839.

[156] Archibald Alison (1792–1867), later (1852) first Baronet, a Tory historian who had made his reputation with a *History of Europe during the French Revolution* (1833–1842).

[157] Dick composed these lines — the initials in the title of which stand for an anagram of his name, Edward Vincory Kent — in 1847 as an invitation to Dr. Brown to visit him at Rothesay. Describing the hospitality that awaits his friend, Dick writes (Brown, *Horæ Subsecivæ,* Ser. III, "John Leech and other Papers," pp. 411–412):

    And I myself have looked into a bin
    Of glass-bound brandy, whiskey, rum, and gin:
    Of these, and those, different, though like in shape,
    Dear prisoned spirits of th' impassioned grape,
    Have noted which for you to disenthral,
    And some fresh claret bought to crown the festival.

very well attended, and I hope he will carry off £300. I wish he could have taken as much from Glasgow, but this has not been found possible. He was so curious about you after reading [158] these verses, which he liked exceedingly. He is 6 feet 3 in height, with a broad kindly face and an immense skull. Do you remember Dr. Henderson of Galashiels? He is ludicrously like him, — the same big head and broad face, and his voice is very like, and the same nicety in expression and in the cadences of the voice. He makes no figure in company, except as very good-humoured, and by saying now and then a quietly strong thing. I so much wish you had met him. He is as much bigger than Dickens as a three-decker of 120 guns is bigger than a small steamer with *one* long-range swivel-gun. He has set everybody here a-reading *Stella's Journal, Gulliver, The Tatler, Joseph Andrews,* and *Humphrey Clinker.* He has a great turn for politics, right notions, and keen desires, and from his kind of head would make a good public man. He has much in him which cannot find issue in mere authorship. — Yours ever affectionately,

J. B.

813.                   TO LADY STANLEY
                       28 DECEMBER 1851

Hitherto unpublished.

> Quite private and confidential
> & only for you & Lord S.
>                     The Grange.  Sunday 28.

My dear Lady Stanley. I thought our young lady looking very nice and pretty, a little thinner perhaps; but it gave me pleasure to see in the Scotch crowd her kind friendly face — and Airlie I thought a handsome young Airlie, elegant looking and good-humoured and my lady rec^d me very kindly, and he seemed pleased that she should see an old friend; and if you must know my sentiment, my sentiment was that I should have liked very much to k—, well, I should upon my word and own it and ain't ashamed.

[158] Peddie prints *sending.*

You see there's something affecting in looking at a pretty young thing just embarked upon that career to w.ʰ all pretty young things are destined with good and evil fortune God knows — Who's to tell what happens when they get away from the home-nest and the real business of life begins for them? I hope this one's inward happiness may correspond to her outward prosperity: and her face looked as if it was so I thought and Lord Airlie looked as if he was proud & pleased and I was very much obliged to them for coming to my Sermon. And I dont intend to forget that friendly row of faces of last July.

The business is so good and yields such hatfulls of money that I shall go on pursuing it in England, and wait for a while before I try *our only ally.* What mayn't happen between this and the next six months? Is Lord Palmerston going to put his flag in advance of the stale old Whig ground? What a fine opportunity M.ʳ Ex-Under Secretary will have now: let him show the world the brains that he has got in him. I long to conspire a little, and if those men are going to show fight on the Liberal advance side, I know a heavy man and hard hitter that would like to take service with them.

I was so disgusted with that caricature w.ʰ appeared in Punch of the Bottleholder [159] that I remonstrated with all my force at the indecency and injustice of attacking the only man who was bottle-holding the liberal cause in Europe and received an answer promising better behavior and in w.ʰ the Editor of the paper said that they intended to be good-natured in the article not wicked, and as no bones were broken, that matter was left to drop. But on coming to London the first thing I see is that iniquitous cut against Louis Napoleon [160] w.ʰ enraged me so that I went in and resigned at once saying that I couldn't and wouldn't pull any longer in a boat where there was such a crew and such a steersman. So you see that political events influence small men as well as big, and I have gone out of office too in my small way.

Now tell me  Do your friends mean anything? Are you going

---

[159] See above, No. 807.

[160] "A Beggar on Horseback; Or, the Brummagem Bonaparte out for a Ride," *Punch,* December 27, p. 275.

forwards? Can I be of any good to Stanley — in a new paper or by going back to the old, or anyhow? Is it preposterous in a mere light littérateur talking in this way? It seems to me *The* Party is to be made in the country: and I want to know if you're of it? You can't go back to the Conservatives: Can you? You dont intend to put up with such a thrashing as you have had? When you hear anything and surtout any mischief please let your humble Serv.<sup>t</sup> know.

My children & I are on a little visit here and the young ones enjoy their first visit to a great house, where everybody is as kind as kind can be [161] — Only the Carlyles [162] & Lady Sandwich here, and a chemist who teaches his art to Lord Ashburton in a private room where they have furnaces and awful experiments. Afterwards about the 2<sup>nd</sup> I go to Erlestoke to Lord Broughton's and then come back for the rest of the month and longer to London. And I wish you a happy New Year, and Lady Airlie twenty such, and send my best respects to Miss Stanley (I mean Alice [163] only I dont like to say so right out) and I am always yours dear Lady Stanley most truly

W M Thackeray

[161] Lady Ashburton wrote to Mrs. Brookfield on January 1, 1852: "Some little people here, Annie and Minnie Thackeray, are vehement in their adoration of Miss Magdalene, who is, we trust, expanding under your tropical sun; they wish much to be remembered to her. As for the Elder Gentleman he is socially tabooed by his assiduous writing of a new novel, and appears only when Nature requires periodical restoration." (*Mrs. Brookfield*, II, 368)

[162] "I had never seen [Thackeray] so well before," Carlyle wrote to his brother on January 3 (*New Letters of Thomas Carlyle*, 2 vols., ed. Alexander Carlyle, London, 1904, II, 122). "There is a great deal of talent in him, a great deal of sensibility, — irritability, sensuality, vanity without limit; — and nothing, or little, but sentimentalism and playactorism to guide it all with: not a good or well-found ship in such waters on such a voyage." Thackeray's biographers, if they mention these strictures at all, commonly assume that they were occasioned by one of Carlyle's attacks of dyspepsia. It may be so. But before the reader accepts the gastric explanation of Carlyle's extravagant judgment as final, he should consider that Thackeray was passing through a period of profound emotional disturbance with which the stern Scottish moralist was peculiarly unsuited to sympathize.

[163] Alice Margaret Stanley (d. 1910), who married Augustus Henry Lane-Fox, later (1880) Lane-Fox-Pitt-Rivers, in 1853.

814.        TO MRS. ELLIOT
                DECEMBER? 1851

My text is taken from a facsimile in *Collection of Letters*, between pp. 142 and 143. The words between daggers were overscored by Mrs. Brookfield.

My dear Madam

It was as I feared on Friday, the little Printers devil barred my door and I could not come out or I should have liked very much to meet † Colonel Croustade: — Colonel Damer † I mean, whom I have already had the pleasure of meeting at your house With an exterior w$^h$ the world would call crusty I know of no person who is inwardly so richly endowed as M de Croustade.

Meeting Kinglake yesterday (no the day before) in the Park, we agreed that I should ask you if you would be so good as to receive me at dinner, or T if your table is full, on Friday: it is the first day I have when I am disengaged.

As I am in the act of writing this very last line the post man brings me your note — but on Wednesday I am going to a party

of authors: and must not be faithless to my friends & brethren.
Is there still hope for me dear Miss Berry? [164]

Always most faithfully yours

W M Thackeray

[For fragments of a letter to Kate Perry, December, 1851, see letter 31, Appendix XXVI.]

[164] Miss Agnes Berry, who died in December, 1851.

# APPENDICES

# APPENDIX VIII

## DIARY 2 FEBRUARY–22 APRIL 1842

Hitherto unpublished. Original owned by Mrs. Fuller.

Feb. 2. 1842. Remember Jawbrahim Heraudee [1] — a good subject in a French tale called Le Croisé de Bigorre. He goes on the crusade is tempted by the devil, who shows him his wife at home on the point of marrying another — the end is rather defective.

Saintine's [2] story 'La Vierge de Fribourg' good idea too. A love-story interwoven with a tour. Something might be done with the Belgian letters perhaps in this way.

Feb 15.

La Journée des Dupes — a family that takes a mysterious stranger for a great man — a dirty, ragged swaggering man. he turns out to be an actor.

Have read in these [days] Capefigue, Louis Blanc, Gallois, & Memoirs & newspapers regarding the restoration: [3] writing a little on the same.

[1] Thackeray's first identified contribution to *Punch* is "The Legend of Jawbrahim-Heraudee" in the issue of June 18, 1842, pp. 254–256.

[2] The pseudonym of Joseph Xavier Boniface (1798–1865), an industrious hack novelist. For the Belgian letters, see above, No. 177.

[3] Thackeray was at work on "The Last Fifteen Years of the Bourbons," an article here first identified as his, which was published in *The Foreign Quarterly Review* for July, pp. 384–420. The books that he mentions are the *Histoire de la Restauration et des causes qui ont amené la chute de la branche aînée des Bourbons* (1831–1833) of Jean Baptiste Capefigue (1802–1872); the *Histoire de dix ans* (1841) of Louis Blanc (1811–1872); and the *Continuation de l'histoire de France d'Anquetil* of Charles André Gallois (1789–1851).

Thackeray's connection with *The Foreign Quarterly Review* began not long after Chapman and Hall bought the magazine from Black and Armstrong late in 1841. On January 19, 1842, Mrs. Carlyle (*Letters and Memorials*, edd. Carlyle and Froude, I, 100–102) wrote to John Sterling that though the old editor, a Dr. Worthington, still retained his position, the management of the venture had been intrusted by the new publishers to Forster, who "is acting gratuitously as Prime Minister, for the mere love of humanity and his own inward glory." " 'Thackeray proposes,' " she continues, evidently quoting Forster, "(remember all this is strictly private, you who accuse me of blabbing) 'offering to keep a hot kitchen (the grand editorial requisite) on a thousand a year. To that there are one or two objections. But he is going to write an article on France and Louis Philippe, which, if he chooses to take pains, none could do better, &c., &c.' " By summer Forster was editor in title as well as in fact. If the appointment rankled, Thackeray did not allow his annoyance to prevent him from contributing to the *Review*. Many of his contributions — and several essays erroneously attributed to him — are printed in *The New Sketch Book*, ed. R. S. Garnett.

Parted on the 9th with my dear wife once more, may God preserve her & restore her.

Feb 25.

Hurried the article on the restoration & sent it off: — have done little else for the last 10 days: but the work seemed to grow bigger as I went on, & got to understand a little more about it.

My wife very comfortable at Chaillot and much better.

A good subject in the 32[d] novel of the Q of Navarre [4] — the faithless lady & the skull — ah says the novelist if all such dames were so served to drink, many a golden cup would be changed for a skull, &c

12th March. Sent off article on Victor Hugo [5] — and between it and the last worked a little on the Opera,[6] hammering out laboriously a song or two.

Painted with Collignon, who gave me plenty of good hints.

April 22 —

L'Hotel des Invalides [7] par Marco Saint Hilaire.

Le Capitaine Bleu an excellent story in Vol II — the young fellow of great spirit with a tinge of madness in his composition, a mania for fighting devils. He has a friend who is equally celebrated — they meet after a long absence, and fight out of fun at first — the Captain kills his friend: excited by a red cloak w[h] he wears —

Hereafter he forswears red, dresses himself in blue from head to foot, and becomes almost mad —

In a café he prevents 2 young officers from fighting & to one of them tells his story — the one turns out to be the son of the friend he has killed. The young man insists on fighting him — & is killed, the Captain goes stark mad.

---

A young lad goes from Spain to Germany in order to see the Emperor. He is a simple fellow believing in gipsies & the stars. A gipsy woman catches hold of him and astonishes him with her predictions.

He is placed as an advance sentinel — the gipsy woman comes to his post at night and tells him that if he will go 1/2 a league off he may see the Emporor. She meanwhile will hold his musquet. She is a spy of the emeny — who advance — confusion & arrival of the Emperor discourse with this boy, his death next day.

[4] In this story from the *Heptaméron* of Marguerite, Queen of Navarre (1492–1549), a certain Bernage surprises his wife with her lover, whom he kills. To punish his faithless spouse he makes her drink every evening from a cup fashioned out of her lover's skull.

[5] "The Rhine, by Victor Hugo," *Foreign Quarterly Review*, April, 1842, pp. 139–167. [6] Nothing is known of this opera.

[7] A novel published in 1841 by Emile Marc Hilaire (1796–1887), whose pseudonym was Marco de Saint-Hilaire.

# APPENDIX IX

## NOTES OF A TOUR IN THE LOW COUNTRIES DURING AUGUST, 1843

The notes that follow are here published for the first time from the manuscript in the Huntington Library. It will be observed that they break into four fragments, to each of which I have given a title. The evening in Rotterdam (as Thackeray's letters show) was that of August 7, 1843, and the other incidents described are to be dated within the next few days.

## I. AN EVENING IN ROTTERDAM

Since the invention of Antwerp & the Belgian & Prussian railroad, Rotterdam has lost most of its charm in the eyes of strangers and land-lords and commissioners are left in a pining & neglected condition. We found only the Smith before mentioned (he turns out to be an American Captain) sitting in the great coffee room, and had the choice of all the apartments in the huge comfortable inn. We fixed upon a neat pavillion, w$^h$ you approach by a brick walk, and w$^h$ has 3 big windows looking out on a shiny green canal, where lie a number of big barges with shining yellow sterns, and little lee-boards, like abortive wings, lying useless by their corpulent sides. Behind the masts, and their multiplicity of white cordage were the quays & trees and buildings of the town, numerous prim streets disappearing into the distance, that looks neat & clean & washed too like the rest of the view. Certain sailors at a capstan are turning the bar in time to a melancholy howling tune, a large square punt goes flapping through the water, a couple of men are cleaning & polishing a greyhound on some piles hard by, and three of the landlords little girls that are fishing out of the pavillion windows start up to make away for the new-comers, & carry off with them (in a broken jug) the results of their evenings sport: viz six pale dropsical unhealthy looking fish of the gudgeon sort & size. *Zez mezzieurs feulent ils rouber* says the little trim German waiter with the tight jacket & glossy boots w$^h$ question is answered according to circumstances.

That American Captain leads the life w$^h$ seems to be not uncommon in seaports. He knows every vessel that comes in and out — the Rhine boats, the Antwerp & Gouda boats, the London & Rhone boats, and is present at their arrival and departure. He is exceedingly anxious if they do not arrive in time, and informs you that he has been expecting you for so many hours. People of our nation generally are very shy of the advances of such strangers & draw away from them with the usual agree-able and supercilious airs w$^h$ makes Englishmen so much beloved on the continent. But why be so shy? the man wants nothing from us; —

only a little sympathy and a few kind remarks about the weather — it
is one's duty to talk to him and say  Sir the wind went to the West in
the afternoon or it grew rather cold towards night & so forth; it is just
as much a part of charity as pence-giving is, to relieve on the high road
poor craving beggars for kindness & sociability and a man has no right
to lock up his courtesy or to hide his fair behaviour under a bushel.

'Come away' says Smith [1] with whom I travel 'I can't bear that impudent forward Yankee' — and so we are obliged to leave the poor
fellow in his desert island of a coffee-room yonder — alone on his raft
of a table, w$^h$ the strange sail might relieve and wont. The poor skipper
gulps a sigh and a glass of Bordeaux down, as Smith & his friend stride
off haughtily, and he falls to reading the old Tuesday's Times w$^h$ he
has by heart, advertisements leading articles, coffee-blotches and all —
Ah for the good Samaritan, that will come and lend a hand to that poor
traveller! — the 2 Pharisees pass on and get their supper in private.

Lying last year alone on a sofa in the smoking-room of the Club, I
remember Snooks came in. We had met before but had never been introduced; we are both partial to cheerful rational conversation and both
I am sure longing to talk.

Hang it says I, it's his business to begin. He is a greater man than I
am. He is rich and I am a poor devil. I can't put myself forward.
Let this man begin the conversation said Snooks (floundering about &
rolling on the opposite sofa) and lighted his cigar, & began puffing it
very majestically.

The end was that we lay each on our cushions for about one hour
& a half, puffing away at the Segars, and as dumb as corpses. Neither,
with a becoming spirit, would one go out of the room before the other.
It would have been a confession of defeat: and thus before the end of
the hour and a half, two men naturally kindly cheerful & well disposed
towards one another, quitted each other boiling with mutual rage and
hatred.

If one or the other had said 'Sir it is a fine day' — we who now hate
each other might have commenced a friendship w$^h$ would have lasted
for life and elicited from either party a thousand good traits, w$^h$ are
all smothered under our abominable mauvaise honte. This is a corollary
to the remarks on the American skipper. My heart bleeds for him, that
is fact, and I have a great mind to quarrel with Smith too. But what
is the use? That broiled salmon is as fresh as a rose; the fresh mixture
of sugar Seltzer and Rhine wine froths up in the cup, in a delicate cool
cream. Smith my boy. Here's your health. Shall we go and take a
stroll through the town?

[1] Stevens.

It is fair time — and the town is illuminated with a hundred thousand of extra lights and swarming with people. Savoyards with organ and monkeys are grinding melodies at the corner of every street; and myriads of happy warm-looking men women and children are grinning & dancing to the same. The art of dancing is here however in its infancy. The girls make lamentable failures at waltzing, at w.<sup>h</sup> failures however the crowd applauds and wonders as much as at more successful efforts.

The people however have a coarse and somewhat ruffianly physiognomy. They look by no means so innocent as a multitude of French or Germans met together for pleasure. The women have bright complexions, twinkling little eyes, and great fresh healthy grinning mouths, w.<sup>h</sup> as they smile upon the passer by shew rows of gleaming white teeth that are more useful than beautiful. A spotless cap of white lace sits closely round these full-moon countenances; and over the head & skull and terminated by a pair of enormous corkscrew ornaments that butt out at either ear like ram's horns, lies a glistening plate of gold or silver — exceedingly fine. A tight sleeved divinity jacket w.<sup>h</sup> descends as far as a pair of enormous hips, and a pair of splay feet paddling in flat shoes and crumpled stockings, completed the costume of the Friezland women who were here by thousands.

Many of these lovely creatures presided in little streets composed entirely of goffre or Fritter shops; w.<sup>h</sup> indeed seemed to form the chief article of commerce in the fair. They had gaudy looking pavillions fitted up with curtains and recesses, where the above named delicacies might be eaten in private. A couple of syrens with the largest grins and jerks of the elbow invite the passer by to enter the booths, and before it straddling over an immense fire and pouring the materials of unbaked fritters into a large iron plate destined to receive it, and perspiring under a large brazen lamp, sits the Fritteress in chief ladling out her goods. She, and they, and the attendant nymphs, looked anything but tempting and indeed there was a great smoke and smell but not much eating of fritters as far as we could see. Perhaps Greenwich fair is a trifle more elegant, and certainly presents more various amusements to those who frequent it.

The fair seemed to contain scarcely any other sort of amusement. You pass through street upon street of goffres, from one frying pan to another, until the delicious amusement begins to pall. There are some shows also to be seen by the curious but these are few in number and not so splendid in appearance as in our own dear country. Vill you go to a dancing-house? says the Jew Commissioner, and leads you through a street that looks like Wapping in a state of festivity. Immense crowding, drumming banging singing flags flying up and down the street liquor shops flowing with light, and sailors and landsmen in commotion.

Three other Jew Commissioners leading three other parties of newly arrived English looking perfectly calm correct & miserable make their appearance too and enter the winged 'Paard' pretty much in company. They do not speak to one another of course, but look respectively as English always do now on meeting their countrymen, with a look that seems to say D— you. What do you do here? & so sit down in respective corners with their respective Jews. About twenty four ladies are walking up & down this saloon, dressed in all the colours of the tulip and flinging about killing glances: and in an orchestra four trumpeters are blowing out the lights with the blasts of immense waltzes.

'Vil you Valtz Sirs?' says the Jew Commissioner, and you feel inclined to knock him down for asking the question. And so starting up nothing abashed, the accomplished rascal seizes one of the ladies and whirls her round the room.

Then you are called upon to pay 3 florins for three glasses of punch: and feeling heartily ashamed of ever having been entrapped into such an abominable place are now at liberty to retire. I had expected to be introduced to a scene the humour of w$^h$ might be somewhat broad it is true, but of a general jovial good-natured sort. A tea-party of Dowagers at Hackney could not behave with more outward correctness, nor could their virtue be more abominably dull than this cold painted leering ogling Dutch vice was. And I could not understand why the lacquais de place into whose hands the helpless traveller falls on his arrival insisted upon taking his prey into this den of vice and dullness until informed that he received half the price of the three glasses of punch w$^h$ he was at liberty to drink too besides.

It was pleasant to get away from the din of the fair and the leers of those hideous ogling gold-plated Friezlanders into the quiet parts of the town, over the tall huge magnificent houses of w$^h$ the moon was shining brilliantly, and lighting up line upon line of dark trees, and long canals and barges and drawbridges. As crowded as the fair was the rest of the city was still — not a footstep was to be heard in the Boompjes and the American Captain sate in the solitude of the coffee room reading Wednesday's Times.

The use of locks and keys has always struck me as a most cruel satire upon the rascality of the world, in w$^h$ as we clap to the hasp of our portmanteau, we show our entire want of confidence — And an especial satire upon us British youth, is the existence of this demoniacal lacquais de place class, one of whom is sure to fasten upon a man on his entrance into a new town.

Our travelling gentry, must be a pretty reputable, elegant high-minded, highly educated class to judge from these fellows: and why not judge by them? You can tell what are the tastes of a country by the wares w$^h$ clever merchants bring to it. They carry over glass beads and iron wares to savages, and French fashions to ladies in the colonies knowing the wants and wishes of those individuals. A planters wife would not bid a high price for an ace-head or a tin of gunpowder, and King Boy on the Quorra would turn up his flat nose (as far as nature permitted) were the trader to propose to him the purchase of a crinoline petticoat or a dozen of white kid gloves from Boivin's. To a pretty sort of wants of our English gentry is that diabolical squinting laughing brazen faced red-haired wretch of a purveyor. In our squeamish days his name is not to be mentioned in plain English — in French it is expressed by the name of a fish [2] that is eaten with fennel sauce — A greater rascal the world never saw dangling at a gibbets end — a more audacious cynical impudence never belonged to any scoundrel Hebrew or Xtian. He lays bare all the rascally qualities of his heart with a great unblushing effrontery, and does not scruple not merely to be but to acknowledge himself a villain. You drive him off with kicks and foul words like a dog, & the fellow comes presently grinning back again to show you the way you have lost in the street, or to place a dish on your table. As he has established a percentage upon all the goods w$^h$ strangers purchase from tradesmen, there is no insult w$^h$ will induce him to let go his hold of you, until your hour of departure is fixed, and he can get money from you no more.

That man must have been more kicked and reviled in his time than an army of martyrs. His villainy is quite a curiosity so enormous and apparent it is . . . But modern politeness forbids the description of such rascals, and will only tell of a rogue whose behavior is as modest as a Quakeress's, and whose vices won't raise a blush to the cheek of the most delicate female' — as the saying is.

So that the agreeable picture of the Jew Commissioner at Rotterdam must not be sketched in this place — Only he has been mentioned here in order that the agreeable truth may be conveyed, that it is the crimes and debauchery of our British gentry on w$^h$ the crimes and debauchery of this rascal fatten. He might have simply swindled in a matter of oranges or sealing wax but our vices were found to be a more profitable trade to cheat and traffic in. And every boat as it comes laden from England with pink-faced lads from college who are trying to give themselves a manly air, or young dragoons with sprouting mustachios empty brains and lacquered boots, brings this watchful villain pupils to introduce into his infernal school, whom he will excite, and corrupt as much as they can be corrupted, and whom he will rob certainly.

They talk about English morality. Psha! there is no vice in the

---

[2] *Maquereau*, which means both mackerel and pander.

world more open, coarse, brutal infamous than that of the English young gentleman — Take that rascal yonder as a criterion. He never thinks of fastening upon a German, and has a thorough almost English contempt for a Frenchman, but he will never leave an Englishman alone. And so *Joseph* (all commissioners are called Joseph Good bye and go and be hanged.

## II. THE UGLY LOVERS

Twelve people take their numbered places in the diligence, most of them with pipes [or] cigars in their mouths. Opposite sit a husband and wife, the former has his arm round his lady's waist, and pokes his head lovingly under her bonnet every now and then, & does not scruple to whiff the smoke into her face. She smiles through the cloud quite comfortable in the midst of it, and you see they are as fond of each other as any two people can be — I am rather glad that they are both so ugly — there is nothing in fancying two handsome people in love with each other. But a man with a face like a guinea-pig, and a little dumpy yellow snub-nosed creature with moist little cork screw ringlets and crumpled ribbons in her bonnet — such a homely little pair evidently in love with each other, and being happy in the midst of the smoke w$^h$ the male emits from his tobacco — is surely a pretty spectacle. Jupiter in the midst of his cloud wooing Imperial Juno is no such pleasing spectacle to the moralist. There is no merit in his falling in love with a superb creature whose charms are decked to the best advantage by means of Venus's cestus and admirable toilette: and as for Juno what can she do but be smitten by the superb imperial Jove; whose αμβροσιαι χαιται (ambrosial whiskers) are enough to set any female heart in a flutter?

A far more touching spectacle to my mind is offered by yon humble ugly pair of lovers. He is not five feet high, he has not even straps to his boots, why do I say boots? — to his bluchers — their children will be squat ugly & pale — their honeymoon w$^h$ is shining on their loves (for I am sure they are just married) is no brighter or more romantic than a fat round greasy Dutch cheese: but they *love*, and good luck to them — see he is just taking out another cigar.

## III. THE MONEY-LENDERS' DINNER

I am sure that poor devil had put his hand to one. He was bowed out with a profusion of compliments, and I thought the mothers good natured eyes turned away somewhat as the above little scene was going on, as if a little ashamed of it. But why ashamed? She has been married these thirty years and has seen such a scene most likely every day. It is a part of my worthy host's creed yonder; far from taking shame he glories in it. I have given my son he said to me twenty thousand guilders to begin the world with, and for whatever more money he wants, *he pays me eight per cent*. Hence to get thirty per cent from any Gentile in need, is I have no doubt not a matter of remorse with him but of exultation. He thinks of it at night as of a good action, and tells his sons, & warns them to profit by his precious examples.

Next day we were invited to a dinner of w^h it behoves me to speak in terms of the greatest respect. There was first a course of fish consisting of marvellous turbots salmon & soles, and then a course of meat & fowls, the whole concluding with a service of pastry w^h no doubt was as good as the courses preceding it. Here were assembled the Melchisedecs of several branches, there was M^rs Zorobabel of Amsterdam, and the two young Melchisedecs of the Hague, & Miss Aaron the Rabbis daughter, and pretty M^rs Manasseh of Leyden. All these ladies were perfectly ladylike pleasing & more than ordinarily clever. They made fun of me & Smith in the most audacious good-humoured merry way possible — of Smith I think especially, though he could not understand their joking, and as I imagined was rather inclined to assert the dignity of an English gentleman. They were fit company, I will not say for Smith & me but for the very best bred society in the world. *Their* lives are not passed in money-getting and discounting and chaffering — their husbands perform that part of the family service, and a pretty opinion must the wives have of them!

But the men — o the men! there was one a young Hebrew dandy with yellow hair, and turned up wristbands & varnished boots, who was said to be a young fellow of enormous wealth and who in the course of dinner handed a paper across the table to another guest. It was a bill of exchange. It ran me through like a carving-knife, not that I have any bills in the market, but why bring out the horrible paper at dinner? Is there no time of enjoyment sacred from it? At the sight of it the salmon turned stale, the wine became flat, the smiles of good natured M^rs Zorobabel became all of a sudden suspicious odious and malignant, as did the jokes of Mynheer Melchisedec (he had plenty of them and out of Joe Miller too for he has lived long and studied in England) and I fancied that his joking and bonhommie was a part of his business. What a number of poor devils has he entertained with those stories, many a faint sufferer has smiled as he told them, they are no more genuine stories than the books on a dentist's table are genuine books, they are decoys, vile stratagems to carry off the patients attention from the Extractor's designs upon him.

Another remark w^h I have to make about this dinner, and w^h fully excuses this criticism upon it, is the following All the while we at our end of the table were drinking the costliest wines I observed Melchisedec

& his family were drinking ordinaire! Can there be any doubt about a
man's intentions after that? Can we suppose for a minute that his
hospitality was real? No. The dinner was a part of his business as much
as a bill of exchange — I was going to say, that I would have drunk
ordinaire myself than submitted to see others drinking it while I had
better fare. That nonsense the reader would not probably believe —
no more do I. But this I swear. I would rather at a feast that others
should fare as well as I and have not the slightest respect for the giver
of an entertainment who arranges matters otherwise.

The only time during w^h Signor Melchisedec appeared to me in an
amiable light was after dinner when we retreated to the drawing room,
when the young people began to frisk and sing, when our noble young
fellow with nothing Israelitish about him played admirably a concert on
the violin, when the yellow-haired dandy before mentioned shrieked
most abominably to the piano a French romance about Madame &
flamme, and J'aime & même, and when Melchisedec himself sate by
quite happy with a long pipe w^h he filled out of a tortoise shell tobacco-
box, not thinking of money but looking on at the happiness of his children
& family.

Next day he came to bid us adieu, and calling down blessings on the
head of Smith told me I might have the tobacco-box a bargain, and I
bought it and have it to this day. His parting words were that I might
have the money back for it whenever I pleased. And we took boat again
and came back to Antwerp.

## IV.  A COACH TRIP

You go to wait for the Hague Coach at a queer old low roofed coffee
house such as coffee houses must have been in England a hundred years
ago. there is no more attempt at ornament than there is in a tavern in
the city. There is a little old billiard table at w^h nobody plays, no swaggering bucks and whiskered dandies frequent the place as in France,
but the guests are for the most part sober fat men with long pipes or
cigars, with large white shirt collars sawing under great raw ears in
w^h very likely a little pair of gold rings are twinkling. They have no
shape to their fat trowsers and no pretensions to a waist. They drink a
power of strong liquors solemnly liquors w^h — I presume to be gin &
cherry-brandy and the like. Behind the plain old counter sits plain old
lady who superintends a little perpetual coffee-boiler, and you are served
in little demure black coffee-pots & milk jugs without any attempt at
finery. Here sit the worthies smoking for ever and ever, and there is a
firepot for lighting the matches w^h never goes out any more than the
flame of the Vestal Virgins.

At last the Coach w^h is called the Vreendschap is ready, a neat inside vehicle, with four rows of benches. Every body who gets in has a segar except the old lady with the child. The young sailor boy is smoking the jolly gentleman with the blue and yellow ribbon is smoking & puffing hugely, the old lady's old gentleman who carries three parasols between his legs and the childs cap on top of one of them, has a segar stuck into a wooden tube w^h — is placed between his thin lips and in w^h he is piping very meekly. All these begin to talk according to the habit of their country, in a language that sounds exactly like English only you can't understand it.

The Vreendschap trots over a brick highway, by many villages, by the handsome city of Delft, by the famous town of Schiedam, and by innumerable flat pastures cow-bespeckled and brilliantly green. The windmills on the most luxurious of mills — vast towns rising from above snug habitations spick and span in the brightest colours, and every one at the door, comfortable and well dressed. Country houses and canals are there beyond calculation, pavillions with dumpy dutch Statues, rows of alders and poplars, bridges, tanks and —— floating on them. On every bridge is a fellow lying on his stomach watching his float w^h hangs in the water below. They are just such figures as you see in the Dutch tiles,[3] and have been bobbing for gudgeons these hundred years — Everybody seems lazy comfortable and prosperous. As for smoking! I saw a little fellow flying a kite who looked up at the kite through clouds of tobacco from the pipe in his little mouth — a little angler with his fishing rods and pail of gudgeon was looking on and smoking too.

It is good to have seen such a scene once, and I think one will always remember this bright picture of ease neatness and plenty, but visit twice and it already begins to pall — To live in the midst of such a landscape would be almost as dismal as to look perpetually at the great sandy desert, or out of a window in Pump Court.

[3] See above, No. 257.

# APPENDIX X

## ACCOUNT BOOK FOR 1844

Hitherto unpublished. Original owned by Mrs. Fuller.

### DIARY, JANUARY 1–DECEMBER 9, 1844

January Cash Received

|  |  |  |  |
|---|---|---|---|
|  |  | 8 | 1 |
|  |  | 25 | 0 |
|  |  | 16 |  |
| 2 | From Stevens | 10 |  |
|  | Bradbury & Evans paid to Lubbock | 10 |  |
| 26 | Drew on Lubbock for 23 1/2 leaving a balance of 20£. |  |  |
|  | Wrote 2–15 Punch | 10 |  |
|  | 3 India letter | 3 | 3 |
|  | 8–11 Novels for Fraser | 9 |  |
|  | 16–20 Barry Lyndon | 12 |  |
|  | 21 Mystères | 4 |  |
|  | 25 Child of Godesberg | 12 |  |
|  | India & America letter | 4 |  |
|  |  | 54 |  |

January Cash Paid

|  |  |  |
|---|---|---|
| Christmas Boxes François 20. Porter 10 | 30 | 10 |
| Inn Bill &c | 15 |  |
| Stevens | 25 |  |
| Sundries | 5 |  |
| Dinner | 35 |  |
| Gilt candlestick & scissors | 25 |  |
| Justin & Flore for children | 20 |  |
| Francois | 20 |  |
| Cabs & sundries | 5 |  |
| Justine's wages | 87 |  |
| Marcellini for law | 95 |  |
| Mrs Hankey for collars | 11 |  |
| Dinner Sundries Cabs &c | 15 |  |
| Mother for wood &c | 40 |  |
| Sundries | 30 |  |
| Porters for wood &c | 20 |  |

| | | |
|---|---|---|
| Sundries | 70 | |
| Lachevardière for dinner &c | 60 | |
| Play & dinner | 10 | |
| Pauline 5 Sundries 5 | 10 | |
| Puzin for Isabella | 210 | |
| | 837 | |
| Sundries | 13 | |

February Cash Received
Cash at Lubbocks 20£
do from Nickisson 22.15/
In pocket 140£
Received from Giraldon 100 f.

| | | |
|---|---|---|
| India & American letter | 3 | 10 |
| Punch | 25 | |
| American letter | 4 | 10 |
| Barry Lyndon &c III. | 12 | 0 |
| Barry Lyndon IV. | 15 | |
| Godesberg. | 5 | |

February Cash paid

| | |
|---|---|
| Puzin for Isabella | 210 |
| Wood | 10 |
| Sundries for Isabella | 30 |
| Tuke | 25 |
| Tuke | 15 |
| Service Wood & Breakfast | 35 |

March Cash Received
At Lubbock 32.10

| | | |
|---|---|---|
| Drew from Bradbury & Evans | 35 | |
| Nickisson | 12 | |
| Nickisson | 20 | |
| Fraser | 9 | |
| C & H | 40 | |
| Drew   4 Paid in | 32 | |
| 10 | 47 | 10 |
| 5 | 20 | |
| 5 | 9 | |
| 8 | 40 | |
| 5 | 148 | 10 |

148
37    111

| | |
|---|---|
| Wrote Preface | 30 |

Chronicle 8
Punch (say) 5

March Cash Paid
    Paid Stevens                                10    0    0
    Left at Home for Isabella                   10    0    0
    Paid Fraser                                      30f
    Lodgings Wood & Service                          75
    journey to London                               100
    Inn bill & Hat box                               50

April Cash Received
    Cash in hand                    110.
                                     43
                                     67
                                     43

        Drew   10 10   0 Reform
                8 10   0 Chappell
                5  0   0 Self
               20 (10.5.5)
                5       Self
                3  5 Shirts
               10
                5

August Cash Received
    Drew on Lubbock 10£ 5£
    Rec^d from Hume 10£
    Hume's letter                                3    0    0

August Cash Paid
    Books                                        2    0    0
    Travelling to London                         3    0    0
    Inn-Bills                                     2    0    0
    Bill at Chaufontaine                         2    0    0
    Paid Daniel                                  2    1    0
    Paid Puzin                                  10    0    0
    Paid London Library                          8    0    0

# APPENDIX XI

## DIARY 13 APRIL–26 DECEMBER 1845

Hitherto unpublished. Original in the Berg Collection of the New York Public Library.

| April | 13. | Tennent 6. |
|---|---|---|
| | 14. | C. 8. |
| | 15. | FitzGerald.[1] Davis Street. |
| | 17. | C. 8. M$^{rs}$ Holland.[2] 63 Portland Place. |
| | 18. | M$^{rs}$ Sartoris T. M$^{rs}$ Prinsep. 7. 37 Hyde Park Gardens |
| | 21. | M$^{rs}$ Holland. 7. |
| | 22. | C. 8 1/2 |
| | 23. | Garrick. Shakespeare.[3] |
| | 24. | India Mail. |
| | 25. | M$^{rs}$ Sartoris T. M$^{rs}$ FitzGerald 1/4 7. |
| | 27. | M$^r$ Young.[4] Denmark Hill |
| | 28. | M$^r$ Hebeler.[5] 6. Tennent to call at 5 1/2 |
| | 30. | M$^r$ Boyd.[6] 7. |
| May | 1. | M$^{rs}$ Holland. T Bradbury & Evans. |
| | 4. | M$^{rs}$ Tennent. |
| | 5. | M$^{rs}$ Crowe. |
| | 6. | M$^{rs}$ Prinsep. |
| | 22. | M$^{rs}$ Procter 7. M$^{rs}$ Milner Gibson [7] T. |

[1] Edward Marlborough FitzGerald, who was living at 45 Davies Street (*Post Office London Directory*, 1847).

[2] Robert Hollond (1808–1877), a wealthy barrister of Anglo-Indian stock who was M. P. for Hastings from 1837 to 1852, lived with his wife at 63 Portland Place (*Royal Blue Book*, 1846).

[3] The annual Shakespeare Dinner at the Garrick Club.

[4] George Young, Denmark Hill, Camberwell (*Post Office London Directory*, 1847).

[5] Bernard Hebeler, Consul General for Prussia and Württemberg (*Post Office London Directory*, 1847).

[6] Possibly Robert Boyd (d. 1883) of Marylebone Hospital, a well-known alienist.

[7] The former Susanna Cullum (1814?–1885), daughter of Thackeray's friend the Rev. Sir Thomas Cullum and wife of the liberal statesman Thomas Milner Gibson (1806–1884). We learn from Serjeant Ballantine (*Some Experiences of a Barrister's Life*, I, 243) that she "at one time gathered around her a large circle, comprising most of those famous in literature, art, and the professions; and here also every foreigner possessing a grievance and an unhappy country was always made heartily welcome." Edmund Yates (*Recollections and Experiences*, I, 253) lists some of the celebrities who frequented her salon.

May       23. M<sup>rs</sup> Sartoris. T.
          28. M<sup>rs</sup> Holland T.

June       6. M<sup>rs</sup> Prinsep.
          22. Boyd's dinner Greenwich 5 1/2.
          23. Brookfield 6.
          24. Hamilton 6 1/2.
          25. Priaulx.[8] Greenwich
          28. James at Richmond.
          29. Easthope [9] —

November 30. Dawdled all day dined at Camberwell.[10]

December  1. Prinsep's dinner. Wrote Alexandria [11] & a little more
           3. Deanery [12] dinner 6.
           4. Reeve's dinner 7.
           8. Dined with my wife
           9. Wrote Punch all day — dined with Ronalds —
          10. Dined with my wife — wrote at night a little
          18. M<sup>r</sup> Lushington [13] 1 Palace Gardens Bayswater 6 1/2
          22. Serjeant Talfourds dinner 6.
          26. M<sup>rs</sup> Pryme 26 Baker S<sup>t</sup> 6 1/2.

[8] Osmond de Beauvoir Priaulx (1805–1891), barrister, writer, and original member of the Reform Club, was long a friend of Thackeray.

[9] Sir John Easthope (1784–1865), first Baronet, proprietor of *The Morning Chronicle* and M. P. for Leicester from 1837 to 1847.

[10] Where Mrs. Thackeray was living in the charge of Mrs. Bakewell.

[11] Chapter 14 of *Notes of a Journey from Cornhill to Grand Cairo.*

[12] We learn from an obituary notice of George Moreland Crawford in *The New York Tribune* (December 13, 1885) that " 'The Deanery' was a snug old-fashioned public house, near St. Paul's . . . [It] derived its name from the fact that it was presided over by Barham, the author of 'The Ingoldsby Legends,' who was a canon of the neighboring cathedral. The dinner[s] cost eighteen pence apiece, and the wine (which was always capital) was drawn out of the tub and cheap."

[13] Charles Lushington was at this time living at 1 Kensington Palace Gardens (*Royal Blue Book,* 1846).

# APPENDIX XII

## ARTICLES NEWLY IDENTIFIED AS THACKERAY'S

As was to be expected, the publication of a comprehensive edition of Thackeray's letters puts the perplexed bibliography of his earlier years on a much firmer basis than it has been heretofore. If his assembled correspondence serves to eliminate certain disputed attributions (such as "Elizabeth Brownrigge" and several papers in *The Foreign Quarterly Review*), it adds a much larger number of articles, which more than compensate for what has been lost.

Chief among these additions is a long series of contributions to *The Morning Chronicle*. I shall not here describe Thackeray's notable work for this journal, for I intend to reprint most of it in the near future, with an introduction showing reason for assigning to him many articles which he does not specifically mention in his letters, but it does seem desirable to list his *Chronicle* articles (exclusive of political leaders) in this Appendix.[1]

In a second list I have brought together a variety of other papers which are for the first time identified as Thackeray's in the notes to this edition. It should be mentioned as well that though nothing is to be gained by endeavoring to ascertain precisely what Thackeray wrote for *Galignani's Messenger* in March, 1838, and for *The Examiner* between March and June, 1845,[2] two very promising areas for bibliographical investigation still remain uncharted: Thackeray's contributions to *The Calcutta Star* between 1843 and 1845 and to an American paper managed by Henry Wykoff in January and February, 1844.[3]

### ARTICLES IN *The Morning Chronicle* NEWLY IDENTIFIED AS THACKERAY'S

1. "*Ireland*. By J. Venedey," March 16, 1844. (See above, No. 274, 23 February, 1844.)
2. "*Ireland and its Rulers, since 1829*," March 20, 1844.

[1] Not included in my list are the following *Chronicle* articles by Thackeray, which were discovered by earlier investigators:

"*A New Spirit of the Age*, edited by R. H. Horne," April 2, 1844.
"*The Life of George Brummell, Esq.* By Captain Jesse," May 6, 1844.
"*Coningsby; or, the New Generation*," May 13, 1844.
"*The Poetical Works of Horace Smith*," September 21, 1846.

[2] See above, No. 119 and No. 302.
[3] See above, No. 241 and No. 275.

3. *"The Three Kingdoms.* By the Vicomte D'Arlincourt," April 4, 1844.
4. "Exhibition of the Society of Painters in Water Colour," April 29, 1844.
5. *"Stanley's Life of Dr. Arnold,"* June 3, 1844.
6. *"Historic Fancies.* By the Hon George Sidney Smythe," August 2, 1844. (See above, No. 274, 22 July, 1844.)
7. *"Egypt under Mehemet Ali.* By Prince Puckler Muskau," March 27, 1845.
8. *"Lever's St. Patrick's Eve — Comic Politics,"* April 3, 1845.
9. *"Sybil.* By Mr. Disraeli," May 13, 1845. (See above, No. 274, 11 August, 1844.)
10. *"Christmas Books. — No.* 1," December 24, 1845.
11. *"Christmas Books — No.* 2," December 26, 1845.
12. *"Christmas Books. — No. III,"* December 31, 1845.
13. *"Carus's Travels in England,"* March 16, 1846.
14. *"Life and Correspondence of David Hume,"* March 23, 1846. (See above, No. 340.)
15. *"Travels in the Punjab. By Mohan Lal,"* April 6, 1846.
16. *"The Novitiate; or, a Year among the English Jesuits.* By Andrew Steinmetz," April 11, 1846.
17. *"The New Timon,"* April 21, 1846.
18. *"The Exhibitions of the Societies of Water Colour Painters,"* April 27, 1846.
19. *"Studies of English Character.* By Mrs. Gore," May 4, 1846.
20. *"The Exhibition of the Royal Academy,"* May 5, 1846.
21. *"The Exhibition of the Royal Academy.* Second Notice," May 7, 1846.
22. *"Royal Academy.* Third Notice," May 11, 1846.
23. *"Haydon's Lectures on Painting and Design,"* June 19, 1846.
24. *"Alexis Soyer, The Gastronomic Regenerator,"* July 4, 1846.
25. *"Moore's History of Ireland; from the earliest Kings of that Realm down to its last Chief,"* August 20, 1846.
26. *"Ravensnest; or the Red Skins,"* August 27, 1846.
27. *"Life at the Water Cure,"* September 1, 1846.
28. *"Diary and Letters of Madame d'Arblay.* Vol. 6," September 25, 1846.
29. *"Royal Palaces.* F. W. Trench," October 5, 1846.
30. *"Meeting on Kennington Common,"* March 14, 1848. (See above, No. 457, 14 March, 1848.)
31. *"Chartist Meeting,"* March 15, 1848. (See above, No. 457, 15 March, 1848.)

ARTICLES IN OTHER PUBLICATIONS NEWLY IDENTIFIED
AS THACKERAY'S

1. "Epistles to the Literati. No. XIV. On French Criticism of the English, and Notably in the Affair of the Vengeur," *Fraser's Magazine*, March, 1840, pp. 332–345. (See *Biographical Memoranda*, Thomas Carlyle.)

2. "The Last Fifteen Years of the Bourbons," *Foreign Quarterly Review*, July, 1842, pp. 384–420. (See above, Appendix VIII, 15 February, 1842.)

3. "The Problematic Invasion of British India," *Foreign Quarterly Review*, April, 1844, pp. 213–229. (See above, No. 279.)

4. "Captain Warner's Discovery," *Punch*, July 27, 1844. (See above, No. 274, 20 July, 1844.)

5. "Lord William Lennox's Readings and Recitations from Joe Miller," *Punch*, August 10, 1844. (See above, No. 274, 23 July, 1844.)

6. "Polk's First Address," *Examiner*, March 29, 1845. (See above, No. 302.)

7. "*Mount Sorel*," *Examiner*, March 29, 1845. (See above, No. 302.)

8. "What Mr. Jones Saw at Paris," *Punch*, September 8, 1849. (See above, No. 621.)

# INDEX OF CORRESPONDENTS

## VOLUME II